# The Arms Race and Nuclear War

# The Arms Race and Nuclear War

David P. Barash
University of Washington

Wadsworth Publishing Company
Belmont, California
A Division of Wadsworth, Inc.

Psychology Editor: Ken King
Production Editor: Deborah O. McDaniel
Designer: MaryEllen Podgorski
Print Buyer: Barbara Britton
Copy Editor: Brenda Griffing
Technical Illustrators: Joan Carol, Alan Noyes
Signing Representative: Karen Buttles

The cover shows a graphic treatment of US and USSR strategic submarine detection and defense systems. The white dots represent the USSR's submarine bases and patrol areas; the yellow dots show US bases and the SOSUS (*Sound Surveillance System*) antisubmarine array. See Figure 2.20 on page 38.

Printed in the United States of America    19

1 2 3 4 5 6 7 8 9 10—91 90 89 88 87

*Library of Congress Cataloging-in-Publication Data*

Barash, David P.
    The arms race and nuclear war.

    Includes index.
    1. Nuclear weapons.   2. Nuclear warfare.   3. Arms race—History—20th century.   I. Title.
U264.B38 1987      355'.0217      86-13257
ISBN 0-534-06846-4

To Judith Eve Lipton,
with all my love

# Contents

# Preface

The Nuclear Age poses problems and opportunities that are in many ways new to the human experience. Although the discovery of nuclear energy is quite recent compared to the discovery of agriculture, the invention of the wheel, or the taming of fire, it is no less historic. With the first nuclear explosions in 1945, the world was changed, perhaps irretrievably.

Along with this change, there has been a change in the nature of information required by citizens in a democracy. Just as literacy is fundamental to informed decision making, the Nuclear Age demands that citizens understand the fundamental issues surrounding nuclear weapons. That is, we must have a minimal level of nuclear literacy if we are to discharge the crucial responsibility of citizenship in a world of nuclear weapons. *The Arms Race and Nuclear War* is directed toward fulfilling this requirement.

This book is intended for beginning and midlevel undergraduates, taking their first (and perhaps, their only) course on the subject. It does not assume any particular background beyond a general high school education. In some ways, it cannot avoid being unsatisfying, since it touches briefly on many different subjects but does not delve deeply into any one. Basic nuclear literacy requires a smattering of physics, history, economics, political science, military doctrine, psychology, and philosophy, with some biology, law, and sociology thrown in for good measure. I encourage students to pursue these various disciplines in relation to nuclear weapons if they have the time and interest; all readers, however, should finish this book with at least a working knowledge of the major issues: what is known and what is controversial, and why disagreements exist.

My original intent was to keep this book brief, as befits a primer. To do justice to the material, however,

a full-sized textbook turned out to be necessary. The present volume could therefore serve as the sole text for an introductory course on nuclear weapons and the arms race. On the other hand, instructors may want to supplement it with outside readings of their choice, presumably reflecting their own professional training and concerns. Courses of this sort are "proliferating" in many universities and a wide range of departments, including humanities, social, physical, and biological science, and even schools of nursing, social work, engineering, law, and medicine. It is my hope that the presence of a beginning level text that pulls together material from a variety of disciplines related to the arms race and nuclear war will encourage instructors to offer a course in this area, even though many issues will likely be outside their training. In addition, *The Arms Race and Nuclear War* is designed to serve as a unifying point for team-taught courses.

Terms are carefully defined and set in **boldface** when they first appear, because one of the confusing aspects of nuclear weapons is the language used to discuss them. If citizens are to participate effectively in the nuclear debate, they must know and understand the language in which it is conducted. Accordingly, once a word or phrase has been introduced, I have incorporated such nuclear jargon into the discussion, in the hope that readers will quickly become conversant not only with the issues but also with the manner in which they are typically presented. Each chapter ends with a list of study questions and a few suggested readings, for those who want to delve deeper.

I have opinions on nearly all the issues raised in this book, in some cases rather strong opinions. These opinions are uniformly "dovish"; that is, I believe that nuclear weapons are enormously dangerous and almost wholly evil, and that the danger posed to the United

States and the world by nuclear war is much greater than the danger posed by the Soviet Union. Other people have other viewpoints, however, and in this book I have tried to present a balanced perspective, clearly distinguishing fact from opinion, and labeling as such the various "hawk" and "dove" arguments that surround various issues. But it is only fair to alert the reader to my preexisting bias, since some of it is unavoidably reflected in the presentation of the material.

The text of each chapter is essentially factual and, I think, basically unarguable. However, when it comes to questions of the arms race and nuclear war, facts lead to diverse interpretations. Except for the first and last chapters, therefore, the main presentation of material is followed by a series of "Policy Issues," providing very brief responses, generally from both a hawkish and a dovish perspective. In writing these, I attempted to present each viewpoint as it is often expressed by devoted partisans; that is, I sought to make a one-sided and sometimes misleading case (as partisans often do), as though I were an advocate of that particular viewpoint. As a result, the reader will find assertions among the various "Policy Issues" that do not agree with other, more objective material in the chapters themselves. When dealing with subject matter as controversial and emotion-laden as the arms race and nuclear war, it seems important to expose students not only to basic information presented in a neutral way, but also to the misrepresentations and confusing rhetoric that often characterize discussions on this topic.

Such material might serve as good starting places for additional discussion, debate, research papers, and so on. Since I have been at pains to keep this book from becoming unwieldy, it has not been possible to cover more than a small fraction of relevant policy issues in this manner. Therefore, I encourage readers to identify additional such questions for each chapter, and to think about the answers. This seems particularly appropriate, since the ultimate answers to questions posed by the arms race and nuclear war remain to be decided.

Many people contributed to this book. I would especially like to thank my students and the following colleagues, who opined helpfully on various chapters: George Modelski, University of Washington; Gerhard R. Barsch, Pennsylvania State University; James Derderian, University of Massachusetts; Robert Ehrlich, George Mason University; Herbert D. Grover, University of New Mexico; David Hafemeister, California Polytechnic University; Conway Leovy, University of Washington; James P. Sterba, University of Notre Dame; and Bruce Russett, Yale University. Also deserving special mention: my tolerant family, who put up with the tribulations of such a project; Ken King, who saw merit in it; and Debbie McDaniel, who helped make it a reality.

David P. Barash

# The Arms Race and Nuclear War

*Part One*

# Nuclear Hardware

The chapters in this section provide an introduction to nuclear weapons: everything you may or may not have wanted to know about them . . . but should. The first chapter is an introduction to basic nuclear physics. The goal is not to teach Bomb Building 101, or to make the reader into a professional scientist, but rather to present the fundamental principles of nuclear weapons, discussing what they are and how they work. Lacking such background, many people feel that they are not entitled to an opinion and tend to leave all related areas to the experts. With the nuts-and-bolts familiarity acquired from Chapter 1, however, the student should gain a sense of competence that will permit informed consideration of the remaining material.

Chapter 2 describes the various long-range delivery systems—that is, missiles and bombers—and then presents a comparative overview of the weaponry possessed by the United States and by the Soviet Union. Chapter 3 considers shorter range delivery systems and provides a very brief review of conventional (nonnuclear) military forces, as well as an introduction to the balance in Europe.

Thus Part One is an introduction to nuclear "hardware," the technology of nuclear weapons. Subsequent sections take up the human side of nuclear weapons: the "software."

# 1 How a Nuclear Bomb Works

*If I had known, I would have been a locksmith.*
Albert Einstein

There are several different kinds of energy, such as energy of position—like the energy available in water about to fall from a height and turn an electric generator—or chemical energy, present in the chemical bonds that hold atoms together. Energy of position is released when something falls; chemical energy is released when something burns or explodes. There is also nuclear energy, present in mass itself and described in Einstein's famous equation $E = mc^2$. Nuclear energy is the stuff of the stars, including our own sun. As we shall soon see, small amounts of nuclear energy are released gradually and naturally, through the process known as "radioactive decay." However, when atoms are split apart or fused together, immense quantities of energy, not otherwise experienced on our planet, are released. This is the stuff of nuclear weapons.

## ATOMIC STRUCTURE

To understand nuclear energy, we must begin with the atom, basic chemical unit of matter. Every element on earth (carbon, oxygen, hydrogen, iron, etc.) is made of its own kind of atom. But even the atoms of different elements are similar to each other, since they are made of the same building blocks, the same kinds of subatomic particles. The atoms of each element, then, are variations on a common theme.

Atoms are composed essentially of different numbers of protons, neutrons, and electrons (Fig. 1.1). A "solar system" model of the sun, although not entirely accurate, provides a good approximation to understanding basic atomic structure. In this model, the protons and neutrons are huddled together in the center

of the atom: the **nucleus.** Therefore, they are called **nucleons.** Electrons are outside, somewhat like planets orbiting the sun. Unlike the planets, however, electrons do not really circle the nucleus; rather, they occupy different energy and probability levels.

**Protons** have a positive electric charge, considered to equal + 1. **Neutrons** are neutral, with an electric charge of 0, and **electrons** have a negative electric charge, considered to equal − 1. Protons and neutrons have weight—more accurately, mass—since this property is independent of the earth's gravity. Electrons are so light that their mass is usually considered to be zero. The mass of a neutron is actually slightly more than that of a proton, and in fact, "neutron" is sometimes defined as a proton combined with an electron.

Since an atom's nucleus contains only protons and neutrons, it is positively charged. This condition is balanced by the negative charges carried by the electrons surrounding the nucleus, making atoms electrically neutral. In theory, atoms can gain positive electric charge by acquiring additional protons; in practice, however, atoms resist changes to their nucleus, and so, if they become more positive, they are likely to do so by losing electrons. Similarly, they can become electrically negative by gaining electrons. Whenever an atom's electrical charge becomes unbalanced because of the addition or subtraction of electrons, it is said to have been "ionized"; that is, the atom has become an **ion.**

The number of protons determines the kind of each atom. If a nucleus has one proton, for example, it is hydrogen; two protons, helium; three protons, lithium, and so on. The **atomic number** of an element is simply the number of protons (the number of positive charges)

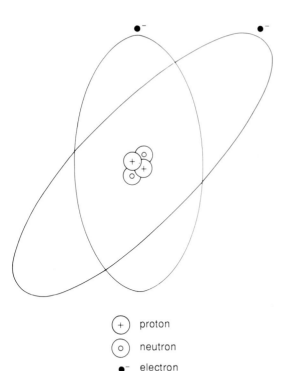

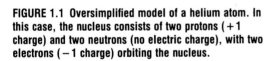

⊕ proton

⊙ neutron

●⁻ electron

**FIGURE 1.1 Oversimplified model of a helium atom. In this case, the nucleus consists of two protons ( + 1 charge) and two neutrons (no electric charge), with two electrons ( − 1 charge) orbiting the nucleus.**

within its nucleus. The atomic number of hydrogen, then, is 1. The atomic number of helium, the next heaviest element, is 2, and so on. Among the very heavy elements, the atomic number of uranium is 92, since there are 92 protons in the uranium nucleus. However, uranium is more than 92 times heavier than hydrogen, because uranium contains a large number of neutrons as well, and as we have seen, neutrons are about as heavy as protrons. So, the atomic number of an atom must be distinguished from its atomic weight. The **atomic weight** of an element is the sum of the protons and neutrons in one atom.

In the case of hydrogen, atomic number and atomic weight are the same—1—because hydrogen has no neutrons; it consists of a single proton in the nucleus, and one electron. But helium, for example, has an atomic

weight of 4, because it consists of two protons plus two neutrons. Oxygen has an atomic number of 8 and an atomic weight of 16: eight protons and eight neutrons. Although the number of neutrons tends to be about the same as the number of protons, this doesn't always hold, especially among the heavier elements, in which the number of neutrons increases more rapidly than the number of protons. The most common form of uranium, for example, has 92 protons and 146 neutrons, for an atomic weight of 238.

When describing an atom, we often want to specify both its atomic number and its atomic weight; this is usually done by writing its atomic number (the number of protons) as a left-hand subscript to the abbreviation for the element, and its atomic weight (the number of protons plus neutrons) as a left-hand superscript. Thus, hydrogen can be designated $^1_1H$, helium as $^4_2He$, and so on. However, since the atomic number specifies the nature of the element, it is redundant with the abbreviation for that element and is often omitted.

It is also possible to add neutrons to an atom (or, more rarely, to subtract them), in which case these changes create an unstable version of the original element. When an element exists in two or more species having the same atomic number but different atomic weights, we call these similar forms, or species, **isotopes.** For example, the usual carbon atom has six protons and six neutrons and can therefore be written $^{12}_6C$ or C-12, in accordance with the convention explained earlier; namely, atomic weight is indicated by a left-hand superscript.* A small proportion of carbon atoms naturally have two additional neutrons, however, and are therefore written C-14. Similarly, most hydrogen exists as H-1, although a small proportion of naturally appearing hydrogen also contains a neutron, and is known as **deuterium** (D), or H-2. Under laboratory conditions, another form of hydrogen can be generated; it contains two neutrons and is known as **tritium** (T), or H-3. Because isotopes differ from the usual form of an element only by containing additional neutrons, they are chemically indistinguishable from the parent element. Thus, two atoms of deuterium can combine with

---

*The left-hand superscript nomenclature, which is found in physics and chemistry texts and in technical publications, is presented here for completeness. For the remainder of the book, however, isotopes are designated in the way they are spoken, that is, using the hyphenated form: "C-12 is the stable isotope of carbon," "H-2 is deuterium," "H-3 is tritium," and so on.

a single atom of oxygen to form "heavy water," or $D_2O$, just as the stable isotope of hydrogen reacts with oxygen to form $H_2O$.

Most of the changes that happen to atoms involve changes in their surrounding electrons. These changes are known as chemical reactions, and when they occur, the nucleus is not changed. Thus, hydrogen can be burned, in which case it combines with oxygen to form water, $H_2O$; the hydrogen and oxygen still exist, however, and in fact the two elements can be separated by other chemical and electrical processes, such as by exposure to an electric current.

However, sometimes changes can be induced in the nucleus of an atom. These **nuclear reactions** are especially likely among unstable isotopes, that is, isotopic forms of an element that because of their added neutron(s) are, in a sense, physically overburdened. We can imagine that depending on its atomic number, each nucleus is designed to carry a certain number of neutrons, usually about equal to the number of protons, but as we have seen, not exactly. So, when extra neutrons are added to the nucleus of an atom, the unstable isotope begins to shift around, throwing off various subatomic particles and other forms of energy as well. Such an atom is **radioactive.**

## RADIOACTIVITY

Very large atoms, with an atomic number of 83 or more, are normally radioactive, even if they are not burdened artificially with extra neutrons. Even small, stable atoms can be made radioactive, however, if they are bombarded with small, fast-moving particles and thereby transformed into unstable isotopes.

Radioactive atoms radiate energy and materials largely in four different forms: **alpha particles, beta particles,** neutrons, and **gamma rays** and X-rays. Alpha particles are essentially helium nuclei, consisting of two protons and two neutrons. They are large, and therefore unable to penetrate very much material: just a few thousandths of a centimeter (cm) of water or body tissue (about the thickness of a sheet of paper), or about 2.5 cm of air. So-called **alpha emitters** can cause serious damage to living things, however, if they are eaten or breathed. This is because as they collide with the molecules of living matter, they transfer their energy to the objects that are struck, leaving a heavy track of ionization, although one that is rather short. The artificially produced element plutonium, for example, is a radioactive alpha emitter, and just a few micrograms

of inhaled plutonium is almost guaranteed to cause lung cancer.

Beta particles can be electrons, emitted when a neutron undergoes "beta decay," producing a proton and an electron. Beta particles can also be "positrons" (like electrons, only positively charged). Beta particles travel farther than alpha particles, but they are readily deflected by the electrons bound to existing atoms.

When an atom has been bombarded by other particles, it may simply emit some of its excess neutrons. Because neutrons lack any electric charge, they do not cause ionization in their surroundings. However, when they crash into other nuclei, they may cause them to be changed, or transmuted, into different elements, and they may also produce injury to living tissue, including modifications in genetic material known as **mutations.** As we shall soon see, under special circumstances, neutrons can be especially important in initiating nuclear fission, hence nuclear explosions. This is because in some cases, the instability caused by an additional neutron striking with high energy is sufficient to induce a nucleus to split.

Finally, gamma rays and X-rays can be thought of as particles of virtually no weight, identical to particles of light, or photons. (Gamma rays, incidentally, are also formed when a positron combines with an electron, after which both disappear, releasing their energy as a gamma ray.) Gamma rays are about a million times more energetic than visible light. They penetrate tissue quite easily and produce substantial ionization because they travel so far. X-rays are much less energetic than gamma rays but are physically similar. Alternatively, these rays are often described as consisting of waves rather than particles. As such, they are a form of **electromagnetic radiation,** which is a kind of wave motion produced when electric charges oscillate and produce an electric field. All radiation of this sort travels at the speed of light. The most familiar kind of electromagnetic radiation is visible light, which can be thought of either as a series of particles (photons) or as an electromagnetic wave. Gamma rays and X-rays have very short wavelengths; accordingly, they vibrate at high frequencies. Their photons are highly energetic compared to other forms of electromagnetic radiation; hence they are capable of doing substantial damage to living tissue. Electromagnetic radiation of progressively longer wavelength takes the forms of ultraviolet (UV) light, visible light, infrared (IR) radiation, radar, and finally, at the far end of the electromagnetic spectrum, radio waves with very long wavelengths, lower frequencies, and relatively little energy per "particle."

When unstable isotopes emit radiation that results in a change in their atomic number, they are transmuted into other species. Each isotope undergoes a pattern of radioactive emission or **radioactive decay** that is characteristic of that isotope. Many of the heavy radioactive elements, such as plutonium and uranium-235, decay by emitting alpha particles. (As a result, their atomic number is reduced by 2 and their atomic weight is reduced by 4.) By a combination of alpha and beta decay, each radioactive element is eventually transformed by a predictable sequence into progressively smaller atoms, until it eventually settles in a stable form, at which point it is no longer radioactive. Sometimes it takes thousands or even millions of years for a radioactive element to be transmuted into a nonradioactive descendant. In other cases, only a few millionths of a second is necessary. The life span of a radioactive substance is measured as its **half-life,** the time it takes, on average, for half the original substance to decay into something else. For example, carbon normally has an atomic number of 12; its radioactive isotope, carbon-14, has a half-life of 5,700 years. Thus, if we start with 8 grams of C-14, after 5,700 years, we will have 4 grams; after 11,400 years, 2 grams, and so on. Plutonium has a half-life of about 26,000 years; strontium-90 (Sr-90) has a half-life of 28 years. Note that a substance with a long half-life is not necessarily any more radioactive than one with a short half-life. In fact, a short half-life may indicate that a large amount of radiation is given off in a very brief time. Radioactivity may therefore be quite intense during this period.

## THE SOURCE OF NUCLEAR ENERGY

All atoms larger than hydrogen contain two or more protons, held close together in the nucleus. Since their positive charges can be expected to repel each other, these protons must be glued together by a very powerful force. This is the so-called nuclear or "strong force," and it operates only over very short distances. This strong force is also referred to as the "binding energy" of the nucleus. If enough energy pries the protons in a nucleus apart, electrostatic repulsion between the protons takes over, and the nucleus flies apart, or undergoes **fission.** With this process of nuclear fissioning, or splitting of the atomic nucleus, enormous amounts of energy are released. But where does this energy come from? And what causes it to be released.?

The energy that is released in nuclear fission can be calculated from Einstein's famous equation, $E = mc^2$. This describes the amount of energy $(E)$ contained within matter, and is worth examining a bit more closely. The constant, $c$, is the speed of light, 186,000 miles per second, and $c^2 = 34,596,000,000$, a very large number indeed. As a result, when it comes to changing matter into energy, a little goes a long way. The amount of mass actually converted into energy via a nuclear reaction is the difference between the mass of the intact nuclei and the masses of the fission products that result after fissioning occurs. When a large nucleus splits, it does so in a variety of ways, producing an array of medium-sized nuclei. The protons and neutrons of such medium-sized atoms as iron, strontium, and cesium are slightly smaller than those making up very large atoms such as uranium and plutonium. As a result, when a uranium atom is split, forming, say, two medium-sized atoms, the protons and neutrons that remain are slightly smaller than they were before; the amount of mass transformed into energy according to Einstein's equation is this difference between the mass before and after a nucleus is split.

To understand why the nucleons of medium-sized atoms are smaller than the nucleons of large atoms, we must consider the strong force, the binding energy of atoms, which keeps the nucleus together. Among very large and also very small atoms, each constituent nucleon has less binding energy than do the nucleons of medium-sized atoms. As a result, they have somewhat more mass, and this difference in mass becomes available for conversion into energy whenever large atoms split (fission) or small atoms fuse into a larger one, in the process known as **fusion** (Fig. 1.2).*

## ATOMIC BOMBS IN THEORY

Chemical energy can often be extracted rather easily. For example, it is not too difficult to start a wood fire, in which the carbon combines chemically with oxygen, releasing heat as well as light. The energy released in a wood fire had been stored in the position and orientation of the element's electrons, not in its nucleus. After a fire, the atoms in question are the same as they

---

*For full source of Figure 1.2 and other figures throughout credited with name(s) and date only, see the source information section at the end of the book.

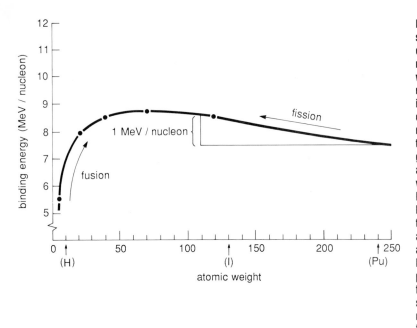

**FIGURE 1.2 The relationship between binding energy, contained in the nucleus, and the atomic weight of various elements. This binding energy is expressed in millions of electron volts (MeV) per nucleon (1 electron volt is the amount of energy gained by one electron accelerating through one volt of electric potential). Note that the maximum binding energy is contained in elements of atomic weight of about 50; as a result, the fission of larger elements such as plutonium (Pu) or the fusion of smaller elements such as hydrogen (H), releases energy.** (Modified from Schroeer, 1984.)

had been before, although they are combined into different compounds with less stored energy. By contrast, nuclear energy is released when an atom is transmuted from one kind to another. The energy released in a nuclear reaction is about one million times ($10^6$) greater per atom involved than in a chemical reaction. Not surprisingly, it is much more difficult to initiate a nuclear reaction than a chemical one—but once begun, the results are far more dramatic.

For nuclear fission to occur, with its enormous release of energy, two things are needed: a bombarding particle and some target material. Neutrons are convenient bombarding particles, since they carry a lot of momentum (much more than electrons or positrons, for example) and, since they have no electric charge, they are not deflected by the charges of the target substance. As for target material, uranium is a good candidate: this large molecule contains enough protons (which spontaneously repel each other) to be made unstable. A half-century ago, the Italian physicist Enrico Fermi (Fig. 1.3) experimentally bombarded various elements—especially uranium—with neutrons and created new, radioactive elements, which themselves underwent spontaneous radioactive decay. During the mid-1930s, however, it was still believed that atoms were indivisible, and Fermi's results were not inter-

preted as the splitting of atoms. In 1938, the German physicists Otto Hahn and Fritz Strassmann observed that new elements appeared to have been produced when uranium was bombarded with neutrons. Shortly afterward, others recognized that uranium had in fact been split and that the substances observed were medium-sized, "daughter" nuclei, newly produced.

The splitting of a small number of atoms releases energy, but not all that much, since the energy liberated by fissioning a single nucleus, after all, is quite small. If one wishes to release large amounts of energy, therefore, it is necessary to split large numbers of nuclei within a very short time. To accomplish this, one must have many highly energetic neutrons flying about. In this respect, uranium possesses certain crucially important characteristics: when uranium splits, it (1) forms several medium-sized atoms (thereby releasing the sought-for energy) and (2) releases additional free-flying neutrons. These free neutrons can bombard other uranium atoms, splitting them and not only releasing the energy liberated in the transformation from large atoms to medium-sized ones, but also producing additional free-flying neutrons that can go on to split yet more nuclei. If, on average, more neutrons escape from the target material or are harmlessly absorbed than are released in the fission process, the reaction cannot be

**FIGURE 1.3 Physicists Enrico Fermi (rear, center) and Niels Bohr (front, left) at a scientific meeting. Fermi is considered one of the great experimental physicists of all time, and Bohr, one of the great theoreticians.** (Photo courtesy of the American Institute of Physics, Niels Bohr Library.)

Fermi. This device began operation in late 1942. Three years later, the first atomic bombs were constructed.

The following chart summarizes some of the main events in the first half-century of modern nuclear physics.

| | |
|---|---|
| 1896 | Henri Becquerel discovers radioactivity, finding that rays coming from uranium ore can expose a photographic plate. (Stimulated by this work, the Curies later isolated the element radium from pitchblende.) |
| 1905 | Albert Einstein publishes his theoretical work on the equivalence of matter and energy. |
| 1911 | Ernest Rutherford discovers the atomic nucleus, suggesting that atoms are largely empty space, with most of their mass concentrated in the center and positively charged. |
| 1913 | Niels Bohr proposes that electrons are arranged around the atomic nucleus in a distinct pattern of shells. |
| 1920 | Rutherford suggests the existence of a subatomic particle without electrical charge. |
| 1932 | James Chadwick discovers the neutron, thus confirming Rutherford's speculation, giving added credence to atomic theory, and providing researchers with a convenient tool for splitting atoms. |
| 1934 | Enrico Fermi unknowingly achieves the world's first nuclear fission by bombarding uranium with neutrons. |
| 1938 | Otto Hahn and Fritz Strassmann recover the elements barium and krypton after bombarding uranium with neutrons. |
| 1938–1939 | Otto Frisch and Lise Meitner deduce that Hahn and Strassmann had in fact caused uranium to fission (Fig. 1.4). |
| 1939 | At the suggestion of Eugene Wigner and Leo Szilard, Einstein writes to President Roosevelt, warning of the possibility of a German atomic bomb, and urging acceleration in the research and development of such a weapon. |
| 1942 | The Manhattan Project is established, under the scientific direction of J. Robert Oppenheimer. |
| 1942 | The first controlled, sustained chain reaction is achieved, by a team at the University of Chicago under the leadership of Enrico Fermi. |
| 1945 | First atomic bombs. |

self-sustaining. It quickly peters out. On the other hand, if for every large nucleus that is fissioned, one neutron is released, which in turn goes on to fission one other nucleus, a **chain reaction** has been produced, and this **self-sustaining** process can continue as long as fissionable ("fissile") fuel is made available. The first chain reaction was achieved in an experimental reactor built at the University of Chicago under the leadership of

In a self-sustaining reaction, the rate of fissioning can be controlled by inserting **control rods,** materials that absorb the free-flying neutrons and therefore can damp the process, much as controlling the rate of airflow into a wood-burning stove controls the speed of the combustion. Nuclear power reactors are based on the controlled fissioning of nuclear fuel, with the released energy used ultimately to generate electricity. Usually the controlled heat of a nuclear reactor is used to vaporize water into steam, which turns electric generators.

But what if the goal is not the controlled release of nuclear energy, but rather, its very rapid, uncontrolled, explosive release? Then, no control rods are used, and the target material must be more tightly packed together, so that very few neutrons escape. Under these conditions, the neutrons that are emitted when a nucleus fissions are likely to be captured by other nuclei, splitting them in turn, and releasing yet more neutrons. If each uranium nucleus, when it splits, produces more than the one neutron needed to split it in the first place, and if this keeps happening, the number of neutrons produced will increase very quickly. The number of fissioning nuclei therefore rises exponentially as well, so that an enormous number of nuclei are split in a very short period of time, releasing a vast amount of energy.

The process is analogous to the compounding of interest, or a population explosion. If, for example, every uranium nucleus, when it splits, releases two neutrons, and every neutron, in turn, splits another nucleus, we get the geometric progression: 2, 4, 8, 16, . . . (Fig. 1.5). As it happens, U-238 is not a suitable candidate for such a process, since it releases fewer neutrons than it absorbs. However, a rare, naturally occurring isotope, U-235, not only splits readily, but when it fissions it releases on average about two neutrons for every one that it absorbs. Each reaction is very quick, taking about 0.00000001 second (10 microseconds). If we begin with a single fissioning nucleus of U-235, it takes only 0.00000002 second for two nuclei to have fissioned, 0.00000003 second for four, 0.00000004 second for eight, and so on. At this rate, in only 0.00000058 second, 58 doublings have occurred, and by this time, $2^{57}$ nuclei will have been split. This is an enormous number, approximately 2 followed by 24 zeros. An entire nuclear explosion of this sort can easily take place in less than a millionth of a second. In this example, the energy equivalent to the explosion of 100,000 tons of TNT will have been released. The yields of fission explosions are typically measured in this way, compared to the amount of energy that would be released by the explosion of various amounts of TNT. Since a **kiloton** (kt) is the energy equivalent to 1,000 tons of TNT, the example above represents a 100-kiloton explosion. By way of contrast, the largest conventional bombs used during World War II averaged about 10 tons of TNT.

**FIGURE 1.4 Physicists Lise Meitner and Otto Hahn. Meitner and her colleague Otto Frisch deduced that Hahn and Strassmann had fissioned the uranium nucleus.** (Photo courtesy of the American Institute of Physics, Niels Bohr Library; from Otto Hahn, *A Scientific Autobiography,* Charles Scribner's, New York, 1966.)

## ATOMIC BOMBS IN PRACTICE

As we have seen, the most abundant natural form of uranium, U-238, is not suitable for fissioning, whereas the naturally occurring isotope U-235, can be used for this purpose. However, U-235 is present in natural uranium ore in a concentration of only about 0.7% (the remaining 99.3% is U-238). Since the two forms are chemically indistinguishable, separating them is extremely difficult. The process of **uranium enrichment** requires enormous amounts of energy. The most common technique employed today is gaseous diffusion (Fig. 1.6), in which the uranium is converted into the gas uranium hexafluoride, $UF_6$. The molecules composed of U-238, being somewhat heavier than those containing the lighter isotope U-235, diffuse a bit more slowly through a porous membrane. By subjecting an initial sample to a large number of such diffusion steps, it is possible to increase the concentration of U-235 to about 3%, which is suitable for use as reactor fuel—or to 90% or more, suitable for use in an atomic bomb.

The next problem is to get enough fissile material together at one time. When the amount is too small, free neutrons escape from the surface and an insufficient number are captured by other target nuclei. With U-235, for example, a lump as big as a golf ball is too small. But a grapefruit-sized lump, weighing about 10

neutron
generation:     1             2             3             4             5

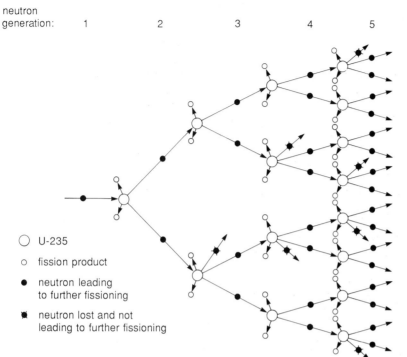

**FIGURE 1.5 A chain reaction involving the fissioning of U-235. In this idealized diagram, 2.5 neutrons are released on average for every splitting of U-235; of these, one out of five are lost (they either are absorbed or escape from the fissioning mass), while the others go on to split additional nuclei.**
(Modified from Schroeer, 1984.)

○  U-235

○  fission product

●  neutron leading
   to further fissioning

✹  neutron lost and not
   leading to further fissioning

kilograms (kg), is large enough to ensure the required energy release: the resulting chain reaction spreads with extraordinary speed once the amount of fissionable material present has exceeded the **critical mass** so that it is not only self-sustaining but geometrically increasing. The actual splitting of a nucleus is essentially instantaneous, so the speed of each doubling in a fission explosion depends on the time required for a neutron to travel from a just-split nucleus to the next nucleus. Since even a very dense material such as uranium is mostly empty space, free-flying neutrons must go on average about 3 cm before striking the next nucleus. But since neutrons travel at virtually the speed of light, it takes only about 0.1 nanosecond (one tenth of a billionth of a second) for this to occur. And because the number of neutrons released and the number of nuclei split doubles every generation, about as much energy is released during the last nanosecond as during all the preceding time. This is why a nuclear explosion results in such a large release of energy, concentrated in a very short time period.

It is important that a supercritical mass of nuclear explosive be reached very quickly. If this fails to occur—because an improper amount of explosive was used—

or because this material was not brought together promptly enough—the bomb will not work. Without enough U-235 in the same place at the same time, an explosion will not occur; with too much material, or if the material is brought together too slowly, a weak, premature detonation will result and the target material will be blown apart by the early stages of the reaction. In the event of a premature explosion, much of the potentially fissionable material never splits and the resulting "fizzle yield" is much below what it could have been. In the Hiroshima bomb, which had a yield of about 13 kilotons, subcritical masses of U-235 were kept at opposite ends of a gun barrel 52 inches long. High-quality gunpowder propelled the smaller mass toward the larger, thereby achieving the critical mass quickly. To help initiate the chain reaction once the U-235 was compressed to supercriticality, a small neutron emitter, made of the radioactive element polonium, was also provided. (Once initiated, of course, the reaction is self-sustaining and needs no further help.)

The man-made element plutonium (Pu) is even more efficient than U-235 as a nuclear explosive. It releases somewhat more energy when fissioned, is more readily fissioned, and releases somewhat more

**FIGURE 1.6 Gaseous diffusion plant at Portsmouth, Ohio, used for uranium enrichment.** (Photo courtesy of the US Department of Energy.)

neutrons as well. Plutonium is one of the by-products of the irradiation of uranium in a reactor; hence it can be extracted (**reprocessed**) from spent reactor fuel or produced in a "breeder reactor," which begins with U-235 and can produce continuing amounts of plutonium from inputs of U-238.

The world's first atomic bomb, exploded near Alamogordo, New Mexico, on July 16, 1945 (Fig. 1.7), was made of plutonium, as was the third such device, exploded over Nagasaki with a yield of about 20 kilotons. These bombs were designed somewhat differently from the Hiroshima bomb, which relied for its explosive power on U-235.

Plutonium is highly unstable and even more difficult to work with than U-235. For example, in addition to the principal isotope, Pu-239, the weapon material invariably contains some Pu-240, which emits neutrons. If neutron emission were to proceed unchecked, spontaneous and premature fissioning would occur before a supercritical mass could be achieved. To prevent this "fizzling," the preferred design of a plutonium bomb consists of a carefully machined sphere of plutonium, surrounded by layers of conventional explosive (Fig. 1.8). The conventional explosives are detonated so as to compress the plutonium uniformly toward the center, "imploding" it to the point of supercriticality. Once

again, a small neutron emitter, made of polonium, is provided to help get the chain reaction started.

To increase the efficiency of atomic bombs, the fissionable explosive is also typically surrounded with a layer of material that reflects neutrons that might otherwise fly out of the system. Both U-238 and the metal beryllium work quite nicely for this, acting a bit like the inner surface of a pressure cooker and keeping the neutrons contained, forcing them to continue to bombard the fissionable fuel. With this additional sheathing, or "**tamper**," the amount of fissile material required is greatly reduced.

The burning of a single atom of carbon—as in coal, oil, or wood—releases about 3 eV of energy (for definition of electron volt, see caption to Fig. 1.2). By contrast, the fissioning of a single atom of uranium yields about 200 MeV. The bomb that destroyed Hiroshima weighed about 10,000 pounds and contained about 25 pounds of uranium (Fig. 1.9). Since this bomb was relatively primitive, it was inefficient, and only about 1%, roughly 4 ounces, of the uranium actually fissioned. Even less was actually converted into energy: less than 1/30 of an ounce! Yet, this was enough to create temperatures of one hundred million degrees, and to kill about 100,000 people. The power of the sun and the stars had been brought to the planet Earth.

## HYDROGEN BOMBS IN THEORY

Atomic bombs are powerful, but hydrogen bombs are more powerful yet. Hydrogen bombs differ from atomic bombs in that they derive part of their energy from **fusion**—the joining together of smaller atoms—rather than just from fission, the splitting apart of larger ones. Physicist Hans Bethe demonstrated in 1937 that the sun's energy is derived from fusion reactions. The first fusion explosion on earth occurred in 1952, following a crash program instituted just two years before.

As we have seen, an enormous amount of energy is released when large nuclei split, producing medium-sized nuclei. A similar process of energy release can also occur when the smallest nuclei are fused into larger ones. Like those of very large nuclei, the nucleons making up very small, lightweight atoms are also somewhat greater in mass than are medium ones: the binding energy of very light nuclei increases with increases in atomic number (see Fig. 1.2). As a result, when two very small nuclei fuse to form a somewhat larger nucleus, the nucleons in question once again lose some mass. And this mass, once again, is released as energy. Fusion also typically releases a neutron, but this is not crucial to maintaining the fusion process itself, since this reaction depends on small nuclei being forced together rather than on neutrons prying large atoms apart, as in fission. (As we shall see, however, there is real significance to the neutrons that are released when small nuclei fuse.)

A great deal of energy is required to cause nuclei to fuse, since the positively charged protons tend to repel each other. The smallest nuclei, containing the fewest protons, are the most fusible. The preferred fuel for nuclear fusion is therefore hydrogen (H-1) and its two isotopes, deuterium (H-2) and tritium (H-3). Deuterium occurs naturally and is stable. It can rather easily be concentrated as heavy water, by diffusion or electrolysis, which separates $D_2O$ from the more common $H_2O$, in a process analogous to the separation of U-235 from U-238. Tritium, on the other hand, can only be produced artificially, by bombarding the element lithium with neutrons; it is radioactively unstable and has a half-life of 12.3 years.

The most convenient fusion reaction involves combining deuterium and tritium, yielding an unstable isotope of helium, which in turn releases a neutron, forming stable helium and also releasing energy:

$$D + T = He\text{-}4 + neutron + 17.6\ MeV$$

**FIGURE 1.7 The world's first atomic explosion, detonated near Alamogordo, New Mexico, on July 16, 1945.** (Photo courtesy of Los Alamos National Laboratory.)

**FIGURE 1.8 The plutonium implosion device, known to Los Alamos scientists as "the gadget" prior to its detonation.** (Photo courtesy of Los Alamos National Laboratory.)

By contrast, the fissioning of a single uranium nucleus releases nearly 12 times more energy: 207 MeV. However, the fusion reaction above requires only five nucleons (two from D and three from T), whereas the fissioning of a very heavy nucleus involves an atom of uranium containing 235 nucleons. The fraction of the reacting substance that is actually converted into energy is therefore greater in the case of fusion than of fission—about 3.5 MeV for each fusing nucleon as opposed to about 0.8 MeV for each fissioning nucleon. (The exploding of TNT, by contrast, releases about 0.2 eV of energy per nucleon involved.) So, fusion is about five times more efficient than fission. And nuclear explosives are more than a million times more efficient than conventional explosives.

## HYDROGEN BOMBS IN PRACTICE

In addition to liberating more energy per mass of explosive, fusion bombs have an added advantage over fission: theoretically, there is no limit to their potential size. Thus, it is difficult to combine more than a certain amount of fission explosive at any one time in any one place without having the device, which has exceeded the critical mass, go off in the bomb builder's face, producing an inappropriately low yield, as well. This vexing problem does not arise with fusion bombs, since

deuterium and tritium do not have a critical mass at which they spontaneously explode; therefore, they can be heaped together in unlimited amounts, and then fused under intense heat and pressure.

However, an opposite problem arises: rather than combining spontaneously, tritium and deuterium will fuse only when subjected to enormous temperatures and pressures. This difficulty is solved by employing a relatively small fission bomb as a trigger to bring the tritium and deuterium up to "kindling" temperature and pressure. Because of this important role of temperature, fusion or hydrogen bombs are also known as *thermonuclear* bombs.

But there is another problem: both deuterium and tritium are gases at room temperature, and fusion is not feasible when there is so much space between the nuclei. Accordingly, the first, primitive fusion explosion used deuterium and tritium that were supercooled to liquid form. This required elaborate and bulky refrigeration devices, which made the entire structure much too large and heavy to be usable as a bomb. Subsequently, it was discovered that such bombs could be miniaturized by an ingenious chemical maneuver using lithium deuteride, a solid compound made by combining deuterium with Li-6, an isotope of lithium. When Li-6 absorbs a neutron, it undergoes fission, yielding helium, energy, and most important, tritium. The tritium can then fuse promptly with the deuterium already

**FIGURE 1.9 A model of the Hiroshima U-235 bomb, known as "Little Boy." It is 28 inches in diameter and 10 feet long.** (Photo courtesy of US Department of Defense.)

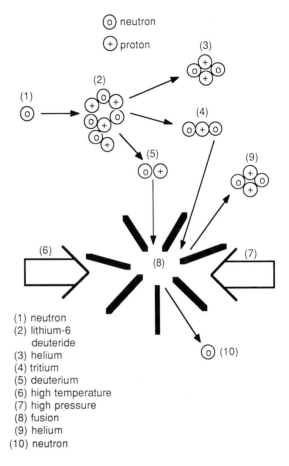

(1) neutron
(2) lithium-6
    deuteride
(3) helium
(4) tritium
(5) deuterium
(6) high temperature
(7) high pressure
(8) fusion
(9) helium
(10) neutron

**FIGURE 1.10 Diagram of the fusion process within a thermonuclear bomb. The exploding of the fission trigger releases energetic neutrons (1), which split lithium-6 deuteride (2), which in turn releases helium (3), tritium (4), and deuterium (5). The tritium and deuterium are forced together by the high temperature (6) and high pressure (7) of the initial fission explosion. They fuse (8), releasing another molecule of helium (9), another neutron (10), and an enormous amount of energy.**

present in the rest of the compound. The necessary neutron, of course, can be provided by the fission trigger. Accordingly, most of the tritium used in a fusion bomb is produced within the bomb itself, during the initial phase of the explosion (Fig. 1.10).

It is also necessary that the lithium, deuterium, and tritium be held together long enough for the high pressures and high temperatures of the fission trigger to squeeze it sufficiently to induce fusion. A hydrogen bomb is therefore further designed to focus the temperature and pressure on the fusion fuel. The intense X-rays of the initial fission explosion are typically focused by a compound of polystyrene foam, not unlike Styrofoam, which vaporizes and explodes, adding enormous pressure to a heavy U-238 tamper, which helps compress and heat the fusion fuel. A rod of plutonium or U-235 is also likely to be inserted within the fusion capsule. When compressed, this material reaches supercriticality and also explodes, thereby heating and compressing the fusion fuel from the inside as well.

There is yet another important aspect to thermonuclear or hydrogen bomb design. We have already mentioned that U-238 is not a suitable fuel for atomic bombs because it is not able to sustain a chain reaction by itself. However, at sufficient heat and pressure, it will fission, releasing great amounts of energy, comparable to U-235 or plutonium. Recall that the fusion reaction releases fast, highly energetic neutrons as well as energy itself. Although some of these neutrons contribute to the production of tritium during the fusion reaction, hydrogen bombs are generally designed to

produce some tritium in the fission trigger as well; these neutrons are not needed for the subsequent fusion process. Accordingly, these neutrons (plus the energy derived from the fusion explosion), can be used to split any U-238 that happens to be nearby.

U-238 is typically used as the tamper for the initial fusion explosion, as already described, and also as a jacket, surrounding the entire bomb and serving as a

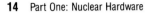

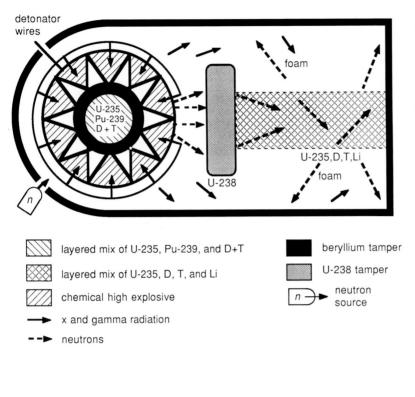

detonator wires

foam

U-235,D,T,Li

foam

U-238

U-235
Pu-239
D+T

*n*

layered mix of U-235, Pu-239, and D+T

layered mix of U-235, D, T, and Li

chemical high explosive

x and gamma radiation

neutrons

beryllium tamper

U-238 tamper

neutron source

*n*

**FIGURE 1.11 A typical hydrogen bomb design. An implosion fission bomb, using both U-235 and Pu-239 (as well as some deuterium and tritium) is at the left. After detonation of the (conventional) high explosives surrounding these materials, the fission device detonates, with the aid of a neutron trigger. The X-rays produced by this explosion are then focused by the foam within the compartment on the fusion components at the right. The pressure wave and heat serve to compress the uranium tamper, within which tritium and deuterium are produced by fissioning lithium deuteride, as shown in Fig. 1.10. The fusion reaction then takes place, after which the U-238 and the casing of the bomb proceed to fission.** (Modified from Schroeer, 1984).

neutron reflector, as with beryllium in an atomic (fission) bomb. This provides an additional bonus, since U-238 is abundant and inexpensive: a ton costs less than $20,000 and can add as much as 20 megatons (Mt) of explosive yield. (One **megaton** is equivalent to the explosion of one million tons of TNT.) Since U-238 is inert at normal temperatures and pressures, there is no limit to how much can be added to a fusion bomb, thereby boosting its yield immensely. Whereas the explosive yield of fission bombs is generally stated in kilotons, fusion bombs can be designed in the megaton range. This is because hydrogen bombs involve not only the more efficient fusion component, but also the splitting of potentially unlimited quantities of U-238. In this sense, a very large hydrogen bomb is usually in fact primarily a uranium bomb.

Fusion bombs are thus actually fission-fusion-fission bombs, although all three explosions take place so quickly that they seem to be a single event (Fig. 1.11).

In a sense, fusion is a relatively "clean" process, since unlike nuclear fission it does not directly generate radioactive products. "Cleanliness," however, is relative, since even in a fusion bomb, some material is irradiated by the neutrons that are released. Moreover, the fission trigger, even if relatively small, produces additional radioactive isotopes among its daughter products. The fissioning of the additional U-238 in a large fusion bomb gives rise to a wide array of extra radioactive by-products, thereby making boosted hydrogen bombs especially "dirty."

In the remainder of this text, we shall use the term "nuclear weapon" to refer to fission or fusion bombs, interchangeably. In the current arsenals of both the United States and the Soviet Union, most weapons are in fact thermonuclear, although some fission weapons also exist.

The earliest hydrogen bombs, produced during the mid-1950s and early 1960s, were exceptionally large: the largest hydrogen explosions in the US and in the

USSR were about 20 and 58 megatons, respectively. For reasons we shall explore later, both sides, especially the US, then reduced the total megatonnage in their arsenals. More recently, however, there has been some tendency to increase the yield of warheads once again. Most US **strategic** warheads—those intended for use against the homeland of the USSR—range from about 50 to 500 kilotons ($\frac{1}{20}$–$\frac{1}{2}$ megaton), whereas Soviet strategic warheads range from about 100 kilotons to 10 megatons. By contrast, **tactical** warheads, those intended for use on a specific battlefield, generally tend to be somewhat smaller: often 1–50 kilotons for the US and perhaps 20 kilotons to 1 megaton for the USSR. It should be noted, however, that large tactical nuclear weapons are larger than many small strategic weapons. The difference between "tactical" and "strategic" refers to their intended targets and their expected role—winning battles or winning wars, respectively—not their size. (We shall discuss this distinction in later chapters.) In general, however, strategic weapons tend to be larger than tactical ones.

## NEUTRON BOMBS

The second fission part of a hydrogen bomb, the final exploding of normally unfissionable U-238, is optional. It is possible to build a fission-fusion bomb that is mostly fusion, by using a small fission trigger to ignite the fusion part and omitting the additional uranium booster. Such a bomb still gives off a great deal of heat and blast (all nuclear weapons do this; see Chapter 4). However, it produces much less radioactive fallout, since its ratio of fission to fusion is very low. In addition, such an explosion produces large quantities of fast-moving neutrons, produced from the fusion of deuterium and tritium.

The result is a **neutron bomb,** also known as an "enhanced radiation warhead," because the amount of energy released as prompt radiation is about 30% of the total energy released, as compared to a traditional nuclear explosion, which gives off only about 5% of its energy in this form. **Prompt radiation** refers to immediate, short-lived, highly energetic radiation produced by the nuclear explosion itself, as opposed to the longer-lived and less energetic radioactive isotopes that eventually settle back to earth along with other debris from a nuclear explosion and are known as **fallout** (see Chapter 5). In the case of the neutron bomb, prompt radiation is released in the form of fast neutrons. Because they lack electric charge, neutrons can penetrate the armor of tanks, killing the crew inside.

Neutron bombs are almost pure fusion weapons, and they tend to be smaller than other hydrogen bombs, or even most fission (atomic) bombs. As such, they cause less **collateral damage:** destruction of noncombatants and property. And as we shall see later, this innovation has been especially appealing to strategists concerned about using nuclear weapons in relatively populated areas, such as Europe. Neutron bombs have been tagged the "ultimate capitalist weapon," since they kill people but are less devastating to property than, say, atomic bombs. It should be remembered, however, that neutron bombs are nonetheless nuclear weapons, and like all nuclear weapons, they produce enormous amounts of blast and heat as well.

## KEY TERMS

To aid the reader in locating individual terms—appearing in boldface in the text—the items are listed in the order in which they appear in the chapter, rather than alphabetically.

| | |
|---|---|
| nucleus | radioactive decay |
| nucleons | half-life |
| protons | fission |
| neutrons | fusion |
| electrons | chain reaction |
| ion | self-sustaining |
| atomic number | control rods |
| atomic weight | kiloton |
| isotopes | uranium enrichment |
| deuterium | critical mass |
| tritium | reprocessed |
| nuclear reaction | tamper |
| radioactive | megaton (Mt) |
| alpha particles | strategic |
| beta particles | tactical |
| gamma rays | neutron bomb |
| alpha emitters | prompt radiation |
| mutations | fallout |
| electromagnetic radiation | collateral damage |

## STUDY QUESTIONS

1. Define the following terms: radioactive, isotope, nucleon, binding energy, alpha particle, critical mass, fission, fusion.

2. What is the relationship of nuclear weapons to Einstein's equation, $E = mc^2$?

3. What is uranium enrichment, and why is it important?

4. Why are hydrogen bombs of potentially unlimited power, whereas fission bombs cannot be made more powerful than about 0.5 megaton?

5. What is the source of most of the tritium that fuels a fusion bomb?

6. What is the difference between neutron bombs and hydrogen bombs?

7. Distinguish between chemical energy and nuclear energy.

8. What are some similarities and some differences between nuclear power and nuclear explosions?

## ADDITIONAL READINGS

Glasstone, Samuel, and R. Lovberg. 1975. *Controlled Thermonuclear Fusion*. Huntington, NY: R. Krieger. A solid, technologically sound exposition for relatively advanced students.

Morland, Howard. 1980. The H-Bomb Secret. In *Time Bomb*. Madison, WI: The Progressive Foundation. An easily understood description of how H-bombs work. The US government attempted to prevent publication of the controversial article that is reprinted in this book.

Schroeer, Dietrich. 1984. *Science, Technology and the Nuclear Arms Race*. Reading, MA: Addison-Wesley. A wide-ranging introduction to the technological issues in the arms race, intended especially for students in the physical sciences.

Segre, Emilio. 1980. *From X-Rays to Quarks: Modern Physicists and Their Discoveries*. New York: W. H. Freeman. An excellent introduction to the major discoveries leading ultimately to nuclear weapons.

# 2 Delivery Systems

*I tell you that in the arts of life man invents nothing; but in the arts of death he outdoes Nature herself, and produces by chemistry and machinery all the slaughter of plague, pestilence and famine. . . . In the arts of peace, man is a bungler. . . . His heart is in his weapons.*
The Devil, in G. B. Shaw's *Man and Superman*

**D**elivery systems are the means whereby nuclear weapons are dispatched against an opponent. Such weapons are generally considered to be either strategic or tactical, although as we shall see in Chapter 3, a third category, somewhat intermediate between these, has recently been introduced. In military and political terms, "strategy" refers to a plan intended to help achieve one's long-range or ultimate goal, whereas "tactics" are the techniques employed to help achieve more immediate, short-term objectives. As indicated in Chapter 1, weapons are generally described as **strategic** if they are designed for possible use against the opponent's homeland; they are assumed to be instrumental in winning a war. **Tactical** weapons, by contrast, are intended for more localized, battlefield use in a specific engagement. Wherever it is located, and whatever its mission, a weapon is said to be **deployed** when it is fully operational and ready to be used. We can therefore speak of ICBMs deployed in missile silos in North Dakota, or of Soviet Backfire bombers deployed for possible use against China.

Controversy over the definition of strategic versus tactical nuclear weapons has arisen based on an important geographic asymmetry between the superpowers: the Soviet Union can be reached by medium-range weapons deployed in Europe and the western Pacific, whereas the United States can be reached only by Soviet weapons of longer range. Accordingly, the USSR defines any weapon that can reach a nation's homeland as strategic, whereas the US restricts this definition to intercontinental weapons. We shall examine the implications of this as well as other disagreements when we consider the problem of negotiating so-called Eurostrategic weapons (Chapter 10). For the present, we adopt the US definition, equating "strategic" with "intercontinental range." In Chapter 3, we shall briefly examine tactical nuclear weapons as well as conventional forces.

Strategic delivery systems are actually quite limited in variety and are divided into two basic kinds: bombers and missiles. Although in theory bombs could be delivered by suitcase or by automobile, in practice, nuclear bombs are generally free-falling gravity bombs, designed to be dropped from high-flying airplanes. By contrast, warheads are nuclear weapons carried on pilotless missiles.

Both American and Soviet strategic delivery systems are divided into a **triad,** or three different modes of delivering nuclear weapons to the other side's homeland. As we shall see, however, unlike the three legs of a stool or a tripod, the three legs of each nation's triad are not necessarily equal. In addition, the US and USSR have each emphasized different parts of their respective triads.

The strategic triad consists of long-range bombers, intercontinental ballistic missiles (ICBMs), and submarine-launched ballistic missiles (SLBMs). More recently, what some people consider a fourth leg is being added: cruise missiles. In this chapter, we shall review these various delivery systems and discuss the strategic balance between the US and the USSR.

## BOMBERS

The only nuclear weapons used in war thus far were gravity bombs dropped by American B-29 strategic bombers. Since World War II, the US has continued to develop a variety of strategic bombers: the B-36, B-47, and B-52, and now, more recently, the B-1 and

**FIGURE 2.1 The B-52 bomber. This model, a B-52H, was photographed in 1979 when it was carrying an experimental air-launched cruise missile under its left wing.** (Photo courtesy of the US Department of Defense.)

Stealth bombers. The B-52 is currently the backbone of the American strategic bombing fleet (Fig. 2.1). It has a cruising speed of Mach 0.77 (77% the speed of sound) and was introduced during the 1950s, with the most recent models produced in the mid-1960s. The age of these airplanes is a bit misleading, however, since they have regularly been upgraded, notably with new engines, electronic guidance systems, and various devices intended to overcome antiaircraft defenses. These devices are known collectively as **avionics.**

In addition, American forces include the FB-111, a supersonic, medium-range bomber that cannot make round trips from US soil to the USSR and back but can easily make round trips from forward bases in Europe. The FB-111 and the new B-1 (Fig. 2.2) have variable geometry wings, which are spread widely at low speeds to provide maximum lift, then retracted at high speeds to reduce drag.

## BOMBER-BASED MISSILES

Traditionally, bombers have been penetrating aircraft, flying over the opponent's territory. In recent years, this role has been diminished by the effectiveness of radar and surface-to-air missiles (the Soviet version of which are known, redundantly, as SAM missiles). As a result, during the mid-1960s and 1970s, the strategic role of B-52s was changed from that of very high overflight, to hedge-hopping missions as low as 50–150 meters above the ground, to duck under defending radar.

B-52s are also equipped with **short-range attack missiles** (**SRAMs,** pronounced "shrams"), effective up to 150 kilometers, and which make it unnecessary for targets to be directly overflown at all. As a result, bombers are rapidly becoming airborne launching pads for missiles. More recently yet, the tendency of bombers to become "launch platforms" for missiles of various sorts has been continued as B-52s have begun to be outfitted with **air-launched cruise missiles** (**ALCMs,** pronounced "al-kems") (Fig. 2.3).

Cruise missiles are small, pilotless jet planes. The V-1 missiles used by the Germans in World War II were cruise missiles, although much less accurate than today's models. Modern cruise missiles are small, about 7 meters long, and relatively inexpensive, costing about $1.5 million apiece. In addition to the air-launched version, there are **sea-launched cruise missiles** (**SLCMs,** pronounced "slick-ems"), and **ground-launched cruise missiles** (**GLCMs,** pronounced "glick-ems"). Cruise missiles have been made possible by two technologic factors: improved small-engine design that enables a range of more than 2,000 kilometers, and the development of computer-aided guidance systems that permit an accuracy of within 50 meters of the target.

Cruise missiles are designed to fly very low over enemy terrain, thereby evading radar. (Since radar tends to "look up" from ground installations, low-flying aircraft are very difficult to detect; on the other hand, cruise missiles might be detectable by such "look-down" technologies as airborn warning and control systems, like the American AWACS airplanes.) The initial stage of a cruise missile's flight is controlled by inertial guidance systems, which use gyroscopes to detect and

**FIGURE 2.2 The B-1 bomber.** (Photo courtesy of the US Department of Defense.)

adjust to deviations from a prepared flight path, as well as signals from navigational satellites. In its final approach to the target, cruise missiles are guided by a terrain-contour matching (**TERCOM**) system. The missile acquires a radar "picture" of the terrain by bouncing signals against the ground and comparing the resulting "echo" with a map stored in its computer memory. From these map readings, the missile corrects its flight path and homes in on the preselected target, with a reputed accuracy of up to 10 meters (Fig. 2.4).

As of 1986, several squadrons of 16 B-52s have been outfitted to carry 12 ALCMs apiece, in addition to 4 SRAMs and 4 gravity bombs. SRAMs, like ALCMs, carry 200-kiloton warheads, and gravity bombs are much larger yet, about 1 megaton. The ALCM program will be temporarily halted after 1,739 ALCMs have been produced; the next generation of cruise missiles, employing so-called Stealth or advanced technology, will eventually replace these ALCMs with missiles that use a combination of techniques to reduce detectability by the opponent's defense. Since radar detection relies on an object reflecting radar waves, it is possible to reduce the radar "cross section" by using nonmetallic surfaces, curved rather than angular design, as well as special radar-absorbing materials. In addition, special baffles can obscure and diminish the heat of engine exhausts, thereby foiling heat-seeking antimissile missiles.

## BOMBER STRATEGIES

### Bomber Types

The B-1 bomber was designed as a follow-on bomber to the B-52. The Carter administration canceled plans for the B-1, however, reasoning that B-52s are equally effective as cruise missile launchers and that, in any event, the B-1 would soon be replaced by the Stealth bomber, which—like its cruise missile counterpart—would be almost invisible to radar. The Reagan administration, however, reinstated plans to construct 100 B-1 bombers, incorporating some Stealth features into a modified version, known as the B-1B. It is planned that 100 B-1B bombers will be deployed in bases within the United States by 1988. In addition, 132 Stealth bombers will be fielded by 1991. These advanced technology aircraft will employ nonmetallic surfaces, engine modifications, and rounded surfaces to reduce the plane's radar cross section.

By contrast with the US, the USSR has never relied heavily on strategic bombing; even during World War II, while Britain and the US devoted substantial resources to strategic bombing, the USSR did not. The mainstay of the current Soviet bombing fleet is the Tu-95 (Tupelov) or Bear bomber (Fig. 2.5). This turboprop airplane, introduced in 1952, was not produced after 1962. A variant of the Bear bomber, however, entered production in late 1983, and about 20 are now active. There

**FIGURE 2.3  An air-launched cruise missile.** (Photo courtesy of the US Department of Defense.)

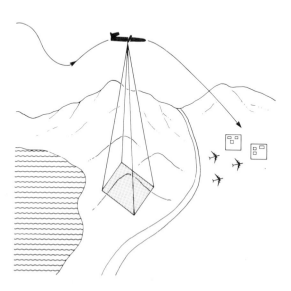

**FIGURE 2.4 TERCOM** guidance in a cruise missile permits it to correct its flight path by comparing the ground terrain with an on-board radar map, then proceeding close to its target (in this case, an airfield).

are also some Mya-4 or Bison bombers, produced in the mid-1950s and entirely jet powered. Some controversy surrounds the third Soviet bomber, the Tu-26 or Backfire. It is in many ways similar to the FB-111, in that it is a jet, larger than a fighter plane but smaller than a full-fledged strategic bomber. Like the FB-111, it has variable geometry wings. The Backfire has nearly twice the range of the FB-111, but only half the **payload** (bomb- and/or missile-carrying capacity).

The controversy is over whether the Backfire bomber should be counted as a strategic bomber. The US claims that it should, since Backfires could reach the mainland if they were refueled in air, if they made one-way suicide missions, or if they landed in Cuba after attacking the US. The USSR claims that the Backfire is of intermediate range only, intended for possible use in Europe, China, or against naval targets. It should be noted that the USSR has never had a significant midair refueling capacity, whereas the US has, and still does. Finally, reports regularly surface regarding a proposed new Soviet strategic bomber, known to the West as the Blackjack. It is believed that some Blackjack deployments may begin during the late 1980s.

The US continues to rely much more heavily on strategic bombers than does the USSR. Whereas only

**FIGURE 2.5 The Soviet Bear bomber.** (Photo courtesy of the US Department of Defense.)

**TABLE 2.1  US-USSR strategic bomber balance, as of 1985**

| Bomber | Payload | Number |
|---|---|---|
| B-52-D | 4 × 1 Mt bombs, 2 × 200 kt SRAMs | 31 |
| B-52-G | 4 × 1 Mt bombs, 4 × 200 kt SRAMs | 135 |
| *US* | | |
| B-52-G | 4 × 1 Mt bombs, 4 × 200 kt SRAMs, 12 × 300 kt ALCMs | 16 |
| B-52-H | 4 × 1 Mt bombs, 4 × 200 kt SRAMs | 90 |
| B-52s | | (187)[a] |
| Total active | | 272 |
| FB-111 | 2 × 200 kt SRAMs | (116)[b] |
| KC-135 tanker | | (646)[c] |
| B-1B | 8 × 300 kt ALCMs, 14 × 200 kt SRAMs; or 24 × 1 Mt bombs | 100[d] |
| *USSR* | | |
| Tu-95 Bear | 3 × 1 Mt | 120 |
| Mya-4 Bison | 2 × 1 Mt | 45 |
| Total | | 165 |
| Tu-26 Backfire | ? | (210)[b] |
| Tu-19 tanker | | (10)[c] |

[a]In inactive storage.
[b]Status as strategic bomber is disputed.
[c]Support aircraft.
[d]Projected.

about 5% of Soviet bombs and warheads are located on bombers, about 25% of the US strategic arsenal is deployed on B-52s and FB-111s. Table 2.1 shows the strategic bomber balance.

## Pros and Cons of Bombers

Since the US has invested much more heavily in bombers than has the USSR, American analysts have vigorously debated the pros and cons of strategic bombing as opposed to other means of delivering nuclear weapons. A bomber on a runway is a relatively **soft target,** that is, it is rather easily destroyed by a surprise attack. As a result, about 30% of B-52s are kept on "ready alert" at all times, able to take off with 15 minutes warning. During times of international tension, this can be increased to virtually 100%. By contrast, Soviet strategic bombers are not maintained on ready alert.

Until the early 1960s, a certain proportion of nuclear-armed B-52s were kept airborne at all times, to prevent their destruction in a surprise attack; this practice was discontinued after several crashes. Bomber survival is greater when response time is short—that is, when the airplanes are able to get off the ground quickly—and when notification time is long. The lowest bomber survival would therefore result from a "depressed trajectory" missile attack, in which incoming missiles, fired from submarines, gained relatively little elevation and therefore reached their targets quickly and with little advance warning. In times of crisis, B-52s would likely be moved to inland bases, where they would be less vulnerable to such an attack. It is currently estimated that virtually all B-52s on "generated alert" would be able to take off following warning of an attack.

Because the backbone of the Soviet strategic bomber fleet consists of Bear bombers, widely acknowledged to be obsolete, Soviet bombers are not considered to pose much threat to the US. The US therefore has only a minimal antibomber defense system. By contrast, the USSR has deployed extensive antiaircraft defenses, including more than 2,000 interceptor aircraft and 12,000 SAM launchers. Because they are relatively slow, bombers are considered to be more capable of being shot down than are ballistic missiles, which are currently invulnerable once launched. However, it is uncertain whether antiaircraft defenses will be effective against radar-evading B-52s coming in at low elevation. During the Vietnam war, for example, B-52s had to enter a very heavily defended perimeter, and yet they suffered an "attrition rate" of

only about 3%, even though the perimeter was relatively small. Because of SRAMs and ALCMs, modern bombers also do not necessarily have to penetrate Soviet airspace to be effective, which further suggests that bombers will be able to function successfully in the future. Finally, assuming that US bombers are to be used in retaliation for a Soviet first strike, they would not arrive at their targets until after US ICBMs and submarine-launched missiles had already arrived, almost certainly destroying airfields, antiaircraft facilities, and radar installations. Therefore, the effectiveness of Soviet antiaircraft systems probably would be greatly diminished. On the other hand, nuclear detonations produce huge quantities of dust (see Chapter 4), which might foul jet engines, thereby incapacitating them; of course, the same should apply to the effectiveness of fighter-interceptors, in which the USSR has invested heavily.

Unlike ballistic missiles, bombers can be retargeted while in the air. Another advantage of bombers is that also unlike ballistic missiles, they can be recalled after takeoff. In a crisis, bombers can be scrambled and sent airborne without irrevocably committing either side to nuclear war. This probably makes it less likely that nuclear war will occur by accident than in cases of missile launch, for example.

The controversies regarding strategic bombers reveal a frequent aspect of disagreement and misunderstanding regarding the US-Soviet military balance: selective attention to certain facts, combined with inattention to others. Thus, those who decry the age of American B-52s typically do not draw attention to their regular modernization and to the even older, less numerous, and much less competent Soviet bombers. Similarly, those who emphasize the superiority of the US bombing fleet tend to ignore the possible strategic role of the Backfire bomber. It can be misleading, for example, to point out that the USSR has greatly outinvested the US in antiaircraft weapons—including both short-range missiles and fighter-interceptors—without also noting that US bombers pose a threat to the USSR that is not reciprocated by Soviet bombers. Looking at the weapons alone, the US-Soviet nuclear balance does not hinge so much on comparisons of each system with its counterpart (bombers with bombers, etc.) but rather, on the question of whether each system is likely to be able to perform its mission (bombers vs. antiaircraft defenses, etc.).

There are many such cases in which fundamental asymmetries make comparison difficult; for example, the USSR can be reached not only by US strategic weapons but also by forward-based systems deployed in Europe, aboard aircraft carriers, or in Korea. The US, by contrast, is not similarly vulnerable to comparable Soviet delivery systems. The US also has several nuclear-armed allies, notably Britain and France, whereas all nuclear-armed nations—including China—are currently opponents of the USSR. On the other hand, the USSR does not have to concern itself about pacifying independent-minded allies, as does the US. The debate goes on, and there may well not be a simple, fixed answer. This makes it all the more important to understand the various sides.

## INTERCONTINENTAL BALLISTIC MISSILES

**Intercontinental ballistic missiles** or **ICBMs** are land-based missiles, located in both the US and the USSR, and aimed at each other. They are large, long-range missiles, capable of reaching speeds of more than 20 times the speed of sound, that is, Mach 20. ICBM flight time from the US to the USSR, or vice versa, is about 30 minutes.

### Operation

**Ballistic missiles** are powered by the initial force that sends them on their way; they do not have engines that operate continuously throughout their flight. Accordingly, they follow a ballistic trajectory that can be calculated knowing the initial momentum and orientation of the object. A thrown ball, an arrow released from a bow, and a speeding bullet all offer familiar examples of ballistic flight paths, which must be distinguished, for example, from the paths of a manned bomber or a cruise missile.

The flight of an ICBM can be divided into three main phases: the rocket-powered initial takeoff or **boost phase,** which carries it through the atmosphere; a **glide phase** above the atmosphere; and a **reentry phase,** as the warhead falls back into the atmosphere and to its target. (A fourth, or **postboost phase,** is sometimes identified between the boost and glide phases.) Since ICBMs are rockets, not jets like cruise missiles, all their fuel is self-contained and they can fly above the atmosphere. The warhead is located in the rocket's nose cone.

The German V-2 rockets of World War II were ballistic missiles, although very inaccurate and of course, conventionally armed. After 1945, German rocket engineers were employed extensively by both the US and the USSR for planning space explorations and designing ICBMs. The range of ballistic missiles increases with their velocity; velocities exceeding 8 kilometers

per second (km/sec) will place an object in earth orbit, whereas velocities exceeding 11.2 km/sec will cause it to escape the earth's gravity altogether. When velocity is less than 8 km/sec, the missile will fall back to earth. Typically, ICBMs, like outer space rockets, are built of several stages, with each stage falling off after its fuel has been used up. During the final reentry phase, only the warhead or **reentry vehicle (RV)** is left (Fig. 2.6A).

Early in the history of long-distance ballistic missiles, each missile carried only one warhead. Then, a new wrinkle was added, placing several warheads, called **multiple reentry vehicles (MRVs),** on a single missile. Typically, three MRVs were placed on one missile, and they separated during the reentry phase, so that three warheads, instead of one, struck the target (Fig. 2.6B). The effect is like throwing three rocks with one hand, or firing a shotgun shell with three pellets. Although MRVs are naturally more destructive than single warheads, they are not especially accurate, and a single MRVed rocket can be aimed at only one target. Neither the US nor the USSR currently maintains any MRVed missiles.

By the late 1960s, research had progressed on **multiple independently targetable reentry vehicles,** or **MIRVs** (pronounced to rhyme with "curves") (Fig. 2.7). MIRVs differ from MRVs in that the warheads are independently targetable—that is, each one is aimed separately. This is accomplished by discharging each warhead or reentry vehicle independently, while the missile is in the high-altitude glide phase. At this point, the booster rockets have fallen away, and the missile consists of its nose cone, or "bus." As the bus glides in its ballistic trajectory, it uses a gas jet or spring mechanism to eject a reentry vehicle, which then continues to follow a ballistic path as it falls back to earth. Meanwhile, back in the bus, small rockets fire, reorienting the bus somewhat, after which another reentry vehicle is ejected, and so on. Each reentry vehicle falls to earth following its own ballistic trajectory determined by the orientation of the bus at the time it was ejected. The bus, in turn, can continue zigging and zagging above the atmosphere, depositing its passengers, and directing each toward a different target, hundreds of miles apart (Fig. 2.6C).

### Accuracy

The destructive effect of a warhead is measured by its explosive force, usually equated to thousands or millions of tons of TNT (i.e., kilotons or megatons). How-

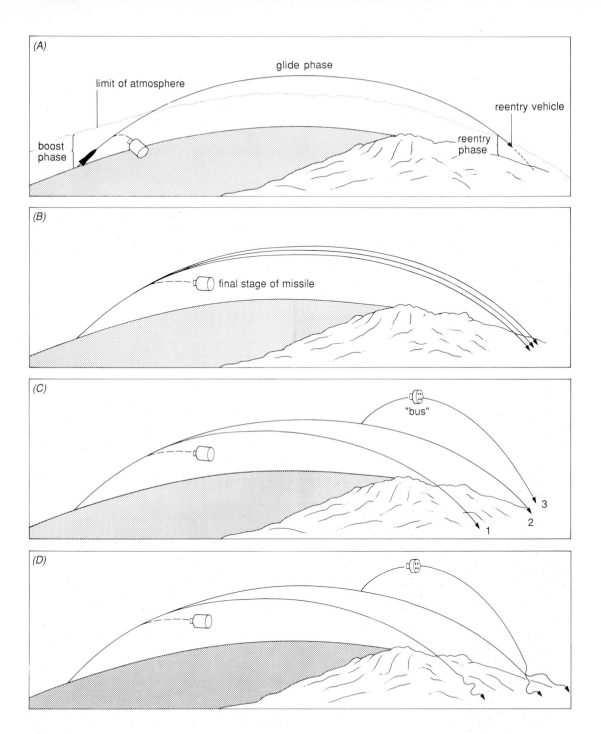

**FIGURE 2.6** The flight phases of an ICBM, also showing different reentry vehicle patterns. (**A**) A single-warhead missile, with just one RV. (**B**) A MRVed missile, with three RVs, which are not independently targeted. (**C**) A MIRVed missile, carrying three RVs, each of which is aimed at a different target. The "bus" delivers the first RV to target 1, reorients itself to permit the second RV to go to target 2, and so on. (**D**) A MARVed missile, carrying three RVs that are independently targeted and also maneuver prior to reaching their target.

**FIGURE 2.7 The nose cone of a Minuteman III missile, showing the three MIRVed warheads that are inside.** (Photo courtesy of the US Department of Defense.)

ever, the effectiveness of a nuclear weapon depends not only on its explosive force, but also on its distance from the target. Missile accuracy is actually defined by a quantity known as **circular error probable** or **CEP.** Imagine a target X, with a number of warheads fired at it. Those warheads will produce a scatter around the target; the greater the scatter, the more inaccurate the missile. CEP is a measure of that scatter, defined as the radius of a circle, drawn among the impacting warheads, such that half the warheads fall within that circle and half outside. In other words, the CEP is the average distance within which 50% of all incoming warheads can be expected to land. Smaller CEPs, therefore, are equivalent to greater consistency, which is generally considered to mean greater accuracy (Fig. 2.8).

In the early years of ICBM design, CEPs were typically measured in miles. More recently, CEPs have been reduced by an order of magnitude, and are now in the realm of a few hundred meters or less. If an ICBM trav-

els 10,000 miles and lands within 100 meters of its target, its aiming accuracy is about 6 parts per million. A football, thrown with comparable precision the entire length of the field, would strike within 0.02 inch of its target. Accuracy like this has profound implications for strategic doctrine, targeting policy, and weapons procurement decisions, as we shall see in Chapter 6. In addition, because of increases in missile accuracy, fears have been raised that each side is developing the ability to destroy the missiles of the opposing side. Since this issue has achieved great prominence during the 1980s, it warrants our special attention.

Increased missile accuracy has been made possible by the perfection of computer-aided **inertial guidance** systems, mounted in each missile: a combination of gyroscopes and accelerometers detects changes in the missile's momentum and corrects deviations from the preprogrammed flight plan by causing small modifications in the rocket exhaust. Greater accuracy yet may be obtained in the near future if ICBMs are connected to **NAVSTAR,** the latest system of navigational satellites. Accuracy also seems likely to be enhanced by techniques that enable missiles in flight to take sitings on stars, and/or from use of high-speed TERCOM systems similar to those of cruise missiles. The results are known as **MARVs,** for **maneuvering reentry vehicles** (Fig. 2.6D). MARVs were supposedly conceived as a means of ensuring that the target was reached by evading defensive weapons expected to be employed by an adversary. However, a terminal maneuvering capability would also convey increased accuracy, especially if the reentry vehicles were equipped to receive last-second navigational information from orbiting satellites. No MARVs have been deployed as of 1986, although they remain a possibility in the near future.

Aside from problems of reliability, substantial uncertainties must still be associated with the possible use of ballistic missiles to disarm an opponent. For example, consider missile **reliability,** which is simply the probability that the device will respond as expected, when and if called upon. The only successful firings of Minuteman missiles have been from specially prepared silos at Vandenberg Air Force Base in California, not from operational missile sites. It is generally estimated that the reliability of US missiles is relatively high, however—about 85%—whereas that of Soviet missiles is considered to be lower, perhaps 70–80%.

In addition, another accuracy factor must be mentioned in discussing the CEP, the so-called bias factor. For example, warheads that are densely bunched

*(A)*

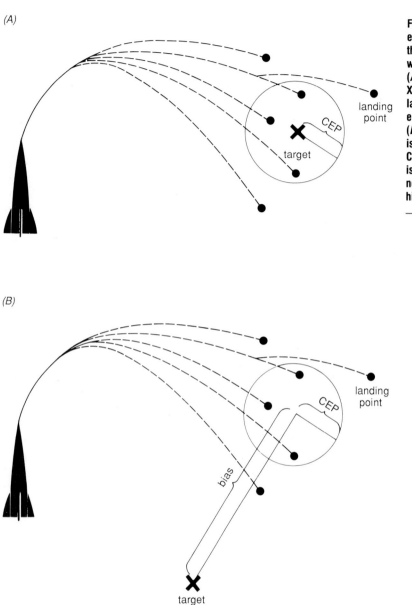

*(B)*

FIGURE 2.8 CEP (circular error probable) for a hypothetical MIRVed missile with six reentry vehicles. (*A*) The RVs are targeted at X, and the CEP is calculated as the radius that encompasses half of them. (*B*) The dispersion of RVs is the same as in *A*, so the CEP is identical, but there is a large bias factor, and not a single warhead has hit the target.

together will have a low CEP, but they may land far from their target, hence being quite inaccurate (Fig. 2.8*B*). The **bias factor,** which is the distance between the center of the circle from which the CEP radius is drawn and the actual target, is particularly difficult to correct for in advance, especially in cases of hypothetical intercontinental attacks, when the missiles would be flying in a northern trajectory, over the North Pole. For

obvious reasons, neither side flight-tests its missiles over the North Pole; in tests, all US missiles fly east to west, from Vandenberg Air Force Base to Kwajalein Island in the Pacific (Fig. 2.9), and all Soviet missiles have been flown west to east, toward eastern Siberia and the Pacific Ocean. Geomagnetic anomalies in the extreme north have been carefully mapped by both nations, but their effect on actual missile navigation

**FIGURE 2.9  Six unarmed Minuteman III reentry vehicles (three from each of two missiles) streaking to their targets near Kwajalein in the western Pacific. Each streak of light is from a different RV.** (Photos courtesy of the US Department of Defense.)

cannot be known for certain . . . until they are actually used.

## Lethality

When calculating the effectiveness of a missile in destroying a heavily armored target (such as another missile in its silo), both accuracy and explosive yield must be considered. Soviet missiles tend to be larger than their US counterparts; they also tend to have greater **throw weight**—the actual weight of the missile's payload, carried in its nose cone. Not surprisingly, throw weight also correlates with megatonnage, the explo-

sive yield of the warhead(s) carried; larger megatonnage requires more throw weight. It should be noted, incidentally, that this correlation is not exact, since with advances in miniaturization, large explosive yields can be concentrated into smaller and smaller packages, a technique that has particularly been mastered by the US.

**Explosive Yield and Accuracy**  As explosive yield increases, the power of the explosion is dissipated in all three dimensions, whereas most targets are located primarily in only two dimensions. As a result, with larger explosive yields, the area destroyed increases less rapidly than does the actual size of the explosion itself. The area destroyed is calculated by raising the yield to the 2/3 power. (That is, taking the cube root of the yield, and squaring it.) This calculation, which is used to determine **equivalent megatonnage,** or **EMT** (Figure 2.10), emphasizes the relative inefficiency of large nuclear explosions.

The total area destroyed by nuclear explosions is greater if those explosions are divided into a relatively large number of "small" blasts instead of many large ones. For example, Figure 2.11 shows the EMT and the area destroyed by blasts totaling 1 megaton, depending on the number and size of the explosions. Note that the equivalent megatonnage and the area destroyed are far greater for a hundred 10-kiloton explosions than for a single 1-megaton blast.

EMT is the appropriate measure when it is expected that destruction (or effectiveness of the explosion) will be determined simply by the amount of area destroyed, such as when a city is targeted. For heavily armored (**hardened**) targets, which can be destroyed only by a large amount of explosive force concentrated in the right place, the parameter known as lethality is calculated. The **lethality** of a nuclear weapon is expressed as a number, which indicates the ability of that weapon to destroy a hard target; the higher the number, the more deadly the weapon. Measures of lethality are used to estimate the theoretical ability of ICBMs to destroy other ICBMs. Not surprisingly, the lethality of an attacking missile increases with increases in the explosive yield of its warheads, and it is also greater the smaller the CEP—that is, the greater the accuracy, the higher the lethality. In the equation used to calculate lethality, $k$, explosive yield appears in the numerator and is measured in equivalent megatons.

$$k = \frac{(\text{yield})^{2/3}}{(\text{CEP})^2}$$

As a result, increases in accuracy are much more important in increasing missile lethality than are increases in megatonnage. On the other hand, increases in accuracy—that is, decreases in the CEP—result in a disproportionate increase in lethality. (Note that as accuracy increases, CEP decreases, since CEP can be seen as a measure of the radius of likely miss.) For example, reducing the CEP by one-half will have the same effect on lethality as increasing the megatonnage eightfold.

Because lethality is so sensitive to differences in CEP, estimates of lethality for different missiles vary

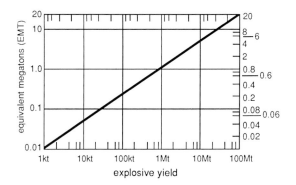

**FIGURE 2.10 The relationship between actual explosive yield and equivalent megatonnage (EMT): EMT = yield$^{2/3}$, with yield and EMT given in megatons. Note that the abscissa is logarithmic. For "soft targets" such as cities, the area destroyed is proportional to the equivalent megatonnage rather than to the actual explosive yield.** (Modified from Schroeer, 1984.)

widely. Although relatively good guesses are available for US missiles, data for the CEP of Soviet missiles are much more difficult to come by: all that can be observed is the dispersion of landing points after Soviet missile tests, since there is no bull's-eye at which the warheads are clearly being fired. Nonetheless, reasonable estimates are available. As a general rule, Soviet missiles have more throw weight than their US counterparts but are somewhat less accurate. It seems likely, in fact, that the Soviet preference for larger missiles with larger throw weight and more megatonnage represents an effort to compensate for relative inaccuracy (Fig. 2.12). Thus, the older, less accurate American ICBMs, such as the Titans, have more megatonnage than more recent models such as the Minuteman. Alternatively, analysts interested in placing the Soviet missile program in its most threatening light have emphasized a "Soviet preference for terror weapons."

In addition to explosive yield and accuracy, missile lethality is strongly influenced by the amount of blast pressure required to destroy the target, which is a function of the **hardness** of the target. It is assumed that a direct hit with a nuclear weapon will destroy any target. Blast pressure is measured in pounds per square inch (psi). Normal frame houses are destroyed at 3 psi. Underground silos for older US and Soviet ICBMs are estimated to be hardened to about 200 psi, whereas the newer silos, built for new missiles, may be hardened to as much as 3,000 psi. Figures of even 5,000

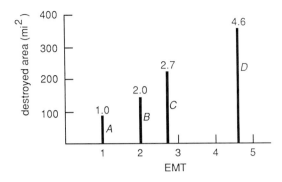

**FIGURE 2.11 Various ways of distributing the destructive power of 1 megaton:** $A = 1 \times 1$ mt, $B = 8 \times 125$ kt, $C = 20 \times 50$ kt, $D = 100 \times 10$ kt. **In each case the explosive power is the same (1 mt), but the EMT and the area destroyed increase with a greater number of smaller explosions.**

psi have been suggested, although it has been questioned whether such degrees of hardening are physically possible.

**Hard Target Kill Probabilities**   There are several important tradeoffs between missile accuracy, warhead yield, and hardness of the target: (1) the more accurate the missile, the less the yield required to destroy a target of a given hardness; (2) the larger the yield, the less accuracy needed to destroy a target of a given hardness, although accuracy is more important than yield; and (3) the harder the target, the greater the accuracy, and/or the greater the yield required to destroy it.

These considerations are especially significant because they have given rise to anxiety, particularly on the US side, over **ICBM vulnerability,** the possibility that American ICBMs may become susceptible to destruction in an initial attack. To understand this argument, it is necessary to understand the calculations involved. First, as we have seen, the lethality of a missile ($k$, for kill probability) is determined by warhead yield and accuracy. Figure 2.13 shows the relationship between missile lethality, target hardness, and the probability that a given hard target (usually assumed to be a missile silo) will be destroyed. Note that for an attack of a given lethality, silos are more likely to be destroyed if they are less hardened: with a missile lethality of 20, for example, there is a 90% probability that a silo hardened to 300 psi will be destroyed, as opposed to only

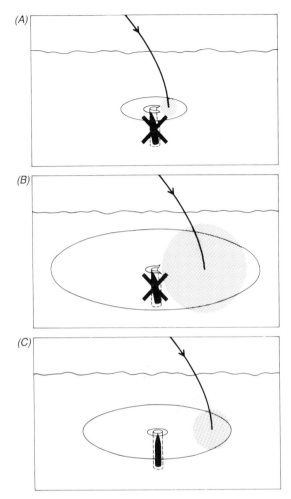

**FIGURE 2.12 The probability that a hardened target will be destroyed by an incoming warhead depends on the accuracy of that warhead and on its explosive yield. (A) A small, accurate warhead can destroy a missile in its silo. (B) So can a large warhead that is inaccurate (i.e., one with a large CEP), although warhead size is less important than is CEP. (C) If a missile's combination of yield and accuracy is inadequate, it cannot be relied on to destroy a hardened target.** (Modified from Scoville, 1977.)

about a 30% probability of destroying a silo hardened to 3,000 psi.

For most calculations, it is assumed that silos are hardened to about 2,000 psi. This generates the following relationship between CEP and the probability of destroying a target (Fig. 2.14). Again, note that greater

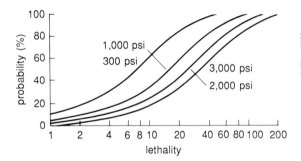

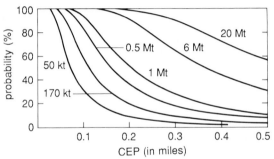

**FIGURE 2.13  The probability (expressed as a percentage) of destroying a missile silo hardened to varying degrees, as a function of the lethality of the attacking warhead. Lethality is determined by considering both EMT and CEP, as discussed earlier.** (Modified from Schroeer, 1984.)

**FIGURE 2.14  The probability of destroying a missile silo hardened to withstand a pressure of 2,000 pounds per square inch (psi), as a function of warhead yields and CEP.** (Modified from Schroeer, 1984.)

accuracy (smaller CEP) correlates with a higher probability of silo destruction. Also, if CEP stays the same, larger warheads (or higher warhead yield) have a higher probability of destroying a given target. By using estimates for lethality and silo hardness, equations are available to calculate the **one-shot kill probability** for each missile system deployed by either side. This is the probability that a warhead from one of these missiles will destroy an opponent's missile silo. To compensate for reliability problems and to increase the probability of a successful attack, however, it is generally assumed that two different warheads will be independently **cross-targeted** on the same silo.

When two-shot kill probabilities are calculated, it is assumed that only the laws of statistics apply. Another important consideration, however, about which very little is known, is **fratricide,** the phenomenon in which a second attacking warhead may be exploded prematurely or thrown off course by the effects of its preceding "brother."

In such cases, the **two-shot kill probability** is easily determined, as in this example: assume a single-shot kill probability of 80% in an attack of 100 warheads on 100 silos. This, by definition, destroys 80 targets, leaving 20. The second wave of attack destroys another 80% of the remaining 20, or 16, leaving 96 silos out of the original 100 destroyed. If the one-shot kill probability is 80%, the two-shot skill probability is therefore 96%. Thus under these assumed, hypothetical conditions, any given target stands a 96% chance of being destroyed if it is attacked with two warheads.

Until the late 1970s, silo kill probabilities were low on both sides. With increased accuracy, however, and to a lesser extent recent increases in warhead yield, such probabilities have become higher, and hawkish American analysts in particular have suggested that US missiles may become vulnerable to attack. There is very little information available as to the degree of Soviet concern over possible vulnerability of their ICBMs. As we shall see, however, such concern may be substantial, since Soviet ICBMs represent a very high proportion of their overall strategic arsenal, and a much smaller proportion of the US arsenal.

### Other Factors in ICBM Performance

ICBM performance is also strongly influenced by the nature of the fuel. Liquid fuels are generally considered to be less desirable than solid fuels, because the former are more corrosive and difficult to maintain. They typically cannot be stored in the missile itself, which must therefore be loaded just before firing. This introduces a potentially long delay, one likely to be especially awkward under the conditions of a nuclear war. The USSR, which has deployed only one solid fuel strategic missile, the SS-13, and that in small numbers, apparently has not mastered solid fuel rocket propellant technology for long-range missiles. By contrast, except for the elderly Titan IIs, which are being phased out, all US missiles are solid fueled.

Missile **readiness** is a final strategic missile quality, and another one that is difficult to measure. Whereas

**FIGURE 2.16 Minuteman missile in its silo.** (Photo courtesy of the US Department of Defense.)

**FIGURE 2.15 Test firing of the Titan II ICBM.** (Photo courtesy of the US Department of Defense.)

"reliability" refers to the probability that a missile will perform when asked to do so (Fig. 2.15), "readiness" refers to the likelihood that once deployed (Fig. 2.16), a missile will be in an active state, ready to be fired. As with reliability, the exact readiness of the superpowers' ICBMs is unknown, but it is widely acknowledged that US missiles are at a higher level of readiness than their Soviet counterparts, both because of technological factors (such as the difference between solid and liquid fuels) and also perhaps because of the Soviet penchant for highly centralized authority. This could produce greater unwillingness to delegate the authority necessary to launch missiles.

Missiles can also be either **hot-launched** or **cold-launched.** A hot launch corresponds to the lay conception of a missile being blasted out of its silo by rocket engines. After a hot launch, the silo itself is typically not reusable. Cold-launching, by contrast, involves popping a missile out of its hardened berth with a puff of gas; only after the missile is airborne do the rocket engines ignite. For obvious reasons, cold-launching is necessary in submarine-launched missiles. It is also used by the USSR in the SS-17 and the SS-18 ICBMs. This has raised the possibility that the Soviets are seeking a significant **reload capacity**—the ability to fire their ICBMs in an attack, then reload and fire again from the same silos. Reloading seems especially inappropriate for liquid-fueled rockets, and it is at least questionable whether such a difficult and delicate maneuver could be carried out while a nuclear war is going on. In any event, cold-launching is planned for America's MX missile.

### The ICBM Balance

When dealing with nuclear weapons, numbers tell only part of the story, and yet, they are typically the focus of most concern. This is especially true of ICBMs, at least partly because certain factors, such as the number of launchers, can be counted accurately, whereas other factors—such as readiness and reliability—cannot be quantified. Moreover, quality factors in general are not included in such numbers, although they may be crucially important.

The largest American ICBMs are also the oldest, the Titan IIs, now being phased out. They are the least accurate, carrying a single, 9-megaton warhead, and they are also deployed in the least hardened silos. The mainstay of the US ICBM force consists of 1,000 Minuteman missiles. Of these, 450 are older Minuteman II missiles, first deployed between 1965 and 1970. These also carry single warheads, about 1.5 megatons, and are significantly more accurate than Titan IIs. During the early 1970s, the US replaced its older Minuteman I missiles with 550 Minuteman IIIs. These are all MIRVed, with three warheads per missile and 170 kilotons per warhead. Since 1979, the warheads of 300 of these Minuteman IIIs were upgraded yet more, to 335 kilotons apiece, and their accuracy was increased. The proposed MX missile, or "Peacekeeper" as the Reagan administration calls it, will be the largest US missile permitted under the terms of the SALT II treaty (see Chapter 10). It is expected to carry 10 MIRVed warheads, each 335 kilotons.

The Soviets now deploy ICBMs in six forms: the SS-11, SS-13, SS-17, SS-18 (at least two different warhead models), SS-19, and the SS-25. The SS-11 and SS-13 are not MIRVed; neither is the older model of the SS-18, the USSR's largest missile. However, some US strategic planners fear that newer models of this missile can threaten US ICBMs. These recent model SS-18s are MIRVed, with up to 10 warheads, although most are believed to carry 8.

Table 2.2 shows the basic US-Soviet ICBM balance. Of the ICBMs deployed on both sides, only the Minuteman III and the SS-18 could be considered "silo busters"—that is, missiles having a two-shot kill probability against hard targets of 90% or more, based on their combination of accuracy and warhead yield. (Soviet strategic bombers, incidentally, are estimated to have a two-shot probability of 77%–97% and US bombers, 99%, but because of their slow speed, bombers are not considered practical weapons for attacks on missile silos.)

The "**strategic posture**" of the USSR (its organization of strategic nuclear weapons) emphasizes ICBMs. Indeed, more than 70% of all Soviet strategic warheads are on ICBMs, as opposed to only about 20% of US strategic warheads. Accordingly, just as a comparison

of strategic bombers alone suggests that the USSR is far behind the US—by about 500 to more than 3,000—a comparison of ICBMs alone suggests that the US is behind the USSR, 2,100 warheads to nearly 6,000. However, the Soviet advantage in ICBMs is sometimes considered especially troublesome, since ICBMs fly much faster than bombers and are more accurate than submarine-launched missiles. Hence, they could constitute a threat to the ICBMs of the opposing side.

Since the US has a smaller proportion of its strategic warheads invested in ICBMs, it is relatively easier to threaten that leg of the triad. However, this also means that even if American ICBMs were entirely destroyed, a smaller proportion of the total US strategic posture would have been eliminated than would be the case for a comparable attack against the USSR's land-based missiles. We shall return to this topic later, when we consider policy issues at the end of this chapter, and then in Chapter 6, when we take up the important concepts of "strategic stability" and "counterforce."

The USSR has lagged behind the US in most technologies associated with nuclear weapons, a notable exception being the construction of large, powerful rockets. During the early 1960s, the US also produced large ICBMs (Atlas and Titan long-range rockets, as well as Thor and Jupiter medium-range rockets), which carried large warheads. However, as we have seen, the weapons designer can make a tradeoff between the needs for explosive size and for accuracy; therefore, as advances in computers and microminiaturization resulted in greater missile accuracy, the US progressively replaced its large ICBMs with smaller, more accurate, and more lethal models. By contrast, Soviet missiles are still somewhat less accurate than US models, and to some degree, this may account for the retention by the USSR of relatively large warheads. The total megatonnage in the US arsenal has been generally declining (even as the total number of warheads has been increasing), because of increases in accuracy. A similar trend appears to hold for the USSR.

In general, the USSR leads the US in "quantitative" ICBM measures—numbers, size, and newness—although it is still behind in accuracy. On the other hand, the US leads the USSR in "qualitative" ICBM measures such as readiness, reliability, efficiency, and miniaturization. ICBMs have certain advantages over other strategic systems: once deployed, they are cheaper to maintain; communications are more secure; the missiles are fast and highly accurate, and there is no defense against them. They also have certain disadvantages: notably, they are easily targeted by the other

**TABLE 2.2 US-USSR ICBM tally sheet[a]**

| Missile | Number | Warheads | CEP (m) | Total warheads |
|---|---|---|---|---|
| *US* | | | | |
| Titan II | 45 | 1 × 9 Mt | 1,300 | 45 |
| Minuteman II | 450 | 1 × 1.5 Mt | 370 | 450 |
| Minuteman III | 250 | 3 × 1.7 Mt | 280 | 750 |
| Minuteman IIIA | 300 | 3 × 3.35 Mt | 220 | 900 |
| (MX) | (50) | (10 × 3.35 Mt) | (80) | (500)[b] |
| *USSR* | | | | |
| SS-11 | 505 | 1 × 0.45 Mt, or 3 MRV | 1,400 | 505 |
| SS-13 | 60 | 1 × 0.45 Mt | 2,000 | 60 |
| SS-17 | 150 | 4 × 0.2 Mt | 450 | 600 |
| SS-18 | 50 | 1 × 10 Mt | 450 | 50 |
| SS-18 | 258 | 10 × 0.45 Mt | 300 | 2,580 |
| SS-19 | 330 | 6 × 0.45 Mt | 300–500 | 1,980 |
| SS-25 | 45 | 1 × ? | ? | ? |

[a]Exact figures for the USSR are not available. In some cases, the number of warheads stated represents an overestimate; I have followed the SALT II convention of estimating that a missile is outfitted ("configured") with the maximum number of warheads for which it has been tested. For example, it has been estimated that as many as 20% of SS-17s are single warhead; since, however, this weapon has been tested with four MIRVs, four are assumed for every SS-17. As of 1986, additional Soviet SS-25 missiles are being deployed; as this happens, a comparable number of SS-11s are being deactivated.
[b]Anticipated.

side, and as missiles become increasingly accurate, land-based ICBMs are becoming increasingly vulnerable, at least in theory, to destruction by preemptive attack.

The USSR, which has invested heavily in ICBMs, must plan around the advantages and disadvantages of these weapons. The US has elected to invest relatively less in ICBMs, and it too both reaps the advantages and suffers the disadvantages of this decision. In particular, the US land-based leg of the triad is relatively more vulnerable than are Soviet ICBMs, in part because the US has somewhat fewer of them. On the other hand, the US also has larger forces deployed invulnerably on the other two legs. Soviet bombers, as we have seen, are not considered especially threatening, and they are also vulnerable. And Soviet submarines, as we shall see, are much more vulnerable and generally less competent than their US counterparts. In addition, increased accuracy on the part of

US submarine-launched missiles, notably the soon-to-be-deployed Trident II (also known as the D-5) will increase the vulnerability of Soviet ICBMs.

## STRATEGIC SUBMARINES

Strategic missiles launched from submarines are known as **submarine-launched ballistic missiles,** or **SLBMs.** SLBMs tend to be somewhat smaller than ICBMs; hence their throw weight and range are somewhat less. As with bombers and ICBMs, both the US and the USSR have gone through several "generations" of SLBMs.

In a sense, the nuclear missile submarines are the most remarkable members of the strategic triad. The feat of firing ballistic missiles from underwater is achieved by cold-launching them from vertically oriented tubes. Modern strategic missile submarines are doubly nuclear: not only do they carry nuclear-armed missiles, but also many are nuclear powered. Nuclear power permits submarines to remain submerged for cruises of approximately 2 months' duration. By contrast, diesel-powered submarines can be submerged for only brief periods because they cannot run their engines while underwater and must rely on short-lived electric storage batteries. The capacity for submarines to remain submerged, hence, undetected, is their major asset as strategic weapons: since they cannot be targeted with present technology, nuclear missile submarines on deep-ocean patrol are considered to be invulnerable. Unlike ICBMs, nuclear weapons deployed on strategic submarines are therefore not considered to be susceptible to a preemptive attack by the other side.

## The US Strategic Submarines

The first US strategic submarines, the Polaris class, were launched in 1960. They were about 120 meters long with a crew of 140 and a top speed of 55 km/hr submerged. They each carried 16 Polaris or A-1 missiles, which had single, 800-kiloton warheads (Fig. 2.17). The warheads were eventually replaced by A-2 and then A-3 versions, the latter being MIRVed with three 200-kiloton warheads. (Note, once again, the tendency to reduce the total megatonnage as warheads are MIRVed, or "fractionated" on a single missile.) The last Polaris submarines were decommissioned in 1982.

Initially deployed in 1963, the second generation of US strategic submarines are known as Poseidons. Somewhat larger than Polaris, they were built to accommodate a larger SLBM, the Poseidon or C-3 missile. Although the range of the Poseidon missile is about the same as the earlier Polaris, it is MIRVed and is typically "configured" with 10 warheads, each equivalent to 50 kilotons (i.e., four times the yield of the Hiroshima bomb). A single Poseidon submarine (Fig. 2.18) carries 16 Poseidon missiles, for a total of 160 independently targetable warheads. As of early 1986 the US had deployed 30 Poseidon submarines, of which 18 carried Poseidon missiles. The remaining 12 Poseidon submarines were refitted with the third-generation American SLBM, the Trident I or C-4.

The third and most recent generation of US strategic submarines, the Tridents (Fig. 2.19), carry 24 launch tubes, as opposed to the 16 of the Polaris and Poseidon vessels. Trident submarines are nearly half again larger than their predecessors, and are also faster as well as quieter. Trident I missiles have longer range and are more accurate than the Poseidons. They can

be MIRVed with up to 14 warheads, but they typically carry 8. As of early 1986, 6 Trident submarines had been commissioned, and at least 20 were planned.

Strictly speaking, Trident submarines are not needed for deploying Trident missiles: Since Trident I missiles have the same dimensions as Poseidon missiles, they fit into Poseidon launch tubes. However, Trident submarines are needed for the fourth generation of SLBMs, the Trident II or D-5. This missile is too large to be accommodated on Poseidon vessels, but it does fit the larger launch tubes of Trident submarines. The Trident II will have greatly increased range and could be MIRVed with 10 or more independently targetable warheads. Eight is generally assumed, however, as with the Trident I. It appears that these warheads will be not only MIRVed, but also MARVed. As we have seen, MARVs can adjust their trajectories even after discharge from the bus. The result seems likely to be accuracy comparable to that of the Minuteman III missile.

## The Soviet Strategic Submarines

The USSR maintains nine classes of strategic submarines and seven models of SLBMs. Some, such as the Golf and Hotel class submarines, are quite outmoded, and more primitive than any US models. They are considered to have a potential role in Europe or China but not as strategic weapons against the US. The Yankee class submarines are similar to the Polaris and were first deployed in 1968, 5 years after the US launched the Poseidons. Soviet Yankee submarines also carry single-warhead missiles comparable to the Polaris. Beginning in 1972, the USSR began deploying its Delta class submarines, roughly comparable to the US Poseidon, and carrying MIRVed missiles. Finally, another generation of Soviet submarines, the Typhoon class, has recently finished sea trials and became operational in the late 1980s. These boats are somewhat larger than the US Trident submarines and carry 20 MIRVed missiles each.

## The US-Soviet Strategic Submarine Balance

Both France and Great Britain maintain strategic submarines, France with five and Great Britain with four. Each of these submarines carries 16 single-warhead or MRVed missiles. Both nations are planning to MIRV their SLBMs, beginning in the late 1980s, Britain by purchasing US Trident submarines. As is the case with other British and French nuclear weapons, these submarine forces are a bone of contention between the

**FIGURE 2.17 The *USS Sam Rayburn,* a Polaris submarine, with its 16 missile tube covers open.** (Photo courtesy of the US Department of Defense.)

**FIGURE 2.18 Poseidon missile emerging from the ocean after being fired from a submerged submarine.** (Photo courtesy of the US Department of Defense.)

US and USSR. From the Soviet perspective, the British and French forces should be counted as part of the US "side," since they are clearly aimed at the USSR; the United States claims (as do Britain and France) that they should not be so counted, since they are independently controlled by sovereign nations. These and other **independent nuclear forces**—notably China—must nonetheless figure in any Soviet strategic calculations (see Chapter 11).

Table 2.3 shows the US-USSR strategic submarine balance as of 1986.

The USSR leads the US in total number of strategic submarines, in number of missile launch tubes, and in total megatonnage carried on SLBMs. However, once again, such numerical measures can be misleading. On balance, there is little doubt that the US is

actually far ahead of the USSR in its submarine-based strategic posture. Thus, US submarine technology is substantially advanced over the USSR. American SLBMs have longer range than their Soviet equivalents, and they are all solid-fueled, whereas all Soviet SLBMs, with the exception of their SS-N-18s and SS-N-20s, are liquid-fueled. This is considered to be a substantial advantage for the United States. The US is also far ahead in MIRVing. As a result, the US has more than double the USSR's number of submarine-based warheads.

In addition, readiness is higher for US submarines, and US submarines spend significantly more "time on station," that is, actually cruising on deep-sea patrol. Whereas approximately 60% of US submarines are on patrol at any given time, only 10–15% of Soviet sub-

**FIGURE 2.19 The *USS Ohio*, a Trident submarine.** (Photo courtesy of the US Department of Defense.)

**TABLE 2.3 US-USSR strategic submarine balance, as of 1985**

| Class | Number of vessels | Number of missiles | CEP (m) | Warheads | Total warheads |
|---|---|---|---|---|---|
| *US* | | | | | |
| Poseidon | 18 | 16 Poseidon (C-3) | 450 | 10 MIRV × 50 kt | 1,880 |
| Poseidon | 12 | 16 Trident I (C-4) | 450 | 8 MIRV × 100 kt | 1,536 |
| Trident | 6 | 24 Trident I (C-4) | 450 | 8 MIRV × 100 kt | 1,152<br>4,568 |
| *USSR* | | | | | |
| Golf III | 1 | 6 SS-N-8 | 1,000? | 1 1 Mt | 6 |
| Hotel II | 6 | 3 SS-N-5 | 2,800 | 1 1 Mt | 18 |
| Hotel III | 1 | 6 SS-N-8 | 1,000? | 1 1 Mt | 6 |
| Yankee I | 20 | 16 SS-N-6 | 900 | 1 1 Mt | 320 |
| Yankee II | 1 | 12 SS-N-17 | 1,500 | 1 1 Mt | 12 |
| Delta I | 18 | 12 SS-N-8 | 1,000? | 1 1 Mt | 216 |
| Delta II | 4 | 16 SS-N-8 | 1,000? | 1 1 Mt | 64 |
| Delta III | 14 | 16 SS-N-18 | 600 | 7 MIRV × 200 kt | 1,344 |
| Delta IV | 1 | 16 SS-N-23 | ? | 7 MIRV ? | 112 |
| Typhoon | 3 | 20 SS-N-20 | ? | 6–9 MIRV × 500 kt | 450?<br>2,548 |

marines are similarly deployed. The remainder are typically being refitted or are simply laying up in submarine bases. As a result, the US maintains approximately 2,800 warheads at all times targeted on the USSR and invulnerable to attack; the USSR, by contrast, maintains about 300 warheads similarly targeted at the US. And as we shall soon see, the invulnerability of even these Soviet SLBMs is in some doubt.

Several other issues are particularly important in assessing the US-USSR strategic submarine balance, notably missile accuracy, communications, and vulnerability.

**Accuracy** US missiles are considerably more accurate than those of the USSR. Single-shot kill probabilities for SLBMs on both sides are currently low, less than 20%. However, the CEP of American SLBMs is significantly less than their Soviet counterparts and going down rapidly; the Trident II, in particular, will have accuracy rivaling that of the newest land-based missiles. Missile guidance for SLBMs is basically similar to that for ICBMs, with the added complication that the location of a submarine at firing must be determined exactly, even if the vessel has been traveling for many weeks, submerged. The submarine's on-board inertial navigation system keeps constant track of the submarine's whereabouts by recording all accelerations. This position information is updated regularly by signals from land-based transmitters and from navigational satellites. Once fired, SLBMs navigate via their own inertial navigation systems. As with ICBMs, substantial improvements in accuracy can be expected in the near future, especially if SLBMs are connected to the NAVSTAR system and/or outfitted with TERCOM guidance.

**Communications** Perhaps the greatest drawback to submarines as strategic delivery systems is the difficulty of communicating with them. Most electromagnetic, radio wave communications use high frequencies. Such energy does not penetrate seawater effectively; therefore, submarines currently must approach the surface to send or receive messages, using a trailing antenna that floats at or near the surface. This, in turn, makes them relatively vulnerable. The US maintains a large number of airplanes that fly near the ocean surface, dragging a long antenna for communicating with submarines. These are the so-called TACAMO planes (for "take charge and move out"). Ground-based low-frequency and very-low-frequency transmitters are also currently in use, permitting some communication

with submerged submarines (the lower the frequency, the deeper the water penetration, but the slower the transmission, and the less information transferrable).

There have also been efforts to develop an **extremely low frequency (ELF)** system, located in Michigan or Wisconsin, which would permit communication with submarines several hundred meters undersea. Such a system would require an enormous antenna, hundreds or thousands of kilometers long, and could send only very simple messages, such as "shoot." If operating, it would provide the opportunity to communicate with all submerged submarines simultaneously. However, the enormous antenna required for ELF would be susceptible to disruption and would almost certainly fail to survive even the initial stages of a nuclear war. Research is also under way to employ blue-green lasers to penetrate seawater at great depths.

**Vulnerability** The particular appeal of strategic submarines is their virtual invulnerability. The SLBMs are the most invulnerable leg of either side's triad. The US is widely acknowledged to have a substantial lead over the USSR with regard to both the invulnerability of US submarines and also the degree to which Soviet submarines are threatened by **antisubmarine warfare (ASW).** Because the USSR is almost completely landlocked, Soviet submarines are very restricted in their outlets to the oceans (Fig. 2.20). They must pass through narrow "choke points," where they are constantly monitored by American radar and sonar stations. By contrast, the US has long, ice-free coastlines as well as servicing ports on Guam and in Spain and Scotland.

The range of SLBMs is particularly important because with longer range, the submarines on patrol have more ocean in which to hide. US submarines, being substantially quieter, are more difficult to track. The existing configuration of US aircraft carriers, helicopters, and long-range surveillance airplanes, as well as fixed monitoring stations, has led some observers to suggest that Soviet submarines can already be tracked throughout much if not all of their active patrol. Submarines can be monitored by "passive" means, which involve listening with delicate underwater microphones, or by "active" detection, by emitting an acoustic or other pulse, and then monitoring the echo. There is much debate, however, over whether ASW efforts have produced a "transparent" ocean, or whether such a thing would be desirable. It seems clear that for now, Soviet submarines are at much greater ASW risk than are US submarines. Given that the US relies relatively

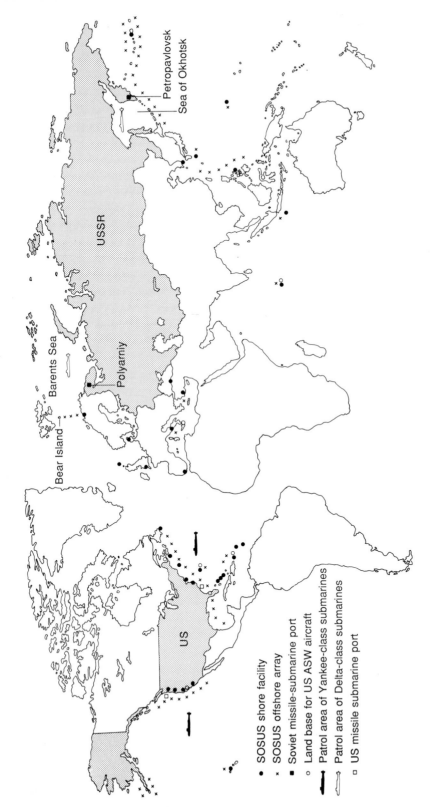

FIGURE 2.20 Geography strongly favors US strategic submarines over those of the Soviet Union. The USSR's ballistic missile submarines are based at Polyarniy, on the Scandinavian Kola peninsula, and at Petropavlovsk, on the Kamchatka peninsula in Siberia. From either location, Soviet submarines must pass through various "choke points" at which undersea "SOSUS" (*Sound Surveillance System*) antisubmarine arrays are set up to detect their passage. By contrast, the US submarine fleet has unrestricted access to the oceans. (Modified from Witt, 1981.)

- SOSUS shore facility
- SOSUS offshore array
- Soviet missile-submarine port
- Land base for US ASW aircraft
- Patrol area of Yankee-class submarines
- Patrol area of Delta-class submarines
- US missile submarine port

more on strategic submarines, any Soviet breakthrough in ASW could be especially troublesome.

In 1984 the United States began deploying the first of 758 nuclear-armed, sea-launched cruise missiles. The USSR is expected to follow suit within a few years. Many submarines currently carry nuclear-armed depth charges and torpedoes, especially the so-called "hunter-killer" submarines. These are important ASW weapons on both sides and are not ballistic missile carriers; rather, they are specially designed to hunt and destroy the other side's strategic submarines. Once again, US hunter-killer submarines are faster, quieter, and technologically superior to their Soviet counterparts.

## COMMAND, CONTROL, COMMUNICATIONS, AND INTELLIGENCE

In a sense, we can identify a different kind of strategic triad, in addition to the usual focus on bombers, ICBMs, and SLBMs just discussed. The three legs of this other triad consist of the nuclear weapons themselves, their delivery systems, and the devices and systems that have been elaborated to command, control, and communicate with them, as well as the intelligence-gathering activities associated with them (Fig. 2.21). This last group is known collectively as **command, control, communications, and intelligence,** or **C³I** (pronounced "see-three-eye"). Actually, a fourth and very important "leg" can also be identified, namely, the doctrine for their use; we shall examine this in Chapter 6.

C³I is substantially less visible than the other aspects of nuclear weaponry, and until recently, it has received virtually no public scrutiny. However, C³I is crucial to nuclear weapons, since it is analogous to the brain and nervous system, without which the nuclear "muscles" on either side could not be flexed. C³I is difficult to describe because it is widespread and diffuse, consisting of a number of different systems and devices, many of which overlap in their functions. Perhaps because it is so important, information concerning C³I also tends to be closely guarded and difficult to obtain. Nonetheless, some general observations can be made.

Nuclear weapons must be under two forms of control: **negative control,** which prevents use unless legitimate orders are given, and **positive control,** which ensures that if commanded, the systems in question will respond as ordered. To some extent, the two forms of control are in conflict insofar as efforts to prevent accidental or unauthorized use (i.e., to achieve nega-

tive control) tend to add obstacles to the firing of nuclear weapons, which increases the possibility that positive control will be impeded. People worried about interference with the ability to retaliate find this worrisome. Similarly, efforts to ensure positive control tend to facilitate actual use, which in turn raises the specter of inadequate negative control, resulting in the use of nuclear weapons without legitimate authority. People worried about possible unintended or unauthorized use of nuclear weapons find this worrisome. As a general rule, we can say that nuclear hawks and nuclear doves tend to emphasize the needs for positive and negative control, respectively. And each considers that too much of the other could be dangerous.

It is useful to divide C³I into three major physical components: warning sensors, command posts, and communications systems.

### Warning Sensors

A set of three satellites is maintained in high-altitude, geosynchronous orbit. These satellites have an orbital speed that matches the rotation of the earth, so they appear to be stationary. One constantly surveys the USSR, alert to ICBM launches; the other two look for SLBM launches—the second surveys the Atlantic Ocean and the third the Pacific. These satellites are equipped with infrared sensors to detect the heat produced by rocket exhaust (Fig. 2.22) about 10 minutes before such missiles would also be detected by a variety of radar systems, such as the older DEW (Distant Early Warning) line in Canada and northern Alaska, to which have been added a number of recently developed radars with acronyms such as BMEWS, PAVE PAWS, and PARCS. Unlike the previous "line-of-sight" systems, newer models include "over-the-horizon" radars, which bounce signals off the ionosphere, hence can operate at distances of thousands of miles. They reputedly have the ability to track hundreds, perhaps thousands, of basketball-sized objects at such ranges. These radars are intended to detect and track incoming missiles and warheads, and to estimate their likely points of impact. Satellites are also outfitted with so-called Vela sensors, which detect and evaluate actual nuclear explosions by sensing the different kinds of energy released. (See Chapter 10 for more on verification technology.)

### Command Posts

Information from the various warning sensors is fed to a number of potential command posts, where decisions to use or not to use nuclear weapons would be

**FIGURE 2.21 The inside of the command post at Strategic Air Command Headquarters in Omaha, Nebraska. The operators at the various consoles receive information regarding reported attacks and would be involved in sending out retaliatory orders, especially to American B-52 bombers.** (Photo courtesy of the US Department of Defense.)

made. The "National Command Authority," authorized to order use of nuclear weapons, resides with the president of the United States, followed in turn by the vice president, and the Speaker of the House of Representatives. Emergency procedures, not made public, have been devised for the delegation of launch authority in the event that the National Command Authority is killed or incapacitated. Reports of nuclear attacks are to be collected at the North American Air Defense Command (NORAD), in Cheyenne Mountain, Colorado, and at the National Military Command Center, at the Pentagon in Washington, D.C. Various alternate land-based command posts also exist, but particular reliance is placed on a specially modified fleet of Boeing 747s, the National Emergency Airborne Command Posts or NEACPs (pronounced "knee-caps"), from which the president or surviving member(s) of the National Command Authority would presumably conduct nuclear war while in flight (Fig. 2.23).

In addition to NEACPs, the US maintains a fleet of "Looking Glass" planes, which fly random patterns over the US in 8-hour shifts, always commanded by a Strategic Air Command (SAC) general. One such plane is in the air at all times, 24 hours a day. These aircraft, like the other command posts, are designed to receive and cross-correlate information during a crisis or attack. Presumably, the Looking Glass planes provide a degree of **redundancy** (repetition of function), which serves as

a backup in case other systems are destroyed or damaged too heavily to be used. The ultimate function of such command posts is to send the orders for nuclear war, the Emergency Action Message.

## Communications

If nuclear weapons are in any sense to be commanded and controlled, the warning sensors must be connected to the command posts and the command posts must be able to communicate with the nuclear weapons themselves. This is the responsibility of various communications systems, many of which are part of the Worldwide Military Command and Control System (WWMCCS, pronounced "wimmecks"). Included here are ground-line telephone links, especially to the ICBM fields and SAC bomber bases, as well as underwater cables, radio systems ranging from low frequency to ultrahigh frequency, and fiber-optic tubes.

Many $C^3I$ systems do more than provide communication. For example, the proposed system of 18 "global positioning" satellites known as NAVSTAR will allow US aircraft and naval vessels to obtain navigational fixes anywhere on the globe, with unprecedented accuracies—measured in the tens of meters. This will not only serve as an aid to navigation, but will also permit unprecedented accuracy for bombers and

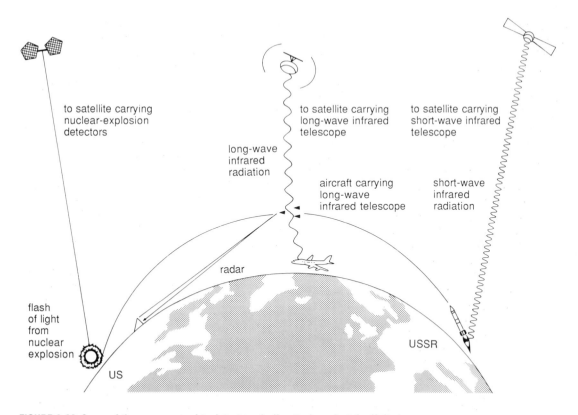

to satellite carrying
nuclear-explosion
detectors

to satellite carrying
long-wave infrared
telescope

to satellite carrying
short-wave infrared
telescope

long-wave
infrared
radiation

aircraft carrying
long-wave
infrared telescope

short-wave
infrared
radiation

radar

flash
of light
from
nuclear
explosion

USSR

US

**FIGURE 2.22 Some of the sensors used to detect a missile attack against the United States. Short-wave infrared sensors, mounted on satellites, would detect the hot exhaust of missiles during their boost phase. Long-range radar would come into play during the glide phase, and satellites sensitive to the characteristic flashes of light produced by nuclear explosions would report on detonations occurring throughout the US. Long-wave infrared sensors now under development are to be mounted on satellites to detect relatively warm warheads against the cold background of space.** (Modified from Carter, 1985.)

missiles once these are equipped to obtain in-flight updating of their position. In addition, the same satellites will be equipped with a special sensor system known as IONDS (integrated operational nuclear detonation detection system). These devices will immediately identify the exact size and location of nuclear detonations occurring anywhere on earth and relay such information back to command centers in "real time"— that is, as the events occur, without having to wait for special processing of their information.

IONDS could have both defensive and offensive implications: it will become an important part of the nation's warning system, since it would inform leaders about the details of an attack against the United States.

Similarly, it will provide the kind of precise, timely information that would be needed to effectively manage a retaliatory strike, or a first strike. Under such conditions, it could be important to receive accurate data about whether one's attacking missiles have functioned as planned, whether they exploded on target, which if any were duds, and so on. Accurate information of this sort can therefore function as a **force multiplier,** greatly increasing the effectiveness of existing weapons for either a retaliatory strike or a first strike.

Very little information is available concerning Soviet $C^3I$, but it seems likely that in this respect the USSR closely resembles the US, except that the US relies relatively more on satellite communications and high-

**FIGURE 2.23 The NEACP plane, from which the president or surviving National Command Authority will, if necessary, conduct nuclear war.** (Photo courtesy of the US Department of Defense.)

speed computers. It also seems likely that compared to the US, Soviet $C^3I$ is somewhat more centralized and that launch authority is less likely to be delegated to local commanders.

It is increasingly agreed that $C^3I$ may well be the weakest link in the entire system of nuclear hardware. Thus, radio transmissions can be jammed, command centers targeted, and satellites are becoming increasingly vulnerable, especially as a result of advances in **antisatellite (ASAT)** warfare. Ionization of the upper atmosphere resulting from the explosion of nuclear weapons could cause radio waves to be absorbed rather than reflected. In addition, among the various effects of nuclear explosions is a powerful **electromagnetic pulse (EMP),** which seriously threatens modern electronic equipment. (More of this in Chapter 4.)

Although public attention is typically focused on the relative numbers of weapons, specialists are increasingly agreed that $C^3I$ constitutes the weakest link in either side's nuclear arsenal. Among the concerns that have been raised are the following.

1. Because of the enormous complexity and huge volume of information to be processed in a very brief time frame, $C^3I$ on either side may fail in time of crisis.

2. The effects of "decapitating" either side's $C^3I$ are simply unknowable. Given sufficient planning and coordination, it may be possible to paralyze the system by inducing chaos. In this case, nuclear war would quickly become totally unmanageable after the first dozen or so nuclear explosions. It is also possible, however, that sufficient redundancy and independent command and control options have been established so that national leaders could manage not only a crisis but a nuclear war as well.

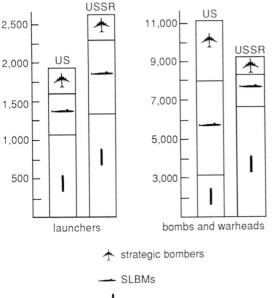

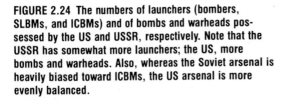

**FIGURE 2.24 The numbers of launchers (bombers, SLBMs, and ICBMs) and of bombs and warheads possessed by the US and USSR, respectively. Note that the USSR has somewhat more launchers; the US, more bombs and warheads. Also, whereas the Soviet arsenal is heavily biased toward ICBMs, the US arsenal is more evenly balanced.**

## SUMMARY OF US-USSR STRATEGIC NUCLEAR BALANCE

1.  The US has several qualitative advantages over the USSR: nuclear allies, superior technology, higher readiness and reliability, greater accuracy, and greater strategic access to the oceans. The USSR has several quantitative advantages: more ballistic missiles (both ICBMs and SLBMs), greater throw weight, and more total megatonnage. On the other hand, the US has more strategic warheads than does the USSR.

2.  The distribution of strategic weapons differs between the two superpowers. The US has a much better balanced triad, with about 50% of its strategic warheads on submarines, 25% on bombers, and 25% on ICBMs. The USSR has about 70% of its strategic warheads on ICBMs, 20% on SLBMs, and 5% on bombers (Fig. 2.24). Although ICBMs are generally more accurate than SLBMs and under better communications, they are also more vulnerable.

3.  The USSR is currently capable, at least in theory, of destroying a high proportion of US ICBMs, whereas the US can destroy only a low proportion of Soviet ICBMs. This will change shortly with deployment of Trident II (D-5) missiles and the NAVSTAR satellite system. The US also has many more warheads deployed invulnerably on submarines and bombers.

4.  The USSR tends to deploy new models, whereas the US tends to modernize existing models.

5.  US missiles are generally more accurate than their Soviet counterparts, especially the SLBMs. Soviet ICBMs are catching up rapidly to their US counterparts in accuracy. The US has a substantial lead in the technology of highly accurate cruise missiles. The USSR has generally compensated for its inferior accuracy by retaining larger megatonnage. A higher percentage of the US SLBM force is MIRVed.

6.  The US and Soviet nuclear arsenals are not directly comparable, since they are configured differently, with somewhat different strengths and weaknesses. Hence, it is unclear that the question "Who is ahead?" can meaningfully be answered.

## Policy Issues

### Should the US continue building and deploying long-range cruise missiles?

**Yes:**  Cruise missiles rely heavily on the technology of electronic microminiaturization, in which the US is far ahead of the USSR. The US can take advantage of this lead by obtaining at low cost effective weapons, which can be deployed on a variety of launchers. If it fails to exploit this opportunity, the USSR will surely continue to develop, improve, and accumulate weapons of this sort. Moreover, because they fly slowly, cruise missiles are not destabilizing; that is, they are not provocative, first-strike weapons.

**No:**  With the addition of Stealth technology, these weapons may become so difficult to detect that they could be potential first-strike weapons. In addition, cruise missiles are so small that they can easily be hidden almost anywhere. As a result, once both sides have deployed them in significant numbers, their presence (or more important, their eventual removal) can never be verified, potentially dooming us to a never-ending arms race. US-built ground-launched cruise missiles have already been deployed in large numbers in Europe, and the US is engaged in deploying large numbers of air- and sea-launched cruise missiles as well. The USSR is currently developing and flight-testing comparable weapons. If we fail to agree to mutual restraint on these weapons the US will have exploited a short-term advantage, but one that everyone will regret eventually.

### Should the US deploy the MX missile?  (Note: In 1985, Congress authorized the purchase of 50, to be deployed in hardened Minuteman silos.)

**Yes:**  The MX is needed to rectify the dangerous "window of vulnerability," whereby the USSR could destroy American land-based ICBMs in a "surgical" preemptive strike causing relatively little civilian damage. Such a first strike would leave the US with only its slow-flying bombers and its relatively inaccurate SLBMs. After attacking US ICBMs, the Soviet leadership could announce that any US retaliation against Soviet cities would lead to destruction of US cities, in effect giving the US the ultimatum of "quit while you are only somewhat behind," whereupon the president would have no choice but to capitulate. Actually, the imbalance in US and Soviet nuclear forces is such that the USSR might not even have to attack our ICBMs first, it might be sufficient just to threaten this action. It is therefore necessary for the US to have weapons that could plausibly retaliate against any missiles that the Soviets have held in reserve, which they would otherwise use to blackmail the US.

Furthermore, the US has not deployed a new ICBM since the Minuteman, more than 10 years ago, during which time the USSR has introduced at least four new models. The MX will be the largest ICBM in the US arsenal, but even so it will be smaller than the large Soviet ICBMs; the MX is desperately needed to correct the unacceptable asymmetry in ICBMs between the US and USSR, although even it will not entirely do the job. In addition, the US cannot expect its European allies to accept new intermediate-range, land-based ballistic missiles (IRBMs), such as Pershing IIs and GLCMs, on their soil if it is not willing to assume its own share of the burden. Such weapons are indeed expensive, but war would be even more expensive yet. The cost of the MX missile must be evaluated against the threat posed by the USSR and the increments it will provide for its security. Moreover, the US cannot realistically hope to persuade the USSR to reduce its missile forces if it unilaterally foregoes a major weapon, independent of any negotiation. Thus, the MX is needed as a "bargaining chip"; only by having it in the arsenal can the US induce the Soviets to give up some of their weapons, notably their heavy ICBMs, such as the SS-18s. To forego the MX would signal a lack of resolve and might effectively hand the USSR a military victory at no cost to them.

**No:** The "window of vulnerability" does not exist. Theoretical calculations of kill probabilities have little relation to the real world, especially since they do not take account of bias factors, polar anomalies, and potential errors of all sorts. It is inconceivable that the USSR could count on thousands of people and millions of components all acting simultaneously and flawlessly the very first and only time. And even if all

American ICBMs were destroyed in a first strike, the US would still have more than sufficient retaliatory forces to wipe out the aggressor: just one Poseidon submarine, for example, carries 160 MIRVed warheads, approximately equal to 640 Hiroshimas. No Soviet leader could ever assume that the US would not retaliate if its ICBMs were attacked. Moreover, after studying 34 different basing modes, no economically and politically acceptable basing mode for the MX has been found that leaves it invulnerable. So even if the "window of vulnerability" was real, which it is not, the MX would not close it. MX proponents cannot have it both ways: either land-based ICBMs are vulnerable, in which case the MX would also be, or they are not, in which case there is no justification for the MX.

By deploying the heavily MIRVed MX in existing Minuteman silos, even if "superhardened," the US would be presenting the USSR with a tempting target, a sitting duck, since a single incoming warhead (or even two) would destroy 10. Because of its combination of MIRVing, accuracy, and warhead yield, the MX is not a retaliatory weapon. Rather, the MX is clearly a silo buster, suitable only for attacking the hardened silos of the other side. As such, it could well precipitate war in the event of a crisis, since the USSR, fearing that war is inevitable and that the US is about to attack their ICBMs with its own, may be led to preempt by attacking the US. The MX may also drive them to a very dangerous "launch on warning" posture, in which missiles are fired on warning of attack. This could lead to nuclear war by false alarm. In fact, the theoretical vulnerability of MX missiles may even force the US to launch on warning. Just because they have large ICBMs does not mean that we should: monkey-see, monkey-do is not good nuclear policy.

Finally, history shows that most bargaining chips, once deployed, are never bargained away; they become part of the arsenal. Rather than leading to Soviet reductions, the MX may just as well lead to Soviet intransigence and the determination to build yet more missiles, thereby reducing the security of both sides. After all, when it builds missiles, the US response is usually to build more yet. When no negotiations were underway, it was claimed that the US needed the MX to "bring the Soviets to the bargaining table." When negotiations are underway, supposedly the US needs the MX "so as not to undercut the negotiators." And presumably if negotiations fail, the need for the MX will be even greater. Isn't it likely that the real governmental commitment is to the MX itself rather than to enhanced security or arms reductions? Rather than planning to build this weapon to ensure success in negotiations, it seems more likely that things have been turned around: the US is negotiating to secure more success in building domestic support for the weapons. The MX is a move in the wrong direction, toward instability and a heightened arms race.

### Should the US build the Trident II (D-5) missile?

**Yes:** The Trident II will provide the US with the same basic advantages as the MX, with the added benefits that these submarine-based missiles will be invulnerable; and since they can be deployed much closer to the USSR, their short flight time will keep the Soviets honest.

**No:** The Trident II will provide the US with the same basic disadvantages as the MX, with the added danger that they will be especially destabilizing because there will be more D-5s than MXs; and because of their short flight time, the D-5 will be even more likely than the MX to provoke a nuclear war in the event of a crisis.

### Should the US build the B-1B bomber as a follow-on to the B-52s?

**Yes:** The B-52s are too old, often older than the crews who fly them. The USSR has deployed increasingly effective antiaircraft defenses, which require increasingly sophisticated airplanes to penetrate Soviet airspace. Bombers can be recalled if necessary and are not as provocative as ballistic missiles, since they are not suitable for a surprise first strike.

**No:** The B-52s have been upgraded and such upgrading can continue, giving them at least another decade of service. Penetration of Soviet airspace is not needed, since bombers are used increasingly as launch platforms for SRAMs and ALCMs. The B-1B would cost many billions of dollars and would quickly be obsolete anyhow, presumably to be replaced by Stealth technology.

---

## KEY TERMS

delivery systems

strategic

tactical

deployed

triad

avionics

short-range attack missiles (SRAMs)

air-launched cruise missiles (ALCMs)

sea-launched cruise missiles (SLCMs)

ground-launched cruise missiles (GLCMs)

TERCOM

payload

soft target

intercontinental ballistic missiles (ICBMs)

ballistic missiles

boost phase

glide phase

reentry phase

postboost phase

reentry vehicle (RV)

multiple reentry vehicles (MRVs)

multiple independently targetable reentry vehicles (MIRVs)

circular error probable (CEP)

inertial guidance

NAVSTAR

maneuvering reentry vehicles (MARVs)

reliability

bias factor

throw weight

equivalent megatonnage (EMT)

hardened target

lethality

ICBM vulnerability

one-shot kill probability

cross-targeting

two-shot kill probability

fratricide

readiness

hot-launched

cold-launched

reload capacity

strategic posture

submarine-launched ballistic missile (SLBM)

independent nuclear force

extremely low frequency (ELF)

antisubmarine warfare (ASW)

command, control, communications, and intelligence ($C^3I$)

negative control

positive control

redundancy

force multiplier

antisatellite (ASAT)

electromagnetic pulse (EMP)

## STUDY QUESTIONS

1. Distinguish between the role of strategic bombers as penetrating aircraft and as missile launch platforms.

2. How do ballistic missiles differ from cruise missiles?

3. Define MIRVing and distinguish it from MRVing.

4. Define CEP and discuss the relationship of accuracy, lethality, and warhead yield.

5. What are some relative advantages of ICBMs over SLBMs? what are some relative advantages of SLBMs over ICBMs?

6. What is meant by the "window of vulnerability"? What are some arguments for and against it?

7. Why are solid-fueled missiles generally considered superior to liquid-fueled ones?

8. In what sense can the US be said to be ahead in nuclear weapons? In what sense can the US be said to be behind?

9. Is there a "megaton gap"? Who does it favor, and why?

10. Compare the vulnerability of US and Soviet nuclear weapons.

11. Why is $C^3I$ considered so important, and yet so vulnerable?

## ADDITIONAL READINGS

Bracken, Paul. 1983. *The Command and Control of Nuclear Forces.* New Haven, CT: Yale University Press. A detailed study of $C^3I$, pointing out the great difficulties of managing nuclear forces during a crisis.

Cochran, Thomas, William Arkin, and Milton Hoenig. 1984. *Nuclear Weapons Databook.* Volume I: *U.S. Nuclear Forces and Capabilities.* Cambridge, MA: Ballinger. An encyclopedic account, complete with photos, of all nuclear-capable weapons in the US arsenal.

Dennis, Jack (Ed.). 1984. *The Nuclear Almanac.* Reading, MA: Addison-Wesley. An edited volume covering many aspects of nuclear weapons, with strong coverage of technical issues.

International Institute of Strategic Studies. *The Military Balance* and *Strategic Survey.* London: IISS. Published annually. Highly regarded, current information on the state of world weaponry, especially nuclear arms.

Stockholm International Peace Research Institute (SIPRI) yearbook. *World Armaments and Disarmaments.* London and New York: Taylor & Francis. Published annually. An excellent compilation of data on the current status of the arms race, including in-depth articles dealing with issues arising during each year.

# 3 Tactical, Theater, and Conventional Forces

*How many divisions has the Pope?*
Josef Stalin to his foreign minister

In recent years, nuclear weapons have become increasingly integrated into the conventional forces of both superpowers. Thus, many short- and medium-range aircraft are **dual capable,** able to use either conventional or nuclear munitions. Hundreds of artillery pieces on each side have sufficient range to fire nuclear shells. In addition, strategic delivery vehicles can be outfitted with conventional weapons as well: cruise missiles, for example. Even strategic bombers are not limited to delivery of nuclear weapons: large numbers of B-52s were employed dropping conventional explosives during the Vietnam war. And finally, with the development of increasingly lethal conventional weapons (notably air–fuel mixtures and cluster bombs) that approach the smaller nuclear weapons in destructive potential, the distinction between nuclear and conventional weapons is blurred still further.

Nevertheless, it is practical to distinguish conventional from nuclear forces. It is also important to make this distinction, because once nuclear weapons are used in combat between nuclear-armed foes, an important psychological "firebreak" will have been crossed, after which escalation to all-out nuclear war might well occur.

When most people think about nuclear weapons, they tend to focus on strategic nuclear weapons, the long-range missiles and bombers. However, there are actually more short- and medium-range weapons in the arsenals of both superpowers. In this brief chapter, we shall first discuss these short- and medium-range nuclear weapons, then quickly examine the balance of conventional forces.

## TACTICAL NUCLEAR WEAPONS

Tactical weapons, designed for use on a battlefield, are typically of short range, and they can be delivered by a wide variety of systems. Nuclear landmines, depth charges, or undersea mines, for example, can be emplaced very much like conventional explosives (Fig. 3.1). For the US, such weapons are typically in the range of 1–10 kilotons. Since nuclear weapons can be made as small as a hundred pounds or so, they can be carried in small rockets, and fired air-to-ground, air-to-air, ground-to-air, ground-to-ground, ship-to-ship, ship-to-ground, and so on. They are also available for use in large artillery. (Note that "nuclear artillery" are nuclear weapons fired by large howitzers, using traditional high explosives; they are not in any way nuclear-powered.)

The navies of both the US and the USSR have deployed a wide array of tactical nuclear weapons, including torpedoes, undersea mines, depth charges, and short-range rockets. A growing proportion of the major warships of both nations carry tactical nuclear weapons of one sort or another. The majority of tactical nuclear weapons on both sides, however, are deployed in Europe. (This has led some people to comment that a tactical nuclear weapon is one that explodes in Germany.) The exact number of Soviet tactical nuclear weapons is unclear, but it is generally acknowledged that the United States, whose ordnance includes a preponderance of 8-inch and 155-mm nuclear artillery shells (Fig. 3.2), has deployed more very-short-range weapons (less than 200 km) than has the USSR. In addition, the US has stockpiled the components for nearly 1,000 enhanced radiation warheads ("neutron bombs") in New York State. A large number of atomic demolition mines—originally intended for possible use in closing mountain passes and thus blocking invasion routes into western Europe—are scheduled to be withdrawn.

When it comes to medium- and long-range tactical nuclear weapons—those with a range of 200–1,000 kilometers—the United States and the Soviet Union have deployed roughly comparable numbers, with the USSR slightly ahead at the longer end, because of somewhat more tactical aircraft.

## THEATER NUCLEAR WEAPONS

Of particular interest and concern is a third category that has only recently been introduced into the simple strategic/tactical distinction: long-range "tactical" nuclear weapons, capable of traveling more than 1,000 kilometers but not reaching true intercontinental distances (i.e., 5,000 km or so). These are sometimes referred to as **theater nuclear weapons, long-range theater nuclear forces (LRTNFs),** or **intermediate-range nuclear forces (INF),** because unlike tactical or battlefield forces, they can be used throughout a wide theater of operations. We discuss the dynamics and current status of theater nuclear weapons in Chapter 10, in connection with negotiated agreements, because these weapons have been the subject of political controversy and prolonged efforts at negotiated settlements.

For now, let us note that the Soviet Union has deployed about 400 SS-20 ballistic missiles; these solid-fueled theater missiles are MIRVed with three warheads apiece and have a range of about 5,000 kilometers. About a third of these are believed to be targeted on China. NATO has deployed 108 Pershing II ballistic missiles in West Germany; these theater missiles are also solid-fueled, and fitted with single warheads. It is expected that in the absence of some negotiated reductions, NATO will also have deployed 464 ground-launched cruise missiles in Europe by 1988. About half this number had been deployed as of 1986 in Britain, Italy, and Belgium. SS-20s, Pershing IIs, and GLCMs are all mobile; this reduces their vulnerability, but adds a level of complexity to nuclear negotiations, since if these weapons are simply removed from the European theater and not destroyed altogether, they can theoretically be brought back in times of crisis. Tables 3.1 and 3.2 summarize US and Soviet tactical and theater nuclear weapons in Europe.

## CONVENTIONAL FORCES

### The Worldwide Balance

Even though our primary focus is on the arms race and nuclear war, the comparative nonnuclear military might of the United States and the Soviet Union is noteworthy. For one thing, a look at conventional forces will help round out our appreciation of the US-Soviet military and political competition. Even more important, perhaps: relative strengths and weaknesses in conventional forces have a strong influence on nuclear weapons policy. In particular, it is widely perceived that the USSR enjoys superiority in conventional forces over the United States; this is the main reason for the US policy of reliance on the threatened use of nuclear weapons in the event of a conventional conflict with the USSR.

There is no simple, meaningful way of comparing the military balance between the United States and the USSR. The population of the USSR, for example, is larger by about 35 million, but the gross national product of the United States is about twice that of the USSR. The United States has a much larger system of more powerful allies, although these allies tend to be feisty and independent. By contrast, the USSR has allies that are more obedient, but are also fundamentally more unreliable—it has been suggested, for example, that Red Army forces in Hungary, Czechoslovakia, and East Germany are there more to act as garrison troops occupying subjugated nations than to defend them against the West or to help launch an invasion. The USSR also has a 4,500-mile unfriendly border with China, to which it has detailed nearly a million soldiers. It is therefore questionable whether Soviet forces in this "theater" could be considered to be available for use elsewhere. And it is uncertain on whose side China should be counted in assessing the worldwide military balance.

In addition to industrial and economic strength, allies, and sheer numbers of personnel and weapons, any meaningful comparison of the two superpowers must take into account the following differences: geographical advantages and disadvantages, the quality of equipment (including capabilities and reliability), morale and dependability of the armed forces, training and proficiency, leadership, alliance cohesiveness,

**FIGURE 3.1 Plume of water produced by underwater detonation of nuclear demolition mine.** (Photo courtesy of the US Department of Energy.)

**FIGURE 3.2 Mushroom cloud rising from the firing of the world's first nuclear artillery shell, at Frenchman Flat, Nevada, 1953.** (Photo courtesy of the US Department of Energy.)

capacity for reinforcement, economic and political ability to support a prolonged conventional armed struggle, and so forth. For example, in one sense the USSR is better situated geographically to fight in Europe because of shorter communication and supply lines; but at the same time its situation is less desirable, since such a conflict would be taking place adjacent to the Soviet homeland. The USSR can accordingly be seen as more threatening to Europe than it is threatened by Europe, or vice versa. Others see Europe as threatened by the nuclear policies of both superpowers.

In general, Soviet military equipment tends to be more basic in design, and thus cheaper and qualitatively inferior to its American counterparts. However, such equipment is generally acknowledged to be rugged and is often produced in larger numbers. The US and its allies have long relied on qualitative superiority

to compensate for inferior numbers. The Soviet armed forces are composed largely of conscripts; by contrast, the US armed forces are recruits and are generally considered to be better trained and more highly motivated. Manpower comparisons between the two nations (as of 1985) are as follows:

| Service | United States | Soviet Union |
|---|---|---|
| Army | 780,800 | 1,840,000 |
| Navy | 564,800 | 490,000 |
| Air Force | 594,500 | 400,000 |
| Marines (US) | 196,600 | |
| Naval infantry (USSR) | | 16,000 |

These figures exclude about 1,135,000 Soviet border guards, internal security, railroad, and

**TABLE 3.1  Soviet nuclear forces in Europe**

| Delivery system | Weapon system Type | No. deployed | Year deployed | Range (km) | Warheads × yield |
|---|---|---|---|---|---|
| *Nonnaval systems* | | | | | |
| Aircraft | Tu-16 Badger | 316 | 1955 | 4,800 | 2 × bombs and ASMs |
| | Tu-22 Blinder | 139 | 1962 | 2,200 | 1 × bombs or ASMs |
| | Tactical aircraft[a] | 2,545 | — | 700–1,000 | 1–2 × bombs |
| Land-based missiles | SS-20 | 414 | 1977 | 5,000 | 3 × 150 kt |
| | SS-4 | 224 | 1959 | 2,000 | 1 × 1 Mt |
| | SS-12 | 120 | 1969 | 800 | 1 × 200 kt–1 Mt |
| | SS-22 | 100 | 1979 | 900 | 1 × 1 Mt |
| | Scud B | 570 | 1965 | 280 | 1 × 100–500 kt |
| | SS-23 | 48 | 1982 | 350 | 1 × 100 kt |
| | Frog | 620 | 1965 | 70 | 1 × 10–200 kt |
| | SS-21 | 120 | 1978 | 120 | 1 × 20–100 kt |
| | SS-C-1B[b] | 100 | 1962 | 450 | 1 × 50–200 kt |
| | Other[c] | n.a. | 1956 | 40–300 | 1 × low kt |
| Artillery | Various[d] | 1,080 | 1974 | 10–30 | 1 × low kt |
| Atomic demolition mines | n.a. | n.a. | n.a. | | n.a. |
| *Naval systems* | | | | | |
| Aircraft | Tu-22M Backfire | 105 | 1974 | 5,500 | 2 × bombs or ASMs |
| | Tu-16 Badger | 240 | 1961 | 4,800 | 1–2 × bombs or ASMs |
| | Tu-22 Blinder | 35 | 1962 | 2,200 | 1 × bombs |
| | ASW aircraft | 200 | | | 1 × depth bombs |
| Antiship cruise missiles | SS-N-3 | 336 | 1962 | 450 | 1 × 350 kt |
| | SS-N-7 | 96 | 1968 | 56 | 1 × 200 kt |
| | SS-N-9 | 200 | 1968 | 280 | 1 × 200 kt |
| | SS-N-12 | 136 | 1976 | 500 | 1 × 350 kt |
| | SS-N-19 | 88 | 1980 | 460 | 1 × 500 kt |
| | SS-N-22 | 36 | 1981 | 110 | 1 × ? kt |
| ASW missiles and torpedoes | SS-N-14 | 310 | 1968 | 50 | 1 × low kt |
| | SS-N-15 | 76 | 1972 | 40 | 1 × 10 kt |
| | SUW-N-1 | 10 | 1967 | 30 | 1 × 5 kt |
| | Torpedoes | n.a. | 1957 | 16 | 1 × low kt |
| Ship-to-air missiles | SA-N-6 | 264 | 1977 | 55 | 1 × low kt |

*Source:* Modified from SIPRI (1985).

[a] Nuclear-capable tactical aircraft models include Su-24 Fencer, Su-17 Fitter, MiG-27 Flogger, MiG-21 Fishbed, Yak-28 Brewer, MiG-25 Foxbat, and Su-25 Frogfoot.

[b] Land-based antiship missile.

[c] Land-based surface-to-air missiles. Nuclear-capable SAMs probably include SA-1, SA-2, SA-5, and SA-10.

[d] Artillery includes 152-mm towed and self-propelled guns and 180-mm, 203-mm, and 240-mm calibres.

**TABLE 3.2  US nuclear forces in Europe**

| Delivery system | Weapon system Type | No. deployed | Year deployed | Range (km) | Warheads × yield |
|---|---|---|---|---|---|
| *Nonnaval systems* | | | | | |
| Aircraft | Various[a] | 2,000 | — | 1,060 / 2,400 | 1–3 × bombs |
| Land-based missiles | Pershing II | 100 | 1983 | 1,790 | 1 × 0.3–80 kt |
| | GLCM | 80 | 1983 | 2,500 | 1 × 0.2–150 kt |
| | Pershing 1a | 144 | 1962 | 740 | 1 × 60–400 kt |
| | Lance | 100 | 1972 | 125 | 1 × 1–100 kt |
| | Honest John | 24 | 1954 | 38 | 1 × 1–20 kt |
| | Nike Hercules | 200 | 1958 | 160 | 1 × 1–20 kt |
| Artillery | Various[b] | 4,300 | 1956 | 30 | 1 × 0.1–12 kt |
| Atomic demolition mines | Medium/special | 610 | 1964 | — | 1 × 0.01–15 kt |
| *Naval systems* | | | | | |
| Carrier aircraft | Various[c] | 900 | — | 550 / 1,800 | 1–2 × bombs |
| Land-attack SLCMs | Tomahawk | 50 | 1984 | 2,500 | 1 × 5–150 kt |
| ASW systems | ASROC | n.a. | 1961 | 10 | 1 × 5–10 kt |
| | SUBROC | n.a. | 1965 | 60 | 1 × 5–10 kt |
| | P-3/S-3/SH-3 | 630 | 1964 | 2,500 | 1 × <20 kt |
| Ship-to-air missiles | Terrier | n.a. | 1956 | 35 | 1 × 1 kt |

*Source:* Modified from SIPRI (1985).
[a]Includes US Air Force F-4, F-16, and F-111, and NATO F-16, F-100, F-104, and Tornado.
[b]There are two types of nuclear artillery (155 and 203 mm) with three different warheads: a 0.1-kt 155-mm shell; a 1–12-kt 203-mm shell; and a 1-kt enhanced-radiation, 203-mm shell.
[c]Aircraft include Navy A-6, A-7, and F/A-18 and Marine Corps A-4, A-6, and AV-8B. Bombs include yields from 20 kilotons to 1 megaton.

**FIGURE 3.3 US Marines test-firing a tube-launched, optically tracked, wire-command-linked (TOW) antitank missile. Precision-guided munitions of this sort are considered to be quite effective against large targets such as war-ships or tanks.** (Photo courtesy of the US Department of Defense.)

construction troops, but include 1,500,000 communications and general support troops for which there is no US equivalent. In addition, many of the tasks performed by military personnel in the Soviet Union (railroad maintenance and construction, assistance with agricultural harvests, etc.) are civilian tasks in other economies. Therefore, the large number of military personnel in the USSR may have, at least in part, nonmilitary significance. The USSR is primarily a continental power, as evidenced by its large army; the United States is more a maritime power, with a far greater array of alliances, foreign military bases, and economic interests spread worldwide. The USSR relies more heavily on manpower; the US, on technology.

Let us take one example of the difficulty of making numerical comparisons: tanks. The USSR and the US have 51,000, and 12,000, respectively. This is consistent with the Red Army's emphasis on large quantities of heavy machinery and its role as a land power. However, many of the Soviet tanks are of World War II vintage. US tanks are faster, better armored, carry more firepower, and provide far better crew conditions and communications. Also, the best defense against a tank is likely to be not another tank, but rather, antitank weaponry, including helicopters and highly accurate precision-guided munitions, in which the US is acknowledged to have a substantial lead. The destruction of the British destroyer *Sheffield* by a single Exocet missile during the Falklands war of 1982 emphasized that large, expensive weapons—such as big naval

vessels or tanks—are increasingly vulnerable to small, inexpensive, precision-guided munitions of this sort (Fig. 3.3).

The Soviet Union has 3,260 tactical combat aircraft; the United States, 3,700. The Soviet Union emphasizes the basing of such aircraft near its borders, especially with Europe and with China. The United States emphasizes mobility, especially the forward basing of aircraft at foreign military bases—in the Philippines, Japan, Korea, Europe, and elsewhere—as well as the use of large aircraft carriers. Historically, the Soviet navy has been almost entirely concerned with its coastal waters; recent years, however, have seen the beginning of a true "blue water navy," capable of "projecting power" away from Soviet shores. The navy of the USSR includes 293 surface combatants; the US navy, 192. However, 152 of the Soviet ships are small frigates, most appropriate for coastal use. The US navy relies heavily on its 14 aircraft carriers, organized into battle groups. These carriers range from 51,000 to 91,000 tons, with most toward the upper end of that size range. The USSR has four very small carriers, of 37,000 tons, carrying relatively few, low-performance, vertical takeoff aircraft. These are all very short-range interceptors, with a restricted airtime.

On balance, the United States is far better equipped for international power projection via its military, because of (1) a much larger and more competent force of marines, (2) many more and larger amphibious landing vessels, and (3) a much more effective airlift capacity,

**FIGURE 3.4 The *USS New Jersey*, a World War II battleship that has been outfitted with sea-launched cruise missiles (SLCMs) in addition to its regular armament including 16-inch guns.** (Photo courtesy of the US Department of Defense.)

featuring well-developed midair refueling. In addition, the United States has begun developing a growing number of refurbished battleship groups, equipped with cruise missiles as well as their enormous, 16-inch guns (Fig. 3.4).

The Soviet Union has more than twice as many attack submarines as the United States (201 to 91), but the US submarine fleet is favored by superior technology, superior training, geographic advantages, and the presence of many maritime allies.

On balance, most observers agree that the United States navy is considerably superior to its Soviet counterpart, that the air forces are comparable, with a Soviet lead in continental defenses and a United States lead in technology and skilled manpower, and that the Soviet army is larger and quite impressive as a land force, making up in numbers and sheer firepower what it lacks in finesse. The USSR has also invested much more heavily than the United States in tanks, heavy armor, and artillery.

### The Balance of Conventional Forces in Europe

The probability of a worldwide conventional war between the United States and the Soviet Union is generally agreed to be vanishingly small (perhaps because of the presence of nuclear weapons). Therefore, comparisons such as the preceding section may be of little value. And because of the pitfalls in comparing numerical data, such evidence may be misleading as well.

However, greater interest and importance attaches to evaluations of the military balance in Europe. It is always possible that US and Soviet forces will directly oppose each other in some third world theater, and in such cases, the relative "power projecting" capabilities of the two nations may prove crucial. It is more likely yet that such conflicts will occur between the troops of one side and third world people from another nation—such as the US and Vietnam, or the USSR and Afghanistan—or that third world troops will oppose each other, with assistance ultimately provided by the superpowers. The most likely site for a direct US-Soviet confrontation appears to be in Europe, where substantial forces from the two contending sides face each other, across a lengthy boundary with a bloody history, and with little in the way of demilitarized buffer zones.

Comparisons of the military balance in Europe require attention to the respective alliances: the North Atlantic Treaty Organization for the United States, and the Treaty Organization (the Warsaw Pact) for the USSR. **NATO** includes the United States, Canada, Great Britain, West Germany, Iceland, Norway, Denmark, Belgium, Luxembourg, the Netherlands, Italy, Greece, Portugal, Spain, Greece, and Turkey. France is part of the political structure of NATO, but maintains an independent military posture. The **Warsaw Pact (WP)** includes the Soviet Union, East Germany, Poland, Hungary, Bulgaria, Romania, and Czechoslovakia (Fig. 3.5).

The NATO nations outnumber the Warsaw Pact in population by about 1.5:1, and in gross national

**FIGURE 3.5 NATO and the Warsaw Pact. NATO countries are shown in a hatched pattern, WP in light gray, non-aligned nations in white. France is a member of NATO's political structure but not its military command. Not shown are NATO members Canada and the United States.**

product by nearly 3:1. There has been much controversy over methods of estimating the Soviet military budget, with critics charging that US government estimates tend to exaggerate that figure (see Chapter 12). However, even taking the US government's own figures, NATO's military spending has consistently exceeded that of the WP. Here is a brief, summarized comparison.

|  | NATO | Warsaw Pact |
|---|---|---|
| Population | 575 million | 375 million |
| Armed forces | 4.9 million | 4.76 million |
| Gross national product | $5.7 trillion | $2.0 trillion |
| Annual military spending | $260 billion | $127 billion |

Some important aspects of the conventional balance in Europe is shown in Table 3.3. These figures do not include the military forces of France.

Certain basic patterns are worth noting.

- *Manpower.* The two alliances are almost precisely equal in armed manpower. NATO has somewhat

more total ground forces, but some of these are deployed in North America, leaving a small WP advantage in continental Europe. The WP has an advantage in the Central Region (Germany), whereas NATO has an advantage in the South (Italy, Greece, and the Balkans). NATO has fewer divisions than the WP, but each division tends to be larger, so comparisons based on number of divisions can be misleading.

- *Armor.* The WP has a substantial lead in tanks and artillery (Fig. 3.6). On the other hand, NATO is acknowledged to lead in **precision-guided antitank munitions.** These small, highly accurate weapons are either wire-guided or directed to their targets by television remote control, infrared light, lasers, or radar. It is generally acknowledged that NATO enjoys a substantial lead both in the technology and numbers of such weapons, having deployed upward of 300,000; exact numbers for the WP are unavailable. Some people interpret the large numbers of WP tanks as threatening a possible inva-

**TABLE 3.3 Comparison of NATO and Warsaw Pact (WP) conventional forces**

| | NATO (excluding US) | US | NATO (total) | Ratio of total NATO to WP | WP (total) | USSR | WP (excluding USSR) |
|---|---|---|---|---|---|---|---|
| *Manpower (× 1,000)* | | | | | | | |
| Total armed forces | 2,888 | 2,136 | 5,024 | 1:1.23 | 6,169 | 5,115 | 1,054 |
| Total reserves | 3,984 | 1,440 | 5,424 | 1:1.31 | 7,119 | 5,300 | 1,819 |
| Total ground forces | 1,916 | 977 | 2,893 | 1:1.1 | 2,657 | 1,840 | 817 |
| Ground forces in Europe | 1,550 | 217 | 1,767 | 1:1.1 | 1,960 | 1,143 | 817 |
| *Ground force equipment* | | | | | | | |
| Main battle tanks | 15,742 | 5,000 | 20,742 | 1:2.4 | 50,500 | 36,000 | 14,500 |
| Artillery, multiple rocket launchers | 9,795 | 670 | 10,465 | 1:1.9 | 19,800 | 13,500 | 6,300 |
| Antiaircraft guns | 5,310 | 100 | 5,410 | 1:1.4 | 7,487 | 4,986 | 2,501 |
| Antitank guided missiles | ? | ? | 4,644 | 2.6:1 | 1,822 | ? | ? |
| *Naval units* | | | | | | | |
| Submarines | 145 | 53 | 198 | 1:1 | 149 | 146 | 3 |
| Aircraft carriers | 7 | 7 | 14 | 4.7:1 | 3 | 3 | 0 |
| Cruisers | 3 | 11 | 14 | 1:1.8 | 25 | 25 | 0 |
| Destroyers | 83 | 38 | 121 | 2.4:1 | 51 | 50 | 1 |
| Frigates | 138 | 43 | 181 | 1.4:1 | 130 | 128 | 2 |
| Corvettes/large patrol craft | 121 | 0 | 121 | 3.7:1 | 30 | 20 | 10 |
| Minesweepers | 261 | 3 | 264 | 1:1.4 | 362 | 285 | 77 |
| Amphibious craft | 212 | 25 | 237 | 2:1 | 118 | 64 | 54 |
| *Naval and maritime aircraft* | | | | | | | |
| Bombers | 0 | 0 | 0 | — | 254 | 254 | 0 |
| Attack planes | 97 | 336 | 433 | 4.2:1 | 104 | 70 | 34 |
| Fighters | 35 | 168 | 203 | — | 0 | | 0 |
| Antisubmarine warfare | 82 | 70 | 152 | 1.2:1 | 130 | 130 | 0 |
| Marine reconnaisance | 97 | 77 | 174 | 1.4:1 | 125 | 115 | 10 |
| Antisub helicopters | 340 | 136 | 476 | 2.8:1 | 170 | 170 | 0 |
| *Land-attack aircraft and fighters* | | | | | | | |
| Bombers | 28 | 0 | 28 | 1:17 | 470 | 470 | 0 |
| Ground attack fighters | 1,768 | 522 | 2,290 | 1:1 | 2,430 | 1,870 | 560 |
| Interceptors | 557 | 96 | 653 | 1:6.9 | 4,500 | 3,200 | 1,300 |
| Reconnaissance | 338 | 38 | 376 | 1:1.8 | 650 | 490 | 160 |
| Armed helicopters | 605 | 330 | 935 | 1:3.4 | 3,150 | ? | ? |

**FIGURE 3.6 Soviet T-72 medium battle tank. The WP leads NATO substantially in the number of tanks deployed.** (Photo courtesy of the US Department of Defense.)

sion of western Europe; others see them as primarily defensive, since Soviet military doctrine calls for an offensive response to aggression. Soviet armor may also be intended to maintain the subjugation of eastern Europe.

- *Navy.* NATO has a substantial lead, especially in large, ocean-going combatants. This is to be expected, given that NATO's membership is spread across the Atlantic.

- *Aircraft.* NATO has a substantial lead in naval and maritime aircraft; the WP has a substantial lead in numbers of land attack aircraft and fighters. On the other hand, the quality of NATO equipment as well as the level of training of NATO pilots is considered to be superior, although this gap is acknowledged to be narrowing.

There are other important comparisons to be made between NATO and the WP, but these are intangible and especially difficult to assess.

- *Reliability and cohesion.* Since NATO is composed of independent nations whose governments are for the most part democratically elected, there is no guarantee of unanimity, either during peace or in the event of armed conflict. It might take days for certain nations to agree on joint military cooperation (Greece and Turkey, for example, are bitter rivals), and others may conceivably refuse to participate. By contrast, alliance cohesion within the WP seems to be a less serious

problem for the Soviet Union during peacetime. But in the event of war, the USSR may not be able to count on the loyalty of Polish, Czech, or Hungarian troops. According to some experts, these Soviet "allies" are more eager to fight the Red Army than to fight NATO.

- *Reinforcements.* NATO would have to rely on lengthy and potentially vulnerable supply lines, across the Atlantic Ocean from the United States. Resupply should not be so difficult for the USSR. However, the Soviets may be hesitant to deplete their forces facing China in the Far East, especially in a wartime climate. In addition, the lengthy overland routes on which the USSR must depend in the event of a European war may be as susceptible to interdiction as are the lengthy over-water routes on which the US would rely.

- *Standardization.* Each NATO member nation tends to use its own equipment, with overall standardization far from a reality. By contrast, WP nations enjoy interchangeability of parts, equipment, and doctrine. The diversity of NATO's military forces, however, might complicate the planning of an opponent.

There is substantial debate over whether NATO's military forces are adequate for their task. Some claim that the Red Army could march to the English Channel any time it wished, in a week or so. Others maintain that NATO has sufficient forces to halt a conventional assault by the WP against western Europe. It is generally agreed, for example, that for an attack to be successful, the aggressor needs a significant numerical advantage over the defender, variously estimated at from 2:1 to 4:1. It has also been argued that the task for NATO is not to defeat an expected WP attack, but rather, to have the ability to render such an action unlikely to achieve its objectives, and to make such an attack unacceptably costly for the attacker. This would presumably deter war by making it not worthwhile to attack in the first place.

Current NATO policy calls for a **"forward defense"** of western Europe, in which forces are deployed primarily along the eastern border of West Germany, to prevent initial penetration by the WP. Many experts consider this strategy to be militarily unwise. It seems to be politically necessary, however, since any plans to allow territory gains by an invading army in heavily populated, heavily industrialized West Germany would be difficult for the NATO public to accept. Alternatives to forward defense include a **"maneuver defense,"** in which invaders are allowed to penetrate and are then harassed within West Germany, or a **"deep strike," offensive strategy** that emphasizes long-range, disruptive attacks against staging areas and reinforcements in eastern Europe and western USSR. Peace movement leaders emphasize, by contrast, the feasibility of non-cooperation and "civilian defense," and they also question whether the WP does in fact have any aggressive designs on western Europe.

In any event, it is the expressed military doctrine of NATO that every effort will be made to repel a conventional assault with conventional forces. Given the potential fragility of its forward defense, however, NATO policy calls for the prompt use of tactical (short-range) nuclear forces, theater (medium-range) nuclear forces, and, if necessary, strategic nuclear weapons against the homeland of the USSR. Since this sequence would undoubtedly trigger retaliation against the US homeland, there is some question whether such a strategy would ever be carried out, or whether it should be.

Perhaps the biggest uncertainties about conventional war in Europe do not deal with the conventional weapons themselves, or with the relative strengths and weaknesses of the two alliances. Rather, they are threefold:

1. Whether the WP actually harbors aggressive designs toward western Europe (the USSR may or may not have similar but reciprocal concerns about NATO and eastern Europe)

2. Whether the use of conventional weapons in Europe would escalate to the use of nuclear weapons

3. Whether the use of tactical nuclear weapons in Europe would result in escalation to the use of strategic nuclear weapons

There is substantial reason to suspect that the answer to items 2 and 3 at least, is yes. Thus, it seems unlikely that leaders on either side would ever sue for peace without resorting to all the weapons available to them. The losing side, in short, would feel strong pressures to escalate. At present, all nuclear bombs and warheads deployed in continental Europe, except those of France, are under US control, whereas the delivery systems themselves typically belong to the various NATO members. Under the existing "two-key" system, both the US political leadership and that of the host country would have to agree to the use of nuclear weapons. However, in the event of war, pressure would almost certainly mount for such authority to be released to field commanders. This would be especially true because of the short range of many tactical nuclear weapons and because many of these weapons are positioned near the east-west borders; as a result, many tactical systems would be in danger of being overrun rather quickly after the eruption of hostilities. Commanders would therefore be faced with a desperate "use them or lose them" situation. Current policy calls for a phased withdrawal of some, but by no means all, US shorter range nuclear weapons in Europe by the early 1990s (Table 3.4).

Majority opinion among NATO military and political leaders is that NATO's conventional forces, taken alone, may be inadequate to stop a Warsaw Pact attack. However, the deliberate first use of nuclear weapons is not considered very credible, because of the likelihood of Soviet escalation, which in turn would probably lead to all-out strategic war. As a result, attention has focused on the potential for accidental or unintended use of nuclear weapons in a European conflict, as a result of $C^3I$ failures during the heat of battle. Some claim that such uncertainty is actually stabilizing, and they point to the benefits of "threats that leave something to chance." Thus, supporters of NATO's current nuclear policy maintain that uncertainty and the threat of nuclear escalation—intentional or otherwise—in the event of conventional war are precisely what is needed to deter such war in the first place. That is, conventional war is made less likely by making it more likely that if war begins, it will "go nuclear."

**TABLE 3.4  Planned changes in US nuclear weapons in Europe**

| Weapon system (warhead) | As of 1985 | Planned withdrawals | As of 1992 |
|---|---|---|---|
| *Stored in Europe* | | | |
| Pershing II | 54 | 0 | 108 |
| Pershing 1a | 231 | 131 | 100 |
| Ground-launched CM | 100 | 0 | 464 |
| Bombs | 1,730 | 0 | 1,730 |
| Lance | 690 | 0 | 690 |
| Honest John | 190 | 190 | 0 |
| Nike Hercules | 680 | 680 | 0 |
| 8-inch (W-33) | 930 | 500 | 430 |
| 8-inch (W-79) | 0 | 0 | 200 |
| 155-mm (W-48) | 730 | 350 | 380 |
| 155-mm (W-82) | 0 | 0 | 100 |
| Atomic demolition mines | 370 | 370 | 0 |
| Depth bombs | 190 | 0 | 190 |
| Total in Europe | 5,895 | 2,221 | 4,392 |
| *Committed to Europe* [a] | | | |
| Carrier bombs | 360 | 0 | 500 |
| Bombs | 600 | 0 | 800 |
| Depth bombs | 140 | 0 | 140 |
| Lance | 380 | 0 | 380 |
| 8-inch (W-79) | 200 | 0 | 200 |
| Total committed | 1,680 | 0 | 2,020 |
| **Total** | **7,575** | **2,221** | **6,412** |

*Source:* Modified from SIPRI (1985).
[a]Does not include tactical naval nuclear weapons.

Opponents point out that such a policy assumes that both sides will remain in complete control of all their forces. This state of affairs may well present Europe and the world with an unacceptably high danger of nuclear war in the event of $C^3I$ failures or if either side becomes convinced that the other is about to escalate. Hence, **"no first use"** advocates argue for much tighter controls over $C^3I$, as well as improved conventional defenses, in the context of an overall "no first use" policy. A similar option, receiving increased attention, is **"no early first use"**—that is, the pullback or elimination of short-range tactical nuclear weapons, to diminish the pressures for early first use, as well as the dangers of error.

## CHEMICAL AND BIOLOGICAL WARFARE (CBW)

More than 100,000 tons of lethal chemicals, mostly chlorine and mustard gas, was used during World War I, resulting in more than a million casualties and nearly 100,000 fatalities. During World War II, the major European combatants did not engage in appreciable chemical warfare, even though newer and more toxic substances had been discovered and stockpiled on both sides. There were two major reasons for this restraint. First, poison gas depends critically on the local weather conditions, notably the prevailing winds. When winds are unpredictable, they can disperse the gas substantially, directing it toward civilians or even

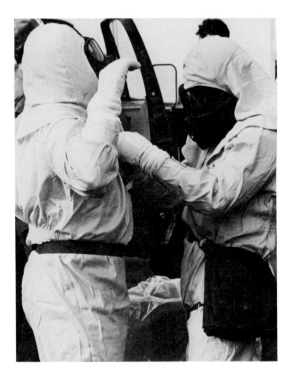

**FIGURE 3.7 US Air Force personnel getting into chemical protective outfits during a practice exercise.** (Photo courtesy of the US Department of Defense.)

one's own troops. Second, since each side had access to such weapons, it was widely recognized that their use would result in retaliation in kind. In short, it appears that mutual deterrence was operating. It is noteworthy that Japan used such weapons against the Chinese, and Italy against the Ethiopians—in both cases, the victims had no ability to retaliate.

There have been numerous international treaties banning the use of poison gas and of other forms of chemical and biological warfare (see Chapter 13). Nonetheless, there have also been technological innovations making CBW nearly as dangerous a prospect as nuclear war. Potential infectious biological warfare agents include such bacterial and viral diseases as tularemia, anthrax, plague, Q fever, and Venezuelan Equine Encephalitis (VEE). The USSR in particular has been accused of maintaining an anthrax research and production facility in the city of Sverdlovsk. Biological toxins that have potential military applications include staphylococcal enterotoxin, shellfish poison (saxi-

toxin), and botulinus toxin (produced by the bacteria causing the fatal disease botulism). A few kilograms of the latter, which could be produced for perhaps several thousand dollars, would contain enough lethal doses for all the world's population, assuming optimum conditions of distribution.

The USSR has been accused of using mycotoxins (fungal toxins) in Afghanistan and of facilitating the use of such materials by its Vietnamese allies in Kampuchea and Laos. However, these charges are controversial, and unproven. For one thing, chemical toxins, unlike biological ones, are not universally banned by treaty. And, the "yellow rain" in which these toxins have been implicated has also been attributed to natural causes, the pollen and feces of tropical bees. Several independent investigations, seeking to corroborate charges of chemical warfare by the USSR, have been unable to produce convincing evidence as of 1986.

The United States employed large amounts of chemical defoliants, notably 2,4-D, in Vietnam. Both the United States and the Soviet Union have also developed and stockpiled large quantities of odorless, invisible, and highly lethal nerve gas. The US currently maintains between 15,000 and 30,000 metric tons of such substances; the USSR, perhaps 300,000 tons. In 1985 Congress approved the production of new, upgraded **"binary" nerve gas** artillery shells. These consist of two chemicals that are nonlethal by themselves but are mixed to form a highly lethal gas when the weapon explodes. Because the two components can be stored separately, they are considered to be safer than current compounds. These include the very deadly agent VX, some of which leaked accidentally from the Dugway Proving Grounds in Utah in 1966, killing more than 6,000 sheep, some of them 45 miles away.

Widespread CBW could, in theory, produce fatalities comparable to nuclear war. Damage to property and structures would of course be much less, and whereas the initial effects of nuclear war would be apparent immediately, CBW agents would act after delays of minutes (for nerve gas and other chemicals) to days (for biological warfare agents). It is generally recognized that if soldiers are adequately trained and equipped, they can be made relatively immune to the effects of CBW. However, their combat efficiency would be greatly reduced by the necessity to wear bulky, heat-retaining respirators and protective suits (Fig. 3.7). Most citizens, on the other hand, are not trained or equipped to deal with CBW and it seems likely that—as in the case of nuclear war—they would bear the brunt of the casualties.

## Policy Issues

### Should NATO initiate a policy of "no first use" of nuclear weapons?

**Yes:**  Most Americans think that US and NATO policy is to make use of nuclear weapons only in retaliation, if the WP uses them first. This isn't true. Instead, the Western powers plan to use nuclear weapons, if necessary, to repel a conventional assault by the Warsaw Pact. This policy makes no sense, because it is either an empty bluff (if NATO wouldn't really use nuclear weapons) or a suicide pact (if it would). Europe cannot be defended by nuclear weapons; it can only be destroyed by them. A "no-first-use" policy would not be a mere declaratory statement; rather, it would be backed up with changes in training, doctrine, and weaponry to make it believable both to the NATO allies and to the WP. It may require some modest beefing up of NATO's conventional strength: greater efficiency of command and communications, prepositioning of supplies, construction of antitank defenses, and so on. But the conventional balance is close enough at present that dramatic increases in military expenditures would not be necessary. The money saved from canceled nuclear expenditures might well be sufficient. Short-range, tactical nuclear weapons are vulnerable to being overrun, and so, in the event of war there would be very great pressure to use them quickly before they were captured. A "no-first-use" policy would involve the removal of such weapons, thereby reducing the hair-trigger danger that now exists. It would also result in greater alliance unity, since disputes over nuclear weapons policy (which many Europeans resent as being dictated by the United States) have been a major internal threat to NATO. Finally, greater reliance on conventional forces would constitute a more effective deterrent, since the threat to use nuclear weapons—that is, to blow up Europe—may not be perceived as credible by Soviet leaders, whereas a no-first-use policy that relied on a realistic conventional deterrent would have more credibility.

**No:**  NATO policy has kept the peace for more than four decades in what had been for centuries one of the most war-torn regions of the world. NATO should be very cautious about changing something that has worked so well, and for so long. The WP has a lead over NATO in conventional forces, and it is entirely possible that it has been restrained only by the fear of NATO's nuclear arms. Having foregone the first use of nuclear weapons, it might be necessary to reinstitute the draft and to multiply the military budget enormously. Moreover, the European allies would have to do the same, and they show no signs of willingness to move in this direction. Removal of the American nuclear umbrella would therefore contribute even more to alliance disunity. Because of simple geography, the USSR is directly adjacent to western Europe; hence it is a palpable military threat that cannot help but have political consequences as well. NATO's European members need the reassurance that American nuclear weapons would be used if necessary, in their defense, if they are to have the confidence needed to maintain their political independence. The American nuclear umbrella therefore serves the important purpose of "coupling" the US to western Europe. Removal of this umbrella might induce NATO nations such as West Germany, which have thus far refrained from developing their own nuclear weapons, to begin doing so. This would be far more dangerous than the current situation.

### Should NATO and the WP agree to a battlefield nuclear weapons free zone in Europe?

**Yes:**  This proposal, first developed by the Palme Commission in 1982, would establish a region, 150 miles to the east and west, along the German-Czech border in central Europe. It would remove nuclear weapons from the immediate "use them or lose them" pressures that might otherwise develop in the event of conventional hostilities. Hence, it would make it less likely that war would escalate to nuclear war.

**No:**  This proposal would play to Soviet advantages in conventional forces. By reducing the ability of NATO to respond to a Soviet conventional assault with battlefield nuclear weapons, a nuclear free zone of this sort would make conventional war more likely to occur in the first place. It would also partially decouple the US from the defense of Europe, which has long been a Soviet ambition.

**Should the US build additional aircraft carriers as part of the goal of attaining a 600-ship navy?**

**Yes:** Aircraft carriers are an arena in which the US has a decided edge over the USSR. These mobile and immensely powerful vessels are ideal for projecting American power throughout the globe. They can be defended by support ships and aircraft. Aircraft carriers are simply one example of the conventional armed forces of the United States that must be strengthened. As a maritime power, the US must have the ability to confront and defeat the Soviet navy anywhere on earth.

**No:** Aircraft carriers are fantastically expensive to produce and to maintain. Given the availability of highly accurate, "smart" weapons, aircraft carriers are also sitting ducks. There is nothing magic or even militarily desirable about a 600-ship navy. Rather, this is simply one example of a narrow-minded obsession with building more weapons, of every sort, without thought to the purpose of these weapons and to whether they really contribute to national security.

**Should the US stockpile additional binary nerve gas?**

**Yes:** The Soviets have about 10 times the chemical warfare materials that the US does. Modernization of this aspect of the arsenal will serve to increase its safety while being stored and to deter use of such weapons in the event of war.

**No:** Such materials are immoral and are not even useful weapons. The US can protect its soldiers by respirators and other protective (defensive) gear. If more weapons of this sort are built, the Soviets will do the same. Far better to negotiate a mutual ban on CBW.

---

## KEY TERMS

dual capable

theater nuclear weapons

long-range theater nuclear forces (LRTNF)

intermediate-range nuclear forces (INF)

NATO

Warsaw Pact (WP)

precision-guided antitank munitions

forward defense

maneuver defense

"deep strike" offensive strategy

no first use

no early first use

chemical and biological warfare (CBW)

binary nerve gas

## STUDY QUESTIONS

1. Why do the USSR and the US differ with regard to the definition of strategic nuclear weapons?

2. What is meant by theater nuclear weapons? What special problems do they pose?

3. Given that our prime concern in this book is the arms race and nuclear war, why are we discussing conventional weapons at all?

4. Why is the European balance of power especially important?

5. Compare NATO and the WP with regard to manpower and weapons technology.

6. Why are precision-guided munitions especially relevant to the European balance of power?

7. What is the difference between power projection and national defense? What similarities might exist between the two?

8. Compare CBW with nuclear weapons.

## ADDITIONAL READINGS

Alternative Defence Commission. 1983. *Defence without the Bomb*. London and New York: Taylor & Francis. A report by a dovishly inclined commission that makes specific suggestions for the nonnuclear defense of NATO.

Cockburn, Andrew. 1983. *The Threat: Inside the Soviet Military Machine*. New York: Random House. An assessment of Soviet military forces (especially conventional forces) making the argument that the widespread image of Soviet military strength is greatly exaggerated.

European Security Study (ESECS). 1983. *Strengthening Conventional Deterrence in Europe*. New York: St. Martin's Press. A report by a dovishly inclined commission, also making specific suggestions for the nonnuclear defense of NATO.

Mansheimer, John. 1983. *Conventional Deterrence*. Ithaca, NY: Cornell University Press. A careful appraisal of the prospects for conventional deterrence, especially in Europe.

US Department of Defense. *Soviet Military Power.* Washington, DC: Government Printing Office. This annual publication emphasizes the size, capability, modernization, and danger posed by the Soviet armed forces.

# Part Two

# Nuclear Weapons Effects

**F**ortunately, it is impossible for anyone to know the exact effects of a large nuclear weapon, exploded on a civilian population. It is equally impossible for anyone to know the exact long-term effects of a nuclear war. However, our understanding of nuclear weapons is woefully incomplete if it is limited to numbers of weapons and the kinds available; we must have some appreciation of what they can do in order to understand why they are so terribly important, and why there is such concern that they should never be used.

There have been hundreds of test nuclear explosions during the decades since 1945, about half of them above ground and half underground. These have provided a large amount of information regarding the immediate or so-called prompt physical effects of nuclear explosions. The actual human, medical, economic, and ecological effects cannot, of course, be known with certainty as a result of such tests, even with the added information obtained from studying the consequences of the atomic bombing of Hiroshima and Nagasaki.

There is even more uncertainty regarding the long-term effects of nuclear war, because of a double unknown. First, there must be uncertainty about what, precisely, will take place during such a war. How many bombs will be used? Of what sort will they be? At what targets will they be aimed? Will they be exploded on the ground or in the air? What will the local and worldwide weather be like at the time? And so on. Second, even if we could have precise answers to the questions just listed, there would be uncertainty over what nuclear war would actually be like. There are many questions that can never be answered with certainty, either from studying past nuclear explosions, from laboratory tests, or from computer simulations. For example, what are the precise effects of large-scale, sudden heat and blast on cities? What is the possibility that nuclear detonations will have certain profound, long-lasting effects on the global climate? It is quite probable that nuclear war, if it ever occurs, will be a singular event; nothing like it has ever happened before in human history.

To some extent, when we study the likely effects of nuclear war, we are like exobiologists speculating about life in outer space—something that, to our knowledge, doesn't exist! But we have a particular responsibility to inform ourselves about the mysterious and fearsome subject of nuclear war, since unlike the case of hypothetical creatures from outer space, what we know—and what we do not know—about the effects of nuclear war may have a bearing on whether it someday becomes a reality.

# 4 Immediate Effects of Nuclear Explosions

*Earth rocks and shudders,*
*The roar of thunder, echoing from the depths bellows beside me.*
*Fiery wreaths of lightning flash, and whirlwinds toss the swirling dust;*
*Blasts of all winds leap forth in dreadful striving.*
*The sky is confounded in the sea.*
Aeschylus *(Prometheus Bound)*

## THE FIREBALL

A nuclear explosion is an exceptionally intense event. "The effects could well be called unprecedented, magnificent, beautiful, stupendous and terrifying," wrote Brigadier General Thomas Farrell, in the official government report concerning the first atomic bomb test at Alamogordo, New Mexico, in July 1945.

> *No man-made phenomenon of such tremendous power had ever occurred before. The lighting effects beggared description. The whole country was lighted by a searing light with the intensity many times that of the midday sun. It was golden, purple, violet, gray and blue. It lighted every peak, crevasse and mountain range with a clarity and beauty that cannot be described but must be seen to be imagined. It was the beauty the great poets dream about but describe most poorly and inadequately. Thirty seconds after the explosion came, first the air blast pressing hard against people and things, to be followed almost immediately by the strong, sustained awesome roar which warned of doomsday and made us feel that we puny things were blasphemous to dare tamper with the forces heretofore reserved to The Almighty. Words are inadequate tools for the job of acquainting those not present with the physical, mental and psychological effects. It had to be witnessed to be realized.\**

Immediately following the detonation, a nuclear explosion's energy is concentrated in a small, rapidly growing volume of immensely heated plasma, known as the **fireball.** With a fission bomb, the fireball is as hot as the center of the sun, approximately 10 million degrees centigrade; with a large fusion bomb, the temperature of the fireball may be 10 times higher, in the range of 100 million degrees centigrade (Fig. 4.1).

At these enormous temperatures, all atoms are completely ionized, stripped bare of their electrons. This includes the atoms of nuclear debris that formerly comprised the bomb or warhead as well as the surrounding air. Under such conditions, immense amounts of X-rays, produced by the explosion, cannot be absorbed by the surrounding air, since the electrons, which typically absorb such radiation, are no longer able to perform this function. The radiation, accompanied by neutrons and gamma rays as well, continues to ionize the surrounding air as the fireball expands rapidly. Then, fractions of a second later, the fireball begins to cool, giving off first X-rays and other invisible forms of radiation, then an intense burst of radiation in the visible spectrum (light), followed by extraordinarily large amounts of thermal radiation (heat). These energies travel at the speed of light, and so, their arrival is virtually instantaneous with the explosion itself (although as we shall see, the heat produced by large nuclear explosions persists for many seconds). Only later do the mechanical effects become apparent: the shock or blast wave traveling at several times the speed of sound, followed by hurricane force winds.

After less than a millisecond (0.001 second), the fireball has cooled to about 350,000°C and is expanding at about the speed of sound. It continues to cool,

*\*From L. Groves. 1962. *Now It Can Be Told.* New York: Harper & Row, 437–438.*

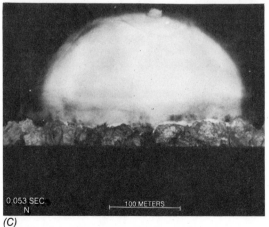

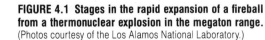

**FIGURE 4.1 Stages in the rapid expansion of a fireball from a thermonuclear explosion in the megaton range.** (Photos courtesy of the Los Alamos National Laboratory.)

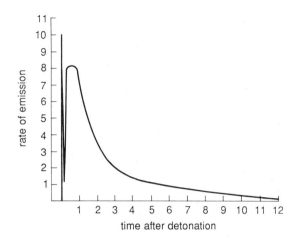

**FIGURE 4.2 The double pulsed pattern of emission of thermal radiation from a nuclear explosion. Both the time after detonation and the rate of emission are in arbitrary units.** (Modified from Glasstone and Dolan, 1977.)

and also to expand, although more slowly than at first. In the case of a 1-megaton explosion, within seconds the fireball has grown to more than a mile in diameter. For a brief period, the superheated, ionized air surrounding the fireball becomes impermeable to visible light; then it cools enough to allow light to escape once more. The result is a characteristic "double flash" of light, which reliably signals a nuclear explosion. Satellites designed to detect such explosions are programmed to recognize this signal, which can be plotted on a graph (Fig. 4.2).

As we have seen, the explosive force of a nuclear explosion is typically measured in kilotons or megatons, indicating that the explosion is comparable in total amount of energy released to thousands or millions of tons of TNT, respectively. However, unlike chemical explosions, whose force is expended almost entirely in blast, nuclear explosions contain a variety of energies. As a general rule, most nuclear explosions release about 15% of their energy as radiation, 35% as heat, and 50% as blast.

## PROMPT RADIATION

Of the roughly 15% of a nuclear explosion's energy that is expended as radiation, approximately 5% appears as prompt radiation, and the remaining 10% as longer lived radioactive fallout. Fallout is carried mechanically some distance from the **epicenter** (the spot where the explosion occurs), or the **hypocenter,** also known as **ground zero** (the place on the ground immediately under the explosion, if it occurred in the air). This fallout is deposited gradually over a period of hours, days, or weeks. We shall consider fallout in the next chapter, under the category of medium and long-term effects.

By contrast, prompt radiation emanates immediately from the explosion, and is over quickly. This radiation consists almost entire of X-rays, gamma rays, and neutrons produced directly by the nuclear explosion itself. Several different measures are used in discussing radiation, and they are a cause of much confusion. Following is a brief list of the units in which radiation is measured.

- *Curie (Ci).* A measure of the degree of radioactivity (the number of nuclear disintegrations per second), of a source, such as a lump of solid, a flask of liquid, or a vial of gas. "One curie," measured for a given source, means that 37 billion nuclear disintegrations are taking place within that source per second. A piece of plutonium, for example, consisting of 100 Ci will have diminished to 50 Ci after 24,000 years (one half-life).

- *Roentgen (R).* A measure of radiation based on the amount of ionization produced when radiation passes through matter. A roentgen is the quantity of radiation required to produce a particular amount of electric charge in air. This unit of measurement is applicable to X-rays and gamma rays only.

- *Rad.* Whereas a roentgen is a quantity of radiation measured at the source (e.g., X-ray machines are rated in roentgens), a rad is an indication of the amount of energy actually absorbed by the target, such as a person or a building. If 1 R is completely absorbed, then we say that the target has received a dose of 1 "radiation unit," or rad.

- *Rem.* The energy absorbed, measured in rads, is not necessarily the same as the damage produced within the target. For living things, different forms of radiation (gamma rays, alpha particles, neutrons, etc.) produce different degrees of damage. One rad of neutrons, for example, produces much more damage than 1 rad of gamma rays. The degree of damage is also "tissue dependent," in that certain types of cells (e.g., those that normally divide rapidly) are more sensitive than others.These differences are taken into account

by the measure known as a "rem" ("roentgen equivalent in man"). Exposure to 100 rems, for instance, produces the same biological effect whether the radiation was in the form of gamma rays, neutrons, or other types. (It takes a larger amount of gamma radiation than of neutron radiation to equal a given number of rems.) For gamma rays, however, 1 rem is taken to equal 1 rad, and for most purposes, the terms "rad" and "rem" are used interchangeably.

In summary, curies and roentgens are measures of radiation intensity, rads are measures of radiation absorbed, and rems are measures of damage done.

In discussing radiation doses, it is also important to specify the time during which a given dose (generally some number of rems) is received. This is because the body is capable of repairing certain amounts of radiation-induced damage; a small dose of radiation, received over a lifetime, may have negligible effects, whereas that same dose, received during a single hour, can have serious consequences. When possible, therefore, dose rate should be distinguished from total dose received. When the intensity of radiation varies over time, such calculations can be difficult, although radiation meters exist for calculating both instantaneous dose rate and accumulated radiation.

As we have seen (Chapter 1), gamma rays consist of electromagnetic radiation, like visible light only with shorter wavelengths. They can penetrate skin and cause damage, but since they can be absorbed by dirt, concrete, or even paper, it is easy to shield oneself against them (assuming sufficient warning). Beta and alpha particles also have little penetrating ability and are more dangerous when they occur as part of fallout, if breathed or ingested. Neutrons are especially important, however, because they penetrate most materials, including steel, until they are absorbed, and they do substantial damage. Radiation damage involves primarily either injury or death of a cell (by ionization of fluids and breakdown of certain proteins), or disruption of the cell's nucleus, sometimes resulting in cancer or in long-term genetic damage.

There is considerable debate over how much, if any, radiation is "safe." Those believing in the "threshold theory" maintain that because of the body's natural repair mechanisms, low-level radiation is essentially harmless as long as it remains below a certain amount, or threshold (in rems per hour). Others maintain that any additional exposure beyond the normal background level is harmful. Exposure to radiation is described relative to the **LD-50,** the lethal dose of radiation that typically kills about half the healthy adults exposed to it, assuming relatively short-term exposures—that is, occurring during about a 24-hour period. Most Americans receive approximately 0.13 rem per year as a result of background radiation (from cosmic rays and natural terrestrial sources) plus medical exposures: a chest X-ray, for example, contributes about 0.05 rem. The result is an average lifetime dose of perhaps 10 rems. For human beings, the LD-50 is taken to be about 450 rems; more than 800 rems is inevitably fatal, regardless of treatment.

Death from radiation sickness is neither quick nor painless. The symptoms include gastrointestinal distress (nausea, vomiting, diarrhea, appetite loss, and cramps) along with thirst and neuromuscular symptoms including fatigue, apathy, fever, headache, and hypertension. Any or all of these symptoms may appear in people exposed to 200 rems up to more than 1,000 rems. These immediate (acute) symptoms typically are followed by a period of remission, lasting several days to several weeks. During this period, people who have been exposed to lethal doses of radiation may feel almost normal. This pattern—acute symptoms followed by a period of remission—is almost identical in victims exposed to 150 rems, from which they will likely recover, or 850 rems, which is inevitably fatal.

As a result, it is very difficult to tell from the initial symptoms whether an exposed victim has received a lethal dose, a sublethal dose that might respond to treatment but would be lethal otherwise, or a minor exposure. This makes it almost impossible to perform medical "triage," the dividing of patients into three groups: those likely to recover without treatment, those unlikely to recover even with treatment, and those able to profit most from medical assistance. This may be especially troubling because in the exposure range from 200 to 600 rems mortality rate rises very steeply with exposure: exposure of 200 rems to the bone marrow, for example, results in an average 2% mortality, whereas a 400-rem bone marrow exposure leads to a mortality rate of 85%.

At very high doses (5,000–10,000 rems), incapacitation is almost immediate. The major symptoms involve the central nervous system, and victims die of the **central nervous syndrome,** probably caused by increased fluid content in the brain and raised intracranial pressure. Severe nausea and vomiting occur within minutes, followed by disorientation, loss of muscle coordination, respiratory distress, diarrhea, seizures, coma, and death. There is no treatment.

Doses of 1,000–5,000 rems also are inevitably fatal within 3–10 days, primarily from a **gastrointestinal syndrome,** made up of severe nausea, vomiting, and diarrhea, leading to dehydration, emaciation, exhaustion, and death. There is, once again, no effective medical treatment, because the syndrome results from the death of the epithelial cells lining the intestines. These cells normally reproduce rapidly, hence, they are especially susceptible to radiation. (This sensitivity of rapidly dividing cells to radiation explains why cancer, which is caused by cells that are dividing out of control, is often treated with radiation.) In addition to uncontrolled fluid loss and inability to absorb nutrients, death of the intestinal epithelium removes an important barrier to infection.

At doses of 200–1,000 rems, people suffer from a **hematopoietic syndrome,** resulting from death of the blood-making cells in the bone marrow. About 3 weeks to a month after exposure, the victim's hair falls out, and he or she suffers chills, fever, fatigue, anemia, and hemorrhages just under the skin (Fig. 4.3). Resistance to infection is greatly reduced, because of the depletion of white blood cells. In a sense, the hematopoietic syndrome produces a condition not unlike the disease AIDS, since the victims' immune system is rendered deficient, and they die of other diseases, notably pneumonia. Blood clotting is also impaired, so that internal hemorrhages complicate the anemia.

About 50% of all healthy adults will die of hematopoietic syndrome after being exposed to 450 rems; young, aged, and infirm people will die in greater proportion. Effective treatment at this level of exposure requires prolonged rest, care, and fluids, and often prolonged maintenance in a germ-free environment. Bone marrow transplantation can also be effective, but this technically difficult procedure is accompanied by a high incidence of complications. As we shall see, it seems unlikely that effective treatment of any sort would be available for the radiation-afflicted survivors of nuclear war. Accordingly, the LD-50 would doubtless be substantially lower than under peacetime conditions, when medical facilities are intact.

For large bombs, however, prompt radiation effects can essentially be ignored. Heat and blast are so great that the lethal radius for these effects alone exceeds that for the prompt radiation. In short, human beings who receive lethal doses of prompt radiation from a large nuclear explosion will die first from other injuries. Another way of looking at it: consider two people, one of them surviving a 1-kiloton explosion and the other surviving a 100-kiloton explosion, each of them at a

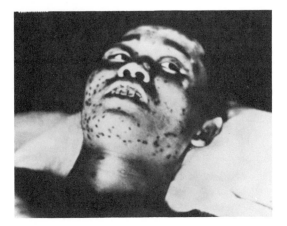

**FIGURE 4.3 This 21-year-old Japanese soldier showing subcutaneous hemorrhaging associated with radiation sickness was exposed about 1 kilometer from the hypocenter and initially appeared relatively uninjured. Symptoms developed more than 3 weeks later. The photo was taken on September 3, 1945, two hours before the young man died.** (United Nations Photo.)

distance such that the blast effects alone are sufficient to kill most but not all people (a blast pressure of 5 psi: see section entitled "Blast," below). The first survivor is about 0.5 kilometer from ground zero, and he or she would receive a lethal dose of radiation; the 100-kiloton survivor, by contrast, is nearly 3 kilometers from ground zero and would receive a sublethal dose of radiation (Fig. 4.4).

For smaller explosions, such as those produced by certain modern tactical weapons, the effects of prompt radiation are more important. Radiation effects were significant at Hiroshima and Nagasaki. These bombs (12.5 and 22 kilotons, respectively) are within the explosive range of nuclear artillery and short-range missiles deployed today. Many people, having survived the blast and heat effects of the bombings of Hiroshima and Nagasaki, died later from **A-bomb disease,** which was subsequently recognized as the gastrointestinal and hematopoietic syndromes of radiation exposure. Several years later, "survivors" began dying of cancers, especially leukemia. At Hiroshima, 31% of the survivors and 16% of those who eventually died of the effects of the bombing showed the initial symptoms of radiation sickness on the day of the explosion.

The use of tactical nuclear weapons alone, for example, in Europe, would presumably result in a sub-

stantial number of radiation-related injuries. Radiation effects are especially important for neutron bombs (or "enhanced radiation warheads"), which as we have seen produce large amounts of fast neutrons that can penetrate the armor of tanks to kill the occupants, while leaving many structures relatively intact. It is noteworthy in this respect that unless tank crews receive upward of 5,000 rems, their death—although certain—may be prolonged by several days, during which time it is unclear whether these "walking ghosts" will be incapacitated or will continue fighting.

## HEAT

About 35% of the energy from a nuclear explosion appears as thermal radiation, or heat. The **thermal pulse** associated with a nuclear weapon travels at the speed of light, and most of it is absorbed within a second of the detonation. But even for a small nuclear explosion (say, 10 kilotons) it takes a few seconds for the brightness of the fireball to subside; for megaton-range explosions, the fireball lasts longer yet. Therefore, unlike a conventional explosion, or the flash from a flashbulb, the thermal flash from a nuclear weapon is persistent: more than 10 seconds for a 1-megaton explosion (Fig. 4.5). Some of the most nightmarish injuries suffered by the residents of Hiroshima and Nagasaki were burns resulting from the intense heat of these explosions (Fig. 4.6). The skin is not normally considered an essential organ; however, without immediate medical care that is both intensive and extensive, severe burn victims eventually die, usually in great agony. Even now, decades later, many burn victims from Hiroshima and Nagasaki suffer from immense quantities of peculiar and disfiguring scar tissue known as "keloid," which results from massive burn injuries.

The severity of burns is characterized by the depth of skin that is destroyed. Most sunburns, for example, are first-degree burns, involving pain and reddening, but no permanent injury to the underlying skin cells. Second-degree burns involve blistering and severe pain, but since the deepest layers of rapidly dividing skin cells are not killed, such burns rarely require substantial medical treatment unless they occur over extensive areas of the body. Third-degree burns involve the death or carbonization of the entire skin layer. They are among the most painful human injuries and require extraordinary, highly skilled, and persistent medical care, especially if they cover a large portion of the body. Burn management requires large quantities of intravenous

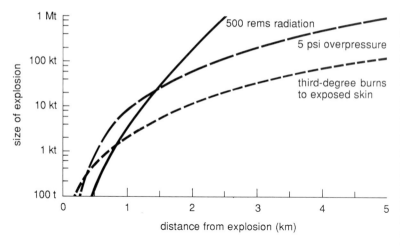

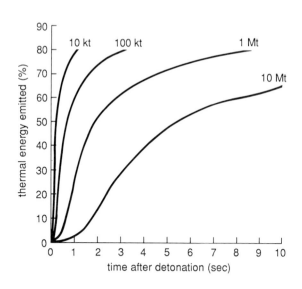

**FIGURE 4.4 The relationship between size of explosion and the distance at which prompt radiation, heat, and blast are likely to be fatal. Note that explosive yield (the ordinate) is logarithmic. From this graph, a 100-kiloton explosion, for example, will expose people to lethal radiation at less than 2 kilometers, lethal blast effects at 2.5 kilometers, and third-degree burns at 4.5 kilometers.** (Modified from Schroeer, 1984.)

**FIGURE 4.5 The percentage of thermal energy emitted from nuclear explosions (airbursts) over time, as a function of size of the explosion. For example, after 3 seconds, a 100-kiloton explosion will have released nearly 80% of its thermal energy; a 1-megaton explosion, 62%; and a 10-megaton explosion, only 27%. Even after 10 seconds, a 10-megaton explosion still has 35% of its thermal energy yet to release.** (Modified from Glasstone and Dolan, 1977.)

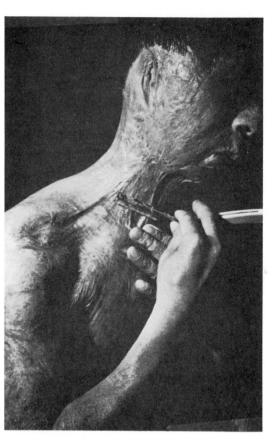

**FIGURE 4.6 Severely scarred burn victim from Nagasaki, 25 years after the bombing.** (United Nations Photo.)

fluids, a sterile environment, skin grafting, and often, numerous elaborate surgical procedures. Second-degree burns covering 30% of the body surface will generally lead to shock and death if untreated; for untreated third-degree burns, 25% body coverage can be fatal. Even with the most modern facilities and mul-timillion-dollar care, third-degree burns over 75% of the body surface are often fatal.

The United States has 1,000–2,000 "burn beds," all of them at specialized institutions. New York City, for example, has a total of about 50 such beds. During certain fires and airplane crashes in recent years, the burn facilities of entire geographic regions were severely strained. The nation's medical facilities for treating such patients would be overwhelmed by even a small fraction of the victims of just one small nuclear weapon. And yet, a general nuclear war would produce easily 100 or even 1,000 times this level of casualties. Even a single nuclear explosion might well produce more severe burns than have occurred worldwide in all recorded history. Moreover, following a nuclear war, a large proportion of the nation's major hospitals would likely be destroyed, since they are located in large cities, which are likely to be targeted.

In the event of a nuclear attack, persons near the epicenter would simply be vaporized by the heat. At both Hiroshima and Nagasaki, there were numerous images left "engraved" on heavy walls or concrete steps, showing where a person had been (Fig. 4.7). At greater distances, death still would be instantaneous (Fig. 4.8), although as the radius from ground zero increases, buildings, walls, and clothing provide shielding from the searing heat. At Hiroshima and Nagasaki, flash-burns to the exposed skin of unsheltered persons frequently led to a burn pattern corresponding to the dark colored (heat-absorbing) fabric of their clothing worn at the time of the explosions (Fig. 4.9). If the bombs had been dropped in winter instead of summer, more people would have been indoors, and in addition, the greater shielding provided by heavy clothing would have reduced the number and severity of immediate burn injuries. However, up to 5 miles from a 1-megaton air-burst, clothing would spontaneously ignite, leading to flame burns that might be even more severe than the instant flashburns from the explosion itself.

The severity of the heat flash would vary with the weather: it would be greater if there were snow on the ground and high overcast because both these conditions tend to reflect the thermal radiation, and it would be somewhat attenuated by heavy fog, which absorbs the heat. With moderate, 10-mile visibility, a 1-megaton

**FIGURE 4.7 The shadow of a man, standing next to a ladder, burnt into a wall in Nagasaki.** (United Nations Photo.)

airburst would cause first-degree burns in all unprotected persons at 7 miles from the epicenter, and even at 8.5 miles, newspapers and dry leaves would ignite; second-degree burns would occur at 6 miles, and third-degree burns at 5 miles. At 4.5 miles, bedding, curtains, and heavy wood also would be ignited (Fig. 4.10). For a 20-megaton bomb, first-degree burns plus spontaneous ignitions of some materials, such as rayon, would occur as far as 30 miles from the epicenter; newspaper would ignite and people would suffer second-degree burns at 21 miles; cotton fabrics and leaves would ignite, and people would suffer third-degree burns at 18.2 miles (an area of 1,040 miles). For a 20-megaton bomb, the sheet metal on auto bodies would melt at 5.2 miles, and at 3.4 miles glass would melt and metals would vaporize (an area of 36 square miles).

Anyone glancing reflexively at the fireball could also suffer retinal burns as far away as 35 miles from a 1-megaton airburst or 50 miles from a 20-megaton airburst. Temporary but disabling "flashblindness" might

**FIGURE 4.8 Corpse of a young boy, killed instantly by the heat of the atomic bomb at Nagasaki.** (United Nations Photo.)

occur 13 miles from a 1-megaton explosion (53 miles at night).

In addition to these direct effects of thermal radiation, numerous fires would be started by the explosion and its massive heat pulse. These indirect or incendiary effects might well be even more severe than the effects of the heat flash itself. Spontaneous ignition of wood, paper, cloth, bedding, carpets, and other combustible materials probably would produce self-sustaining fires that developed in intensity several minutes to hours and even days after the initial explosion. Natural gas lines, gasoline tanks, storage facilities, and industrial and chemical stockpiles would likely ignite, as well as forests, houses, and automobiles. There would almost certainly be no opportunity to combat these fires, since streets would probably be impassable, fire equipment destroyed, water pressure unobtainable, and most potential firefighters killed or injured.

Two kinds of mass fires are possible if the various and inevitable spot fires coalesce into an exceptionally large blaze: firestorms and conflagrations. A **firestorm** occurs when strong updrafts draw the heated air vertically, as a result of which powerful winds (up to 100 mph) blow inward, toward the fire from the periphery, causing it to roar like a blast furnace, reaching great temperatures. Because of these inrushing winds, firestorms tend to be relatively immobile. A firestorm was created at Hiroshima (Fig. 4.11) and also during the nonnuclear firebombings of Tokyo, Hamburg, and Dresden. In such cases, even blast shelters became

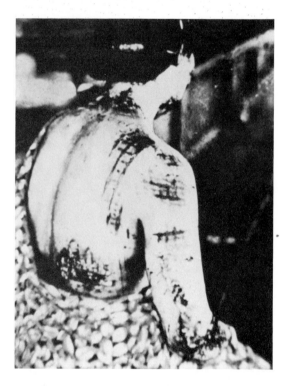

**FIGURE 4.9 Hiroshima woman showing burn patterns produced by the dark (heat-absorbing) pattern of the kimono she was wearing at the time of the explosion.** (United Nations Photo.)

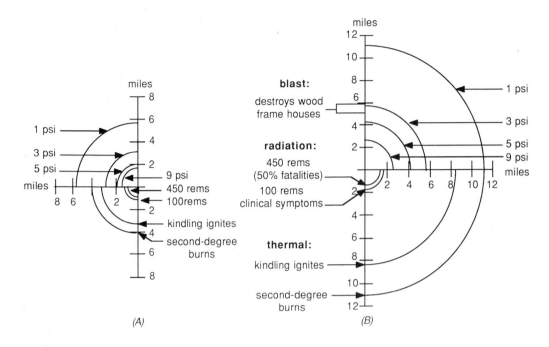

**FIGURE 4.10  A comparison of the radiation, thermal, and blast effects for explosions of 100 kilotons (*A*) and 1 megaton (*B*).** (Modified from Katz, 1982.)

**FIGURE 4.11  The firestorm at Hiroshima, photographed from the ground about 3 hours after the bombing.** (United Nations Photo.)

**FIGURE 4.12 The remains of a wristwatch found in the ruins of Hiroshima. Its wearer was never identified.** (United Nations Photo 149443 by Yuichiro Sasaki.)

so hot that many were turned into crematoria. A **conflagration,** by contrast, is driven by horizontal winds present before the fire, not produced by the blaze itself. Conflagrations move horizontally, at speeds that depend on the prevailing ground winds. The Great Chicago Fire was a conflagration. Mass fires of either sort produce enormous heat, in the neighborhood of 1,000°C, hot enough to melt glass and most metals (Fig. 4.12). Mass fires also produce large amounts of carbon dioxide; this gas settles into cellars and underground tunnels, where it may asphyxiate any who have survived the fire.

It is estimated that a firestorm or conflagration increases the lethal radius of a nuclear explosion by as much as fivefold. Experts disagree, however, whether the density of combustible materials in most US and Soviet cities is high enough to permit the development of either conflagrations or firestorms. It is generally estimated that for a firestorm, this density ("fuel loading") must equal at least 8 pounds per square foot (lb/ft²); Hamburg had 32 lb/ft², whereas a neighborhood of

two-story brick houses in the United States has a fuel loading of about 5 lb/ft². There is also some debate over whether the blast effects of a large nuclear explosion (see the next section) will tend to blow out certain fires. The blast with its resulting winds will arrive several seconds after the intense heat flash; thus it is also possible that this intense rush of air will act instead to fan the flames. As we shall see in the next chapter, the incendiary effects of nuclear weapons may also have important long-term effects on the earth's climate.

## BLAST

The largest proportion of the energy from most nuclear explosions (about 50%) is released as blast and shock. This constitutes, at least initially, the most destructive effect of such an explosion. Because of the extremely high temperatures and pressures of the explosion itself, all nearby materials are vaporized, becoming part of the rapidly expanding fireball. As these gases expand, they push and heat the air molecules and other atoms in front of them. This expanding wall of air and gases is known as the **shock front.** Close to ground zero, it travels several times faster than the speed of sound, but much slower than the prompt radiation and the thermal pulse, which move at the speed of light. Slow motion movies of test nuclear explosions show that nearby structures first start melting, char, or catch fire several seconds before the immense blast wave flattens them (Fig. 4.13).

A nuclear blast comes in two parts: static overpressure and dynamic overpressure. **Static overpressure,** which is unique to nuclear explosions, consists of a steady, sustained pressure due to the powerful, convulsive expansion of the fireball and the compression it produces. Unlike a clap of hands or of thunder, however, static overpressure is like an enormous hand that presses against all surrounding objects, and keeps pressing for several seconds. Much of the immediate destructiveness of nuclear explosions derives from this phenomenon. Static overpressure is measured in pounds per square inch (psi). Normal atmospheric pressure is 14.7 psi; anything above that constitutes *overpressure.* By contrast, **dynamic overpressure** consists of winds, often hurricane force and greater, measured in hundreds of miles per hour, which arrive shortly after the static overpressure of the shock front. Eight miles from a 1-megaton airburst, these winds can hurl a 180-pound adult at several times the force of gravity.

(A)

(B)

(C)

(D)

**FIGURE 4.13 Destruction sequence of a frame house, 3,500 feet from a kiloton-range test explosion at Yucca Flat, Nevada. The time from the first to the last photo is only 2.33 seconds.** (Photos courtesy of the US Department of Energy.)

Many people in modern office buildings at this distance would likely be blown out of the windows.

The larger the explosion, the greater the overpressure and the longer it lasts. For example, a 20-kiloton airburst produces overpressures at 1–2 miles that last from 1 to 1.5 seconds; the overpressure from a 1-megaton airburst at the same distance would last 2.5 seconds. The unit of measurement, psi, gives a deceptively low impression of the forces involved. "One pound per square inch"—1 psi—may sound like a very small pressure, but it equals 144 pounds per square foot, or 1,296 pounds per square yard. Since an average window measures about 2 square yards, 1 psi produces 2,592 pounds of additional pressure, easily enough to shatter the average window. Similarly, the outside wall of a house measuring 15 feet × 30 feet would sustain 64,800 pounds of overpressure if it was exposed to a 1-psi blast.

The human body is quite resistant to static overpressures, although pressures in excess of 8 psi can produce lung damage, and 15 psi will rupture most eardrums. The destructive effects of overpressure, however, generally occur indirectly, through its role in demolishing structures and turning objects into small missiles. As we have seen, ICBM silos may be superhardened to withstand several thousand psi; essentially, they require a direct hit to be destroyed. An ordinary frame house, however, will collapse at a "mere" 5 psi, and most concrete structures, at 10 psi.

Shortly after the static overpressure, a 1-megaton airburst will produce winds on the order of 300–600 mph within the 10-psi zone; 4.4 miles from ground zero, the same explosion will generate winds in excess of 160 mph. Such dynamic overpressures will throw buildings, vehicles, and people great distances, causing further damage. After these winds have swept away from ground zero, they create a low-pressure zone at the center. As the fireball begins to fade, the winds that had been blowing outward reverse, rushing back toward the center, carrying dust, debris, and possibly, people. Thus in less than 2 minutes a 1-megaton airburst has demonstrated an extraordinary range of effects (Fig. 4.14).

## GROUNDBURSTS VERSUS AIRBURSTS

Nuclear weapons may be exploded in the air (**airburst**) or on the ground (**groundburst**). Groundbursts are preferable for destroying hardened targets. This is because they concentrate their destructive force directly on the target, vaporizing any known materials, and producing a crater where the target used to be. When a nuclear weapon is exploded at the surface, about 10–15% of its energy is coupled directly to the ground; the result is a large crater, plus tremors that resemble those produced by an earthquake. For example, a 1-megaton groundburst will excavate a crater with a diameter of 400 meters, and about 70 meters deep.

However, the overpressures produced by groundbursts do not extend as far as those produced by airbursts, simply because some of the energy of groundbursts goes into the ground. Therefore, when seeking to destroy "soft targets" such as cities—which can be demolished with much less than thousands or even hundreds of psi—it is most efficient to employ airbursts. Overpressures of 5 psi are likely to be sufficient for this task, and by using airbursts at the optimum altitude, such destruction can be produced over the widest possible area. There are predictable relationships between size of the explosion, the height of the detonation above ground, and the overpressure contours produced. As the altitude of an explosion is increased, the overpressure directly under the bomb decreases, but at the same time, the area exposed to a given overpressure increases. For every size of explosion, there is an altitude that maximizes the blast effect. If the goal is to produce, say, 5 psi across the largest possible area, the larger the explosion, the higher the optimum detonation. A smaller bomb would have to be exploded closer to the ground to have the same effect as a larger bomb, exploded higher in the air.

Airbursts are generally more destructive of "soft" targets such as cities than are groundbursts. This is especially true of blast effects generally, since in the case of an airburst, the direct, "incident" shock front, emanating from the explosion itself, is reinforced by additional shock waves reflected off the ground (refer to Fig. 4.14).

An attack on superhardened silos would likely use groundbursts. If the goal were to destroy industrial facilities (maximize the area subject to 10-psi overpressure), a 1-megaton bomb would optimally be exploded at 7,500 feet. To destroy civilian structures (maximize 5 psi overpressure), the optimal burst height would be higher yet. At such heights, of course, the surface area exposed to very high overpressures would be reduced.

As we have seen, the destructive radius of a nuclear explosion is roughly proportional to the cube root of the yield. As the yield increases 1,000-fold, for example, from 1 kiloton to 1 megaton, the energy released during the explosion can fill a volume roughly 1,000 times as large. But the radius of a 1-megaton sphere is only about 10 times larger than one of 1 kiloton. So, the region destroyed via overpressure increases more slowly than does the size of the explosion. In addition, the effective radius for prompt radiation effects goes up even more slowly, because the neutrons and gamma rays are absorbed by the surrounding air.

The immediate devastation that extends out from a nuclear explosion is most intense at ground zero, diminishing at greater distances. As a rule of thumb, the distance from the epicenter at which an overpressure of 5 psi is produced is taken as the **lethal radius** of that nuclear explosion; the larger the explosion, the larger the lethal radius, although as we have seen, the lethal radius increases more slowly than does the size of an explosion. The lethal radius will not be lethal for everyone: some people will doubtless survive an initial blast within the 5-psi radius, just as some people will die outside this distance (Fig. 4.15). However, on balance the number of survivors within this "lethal area" is estimated to equal the number that will be killed outside it. Therefore, for such purposes as estimating the likely effects of a bomb of a given size exploded over a given city, it is often assumed that everyone within the 5-psi radius will be killed, and everyone outside it will survive. (Such calculations refer to immediate fatalities only; subsequent deaths from infection, exposure, starvation, dehydration, or the effects of fallout are not included.) The 5-psi lethal radius for a 100-kiloton airburst is considered to be 2.5 kilometers; for 500 kilotons, 5 kilometers; and for 1 megaton, 5.8 kilometers. Thus, a 100% increase in explosive yield, from 500

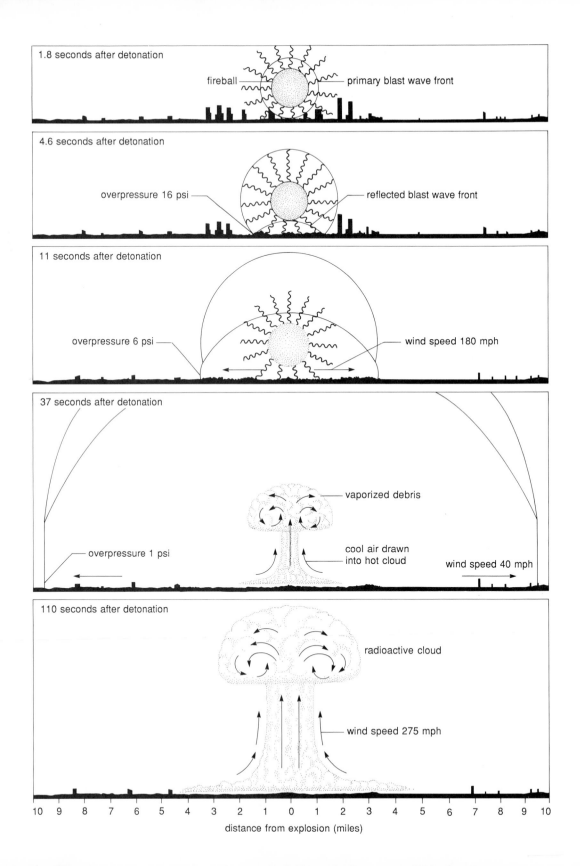

1.8 seconds after detonation

fireball — primary blast wave front

4.6 seconds after detonation

overpressure 16 psi — reflected blast wave front

11 seconds after detonation

overpressure 6 psi — wind speed 180 mph

37 seconds after detonation

vaporized debris

overpressure 1 psi

cool air drawn into hot cloud

wind speed 40 mph

110 seconds after detonation

radioactive cloud

wind speed 275 mph

10  9  8  7  6  5  4  3  2  1  0  1  2  3  4  5  6  7  8  9  10

distance from explosion (miles)

**FIGURE 4.14 (opposite) Sequence of effects produced by a 1-megaton explosion, detonated at 6,500 feet. At about 1.8 seconds, the front of the blast wave would be 0.5 mile ahead of the fireball. Prompt radiation is indicated by the wavy lines; thermal radiation, by the darkened background. Depending on the size of the explosion and its height above the ground, at a certain distance the direct and reflected blast fronts fuse at the surface, forming a single, reinforced "Mach front," spreading outward and gradually weakening. In less than 2 minutes the fireball cools sufficiently to allow the hot gases to rise, drawing air in and forming the characteristic mushroom-shaped cloud, which in this example would rise to about 14 miles.** (Modified from Lewis, 1979.)

kilotons to 1 megaton, increases the lethal radius by only $0.8/5 = 16\%$.

Most deaths and injuries due to blast would result from structures collapsing and from objects being blown onto or against people, as well as people being blown out of or against structures. A collapsing, obliterated city would suddenly be transformed into a huge fragmentation grenade, with small dartlike pieces of wood, metal, concrete, and glass, and also enormous chunks including whole buildings—all traveling at lethal speeds and perhaps on fire as well. Objects striking human

bodies would produce innumerable puncture wounds, as well as lacerations, fractures, crushing injuries, and the entire gamut of internal injuries, plus shock. In some ways, it would be like many hundreds of thousands—perhaps millions—of people all experiencing a very high speed head-on automobile accident, simultaneously . . . with high temperatures and radiation thrown in for good measure.

## COMBINED EFFECTS

For convenience of thought, we have focused separately on each of the immediate effects of nuclear explosions. However, most people injured by radiation, burns, and blast would suffer from several of these agents simultaneously: radiation and burns, burns and blast, radiation and blast, or combinations of all three. Estimates of nuclear explosion casualties are likely to be underestimates, since these effects will almost certainly be cumulative at the least; more likely, one effect will multiply the consequences of another. For example, radiation exposure reduces dramatically the ability to resist infection, and infection is a particular threat to victims of puncture and laceration wounds, and especially to those with severe burns. An additional 100 rems to victims with standard burn injuries increases their mortality eightfold. It also seems likely that the LD-50 will be substantially lower for patients already suffering other injuries. People who have experienced lacerations, internal injuries, or other trauma in addition to severe burns may well succumb, even when the burns alone or the lacerations alone would not have proved fatal. Many victims trapped in collapsing buildings will probably die in fires from which they will be unable to escape. The low probability of effective rescue will also increase mortality among people who were not immediately killed by their injuries.

A 1-megaton airburst would totally destroy the entire downtown areas of such major cities as Boston, Tulsa, St. Louis, and Cleveland. A 100-kiloton airburst would do the same to medium-sized cities such as Abilene, Texas, Camden, New Jersey, or Tacoma, Washington. It has been estimated that a single 20-megaton explosion above New York City would destroy all buildings in Manhattan, the Bronx, Brooklyn, Queens, and Staten Island, as well as Jersey City and Hoboken. There would probably be 5 million to 10 million casualties. A single 1-megaton airburst over an average American city would kill about 25% of the population immediately and injure another 25%. Subsequent mor-

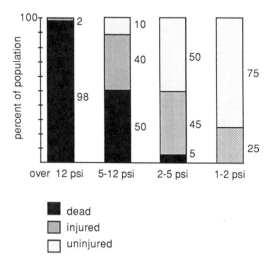

**FIGURE 4.15 The likely vulnerability of human populations in various zones of overpressure.** (From the Office of Technology Assessment, 1979.)

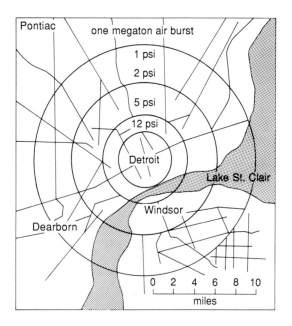

**FIGURE 4.16 Effect of a 1-megaton airburst on Detroit. The concentric rings indicate different overpressures.** (From the Office of Technology Assessment, 1979.)

tality would presumably be higher yet. Estimates can be made by superimposing population density maps on a series of concentric circles indicating the predicted overpressure and heat effects. This requires making assumptions about the height of the explosion, the number of explosions, the visibility (important for thermal pulse transmission), the season (which influences the proportion of people outdoors, as well as the type of clothing worn), and the time of day (which influences how many people are at home rather than at work). Other critically important variables may be whether the explosions occur with no warning, and whether effective efforts at sheltering or evacuation have occurred (see Chapter 7).

## ONE BOMB ON ONE CITY: DETROIT

The congressional Office of Technology Assessment (OTA) carried out a detailed analysis of the likely effect of nuclear explosions on Detroit and on Leningrad. The study examined various possibilities in detail: a 1-megaton airburst, a 1-megaton surface burst, and a 25-megaton airburst in each case. Figure 4.16 depicts

the case of a 1-megaton airburst, 6,000 feet over Detroit. Other assumptions include: no warning, nighttime detonation, and clear weather with 10-mile visibility.

If one were able to watch the city's destruction from nearby, one would see it first melt, then char, then be blown down and collapse. What is left of the buildings rapidly fills up what is left of the streets. The rubble roars into flames. Within the 12-psi zone, essentially all structures, including reinforced concrete, are destroyed. Virtually everyone present is killed outright.

Within the 5-psi zone, lightly constructed commercial buildings and typical residences are destroyed; heavier construction is severely damaged. Exposed skin receives third-degree burns (charring) and clothing ignites spontaneously; even without mass fires, this area will likely be totally burned over from the heat flash alone. In this zone, about 50% of the inhabitants are killed promptly, 35% seriously injured, and 15% slightly injured or uninjured.

Within the 2-psi zone, residences are severely damaged and winds cause flying debris and flying bodies that are lethal to those caught in the open. Exposed skin receives second-degree burns. It is estimated that out to the 2-psi zone (8.5 miles in our hypothetical case), 15% of the population will be killed promptly, 40% seriously injured, and 45% slightly injured or uninjured. The fate of the survivors will depend critically on the availability of outside assistance, hence, on whether the hypothesized explosion is an isolated one, or part of a general nuclear war.

Because, as we have seen, smaller explosions are more efficient than larger ones in destroying "soft" targets such as cities, it seems likely that cities will be attacked with a relatively large number of smaller warheads.

## ELECTROMAGNETIC PULSE

Another immediate effect of nuclear explosions, although one that is not believed to be directly harmful to people, is **electromagnetic pulse** or **EMP**. In 1962 the United States exploded a thermonuclear warhead 250 miles above Johnston Atoll in the Pacific Ocean. Immediately afterward, street lights failed, alarms sounded, and electrical systems went haywire in Hawaii, 800 miles away. EMP, previously unknown, was thus revealed. Gamma rays colliding with air molecules ionize them by knocking the electrons away from the positively charged nucleus. When these electrons spiral in the earth's magnetic field, they emit a powerful surge of electromagnetic energy, much like that created by a lightning bolt. However, EMP is much faster than lightning (1 hundred-millionth of a second vs. 1 millionth of a second), and it can be thousands of times stronger. It causes a split-second surge in voltage in any electrical conductor. EMP effects are measured in volts per meter (V/m), and they depend on the strength of the EMP itself as well as the length of exposed conductor. Voltage surges on the order of 25,000−50,000 V/m are not unlikely; this could produce 250,000−500,000 volts along a 10-meter conductor (such as an ICBM or a radar antenna).

EMP is of short range when explosions occur at ground level or in the low atmosphere; however, when an explosion takes place at very high elevations, the gamma rays travel long distances before striking air molecules throughout a very large region. As a result, this generates an intense EMP that covers a very wide area. A single 1-megaton weapon, for example, exploded several hundred miles over the central United States, could blanket most of the lower Forty-Eight and parts of Canada and Mexico with EMP on the order of 25,000−50,000V/m (Fig. 4.17).

Compared to the electronic circuitry used in 1962 when EMP was discovered, modern solid state circuits rely heavily on transistors rather than vacuum tubes. And compared to the older systems, modern components are substantially more sensitive to electrical surges of the kind caused by EMP. There is no evidence that EMP is directly dangerous to human beings. It could have important social, economic, and strategic effects, however, since a single EMP could severely damage solid state circuits and satellites, and perform electronic lobotomies on computers. It would presumably shut down the nation's electric power grid and knock out all unprotected communications equipment. Susceptible materials can be shielded against EMP by wrapping them in a layer of metallic conductor. In other cases, wire cables are being replaced by fiber-optic tubes, which are not affected by EMP. However, the exact occurrence of EMP, as well as the effectiveness of various protective measures, remains a major mystery in any effort to predict and prepare for the events of a nuclear war (Fig. 4.18).

## HIROSHIMA AND NAGASAKI

The experiences of Hiroshima and Nagasaki are not good indicators of the likely effects of nuclear weapons used in the 1980s and beyond. This is because the

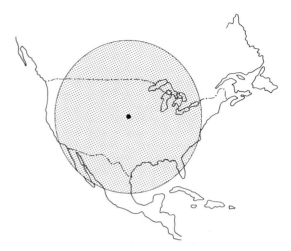

**FIGURE 4.17 The likely EMP coverage that would result from a single megaton-range explosion detonated 200 miles above SAC headquarters in Omaha, Nebraska. The area circled would experience electrical surges in the realm of 25,000−50,000 V/m.** (From the Office of Technology Assessment, 1979.)

12.5- and 22-kiloton bombs dropped on Japan were very small by modern standards, more on the order of tactical than strategic nuclear weapons. In addition, an outside world existed. After the Japanese surrender, American recovery aid was available, as well as medical and reconstruction teams from other, unbombed regions. Hiroshima and Nagasaki were rebuilt. It is not at all clear, however, that anything similar could occur after an all-out nuclear war. The events of Hiroshima and Nagasaki are nonetheless important, both as a real-life laboratory for studying the effects of two small, isolated nuclear explosions, and also because they serve to impart psychological reality to the consequences of nuclear war, albeit on a very small scale.

Exact figures on the deaths and injuries in Hiroshima and Nagasaki are unavailable, at least partly because the destruction was so thorough (Fig. 4.19) that many records were lost and thousands of people unaccounted for. There are substantial disagreements with respect to the death rates. The city of Hiroshima officially estimates that of approximately 300,000 people living there at the time of the bombing, between 130,000 and 150,000 had died by December 1945. By 1950, delayed deaths attributable to the bombing had reached about 200,000. The US government, on the

**FIGURE 4.18 An enormous wooden platform at Kirtland Air Force Base in New Mexico, constructed with no metal, is used to test the "hardness" of B-52 bombers against simulated EMP effects.** (Courtesy of the US Department of Defense.)

other hand, estimates total deaths at 78,000. The number of dead and injured at Nagasaki was considerably lower: the United States estimates 40,000 killed, whereas the city of Nagasaki estimates 75,000 killed and another 75,000 wounded. The lesser destruction of Nagasaki is attributable to two circumstances: (1) the bomb was somewhat off target, and (2) unlike Hiroshima, which is built on a flat river delta, Nagasaki is a city of hills, which tended to confine the explosion's impact to one valley.

If a person survived within 1 kilometer of the hypocenter at Hiroshima, more than 90% of those around him or her were fatalities. The heaviest casualties were among children, especially those who were outside in schoolyards. Many also died in the firestorm after the blast, which had developed by afternoon. Many others drowned in the rivers, seeking water and relief from their burns. Approximately 50% of the fatalities were due to burns of one sort or another, and about 30% had received lethal doses of radiation as well. It is not known how many people died as a direct result of prompt radiation.

Although technical knowledge is important, such sanitized data are inadequate for conveying the full horror of nuclear war. There is another kind of knowing that is equally important, if not more so. This knowing comes from direct accounts, and it speaks to our emotions through imagery rather than facts and figures. Such knowing, painful as it may be, is essential if something of the awesome reality of nuclear weapons is to penetrate our consciousness. Consider the following descriptions of the initial bombing of Nagasaki:

> *For some 1,000 yards, or three-fifths of a mile, in all directions from the epicenter . . . it was as if a malevolent god had suddenly focused a gigantic blowtorch on a small section of our planet. Within that perimeter, nearly all unprotected living organisms—birds, insects, horses, cats, chickens—perished instantly. Flowers, trees, grass, plants, all shriveled and died. Wood burst into flames. Metal beams and galvanized iron roofs began to bubble, and the soft gooey masses twisted into grotesque shapes. Stones were pulverized, and for a second every last bit of air was burned away. The people exposed within that doomed section neither knew nor felt anything, and their blackened, unrecognizable forms dropped silently where they stood.\**

At greater distances, people survived at least for a time. There are harrowing accounts of infants seeking to nurse at the corpses of dead mothers; people with empty eyesockets, the eyeballs having melted; burn victims with the skin of their arms and bodies hanging down in long, loose strips; and family members seeking to rescue relatives trapped helplessly under their

---

\*From F. Chinnock. 1969. *Nagasaki: The Forgotten Bomb.* New York: World.

**FIGURE 4.19 The remains of the Prefectural Industry Promotion Building surrounded by some of the devastation of Hiroshima nearly 2 months after the bombing. The bridge just beyond this building, which has been preserved as Hiroshima's "A-Bomb Museum," was ground zero.** (United Nations Photo by Eiichi Matsumoto.)

demolished and burning homes. A survivor from Hiroshima gave this painful account:

> *The sight of the soldiers was more dreadful than the dead people floating down the river. I came upon I don't know how many, burned from the hips up; and where the skin had peeled, their flesh was wet and mushy. . . . And they had no faces! Their eyes, noses, and mouths had been burned away, and it looked like their ears had melted off. It was hard to tell front from back.*

Finally, a Hiroshima physician describes the behavior of some other survivors leaving the city. His account is of particular interest for its insight into the overwhelming psychological effects of nuclear explosions, some of which we shall explore in greater detail in Chapter 14:

> *Those who were able walked silently toward the suburbs in the distant hills, their spirits broken,*

*their initiative gone. When asked whence they had come, they pointed to the city and said, "that way"; and when asked where they were going, pointed away from the city and said, "this way." They were so broken and confused that they moved and behaved like automatons. Their reactions had astonished outsiders who reported with amazement the spectacle of long files of people holding stolidly to a narrow rough path when close by was a smooth, easy road going in the same direction. The outsiders could not grasp the fact that they were witnessing the exodus of a people who walked in the realm of dreams. . . . A spiritless people had forsaken a destroyed city.\**

---

\*From M. Hachiya. 1955. *Hiroshima Diary.* Chapel Hill, NC: University of North Carolina Press.

---

## Policy Issues

---

### Should people be taught about the effects of nuclear war in gruesome detail, as partly accomplished in this chapter?

**No:** By obsessively dwelling on the horrible consequences of nuclear war, we encourage not only mor-

bid fascination, but also a revulsion that might contribute to reluctance to support the maintenance of adequate nuclear arsenals. Such information, by emphasizing the horror of it all, tends to obscure clear thinking about the subject. It should, at minimum, be balanced by data as well as first-person accounts of Soviet repression and the horrors of Soviet prison camps (the "gulag"), because we must endure the possibility of nuclear horror in order to stave off the horror of Soviet domination. In addition, material of this sort could lead to a diminution of respect for government authority and in the ability of government to protect its citizens.

**Yes:**   Awful as they are, these are the facts. They will

not go away by our ignoring them. We have no choice but to face the pain and seek to understand—both intellectually and emotionally—what nuclear war would be like, to be able to appreciate the importance of preventing it. Otherwise, as people avoid information that is unpleasant, they are more likely to develop a somewhat tolerant attitude toward nuclear war. Such an attitude could be suicidal.

## KEY TERMS

| | |
|---|---|
| fireball | A-bomb disease |
| epicenter (ground zero) | thermal pulse |
| hypocenter | firestorm |
| curie (Ci) | conflagration |
| roentgen (R) | shock front |
| rad | static overpressure |
| rem | dynamic overpressure |
| LD-50 | airburst |
| central nervous syndrome | groundburst |
| gastrointestinal syndrome | lethal radius |
| hematopoietic syndrome | electromagnetic pulse (EMP) |

## STUDY QUESTIONS

1.  What are the three major prompt effects of nuclear weapons?

2.  Describe briefly the medical effects of radiation exposure.

3.  Distinguish between static and dynamic overpressure.

4.  Distinguish between firestorms and conflagrations on the one hand, and thermal pulse on the other.

5.  Why are airbursts more effective than groundbursts for destroying cities?

6.  What is meant by the lethal radius of a nuclear explosion?

7.  What is EMP, and why is it considered different from the other prompt effects of nuclear explosions? Why does it introduce uncertainties into plans regarding nuclear war?

8.  In what ways are the experiences of Hiroshima and Nagasaki important for understanding the effects of nuclear war? In what ways are they potentially misleading?

## ADDITIONAL READINGS

The Committee for the Compilation of Materials on Damage Caused by the Atomic Bombs in Hiroshima and Nagasaki. 1981. *Hiroshima and Nagasaki.* New York: Basic Books. An encyclopedic account of the physical, medical, and social effects of the atomic bombings.

Glasstone, Samuel, and Philip J. Dolan. 1977. *The Effects of Nuclear Weapons.* Washington, DC: Government Printing Office. The standard government reference regarding nuclear weapons effects, based especially on rigorous analyses of nuclear test explosions.

Office of Technology Assessment. 1979. *The Effects of Nuclear War.* Montclair, NJ: Allanheld, Osmun & Co. An official report, made by the OTA at the request of the Senate Foreign Relations Committee, that examined the consequences of a wide range of attack scenarios: airbursts and groundbursts of various sizes on various cities, and so on.

# 5 Medium and Long-Term Effects of Nuclear Explosions

*A very large nuclear war would be a calamity of indescribable proportions and absolutely unpredictable consequences, with the uncertainties tending toward the worse (sic). . . . All-out nuclear war would mean the destruction of contemporary civilization, throw man back centuries, cause the deaths of hundreds of millions or billions of people, and, with a certain degree of probability, would cause man to be destroyed as a biological species.*
Soviet physicist Andrei Sakharov

Since time itself is continuous, not broken up into discrete bundles, it is artificial to divide the effects of nuclear weapons into those acting immediately (Chapter 4) on the one hand, and medium and long-term effects (this chapter) on the other. Moreover, some "immediate" effects, including firestorms and conflagrations, typically take many hours to develop, whereas some "medium" effects, such as short-term fallout, occur more quickly. It is conceptually useful, however, to distinguish the events that follow directly upon the explosion itself, and others that make their full weight felt only later. In this chapter, we shall consider these slower acting effects.

The Office of Technology Assessment, in its study of the effects of nuclear war, concluded that "the effects of a nuclear war that cannot be calculated are at least as important as those for which calculations are attempted. Moreover, even these limited calculations are subject to very large uncertainties." This suggests that we should be wary of any categorical statements about the effects of nuclear war, whether tending to downplay its likely seriousness (a frequent habit of hawks) or to emphasize it (a frequent habit of doves). On the one hand, it may be argued that by accepting a "doomsday" view of nuclear war, and one that may be exaggerated, we undercut deterrence by signaling a lack of resolve on our part. This could conceivably encourage the USSR to engage in activities from which it might otherwise refrain. But it can also be argued that by taking seriously the apocalyptic possibilities inherent in nuclear war, we err—if at all—on the side of safety, which is only prudent given the possible

catastrophe if we have underestimated those effects. It is at least possible that an underestimate of nuclear weapons effects will result in a somewhat more cavalier attitude toward them, thus making nuclear war more likely. Conversely, an overestimate may conceivably result in a degree of self-defeating timidity in international relations.

Ideally, of course, we would neither overestimate nor underestimate the effects of nuclear war; perfect accuracy in this regard, however, may be impossible. And when it comes to medium and long-term effects, as we shall see, our estimates are likely to be even more inexact than in the preceding chapter.

## FALLOUT

### Basic Principles

Roughly 15% of the explosive power of a nuclear weapon is expended in radiation products. Of this, 5% is expressed as prompt radiation; this means that twice as much energy (10% of the total yield) is contained in the longer lived radiation known as fallout.

Nuclear explosions produce a witches' brew of radioactive elements, notably the various fission products of U-235 and/or plutonium. In the case of large fusion bombs, in which U-238 is also fissioned, the diversity and abundance of such radioactive products is even greater. Some of the most significant of these "daughter" elements are as follows:

| Isotope | Half-life | Biological significance |
|---------|-----------|-------------------------|
| Strontium-90 | 28 years | Acts chemically like calcium, concentrating in milk and subsequently, in bone |
| Iodine-131 | 8.1 days | Acts like normal iodine, concentrating in the thyroid gland |
| Cesium-137 | 30 years | Acts like normal potassium; of unknown significance |
| Plutonium-239 | 24,000 years | Produces lung cancer if inhaled |

Tritium is produced by fusion bombs and is a component of fallout as well. However, since it is chemically identical to hydrogen, tritium combines into water molecules and is thereby diluted; thus it is neither biologically concentrated nor considered to be especially important as a radioactive by-product. In general, fission products are radioactively "dirty," whereas fusion products are relatively "clean." The amount of fallout produced by an explosion depends partly on the ratio of fission to fusion in the bomb design.

Isotopes with short half-lives, such as iodine-131, are radioactive for relatively brief periods, compared with long-lived materials such as plutonium. By definition, however, short-lived radioactive substances are likely to be more intensely radioactive during their (briefer) existence, since they lose half their radioactivity during a shorter time period. The biological effect of radioactive fallout is considered to be similar to that caused by prompt radiation. Hence, units of measurement such as rads and rems are employed, and the interpretation of exposures to given dosages is identical to that discussed previously. Unlike prompt radiation, however, fallout involves the production of relatively large amounts of **internal emitters,** radioactive particles that are either ingested or inhaled and then cause damage by radiating the body from inside.

When a nuclear explosion is airburst and does not make contact with the ground, the radioactive products of the explosion rise into the upper atmosphere. Because of their very small size, these particles descend to earth

very slowly, after days, weeks, even months or years. (The smaller the particle, and the higher it has gotten into the atmosphere, the longer it takes to descend.) As a result, in the case of high-altitude airbursts, the short-lived radioisotopes are not considered to be a significant problem because they lose much of their radioactivity before settling. Unless the amount of such fallout is extraordinarily high, as might occur in a very large-scale nuclear war, it is generally assumed that airbursts—even airbursts of large numbers of large weapons—will not make a significant contribution to the worldwide background radiation levels.

Groundbursts, on the other hand, are very different. If a fireball touches the ground, and particularly if it explodes directly on the ground, enormous amounts of finely pulverized dirt and other substances are scooped up in the mushroom cloud, which can extend upward for many miles. Radioactive fission products adhere to these particles, and to some extent, neutron activation renders the particles themselves radioactive. The resulting **induced radioactivity** comprises much of the fallout hazard resulting from groundbursts. Being larger and heavier than the naked isotopes produced by the explosion, these particles fall much more rapidly. (Note, however, that groundbursts generally produce many more fine particles than do airbursts.) Radioactive particles that rise up only partway into the "stem" of a mushroom cloud fall back to earth relatively quickly, in minutes. Such fallout is not considered to be particularly significant, largely because it affects areas near the hypocenter, within which people have already been killed by the blast and thermal effects, if not by the prompt radiation as well.

Larger explosions generate more radioactive by-products and pulverize larger amounts of ground (Fig. 5.1). Unlike the lethal radius, the amount of fallout produced by a nuclear explosion is considered to vary in a linear relation to its explosive size. A 1-kiloton surface burst, for example, will contaminate about 2 square kilometers with 500 rems (long-term exposure); 10 kilotons will similarly contaminate 20 square kilometers; and 1 megaton will contaminate 2,000 square kilometers.

Larger explosions also produce stronger updraft winds within the mushroom cloud, on the order of hundreds of kilometers per hour. The height of the mushroom cloud increases with the size of the blast. For explosions below about 100 kilotons, the mushroom cloud remains within the lower region of the atmosphere (the **troposphere**); hence fallout is unlikely to be distributed worldwide, nearly all of it settling to the

**FIGURE 5.1 Large mushroom cloud produced by a thermonuclear explosion in the multimegaton range. Such explosions, when groundburst, produce very large amounts of radioactive fallout. Because of the height of the cloud, they also introduce materials into the stratosphere.**
(Courtesy of the US Department of Defense.)

ground within hours, or at most a few days. The top of a 1-megaton mushroom cloud, on the other hand, reaches about 20 kilometers. The **tropopause** (the boundary between the lower and upper atmosphere, between the troposphere and the stratosphere) occurs at about 12 kilometers, or 40,000 feet. The mushroom cloud of a large fusion bomb extends well past this boundary; hence, most of the radioactive fission products for bombs greater than 1 megaton are deposited in the stratosphere. They therefore have a long settling time and widespread distribution (Fig. 5.2).

The boundary between troposphere and stratosphere is relatively difficult to cross. Vertical transport of materials airborne in the troposphere is relatively fast, whereas for substances injected into the stratosphere such transport is very slow. Unlike material in the troposphere, which settles to earth by gravity and is also washed out by rain, substances in the stratosphere remain aloft for prolonged periods of time during which they are circulated worldwide. Because it may take weeks or even months for such products to settle to earth, most short-lived isotopes decay without ever reaching ground. Only long-lived isotopes are therefore accorded significance in cases of global fallout distribution.

## Distribution and Decay of Fallout

Radioactive particles within the troposphere settle out within hours or days, producing contamination that can be lethal to unsheltered or unprotected people, animals, and plants. The size of the explosion and the local weather (e.g., raining or not raining) are important factors in influencing local fallout patterns. Wind direction and velocity are also especially critical. Assuming constant wind direction, constant wind velocity, and stable weather, fallout is distributed in a cigar-shaped pattern, extending downwind of ground zero. Idealized contour diagrams of this sort have been established, depending on explosive size and wind speed (Fig. 5.3). Certain general relationships are worth pointing out.

1. Larger explosions result in greater quantities of fallout.

2. Stronger winds result in thinner, longer plumes; gentler winds produce fatter, shorter plumes.

3. Higher radiation doses are found closer to ground zero.

The dose contours must be interpreted with caution because they vary substantially depending on what

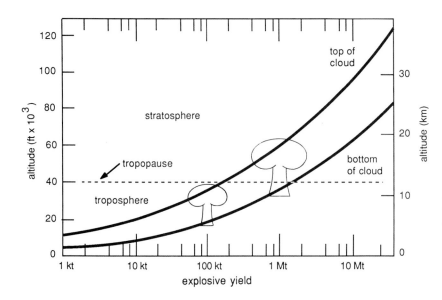

**FIGURE 5.2 The relation between explosive yield and the altitude reached by the top and bottom of a mushroom cloud, for groundbursts. Note that explosions larger than 100 kilotons introduce material into the stratosphere; above 1 megaton, a very large proportion extends beyond the tropopause.** (Modified from Glasstone and Dolan, 1977, and Schroeer, 1984.)

temporal pattern of dose they assume: for example, whether they are based on acute exposure, or on 24-hour, 7-day, or lifetime accumulated exposure, of the sort that would be experienced by someone who remained indefinitely at the site.

The fallout plume will depend almost entirely on wind direction. For example, Figure 5.4 shows the estimated fallout resulting from a 1-megaton surface burst on Detroit. In this case, the dose levels assume 7-day accumulated levels in the absence of shielding. It also assumes constant 15-mph winds blowing from the southwest. Carried downwind, the fallout in this case would largely affect rural Ontario, a region of Canada in which the population density is relatively low. But if the winds were from a different direction, a different geographic—and demographic—pattern would result. As shown in Figure 5.5, if the wind were blowing from the northwest, the fallout from Detroit would land on heavily populated areas, including Windsor (Ontario), Cleveland, Youngstown, Pittsburgh, and possibly Akron.

Fallout looks like a fine coating of dust. Its radioactivity decays over time, such that roentgen levels after 2 days are 1/100 their original levels, and after 2 weeks, 1/1000. As a rough estimate, radiation from fallout declines by a factor of 10 for every sevenfold increase in hours from the explosion. So, if at 1 hour the radiation dose intensity from fallout is 1,000 rems per hour, at 7 hours it will be 100, and at 49 hours (7 × 7), it will be 10 (Fig. 5.6). Nonetheless, cumulative

levels—not instantaneous rates—are critical here. Assuming that just over 50% of the fallout descends to the ground in about 1 hour after the explosion, it is possible to calculate the total accumulated dose, given the hourly dose rate. The total integrated dose received by an exposed person, for example, is about 4.5 times the dose rate at 1 hour after the explosion: if the dose rate 1 hour after an explosion is 400 rems, the total fallout dose received would be 1,800 rems (400 × 4.5). One-quarter of this total is received during the first 4 hours after the explosion, the next quarter during hours 4–17, the third quarter between 17 hours and 1 week, and the last quarter after a week, with hourly doses falling off rapidly. This exponential rate of decay is the basis for the general assumption that fallout sheltering will be necessary for at least a week, longer in more heavily contaminated areas, but in most cases not significantly longer than that. It should be emphasized, however, that total dosage accumulates substantially, even many days or weeks after an explosion.

If repeated bombardments occurred over a period of time, the fallout dose patterns would recur. And of course, lifetime exposure levels would be cumulative. The higher the radiation level, the longer it would take for exposure rate to return to tolerable levels. Thus, for the one-time hypothetical fallout scenario presented above for Detroit, decay to a "safe" radiation level would take years:

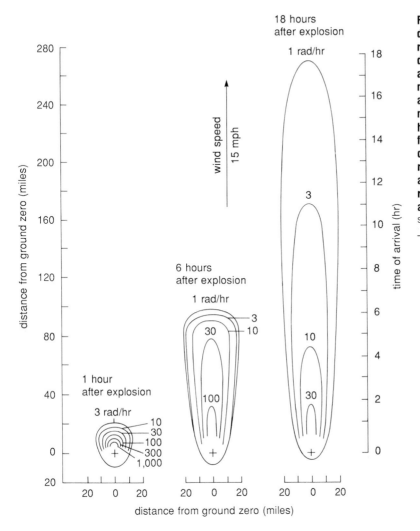

**FIGURE 5.3 Theoretical diagram showing the radiation contours produced 1, 6, and 18 hours after detonation of a 2-megaton surface burst, assuming constant, 15 mph wind. Note that the highest dose rates are found in the most interior contours and that these rates diminish over time, although the remaining radiation also covers more area.** (Modified from Glasstone and Dolan, 1977.)

| Initial radiation dose | Time required for decay to 0.5 rem/year |
|---|---|
| 3,000-rem contour | 8–10 years |
| 900-rem contour | about 6 years |
| 300-rem contour | 3–4 years |
| 90-rem contour | about 3 years |

Survivors seeking to cope with the "postattack environment," would doubtless have to emerge from shelter long before radiation levels considered safe in the preattack would had been reached.

Rain would wash out some fallout particles, causing them to be distributed short of their predicted distances. However, this would also produce local "hot spots" in which the radiation dosage was especially high.

The effect of unpredictable wind patterns was shown by the 15-megaton hydrogen bomb test code-named **Bravo,** which eliminated the tiny Pacific island of Elugelab (part of the Eniwetok chain) in 1954. This test also provided the world with the first clear demonstration of the danger of fallout. The wind changed direction during the test, and as a result, the fallout did not settle in the pattern that had been expected. Natives of the island Rongelap, about 100 miles downwind, were outdoors in the fallout for up to 48 hours before

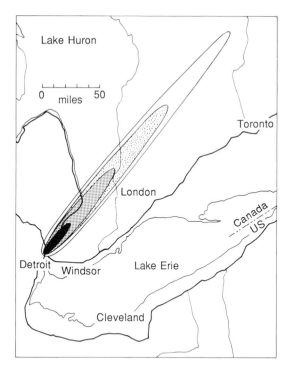

**FIGURE 5.4  Predicted fallout pattern for a nuclear attack on Detroit, as described in text. The four radiation contours show these 7-day accumulated dose levels, from the inside out: 3,000, 900, 300, and 90 rems.** (From Office of Technology Assessment, 1979.)

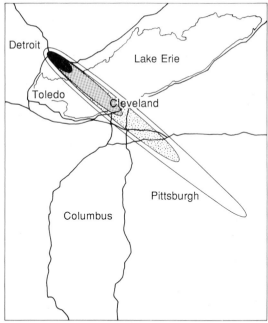

**FIGURE 5.5  Predicted fallout pattern similar to that in Figure 5.4 but with the wind blowing from the northwest.** (From Office of Technology Assessment, 1979.)

being evacuated. Radiation doses up to 175 rems were received; had these people been 20 miles or so closer, many would have died (Fig. 5.7). The crew of the Japanese trawler *Lucky Dragon* received doses of approximately 200 rems. All became ill, and one man died. In addition, some of the radioactive fallout that hit the ocean was concentrated in plankton, and in turn, more concentrated yet in the body tissues of fish caught by Japanese fishermen shortly thereafter. This caused widespread anxiety, even panic, in Japan. It also demonstrated how ecological food chains can concentrate certain radioactive fallout. Human beings, who tend to eat "high up" in such food chains, are especially susceptible to concentration effects of this sort. In the aftermath of these events, worldwide concern about fallout from atmospheric nuclear testing grew rapidly, culminating in the partial test ban treaty of 1963 (see Chapter 10).

## Long-term Effects of Fallout

It is virtually impossible to estimate reliably the long-term consequences of radioactive fallout resulting from a nuclear war. This is because of unresolved scientific controversies regarding the effects of radiation exposure, particularly when this exposure occurs over a prolonged period, and even greater uncertainties about the nature of the hypothesized nuclear war itself: the number of bombs, the proportion of airbursts and groundbursts, weather conditions, degree of warning and sheltering for the population, and so on. Nonetheless, some general statements can be made.

A large-scale nuclear war (with the explosion of about half the superpower strategic arsenals, which would be roughly 5,000 megatons) would probably produce about 20 rems of whole-body exposure per inhabitant of the Northern Hemisphere, most of this

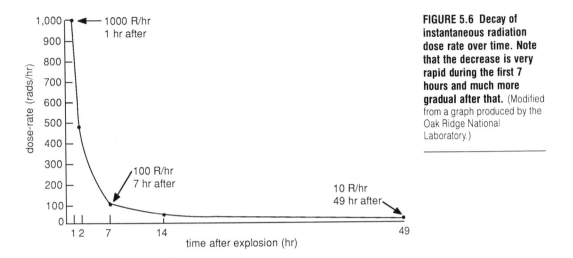

**FIGURE 5.6 Decay of instantaneous radiation dose rate over time. Note that the decrease is very rapid during the first 7 hours and much more gradual after that.** (Modified from a graph produced by the Oak Ridge National Laboratory.)

accumulated during the first month or so. Another 20 rems would be ingested and inhaled from contaminated materials: total, 40 rems/person. It must be emphasized that such dosages are averaged over the world population; in reality, inhabitants of the Northern Hemisphere and those downwind of targets, especially groundbursts, would receive much more than this, and inhabitants of the Southern Hemisphere, much less. It is also noteworthy that recent trends in targeting and warhead design have exacerbated the fallout danger: because older arsenals contained multimegaton weapons, much of the fallout they were capable of generating would have remained in the upper atmosphere, losing some of its radioactivity before settling to earth. By contrast, the smaller yield, ground-targeted weapons of the 1980s would produce more fallout, injecting it into the troposphere only; it would fall to earth relatively soon, thereby generating substantially more long-term radiation exposure.

Inhabitants of the United States, especially those who were located near targeted areas, would certainly be exposed to levels that were higher than the world-wide average. The federal government has estimated that 65% of Americans live within 20 miles of at least one prime military or industrial target and that 95% live within 100 miles. According to a conservative estimate, most survivors would experience at least 100 rems/person. A short-term dose of 250 rems produces acute radiation sickness, but with a high probability of recovery. However, "recovery" means simply that one does not immediately die; it does not necessarily mean a return to full health. In addition to greatly increased susceptibility to disease and infection, the two best-

known effects of chronic radiation exposure are cancer and possible genetic defects.

Here, as elsewhere when discussing the likely effects of nuclear war, we must speak statistically. Thus, whereas some individuals will be affected, others will not; not everyone will be affected equally. If radiation doses are held constant but a larger population is exposed, effects will be more frequent and more severe in certain individuals. Alternatively, if the exposed population is held constant but the average dose increases, roughly the same effect should occur. It is generally estimated that when a million people receive 100 rems apiece, about 12,500 cancer deaths result. At such high doses, the relationship of cancer rates to radiation exposure is approximately linear: twice as many cancers in the population (or alternatively, twice as high a probability of cancer in any given individual) at 200 rems as at 100 rems. Hence, we might expect roughly 2 million additional cancer deaths to occur in the United States within about 40 years after a general nuclear war (assuming that a large population survives that long).

There would almost certainly be a substantial increase in the number of spontaneous abortions (i.e., miscarriages) due to chromosomal damage, as well as abnormal genetic effects present in subsequent generations. Order-of-magnitude estimates for the United States following a general nuclear war range from 500,000 to 15 million spontaneous abortions plus genetic defects during the succeeding 40 years. Pregnant women whose fetuses were exposed to radiation in utero at Hiroshima or Nagasaki gave birth to a large number of severely deformed offspring, many of them

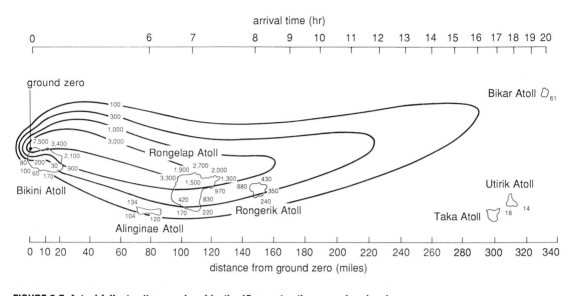

**FIGURE 5.7  Actual fallout pattern produced by the 15-megaton thermonuclear bomb test "Bravo" in the South Pacific in 1954. The contours show the integrated radiation dosage received by an unshielded person during the first 48 hours following the detonation.** (From Glasstone and Dolan, 1977.)

suffering from anencephaly ("no brain"). However, no clear evidence of increased genetic mutations has yet been documented among the survivors themselves.

Even in the event of a full-scale nuclear war, it is very unlikely that a race of mutated monsters would be produced, since those who are the worst afflicted seldom survive to reproductive age. In addition, the overwhelming majority of mutations are carried in recessive genes (and thus are apparent only if such recessive genes are contributed by both parents). Some people—mostly partisans of nuclear testing such as Edward Teller, widely considered the father of the hydrogen bomb—have even suggested that the increased mutation rate associated with radioactive fallout could turn out to be beneficial because it might speed up the rate of human evolution. This is equally unlikely to be correct: the overwhelming majority of mutations are in fact harmful. Moreover, evolutionary rates are determined by selection pressures, not by the availability of genetic variation. Normal mutation frequencies, plus sexual recombination, provide all the genetic diversity that is needed.

Although it cannot be known for certain, it seems unlikely that there will be substantial long-term genetic effects of a nuclear war on the surviving population; it

is virtually inconceivable that a race of two-headed mutant monsters would result. It is even more unlikely that the human species would be improved. In any event, the medical and genetic effects of nuclear war, although horrific by themselves, would be dwarfed by the immediate fatalities, and almost certainly, by other long-term consequences.

Cancer and genetic effects would be increased substantially if an attacker deliberately sought to produce them by detonating a large number of groundbursts, or if many groundbursts occurred in the course of a "counterforce war" against each other's missile silos, regardless of whether such fallout effects were intended. (The US and Soviet policy of hardening strategic "assets" such as ICBM silos has a side effect of encouraging an attacker to do precisely this.) A groundburst targeting policy would also have the more immediate effect of rendering large regions of the victims' homeland uninhabitable. Nuclear reactors and waste storage sites could also be targeted.

All the preceding discussion has assumed that fallout products were those produced by nuclear explosions themselves. But nuclear reactors generate large amounts of radioisotopes that are exceptionally long-lived, surviving much longer than those produced by

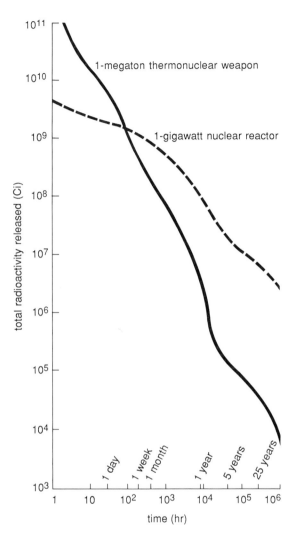

**FIGURE 5.8 Projection of the total radioactivity released after the detonation of a 1-megaton explosion and after the destruction of a long-operating 1-gigawatt (1-billion-watt) nuclear reactor. One hour afterward, the weapon has released 1,000 times more radioactivity. However, the radiation released by the reactor contains longer-lived isotopes, which take much longer to decay. One year later, therefore, the reactor is releasing about 100 times more radioactivity, and this difference increases over time.** (Modified from Fetter and Tsipis, 1981.)

a typical nuclear explosion. If the containment vessels of reactors and high-level storage sites were breached, and their radioactive products dispersed over the countryside, the background level of radioactive fallout would be increased many times, perhaps reaching levels of 300 rems or more for any survivors in North America (Fig. 5.8). It has been estimated that with widespread exposure of 300 rems, just about everyone who lived long enough could be expected to develop cancer; perhaps 50–75% of those afflicted would die of the disease, given reduced availability of medical care.

As we have seen, "normal" fallout is expected to decay exponentially in virulence, such that significantly lower levels might be obtained over a period of weeks, at least in areas that were not particular hot spots. But if the nuclear core of a long-operating reactor were vaporized, the radiation released would pose a persistent radioactive hazard for thousands of years. On the one hand, an aggressor might be expected to refrain from attacking such a facility because of the global havoc this action would wreak. However, it is also possible that the temptation to strike an opponent in such a devastating way would be irresistible. In addition, since nuclear facilities are widely recognized to have bomb-building potential (see Chapter 11), they may well be targeted for this reason alone.

## HYPOTHESIZED ATTACKS

### A Counterforce Attack

There have been numerous efforts to model the likely effects of different kinds of nuclear attack, especially on the US and the USSR. The results depend strongly on the assumptions made; that is, they vary greatly depending on the number and kind of explosions one assumes, on whether the population is assumed to have received warning and to have evacuated or taken shelter, and so on. Moreover, ulterior motives often exist for the choices of different assumptions as starting points. Hawks generally are inclined to understate the effects of nuclear war and doves, to overstate them. Zbigniew Brzezinski, President Carter's hawkish National Security Adviser, stated that "If we used all our nuclear weapons and the Russians used all of their nuclear weapons, about ten percent of humanity would be killed . . . it's not the end of humanity." Dr. Teller has expressed similar sentiments, emphasizing the resilience of the human species in the face of various natural and man-made disasters.

On the other hand, Jonathan Schell has written that "It has sometimes been claimed that the United States could survive a nuclear attack by the Soviet Union, but the bare figures on the extent of the blast waves, the thermal pulses, and the accumulated local fallout dash this hope irrevocably."* And John F. Kennedy said: "The human race must do away with nuclear weapons, or nuclear weapons will do away with the human race."

By downplaying the possibly disastrous consequences of resort to nuclear weapons, hawks hope to make the United States less likely to back down in the face of what they see as the greater danger: the aggressive designs of the USSR. They argue that the US must be more assertive in its interactions with the Soviet Union, and to achieve this, hawks feel that it is necessary to avoid paralysis of American foreign policy due to excessive fear of nuclear war and/or its consequences. On the other hand, by emphasizing the possibly negative consequences of nuclear war, doves are seeking to diminish what they see as the greater danger: a willingness to risk nuclear war in the furtherance of foreign policy goals.

A major area of disagreement has concerned the likely effect of a so-called **counterforce attack** against the stragetic nuclear weapons of the United States. Such a scenario has particular importance for deterrence and for strategic nuclear doctrine. If a counterforce attack can be carried out successfully, and with minimal civilian casualties (a so-called surgical strike), there might be strong pressures on the victim country to do nothing, since retaliating would simply make a bad situation worse. If the hypothesized counterforce strike left a victim somewhat disarmed but with its civilian population basically intact, it would be especially foolish to retaliate, since this would expose one's population to devastating counterretaliation.

Hawkishly inclined analysts, politicians, and military figures, who warn that a surgical counterforce attack is possible, have used this contingency as a justification for further nuclear "modernization." The alternative view is that such an attack would lead to death and destruction on a scale so unprecedented that no sane Soviet leader could assume that an American president would fail to retaliate. As a result, in the curious twisted logic of nuclear strategy, hawks have emphasized that the US might suffer a minimally destructive counterforce attack. Since in their view, such an attack would not be catastrophic, it is accordingly more likely.

*From J. Schell. 1982. *The Fate of the Earth*. New York: Knopf.

By contrast, doves rely on the probability that such an attack would be terribly destructive, and is therefore unlikely. ICBM vulnerability (see Chapter 2) is of more concern if it can be demonstrated that an attack that destroyed one's ICBMs would not simultaneously cause additional destruction, since in theory this would make retaliation more uncertain.

During the mid-1970s, Defense Secretary James Schlesinger (Fig. 5.9) reported to Congress that a Soviet counterforce attack could produce "only" 800,000 civilian deaths, thus lending theoretical credibility to such an attack by the USSR. In response to this assertion, the Office of Technology Assessment report, to which we have already referred, was commissioned. It yielded very different conclusions, with an estimated range of civilian deaths from about 1 million to 20 million, depending on winds and whether evacuation or sheltering was attempted. The differences in these two estimates reveal the degree to which such analyses depend on the assumptions made.

| *Schlesinger's assumptions* | *OTA's assumptions* |
| --- | --- |
| Only ICBMs targeted | ICBMs, bomber bases, and submarine bases targeted |
| One airburst per target | Two groundbursts, or one groundburst and one airburst per target |
| Little or no wind (little fallout) | Moderate wind (wider fallout distribution) |

Figure 5.10 depicts the possible fallout contours for an estimated counterforce attack against the United States. Whereas the targets tend to be in relatively unpopulated areas, fallout would be distributed across many urban areas. The fallout from an attack on the ICBMs at Whiteman Air Force Base, for example, would blanket St. Louis, and that from the Bangor Submarine Base (home of the Trident fleet) would cover Seattle. $C^3I$ installations, many of which are located in populated areas, would doubtless be prime targets. Groundbursts, which produce large amounts of fallout, seem most likely as a means of destroying hardened targets. Hypothesized US attacks on comparable Soviet counterforce targets result in somewhat lower casualties, but of the same order of magnitude.

Since ICBMs tend to be sited in highly productive agricultural areas, the long-term impact on farm production of a counterforce attack probably would be substantial. The season of the attack would be especially important: if it occurred during the spring or summer, large portions of that year's crop would be lost.

**FIGURE 5.9 Defense Secretary James Schlesinger conferring with his predecessor, Elliot Richardson, in 1973.** (Courtesy of the US Department of Defense.)

Early in the growing season, crops are especially sensitive to radiation because they are young and growing rapidly. Later in the summer, the fallout hazard would preclude harvesting. Attacks during the late fall or winter would be less destructive. In general, farm animals are about as sensitive to radiation as human beings are (perhaps a bit more resistant). Most crops are significantly more resistant, although there is a great range of sensitivity: yields are reduced by 50% following exposure of peas to 1,000 roentgens whereas the comparable figure for squash exceeds 16,000 roentgens.

Perhaps the greatest uncertainty surrounding a counterforce attack, however, involves its political and military effects: whether the victim will retaliate, and if so, how, and whether such retaliation will lead to all-out nuclear war.

## All-out Nuclear War

There have been at least as many hypothesized scenarios for all-out nuclear war as for various limited versions. The Office of Technology Assessment, for example, examined a presumed attack on both military and urban-industrial targets in each nation; estimated fatalities if the attack came without warning were 155 million to 165 million Americans and 100 million Soviets. With warning and evacuation of cities, American fatalities were set at 20 million to 55 million, and Soviet fatalities between 25 million and 35 million. All these projections assumed no mass fires, and casualties were estimated during the first 30 days postattack only. It must be emphasized that survival for one month after such an event does not insure long-term survival, or success.

An independent study, conducted by strategic analyst Arthur Katz, assumed somewhat different attack parameters: five hundred 1-megaton warheads on 71 US metropolitan areas, plus three hundred 100-kiloton warheads on 34 industrial regions. The result: 50 million to 60 million fatalities plus 20 million to 30 million moderate to severe injuries (again, prompt casualties only, no mass fires). If the goal of the attack had been civilian destruction rather than military and industrial damage only, the casualty rate would have been significantly higher. It is noteworthy that this scenario involved the total explosion of only 800 bombs, comprising only about 530 megatons; since the Soviet arsenal is more than 10 times this magnitude, these estimates seem likely to be conservative.

A third study, by the Defense Civil Preparedness Agency, supposed an attack of 6,559 megatons (the

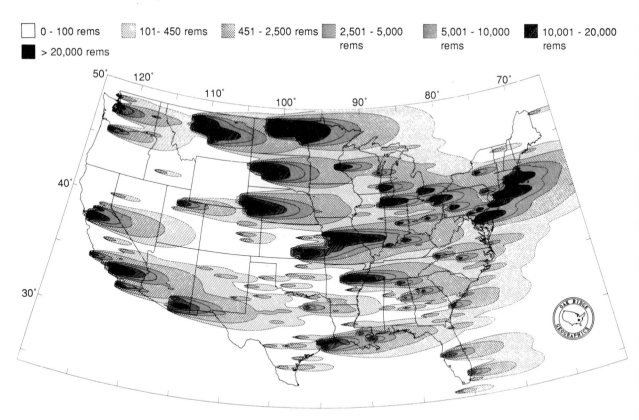

□ 0 - 100 rems   ▨ 101- 450 rems   ▨ 451 - 2,500 rems   ▨ 2,501 - 5,000 rems   ▨ 5,001 - 10,000 rems   ▨ 10,001 - 20,000 rems

■ > 20,000 rems

**FIGURE 5.10 Fourteen-day integrated radiation exposure doses following a hypothe-sized counterforce attack, assuming a west wind at 20 mph.** (From the Oak Ridge National Laboratory.)

equivalent, in explosive force, of 524,720 Hiroshima bombs). This was assumed to be aimed at military targets, industrial facilities, and all population centers of 50,000 or more. The results: within a few minutes, 40% of the US population—86 million persons—would be killed instantly, with another 27%—34 million persons—seriously injured. Fifty million more people would die within the next few months, for a short-term total of 133 million deaths. Another 30 million would remain alive, but with moderate injuries. About 60 million Americans would be more or less uninjured, and only moderately irradiated. It therefore seems not unreasonable to conclude that in the immediate aftermath of a large-scale nuclear attack, a substantial fraction of the US citizenry will be crushed, smashed, irradiated, minced, sliced, diced, battered, blinded, punctured, lacerated, fried, baked, and broiled.

In Chapter 7 we shall briefly review and compare presumed US and Soviet nuclear vulnerabilities and the potential for postattack recovery. It seems very likely, however, that social disruption and economic chaos would be extreme in both nations, and perhaps in the world. Indeed, once the fires have burned themselves out and most of the victims of blast and burns have either died or somewhat recovered, the surviving population will have to confront the psychological and emotional impact of the event. We shall treat this circumstance briefly in Chapter 14, but it is worth noting here that such effects are difficult, perhaps impossible, to predict. During the saturation bombings of World War II, there were intervals between attacks during which a sense of continuity and sometimes even normality was achieved, even amid terrible destruction. By contrast, the likely suddenness of a nuclear war, combined with extraordinary chaos and the catastrophic effects suggested above, will present the human species with a situation that is unprecedented in its history. Never have millions of people died within minutes. It is possible that the shredding of the social fabric plus intense psychological trauma will leave permanent and crippling scars. It is also possible, of course, that as supporters of civil defense programs claim, "When the going gets tough, the tough will get going." Maybe survivors will function with determination and effectiveness, within the limits of resources available to them.

Electricity was restored in some of the less badly damaged areas of Hiroshima the day after the attack; train service to the city also resumed the next day, and in the outskirts, limited streetcar service was available on day 3, with some telephone lines operating within 10 days. This was because of assistance from undamaged areas, and because the single bomb that fell on Hiroshima was a very small one by today's standards. In a widespread nuclear war there probably will be no "outside," and the prospect of assistance may be remote. Almost certainly, targeted cities that have not burned will have their streets blocked by debris; aside from this, would-be rescuers would likely be deterred by fallout hazard.

In the virtual absence of long-distance transportation and communication, it may be difficult or impossible to maintain a society, an economy, or any form of political organization that resembles current systems. Oil refining, electric generating, pharmaceutical manufacturing, large-scale food growing and processing, as well as the distribution of any such products, would be difficult, and maybe impossible for unpredictable periods, perhaps many years or even forever.

Food storage near urban areas and other targets will be destroyed and remaining grain will be concentrated in rural areas where there are few people. Since oil refineries are very vulnerable and also likely to be targeted, it seems unlikely that fuel supplies will be adequate to permit large-scale distribution of food to the survivors, even assuming that the social, economic, and political structures exist to organize such activities.

Simple barter would probably replace a money economy. Standards of sanitation and basic hygiene will plummet; cold and starvation will become major concerns. In the absence of rigid police-state techniques, anarchy may result. The federal government may not retain enough authority and resources to reconstitute itself.

A demoralized and weakened population, crowded into makeshift shelters with inadequate hygiene, would provide the ideal conditions for the spread of serious epidemics. According to some estimates, communicable diseases may well strike one-quarter of the survivors, with likely plagues of radiation-resistant bacteria and viruses, carrying typhoid, typhus, cholera, tuberculosis, and influenza. Some of these will spread via insect vectors, which in turn will feast and breed on the millions of unburied, rotting human and animal corpses. The surviving population will almost certainly be susceptible to such onslaughts, especially because antibiotics will be in short supply or unavailable and most major hospitals destroyed, along with a large proportion of the nation's health care professionals.

The Office of Technology Assessment is quite clear that following a general nuclear war, things would get progressively worse, not better, for an unknowable period of time. There would be a race between the consumption of existing food, fuel, and medical supplies, and society's ability to produce these essentials. American agriculture, for example, is very energy intensive, depending on mechanized equipment requiring large amounts of refined petroleum, fertilizers and pesticides (which are manufactured at vulnerable chemical plants), and artificial irrigation, which requires energy to pump water from underground aquifers. Planting and maintenance of fields will be rendered very difficult, as will harvesting, storage, and distribution.

"And when it is all over, what will the world be like?" asked Lord Louis Mountbatten.

> *Our fine great buildings, our homes will exist no more. The thousands of years it took to develop our civilization will have been in vain. Our works of art will be lost. Radio, television, newspapers will disappear. There will be no means of transport. There will be no hospitals. No help can be expected for the few mutilated survivors in any town to be sent from a neighboring town—there will be no neighboring towns left, no neighbors, there will be no help, there will be no hope.\**

There is also another view, expressed particularly during the early years of the Reagan administration, that emphasizes the potential survivability of nuclear war. During his confirmation hearings for the directorship of the Arms Control and Disarmament Agency

---

\*From speech delivered in Strasbourg, May 1979.

(1981), Eugene V. Rostow was asked if he felt that either the US or the Soviet Union would survive a nuclear war. He answered:

> *Well, there are ghoulish statistical calculations that are made about how many people would die in a nuclear exchange. Depending upon certain assumptions, some estimates predict that there would be ten million casualties on one side and one hundred million on another. But that is not the whole of the population.*

The rest of the world, too, has studied the subject and has offered speculations. In 1983, for example, the Royal Swedish Academy of Sciences advanced a scenario for all-out, global nuclear war (cited in Additional Readings for this chapter as AMBIO). It was assumed that 14,747 bombs and warheads, totaling 5,742 megatons, would be detonated. The targets were: all major industry and military installations in the US, the USSR, and their major allies; all cities of 100,000 or more in the major industrialized nations aligned with one bloc or the other, and cities of 500,000 or more in other nations of the Northern Hemisphere. The results: 750 million killed promptly and 340 million seriously injured, out of an urban population of roughly 1.3 billion in the Northern Hemisphere. It was further estimated that of the 200 million urban survivors that were initially uninjured, many would succumb to exposure, starvation, dehydration, epidemics, violence in the wake of civil unrest, and latent radiation injury. It is at least possible that modern civilization, with its interconnections, amenities, and complexities, would collapse altogether, on a worldwide scale.

Soviet Premier Nikita Khrushchev once prophesied that in the aftermath of a nuclear war, the living would envy the dead. If we are fortunate, we shall never find out whether he was correct.

## OZONE DEPLETION AND ULTRAVIOLET LIGHT

Any discussion of survivors and the possible reconstitution of society assumes that the ecological fabric conducive to human life will be preserved after a large-scale nuclear war. Logicians might say that a fundamentally intact world ecosystem is not a sufficient condition for postattack recovery, but it is a necessary one. Aside from the possibility of toxic levels of worldwide fallout, the two major areas of concern are depletion of the ozone layer and drastic darkening and cooling of the world climate (nuclear winter). Although these effects, if they occur at all, are likely to be concentrated in the Northern Hemisphere, they are essentially global in extent, thus including all nations of the world, not just the superpowers.

It is generally agreed that high-intensity ultraviolet (UV) light, striking the earth's surface billions of years ago, helped stimulate the chemical reactions that produced the first life. (In this and further discussions, we shall be referring to the biologically important component of UV radiation, also known as UV-B.) This form of electromagnetic radiation is so toxic to living cells that surgical instruments are often sterilized by UV lamps. UV radiation is responsible for producing sunburn, and in extensive and prolonged doses, it causes skin cancer and can result in blindness as well. Such negative effects are ameliorated in the world today because plants release molecular oxygen ($O_2$), some of which rises into the stratosphere and is converted into ozone ($O_3$). This ozone shields the earth's surface from much of the UV light that would otherwise fall upon it.

Nuclear explosions produce large amounts of nitrogen oxides, chiefly NO and $NO_2$. For smaller nuclear weapons (less than 0.5 megaton or so), these chemicals remain in the troposphere and have minimal impact on stratospheric ozone. However, larger explosions inject immense quantities of the oxides of nitrogen into the stratosphere, where by a series of complex chemical reactions, they catalyze the conversion of ozone back into molecular oxygen. If this cycle were to proceed on a large scale, it would allow large amounts of UV light, which otherwise would be blocked by the ozone, to reach the surface of the earth. Depletion of the ozone layer is unlikely to be a permanent effect, since eventually the molecular oxygen will be reconverted to ozone, just as it was long ago when oxygen first became abundant in the earth's atmosphere. However, current estimates are that the recovery of the earth's ozone layer would take at least several years. The amount of depletion would depend on how much ozone was destroyed, which in turn would depend on the number of explosions and their size (Fig. 5.11). Recovery time would also depend on the time required for the excess nitrogen oxides to be removed from the stratosphere by wind systems and/or naturally occurring turbulence.

In 1975 the National Academy of Sciences (NAS) reported on a study examining the possible worldwide effects of a general, 10,000-megaton nuclear war in the Northern Hemisphere, using weapons of 1, 3, and 5 megatons. The NAS concluded that such an event could significantly deplete the ozone layer: "A 30–70% reduction in the ozone column in the Northern Hemisphere and 20–40% reductions in the Southern Hemisphere, with a recovery time of two to four years, are possible." The relationship between ozone depletion and UV penetration to the ground is not simple: a 20% ozone depletion would increase UV incidence somewhat more than 2-fold, a 40% depletion would result in about a 5-fold increase, and an 80% depletion would produce approximately a 23-fold increase. A 30–70% ozone reduction, as estimated by the NAS, would produce an increase in UV penetration of about four to eight times normal levels. More recently (1985), the NAS calculated that a 6,500-megaton war—detonating just over a half of the superpower arsenals—would produce a 17% ozone depletion after 8 months, increasing UV radiation by a factor of 2–4.

The effects of increased UV penetration are uncertain and somewhat controversial. Certain plants, especially aquatic plants, are believed to be near the upper limit of their UV tolerance; substantial increases in UV could therefore kill or injure many such plants. Human beings would be at greatly increased risk of sunburn, especially in the tropics. With 50% depletion (a seven-fold increase in UV penetration), for example, light-skinned persons would suffer second-degree sunburn after just 30 minutes of direct exposure. The NAS also estimated that a 50% ozone depletion would produce a 10% increase in skin cancer over the next 40 years; about 1% of skin cancers are fatal. "Snow-blindness" would also be a real danger. Both these risks could be diminished by wearing protective clothing and sunglasses.

There is greater doubt about the effects of increased UV on animals, especially the possibility of blinding, since animals—particularly wild animals—cannot readily be induced to wear protective clothing or sunglasses. Some authorities claim that animals would not be severely impaired or threatened. Others, like MIT physicist Kosta Tsipis, maintain that the ozone layer depletion that would result from the explosion of only 10% of the world's arsenals would cause the blinding, hence the extinction, of many of the world's animals. Certain animals have a crucial role in the worldwide ecosystem: the pollinating activities of many insects are one example. It is therefore conceivable that the combined effect of ozone depletion on terrestrial plants, oceanic plankton, and certain animals could lead to worldwide biological collapse. On the other hand, the NAS scenario is based on the use of very large nuclear explosions. With the US and Soviet emphasis on some-

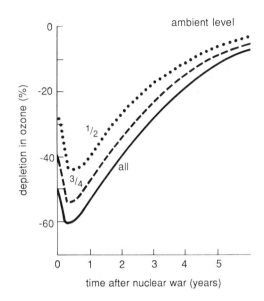

**FIGURE 5.11 Predicted depletion of stratospheric ozone in the Northern Hemisphere following a nuclear war in which the indicated combined proportions of the US and Soviet strategic nuclear stockpiles were detonated. Maximum ozone depletion would occur about 6 months after a nuclear war, and recovery would take several years.** (Modified from Ehrlich, 1984.)

what smaller, more accurate nuclear weapons, the danger to the world's ozone layer is now doubtless less than it was in the 1960s—although it may still be substantial.

## NUCLEAR WINTER

*Our most thoughtful projections show that a major nuclear exchange will have, among its plausible effects, the greatest biological and physical disruptions of this planet in its last 65 million years.*[*]

During the 1950s and 1960s, the diffuse global effects of nuclear war seemed limited to worldwide fallout (the book and movie *On the Beach,* in which survivors ultimately died of radiation, illustrated this in extreme form). During the late 1960s and 1970s, attention shifted somewhat to ozone destruction and toxic

---

*Stanford University president Donald Kennedy. From P. Ehrlich, C. Sagan, D. Kennedy, and W.O. Roberts. 1984. *The Cold and the Dark.* New York: W.W. Norton.

levels of UV light. In the 1980s, concern has focused especially on possible adverse global climatic changes, known as nuclear winter.

The NAS study referred to above concluded that despite the possibly dangerous effects of ozone depletion, a large-scale nuclear war probably would not result in the extinction of *Homo sapiens*. But more recent studies have taken a much more somber view, based on the chances that dust and soot, lofted into the upper atmosphere, would block out substantial amounts of light and warmth, resulting in catastrophic changes in the global climate. The most renowned of these studies, published in 1983, is known as the **TTAPS report,** from the last names of its five authors (Turco, Toon, Ackerman, Pollack, and Sagan). It is noteworthy that the possibility of serious long-term effects of nuclear dust and smoke were not even suspected until 38 years into the Nuclear Age. The TTAPS report coined the phrase **nuclear winter,** referring to a prolonged period of intense, worldwide cooling and darkening predicted as a consequence of nuclear war. This study, and the many others that have come after it, used computer models to simulate the production of dust and soot, the movement of these particles through the atmosphere, and their likely effects in depressing temperature and light levels at the surface.

The discovery of nuclear winter as a likely effect of nuclear war correlates with the theory that the extinction of dinosaurs and marine invertebrates may have been caused by the impact of a large meteor on the earth, which lofted huge amounts of dust that in turn may have dramatically altered the planet's climate. Similarly, in 1815 the volcanic eruption of Tambura, in what is now Indonesia, affected the earth's climate for an entire year: crops later failed throughout North America and Europe, and 1816 was known as the "year without summer." The dust produced by this eruption appears to have lowered average temperatures by 1°C; even this seemingly modest reduction produced widespread famines and deprivation. The eruption of Mount Krakatoa in 1883 also made the planet colder and darker, and in this century dust from the eruption of Mount St. Helens (Fig. 5.12) caused darkness over three northwestern states.

Volcanic dust alone seems unlikely to produce the catastrophic effects implied in the phrase "nuclear winter." The dust produced by nuclear groundbursts, however, would be more effective than volcanic debris, because the particles generated by nuclear explosions are more absorptive. As a result, they would block sunlight more efficiently, so that the effect of nuclear dust

would be more intense as well as more prolonged than that of volcanic dust. However, even nuclear dust does not seem likely to be the major cause of nuclear winter. Smoke is the real culprit.

In addition to dust, nuclear war would produce vast quantities of smoke and soot, from burning wildlands and cities (Fig. 5.13). Smoke particles differ from dust particles in that they are much more prone to absorb incident sunlight. As a result, the effect of smoke in contributing to nuclear winter differs from that of dust in that whereas dust tends to scatter sunlight, smoke is blacker and therefore more effective in absorbing it, across all wavelengths. Smoke will therefore cause greater darkness and lower temperatures at the surface than an equivalent amount of dust. But since smoke particles generally do not rise as high as dust, smoke may be more likely to be washed out of the troposphere by rain. Groundbursts—the preferred targeting strategy for destroying ICBM silos and other hardened targets—produce large amounts of dust. Airbursts, the preferred targeting strategy for destroying cities and other "soft" targets, produce large amounts of smoke because they are more likely to cause widespread secondary fires.

Energy from the sun reaches the earth in many different forms. Much of it arrives in a form visible to the human eye; we call it light. Since the earth's atmosphere is relatively transparent to these wavelengths, such energy tends to pass through the atmosphere, warming the earth itself. Additional energy is reflected back away from the ground as infrared radiation. If the earth lacked an atmosphere, it would soon become too cold to support life, as its heat was radiated back into space. However, the atmosphere is less transparent to infrared than to visible waves, so heat that is radiated by the earth is absorbed by the planet's atmosphere. It is this **"greenhouse effect"** that tends to warm the earth's surface, causing air temperatures to be higher closer to the ground, and to decrease at higher altitudes. Like the glass of a greenhouse roof, the cool upper atmosphere intercepts some of the reflected infrared radiation coming from the warm ground and reradiates it to space less effectively because the "roof" is cooler than the ground. (This behavior also explains why cloudy nights in the winter are typically warmer than clear nights—namely, because clouds are much more efficient than clear air at intercepting the radiation from the ground.)

In any event, the predictions of nuclear winter are based on the likelihood that with immense amounts of smoke and dust in the upper atmosphere, the normal

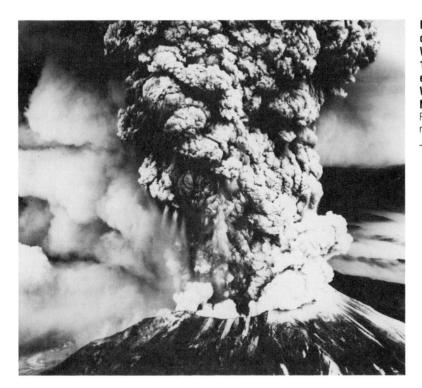

**FIGURE 5.12 The eruption of Mount St. Helens, in Washington State, during 1978. The dust from this eruption darkened much of Washington, Idaho, and Montana.** (Courtesy of the Federal Emergency Management Agency.)

**FIGURE 5.13 Massive amounts of smoke produced by a medium-sized forest fire.** (Courtesy of the US Forest Service.)

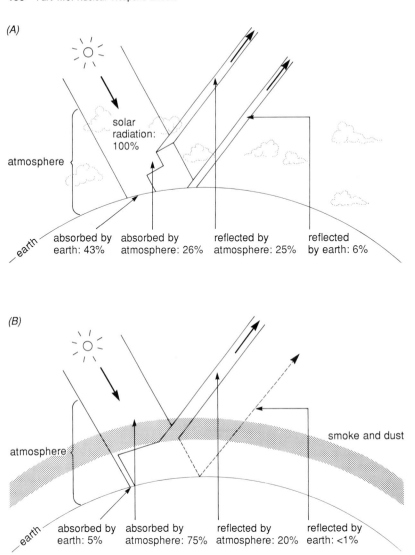

*(A)*

solar
radiation:
100%

atmosphere

earth

absorbed by
earth: 43%

absorbed by
atmosphere: 26%

reflected by
atmosphere: 25%

reflected
by earth: 6%

**FIGURE 5.14 The earth's energy balance (*A*) under normal conditions and (*B*) in the aftermath of nuclear war according to the nuclear winter calculations. Normally, solar radiation warms the earth, which absorbs 43% of it; during nuclear winter, however, 75% of the incoming solar radiation would be absorbed by the soot and dust in the atmosphere, and only about 5% by the earth.**

*(B)*

smoke and dust

atmosphere

earth

absorbed by
earth: 5%

absorbed by
atmosphere: 75%

reflected by
atmosphere: 20%

reflected by
earth: <1%

energy budget of the earth would be severely disrupted (Fig. 5.14). Instead of reaching the ground, most of the sun's energy would be absorbed by vast amounts of these tiny particles, suspended at high elevation. These particles of dust and smoke would then radiate their heat back into space, with relatively little of it ever reaching the ground. At the same time, tiny smoke and dust particles, which are too small to intercept infrared radiation, would not contribute to greenhouse-type warming of the surface. A massive temperature inversion would result, with colder temperatures near the

ground, and warmer, particle-laden air at higher altitudes.

Just as with other efforts to anticipate the effects of nuclear war, analyses of nuclear winter are strongly dependent on the assumptions that are made. The TTAPS study analyzed several hypothetical nuclear war scenarios, making various assumptions about the amount of smoke and dust produced, their duration in the atmosphere, and their effects in blocking sunlight. The results for four of these scenarios are presented here (Fig. 5.15). Scenario 1, the "baseline" case, sup-

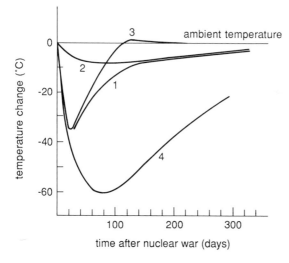

**FIGURE 5.15  Decreases in temperature at the earth's surface as a function of time, following nuclear war scenarios 1–4. See text for details.** (Modified from TTAPS, 1983.)

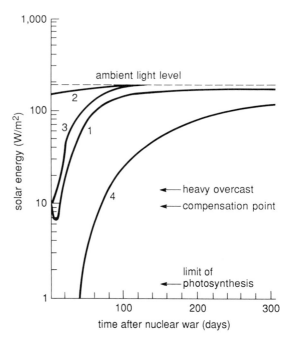

**FIGURE 5.16  Decreases in light levels at the earth's surface as a function of time, following nuclear war scenarios 1–4 as depicted in Figure 5.15.** (Modified from TTAPS, 1983.)

poses 5,000 megatons, 80% of which is directed at military sites, and 20% against urban and industrial targets. Scenario 2 is a 3,000-megaton counterforce attack, consisting of groundbursts at missile silos and other military targets. Scenario 3 is a 100-megaton attack, directed at cities and using only airbursts. Scenario 4 is a worst-case estimate, assuming 10,000 megatons—unlikely at present, but conceivable if the superpower arsenals grow and if a large proportion is actually used in a war.

Several aspects of these findings are notable.

1.  In scenarios 1 and 3, land surface temperatures would drop from the continental mean of 13°C to −23°C. Temperatures would remain below freezing in the baseline case (1) for 95 days and in the cities-only case (3) for 70 days. In the cities-only case, more than 3 months would elapse before near-normal temperatures would resume; in the baseline case, 10 months would be required.

2.  Along with depressed temperatures, nuclear winter would entail substantial reductions in ambient light. Perhaps as much as 95% of the light that normally reaches the ground would be absorbed and/or reflected by the dust and soot aloft; light

levels at midday would be roughly equivalent to that now found at full moon (Fig. 5.16).

3.  All these scenarios generate substantial drops in temperature. It has been claimed that an average drop of just 1°C would incapacitate wheat growing in Canada. The effects of depressing temperature by many degrees may be calamitous.

4.  The counterforce attack produces the smallest temperature change, but one that is relatively long-lasting. This is because it is produced primarily by dust. Although less effective than smoke in blocking sunlight, dust is more persistent.

5.  The 100-megaton city attack, despite its relatively small total explosive power, produces climatic effects that are not dramatically different from those of the 5,000-megaton baseline scenario. This is because of the significance of large amounts of

smoke (produced especially by airbursts). The TTAPS study shows that number of warheads is more important than their explosive yields. It also suggests the striking finding that a threshold effect for worldwide climatic catastrophe may exist, and that this threshold may be as low as 100 megatons, which is a very small fraction of the world's arsenals.

6. The cooling effects are most dramatic in the spring and summer, and in the Northern Hemisphere.

A very small worldwide cooling and darkening could be catastrophic, even if this happened in the absence of nuclear war. Living things are rather precisely calibrated to the normal seasonal variations in temperature. Resistance to extreme cold is most poorly developed in tropical organisms, and sudden plunges of many degrees, for prolonged periods, might cause substantial destruction of tropical ecosystems. Even at the middle and high latitudes, resistance to winter conditions develops over a period of time, usually cued by progressive decreases in day length during autumn. Precipitous drops in temperature might well cause the death of many temperate and even arctic organisms as well.

Nuclear winter could also have a severe impact on the chances of human survival in the postattack environment, in several other ways.

1. The cold would greatly exacerbate the morbidity (sickness) and mortality (deaths) otherwise associated with the aftermath of nuclear war.

2. As we have seen, in addition to the environmental temperature changes, the nuclear winter scenario calls for substantial darkening of the planet. If this darkening of the earth's surface were sufficient to impair photosynthesis, the basic energy cycle on which living things depend would be seriously disrupted. Thus, in addition to posing the monumental problem of keeping warm, nuclear winter would greatly complicate the chances that survivors would be able to grow or raise sufficient food. Perhaps most critically, depressed temperatures and light levels could make effective agriculture substantially more difficult, and in some scenarios, impossible.

3. Substantial quantities of the Northern Hemisphere's inland fresh waters would be likely to freeze at least temporarily, and wild animals as well as people might be unable to obtain usable water for prolonged periods. It has been estimated that freshwater sources could be covered with 1–2 meters of hard ice, which, in the absence of heavy machinery or high explosives, might be inaccessible to people, plants, or animals. Without electricity or fuel to run pumps, groundwater supplies may also be unavailable, adding thirst to the likely famine.

4. Marine ecosystems would be less susceptible than terrestrial environments to catastrophic cooling because of the greater heat-holding capacity of the oceans. However, the darkness of nuclear winter could be especially troublesome for oceanic life forms. Marine phytoplankton are major generators of atmospheric oxygen, as well as being the building blocks of oceanic ecosystems. If sunlight were eliminated or drastically curtailed for several weeks, these oceanic algae could be decimated, and since many have life cycles of only several days or even hours, the disruption might be pronounced. To some extent, the effect of ozone depletion (notably, increases in UV light) would be offset by the dust and soot clouds. However, this nuclear pall is expected to clear one or more years before the stratospheric ozone is reconstituted. As a result, UV penetration could become a particular problem after the immediate effects of nuclear winter had largely run their course. Also, since oceanic phytoplankton are very sensitive to UV light, they might be killed in large numbers when nuclear winter was over but the ozone not yet reconstituted; after a nuclear winter, there would be an ultraviolet spring.

5. Depending on its duration, global darkening could seriously impair the survival of certain terrestrial green plants, if light levels remain below what is necessary for plants to carry out photosynthesis. The effect on the planetary food chain would be disastrous.

6. The predicted cold and dark is also expected to greatly reduce rainfall patterns by interfering with widespread evaporation. The resulting droughts could prove to be as harmful as the cold and the dark.

7. The large-scale burning of synthetic materials at industrial and urban sites would release large quantities of toxic fumes (dubbed "pyrotoxins") such as cyanides, carbon monoxide, nitrogen oxides, dioxins, and furans. These gases could

blanket much of the Northern Hemisphere for days, weeks, or even months, causing unknown and currently unknowable problems.

8.  With high-tech agriculture likely to be unavailable, survivors might be forced to rely heavily on natural ecosystems at precisely the time when fallout, cold, and dark may have made the nonliving natural environment extraordinarily hostile to human existence. In addition, the biosphere will have been decimated by the widespread climatic effects just described.

Certain intangible factors might also be significant as far as the surviving human population is concerned: the profoundly depressing effects of darkness and cold, especially, as well as the grotesque destruction of most of what had constituted natural beauty. Combined with the widespread, direct devastation of nuclear war itself, nuclear winter suggests that the recovery of civilized human society, especially in the Northern Hemisphere, may be much less likely than even the most pessimistic earlier analyses have suggested. Even the survival of the human species (as well as many other species) is rendered problematic.

There have been many efforts to cross-check and verify the nuclear winter projections. The first analysis, by TTAPS, was relatively simple. It used a one-dimensional model of the atmosphere in which smoke and dust were assumed to move vertically but not horizontally. Subsequent efforts by Soviet and American scientists have been more sophisticated, adding the likely effects of winds and of the oceans. For example, since water has a very high heat-holding capacity, the temperature drop over the oceans and in coastal areas is likely to be less extreme than inland, over the continents. The enormous and unprecedented temperature differentials between coastal and inland regions can be expected to generate extraordinarily stormy and unstable weather. This will probably make life in such areas highly stressful, and fishing efforts or maritime trade may become very hazardous, perhaps impossible.

Many other uncertainties remain, even beyond the "usual unknowns" such as the size of the hypothesized war and the mix of weapons exploded. For example:

- *How much smoke would be generated by a nuclear war?* The baseline scenario evaluated in the TTAPS study made the assumption that 240,000 km² of urban areas would burn and 500,000 km² of grassland, shrubland, and forests, producing a total of about 225 million tons of soot. An evaluation of the nuclear winter study by the NAS concluded that 180 million metric tons of smoke could produce nuclear winter; however, estimates of the amount of smoke likely to be produced by a nuclear war vary enormously, from 30 million to 650 million metric tons. This is because of uncertainty about the amounts of fuel in cities, the fraction of the fuel that would be converted to smoke, whether firestorms would occur, and if so how many and where, what sort of soot and dust would be produced, whether blast effects would put out some fires, how long the various fires would burn, and whether any significant efforts could or would be made to extinguish them.

- *How much smoke would remain in the atmosphere long enough to have the needed effect?* Smoke particles would be washed to earth with rain, and the hot gases of nuclear explosions tend to produce local rainstorms: a "black rain" of fallout, soot, and dust fell on Hiroshima and Nagasaki shortly after the bombings. Other models suggest, however, that under conditions of great heat, nearly 40% of the smoke produced would be warmed sufficiently to be lofted into the stratosphere. At such high altitudes (above 12 kilometers or so) these pollutants would be invulnerable to washout, since day-to-day weather takes place in the troposphere, closer to the ground. As in the cases of ozone depletion and worldwide fallout production, larger explosions would inject a larger proportion of their substance above the tropopause (the upper boundary of the troposphere) and into the stratosphere. It is also true, however, that for a given number of total megatons, smaller weapons igniting fires are more effective than large ones, and ultimately, it appears that the amount and the nature of the fires produced are more critical than the actual size of the nuclear explosions.

- *Would the smoke be of the right sort to absorb or reflect sufficient quantities of sunlight?* Different materials, when burned, produce different kinds of smoke. It is unknown what proportion of the smoke produced would come from wildland fires and what proportion from cities, at least partly because the flammability of cities under nuclear war conditions is simply unknown.

Despite all these uncertainties, the basic nuclear winter projections have thus far been quite robust. It must be concluded that in the event of nuclear war, the use of even a small proportion of both superpowers' arsenals could result in very severe worldwide climatic effects, with potentially disastrous consequences for much of life on earth.

## STRATEGIC IMPLICATIONS

There are several major inferences to be drawn from the nuclear winter studies, some supporting doves, others, hawks. The dovish principal inference is that the prospect of nuclear winter is reason enough to oppose the conduct of nuclear war for any reason. Indeed, it appears unlikely that a limited nuclear war is possible, since even the smallest scale TTAPS scenarios generated catastrophic global consequences; for the same reason, a counterforce attack cannot be considered to be a realistic possibility. Moreover, all the world's people, as well as other life forms, seem likely to be involved in the consequences of a nuclear war—not just the combatants. Thus nuclear winter presents us with compelling reasons for mutual agreements to reduce the size of nuclear arsenals, at least below the nuclear winter threshold level. If nothing else, this would ensure that if worse comes to worst, life on earth would have a good chance of surviving.

Two principal hawkish inferences are as follows. (1) The prospect of nuclear winter makes it especially desirable to "modernize" the arsenal, emphasizing relatively small, accurate warheads that presumably would be targeted on military forces (including missile silos). Groundbursts and earth-penetrating warheads would be preferred to airbursts, to minimize possibly adverse climatic effects. (2) With our growing appreciation of the potentially dire consequences of nuclear war, deterrence ought to be, if anything, more secure than ever. The paradox, for doves, is that a military posture emphasizing small, highly accurate warheads would seem to make nuclear winter less likely, but nuclear war more likely. This is because such a posture can be seen as threatening an opponent's ability to retaliate (see Chapter 6), and it suggests that one side is seeking to configure its forces in a way that permits a first strike against the other side, while minimizing the global consequences for the attacker. In any event, the argument can be made that with nuclear winter a real possibility, the superpowers have in effect wired the planet to a "doomsday device." Retaliation (hence, deterrence) seems to have less credibility as a result. But at the same time, it can also be argued that deterrence is strengthened, since a first strike from either side should be even less likely.

It remains to be seen how—or whether—the rest of the world, outside the superpowers, responds to the threat of nuclear winter.

## WOULD *Homo sapiens* SURVIVE?

The global effects of nuclear war could well be catastrophic. But it must be emphasized that the probability of the events described above remains unknown. Given present knowledge, it seems likely that some representatives of the human species would survive, possibly with a moderately advanced level of civilization, at least in the Southern Hemisphere. There are relatively few strategic targets in the Southern Hemisphere, and although many of the worldwide, long-term effects would be harmful to the entire world, there is good reason to think that they would be less severe in the South than in the North.

1. Unless very large amounts of long-lived radioactive products are injected into the stratosphere, as by the targeting of nuclear reactors, fallout in the Southern Hemisphere may average only about 5% of the levels found in the Northern Hemisphere. This is because during the time required for fallout to move from the North to the South, substantial radioactive decay would have taken place.

2. Depletion of the ozone layer would be less pronounced in the Southern Hemisphere, perhaps only one-third the levels in the North.

3. Nuclear winter effects in the Southern Hemisphere—notably temperature reductions—will be perhaps only 25% of conditions found in the North.

However, such projections are speculative; many are based on additional assumptions regarding worldwide atmospheric airflow, which involves many more unknowns. In addition, since much of the Southern Hemisphere is not self-sufficient in food, and it is inconceivable that the North will be exporting food in the aftermath of a nuclear war, it seems likely that famine and epidemics will be widespread in the south as well. The Scientific Committee on Problems of the Environment (SCOPE), a branch of the International Council of Scientific Unions, studied a hypothetical war involving 12,600 weapons, which produced an estimated 150 million tons of smoke. In addition to confirming the basic nuclear winter scenario, this SCOPE study also concluded that even regions not subjected to direct attack

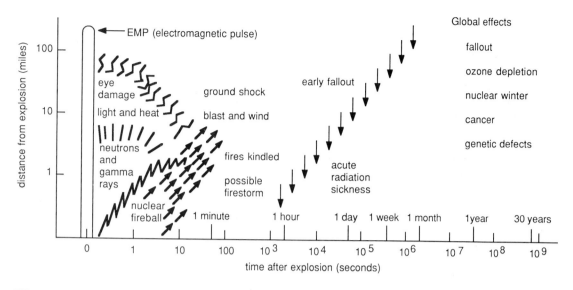

**FIGURE 5.17 Time scale for prominent nuclear war effects.** (Modified from Dennis, 1984.)

would suffer in the massive worldwide starvation that would occur because of disrupted agricultural production.

The long-term picture following a nuclear war must be considered to be profoundly unpleasant and possibly catastrophic, on a global level as well as a superpower, national level. It is also profoundly unknown. Figure 5.17 depicts a time scale for roughly a dozen effects of nuclear war; Table 5.1, which is somewhat more specific, includes general estimates of the world areas at risk and the magnitude of those risks. The survival of human beings in at least limited numbers in isolated geographic regions, may well occur, although even this cannot be assured. We can have even less confidence in the ultimate survival of modern civilization, which is assuredly more delicate than the biological species *Homo sapiens*.

## Policy Issues

### Does the possibility of nuclear winter require rethinking of nuclear weapons policies?

**No:** There are numerous uncertainties in any nuclear winter scenario. Until these are resolved (and they may never be), we must base strategic doctrine on what we know to be true—especially, the importance of maintaining a sufficient arsenal to deter any opponent from threatening vital national interests. Moreover, if the US reduces its arsenals and the USSR does not have equal respect for the possibility of worldwide catastrophe, they may behave more aggressively and recklessly than the US, as a result of which they would profit from US timidity. So, regardless of the unknowns and potential dangers, the US must be prepared to use nuclear weapons in retaliation, that is, as a deterrent.

**Yes:** What nations prepare to do may have some direct bearing on what they actually do. When wars occur, nations have a strong tendency to use whatever is in their arsenals, and if the US and/or the Soviet Union have sufficient firepower to destroy the world, no one can be confident that such firepower

**TABLE 5.1 Approximate magnitude and timing of major direct and indirect effects of a general nuclear war**

Time after nuclear war scale: 0, 1 hr., 1 day, 1 wk., 1 mo., 3 mo., 6 mo., 1 yr., 2 yr., 5 yr., 10 yr.

| Effect | Time after nuclear war (graphical) | Population at risk[a] — US | NH | SH | Casualty rate for those at risk | Potential global deaths[b] |
|---|---|---|---|---|---|---|
| Blast | | H | M | L | H | M–H |
| Thermal radiation | | M | M | L | M | M–H |
| 1° Ionizing radiation | | L | L | L | H | L–M |
| Fires | | M | M | L | M | M |
| Air pollution | | H | M | L | L | L |
| Stratospheric O₃ reduction | | H | H | M | L | L |
| Light reductions | | H | H | M | L | L |
| Temperature reductions | | H | H | H | H | M–H |
| Frozen water supplies | | H | H | M | M | M |
| Food shortages | | H | H | H | H | H |
| Medical system collapse | | H | H | M | M | M |
| Diseases Contagious (shelter period) | | M | M | L | H | M |
| Epidemics (pest vectors) | | H | H | M | M | M |
| Psychological/societal stress | | H | H | L | L | L–M |
| Radiation | | H | H | L–M | M | M |

Source: Modified from Harwell, 1984.
[a]US = United States, NH = Northern Hemisphere, SH = Southern Hemisphere.
[b]L(ight) = 0–10⁶, M(edium) = 10⁶–10⁸, H(eavy) = 10⁹.

will not be used. If one side uses nuclear weapons, knowing full well that the other side possesses retaliatory capacity—an act of extraordinary irrationality—what basis do we have for assuming that in the midst of such unreason, good judgment will suddenly prevail? Remember that if the nuclear winter studies are correct, a very small fraction of superpower arsenals could virtually extinguish life on earth. This means that if these results are understood, either side should (indeed, must) be deterred from initiating an attack in the first place, because in the ensuing nuclear winter, the attacker would be destroyed along with the victim, even if the victim does not retaliate!

## KEY TERMS

internal emitters

induced radioactivity

troposphere

tropopause

Bravo

counterforce attack

TTAPS report

nuclear winter

greenhouse effect

## STUDY QUESTIONS

1. Why would attacks on missile silos produce more fallout than attacks on cities?

2. Discuss the role of wind and rain in influencing fallout patterns.

3. Describe some similarities and some differences between the effects of prompt radiation and radiation due to fallout.

4. What are some of the important uncertainties in estimating the effects of all-out nuclear war?

5. Compare the influence of large and small nuclear explosions in possibly depleting the ozone layer.

6. Compare attacks on cities with attacks on missile silos in terms of the likelihood of bringing about a nuclear winter.

7. What are some of the important uncertainties in the nuclear winter scenario?

## ADDITIONAL READINGS

AMBIO (Royal Swedish Academy of Sciences, edited by J. Peterson). 1983. *The Aftermath*. New York: Pantheon. Presents the results of a study examining the worldwide effects of a hypothesized large-scale nuclear war.

Ehrlich, Paul R., Carl Sagan, Donald Kennedy, and Walter Orr Roberts. 1984. *The Cold and the Dark*. New York: W. W. Norton. Presents the basic nuclear winter findings in book form, including the proceedings of the first major conference describing the phenomenon.

Harwell, Mark A. 1984. *Nuclear Winter*. New York: Springer-Verlag. A concise examination of the possible human and environmental consequences of nuclear war.

Katz, Arthur M. 1982. *Life After Nuclear War*. Cambridge, MA: Ballinger. A careful, detailed, data-filled analysis of the social and economic effects of a moderate nuclear attack on the United States.

Pollack, D., T. Ackerman, P. Crutzen, M. MacCracken, C. Shapiro, and R. Turco. 1985. *The Environmental Consequences of Nuclear War: Vol. 1. Physical and Atmospheric Effects*. New York: John Wiley. The first of a series of reports on worldwide environmental effects of nuclear war. This study presents impressive data on the likely impact of nuclear war even on untargeted areas, especially via nuclear winter and disruption of food production.

# Part Three

# Strategic Doctrine

**W**e have examined the nature of nuclear weapons and their delivery systems (Part One) and the effects of these weapons (Part Two). Against this background, we now consider the concepts and strategies that underlie the nuclear weapons regime.

First, we shall look at deterrence and nuclear strategy (Chapter 6). In Chapter 7 we move on to explore the controversial notions of civil defense and strategic defense ("Star Wars"). Our consideration of strategic doctrine ends with Chapter 8, which reveals the possible ways deterrence might fail.

# 6 Deterrence

*Safety will be the steady child of terror, and survival, the twin brother of annihilation.*
Winston Churchill

To a great extent, nuclear weapons have changed the way governments think about war—at least, governments of the two nuclear superpowers, the US and the USSR. Conventional (i.e., nonnuclear) weapons are still maintained by both nations, and in large numbers. In fact, expenditures on nuclear weapons actually represent only about 20–25% of the military budgets of both. Nonetheless, because of their extraordinary destructiveness, nuclear weapons have had a special role in the purpose and limits of military force. To understand the Nuclear Age, it is necessary to understand the weapons themselves and their possible effects. It is no less important, however, to understand the plans and doctrines for their use. These plans and doctrines have an important role in influencing procurement policies, deployment decisions, geopolitical activities, and most important, the probability that nuclear weapons will actually be used.

In a sense, nuclear strategy is an exercise in abstract theory, since except for Hiroshima and Nagasaki, nuclear weapons have never been detonated in anger. As we shall see, much of nuclear strategy involves concocting **scenarios,** anticipated events of the sort: "If the other side does this, then we will do that, then the other side will do something else," and so forth. There are colossal uncertainties, not only in seeking to anticipate the behavior of another nation, but also in trying to plan for events that, if they occurred, would have effects that are literally unknowable in advance.

Although strategic doctrine is merely theory, and—according to many critics—questionable theory at that, it is nonetheless real in its impact on events. A basic understanding of nuclear strategy is therefore crucial to understanding how we have gotten where we are, and where we will go in the future.

## THE FIRST PHASE: AMERICAN NUCLEAR MONOPOLY

The US emerged from World War II as the strongest nation on earth. Europe was a shambles, and the old colonial empires were about to be dismantled. The USSR had lost 20 million people, and her economy was devastated. By contrast, the US had lost about 400,000 soldiers, and except for Pearl Harbor, had not had to fight on her own soil. The US was also the only nation that possessed nuclear weapons.

The American nuclear monopoly resulted from a top-secret research and engineering effort known as the Manhattan Project. It was begun at the urging of several nuclear physicists, including Albert Einstein, who feared that Germany would obtain nuclear weapons before the Allies. However, the Project was continued at full speed even after Hitler's defeat, culminating in the atomic bombing of Hiroshima and Nagasaki.

President Truman's decision to use nuclear weapons in 1945 is a highly controversial one. Some argue that this action was necessary and appropriate, to end World War II and to save American lives and, ultimately, Japanese lives as well. Others maintain that Japan was on the verge of defeat anyhow and that the atomic bombs were actually used to intimidate the Soviet Union. (A brief history of US–Soviet relations will be presented later, when we discuss the history of the arms race in Chapter 9.)

In any event, following World War II, it was widely perceived that nuclear weapons changed the uses of military power. A new group of specialists emerged, concerned with developing a strategy for the proper use (or nonuse) of these novel weapons. As emphasized especially by one of these strategists, Bernard Brodie, the role of military force had changed fundamentally: before 1945, military force was intended to fight wars. With nuclear weapons, its role could only be to prevent them. In this way, the basic concept of **nuclear deterrence** was born: seeking to prevent or "deter" war by the threat of unacceptable damage to an aggressor.

Most nations, including the US, demobilized large segments of their armed forces after World War II. The USSR also demobilized, but to a lesser extent than the US, and it maintained about a 4:1 superiority in the number of men under arms. The USSR did not withdraw from the countries of eastern Europe that it had liberated and then occupied during the final stages of the war. Josef Stalin also continued to maintain a repressive dictatorship. Although the US and the USSR had been allies against Hitler, relations between the two nations quickly grew strained. From the American perspective, the USSR's large armed forces required that the US maintain and further develop nuclear weapons; from the Soviet perspective, American nuclear weapons required the maintainance of a large armed force. Europe quickly assumed a crucial role in the growing East–West confrontation in that the West came to fear the large and powerful Red Army, whereas the USSR, lacking nuclear weapons, used conventional forces to hold western Europe hostage against the possibility of an American nuclear attack on the Soviet Union.

Some scientists claimed that it would be decades before the USSR developed nuclear weapons. However, the Soviet Union detonated its first atomic explosion in 1949. Even then, the US maintained an effective nuclear monopoly, since the USSR lacked large numbers of delivery systems, whereas the US had a massive bomber fleet and had circled the USSR with overseas bases. By the mid-1950s, however, the USSR had begun producing long-range bombers, and for the first time, the perception grew that the US homeland might be vulnerable to nuclear attack.

### THE SECOND PHASE: US BOMBER SUPERIORITY AND "MASSIVE RETALIATION"

As the Cold War became more intense, US government leaders became increasingly alarmed about Communist expansionism (Fig. 6.1). President Dwight Eisenhower was reluctant to authorize massive military expenditures, and it was decided to rely increasingly on nuclear weapons. Eisenhower's "New Look" substi-

**FIGURE 6.1 President Dwight Eisenhower conferring with Secretary of State John Foster Dulles. American nuclear strategy at this time of overwhelming US nuclear superiority emphasized massive retaliation.** (Courtesy of the Dwight D. Eisenhower Library.)

tuted nuclear technology for manpower and conventional weapons. Under this program, and under the sponsorship of Secretary of State John Foster Dulles, the US developed the policy of **massive retaliation,** under which the government threatened that in the event of Soviet aggression, the US would devastate the homeland of the USSR with nuclear weapons.

How had this policy developed? Even though the USSR was emerging as a nuclear power in the early 1950s, the US had overwhelming nuclear superiority, by a ratio of perhaps 100:1. The Korean War ended in July 1953, and shortly afterward Dulles announced that American nuclear weapons would be employed, massively, "at times and places of our own choosing," if need be. There was a great reluctance to be drawn into another land war, and yet, also a great fear of Communist expansionism. For understandable reasons, many of the specifics of massive retaliation were left unstated and thus, ambiguous. The policy of nuclear brinkmanship involved willingness to go within inches of nuclear war in the event of Soviet misconduct, but precise limits of misconduct that would be tolerated were not specified; presumably, an official indication of exactly what provocation would lead to what response would have been a virtual invitation to go just up to that point. As it was, Dulles hoped that the uncertainty, as well as the dire consequences of a misstep, would deter any Soviet provocations in the first place.

## LIMITED WAR: AN UNDERCURRENT

Although massive retaliation remained the official American nuclear doctrine throughout the Eisenhower years, there were dissenters, even within the strategic community. Massive retaliation was in a sense a product of the Korean War, since American officials vowed not to become involved again in a drawn-out land war. Rather, the US decided to exploit its technological advantages, especially in nuclear weapons, to avoid a repetition of this conflict. But critics of massive retaliation argued against such reliance on nuclear weapons by pointing out that the Korean War had taken place despite America's existing nuclear monopoly. Moreover, it had been fought in a "limited" manner: that is, without use of nuclear weapons. When United Nations forces crossed the 38th parallel and advanced up to the Yalu River, a major land was precipitated. Even then, Chinese forces maintained a hands-off attitude toward American staging areas in Japan. And for their part, US forces studiously refrained from bombing north of the Chinese–North Korean border, to avoid provoking an even more vigorous Chinese response or possible Soviet involvement. Taking Korea as a pattern, it seemed likely that the US could not realistically rely on the threat of massive retaliation to deter future conflicts. It seemed necessary to possess the ability to wage "brushfire" conventional wars as well.

Folowing the lead of MIT political scientist William Kaufmann and Harvard economist Thomas Schelling, analysts began to develop plans for limited, conventional wars, since it appeared that the mere presence of nuclear weapons would not necessarily inhibit such conflicts. Military leaders, many of whom had been restive about Eisenhower's "New Look," also rallied to the call for maintaining effective conventional forces. It was hoped that if challenged, the US would not be confined to the choice of escalating massively with nuclear weapons or giving up altogether.

## THE THIRD PHASE:
## THE BEGINNINGS OF PARITY
## AND THE PROBLEM OF CREDIBILITY

In the early 1950s, American strategic nuclear weapons were the responsibility of the Strategic Air Command, whose plans for nuclear war involved basically an all-out, devastating strike against any would-be opponents—assumed to be the USSR or China or both. Concerns were raised that such an attack would be immoral, hence not believable, or *credible*. A threat that is literally incredible is not likely to be effective.

The credibility of early American nuclear doctrine was even more strongly undermined by the mid-1950s as the USSR deployed strategic bombers, giving the Soviets the ability to bomb the US mainland. Combined with the Soviet discovery of hydrogen bombs and an intensifying Cold War, this was a time of extensive "duck and cover" and shelter drills in the American schools, and of mounting concern about civil devense. Even more important, perhaps, the prospect of nuclear parity between the US and the USSR resulted in some glimmerings of change in strategic doctrine, based on the growing problem of credibility. The problem was simply this: Whereas the threat of massive American nuclear retaliation against the USSR might have been credible when the US was effectively immune to Soviet counterretaliation, as the USSR became a nuclear power in its own right, with the ability to devastate the US, American nuclear threats became hollow, and also, perhaps, inadequate to keep the peace.

Some analysts, among them a little-known professor of government named Henry Kissinger, accordingly developed the concept of **limited nuclear wars.** The idea was that the only way to deter aggression and war by the threat of using nuclear weapons was for the US to have the capability and the plans for employing nuclear weapons selectively (i.e., in a limited way), without presupposing that such use would escalate to all-out strategic war.

Toward the late 1950s, American strategic doctrine moved somewhat to accommodate these concerns, especially because of the growing Soviet nuclear arsenal. Thus, although the US maintained a commanding lead in numbers of nuclear bombs and an even greater lead in strategic bombers for delivering them, the Soviet development of hydrogen bombs and of bombers meant that for the first time, the US homeland could be attacked. And the unique destructive power of nuclear weapons meant that even a "small" nuclear attack would be devastating. This, in turn, made the threat of massive retaliation less and less credible. Specialists therefore worried that it could no longer be relied on for deterrence. Short-range, tactical nuclear weapons were introduced into Europe, and official policy allowed that a strictly local conflict might result in the use of tactical nuclear weapons rather than escalating immediately to strategic war. The concept of

**graduated deterrence** was born, whereby the threshold of strategic attack was raised somewhat and the gap filled by the prospect of limited, or tactical nuclear war.

This, in turn, introduced one of several paradoxes of deterrence theory: nuclear war was to be made less likely by making it more likely. That is, by developing weapons as well as doctrines for their use that will not necessarily result in mutual suicide, and are therefore credible, it was (and is) hoped that the need to use them will be reduced. Such thinking gave rise to a proliferation of plans for fighting limited nuclear wars, elaborate scenarios of move and countermove, all presumed to be conducted with cool rationality and short of nuclear holocaust. For example, in his controversial book *On Thermonuclear War,* physicist-turned-strategist Herman Kahn, the celebrated "thinker about the unthinkable," developed no fewer than 44 "rungs" of potential nuclear escalation. On the other hand, critics began pointing out, and have been pointing out ever since, that by designing strategy that is intended to make nuclear war less likely by making it more likely, some of the inhibitions against nuclear war may be removed, thereby actually increasing the chances that war will occur. According to such critics, notably those in the antinuclear peace movement, this trend has become especially dangerous in the 1980s, since the doctrines of limited war have been augmented by highly accurate weapons and delivery systems.

Regarding the possibility of keeping a nuclear war limited, Secretary of Defense Harold Brown reported in 1980:

*My own view remains that a full-scale thermonuclear exchange would constitute an unprecedented disaster for the Soviet Union and for the United States. And I am not at all persuaded that what started as a demonstration, or even a tightly controlled use of the strategic forces for larger purposes, could be kept from escalating to a full-scale thermonuclear exchange. (Annual Posture Statement of US Defense Department.)*

He went on, however, to explain one rationale for maintaining the capability of using nuclear weapons in some sort of limited way: "But all of us have to recognize, equally, that there are large uncertainties on this score, and that it should be in everyone's interest to minimize the probability of the most destructive escalation and halt the exchange before it reached catastrophic proportions." Damage limitation was therefore added to credibility, as another reason for possessing the ability to wage limited nuclear wars.

And yet, in 1983, former Defense Secretary Robert McNamara emphasized that in his view, nuclear weapons can serve only for large-scale deterrence, not for effective military use:

*I do not believe we can avoid serious and unacceptable risk of nuclear war until we recognize—and until we base all our military plans, defense budgets, weapon deployments, and arms negotiations on the recognition—that nuclear weapons serve no military purpose whatsoever. They are totally useless—except only to deter one's opponent from using them.*

By the time John F. Kennedy was inaugurated President of the United States in 1961, the Soviet Union had a very small number of ICBMs, which nonetheless constituted a force to be reckoned with. A remodeled form of graduated deterrence quickly came to replace massive retaliation, under the name of **flexible response** (Fig. 6.2). Flexible response accepted the existence of a nuclear stalemate: even though US strategic nuclear forces were still substantially stronger than the USSR's, Soviet nuclear strength was such that no more unilateral advantage was expected. Flexible response emphasized that the forces of each side countered those of the other: strategic weapons deterred strategic weapons, tactical weapons deterred tactical weapons, and conventional weapons deterred conventional weapons. Flexible response also meant relying heavily on the ability of the other NATO countries to bear a greater military burden, and on technological innovations that resulted in greater "flexibility" in the control and functioning of battlefield weapons, such as greater precision and accuracy.

## THE PROBLEM OF VULNERABILITY

Unease, legitimate or not, about the "window of vulnerability" did not begin with the deployment of large Soviet SS-18 missiles in the mid-1970s. Rather, it has a longer history in the development of American strategic thought. During the 1950s, when the US nuclear posture relied entirely on its bomber forces, there was growing concern, led by strategic analyst Albert Wohlstetter, that America's SAC bases were becoming vulnerable to a preemptive Soviet attack. The argument was that in the event of hostilities, or even a serious crisis, if the USSR became convinced that the US was about to attack, the Soviets might be tempted to initiate a preemptive strike against American bombers.

**FIGURE 6.2 Secretary of Defense Robert McNamara conferring with General Maxwell Taylor and President John F. Kennedy. American nuclear strategy at this time underwent several changes, while the USSR acquired a substantial nuclear capability.** (Courtesy of the John F. Kennedy Library.)

Such temptation seemed to be all the greater in proportion to the vulnerability of these bombers: that is, to the extent that the bombers were capable of being destroyed in a surprise attack and thus unable to retaliate. This anxiety was enhanced by the short-lived Soviet lead in ICBM technology following their orbiting of Sputnik in 1957. (*Note:* Our goal in this chapter is to review the evolution of nuclear strategy: in Chapter 9 we shall take up the history of the nuclear arms race in greater detail.)

The concept of **first-strike capability** had been born. In a sense, a first strike occurs whenever someone attacks first, and first-strike weapons are therefore any weapons that are used in such an enterprise. Thus, a butcher knife could be a first-strike weapon. But in dis-

cussions of nuclear strategy, first-strike capability has a very specific meaning: the ability to attack an opponent and in the process, make retaliation impossible. A first-strike capability is thus the capacity to perform a disarming first strike. It is generally assumed that in a nuclear-armed world, stability is desirable. **Stability,** in this sense, is the failure of either side to use nuclear weapons, or if such use occurs, it is the ability to prevent hostilities from escalating. Stability is enhanced when neither side has a first-strike capability.

It is also important to distinguish first strike from first use of nuclear weapons. The first use of nuclear weapons during a conflict or crisis may well take place in an attempted disabling first strike, especially if strategic stability does not exist. However, first use need not necessarily be part of a first strike. Ever since tactical nuclear weapons were introduced into Europe, along with the developing strategy of graduated deterrence (later adopted officially by NATO in 1967 as flexible response), NATO and the US have relied explicitly on the following announced policy of **first use**: namely, that a conventional assault in Europe will be met initially by conventional means, but if this fails, nuclear weapons will be employed. That is, NATO and the US explicitly state that they will, under certain circumstances, make "first use" of nuclear weapons, to halt a Soviet attack. There have, in fact, been numerous cases of threatened first use: that is, efforts to gain diplomatic leverage by the threat of using nuclear weapons (see Chapter 8). However, both the US and the USSR claim that neither a first strike nor a first-strike capability is in their strategic plans.

Most deterrence theorists assume that when either side has a first-strike capability, the resulting situation is unstable. This instability can occur in at least two ways: (1) the side with a first-strike capability may be tempted to exercise it, especially in times of crisis when an attack by the other side might seem likely, and (2) the side lacking a first-strike capability may feel anxious that the other side will preempt (i.e., embark on condition 1) and may therefore feel constrained to limit the likely damage by preempting the opponent's preemption. This system can be multiplied indefinitely, with efforts to preempt the preemptive preemption, and so on. During a crisis, vulnerability can give rise to the **"use it or lose it" syndrome,** in which the vulnerable side fears not only that its deterrent no longer works, but that it is likely to draw an attack from the opponent. As a result, there is pressure to use the weapons promptly, before they are destroyed by the opponent's first strike.

## SECOND-STRIKE CAPABILITY

Much of strategic analysis has become the study of situations that promote stability by avoiding such pressure to preempt. And much of this concern has focused on promoting stability by denying either side a first-strike capability: that is, by maintaining a second-strike capability. A **second-strike capability** is therefore not the ability to follow up a first strike with another, or simply to retaliate when attacked: rather, it is the ability, after being attacked, to retaliate with force sufficient to make it unprofitable for the attacker to have initiated hostilities in the first place. It implies the ability to "ride out" an opponent's attack and still respond effectively. When one side has a secure second-strike capability, the other, by definition, does not have a first-strike capability. It is generally assumed that by maintaining a secure second-strike capability, both sides reduce the chances of war, because there can then be no advantage of striking first. And if no one attacks first, no one attacks at all.

If it is accepted that the purpose of nuclear weapons is to prevent wars rather than to fight them, the important factor in evaluating either side's nuclear arsenal becomes not the number of weapons present, but rather, the number that would be **survivable**; that is, a nation's remaining functional arsenal after it has been attacked. Estimates of how many and what kinds of nuclear forces will survive an attack depend on many assumptions including the following.

| Attacking forces | Side attacked |
|---|---|
| Number of warheads/bombs | Number of targets |
| Lethality | Hardening of ICBM silos; detectability of submarines; alert status of bombers |
| Warning time | Readiness |
| Reliability | Reliability |
| Fratricidal effects; targeting policy (cross-targeting, ground- or airbursts, etc.) | $C^3I$ effectiveness |

To some extent, both the US and the USSR maintain forces much in excess of what seems to be needed to destroy each other, because each side determines its force needs by calculating what would remain after it had been attacked. (As we shall see in Chapter 9, other factors also drive the arms race.)

A distinction should here be made between nuclear forces on day-to-day alert (for the US: all ICBMs, about

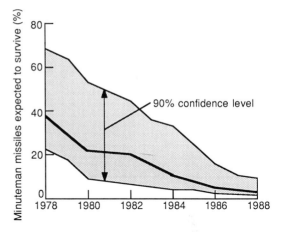

**FIGURE 6.3 The percentage of US Minuteman missiles expected to survive a hypothetical Soviet first strike, according to the 1980 posture statement of the Department of Defense. Although the 90% confidence level, indicated by the shaded band, was quite wide at the time the posture statement was produced, it tends to narrow with time, just as the expected survival decreases.**

60% of submarines, about 30% of bombers) and those that could be placed on generated alert if the entire functional triad is prepared for possible use. When estimating the effects of a Soviet attack in reducing the ability of US forces to retaliate, it therefore makes a difference whether such an attack occurred as a "bolt out of the blue"—a so-called BOOB attack, generally considered to be the least likely of all—or whether it came after a period of increasing tensions and perhaps conventional hostilities. The latter case would result in a **generated alert,** with bombers ready to take off or actually in the air and submarines leaving their berths to go on ocean patrol. Under these conditions, an attack would destroy a smaller proportion of the victim's forces, leaving more to retaliate.

Estimates show that the number of US land-based ICBMs surviving a Soviet attack can be expected to decline rapidly during the 1980s (Fig. 6.3). Similar estimates show that the number of surviving Soviet land-based ICBMs will also decline during the 1980s, but less precipitously. Such arguments have been used to support the deployment of additional American ICBMs and to emphasize the issue of ICBM vulnerability. However, it has also been pointed out that ICBMs are only one component of both nations' respective strategic triads. Since these missiles represent a large proportion of the Soviet strategic forces but a much smaller proportion of US forces, threats to American ICBMs pose less overall danger of destabilization than do threats to the Soviet ICBMs.

Figure 6.4A shows Defense Department estimates of the total US and Soviet forces before any attack. Lines below the 1:1 equilibrium show a Soviet advantage: lines above this equilibrium show a US advantage. Figures 6.4B and 6.4C show the **dynamic balance** in these strategic ratios, that is, the likely situation after a hypothesized Soviet counterforce attack against US strategic forces followed by US retaliation. These estimates suggest that after such an exchange, the US would have an advantage in remaining warheads and the USSR would have an advantage in equivalent megatons. Note that a first strike depletes not only the arsenal of the victim, but also that of the attacker. Also, hypothesized attacks are more effective in disarming an unsuspecting victim than one that is on generated alert.

## HOW TO REDUCE VULNERABILITY

Critics of the vulnerability concept claim that such analyses come from a dream world, far removed from realities. Thus, such calculations can be seen to suffer from what the philosopher Alfred North Whitehead called "the fallacy of misplaced concreteness," the error of thinking that anything with numbers attached to it must be precise. Vulnerability skeptics emphasize the enormous uncertainties associated with an attempted first strike, also pointing out that strategic analyses assume that either side will attack simply if it can get away with it. This, in turn, can become a self-fulfilling prophecy. They also observe that alarms about strategic vulnerability have regularly served to pave the way for more weapons, on both sides.

Proponents of the vulnerability argument claim that theoretical vulnerability is a potentially serious, destabilizing development and must be addressed. Whatever one's personal judgments, it is clear that the question of vulnerability has had substantial impact on deterrence theory and on weapons policy and procurement decisions. In examining vulnerability, our goal is not to endorse or to refute the arguments, but rather to understand them and their consequences.

Both sides have taken the following steps (not necessarily in this order) to reduce presumed vulnerability of their weapons:

- Deploying weapons on submarines

- Hardening ICBM silos

- Dispersing targets

- Increasing the number of potential targets

- Investigating the possibility of land-based mobile ICBMs

- Improving $C^3I$, especially by hardening facilities against EMP

At least partly as a response to concern about possible vulnerability of US forces to a Soviet first strike, the US developed the Polaris nuclear submarine fleet and began placing ICBMs in underground silos, which were hardened to perhaps 2,000 psi. Older ICBMs such as the Atlas missile had been deployed at above-ground launching stations. Also previously, the navy had not been involved with strategic nuclear weapons, which had been solely the province of the air force.

Other suggestions have been made to further reduce vulnerability by enhancing each side's second-strike capability.

- *Establish strategic submarine sanctuaries for both sides.* That is, designate areas of the oceans in which ASW would be prohibited (Fig. 6.5).

- *Develop and deploy ICBMs that are somehow mobile;* hence very difficult for an opponent to target. This was the original preferred "basing scheme" for the MX missile (Fig. 6.6). Since no satisfactory mobile basing mode has been identified for the MX, it now appears that this missile will be deployed in fixed, superhardened Minuteman silos. Mobility is planned, instead, for a new, small single-warhead missile officially known as SICBM (small ICBM), but more widely dubbed "Midgetman" (Fig. 6.7).

- *Eliminate the land-based ICBM leg of the strategic triad altogether.* Advocates maintain that if ICBM vulnerability is part of the problem, ICBMs should be scrapped in favor of bombers and submarines, which are more survivable. After all, it is said, the triad is not the Trinity. Supporters of ICBMs, in turn, point to possible advantages of maintaining as diverse a deterrent as possible, arguing that by

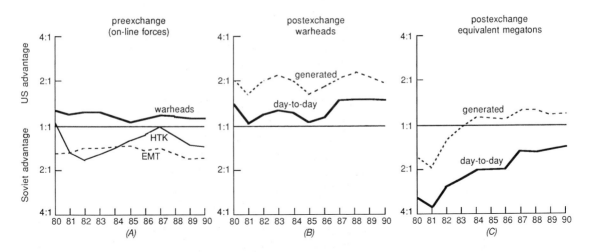

**FIGURE 6.4 US–Soviet strategic balance indicators before and after an estimated Soviet attack on the United States.** (*A*) The relative number of warheads, equivalent megatonnage (EMT), and hard target kill (HTK) capacity before any attack. (*B*) and (*C*) The relative numbers after a hypothesized Soviet attack followed by an American counterattack, comparing the situations of an initial Soviet attack occurring by surprise (day-to-day alert) and during a time of crisis (generated alert).

**FIGURE 6.5 A P-3C Orion antisubmarine aircraft on patrol. ASW activities threaten the survivability of the SLBMs on the other side.** (Courtesy of the US Department of Defense.)

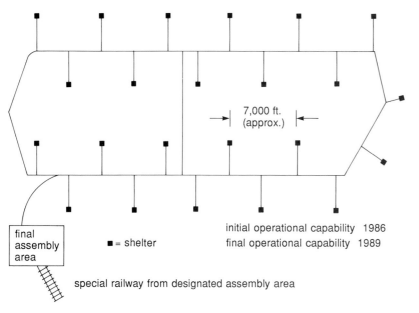

FIGURE 6.6 Artist's conception of the "racetrack" basing mode that was seriously considered for the MX missile. According to this plan, each of 200 MX missiles would have been shuttled by heavy-duty transporter vehicles among 23 different hardened launching structures (shelters) about 1.5 miles apart. There would have been 4,600 hardened structures: 200 closed loops, each with one missile and 23 structures per loop. (Courtesy of the US Department of Defense.)

7,000 ft. (approx.)

final assembly area

■ = shelter

initial operational capability 1986
final operational capability 1989

special railway from designated assembly area

keeping all three legs of the triad, the US greatly complicates the timing and nature of any hypothesized Soviet attack. It is claimed that deterrence might be diminished if the US placed too many of its eggs in only two baskets: bombers and submarines.

## STRATEGY IN THE 1960S

### Flirting with Counterforce, Marrying MAD

Nuclear attacks against cities and industry are referred to as **countervalue**; that is, attacks against what the other side particularly values. On the other hand, attacks against the other side's military forces, especially its nuclear forces, are known as **counterforce.** During the Eisenhower and early Kennedy years, strategists at the RAND Corporation (a civilian "think tank" supported initially by the air force), developed the theory of counterforce. They reasoned that with each side capable of destroying the other, strategic countervalue targeting would be suicidal. If the US responded to a Soviet attack in Europe or the Middle East with an attack against Soviet cities, the USSR might well blow up US cities in return. Far better, they argued, to attack only selected military targets and refrain from attacking Soviet cities as long as the USSR refrained from attacking American

cities. The theory of counterforce therefore developed from much the same concerns that produced doctrines of limited nuclear war.

Counterforce added another mission to America's nuclear weapons, **damage limitation.** Theoretically, in the event of war, damage to the homeland could be limited in two ways, defensively and offensively. We consider strategies of defensive damage limitation (civil defense and so-called strategic defense, or "Star Wars") in Chapter 7. Offensive damage limitation, by contrast, involves destroying the opponent's weapons before they are launched.

A strategy of damage limitation requires speed and accuracy (Fig. 6.8), and was ideally suited to the air force, since the navy's SLBMs, although invulnerable, were not accurate enough for counterforce. As of the 1980s, SLBMs are still too inaccurate to have a counterforce mission, although as we have seen, this will change with the deployment of the Trident II, or D-5 missiles. And although bombers were sufficiently accurate, they were too slow to attack the other side's nuclear striking forces. Counterforce for damage limitation therefore fit with the development of ICBMs, which were deployed in large numbers during the 1960s. ICBMs were fast and potentially accurate. Counterforce also required a great increase in the number of deliverable warheads, since although there are only about 220 Soviet cities with populations exceeding

**FIGURE 6.7 Artist's conception of SICBM (small ICBM) or "Midgetman." As currently conceived, these small single-warhead missiles will be fully mobile, carried on specially designed, tracked vehicles built to withstand substantial overpressures and capable of launching the missiles directly.** (Courtesy of the US Department of Defense.)

**FIGURE 6.8 Artist's conception of one of the 24 satellites to be part of the US Global Positioning System beginning in the late 1980s. These satellites will provide greater accuracy for navigation, and possibly, for missiles as well.** (Courtesy of the US Department of Defense.)

100,000, there are many more military targets: ports, airfields, staging areas, command and control centers, and so on, as well as individual ICBMs.

Secretary of Defense Robert McNamara endorsed counterforce early in the 1960s. However, he became disillusioned with it once the USSR began building its own SLBM fleet as well as deploying ICBMs in hardened silos (as the US had done a few years before). These developments meant that some of the USSR's nuclear forces would almost certainly survive a counterforce attack and would therefore leave the US open to Soviet retaliation. McNamara had attempted to promote a "no cities" doctrine as a type of gentlemen's agreement with the USSR, but Soviet leaders were not

responsive. Finally, it also became apparent that counterforce leads to a never-ending arms race if each side simply deploys more missiles in direct response to the deployment of missile-threatening missiles by its opponent.

In a sense, however, counterforce has never been completely abandoned, since US targeting policy has always emphasized attacks on military rather than civilian targets (Fig. 6.9). That is, the **single integrated operational plan,** or **SIOP** (pronounced "sigh-op"), the top-secret targeting scheme for actual use of nuclear weapons in World War III, is known to concentrate on military forces rather than on civilians per se. Counterforce gained special public attention during the late

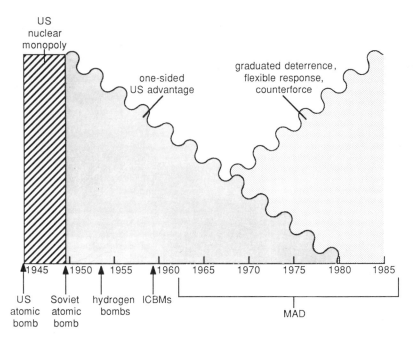

US
nuclear
monopoly

one-sided
US advantage

graduated deterrence,
flexible response,
counterforce

**FIGURE 6.9 Variation in US strategic nuclear policy since 1945.**

1945  1950  1955  1960  1965  1970  1975  1980  1985

US
atomic
bomb

Soviet
atomic
bomb

hydrogen
bombs

ICBMs

MAD

1970s with Jimmy Carter's **Presidential Directive 59 (PD 59),** which specified the targeting of Soviet military forces. However, some degree of counterforce rather than countervalue has been the prime focus of the SIOP at least since the mid-1960s. The difference may be academic anyhow, since many military targets are closely associated with civilian areas; it may be that nuclear weapons could be employed with negligible damage to civilians only in the cases of naval forces fighting at sea or satellites in outer space.

As mentioned earlier, Herman Kahn imagined alternative courses of action by all parties for different "kinds" of nuclear war, including a great variety of imagined counterforce attacks and responses. It is widely assumed that countervalue attacks are likely to lead to prompt and uncontrolled escalation, whereas counterforce attacks, leading to presumed counterforce responses, are more often involved in elaborate strategic scenarios.

In his Annual Report for 1980, Secretary of Defense Harold Brown wrote:

> It has never been US policy to limit ourselves to massive countercity operations in retaliation, nor have our plans been so circumscribed. For nearly 20 years, we have explicitly included a range of employment options—against military as well as nonmilitary targets—in our strategic

nuclear empoyment planning. . . . In particular, we have always considered it important in the event of war to be able to attack the forces that could do damage to the United States.

Critics worry that counterforce is destabilizing precisely because it threatens to deprive the opponent of an assured second-strike capability. The advocates of counterforce, however, claim that the USSR would not be tempted to a first strike if we stayed far enough ahead, and neither side could feasibly carry out a disarming first strike anyhow.

By the mid-1960s, because of the difficulties with counterforce, US strategic doctrine began to reemphasize counter value and what we might call plain, old-fashioned deterrence: the notion of "assured destruction" was mentioned prominently. It quickly became transmuted into **mutually assured destruction,** or **MAD.** Under MAD, the populations of both the US and the USSR are essentially held hostage to each other. In articulating "mutually assured destruction," American deterrence strategists in the 1960s were not so much designing a new strategy as they were describing the situation as it existed, once the US and the USSR had developed sufficient nuclear weaponry to be able to destroy each other. Policy or not, MAD became reality.

## How Much Is Enough?

In addition to credibility and vulnerability, deterrence must face a third, thorny problem. Counterforce targeting, as we have seen, not only requires a very large number of warheads, it may also give rise to a never-ending increase in this number. This is because acquisition of additional weapons on one side seems likely to directly stimulate the deployment of more weapons on the other because of fears for the latter's vulnerability. MAD, on the other hand, could theoretically lead to a rational limit. Thus, one result of MAD is that "nuclear superiority" becomes meaningless. Once each side retains the ability to absorb a first strike and still destroy the opponent, it no longer matters which side has more.

Nuclear sufficiency therefore becomes a more realistic goal. **Nuclear sufficiency** is achieved when a nation has nuclear forces sufficient to deter an attack, regardless of an opponent's arsenal.

However, even nuclear sufficiency is not easy to define, since it depends not on some objectively determined quantity, but rather, on the perceptions of one's opponent. The amount of nuclear weaponry necessary to achieve **minimal deterrence** is therefore the smallest amount that will serve to deter an opponent. Unfortunately, this quantity cannot be calculated with certainty. It may well be, as some have argued, that the leaders of the USSR are so cautious and averse to strategic war that the threat of one or a handful of strategic nuclear explosions would constitute an effective deterrent. On the other hand, perhaps more is needed; for better or worse, most strategists have felt that prudence dictates making this assumption. Seeking to obtain a workable answer, Secretary McNamara commissioned a study that examined the likely effects on the USSR of various levels of countervalue nuclear attack (or retaliation) by the US. It was found that beyond a certain point, the principle of diminishing returns begins to operate: the difference between the second bomb and the first is much greater, for example, than that between the thousandth and nine hundred ninety-ninth. (Winston Churchill commented during World War II that after a point, one simply "made the rubble bounce.")

In McNamara's nuclear calculations, the rubble-bouncing inflection point—at which this shift in damage-producing efficiency takes place—was especially pronounced after about 400 equivalent megatons. With this intensity of attack, roughly one-quarter of the population and two-thirds of the industry would be destroyed (Fig. 6.10). It was then decided that to assure sufficient redundancy, each leg of the strategic triad should be designed conservatively, with the ability to deliver independently at least this deterrent level of attack, (i.e., 400 equivalent MT each by bombers, ICBMs, and SLBMs).

For various reasons, outlined in Chapter 9, each leg is currently much more powerful than this. We have already seen that the three legs of the triad have different strengths and weaknesses. Beginning in the 1960s, maintenance of the triad became part of the bedrock of American deterrence theory, and it has remained so.

During the 1960s, the US and the USSR gradually became about equally capable of destroying each other. With the two nations having achieved this state of essential strategic equivalence, or **parity,** deterrence theorists turned their attention increasingly to arms control. (We shall turn our attention to arms control in Chapter 10.) Note that "parity" implies equivalence for all practical purposes, not necessarily exact equality—two sides can be at parity even though one side is ahead in some respects and the opposing side leads in others.

## The Strategic Implications of MIRVing

Just when strategic stability appeared to be ensured for the foreseeable future, instability raised its head, or rather, its many heads, in the form of the hydralike MIRVs. The US and the USSR began MIRVing in 1970 and 1974, respectively. It is important to understand how this process has reduced strategic stability.

Consider, for example, two nations facing each other, each armed with 100 single-warhead missiles. If one side were to attack the other's missiles, it would have to use all its own, and even then some would likely fail (because of inaccuracy, unreliability, etc.). The **exchange ratio**—the ratio of enemy launchers destroyed to every one of the aggressor's missiles used up in the attack—could never be higher than 1 and would almost certainly be less. As a result, under such conditions, even a "successful" first strike would not leave the attacker any better off than the victim. If the attacker used all its 100 missiles and destroyed 95 of its opponent's (a very good exchange ratio of .95), the opponent would be left with 5 missiles with which to retaliate against the attacker's cities. As a result, such a starting condition is considered to be strategically stable, since neither side has an incentive to attack first.

By contrast, imagine once again that two nations are armed with 100 missiles each, but now let us say

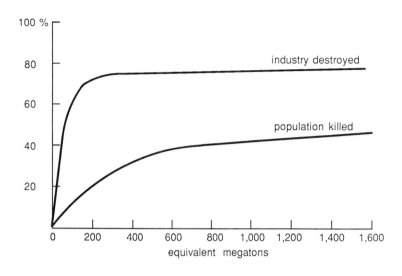

FIGURE 6.10 Curves used by Defense Secretary Robert McNamara in estimating criteria for "assured destruction" of the USSR. It is apparent that beyond 400 equivalent megatons, additional explosives produce relatively little increase in destruction.

that each missile is MIRVed with five warheads. Let us further suppose that the single-shot kill probability is the same as above (.95). Now, by firing just 20 of its missiles, either side can theoretically destroy 95 of its opponent's missiles, an exchange ratio of 95/20 = 4.75. If the attacker then used just two of its 80 remaining missiles, it could cross-target the five surviving enemy missiles with two warheads each, giving it a very high probability of destroying all the victim's missiles while still retaining 78 of its own. Or alternatively, the attacker could cross-target all 100 of the opponent's missiles in the initial attack, in which case it would take only 40 of its own missiles to attack its opponent with two warheads each (40 missiles × 5 warheads each = 200 warheads).

This, then, is the problem introduced by MIRVing. With single-warhead missiles, by contrast, an aggressor can never destroy more of the other side's missiles than are used in the attack. Deterrence rests on the notion that neither side will gain an advantage by striking first, but MIRVing changes this—at least in theory (Fig. 6.11). Furthermore, MIRVs are doubly provocative, first because they produce a high exchange ratio for a would-be attacker even if the other side is not MIRVed (you might want to convince yourself of this), and second because if both sides are MIRVed, the familiar fear of preemption is magnified. An opponent, worried that he will be attacked, might elect to strike first. The larger the number of MIRVs per missile, the greater the temptation to strike first and also, the greater

the fear that the other side might yield to the same temptation, since by doing so an attacker could destroy a larger number of warheads. A heavily MIRVed missile is a tempting target, especially if it is vulnerable.

The US took an early lead in MIRVing and remains far ahead in MIRVing of SLBMs. However, the USSR has surpassed the US in MIRVing of ICBMs. Who is ahead overall in the instability resulting from MIRVing? The USSR might seem to be ahead in that it has a larger number of heavy ICBMs with large payloads, which have already been MIRVed and could, in theory, be MIRVed yet further. Each SS-18, for example, might be able to carry as many as 40 independent warheads. On the other hand, one could argue that the US is ahead, not only because of its advantage in MIRVing its SLBMs, but also because unlike the USSR, which has the bulk of its strategic forces on theoretically vulnerable ICBMs, most US warheads are on submarines (Fig. 6.12), hence are hedged against the destabilizing effects of MIRVing. It seems reasonable to conclude that neither side is ahead; both are behind.

MIRVing also resulted in a dramatic increase in the overall number of strategic warheads, since it is cheaper to build warheads than missiles, and of course with MIRVing, many warheads can be mounted on a single missile. As we shall see in Chapter 9, MIRVing was first justified, ironically, as a way of preserving deterrence, by promising to penetrate Soviet missile defenses. Instead, it has resulted in a great challenge to strategic stability.

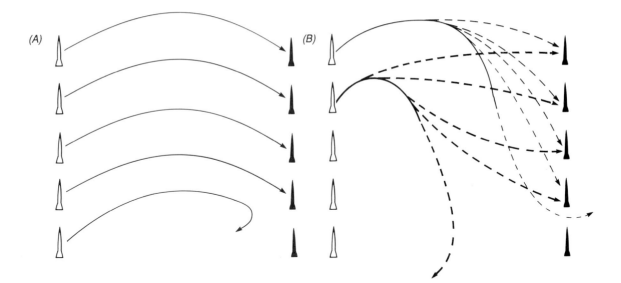

FIGURE 6.11  The effects of MIRVing on strategic stability. (*A*) With single-warhead missiles on each side, one attacking missile is needed to destroy one of the opponent's missiles. Therefore, the attacker's exchange ratio is never more than 1; given the likelihood that some attacking warheads will malfunction or go astray, the exchange ratio almost surely will be less than 1. (*B*) If each missile is MIRVed with five warheads, the exchange ratio favors the attacker, even if some warheads malfunction. Thus in this hypothetical case the attacker is left with three missiles, which should be more than sufficient to disarm the opponent's single remaining missile.

FIGURE 6.12  The *USS George Washington*, strategic missile submarine. Submarine-based missiles are currently invulnerable while submerged in the open ocean; hence, they are believed to contribute to strategic stability. (Courtesy of the US Department of Defense.)

# GAME THEORY AND THE PRISONER'S DILEMMA

In their efforts to understand strategic stability and instability, analysts have relied heavily on a mathematical technique known as **game theory,** or the analysis of carefully described interactions between a limited number of participants ("players"), after which the outcomes ("payoffs") are divided according to predetermined rules. Rather than going into the arcane details of game theory, we shall describe its basic assumptions and give the reader a feeling for the kind of analysis that is performed.

Most competitive events are **zero-sum games** in which success by one player is exactly balanced by failure on the part of another: I win/you lose, or vice versa. On the other hand, many interactions are **non-zero-sum games** in which both players can win, or both can lose. For example, avoiding nuclear war would constitute a positive outcome for both sides, whereas World War III would likely mean that both sides would lose, since it is generally agreed that no one would "win" a nuclear war.

In the simplest games, there are only two players. Each player makes a "move," which results in some combination of consequences ("pay offs": points earned, punishments avoided, etc.). A crucial aspect of such games is that payoffs are determined not simply by what a player does, but by what the player does *and* by what the opponent does. If each player can choose from two different moves, there are four possible payoff combinations. For a very simple example, let us consider two nations, facing each other with weapons. Each can attack, or wait. Let us assume that there is a payoff to each if both wait; that is, if neither one attacks. There is also a payoff to each, presumably a very negative payoff, if both attack. But the catch is that there may also be a payoff, possibly the highest of all, to attacking while the other one waits. Similarly, let us assume that there is a low payoff—the lowest of all—to waiting while the other one attacks. Each side must decide what to do, and that decision, if made "rationally," will be based on the payoffs available in conjunction with each side's judgment of what the other will be doing. Thus, for example, if you think the other side will wait, it may be best to wait; but if you think the other side will attack, it may be best to attack first.

Symbolically, the interaction can be represented in a payoff matrix such as the following:

|  |  | side 2 | |
|---|---|---|---|
|  |  | wait | attack |
| side 1 | wait | R, R | S, T |
|  | attack | T, S | P, P |

In the standard notation

R = the reward for waiting

P = the punishment for attacking and being attacked in turn

T = the temptation to attack if the opponent does not or cannot attack in return (i.e., if he "waits")

S = the sucker's payoff for waiting when the opponent attacks.

The first letter in each box represents the payoff to side 1, and the second letter to side 2. Thus, if both sides attack, both receive P, the punishment of being attacked in return for attacking. If both wait, and refrain from attacking, both receive the higher payoff R, the reward for restraint. If one attacks while the other waits, the attacker receives the highest payoff of all, T, the temptation to preempt the opponent. In this case, the one who waited and was attacked without being able to retaliate received the lowest payoff of all, S, the sucker's share.

Of course, in the real world, each side has many more options, and most such "games" are played many times, so the final payoffs for both players do not depend on a single outcome. It is also impossible to assign realistic payoff values to each option. In addition, given the disastrous consequences of nuclear war, there may be little reason to expect that P would be any more desirable an outcome than S. And in the event of worldwide climatic catastrophe, there may in fact be no real difference between payoffs P, T, or S. (There are many other drawbacks to game theory in the context of strategic doctrine and deterrence; you might want to try identifying them.) Nonetheless, game theory does help to identify some of the key issues in the maintenance of strategic stability, and it has been used extensively by mathematically minded analysts.

A situation can be stable if R is sufficiently high, and if P is sufficiently aversive. In practice, the reward of continuing to avoid nuclear war is rarely evaluated as such; rather, it is taken for granted. Deterrence theory seeks to maintain stability by keeping P, the punishment of mutual attack, dauntingly great. This, in turn, is achieved by maintaining a secure second-strike capability. Instability arises if T, the temptation to strike first, is high enough. This may occur if—for example, by MIRVing—it becomes theoretically possible that by attacking, the aggressor greatly diminishes the opponent's ability to retaliate, in effect forcing him to accept S, the sucker's payoff. Instability can also occur even if the temptation to strike first is low, if one player becomes convinced that the other is about to strike first. That is, if either side, pushed to the wall, would rather accept P than S, perhaps for emotional, religious, or ideological reasons, it can "pay" to attack even if, by attacking, both sides get P.

One might say that deterrence seeks to keep both players in the R,R corner. The goal is that even in very tense situations, when each side may think the worst of its opponent, crisis stability will be maintained; when **crisis stability** exists, neither side will strike first. By contrast, **crisis instability** obtains when either side calculates that there may be an advantage in going first—that is, in getting the payoff T. It is relatively easy to have stability when relations are smooth. The goal of deterrence is to maintain crisis stability as well.

Both players face a special bind, called a **Prisoner's Dilemma,** when the relations among the payoffs are such that T is greater than R, R is greater than P, and P is greater than S (in mathematical shorthand, this sequence is expressed T > R > P > S). In such a case, each player is tempted to attack and is fearful of being suckered. Each player reasons as follows: "My opponent can either attack or wait. If he attacks, I had better be attacking too, to prevent being suckered. If he waits, I still would do best to attack, so I can sucker him. So, whatever he does, I have to attack." The dilemma is that both players wind up attacking and getting the low payoff P, whereas they could have gotten a much higher payoff R if they had figured out some way to cooperate.

## THE GAME OF CHICKEN

Prisoner's Dilemma may be an appropriate model for some kinds of arms race (see Chapter 9). For nuclear diplomacy and deterrence during a crisis, a different payoff arrangement may be more relevant. **"Chicken"** is named after the 1950s teenage "game" involving two automobiles on a collision course. Each has two moves: go straight (equivalent to attack, in our previous game) or swerve (equivalent to wait). The payoff matrix, however, is not a Prisoner's Dilemma; rather, it is closer to nuclear war, because the payoff if both players go straight ahead is very low indeed. If both cars swerve—assuming they don't swerve in the same direction!—no one loses, but also no one wins. If one goes straight while the other swerves, the one going straight wins and the one who swerves loses. The crucial point is that the driver who swerves has indeed "lost," but not nearly as badly as if neither had swerved. Following is a hypothetical payoff matrix for the game of Chicken.

|  | side 2 | |
|---|---|---|
|  | swerve | straight |
| side 1 — swerve | -2, -2 | -20, +20 |
| side 1 — straight | +20, -20 | -1,000, -1,000 |

In a situation of stable deterrence, it pays each player to wait, confident that the opponent will do the same. In Prisoner's Dilemma, each player is constrained to attack, regardless of what the other side does. In Chicken, it pays to go straight, but only if the other player swerves. If you are convinced that the other side will go straight, it pays for you to swerve. As a result, when playing stable deterrence, each player has an interest in convincing the opponent ("partner"?) that it will behave cooperatively, to encourage the other to do the same. But when playing Chicken, both sides find it in their interest to try to induce the other to swerve. When playing Chicken, therefore, each player is likely to send signals indicating "resolve," the determination to go straight, although in the end, if both go straight, both are worse off.

This impression of resolve can be achieved by developing a reputation as someone who does not swerve, by driving a large and heavily armored vehicle, or perhaps by throwing the steering wheel out the window, thereby indicating that you cannot swerve, so the opponent had better be the chicken. After the Cuban missile crisis, for example, Secretary of State Dean Rusk observed that we had been "eyeball to eyeball, and the other guy blinked." It is widely believed that Soviet premier Nikita Khrushchev swerved that time because the

US had overwhelming nuclear and conventional superiority; that is, President Kennedy was driving a much stronger vehicle. Now that both sides have achieved **strategic parity,** a generally acknowledged equivalence in military strength, it is not clear who would back down in a crisis. (The danger is that under such circumstances, with each side determined to go straight, insisting that the other must be the one to swerve, games of Nuclear Chicken could result in fried chicken.)

## LAUNCH ON WARNING

In the movie *Dr. Strangelove, or How I Learned to Stop Worrying and Love the Bomb,* we are introduced to a fictional situation in which the USSR, hoping to deter an American attack, has made a doomsday device that will destroy the world. It is set to go off automatically if any nuclear weapons explode on Soviet soil. In a sense, it is the ultimate deterrent, designed to prevent attack by threatening total retaliation. In itself, such a doomsday device would clearly lack credibility, because in the event of an actual attack—that is, if deterrence did fail—there would be no benefit to the victim in implementing the planned retaliation. Given what we are now learning about nuclear winter, retaliation looks even more illogical, hence, lacking in credibility. Therefore, the doomsday machine in the movie was taken out of human control. This is analogous to throwing away the steering wheel in a game of Chicken. It is a way of saying: "Do not doubt the credibility of my retaliation, even if it seems suicidal, because in fact I can not control it." Understanding this, the opponent should be permanently deterred.

Ironically, then, a system that guarantees retaliation, even if such retaliation is itself irrational, is a possible "rational" way to enhance the credibility of deterrence. As we have seen, in addition to credibility, vulnerability is a problem for deterrence theory, a problem that has grown with the development of increased missile accuracy as well as MIRVing. Also as we have seen, vulnerability can be reduced—and thus, stability increased—by a variety of techniques, including increased alert status. ICBMs in particular could be made maximally invulnerable if it were known that they would be launched before any attacking warheads could arrive. The idea is that if an opponent knows that any attack will precipitate launch of the other side's missiles before they can be destroyed, the opponent will be deterred from attacking in the first place.

One potential solution, therefore, to the crisis instability that results from declining credibility and increasing vulnerability is a strategic posture of **launch on warning.** In this posture, retaliatory missiles would be launched when *warning* of an attack was received, without waiting for absolute confirmation that an attack was under way (by which time it might be too late). The current policy of both the US and the USSR is either to "ride out" any presumed attack before responding, or to **launch under attack,** that is, to launch missiles during an attack, but not before. As long as both sides have a secure second-strike capability, neither fears that its ability to retaliate—hence, to deter an attack—is dangerously compromised. However, if and when deterrence is sufficiently eroded, launch on warning may seem more attractive. Because of the very brief response time that would be involved, launch on warning is often assumed to be automatic, with launch authority vested in automatic sensors and computers (hence the similarity to the doomsday device in Kubrick's movie, which was out of human control). However, launch on warning could in theory still involve a human decision, as long as the same guidelines are observed.

## EXTENDED DETERRENCE

Many Americans think that US nuclear weapons are maintained solely to deter nuclear attacks against the US. This is not the case. In 1980 Secretary of Defense Harold Brown stated:

> . . . [d]eterrence must restrain a far wider range of threats than just massive attacks on US cities. We seek to deter any adversary from any course of action that could lead to general nuclear war. Our strategic forces also must deter nuclear attacks on smaller sets of targets in the US military forces, and be a wall against nuclear coercion of, or an attack on, our friends and allies. And strategic forces, in conjunction with theater nuclear forces, must contribute to deterrence of conventional aggression as well.

Deterrence, in short, has been extended to cover attacks anywhere the US government perceives that it has a vital interest, notably Europe, the Middle East, Korea, and more recently, the Persian Gulf. **Extended deterrence** therefore is proposed as a means of keeping the peace and maintaining US strategic interests worldwide. Critics point out that by extending deterrence, we also extend the possibility that some confrontation, somewhere, will result in nuclear war; supporters maintain that the goal is to prevent all war, not just nuclear war.

Extended deterrence relies on an ability to play aggressive poker, to meet any level of violence and raise the ante to a higher level if needed. To make this credible, it is said that the US must furthermore have the ability to defeat the USSR at every rung of the "escalation ladder," from conventional skirmishes in third world nations to full-scale nuclear war. Richard Perle, Assistant Secretary of Defense for International Security Policy in the Reagan administration, described **escalation dominance** this way:

*I've always worried less about what would happen in an actual nuclear exchange than about the effect that the nuclear balance has on our willingness to take risks in local situations. . . . I worry about an American president feeling he cannot afford to take action in a crisis because Soviet nuclear forces are such that, if escalation took place, they are better poised than we are to move up the escalation ladder.*

According to this view, if the USSR had this ability to dominate conflict at all levels of violence, it could intimidate the US. If the US, on the other hand, had the capacity to achieve escalation dominance, the USSR would be much more cautious and would lack the incentive to escalate or even to threaten escalation in the first place.

If both sides play Chicken with escalation dominance and keep upping the ante, both sides could find themselves at the topmost rung of the ladder of nuclear violence. Then, according to the Department of Defense 1982 Defense Guidance document: "Should deterrence fail and strategic nuclear war with the USSR occur, the United States must prevail and be able to force the Soviet Union to seek earliest termination of hostilities on terms favorable to the United States." In other words, escalation dominance is still the goal. The strategies identified for achieving this include civil and strategic defense to limit damage (see Chapter 7), and "decapitating" strikes against the Soviet leadership. Supporters claim that by credibly threatening what the opponent most values, the US can deter war in the first place. If deterrence fails, they hope to restrict the USSR's ability to command, control, and communicate with its military forces, thereby further limiting damage to the US.

*R. Scheer. 1982. *With Enough Shovels*. New York: Random House.

Critics point out that such threats add to a possible "hair-trigger" situation in which each side nervously fears that the other might strike first. They also ask how the USSR will be able to seek termination of hostilities on any terms whatever, once their leadership (as well as that of the US) has been "decapitated."

For better or worse, public government advocacy of "prevailing" at any level of nuclear hostility is a relatively new one for US strategic doctrine. Although it gained popularity during the mid-1970s and was enunciated in PD 59, the policy of "prevailing" in a "limited nuclear war" had not been openly pursued since the threat of massive retaliation in the 1950s was perceived to lack credibility.

## EUROPE: A SPECIAL CASE

Strategic doctrine applies generally throughout the world, although both the US and the USSR make special provision for regions in which conflict seems most likely and their vital interests are engaged. In this respect, Europe is a special case. A large proportion of the military budgets of both sides are directed toward the "defense" of Europe, each against the other. It is widely acknowledged that no one has anything to gain from war in Europe, but each claims that the other might not realize this.

The present European boundaries were essentially established at the end of World War II, and to some degree, the difference in East–West military forces during the late 1980s are similar to those in the late 1940s: some quantitative advantages to the East, some qualitative advantages to the West. We have already examined some specifics of the NATO–WP balance in Chapter 3. Our purpose here is to relate this to nuclear strategy.

Perhaps more than anywhere else, western nuclear strategy in Europe is bedeviled by the problem of credibility. Thus, because it is so densely populated, the continent of Europe probably lends itself less to being defended by nuclear weapons than anyplace else on earth. There is some truth in the observation that towns in Germany are "about a kiloton apart." Hence, many people consider that the plan to defend Europe with nuclear weapons is a gigantic bluff.

As we have seen, confidence in the US "nuclear umbrella" was increasingly eroded as the USSR achieved nuclear parity. European leaders in particular wondered aloud whether an American president would sacrifice Chicago, for example, to save Hamburg. Such concern was instrumental in the withdrawal of France from the integrated military command of NATO to establish its own independent nuclear force. It also led strategists to emphasize the concept of flexible response, applied especially to Europe. The argument went as follows: if an American strategic response to a Soviet invasion of Europe is no longer credible because the US homeland is at risk to Soviet retaliation, perhaps the use of tactical nuclear weapons, in Europe itself, would be. Flexible response became official NATO doctrine in 1967.

However, not all Europeans were reassured. There has long been an undercurrent of concern that the US seeks to decouple its security from that of Europe. **Decoupling,** to the Europeans, could mean either that the US would not seek to defend Europe in the event of a Soviet attack, or that the US and the USSR would fight a limited nuclear war in the European "theater." In the first case, western Europe might be susceptible to invasion from the East, or to political intimidation. In the second, the US and the USSR might fight each other to the last European, a prospect about which the Europeans have not been enthusiastic. The argument for coupling the US and western Europe is that once it became sufficiently clear that US strategic forces would necessarily be engaged in any East–West hostilities in Europe, both the US and the USSR would exercise restraint and the nations of western Europe could also be free of Soviet intimidation. On the other hand, if the fate of the US were decoupled from the defense of Europe, the USSR (and the US) might behave less responsibly than if their respective homelands were likely to be involved. This is why many Europeans were very upset when President Reagan said in 1981 that he thought tactical nuclear war might occur in Europe without causing all-out strategic nuclear war.

The perceived danger of decoupling is that it might tempt an aggressor. Precisely to prevent the perception of decoupling, US military forces have long been stationed in West Germany. Since the early 1950s, they have been there not so much as an occupying force or even for their actual fighting ability, but as a "trip wire." It is reasoned that if US forces are under attack, the US would make good on any additional military commitment necessary to protect European allies. Those supporting the deployment of American Euromissiles (Pershing IIs and GLCMs) further argue that such intermediate-range forces will plug the gap between conventional and short-range tactical nuclear weapons (such as nuclear artillery) and US strategic forces, thereby preventing decoupling.

Some Europeans, especially those in the peace movement, worry that the danger to Europe is not decoupling but being too tightly coupled. They fear that Europe will serve as a battleground between the US and the USSR, and that deploying weapons that are provocative to the USSR increases the chances of this happening. (We shall examine the history of Euromissile deployments and the arguments on either side as part of our review of the arms race, in Chapter 9.)

Finally, the problem of the credibility of nuclear weapons in Europe is directly associated with the controversial neutron "bomb," or enhanced radiation warhead. As we have seen, neutron bombs are nuclear weapons that produce relatively less blast and heat, and more neutrons. It has been argued that to deter aggression in Europe, it would be helpful to have small nuclear weapons, which could be used selectively against attacking forces (especially tank crews), but whose use would be credible because unintended destruction of civilians—so-called collateral damage—would be relatively low. It has been calculated that a 1-kiloton neutron bomb would kill twice as many tankmen as would a 10-kiloton fission weapon, but with only one-fifth the blast damage. The generation of prompt radiation by the two types of weapon is compared in Figure 6.13.

Neutron bombs would seem to reduce the clarity of the **nuclear firebreak,** a psychological barrier between using conventional and nuclear weapons. Supporters claim that this makes it less likely that any war, conventional or nuclear, will be started, once again because of the enhanced credibility of NATO's response. Opponents claim that by blurring the distinction between nuclear and conventional weapons, neutron bombs erode this crucial firebreak, thereby making it more likely that if hostilities start, nuclear weapons would be used.

The Carter administration first pressured European leaders to support deployment of neutron bombs, then thought better of it. The Reagan administration has resumed production of these weapons, which are currently stored in the US.

Supporters of a nonnuclear defense of Europe often emphasize the potential for high-technology, "smart" weapons to provide a nonprovocative defense, especially against tanks and other relatively large targets. It has been suggested that NATO undertake a **"no first use" policy,** in which it pledged never to initiate the use of nuclear weapons. (The USSR has unilaterally announced such a policy.) If adopted by NATO, this would presumably be more than mere words, since "no first use" would require that NATO accentuate its reliance on conventional weapons and other defenses. Critics of "no first use" point out that with nuclear weapons, Europe has been able to purchase defense very cheaply and that it has been unwilling to increase military expenditures. The exact requirements for a credible no-first-use policy in Europe are being actively debated. Contributing to this debate are the disagreements we have already seen (Chapter 3) regarding the actual military balance in Europe, as well as disagreement over the extent to which the Soviet Union actually harbors ambitions to conquer Europe.

In any event, the special case of Europe remains central to questions of nuclear deterrence, to the relation between conventional and nuclear weaponry, and to the relation between historical, political, and military issues.

## THE SOVIET VIEW OF DETERRENCE

Just as it takes two to tango, it takes two to play the "game" of deterrence. Hence, the USSR's attitude toward nuclear doctrine is crucial. Yet information about this attitude is limited and hotly debated. Advocates of greater western deployment of nuclear weapons emphasize what they see as the Soviet Union's belief that it can fight and win a nuclear war—that is, the USSR's refusal to accept western concepts of deterrence. Others take a more moderate view of Soviet policy, emphasizing certain fundamental similarities with US doctrine and a shared commitment to avoiding nuclear war.

Communist doctrine has always called for worldwide victory over capitalism, and Karl Marx preached the "inevitability" of class conflict and war. When Stalin triumphed over Trotsky, however, he emphasized the need to establish "socialism in one country." Khrushchev officially embraced "peaceful coexistence," emphasizing that because of nuclear weapons, war would be mutual suicide. This ideological shift has not been repudiated. Communist doctrine continues to profess faith in the historical inevitability of the triumph of Marxism–Leninism and to support foreign "liberation movements." According to official Soviet pronouncements, however, war between the US and the USSR is no longer considered to be inevitable.

Soviet military doctrine tends to be closely tied to ideology, and accordingly, it rejects much of western deterrence theorizing as a type of metaphysical scho-

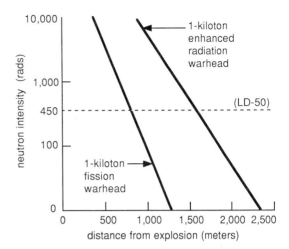

**FIGURE 6.13  The effectiveness of fission warheads compared with enhanced radiation warheads ("neutron bombs") in releasing prompt radiation. Note that a 1-kiloton enhanced radiation warhead will generate 450 rads (the LD-50) 1,500 meters from the explosion, whereas a 1-kiloton fission warhead will produce this radiation intensity for only about 750 meters.** (Modified from Kaplan, 1978.)

lasticism that obscures the real causes of war. These are seen to involve class conflict and imperialist adventuring on the part of the West. Soviet theory therefore does not accept the need for the USSR to be deterred, but it does accept the need to prevent war-making by the West. Soviet doctrine has emphasized a war-fighting capability to a degree that has exceeded US doctrine, a tendency that has disconcerted many western analysts. Whereas the West is more disposed toward **deterrence by punishment,** the notion that deterrence can be achieved by the threat of unacceptable retaliation on an aggressor, the USSR's policy is better described as **deterrence by denial,** a strategy that relies on striking first when and if an attack is imminent.

This comes close to a strategy of preemptive attack: if they become convinced that the US is about to strike first, they will preempt. Western analysts who take a dim view of Soviet strategic doctrine tend to emphasize the USSR's heavy investment in increasingly accurate, MIRVed, land-based missiles, and the seemingly lesser Soviet concern about retaining a second-strike capability. Thus, the Soviet nuclear configuration can be seen as closer to a first-strike doctrine than to the western view of stable deterrence. Critics also point out that the

USSR lost 20 million people during World War II, yet the Soviet Union emerged as a great power. This is seen as evidence that the USSR might be willing to endure a similar cost again. There is also the Soviet civil defense effort (which we shall consider in the next chapter), as well as Soviet military manuals, notably *Military Strategy,* edited by Marshal V. Sokolovsky, which emphasizes continuity between prenuclear and nuclear strategy.

On the other hand, the Soviets have indicated quite clearly that their perception of nuclear war is not very different from that of the West, as seen in this officially cleared statement early in the SALT negotiations: "We all agree that war between our two countries would be disastrous for both sides. And it would be tantamount to suicide for the ones who decided to start such a war." Soviet scientists have been actively researching the nuclear winter scenario, and Soviet physicians have appeared on Soviet media to warn of the catastrophic effects of nuclear war. Those who take a more benign view of Soviet strategic policy emphasize that the USSR suffered immensely in World War II, much more than did the US. Hence, it can be argued that the USSR is if anything more averse to war than is the US. Moreover, World War II was forced on the Soviets by a massive surprise attack by Germany; it was not something they chose. One can also point to western military manuals, which, like their Soviet counterparts, appear to take a rather cavalier view of nuclear war-fighting. Military manuals, on both sides, are not given to outlining the horrors or unwinnability of war. Rather, they emphasize what is to be done in the event of war, and they do not counsel defeat.

The Soviet experience during both world wars seems to be important in setting their current attitude toward possible nuclear war. Thus, they are reluctant to tie their security to the behavior of an adversary. They believe, instead, that strategic war can be prevented by retaining the ability to fight one. In this sense, Soviet strategy has resembled the war-fighting doctrines which, during the late 1970s and 1980s, have become US policy as well. Citing the costs of World War II, Soviet doctrine clearly states that any future wars will be fought on the aggressor's territory, not on their own. The result is a "forward-based" military posture that might well be intended to be defensive but looks ominously offensive to some western experts.

Unlike recent US strategy, Soviet doctrine is quite discouraging about the prospects of fighting limited or controlled nuclear wars. This is consistent with the nature of the USSR's strategic weaponry, hobbled by somewhat inferior technology as it is, which has emphasized large, less accurate and less precisely controllable weapons. It also makes plans for flexible response and escalation dominance appear less feasible; that is, if precise, tactical use of nuclear weapons by the West were to precipitate an unrestrained response by the USSR, the value of such strategies by the West would be called into question.

Finally, the possibility also exists that both US and Soviet doctrines in this respect are merely bluffs: maybe NATO will not respond to a conventional conflict by limited use of tactical nuclear weapons. And maybe the USSR would not respond to tactical nuclear war by escalating to the use of strategic nuclear weapons. It is to be hoped that we shall never find out.

## STRATEGY IN THE 1980S

There have been no major conceptual innovations in nuclear strategy since the late 1960s. The three basic problems appear and reappear: "credibility," "vulnerability," and "how much is enough?" Accordingly, debates are regularly resumed over counterforce, limited nuclear war, windows of vulnerability, and minimum deterrence. During the 1970s and 1980s it appears that technological advances have driven strategy, rather than vice versa. Developments in weaponry should ideally occur in response to decisions about what is desirable for national or mutual security. However, the weapons seem to be coming first, followed by efforts to justify or plan for them. Of course, it can be argued that this has always been the case in the Nuclear Age, beginning with the invention of nuclear weapons themselves: once the weapons were available, it was necessary to figure out what to do with them. In a sense, the technological tail has been wagging the policy dog.

This is especially true with regard to growing anxiety about the increasing accuracy and diminishing flight time of counterforce weapons, which in turn has been shortening the response time available for a nation under attack. As we have seen, this has made the option of launch on warning increasingly attractive to some strategic planners.

Strategic doctrine in the 1980s seems to have become especially entwined with strategies of counterforce and war-fighting. Thus, old-fashioned deterrence requires neither accuracy nor speed. The weaponry of the 1980s, however, emphasizes both these qualities. With the possible exception of cruise missiles, there can be little doubt that the major strategic weapons of both sides are moving toward an increasing counterforce capability: the MX, Trident II, and Pershing II missiles on the US side, and the SS-18s and Typhoon SLBMs on the Soviet side. Along with these weapons, war-fighting and war-"prevailing" doctrines have become increasingly convergent, with the avowed US strategy coming to resemble that of the USSR. The effect of these developments on strategic stability remains to be seen. (Fig. 6.14).

The possibility of "nuclear winter" has introduced a new potential twist into strategic thought. As Chapter 5 demonstrated, even the limited use of nuclear weapons, by either side, might spell doom not only for the victim but for the attacker, as well. This concern has not yet been incorporated into deterrence theory. On the one hand, if the nuclear winter scenario turns out to be valid, both sides should be self-deterred, with much of the anxiety regarding preemptive strikes and windows of vulnerability becoming fatuous. It can then be debated whether both sides should vigorously seek to reduce arsenals below the threshold levels likely to bring about nuclear winter. Fundamental sanity would seem to dictate that we reject the possibility of destroying our planet. But should this mean striving to make our mutual arsenals "safe" so that nuclear war can occur without triggering nuclear winter? Remember that nuclear winter seems most likely to result from many airbursts over cities; therefore, a strategic posture that emphasized relatively more groundbursts at military targets such as ICBM silos (more fallout, but fewer smoky fires) would be one possible response to the specter of nuclear winter. It is ironic that such a posture might threaten deterrence, whereas one less threatening to strategic stability seems more likely to threaten nuclear winter. Therefore, it may be that policies less likely to result in nuclear winter may be more likely to precipitate nuclear war in the first place.

Alternatively, is it possible that after determining the threshold level of megatonnage likely to bring about nuclear winter, one side might use just less than that amount in a first strike, leaving the victim nation unwilling to retaliate? As of 1986, the official US doctrinal response to the possibility of nuclear winter has been to point out that this highlights the need to reduce the nuclear arsenals of both sides, and the appropriateness of current national policy.

**FIGURE 6.14 Coordinated multiple launch of Minuteman III missiles from Vandenberg Air Force Base, California. Such coordinated launches have been attempted only rarely by either side. A first strike would require a massively and precisely coordinated multiple launch, by thousands of warheads.** (Courtesy of the US Department of Defense.)

## A CAUTIOUS CONCLUSION

To some extent, deterrence has been around for a long time, as long as the phenomenon of threat in animals. Aside from any moral problems, however, nuclear deterrence has some theoretical difficulties. Critics claim that deterrence has become an excuse for justifying the nuclear arms race and that its own momentum is resulting in progressively more instability. Supporters claim that it has kept the peace, despite its dangers and peculiar illogic. According to former presidential adviser McGeorge Bundy, deterrence does not work in theory; only in practice, because regardless of the theoretical niceties, neither side is willing to take the risk of immense losses. Strategic analyst Leonard Freedman notes that "the Emperor Deterrence has no clothes, but he is still the emperor."

## Policy Issues

### Does nuclear deterrence work?

**Yes:** Despite varying levels of hostility since 1945, the US and the USSR have not fought a war. Because of the nuclear weapons on both sides, the two nations have ample reason to back off from any serious confrontation. Although a world free of the threat of nuclear war would be highly desirable in itself, the elimination of nuclear weapons—even if it were possible—might not be desirable. Thus, conventional weaponry has become increasingly lethal, and without the inhibitions provided by the presence of nuclear weapons in an adversary's arsenal, international events could well be more tense and bloody than at present. Deterrence may not be lovable, but it is livable, and essential to keeping the peace. Our responsibility in the Nuclear Age is to maintain and strengthen deterrence, to see that it is not eroded.

**No:** The assertion that deterrence works is counterfactual and cannot be checked, since we know only that something didn't happen—we don't know why it didn't happen. It may well be, for example, that the USSR has not had any interest in attacking the US, nuclear deterrence aside. We cannot prove that the USSR has been deterred by US nuclear weapons, any more than the Soviets can prove that their nuclear weapons have deterred the US. The fact that something has not yet happened does not mean that it will not; indeed, you can just as well conclude that you will never die, because you haven't yet. Europe went through decades between World War I and World War II, longer yet between the Franco-Prussian War and World War I, and so on, but the next war always came. It is inconceivable that the world will go on indefinitely without nuclear deterrence failing somehow, somewhere. Moreover, deterrence has become an addiction, demanding ever more weapons. Our responsibility in the Nuclear Age is to get out from under deterrence as soon as we can.

### Should the US plan for limited nuclear wars?

**Yes:** The goal is to prevent war, all war: whether conventional or nuclear. The most effective way to do this is for the US to be able to respond to potential

provocations in ways that inhibit such behavior in the first place, or failing that, to seek to limit the conflict as much as possible. It is absurd and dangerous for us to have no options other than conventional war or all-out nuclear destruction. Failing to plan for the in-between contingency, the US may be faced with the choice between holocaust and surrender. By having forces that are ready to be used and flexible enough to be used in a variety of ways, we strengthen deterrence and ensure that these forces are not in fact used. Moreover, by maintaining a war-fighting option, the US can employ the plausible threat of nuclear force in its national interest. As strategic analysts Colin Gray and Keith Payne put it, "If American nuclear power is to support US foreign policy objectives, the United States must possess the ability to wage nuclear war rationally." It is even possible that a nuclear war could be limited and fought successfully.

**No:** Limited nuclear wars are virtual impossibilities, like being half-pregnant or—more to the point—half-dead. After the first few nuclear explosions have gone off, it is very unlikely that either side will have any ability to command, control, or communicate with its weapons. In fact, the EMP effects of a single high-altitude nuclear weapon would likely destroy most of the sophisticated devices needed to control such a war. Military actions of all sorts have to cope with extreme cases of Murphy's law: anything that can go wrong, will. This would be particularly true of efforts to fight a limited nuclear war. In addition, having just suffered millions of casualties, it is unlikely that either side would surrender while it had unused weapons. With the leadership on both sides likely to be destroyed, any attempt to limit nuclear war would quickly deteriorate into a suicidal slugfest. By planning for limited nuclear wars, and developing doctrine and weapons for fighting them, we go from MAD to worse, by making nuclear war thinkable, hence doable. Deterrence is bad enough; the concept of limited nuclear wars undermines deterrence. It is absurd to assume that national leaders, after committing the fundamental irrationality of using nuclear weapons, will suddenly turn rational and limit their use, especially in view of the confusion, anger, and other passions that will have been aroused. Because of the high probability that nuclear warfare will rapidly get out of hand, it is fundamentally irrational to plan to conduct it.

## Should the US adopt a policy of "minimal deterrence" rather than maintaining current levels of "overkill"?

**No:** It is indeed true that current nuclear arsenals equal the equivalent of about 4 tons of TNT for every person on earth, but this is misleading. Megatonnage cannot be distributed evenly to each person; nuclear weapons necessarily concentrate their force in a relatively small number of large explosions. In addition, overkill is really a fail-safe redundancy. By maintaining nuclear destructive potential that is presumably greater than actually needed, we are hedging our bets against a possible preemptive strike, or against a technological breakthrough that might render one or more legs of the triad vulnerable. An arsenal suited for minimal deterrence only would also be insufficient to achieve various patterns of limited nuclear war in the service of escalation dominance; therefore, it would be a less credible posture, and less likely to deter the other side. It would also be less useful if limited nuclear war actually occurred. Finally, there is no way to know exactly what would constitute a "minimal" deterrent—how much is needed to deter our opponents—and it would be tragic if we were to elect a low level, thinking it to be sufficient, only to find that it was not.

**Yes:** Nuclear arsenals on both sides have become grotesquely bloated. The USSR has only 220 cities with a population of 100,000 or more. Two of the older Poseidon submarines, 320 warheads, could effectively destroy the USSR, possibly for all time. To allow for malfunction and so on, perhaps as many as a half dozen Poseidons could be maintained. Any more is wasteful, unnecessary, and provocative. Nuclear weapons are not really weapons at all; they can serve no rational purpose, whether military or political, except perhaps to deter an opponent from using nuclear weapons against us. Since the use of nuclear weapons in even a "limited" manner is almost certain to result in nuclear holocaust, we are ill advised to plan for such a contingency. There is, at present, no prospect for halting the arms race short of some concept of minimal deterrence. By adopting it, we could possibly end this madness, calling a halt

to the arms spiral that now threatens to become a whirlwind.

## Should the US deploy counterforce weapons?

**Yes:** The most effective way that the US can restrain Soviet adventurism is to have the potential of destroying the Soviets' weapons and their ability to command and control them. By a kind of "stability produced by instability," the USSR will be less likely to act provocatively in other ways, notably in the third world, if it knows that its missiles are threatened by US warheads. It is also morally preferable to attack the other side's military forces instead of its civilians. The USSR would be further deterred from attacking if the leadership knew that the US could retaliate with strikes against their remaining weapons; if, alternatively, the US had only relatively inaccurate weapons, suitable only for destroying cities, the US would be susceptible to Soviet postattack blackmail. They could attack US ICBMs and the US wouldn't dare retaliate against their cities, since this would almost surely bring about a counterretaliation against our cities, which up to this point would not have been touched. But if the US could respond against their missiles and leadership, such retaliation would be appropriate and credible. The USSR has been deploying counterforce weapons, and so the US must too. Perhaps by doing so, the US will force them to reduce their increasingly threatening arsenal.

**No:** Counterforce weapons are inexcusably dangerous. Perhaps the most useful commandment for the Nuclear Age is "Thou shalt not target thy neighbor's deterrent," because by doing so, one directly undermines deterrence itself. Deterrence relies on the ability of each side to maintain a secure second-strike capability. It actually makes us less safe to place Soviet missiles at risk, because it makes the Soviet leadership worry that we might preemptively attack them. This would make them more likely to interpret a false alarm as a real attack, or to strike first during times of international tension. When the US builds increased numbers of more threatening missiles, the Soviets could respond by building more such "bargaining chips," as they have so far, and as the US responded to their deployments. Counterforce is a trap, likely to keep driving the arms race, and worse yet, to erode crisis stability.

## KEY TERMS

scenarios

nuclear deterrence

massive retaliation

limited nuclear wars

graduated deterrence

flexible response

first-strike capability

stability

first use

"use it or lose it" syndrome

second-strike capability

survivable

generated alert

dynamic balance

countervalue

counterforce

damage limitation

single integrated operational plan (SIOP)

Presidential Directive 59 (PD 59)

mutually assured destruction (MAD)

nuclear sufficiency

minimal deterrence

parity

exchange ratio

game theory

zero-sum games

non-zero-sum games

crisis stability

crisis instability

Prisoner's Dilemma

Chicken

strategic parity

launch on warning

launch under attack

extended deterrence

escalation dominance

decoupling

nuclear firebreak

"no first use" policy

deterrence by punishment

deterrence by denial

## STUDY QUESTIONS

1. Explain the relationship between massive retaliation and the overwhelming US nuclear superiority of the 1950s.

2. What led to concern about the credibility of deterrence?

3. What was the doctrinal response?

4. Distinguish between minimal deterrence and overkill.

5. Why is vulnerability a major problem for deterrence theory?

6. How have US strategists attempted to reduce vulnerability?

7. What is the relationship between credibility and limited nuclear war-fighting?

8. In what sense is "mutual assured destruction" less a policy than a fact of life?

9. Distinguish between counterforce and counter-value.

10. What is meant by secure second-strike capability?

11. Why is vulnerability of each side's population considered to be stabilizing in the Nuclear Age, whereas vulnerability of each side's weapons is considered to be destabilizing?

12. What are some aspects of game theory that make it appropriate for modeling nuclear deterrence? What are some aspects that make it inappropriate?

13. What is meant by "decoupling" US from European security?

14. Why is it generally agreed that MIRVed missiles are more destabilizing than single-warhead missiles?

## ADDITIONAL READINGS

Brodie, Bernard. 1959. *Strategy in the Missile Age.* Princeton, NJ: Princeton University Press. A classic statement of deterrence thinking in the 1950s.

Freedman, Lawrence. 1981. *The Evolution of Nuclear Strategy.* New York: St. Martin's Press. An encyclopedic review of the history and major ideas of deterrence.

Kaplan, Fred. 1983. *The Wizards of Armageddon.* New York: Simon & Schuster. A very readable account of the personalities and history of those responsible for American strategic doctrine.

Russett, Bruce. 1983. *The Prisoners of Insecurity.* New York: W. H. Freeman. A handy, convenient, easy-to-read guide to many salient issues in the arms race, nuclear war, and deterrence; particularly good coverage of crisis stability and the Prisoner's Dilemma.

Schelling, Thomas. 1960. *The Strategy of Conflict.* Cambridge, MA: Harvard University Press. An enormously influential work on escalation and limited war; one of the major works on deterrence theory.

# 7 Civil Defense and Strategic Defense ("Star Wars")

*I have set before you life and death. . . . Choose life. . . .*
Deuteronomy 30:19

We have seen that nuclear weapons policy relies basically on deterrence, the prevention of nuclear war by threatening that the consequences of initiating one will be so severe that each side will refrain from doing so. Reliable or not, it is clear that deterrence is quite different from defense. Deterrence relies on manipulating the behavior of an opponent, hence, it is hostage to the other side's behavior and perceptions. Not surprisingly, some people in both the US and the USSR have also sought to achieve defense more directly. In this chapter, we shall review the two major governmentally sanctioned attempts at achieving defense in the Nuclear Age: civil defense (CD) and so-called strategic defense, more commonly known as "Star Wars."

Like so many other aspects of the arms race, both civil defense and strategic defense have been controversial, with the debate revolving around such questions as: Will it work? (i.e., Is it technically feasible?) and Will it be economically feasible? (i.e., Is it an appropriate expenditure, or would the funds and effort be better spent elsewhere?). In addition, defensive strategies cannot be divorced from the deterrent postures of both superpowers. It must therefore be asked whether civil and/or strategic defense activities represent efforts to prepare to fight a nuclear war, as critics claim, or to mitigate the effects if nuclear war occurs despite every effort to prevent it, as supporters maintain. Finally, and perhaps most important, it is crucial to ask about the likely effect of civil and/or strategic defense on deterrence itself. Will such efforts bolster or undermine deterrence? If they threaten to undermine deterrence, are there additional benefits that might balance this effect, thereby making the effort worthwhile nonetheless?

The goal in this chapter, as throughout the book, is to explain the issues as informatively and impartially as possible, so that students will be able to start answering such questions for themselves.

## CIVIL DEFENSE IN THE UNITED STATES

### Sheltering

Civil defense became an issue in the United States when the Soviet Union developed nuclear weapons and especially, the ability to attack the US with them, by strategic bombers in the mid-1950s and by ICBMs in the late 1950s and early 1960s. Spurred on by the Berlin crisis of 1961 and the Cuban missile crisis of 1962, as well as fears of a "missile gap" favoring the USSR, civil defense became a popular topic—almost a craze—in the United States during the early 1960s. President John F. Kennedy was an ardent supporter. Many houses constructed at that time contained family shelters (Fig. 7.1), and public shelter space, ostensibly capable of maintaining millions of people, was identified, especially in large urban areas (Fig. 7.2). However, as the Soviet arsenal grew, serious doubts were raised about the likely effectiveness of civil defense, about the cost, and about the morality of defending one's shelter at gunpoint against fellow citizens seeking entrance (to mention one disturbing possibility).

There are basically two aspects to civil defense in the US: shelters and evacuation. Both are intended to help the civilian population survive a nuclear war. Shelters, in turn, are of two basic kinds: against blast and against fallout. **Blast shelters** are supposed to provide protection against the extreme overpressures of nuclear attacks and can be hardened to 50–100 psi without Herculean efforts. **Fallout shelters** are less blast resistant and are intended for long-term occupancy when the goal is to avoid exposure to radioactive fallout. The effectiveness of fallout shelters in providing insulation from outside radioactivity is measured by their **protection factor,** the degree to which radiation exposure is reduced by the shelter itself. Thus, a protection factor of 100 means that the occupants experience 1/100 the level of radiation that is present outside. A typical home basement provides protection factors ranging from about 10–20, and fallout shelters, about 100.

CD supporters point out that less than 0.05% of the area of the US would be exposed to overpressures of 50 psi or more, making even blast shelters feasible. Opponents emphasize that people are concentrated in cities, and in the likely event of a conflagration or firestorm, blast shelter residents would be incinerated, and their oxygen supply sucked out by the intense fires. It would be a daunting problem to equip such shelters with self-contained sanitation and ventilation facilities, as well as supplies of food and water.

CD supporters point out that radioactive fallout tends to decay rapidly: 2 days after an attack, it is reduced to about 1/100 of its initial level, and after 2 weeks, to 1/1000. Combined with the substantial protection factors available even in rudimentary shelters, it is conceivable that survivors could emerge after several weeks underground. On the other hand, cumulative radiation levels are more important than acute exposure, and since submarines remain invulnerable for weeks on end, repeated attacks over a period of weeks or even months would be quite feasible. This would be especially true if plans for fighting a "prolonged nuclear war" became reality.

Opponents also maintain that effective sheltering is impossible; CD supporters argue that a workable program might save millions of lives and that the government is obligated to try to establish one.

ICBMs could begin striking the United States 30 minutes after launch. Allowing perhaps 10 minutes for the missles to be detected and confirmed, and another 10 minutes for the various emergency notification procedures to be instituted, about 10 minutes would remain between the sounding of air-raid sirens and activation of the Emergency Broadcasting System, and the first detonations. For SLBMs launched closer to the mainland, this warning time would be even briefer. As a result, most people, including CD supporters, agree that sheltering alone is not practical. As MAD became widely understood, if not embraced, interest in civil defense therefore declined precipitously in the United States throughout the 1960s and 1970s.

**FIGURE 7.1 Official Civil Defense photo from the 1950s: a family living happily in their home fallout shelter.** (Courtesy of Fossil Films and Photos.)

## Crisis Relocation

Beginning with the Reagan administration in 1981, however, the concept of civil defense was revived, this time with special emphasis on **crisis relocation,** the evacuation of cities and other high-risk areas if governmental authorities decide that nuclear war is imminent. Plans for crisis relocation, and other aspects of civil defense, are administered by the **Federal Emergency Management Agency (FEMA),** which was formed in 1979 to replace the Civil Defense Administration. FEMA was given charge of the sheltering plans as well as the crisis relocation program. FEMA has drawn up scenarios for the evacuation of all urban and other "high-risk" populations, and for quartering the evacuees in "host" communities considered to be at low risk of direct attack. For the purposes of such plans, it is assumed that a superpower crisis will develop over a period of at least several days, which will provide enough time for the government to order citizens to evacuate, and for that evacuation to be carried out (Fig. 7.3).

Crisis relocation has been bitterly opposed by some and strongly supported by others. In the early 1980s,

**FIGURE 7.2 Official Civil Defense photo from the 1950s: a typical "take cover" exercise for public school students. Such activities gradually lost favor as a means of civil defense.** (Courtesy of Fossil Films and Photos.)

many urban areas refused to participate in such plans, as did many designated host regions, finding the concept offensive, ludicrous, and/or dangerous. There was confusion over whether a given community was likely to be a target of Soviet warheads—hence a candidate to be evacuated—or more appropriate as a host for evacuees arriving from elsewhere. Serious doubts were raised about the feasibility of evacuating large and medium-sized urban areas. The availability of shelter and provisions for large number of evacuees has seemed grossly inadequate, and providing such facilities unacceptably expensive. Public education activities, especially by a group known as Physicians for Social Responsibility, made many people acutely aware of the inadequacy of medical care in the aftermath of a nuclear war, and gave a Strangelovian tone to arguments supporting crisis relocation. Many people accordingly suggested that effort spent on crisis relocation was misplaced and that attention should be directed toward preventing nuclear war rather than preparing for it. As of 1985, crisis relocation—and civil defense in general—had once again receded in American nuclear doctrine, largely for budgetary reasons and because of widespread public apathy as well as occasional outright antagonism.

Some Americans have taken substantial personal steps toward what they define as their own private civil defense. These self-styled **survivalists** appear to be

**FIGURE 7.3 Portland, Oregon, virtually deserted following evacuation exercise ("Operation Greenlight") in 1957.** (Photo by Rollie Dobson, *Portland Oregonian,* courtesy of the Federal Emergency Management Agency.)

convinced of the likelihood of nuclear war and of the possibility that they could survive, as individuals and families if not as part of society, if they are properly trained and equipped. Survivalists are currently very much a minority.

## CIVIL DEFENSE IN THE SOVIET UNION

Concern about American inadequacy in civil defense measures is typically expressed by those who point to the more vigorous Soviet effort. Others emphasize that "adequacy' or "inadequacy" in this respect should be determined by whether the measures in question are likely to work, not by what the other side is doing. In any event, it is generally acknowledged that the USSR has a more active civil defense program than does the US. The Soviet CD program, with an annual budget of $1 billion, employs about 100,000 persons and has constructed about 30,000 blast shelters. It is emphasized, however, that comparisons of Soviet and American expenditures are always questionable, since they typically involve calculating the Soviets' costs as if the US were to purchase comparable goods and services in the American economy, with American dollars. Nonetheless, the USSR's civil defense effort seems far more substantial than that of the US. Soviet adults as well as school children receive CD instruction, for example. It remains uncertain, however, whether the program is meaningful or largely cosmetic.

As in the US, crisis relocation is emphasized in Soviet CD plans. Hawkish analysts see the Soviet CD program as further confirmation of the USSR's plans to fight and win a nuclear war. Others, opposed to a substantial American CD effort, emphasize the likely inadequacy of Soviet sheltering and evacuation schemes. They also point to the Russian historical experience of being invaded and attacked, suggesting that this may have led to a determination to protect the nation from future incursions even if the "protection" is only a sham. The Soviet CD effort looks relatively impressive on paper; whether it would work is unknown. The American CD program also looks good on paper, and it may provide grist for Soviet CD officials, eager to enlarge their professional role by pointing to "the American CD challenge." A study of Soviet civil defense by the CIA in 1978 concluded that the' Soviet Union's CD effort is unlikely to provide significant protection in the event of a nuclear war. Nonetheless, the likely effectiveness of Soviet CD is hotly debated.

## COMPARING CIVIL DEFENSE VULNERABILITIES

It is clear that a nuclear war would be an unprecedented disaster for the nations involved, and perhaps for the entire planet. It therefore seems especially mean-spirited to worry about relative "advantages" in surviving such a war. However, such comparisons are implicit in any examination of US–Soviet civil defense efforts. The possibility also exists that a disparity in civilian vulnerability might make the side that is less vulnerable more likely to risk a crisis, and even, perhaps, a nuclear war. A reasonably convincing case can be made that either side is the more vulnerable.

- *Greater US Vulnerabilities.* The USSR has a better developed civil defense program and a much larger land area over which to disperse its population. The people are used to following orders and making sacrifices without question, and are accustomed to a lower standard of living. Being less highly industrialized, the USSR would be able to rebuild to its current level more easily than could the United States. Being more centralized, the Soviet government could more easily organize not only mass evacuation, but also recovery afterward. The US has a relatively large number of people whose professional skills would be virtually useless in a postwar world (insurance salesmen, realtors, etc.), whereas the USSR has more manual laborers as well as more engineers. US cities are highly dependent on automobiles, which would almost certainly become unusable after a nuclear war, whereas the USSR's cities are more dependent on mass transportation, and because they are more compact, they offer better prospects for life in a postattack world.

- *Greater USSR Vulnerabilities.* Although the USSR is geographically larger than the US, much of it is uninhabited Siberia. Strategic targets in the USSR are at least as concentrated as those of the US (Fig. 7.4). The Soviet population occurs largely in western, European USSR. Moreover, the Soviet urban population is actually more concentrated than its US counterpart: 131 million American urbanites inhabit roughly 47,000 square kilometers, whereas 126 million Soviet urbanites occupy only about 18,000 square kilometers. Breaking this down further, we find that about 40% of the Soviet population occupies 7,500 square kilometers, and to destroy such an area would require 100 explo-

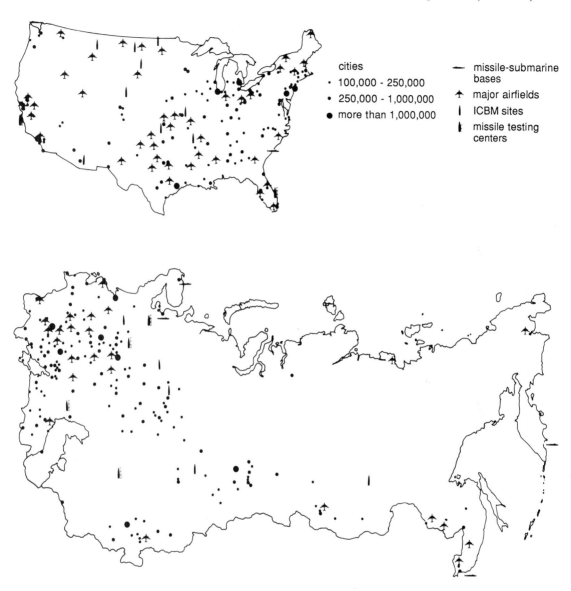

cities
- · 100,000 - 250,000
- · 250,000 - 1,000,000
- ● more than 1,000,000

— missile-submarine bases
✈ major airfields
| ICBM sites
| missile testing centers

**FIGURE 7.4 Relative concentrations of major military targets and population centers in the US and the USSR. Such targets are, if anything, more concentrated in the USRR.** (Modified from Lewis, 1979.)

sions of 1 megaton each (top curve, Fig. 7.5). In the US, however, only about 20% of the population occupies 7,500 square kilometers; to kill 40% of all American citizens, an attacker would have to cover 22,500 square kilometers, which would require 300 EMT (bottom curve, Fig. 7.5).

Soviet citizenry generally live closer to their workplaces than do Americans; hence, attacks against Soviet industry are more likely to destroy civilian homes and lives as well. Industry is highly concentrated due to a Soviet penchant for industrial gigantism. As a result, the economy of the

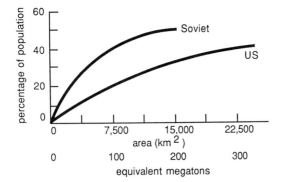

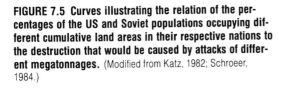

**FIGURE 7.5 Curves illustrating the relation of the percentages of the US and Soviet populations occupying different cumulative land areas in their respective nations to the destruction that would be caused by attacks of different megatonnages.** (Modified from Katz, 1982; Schroeer, 1984.)

USSR is much more vulnerable than is the US. There are generally a small number of enormous chemical plants, manufacturing centers, power generating stations, etc. Even in peacetime, the Soviet economy is subject to massive bottlenecks because it is so highly centralized and inefficient; after a nuclear war, it would almost certainly collapse altogether. Even in peacetime, the USSR is not self-sufficient in food; after a nuclear war, it would doubtless be worse off. The USSR is an empire of many ethnic minorities, which might be totally ungovernable after a nuclear war, especially if—as seems likely—ethnic Great Russians bear the brunt of the casualties. Finally, the USSR's climate is much more severe than that of the US, particularly because of its long, cold winters and difficult, muddy springs.

It is at least possible that the somewhat greater Soviet concern with civil defense represents an effort to compensate for their own self-perceived vulnerabilities vis à vis the United States.

## COULD CIVIL DEFENSE "WORK" FOR EITHER NATION?

Some studies have suggested that US casualties could be reduced from 48–75% of the population without

civil defense to 10–26% of the population with civil defense. Common sense tells us that even when dealing with a terrible catastrophe, it is better to have some plans than none at all. The basic technology needed for constructing shelters, evacuating people, and so on is currently available and in that sense, feasible. Mass civilian evacuations during disasters such as hurricanes have proceeded with very little panic.

On the other hand, a nuclear war is beyond the reach of previous experience; people may very well fail to respond to the threat or the reality of nuclear war as they have in the past to domestic disasters. The Soviet evacuation plans call for millions of urban residents to leave their cities on foot, and to build their own "expedient" shelters, a doubly difficult task, especially in winter.

Relocation plans can be vulnerable to retargeting by the other side, especially with the creation of vast amounts of fallout by aiming large groundbursts upwind of relocation areas. Perhaps most important, and most unknowable, are the long-term effects of nuclear war, which we have reviewed in Chapter 5. It is at least possible, and perhaps likely, that any short-term survivors will emerge into a freezing, darkened, poisoned wasteland, rendering previous efforts at civil defense useless. Civil defense plans, now so disdained, might nonetheless be dearly wished for in the event of an actual nuclear war, especially if such a conflict turns out to be limited, hence at least potentially survivable. Moreover, it is possible that the probability and/or the severity of nuclear winter have been exaggerated. Some devotees of civil defense also maintain that even if nuclear winter is a real possibility, this simply makes civil defense and the stockpiling of food, water, and fuel all the more important.

## IS CIVIL DEFENSE DESIRABLE? YES

There are two primary arguments in favor of civil defense. The first depends on the assertion that it would work; that is, civil defense might save millions of lives in the event of nuclear war. If true, this alone may be a sufficient justification for CD. It would not be necessary for all, or even a significant proportion, of a nation's population to be saved, although presumably, the more the better.

One of the most important responsibilities of government is to provide for the protection of the citizens. It therefore seems reasonable to expect governments to make all possible provision for saving as many lives as possible in the event of nuclear war. It should be noted that according to some estimates, postwar recovery would be facilitated by having fewer survivors, rather than more, because there would be fewer mouths to feed and fewer demands on drastically limited medical, transportation, and other facilities. Other analyses reach the opposite conclusion: since a postwar world, if survivable at all, would be one of much simpler, "labor-intensive" technology, recovery would be most likely if a relatively large work force were available.

CD supporters maintain that with hardening of key industries and the storing of food supplies, the American civilian economy could return to prewar levels within a few years. In some cases, these arguments have been carried to extremes, such as the claim by Deputy Undersecretary of Defense T. K. Jones in 1982 that "Everybody's going to make it if there are enough shovels to go around. . . . Dig a hole, cover it with a couple of doors and then throw three feet of dirt on top. It's the dirt that does it."* Although most civil defense advocates are somewhat less optimistic about the prospects of survival after a nuclear war, they emphasize that in the face of so many uncertainties, it makes sense to plan as though recovery might be possible. If deterrence fails, their argument goes, any survivors will be profoundly grateful for whatever civil defense, advance planning, and stockpiling has occurred. Civil defense, realistically assessed, may thus be seen as a form of insurance or prudent foresight.

The second major argument in favor of civil defense is not concerned directly with its likely effectiveness, but rather, with the possible effect of CD in helping maintain a stable strategic balance; that is, it is argued that CD will help bolster deterrence. Advocates of this approach like to compare the US and Soviet civil defense plans, pointing to what they see as a Soviet advantage and a greater US civilian vulnerability. If one side perceives that it is significantly less vulnerable than the other to nuclear war, such confidence may lead to a weakening of deterrence. This might lead to nuclear war.

Many CD supporters argue that an even more likely result of a US–USSR civil defense imbalance is US susceptibility to nuclear blackmail. If the Soviets come to feel that the USSR is likely to emerge from a nuclear

war with fewer casualties than the United States and a greater probability of rebuilding its society, they might be less deterred than otherwise. They might also be less deterred than the United States would be. Furthermore, CD supporters ask, what if the USSR evacuated its cities, thereby reducing Soviet vulnerability, and the US was unable to respond in kind? The Soviet leadership could then threaten war, with both sides knowing that if it occurred, the US would suffer more grievously than the USSR. As a result, the Soviet Union could make demands without firing a shot, and the United States would have to give in.

Civil defense does not violate any treaties. Rather than promote a false sense of security, it might produce a realistic sense of the dangers of nuclear war by making the issue more real to most citizens. It could also diminish the paralyzing sense of anxiety felt by so many people, freeing their minds to think clear-headedly about nuclear war. The per capita costs of CD would be very low. Switzerland, for example, has been spending about $50 per capita per year on CD; all new Swiss construction, by law, must include blast and fallout shelters. Within a few decades, every Swiss citizen will have designated protection. The USSR spends about $4 per year per capita and the US, perhaps 50 cents.

## IS CIVIL DEFENSE DESIRABLE? NO

Civil defense opponents argue that nuclear war is unlikely to be survivable, and even if it is—for some people in some places—its consequences would be so severe that we are obliged to exert ourselves to prevent it, not to seek to mitigate its effects. According to this viewpoint, civil defense fosters the illusion of survivability. As a result, citizens are likely to be lulled into a sense of false security. In turn, this dulls citizen concern with preventing nuclear war. CD also has the pernicious effect of making nuclear war "thinkable": once we consider possible ways and means of surviving, then subtly, nuclear war becomes more tolerable, hence an acceptable option.

At the level of strategy, CD can also be criticized. A flood is not made more likely by stockpiling sandbags, nor does one hasten one's death by buying life insurance. But unlike other kinds of disaster planning, civil defense may actually make nuclear war more likely. Thus, deterrence rests, however uncomfortably, on mutual vulnerability. Anything that renders either side's population less vulnerable therefore undermines

---

*From R. Scheer. 1982. *With Enough Shovels*. New York: Random House.

deterrence. It is not destabilizing for the Swiss to practice civil defense because they do not control nuclear weapons and can only be victimized by them. It is dangerously deluding, however, for either superpower to think itself safe from the intolerable devastation of nuclear war, or to think that damage to itself might be low enough to make nuclear war a tolerable option. The unavoidable reality is that both sides are profoundly vulnerable and will remain vulnerable as long as nuclear weapons exist. Any significant increase in CD efforts by either side would more likely lead to a further increase in the arsenals of the other. This in turn would simply result in a stalemate at higher levels of destructiveness, even more likely to bring about a nuclear winter.

Opponents of crisis relocation emphasize that for either side to evacuate its cities would be an extraordinarily dangerous and provocative move. This is because evacuation would suggest to the other that the evacuating side is preparing for a first strike. It could produce dangerous crisis instability, since the other side might feel pressured to preempt before the evacuation was completed. Even if successful evacuations saved some lives in the event of war, opponents of these measures believe that this benefit is more than canceled by the possibility that the evacuation itself would lead to war. Hence, it is essential that such destabilizing evacuations not take place. If governments make serious crisis relocation plans, they are more likely to use them someday. Civil defense opponents emphasize that when there is no cure for a disease, all one's attention must be given to prevention. And CD, they charge, is worse than a quack cure: it may even help bring on the disease.

Civil defense is essentially passive. Its goal is to reduce the effects of an attack. By contrast, defensive strategies can also be active, designed to intercept and somehow parry a nuclear attack. In Chapter 6, we examined counterforce, which has occasionally been justified as another form of active defense; namely, damage limitation. In the remainder of this chapter, we turn to the concept of clear-cut defenses: first antiaircraft and early antimissile systems, then a review of one of the most controversial programs of the 1980s, President Reagan's Strategic Defense Initiative (*SDI*), more commonly known as Star Wars. (We shall use both phrases, where possible referring to the former when being supportive of the program and the latter when being critical, since this has become the usual practice during public debate on this issue.)

## ANTIBALLISTIC MISSILES

### A Brief History of ABMs

Both the US and the USSR have consistently sought active defenses against nuclear attack. In fact, the debate over strategic defense in the 1980s repeats many of the issues raised in earlier decades. Accordingly, it is especially important to understand the recent history of active strategic defense.

As we have seen, the United States has a history of strategic bombing, and the USSR of antiaircraft defenses. However, during the 1950s the US also developed and deployed antiaircraft defenses, including interceptor aircraft and notably, a nuclear-armed antiaircraft missile, the Nike-Ajax, under the auspices of the army. Soon it became clear, however, that the Soviet Union was investing much more heavily in ICBMs than in bombers, so the United States began to develop missiles that could shoot down attacking missiles, that is, *antiballistic missiles* or ABM missiles, typically called simply ABMs. Missiles are much more difficult to intercept than are bombers because they are so much faster: Mach 10–15 rather than Mach 1. As a result, missiles would also arrive with significantly less warning time, under 30 minutes rather than 6–8 hours, and less warning yet for SLBMs.

The first ABM system proposed for the United States was the Nike-Zeus, an upgraded version of the old Nike-Ajax. The Nike-Zeus was designed to counter the first generation of Soviet ICBMs in the late 1950s. However, most experts concluded that the Nike-Zeus could not do the job, so a new version, the Nike-X, was proposed in 1963. The Nike-X consisted of a two-tiered system, with long range rockets first intercepting incoming missiles in their stratospheric glide phase, and short-range rockets intercepting any surviving warheads after they had reentered the atmosphere.

However, by this time the pendulum had begun swinging against ABM systems: after flirting with the "no cities" doctrine, as we have seen, the US Department of Defense, following the lead of Robert McNamara, was settling down to the recognition of mutual assured destruction (MAD) as a fact of life. Advances in Soviet rocketry seemed to guarantee that any American ABM system could easily be penetrated by Soviet ICBMs, especially once the latter were fitted with **penetration aids** to confuse radar and/or provide greater shielding to the attackers, thereby assuring that warheads would penetrate defenses. The US also con-

**FIGURE 7.6 Soviet "Galosh" ABM missile in its transporter/launcher canister displayed during the May Day parade in Moscow, 1982. The existence of these missiles, despite their limited capability, was a major stimulus for US development of an ABM system.** (Courtesy of the US Department of Defense.)

cluded that superpower ABM competition would serve as a never-ending spur to the arms race and would be ruinous to both sides. The Nike-X program was accordingly canceled.

But beginning in 1966, the USSR began installing around Moscow an ABM system (known to the West as "Galosh") (Fig. 7.6). Although it was widely conceded that Galosh was of very minimal capability, pressure mounted for the United States to have at least a matching ABM system. In 1967, therefore, Secretary McNamara announced that the two-layered Nike-X system was being resurrected, under a new name, Sentinel.

The distinction between area defense and point defense is important. **Area defense** is the ABM equivalent of countervalue missiles; it is intended to defend relatively large areas, usually containing cities and other regions of civilian value. **Point defense,** by contrast, is the ABM equivalent of counterforce missiles; it is intended to defend much smaller areas (points), generally hardened ICBM silos. Area defenses are much more difficult to achieve, since the region being defended is larger and also, penetration of a city by only a very few attacking warheads would be catastrophic. Area defenses, therefore, must be virtually perfect to be effective, whereas point defenses can be leaky and yet still effective. In addition, as we shall see, area defenses are more likely to undermine stable deterrence.

Point defenses are technically easier to achieve, because they can ignore all warheads except those that are precisely aimed at a given silo. And furthermore, with hardened silos, defenders need worry about only direct hits. Moreover, defense of a fixed silo need not be continued for a prolonged period, just long enough to permit its missile to be fired in retaliation, as

opposed to a city, which presumably must be defended indefinitely. Point defenses are often considered to be strategically stabilizing, since they help maintain a secure second-strike capability. However, they are typically harder to justify politically, since the unpleasant reality is that with a point defense, weapons are defended directly while people are not.

Sentinel, as proposed by McNamara, was to be a "thin" area defense, useless against a determined Soviet attack, but possibly effective against an accidental Soviet assault, or against a small number of Chinese ICBMs, which were then anticipated within 5–10 years. To the surprise of many, the Sentinel decision precipitated a storm of protest, including not only scientists who doubted its effectiveness and warned that Sentinel would be dangerously destabilizing, but also urban residents. The city-defending ABM system required that missile sites be constructed near the cities in question, and many residents objected to having "missiles in their backyard," for fear that it would make them guaranteed targets.

Recently elected President Richard Nixon canceled Sentinel in 1969 and proposed to change it to a point defense system, centered around the newly constructed Minuteman ICBM fields in the more sparsely populated western states. Although this decision made more strategic sense in terms of the classic formulations of deterrence, the controversy was intense. The "great ABM debate" of the late 1960s was resolved in 1969, when Vice President Spiro Agnew broke a 50–50 tie in the Senate, and construction began the following year on the only ABM system the US has ever deployed, known this time as Safeguard.

However, concern remained about whether such a system would work, and also about its effects on strategic stability and on the arms race. These con-

**FIGURE 7.7 Full-scale mockup of a Spartan long-range, interceptor ABM.** (Courtesy of the US Department of Defense.)

**FIGURE 7.8 The "PAVE PAWS" phased array radar site, at Otis Air Force Base, Massachusetts. Devices like this, which are easier to harden than conventional radars, detect objects in space as well as incoming missiles.** (Courtesy of the US Department of Defense.)

cerns led to one of the most important nuclear weapons treaties between the US and the USSR, the ABM Treaty of 1972. Before we discuss this treaty, however, it is appropriate to review the anatomy and vulnerability of ABMs at that time, as well as their strategic significance.

## ABM Anatomy

The two-layered Safeguard ABM system of the late 1960s involved long-range interception by large three-stage missiles known as Spartans (Fig. 7.7), followed by short-range interception of any surviving attackers by very fast, two-stage missiles known as Sprints. This system had been made possible by advances in solid fuel technology, in computer guidance, and in radar. Radar had been—and to some degree, remains—one of the weakest links in the ABM chain, because radar stations with their large, delicate, movable dish-shaped antennae, are very difficult to harden against attack. Modern ABM technology employs phased array radars, which are more accurate and less vulnerable than the old style. The **phased array radars** do not move mechanically; rather, they have fixed faces, employing a large number—an "array"—of subordinate tracking antennae, which electronically compare the time of arrival of radar signals at the various components. Such radars

can be hardened to about 20 psi, compared to only 2 psi for older, mechanical tracking devices (Fig. 7.8).

The long-range Spartan missiles were directed by long-range radars. Known as **perimeter acquisition radars (PARs),** these outward-oriented tracking devices were designed to detect attacking missiles 3,500–4,000 kilometers away, about 10 minutes before intended impact. The Spartan missiles would then be fired, being directed by their PARs to perform **exoatmospheric intercepts,** destroying the attackers with nuclear warheads perhaps 500 kilometers from their targets. The Spartans, with their relatively long-range radars, were backed up by short-range Sprint missiles, suitable for **endoatmospheric intercepts** (see Fig. 7.9). The Sprints were directed by **missile site radars (MSRs),** which were shorter in range but more accurate. Unlike PARs, which are directed only outward, missile site radars scan electronically in all directions. The only completed Safeguard system was built to defend the Minuteman missile base near Grand Forks, North Dakota. It consisted of 30 Spartans and 70 Sprints along with their associated radars, and it cost $5.6 billion.

Although both Spartan and Sprint carried nuclear warheads to destroy their targets, they differed signif-

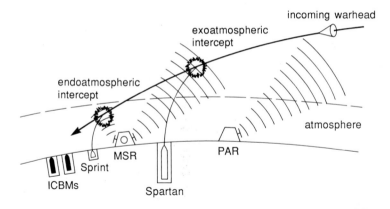

**FIGURE 7.9 Schematic diagram of a two-layered Safeguard ABM system for the protection of ICBMs. Long-range perimeter acquisition radar (PAR) tracks incoming warheads for the long-range Spartan missiles; shorter range missile site radar (MSR) provides information to be used by short-range Sprint missiles.** (Modified from Schroeer, 1984.)

icantly in their intended functioning. For example, since blast effects would be greatly reduced above the atmosphere, in the absence of air to transmit the shock wave, Spartans were armed with large (1-megaton) warheads, which relied on the X-rays and fast neutrons released during a nuclear explosion to destroy the incoming warheads. Enhanced radiation warheads (or "neutron bombs") were therefore designed for these missiles. The lower elevation Sprint missiles, however, were able to create significant blast effects as well.

## ABM Weaknesses

It has been said that the task of an ABM system is to hit a bullet with a bullet. Although this is an exaggeration, when it comes to nuclear weapons it is nonetheless much more difficult to construct an effective defensive system than an offensive one. In addition, ABM systems are vulnerable to a variety of countermeasures. Following is a brief list of some of the strategies that could be used to allow attacking missiles to overcome an ABM defense.

- Build an offensive force large enough to overwhelm the defenders, by increasing the total number of missiles and/or by MIRVing.

- Aim the attacking missiles in a low trajectory. Not only would they arrive at the target sooner, they would also provide less opportunity for detection and response, since a low arc would not be detectable until it was relatively close to the target.

- Set numerous large fires at the time of an attack, to confuse the infrared satellite sensors and make tracking difficult.

- Harden the reentry vehicles by use of paraffin (an efficient neutron absorber) or various shock-absorbing devices.

- Employ maneuverable reentry vehicles (MARVs), which can take unpredictable evasive action. (After ABM radars detect an incoming reentry vehicle, they calculate its course assuming that it will follow an unchanging ballistic trajectory.) Many different reentry vehicles, each maneuvering rapidly and randomly while approaching its target, would be virtually untargetable by the defender.

- Use penetration aids to confuse and/or blind the ABM's radar (Fig. 7.10). Other tactics include the use of wire-metal chaff, either made to resemble individual reentry vehicles or formed into a radar-impermeable cloud to hide the actual warheads. Radar jamming devices could also be included among the incoming warheads. Most effective among these would probably be a small number of very high altitude nuclear explosions, which would produce EMP and also ionize the higher atmosphere, blacking out the defender's radar.

In addition to such potential countermeasures by an attacker, ABM defense poses some enormous problems for itself. Thus, it would require the perfect or near-perfect functioning of millions of different components, all superbly coordinated. Since such an immensely complex operation could never be tested in advance of use, the possessor of an ABM system could never be entirely confident that it would work. Moreover, such an extraordinarily complex operation would have to be carried out in a matter of minutes, under chaotic wartime conditions. Finally, the explosion of even a single nuclear weapon above the atmo-

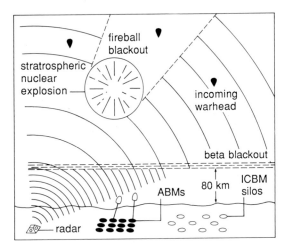

**FIGURE 7.10 Possible ways of interfering with radar tracking of incoming warheads. Exploding a warhead in the stratosphere would produce "beta blackout" via the fission products themselves, as well as "fireball blackout" immediately in the shadow of the explosion.** (Modified from Schroeer, 1984.)

sphere, by either the defender or the attacker, would ionize the atmosphere, possibly blocking radar transmissions, and would in addition produce EMP (see Chapter 4) which might very well render useless all the elaborate electronic machinery needed for ABM functioning. This would wipe out the radar and communication systems, and possibly the guidance mechanisms of the ABM missiles.

It has generally been admitted that offensive nuclear countermeasures are cheaper and more easily designed than defensive techniques. During World War II, for example, the Royal Air Force won the Battle of Britain by shooting down about 10% of the attacking German bombers; thus, although on average 90% of the attacking Luftwaffe got through, Britain not only survived but triumphed. But because of the unique destructive power of nuclear weapons, the demands of a nuclear defensive system are much more severe. For an area defense ABM system to be "successful," nearly all the attacking warheads would have to be destroyed, and even then the defender might lose. For example, imagine an attack involving 5,000 warheads (about half the Soviet strategic arsenal), of which a sharp-shooting defense shot down 95%. This phenomenally successful result means that 250 warheads would

still get through, enough to devastate the victim's homeland. Such considerations, combined with the options open to would-be attackers, led most observers to conclude that active strategic defense was an impossible task.

### ABMs and Strategic Stability

In addition to questioning whether ABMs would work as intended, many scientists and government officials have worried about the effect of ABM systems on strategic stability. Two considerations are at issue here: arms race stability and crisis stability. **Arms race stability** refers to the potential for ending or at least greatly restricting the superpowers' nuclear competition in the arms race. **Crisis stability** refers to the potential for maintaining stability—that is, avoiding war—during any particular crisis. Arms race stability is enhanced when neither side perceives that it could gain an advantage by proceeding with a new round of armaments; crisis stability is enhanced when neither side perceives that it could gain an advantage by striking first in a crisis. ABM critics claim that ABM systems threaten both forms of stability.

It seems likely that as either side proceeded to deploy an ABM system, or even planned to do so, the other would feel a need to counter that system. This could involve additional offensive forces: in fact, as we shall see in Chapter 9, MIRVing was first justified as a response to the USSR's initial ABM deployments. In reaction, the defending side could be expected to increase its ABM plans, leading to yet more offensive plans, and so on. The ABMs on one side would therefore lead to a proliferation of offensive countermeasures (chaff, jamming, decoys, etc.), which would lead in turn to new defensive counter-countermeasures, and so on, with no end in sight.

Crisis instability is perhaps a greater concern than arms race instability. We have seen that even an ABM defense capable of destroying 95% of attacking warheads (a capability that does not exist), would not really "protect" a nation. An ABM system could not realistically defend against a full-scale attack. It could, however—at least in theory—substantially blunt retaliation by a nation that had been massively attacked. Let us assume that a first strike has destroyed at least some of the victim's retaliatory force and that the attacker's ABM system has been somewhat successful in intercepting whatever the victim was able to launch in retaliation. In conjunction with a preemptive first strike, even a partially successful ABM system could—again, in theory—provide the promise of a sufficient shield to tip the scales in favor of a first strike. In short, an ABM system could be destabilizing, especially in a crisis, if either side becomes convinced that war is inevitable anyway.

To see this, imagine a first strike conducted by a nation that has its own ABM system. If the victim begins with 10,000 warheads and 95% are destroyed in the attack, this leaves 500. Let us further assume that the victim retaliates with the 500 warheads and that the attacker's ABM system destroys 95% of these, leaving 25. Admittedly, 25 nuclear weapons exploding on one's homeland would constitute an immense catastrophe, but the damage would have been much worse if the ABM system had not been installed. It is quite likely that the original victim's ABM system would be overloaded by the attack with 10,000 warheads and would almost certainly fail completely. In our hypothetical example, however, the victim was nevertheless able to retaliate, with "only" 500 warheads—a so-called **ragged retaliation.** If the original attacker possesses an intact and moderately effective ABM system, such a scaleddown retaliation from its victim is less likely to be devastating. On balance, then, it is just possible that an ABM system, by promising to "degrade" sufficiently the opponent's retaliation, could make a preemptive strike attractive, while without an ABM system, it would not be.

Let us further assume that even if the US had a moderately reliable ABM system, its leadership would be immune to such a temptation and would never launch a first strike. Although this seems reasonable to most Americans, Soviet leaders may be less confident of US intentions. When it comes to nuclear weapons, often the important thing is not reality itself, but the perceptions of reality held by either side. As a result, critics point out that the possession of an ABM system by the United States might induce the USSR to strike first in crisis situations, out of fear that the US was planning a strike. As we have seen, preemptive strikes of this sort appear to be part of the Soviet conception of nuclear deterrence. And the temptation might be even greater because such a defensive system—although theoretically effective against a ragged retaliation—would almost certainly be ineffective against a determined first strike.

As we have just seen, a fully deployed ABM system could generate crisis instability. Beyond this, the mere threat to deploy an ABM system could be destabilizing enough to produce a crisis because the potential victim might fear that by waiting for the system

to become functional, it would be vulnerable to nuclear blackmail, or worse yet, to a preemptive attack. Under such conditions, initial attempts to deploy an ABM system could lead to a "preventive" first strike by the other side.

On the other hand, it is possible that a point defense ABM system could help stabilize deterrence. This is because if such a system were limited, for example, to the defense of ICBM silos, it could in theory increase the survivability of these ICBMs in the event of a first strike by the other side. Thus, a point defense ABM system could help guarantee a secure second-strike capability. It would not in itself threaten the other side's missiles; and since it did not defend cities, it would not interfere with the other side's ability to retaliate if it was attacked. Supporters have also argued that such a system would complicate the planning of any attacker, since it would introduce substantial uncertainties with respect to whether a first strike would work as planned. However, skeptics have countered that even such a point defense would be unlikely to work, would be terribly expensive and wasteful, would simply encourage the USSR to engage in appropriate countermeasures, and could never reliably be distinguished in an adversary's mind from destabilizing area defenses.

There were, in short, many concerns about the wisdom of ABM systems, about their likely effectiveness, and also about the strategic consequences of deploying them—consequences both for the arms race and for crisis stability. These concerns led ultimately to the ABM treaty of 1972.

## The ABM Treaty

On May 26, 1972, the United States and the Soviet Union signed the Treaty on the Limitation of Anti-Ballistic Missile Systems, generally known as the **ABM treaty.** Quickly ratified by the US Senate, this treaty was an important part of the first round of **Strategic Arms Limitation Talks,** or **SALT I,** which we shall review in greater detail in Chapter 10. As we shall see, the ABM treaty was accompanied by a protocol that somewhat limited the kinds and numbers of offensive nuclear weapons. Unlike the SALT I protocol, however, which had a fixed expiration date, the ABM treaty was intended to be of "unlimited duration," although it was to be reviewed for possible amendment every 5 years. Such reviews occurred in 1977 and 1982, but there were no amendments.

The ABM treaty allowed each side to maintain only two ABM sites each, one associated with its capitol and the other to defend one designated ICBM installation. This was modified by mutual agreement in 1974 during a meeting in Vladivostok between President Gerald Ford and Soviet premier Leonid Brezhnev to include only one fixed, land-based ABM system for each side. The USSR designated its site around Moscow, based on its early Galosh ABM system. By 1986 these 64 missiles were increased to 100. For its part, the US completed construction of the Safeguard ABM site intended as a point defense for the Grand Forks, North Dakota, Minuteman field. However, even this system was perceived to be ineffective and was abandoned in 1975.

In addition to limiting the kind and number of fixed land-based ABM systems available to each side, the ABM treaty prohibits either side from developing, testing, or deploying mobile ABM systems or components that are based on land or sea, in the air or in space. The treaty also forbids the deployment of **exotic ABM systems,** such as particle beam and laser weapons, which are based on physical principles other than interceptor missiles with their associated radar tracking stations. Laboratory research on ABM technologies is permitted under the ABM treaty, however, because it was generally agreed that there was no dependable way to monitor such activities. But field testing of any prototypes (experimental models intended for further development) is prohibited.

It was also agreed that in the case of exotic new technologies, both sides would discuss "specific limitations." This was interpreted by some Star Wars/SDI advocates within the Reagan administration as indicating that the ABM treaty approves and authorizes such technologies. However, the treaty states clearly that the purpose of "specific limitations" on exotic technology is "to ensure fulfillment of the obligations not to deploy ABM systems and their components except as provided in Article 3" (the ground-based ABMs already discussed). The treaty also restricts the location and number of radar installations permitted; as we have seen, such systems are crucial to any successful ABM defense. Like most such agreements, the treaty includes a provision that either side may withdraw with 6 months prior notice "if it decides that extraordinary events related to the subject matter of [the] Treaty have jeopardized its supreme interests."

The ABM treaty was in some ways a watershed of strategic nuclear doctrine in that it formalized a recognition by both sides of the concept of mutually assured destruction. Thus in the ABM treaty, each side pledged, in effect, not to seek active defense of its population.

Previously, the Soviet leadership had argued that defending one's own population was more acceptable than seeking to destroy one's enemy, while the United States leadership had argued for a mutual ban on such defenses. The Soviet Union eventually came around to the US position. In the 1980s, ironically, this situation has been reversed, and the United States has begun to champion the prospect of active missile defense.

## BALLISTIC MISSILE DEFENSE AND STAR WARS/SDI: HOW IT MIGHT WORK

Research on active missile defense continued throughout the 1970s and early 1980s. Initially, there was relatively little public notice, despite annual budgets in the hundreds of millions of dollars. The primary focus of the research changed, however, from ABMs to the more inclusive ballistic missile defense. **Ballistic missile defense (BMD)** includes such traditional ABM concepts as the use of ballistic missiles to intercept attacking missiles, especially at short range, but it embraces other technologies as well. Among the more "conventional" ABM concepts, of special interest is the latest version of Sprint, known as **low-altitude defense systems,** or **LoADS.** The problems of electromagnetic pulse had not been fully appreciated at the inception of ABM programs during the late 1950s and 1960s. As a result, the Nike-Zeuss and Nike-X programs, as well as Sentinel and Safeguard, were designed to use nuclear explosions in defending against incoming missiles. By contrast, the LoADS designs of the 1970s and 1980s generally employ nonnuclear interception, typically with heat sensors, optical sensors, and/or quick-responding radar to direct defending missiles armed with metal shrapnel or the equivalent into a physical collision with attacking warheads.

By the time reentry vehicles have actually reentered the atmosphere, they are at most only a few minutes from their targets. Moreover, because of MIRVing, the number of warheads is likely to be very great. It is therefore generally agreed that LoADS, and indeed, atmospheric interception in general, would not be practical for defense of cities, although it is still being investigated as a final stage in "layered systems" providing possible point defense, notably of MX missile silos. (As we have seen, although the MX was initially proposed as a solution to presumed Minuteman vulnerability, there has been continued anxiety that the MX might itself be vulnerable, and thus, in need of some form of point defense. This may be especially true once the MX is based in fixed Minuteman silos.)

In March 1983, President Reagan announced that he was giving special, urgent priority to an effort to develop active defenses against nuclear missiles, with the goal of eliminating deterrence altogether and making nuclear weapons "impotent and obsolete." There has accordingly been a substantial increase in expenditures for research on missile defense, with the administration requesting $27 billion over a 5-year period. This program is known officially as the **Strategic Defense Initiative (SDI).** It is also known, generally to its detractors, as **Star Wars,** because it depends heavily on the possible use of exotic technology, especially so-called **directed energy weapons** such as particle beams and lasers, to "zap" enemy missiles in flight. In addition, much of the actual weaponry for Star Wars/SDI would be located in, and controlled from, space. To its supporters, SDI offers the possibility of ending the nuclear arms race, or at least of stabilizing deterrence. To its critics, Star Wars is science fiction, and dangerous as well—since it threatens both to accelerate the arms race and to generate crisis instability.

Much of this research effort has been concerned with destroying attacking missiles during their initial lift-off, or boost phase, when the main rocket engines are propelling the missile through the atmosphere. Because the surface of the earth is curved, it is not possible to monitor and attack opposing ICBMs from the other side of the planet. However, with the advent of sophisticated earth satellites, it becomes theoretically feasible to "look down" at missiles as they are being launched.

Boost phase interception is particularly appealing for a number of reasons. First, missiles are easiest to detect at this point, owing to the hot exhaust of the main rockets. Missiles are about 10 meters long, whereas reentry vehicles average about 1 meter; missiles are therefore about 10 times easier to hit. Missiles are also traveling much more slowly when they are just beginning to accelerate. A final advantage to boost phase interception is that by destroying an attacking missile before its many warheads are dispersed during the exoatmospheric glide phase, it would be possible to destroy many MIRVed birds with a single stone. On the other hand, boost phase takes only about 500 seconds (8 minutes or so), of which the missile remains within the atmosphere for about 2 minutes. As a result, there is not much time for a BMD system to work.

Whereas boost phase interception is especially attractive, current Star Wars/SDI plans envision attacking missiles during the postboost and glide phases as

well. These periods last longer than the boost phase, providing more opportunities for attack, although the technical difficulties of postboost and glide phase attack appear to be more formidable because during these midcourse stages the targets are traveling very rapidly, are difficult to track, are smaller—consisting of warheads and buses, rather than whole missiles, and are likely to be accompanied by decoys of many sorts (Fig. 7.11).

Because of considerations of cost and feasibility, it seems likely that any strategic defense in the foreseeable future will emphasize variants in existing "on the shelf" technology: especially LoADS plus the emplacement of miniature rockets on satellites, to be fired directly at attacking ICBMs. On the other hand, critics question whether such systems could be made to react quickly enough to be effective, especially in the face of a massive, coordinated attack. The new-found American enthusiasm for strategic defense derives in particular, however, not from modifications of existing weaponry, but rather, from the possibility of technological innovations. Thus, in addition to the availability of satellites as well as improvements in computer and radar design, perhaps the major technological impetus for Star Wars/SDI is the prospect of using exotic technologies, notably directed energy weapons—particle beams and lasers—rather than ABMs. This approach is appealing because whereas ICBMs travel at 7–10 km/sec, directed energy weapons travel at virtually the speed of light (300,000 km/sec). In theory, this permits a would-be defender to shoot, correct the aim, and shoot again, many times if necessary during just a few seconds.

Star Wars/SDI is not a single program, but rather an effort to explore a variety of possible antimissile weapons and systems. Many different technologies are being investigated.

## Particle Beams

**Particle beams** are streams of atomic or subatomic particles, such as electrons, protons, neutrons, and hydrogen atoms. They are produced by a variety of techniques, of which "particle accelerators" are the best known. These devices are generally very large and require enormous amounts of energy as well. It is estimated that space-based particle beam weapons would have to be about 80 feet long and would weigh 50–100 tons. Particle beams would inject their energy under the target's skin, thus disrupting its inner workings, notably the electronic components. As a result, how-

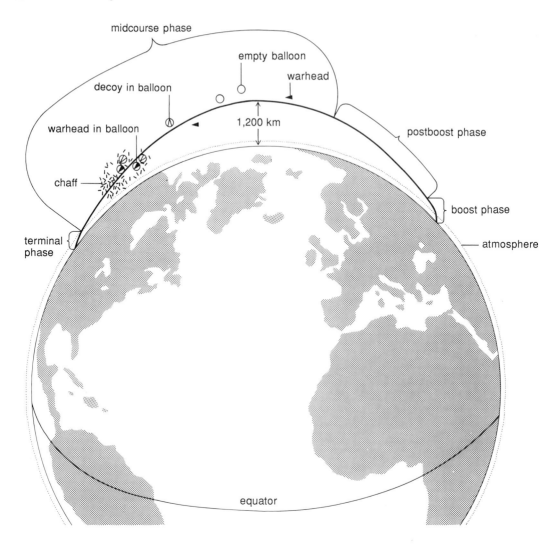

**FIGURE 7.11 Four phases of an ICBM flight: boost, midcourse, postboost, and termi-
nal or reentry. The boost phase carries the missile above the atmosphere; MIRVs are
released during postboost; the midcourse or glide phase is the longest and is followed by a brief terminal phase back through the atmosphere. If the side being
attacked had a Star Wars/SDI system, the attacking bus would be able to produce a
large "threat cloud" by releasing an array of penetration aids including decoy balloons, fake decoys (with warheads inside), and radar-blocking chaff.** (Modified from
Bethe, Garwin, Gottfried, and Kendall, 1984.)

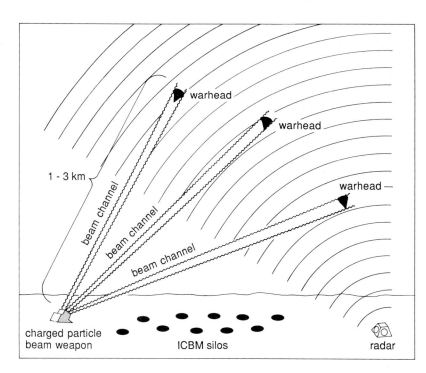

**FIGURE 7.12 Schematization of a land-based charged particle beam system, which might be used for "terminal defense" of ICBM silos.** (Modified from Schroeer, 1984.)

ever, it would be difficult to determine from a distance when a "kill" had been made.

There are basically two kinds of particle beam, charged and neutral. **Charged particle beams,** involving a stream of electrons or protons for example, are not suitable for use in space because the like-charged particles repel each other, resulting in a widely spread, unfocused beam that is too weak to damage its target. Such beams are also subject to unpredictable bending by the earth's magnetic field as well as other physical effects analogous to kinking and coiling. These difficulties appear to make long-range firing of a charged particle beam difficult and—according to some physicists—perhaps impossible.

After repeated firings, however, charged particle beams could theoretically bore low-density channels in the air, which would permit passage of the particles, notably electrons or hydrogen atoms. In addition, a sheath of oppositely charged air particles would be formed, thereby helping to keep the particle beam more narrowly focused than is possible in the vacuum of outer space. Nevertheless, their range is likely to be limited, and it is not known whether such beams could be propagated for the distances needed (at least several kilometers).

**Neutral particle beams** can be produced by adding an extra electron to a hydrogen atom, making it $H^-$. The negatively charged ions are accelerated in a magnetic field and stripped of their extra neutrons as they depart the accelerator. Such neutral beams are less susceptible to bending and other disruption, but they are more difficult to generate and to control. It seems likely that neutral particle beams, if they are ever to be feasible weapons at all, would be stationed in space, mounted on huge satellite battle stations, to be used against warheads during the attacker's exoatmospheric glide phase.

It is thought that whereas neutral particle beams would be based in space, charged particle beams could conceivably be based on the ground. If so, the latter would be part of a "terminal defense" of fixed sites (missile silos, command posts) after the warheads had reentered the atmosphere and were within a few kilometers of their targets (Fig. 7.12).

## Lasers and Other Devices

**Lasers** are currently considered to be the most feasible of directed beam weapons. These extremely intense, narrowly focused beams of light are produced when

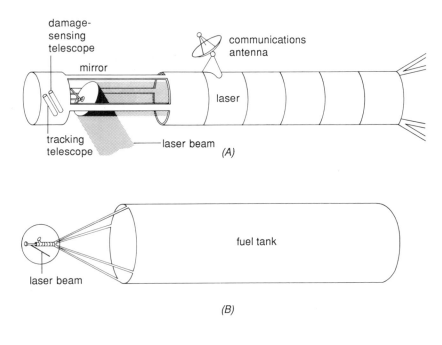

**FIGURE 7.13** In a space-based laser battle station, communications antenna would connect with relay satellites and/or ground-based control stations. (*A*) Optical or infrared telescopes would track the targets, and a hinged mirror—large, optically perfect, resistant to destruction—would direct the laser beam, produced in the laser itself. Another set of telescopes would measure miss distance and/or assess damage. (For simplicity, only one telescope of each kind is shown.) (*B*) These operational components (circled) would be dwarfed by the fuel system. (Modified from Tsipis, 1981.)

many electrons, each of them highly energetic, are induced to give up some of their energy simultaneously and in synchrony, in the form of electromagnetic radiation (in this case, light). Unlike particle beam weapons, lasers deliver their energy to the surface of a target. If focused continuously, they burn through their target; if pulsed, they thump on it like a sledgehammer. There are many ways of generating laser beams.

**Chemical lasers** are the most powerful lasers now available. A variety of laser-generating techniques are being investigated. Perhaps the most promising is the hydrogen fluoride laser, which combines hydrogen and fluorine gases to produce hydrogen fluoride molecules, stimulating the simultaneous emission of highly energetic photons, which are focused by special mirrors. Laser beams could also be produced by the very rapid cooling of hot gases (e.g., carbon dioxide). Such lasers produce infrared energy which, like neutral particle beams, is unlikely to be effective for long-distance use in the lower atmosphere (the troposphere), since the stream of high-energy photons would be absorbed and dispersed by rain, fog, clouds, or smoke. Accordingly, chemical lasers are generally considered to have more potential if generated by orbiting laser battle stations above the atmosphere (Figs. 7.13 and 7.14).

Two other forms of light laser beams are theoretically possible: the so-called **free-electron lasers,** which pass electrons through an array of wiggling magnets, and **excimer lasers,** which use chemically inert gases (argon, neon, etc.). Such lasers would produce short-wavelength, ultraviolet energy that could destroy a target more quickly than the chemical, infrared models. In addition, these emissions could penetrate the atmosphere, although they would be critically dependent on an ability—not yet demonstrated—to bore through clouds, and possibly the smoke and dust of nuclear war. Such a capability, in turn, would call for vast amounts of energy, suggesting that free-electron and excimer lasers, if technically feasible, probably would be ground based. In this mode, their intense energy could be reflected off huge mirrors mounted on satellites and directed toward targets during the boost or glide phase (Fig. 7.15). Because the satellites would be in **geosynchronous orbit**—that is, their orbital velocity would match the rotation of the earth—the ground-based and space-based components of the weapon would always be in phase and ready for use.

Finally, there is growing interest in **X-ray lasers,** which are obtained by surrounding a thermonuclear explosion with rods pointed at a target. The explosion pro-

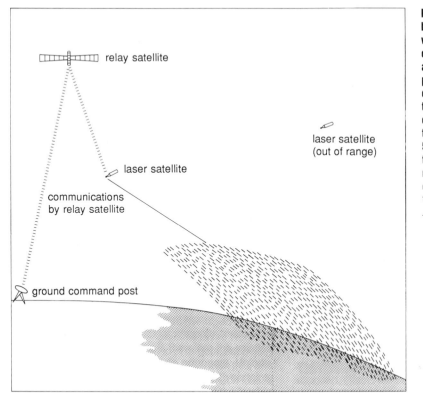

relay satellite

laser satellite
(out of range)

laser satellite

communications
by relay satellite

ground command post

**FIGURE 7.14 A space-based laser probably would orbit at an altitude of about 1,000 kilometers, and since most targets presumably would be out of firing range at any given time, each laser must be capable of dealing with up to 1,000 missiles during 500 seconds or less. In this diagram, we assume a relay satellite, and no countermeasures.** (Modified from Tsipis, 1981.)

duces an intense burst of X-rays directed along the rods, toward the target. These weapons would be one-shot affairs, destroying themselves as they are fired. X-ray lasers could be orbited in satellites, but it seems unlikely that the public would tolerate nuclear-armed satellites regularly circling the earth. Thus the most likely use of X-ray lasers would be as "pop-up" weapons on submarine-based, quick-response missiles following warning of enemy attack (Fig. 7.16). The time constraints for such a system would be very tight, and there is also concern that use of high-altitude nuclear explosions might destroy friendly space-based systems nearby.

Another new technology being investigated involves **rail guns,** which would use electromagnetic energy to fire conventional pellets at extremely high velocity, several times faster than conventional bullets. It has been proposed that these projectiles would be somehow self-aiming, making them "smart rocks." As with beam weapons and orbiting lasers, it seems likely that such weapons would not become functional until the twenty-first century, if then.

The Soviet Union has been pursuing research on its own system of missile defense and is believed to lead the US in certain areas, notably the production of high-energy particle beams. However, it is widely acknowledged that the USSR's program in this respect is significantly more crude than that of the United States and is especially far behind in the all-important technologies of computer hardware and software, as well as sensing mechanisms.

## WILL STAR WARS /SDI WORK?

### Internal Problems

Any scheme for active strategic defense faces technical problems of two kinds. First are the difficulties inherent in the system itself; second are the problems posed by likely countermeasures invoked by an attacker.

Even with new technology, defense against nuclear-armed ballistic missiles is a formidable task; according to many scientists, it may be impossible. Most of the

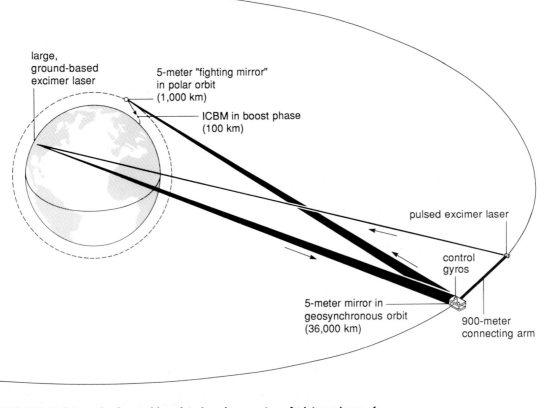

**FIGURE 7.15 Schematic of ground-based excimer laser system. An intense beam of UV light is directed to a 5-meter geosynchronous mirror, which in turn reflects the energy to a low-orbit "fighting mirror," which redirects the energy yet again onto attacking ICBMs. In this representation, the geosynchronous mirror is equipped with a much smaller, pulsed laser, directed at the ground station, which provides infor- mation allowing the ground laser's outgoing beam to compensate instantaneously for atmospheric conditions.** (Modified from Bethe et al., 1984.)

technical obstacles to Star Wars/SDI are the same as those that were judged insurmountable for its prede- cessor, which consisted of the various ABM systems. Here are some of the major problems.

- *An enormous amount of information must be obtained, processed, and acted on in a very brief time.* It is necessary first to identify missiles and/ or reentry vehicles and then to plot their course with great accuracy, that is, to perform **target acquisition.** Then, weapons must be fired and their effect assessed, so that firing is continued if the target is not destroyed, reaimed if the beam missed

altogether, or aimed at the next target until all are accounted for. This whole process is known as **battle management.** Every complex computer pro- gram contains many errors or "bugs," which can be corrected only by repeatedly testing the pro- gram. The target acquisition and battle manage- ment computer programs for Star Wars/SDI would be the most complex ever written, and yet, they could never be tested prior to use. Hence, it is questionable whether they ever could be relied on. During the final minutes of a space shuttle launch, about 88,000 instructions must be trans- mitted; by contrast, in a fraction of this time, about

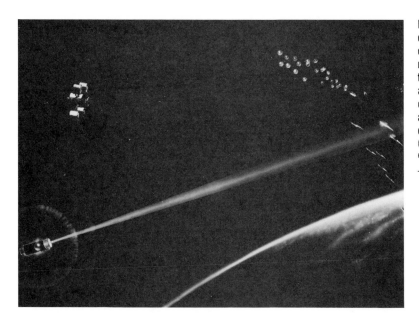

**FIGURE 7.16 Artist's conception of an X-ray laser in operation. The laser receives information from the orbiting satellite shown above it; among the attackers, at least one "bus" has already released a cloud of decoys and warheads.** (Courtesy of the Lawrence Livermore National Laboratory.)

10 million messages would have to be processed, accurately, by a Star Wars/SDI system.

- *As the complexity of a system increases, its reliability and its readiness generally decrease.* For example, F-14 and F-15 interceptors are ready only about 50% of the time. And yet a Star Wars/SDI system would have to be not only tremendously complex, but also absolutely reliable and ever-ready.

- *The sheer magnitude of Star Wars/SDI may render it unfeasible* (Fig. 7.17). Estimates of the number of satellite battle stations required range from a low of about 50 to as many as 2,400, depending on assumptions regarding the feasible range and coverage of each. Because many (in fact, most) of these satellites would have to be assumed to be out of position when an actual attack occurred, every one might have to be equipped to detect, process information about, and shoot down a substantial proportion of an attacking force composed of thousands of missiles, reentry vehicles, decoys, and so on. The physical requirements of command, control, and communications alone may exceed the possibilities for individual satellites. In addition, the fuel requirements—using current technology for hydrogen fluoride lasers, for example—involve millions of tons of fuel in the various

satellites. Ferrying fuel alone would require tens of thousands of space shuttle flights.

- *The technology is mind-bogglingly expensive.* As of the mid-1980s, it costs more money to transport an item into space than to plate it with gold: about $1,500 per pound of payload. Unless this cost can be reduced by an order of magnitude, Star Wars/SDI may be unaffordable, even if it proves to be feasible. A complete system will doubtless cost hundreds of billions of dollars.

- *The technology may be unachievable in the foreseeable future.* It is at least debatable whether lasers and/or particle beams of sufficient power can be built, whether adequate computers can be built, whether sufficient communications between computers and weapons can be achieved, and whether laser or particle beams can be stably and reliably propagated long distances through the atmosphere and/or space, since being subject to "magnetohydrodynamic instabilities," they have disconcerting tendencies to kink and coil like a garden hose, or to pinch together like a string of sausages. Many experts also doubt whether sufficiently large, optically perfect mirrors can be orbited in satellites, deployed on demand, and adjusted accurately and in time to permit the reaiming of lasers at multiple attacking ICBMs. It

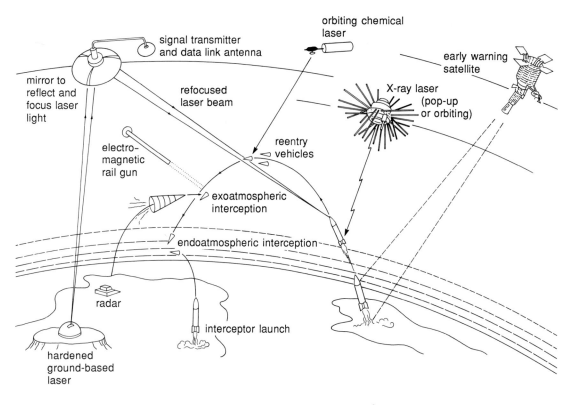

**FIGURE 7.17 Diagram of some of the components of a Star Wars/SDI system; C³I aspects are not shown, nor are various possible countermeasures.** (Modified from SIPRI, 1985.)

is further uncertain whether such a delicate and exquisitely complex system, even if it could be constructed, would be able to operate in a nuclear war environment, with the resulting EMP, dust, smoke, gamma and X-ray radiation, and radar and optical blackout, as well as a wide array of thermal and geomagnetic anomalies, many of which could not be planned for in advance.

- *Everything must work in a very demanding time frame of several minutes.* In most cases, only a few seconds will be allowed for the destruction of each target. Unlike conventional and nuclear explosives, directed energy weapons have no "kill radius." To be effective, they must score direct hits. Taking an average ICBM to be about 10 meters long, and average firing distance of defending weapons about 1,000 kilometers (i.e., a million meters), this means that aiming accuracy must be

within 1 part in 100,000 (10 meters/1 million meters = 1/100,000). Furthermore, the beam must be kept on target in most cases for several seconds. Since some of the proposed weapons (e.g., particle beams) rely on invisible energy, it is unclear what sort of feedback will permit an assessment of the initial firing error so that the beams can be reaimed as needed.

- *Detection of an attacker's warheads would be extremely difficult.* Although missiles are easily spotted during their boost phase, when they are hot and moving relatively slowly, it is very much harder to detect and track many thousands of dark, cold, fast-moving warheads and decoys against the similarly cold and dark background of space.

As we shall now see, many of these difficulties, inherent in missile defense, can be magnified by an adversary's countermeasures.

## The Empire Strikes Back

If either side were to employ a defensive system, it is unlikely that a potential attacker would be any less determined to foil it. This is especially logical because a wide range of countermeasures would be available to the offense. Unlike Star Wars/SDI, these counter-measures are based on proven, reliable technology, as illustrated by the following list.

- Missiles and reentry vehicles can be made to reflect 96% and more of laser light simply by making them shiny. Moreover, by rotating missiles as they are launched, the difficulty of maintaining a directed energy beam on the same spot of a missile's exterior is greatly increased, thereby making it necessary to heat a much larger area if the missile is to be incapacitated.

- Missiles and reentry vehicles can be built of reinforced outer materials or ablative substances that melt and disperse the energy of attacking beams, and/or electromagnetically disrupt incident particle beams.

- Rapidly accelerating "quick-burn" launcher rockets could reduce the duration of the boost phase to as little as 50–100 seconds. This would greatly diminish the time spent in the most vulnerable phase, placing the defense under enormous time pressures for rapid response, and forcing a defender to cope with the more difficult postboost and glide phases. Depressed trajectories could further reduce the time available for the defender.

- Star Wars/SDI would offer no real protection against cruise missiles or other endoatmospheric methods of attack.

- A Star Wars/SDI defense would seem to be vulnerable to the same array of countermeasures that threatened the ABM systems of the 1960s and 1970s: overwhelming the defense with increased numbers of attacking objects, as well as many thousands of decoys including small, metallic Mylar balloons. Real warheads could be placed in such balloons. Radars could be confused by chaff, and other sensors could be readily blinded with high-altitude nuclear explosions and/or jammed with electromagnetic radiation, as discussed earlier.

- Satellite battle stations would seem to be especially vulnerable to direct attack, since their orbits are more predictable and easier to track than the trajectories of ballistic missiles. It should be possible to attack Star Wars/SDI satellites by launching missiles in head-on, counterrotating orbits, by deploying "space mines" that orbit near a satellite and can be designed either to be detonated by remote control or to explode automatically if efforts are made to disarm them. Satellites can even be attacked by other directed energy weapons, based on the ground or on other satellites. As we have seen, the extensive demands placed on satellite battle stations would require enormous complexity and delicacy just to shoot down an ICBM and SLBM attack; it would be a substantial and perhaps intolerable burden for the same satellites also to defend against a dedicated attack directed at themselves as well. Such a defensive capability might require cumbersome shielding and/or maneuverability apparatus, which would interfere with the delicate tasks of target acquisition, battle management, and so on.

To these criticisms, supporters respond that we will find out whether such accomplishments are possible only if we aggressively pursue the necessary research.

## SOME STRATEGIC IMPLICATIONS OF STAR WARS/SDI

As with the debate over ABMs 20 years ago, the advent of Star Wars/SDI has raised concerns about the impact of strategic defense on both arms race stability and crisis stability. Thus, assuming that Star Wars/SDI is technically feasible, would it be desirable? The arguments are very similar to the earlier ABM debate: advocates maintain that defense is preferable to retaliation, while opponents claim that defense will stimulate a potentially unending series of new rounds in the arms race, as well as generating crisis instability. The likely effect of strategic area defense (or civil defense) on deterrence is a cyclical one: with increasing effectiveness of area defense, more offensive weapons will be required by the other side to maintain deterrence. Supporters of strategic defense claim that this policy will discourage the Soviet Union from investing in offensive missiles and will make the USSR more likely to consider reductions. Opponents argue exactly the opposite: that strategic defense will cause the USSR to increase its offensive arsenal.

Advocates of strategic defense favor developing such a system for a variety of reasons. Thus, President Reagan has emphasized that a defense-oriented posture could eventually enable both sides to move away from the horrors of deterrence. According to this view, the Strategic Defense Initiative promises a future free of the fear of nuclear weapons, and possibly, free of the weapons themselves. SDI, it is claimed, would also be more moral than a continued reliance on deterrence, since SDI would rely on the prospect of defending lives rather than avenging them. Indeed, President Reagan even proposed that once it was developed, the United States might someday share such a defensive system with the Soviet Union, in the interests of crisis stability. Secretary of Defense Caspar Weinberger, by contrast, has noted the possible coercive benefits of possessing an impermeable strategic shield, as well as the possible dangers if the Soviet Union outmatches the US in SDI competition. Both these approaches presuppose an eventual system of area defense, protecting the entire United States.

Even among the scientists who support Star Wars/SDI, it is generally conceded that effective area defenses are unlikely in the foreseeable future and perhaps are impossible. They emphasize the prospect of developing point defenses, which would presumably enhance deterrence rather than supersede it. Nuclear strategist and Reagan adviser Paul Nitze has argued that eventually, when point defenses have been perfected, area defenses might be phased in—carefully and gradually, to avoid upsetting strategic stability in the process. The result would be movement toward a defense-dominated future. In any event, limited testing of orbiting laser battle stations could begin in the early to mid-1990s.

Opponents point out that both superpowers have great difficulty in negotiating even straightforward arms control, never mind reductions. They could hardly be expected to share highly sensitive technology or to arrange delicate and potentially dangerous switching among systems, which would be much more difficult to achieve. They also argue that Star Wars is fatally flawed, not only because of insurmountable technical obstacles but because it is much easier to overcome such a system than to construct one, just as critics argued earlier about ABM defenses. It is also pointed out that the Soviet Union is most unlikely to agree to reduce its stock of offensive weapons if the US is threatening to render even the existing Soviet arsenal ineffective. Critics therefore claim that rather than ending the arms race, Star Wars will intensify it. A report

by the nonpartisan Office of Technology Assessment also pointed out that in a world of imperfect US–Soviet strategic defenses, US retaliatory forces would probably be less effective than they are today. This is because even though presumed US defenses might intercept a proportion of Soviet attacking warheads, presumed Soviet defenses would also blunt any US retaliation. This could make deterrence more unstable. In addition, Star Wars critics point out that an unreliable defensive system would do better at defending hard point (military) targets than cities, since the latter are easier game; therefore, Star Wars would increase the incentive for the Soviets to aim at American cities, which they could be more confident of hitting.

American allies have given the Star Wars/SDI concept a mixed reception. There is interest in participating in research and development efforts, but hesitation with respect to the strategic wisdom of deploying such a system, if it can be developed. Supporters claim that with a defensive system in place, the US would be more willing to come to the aid of its European allies, since SDI would overcome the credibility problem of whether the US would risk New York to save Hamburg. Hence, "coupling" of the defense of Europe to that of the US would be strengthened. But opponents point out that a vigorous effort by the US would almost certainly stimulate a comparable effort by the USSR, which would result in deployed systems that although useless against either superpower's large arsenals, would be potentially effective against the much smaller forces of France or Britain, thereby weakening the effectiveness of these deterrents. In addition, fear has been expressed that if both the US and the USSR could hide behind their respective defensive shields, both would be freer to engage in "theater nuclear wars" in other regions, such as Europe. It would be even more difficult to extend active strategic defense to Europe than to North America, because Europe is so much closer to launch sites in the USSR; nonetheless, Reagan administration spokespeople claim that ultimately such protection would be attempted. Some Europeans, notably the French, have begun efforts to research independent Star Wars/SDI counterparts.

## ANTISATELLITE WEAPONS

### History and Hardware

Antisatellite (ASAT) warfare is conceptually distinct from ballistic missile defense in that ASAT warfare involves the destruction of the adversary's satellites rather than its nuclear missiles. However, there are numerous similarities. Satellites are relatively small, and they travel rapidly. As a result, some of the technology developed for attacking satellites can be transferred for use in attacking warheads, and vice versa. Most important, both ASAT and Star Wars/SDI involve the military use of space.

As of 1985, there were no treaty restrictions prohibiting ASAT activities that do not involve the explosion of nuclear weapons in space or the placing of nuclear weapons in earth orbit. During the 1960s, both sides

deployed primitive ASAT systems using nuclear warheads; the US version was mounted atop an Atlas rocket. The United States then dismantled its ASAT capability and argued that the national security of both superpowers would be best served by mutual restraint in ASAT weapons. Nonetheless, the USSR persevered in developing an ASAT of its own, first testing a limited, nonnuclear system in 1967. The Soviet ASAT involves a conventional explosive mounted atop a modified SS-9 ICBM. In a maneuver known as **co-orbital interception,** the missile launches its satellite based on programmed calculations that enable it to track the target for one or two orbits. At the appropriate orbital position (boxed area, Fig. 7.18A), the nose cone is directed by radar to within attacking range of the enemy satellite, whereupon it explodes, destroying or disabling the target by shrapnel (Fig. 7.18B). The Soviet ASAT is still designed to operate in this manner; it has failed about one half of its field tests.

Later, during the Carter administration, the United States adopted a two-track approach: (1) develop a new ASAT while (2) trying to reach a negotiated agreement with the USSR, either restraining the development of such weapons or banning them altogether. In 1983 the USSR announced a moratorium on tests of its own ASAT and presented to the United Nations a draft treaty banning space weapons. The Reagan administration, however, has insisted that compliance with such a ban could not be verified reliably and has proceeded with ASAT development and testing. (Congress, meanwhile, has sought to impose restrictions.)

*(A)*

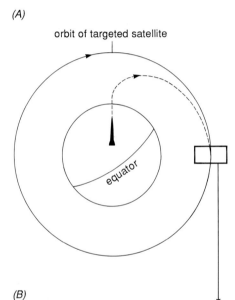

orbit of targeted satellite

equator

*(B)*

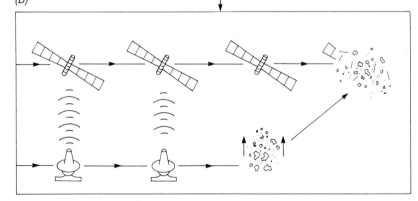

**FIGURE 7.18 The Soviet ASAT system uses co-orbital interception (A). (B) After homing in on its target via radar, the attacking satellite (bottom) self-destructs, taking the target with it.**

**FIGURE 7.19 An F-15 interceptor carrying an ASAT missile under the fuselage.** (Courtesy of the US Department of Defense.)

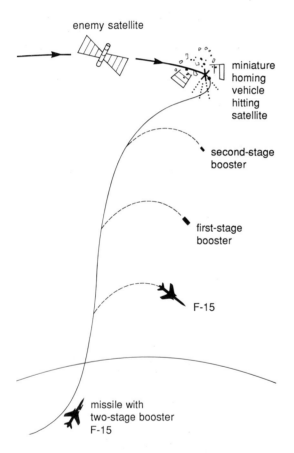

enemy satellite

miniature homing vehicle hitting satellite

second-stage booster

first-stage booster

F-15

missile with two-stage booster F-15

**FIGURE 7.20 In the United States ASAT system, an F-15 carries the missile to about 40,000 feet, after which the two booster stages power it higher yet. Finally, the miniature homing vehicle is guided by infrared sensors to collide directly with the target satellite.**

The American ASAT is quite different from its Soviet counterpart. It involves a small two-stage rocket that is carried by a high-altitude F-15 jet (Fig. 7.19). Final interception is accomplished by a miniature homing vehicle that uses infrared sensing telescopes to detect its target, then maneuvers to collide with it at very high speeds (Fig. 7.20).

## The ASAT Balance

Military satellites are used by both sides for many purposes. These include, most notably: photoreconnaissance (spying and treaty verification), early warning of missile attack, and long-distance communications. Photoreconnaissance is achieved largely by satellites in low earth orbit, up to about 1,000 miles. The most crucial functions (early warning and long-distance communications) are performed by US satellites circling the earth in geosynchronous orbit at about 42,000 kilometers above the equator. By contrast, the most important Soviet early warning and communications satellites are in highly elliptical "Molniya" orbits, approaching geosynchrony high over the North Polar regions and swooping as close as several hundred miles from Earth near the South Pole (Fig. 7.21).

The USSR launches a larger number of satellites than does the US. However, this does not prove that the Soviet Union's space program is more advanced; rather, Soviet satellites tend to fall out of orbit and/or to cease functioning more rapidly than do their US counterparts. In addition, the Soviet satellites lack the versatility of US satellites, most of which are multipurpose. The United States—a maritime power with far-flung security interests and military forces—relies on satellites to carry about 70% of all long-haul communications. By contrast, the Soviet Union—a continental power whose forces are concentrated in the Eurasian landmass—relies less heavily on satellites and makes more use of ground communications.

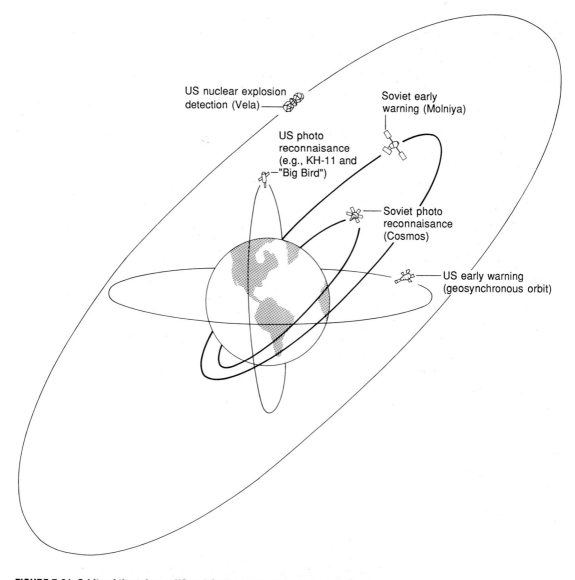

**FIGURE 7.21  Orbits of the primary US and Soviet military satellites. Photoreconnaissance satellites tend to be in roughly circular, low orbits (between about 150 and 2000 km); those in geosynchronous orbits remain in fixed positions above the equator, at about 36,000 kilometers; Soviet "Molniya" are highly elliptical, from several hundred kilometers at the South Pole to 40,000 kilometers at the North Pole.**

It would be especially provocative if either side were to attack the communication and early warning satellites of the other, since these are an integral part of each nation's $C^3I$ apparatus, vital to any retaliatory action that might be called for. As of the mid-1980s, the USSR is considered to have an operational ASAT system in place, whereas the United States does not. However, the Soviet ASAT, with its large rockets and fixed launch sites, is acknowledged to be cumbersome, unreliable, very difficult to aim, and slow to react. The American ASAT system, which is judged to be superior, is technologically sophisticated, small, and maneuverable. But it is not yet deployed. If no ASAT treaty is reached, initial deployment of the American ASAT is scheduled to begin around 1988–1989. Nei-

ther nation has the ASAT capability to threaten the other's satellites higher than about 2,600 kilometers, although the low-altitude phase of Soviet orbits makes them somewhat more vulnerable.

It seems likely that in a technological duel between satellites and ASATs, the latter will win. It is also worth noting that ASAT research and development can serve as a cover for ABM research and development, which is prohibited under the ABM treaty. Also, further elaboration of Star Wars/SDI might well lead to reduced interest in an ASAT treaty, since ASAT weapons might eventually seem attractive for use against the orbiting battle stations envisioned in the various schemes for ballistic missile defense.

## Policy Issues

### Should the US devote more effort to civil defense?

**Yes:** Civil defense is relatively inexpensive and could possibly save many lives. Unlike Star Wars/SDI, for example, civil defense relies on proven technology. It is also relatively nonprovocative. And finally, a more vigorous US civil defense program is necessary to offset the Soviet Union's activities in this regard.

**No:** Civil defense is a waste of time and money, likely to produce a false sense of security and the illusion that nuclear war might be survivable. This, in turn, could make leaders consider that nuclear war itself is a viable policy option. Soviet civil defense efforts have been greatly exaggerated by American advocates of civil defense.

### Should the US actively pursue Star Wars/SDI?

**Yes:** There have always been nay-sayers. It was claimed, for example, that steam power would never replace sails, that nuclear energy could never be tapped, that we would never place a man on the moon. We shall never know whether the SDI is feasible unless we explore its possibilities. It may well offer real hope for a nonnuclear world, because after nuclear missiles have been rendered obsolete, they can be dismantled without endangering the nation that did so. In the meantime, the US has a substantial

lead in the kind of high technology employed in the SDI; we would be foolish to inhibit ourselves from competing in just that area in which we are most ahead. Far from being destabilizing, SDI is only a research program at present, and moreover, the USSR has been actively researching missile defense systems for years.

If the SDI leads to a new form of arms race, better a defensive one than an offensive one, and if worse comes to worst, better a war in space than on earth. And it should not be forgotten that if it is successful, the SDI holds out the possibility of ending the arms race altogether. A credible SDI could even make nuclear disarmament possible, since it wouldn't matter if an opponent cheated and kept a small number of nuclear weapons (a few bombs or warheads wouldn't be decisive for a nation that is defended). By contrast, without such a system, neither side is likely to be persuaded to give up its nuclear weapons, ever. Finally, isn't it inconsistent to claim that SDI couldn't work, and then to warn that it might precipitate war because the Soviets would take it seriously? Given the Soviets' clear concern about our SDI, however, perhaps we could exact concessions from them by way of reductions in their heavy ICBMs. General Secretary Mikhail Gorbachev has already indicated that this might be the case.

**No:** Star Wars is pie in the sky, a pipe dream by people who are naive about the limits of technology, who dream unrealistically about a technological fix. Support of SDI has become a litmus test for ideological support of President Reagan rather than a reflection of considered technical and political judgment. It is also, not surprisingly, supported by scientists who stand to make a lot of money researching systems that current knowledge strongly suggests will not work. Most independent scientists oppose it. Most programs begin as research, then develop a momentum of their own as contractors become dependent on the income received; once funded, such programs become difficult to stop, regardless of their merits. Furthermore, Star Wars is more than research; it has been heralded as a messianic national commitment.

The Manhattan Project and the space program are not analogous to the proposed Star Wars research effort: the former had to cope only with nature, not with human countermeasures as well. Despite the virtual certainty that Star Wars would not work, the Soviets will be forced to take it seriously, to devise countermeasures, and above all, to refuse to reduce their offensive arsenal. Rather than ending the offensive arms race, Star Wars would stimulate it to new levels. Because we could never be confident that Star Wars would work, we would be almost forced to complement it with augmented offensive arsenals. Star Wars would be ineffective as defense against a determined first strike but possibly useful in defending against a ragged retaliatory attack. It therefore looks suspiciously like part of a first-strike strategy by the US, hence is dangerously destabilizing. There is nothing inconsistent about worrying that a weapon might have dangerous effects even though it couldn't actually work: for example, try pointing a realistic-looking toy gun at a policeman! A first strike would constitute a "rational" option if and only if the other side deployed a moderately successful Star Wars system. Rather than substituting for or preventing war on earth, Star Wars would make war more likely, with war in space as a prelude.

### Should the United States abrogate the ABM treaty?

**Yes:**   The security interests of the United States are not served by agreements that restrict our ability to defend ourselves. This is especially true when the USSR fails to abide by this treaty, as for example, by constructing a large phased array radar at Krasnoyarsk, Siberia. The ABM treaty specifically prohibited such radars, which can be used as part of an ABM system. The ABM treaty has been a failure; it did not lead to constraints in the offensive arms race, despite its supporters' predictions. Thus, although the United States had given up strategic defense and left its cities vulnerable to nuclear attack by the USSR, the Soviets did not settle for "minimal deterrence." Rather, they embarked on a massive buildup during the 1970s. In any event, the Strategic Defense Initiative will ultimately require us to abrogate the ABM treaty, or at least modify it significantly. When such an agreement gets in the way of national security, we have a right—even a duty—to act independently of it. We should do whatever is best to defend our nation, going so far as to abrogate treaties if necessary, especially when we are the only party adhering to such agreements.

**No:**   The ABM treaty is one of the most effective arms limitations yet negotiated. It has saved both sides billions in wasted money and has prevented destabilizing developments. It is the most dramatic example of potentially dangerous new technologies being effectively short-circuited by mutual agreement. Hence, it is very valuable, both substantively and symbolically. The Krasnoyarsk radar is not necessarily a treaty violation: the USSR claims that the contested radar is for tracking satellites. The treaty forbids phased array radars except those at each nation's periphery and oriented outward; that is, early warning and satellite tracking systems are permitted. The Soviets claim, in turn, that our new, large "PAVE PAWS" phased array radars are also in violation of the treaty. There is a mechanism available for resolving such disputes, the Standing Consultative Commission (see Chapter 10). Instead of seeking to score propaganda points and using alleged violations as excuses for throwing out a very precious agreement, we should investigate the disputed situations, and then seek to clarify and strengthen the treaty, to the benefit of both sides.

### Should the United States seek a treaty that prohibits ASATs?

**No:**   The USSR has already tested and deployed a workable system. We must not stop now, while they are ahead. Besides, an ASAT ban could not be verified. The nation that controls space will also control the earth; this is an area in which superior technology can serve the US well. Space is the new, high frontier for human exploration and like it or not, for superpower competition as well. Given our substantial reliance on satellites, we must at minimum retain the ability to threaten Soviet satellites so as to deter the USSR from attacking ours.

**Yes:** The Soviet system is far less capable than ours. We have more valuable space assets than they, and so, we would lose more than the Soviets if satel-lites become vulnerable, as will doubtless happen if ASAT competition is unrestrained. Effective ASAT weaponry on both sides would add a new dimension of hair-trigger instability; it also would make breakout from the ABM treaty more likely. Compliance with an ASAT ban could be monitored by restricting field tests, which are easily verified.

## KEY TERMS

blast shelters

fallout shelters

protection factor

crisis relocation

Federal Emergency Management Agency (FEMA)

survivalists

penetration aids

area defense

point defense

phased array radars

perimeter acquisition radars (PARs)

exoatmospheric intercepts

endoatmospheric intercepts

missile site radars (MSRs)

arms race stability

crisis stability

ragged retaliation

ABM treaty (1972)

Strategic Arms Limitation Talks (SALT I)

exotic ABM systems

ballistic missile defense (BMD)

low-altitude defense system (LoADS)

Strategic Defense Initiative (SDI)

Star Wars

directed energy weapons

particle beams

charged particle beams

neutral particle beams

lasers

chemical lasers

free-electron lasers

excimer lasers

geosynchronous orbit

X-ray lasers

rail guns

target acquisition

battle management

co-orbital interception

## STUDY QUESTIONS

1. Distinguish between blast shelters and fallout shelters.

2. What is crisis relocation? In what way can crisis relocation be seen as stabilizing? Destabilizing?

3. Distinguish between area defense and point defense. Why are they often considered to be de-stabilizing and stabilizing, respectively?

4. Compare the likely vulnerability of the US and the USSR to the effects of nuclear war.

5. Why did the two superpowers agree to the ABM treaty?

6. Describe some of the technical problems inherent in active strategic defense. Describe some advances that make strategic defense more attractive than it was when the ABM treaty was negotiated.

7. In what ways is the current debate over Star Wars similar to the earlier one over ABMs? In what ways is it different?

8. Distinguish between lasers and particle beam weapons.

9. Describe the various arguments by which strategic defense is considered to be (a) a way of eliminating deterrence, (b) a way of coercing the USSR, (c) a way of avoiding being coerced by the USSR, and (d) a way of strengthening deterrence.

10. Describe the various arguments by which strategic defense is considered likely to contribute to arms race instability; to crisis instability.

11. Draw up a balance sheet showing US and Soviet advantages in ASAT competition.

12. What are some similarities between ASAT weaponry and Star Wars/SDI? Some differences?

## ADDITIONAL READINGS

Chayes, Abraham, and Jerome Wiesner (Eds.). 1969. *ABM: An Evaluation of the Decision to Deploy an Antiballistic Missile System*. New York: Harper &

Row. A collection of articles describing the technical and political issues raised in the ABM debate of the 1960s.

Goure, Leon. 1976. *War and Survival in Soviet Strategy*. Coral Gables, FL: Center for Advanced International Studies. An expert on Soviet civil defense argues that the USSR has a substantial civil defense capability and that we should respond with one of our own.

Jastrow, Robert. 1985. *How to Make Nuclear Weapons Obsolete*. Boston: Little, Brown. A noted astrophysicist makes the case for Star Wars/SDI.

Kearny, Cresson H. 1980. *Nuclear War Survival Skills*. Coos Bay, OR: NWS Research Bureau. A nuclear war survival manual.

Leaning, Jennifer, and Langley Keyes (Eds.). 1984. *The Counterfeit Ark*. Cambridge, MA: Ballinger. A series of articles severely criticizing crisis relocation and other civil defense plans.

Tirman, John (Ed.). 1984. *The Fallacy of Star Wars*. New York: Vintage Books. Articles opposing the technology, politics, and strategic implications of Star Wars, primarily by a group of renowned physicists associated with the Union of Concerned Scientists.

# 8 How Deterrence Could Fail

*Every man, woman, and child lives under a nuclear sword of Damocles,*
*hanging by the slenderest of threads, capable of being cut at any moment by*
*accident, miscalculation, or madness.*
John F. Kennedy

The thread has held since August 9, 1945, when Nagasaki experienced the second—so far—nuclear explosion in wartime. In this chapter, we conclude our examination of strategic doctrine by briefly considering some ways in which that doctrine might fail, and the "nuclear sword of Damocles" might fall. It should be emphasized that since a nuclear war has not occurred, all the scenarios described below are hypothetical. Moreover, there is no way of knowing precisely what course any of them might take, hence whether prompt conclusion of hostilities or escalation to worldwide holocaust would result.

## A BOLT OUT OF THE BLUE

The most frequent lay perception of nuclear war is an all-out surprise attack, launched massively against all targets on the other side—both civilian and military—and without any apparent provocation. Such a **bolt out of the blue** (or **"boob"**) **attack** is, however, generally regarded as the least likely of all. It would fly in the face of rationality, since it would doubtless result in destruction of attacker and victim alike.

A counterforce "boob" attack is also acknowledged to be extremely unlikely, although perhaps somewhat less unlikely than a countervalue scenario. This is because a counterforce attack presumably would reduce somewhat the victim's ability to retaliate. Nonetheless, even assuming for the sake of argument that either side had motivation for such an attack, deterrence appears to be robust enough to prevent such an option from becoming attractive. Opponents of counterforce weaponry emphasize the dangers of modernizing the arsenals of each side with weapons

that have the combination of accuracy and yield that might eventually tempt either side to try a surprise first strike. Supporters of counterforce weaponry emphasize that by targeting the weapons of the other side, we protect ourselves against nuclear blackmail, while also enhancing the credibility of our response, which in turn might strengthen deterrence.

## CRISIS CONDITIONS

Behavior that would be very unlikely in times of tranquility may occur in periods of crisis. Even though a rational analysis suggests that both sides would be losers in any nuclear exchange, either side nonetheless might become convinced that war is inevitable, perhaps because of ideological bias, false information, or conviction that the opponent is irrational. Alternatively, under some conditions, war may in fact be on the agenda of the other side, in which case striking first may seem less unattractive than waiting and being struck preemptively. The goal of deterrence is to ensure that getting in the first blow confers no advantage. However, once either side expects the other to strike first, there may be a relative advantage in preempting, even though in absolute terms, both sides would be better off if neither attacked at all.

Under conditions of crisis, each side may be expecting the other to do things that normally would not be anticipated, and each side might therefore be provoked by acts that otherwise would not be interpreted as provocative. For example, the president leaving the White House for a weekend is not in itself a cause for alarm. However, imagine that an American aircraft carrier is destroyed by an accidentally fired

**FIGURE 8.1 First test of the US–USSR Hot Line, in 1961; William Foster, first director of the Arms Control and Disarmament Agency (elbow toward camera) looks on.** (Courtesy of the US Arms Control and Disarmament Agency.)

Soviet missile, and the president immediately departs Washington, DC. This movement could signal to nervous Kremlin officials that the United States was planning a nuclear retaliation, perhaps precipitating a preemptive attack. This admittedly hypothetical example illustrates how in times of crisis, seemingly innocent actions may be interpreted according to worst-case scenarios.

In recognition of this potential for overreaction, the **Hot Line** communications system was established to connect American and Soviet leaders by teletype. Begun soon after the Cuban missile crisis in 1962, the Hot Line was improved in 1971, and again in 1980, with the addition of satellite links providing nearly instantaneous communication. Suggestions have been made to upgrade the Hot Line (Fig. 8.1) and also to establish a "crisis control center," manned at all times by high-level US and Soviet military and diplomatic personnel, to permit rapid communication and clarification of possible misunderstandings.

In some cases, the actions of parties to international disputes have had unintended and tragic consequences. An accelerating spiral of actions and reactions, lubricated by growing mutual distrust, occurred immediately before World War I, a war that most historians agree was not really desired by the major belligerents. Thus, when the Archduke Ferdinand of Austria was killed by a Serbian, Austria mobilized its military

forces, to make known its degree of irritation, and hoping by this show of resolve to keep Russia (tiny Serbia's ally) out of any conflict. But Russia mobilized in turn, worried that Austria might have designs on Russia as well. Germany then mobilized to show support for Austria; France mobilized in case the German armies went west instead of east, and Britain mobilized to show support for France. Although World War I appears to have been an outcome that no one wanted, strictly speaking, it was not the result of an accident, or even a series of accidents: rather, everything functioned as it had been planned when the European alliances were first established. The tragedy of World War I—and perhaps the lesson for the Nuclear Age—is that a cascade of events produced a very undesirable yet ultimately irresistible sequence, with enormous momentum and a feeling of intense time pressure.

Just as doves point to World War I as a warning for the Nuclear Age, hawks point to World War II. Events preceding Hitler's invasion of Poland in 1939 suggested once again that questionable judgments and misreadings of events were involved: Hitler's appetite had been whetted by his ability to build up military forces in violation of the Treaty of Versailles, which ended World War I, by his success in militarizing the Rhineland without British or French opposition, and by the seeming willingness of the great democracies to condone his aggressive designs against Czechoslovakia.

Although World War II did not involve the fast-moving crisis miscalculations of World War I, it did result in part from insufficient resolve under conditions of great stress, which led Adolf Hitler to overestimate his power and to underestimate the Allies' willingness to fight. It is widely believed that Hitler did not expect his invasion of Poland in 1939 to result in a declaration of war by Britain.

In the 1980s, communications are much better, but it is not clear that errors and misperceptions are any less likely. Moreover, both the US and the USSR are in effect already "mobilized" in that a nuclear response could take place in a matter of minutes. There is therefore a danger of **interacting alerts,** in which each side goes on alert and interprets the other's defensive alert procedures as threatening. Once either side becomes convinced that the other is about to attack, pressures will develop for mounting a preemptive attack to limit the damage and gain whatever advantage may accrue to striking first. Then nation A, fearing that nation B is about to attack, plans to preempt, whereupon nation B, fearing that A is about to preempt, plans to preempt that preemption, whereupon nation A. . . .

## ESCALATED CONVENTIONAL WAR

According to the United Nations, approximately 20 million people have died in wars since World War II, about half as many as died during that war. Thus, although there has never been a nuclear war, the world has not exactly been at peace. According to one report, the United States employed a military "show of force" 215 times between 1945 and 1977, nearly seven times per year. It appears that analogous figures for the USSR are somewhat lower, since that country has fewer widespread economic, military, and political commitments. Its coercive military presence in Eastern Europe, however, can be seen as an ongoing military show of force.

Both the US and the USSR have been engaged in conventional warfare since 1945, although not against each other. Nuclear weapons were not used by the United States in Korea, where the US eventually settled for a stalemate; nor were they used in Vietnam, where the US was defeated. Similarly, the USSR did not use nuclear weapons in Hungary (1956) or Czechoslovakia (1968), and has not done so in Poland (1981) or Afghanistan (1979–present). Examples of Soviet threats to employ nuclear weapons have not been clearly documented, although there are claims to this effect for the Suez war in 1956. Shortly after the launching of Sputnik in 1957, Soviet Premier Khrushchev threat-ened to use nuclear missiles against Turkey (scheduled to become the basing site for US medium-range nuclear missiles). Most dramatically, there was the mutual threat to use nuclear weapons during the Cuban missile crisis of 1962, as well as implied nuclear threats by both the US and the USSR during the 1973 Yom Kippur war in the Mideast. There have been many cases in which the United States seriously considered or at least threatened the intentional use of nuclear weapons. Some examples:

- President Truman is said to have threatened use of nuclear weapons unless Stalin withdrew his troops from Iran following World War II; the troops were withdrawn.

- Nuclear weapons were offered to the French in 1954, for defending Dien Bien Phu, and possibly, attacking China.

- In the defense of the islands of Quemoy and Matsu, held by Taiwan and being bombarded by China in 1958.

- Against the Pathet Lao in Laos, in 1961.

- During the Berlin crisis of 1961.

- During the siege of Khe Sanh, in Vietnam, in 1968.

- Following the Soviet invasion of Afghanistan in 1979, President Carter made it clear that any perceived threat to the Persian Gulf region by the USSR could bring about nuclear war.

It is unclear whether use of nuclear weapons by either superpower against a nonnuclear weapons state would result in a superpower confrontation, although clearly, it would cause enormous destruction and would heighten tensions extraordinarily. In fact, US and Soviet armed forces have not fought each other in many decades. And for whatever reason, the "firebreak" between conventional and nuclear war has held thus far. China did not use its nuclear weapons during a brief conventional border war with India, which at that time lacked such weapons. Britain did not employ nuclear weapons against Argentina during the Falklands war of 1982. But on the other hand, the knowledge that Britain possessed nuclear weapons did not deter Argentina from initiating that war. It is always possible that a conventional conflict between US and Soviet armed forces would escalate rapidly to the use of nuclear weapons, especially since the side that was losing would be under strong pressure to use its nuclear weapons to redress any battlefield disadvantages. It is also conceivable

**FIGURE 8.2 Meeting of the Executive Committee during the Cuban missile crisis, October 1962. President Kennedy is flanked by Secretary of State Dean Rusk and Secretary of Defense Robert McNamara. Attorney General Robert Kennedy is across the table.** (Courtesy of the John F. Kennedy Library.)

that the threat of such an occurrence has inhibited direct confrontations of this sort in the first place.

The possibility always exists that either superpower would be tempted to use nuclear weapons if it were fighting a conventional war and losing, regardless of whether the opponent possessed nuclear arms. (This is explicit NATO doctrine for the defense of Europe.) In addition, as we have seen, a crisis atmosphere may color events in ways that maximize their threatening aspects.

Escalation of conventional conflicts to possible nuclear war can resemble the game of Chicken, which we have already reviewed. Perhaps the most dramatic example of nuclear Chicken occurred in October 1962, when the US discovered that the USSR had been seeking to deploy medium-range, land-based missiles in Cuba. The US demanded that the weapons be withdrawn and initiated a naval and air "quarantine," which amounted to a blockade. Soviet ships bearing offensive military equipment eventually turned back, avoiding a confrontation on the high seas, and Premier Khrushchev agreed to dismantle the Cuban installations. During the very tense period that preceded this dénouement, President Kennedy and his advisers (Fig. 8.2) had been examining the following options, some of them in combination.

- A preemptive strike (either nuclear or conventional) against the missile sites in Cuba

- An invasion of Cuba

- Preemptive strikes against Soviet nuclear weapons in the USSR

- A massive, preemptive strike against the USSR

Although the last two possible courses of action do not appear to have been very seriously planned for,

they were favored by certain high-ranking officials, both military and civilian. It was also conceded that either of the first two options would probably precipitate a Soviet counterstrike against US medium-range missiles then stationed in Turkey. President Kennedy estimated that at the time, the chances of nuclear war were between 1 in 3 and 1 in 2.

During a contest of escalation, the weaker side is the more likely to back down. (This is generally acknowledged to have happened during the Cuban missile crisis; the Soviet Union was weaker not only in terms of nuclear weapons but also with respect to conventional forces available for possible use in the Caribbean.) However, sometimes national resolve is more important than military power as such: for example, the United States was undoubtedly more powerful than North Vietnam and the Viet Cong, but was also less committed to obtaining a military victory.

It is generally assumed that when two sides are about equally strong and both are lethally armed, as is now the case for the US and the USSR, games of Chicken will be avoided because they are so dangerous. However, if contests of escalation take place, for whatever reason, it is always possible that deterrence will fail simply because each side is determined not to swerve. This might be especially likely if leaders perceived that national or personal prestige was at stake; it is widely acknowledged, for example, that Khrushchev's humiliation after the Cuban missile crisis was instrumental in his fall from power two years later.

As of the mid-1980s, the United States has articulated a policy of **horizontal escalation;** that is, in the event of a conventional war, the US would escalate hostilities in areas where the country enjoys a military advantage. It has been widely assumed, for example, that a conventional war in western Europe might induce the US to use its carrier-based aircraft and other naval forces to attack the Soviet navy, which would be seriously outgunned and under substantial geographic disadvantages. Such a declared policy might enhance deterrence by making initial military adventurism on the part of the USSR less likely; however, it might also increase the dangers of nuclear confrontation if hostilities were to erupt. It might also increase the Soviet anxiety level, leading to possible misconstruing of otherwise routine or defensive precautions by the US or one of its allies.

## CATALYTIC WARS AND PROXY WARS

Except for occasional showdowns such as the Cuban missile crisis, the US and the USSR have tended to avoid direct confrontations. However, each nation has been involved in numerous military confrontations with other nations, which in turn have been allied with the other side. For example, while Vietnam was fighting the US, it received substantial military aid from the USSR, and Afghan rebels currently receive US aid. The situation in Central America offers even more complex examples. In addition, the many nonsuperpower wars often involve allies of one side arrayed against allies of the other. Especially in the case of third world military struggles, one or both parties may also be serving as proxies for the superpowers, whose prestige—and sometimes, even, strategic interests—rest on the outcome. The Soviet Union's status in the Middle East fell substantially, for example, following the Israeli invasion of Lebanon in 1982, when Israel, using American-made military equipment, inflicted heavy losses on Syria, which had been equipped by the USSR. The American invasion of Grenada did not produce Soviet casualties; a similar action in Nicaragua, on the other hand, might well have this effect, with serious consequences. In such cases, there is the possibility of **catalytic war,** in which hostilities among other nations can serve ultimately to drag in the superpowers as well.

The Middle East appears to be especially dangerous in this respect. For example, it is generally agreed that early in the 1973 Yom Kippur war, Israel assembled its nuclear arsenal for possible last-ditch use against Egypt and/or Syria. The USSR was then thought to have provided a nuclear guarantee to the Arab powers, whereupon the United States ordered a worldwide nuclear alert (Fig. 8.3). Israel turned the tide using conventional weapons, however, and seemed about to destroy the Egyptian armed forces. At this point the USSR is believed to have alerted several of its divisions, and the US again responded with a nuclear alert. This time the situation was defused by the United Nations. Whereas the Cuban missile crisis shows how superpower confrontations carry a risk of nuclear war, events in the Middle East demonstrate how such a risk can develop even when neither superpower is directly engaged. In other cases, as with the Iran–Iraq war, both superpowers appear to have successfully avoided direct involvement, but it remains possible that any dramatic turn of events, if followed by the engagement of either the US or the USSR, would precipitate a response by the other nation.

There are many other possible trouble spots, situations of local conflicts and antagonisms in which one or both of the protagonists also have superpower patrons: Central America and the Caribbean; North and South Korea; Kampuchea and Vietnam; Afghanistan and Pakistan; Israel, Lebanon, and Syria; the Horn of Africa (Ethiopia and Somalia). Any such regional tinderboxes could serve as catalysts for superpower involvement, and thus, nuclear war. One scenario, considered likely by some experts, goes roughly as follows: widespread civil unrest in East Germany leads to a Soviet military crackdown on the dissidents. The USSR's tanks are met with Molotov cocktails and substantial loss of life on both sides, whereupon West German military forces cross the border into the East, to "keep order." (Or alternatively, the Soviet Union, provoked by West German efforts to aid their fellow Germans against the Red Army, invades the West "to prevent further provocations.") It should be clear that in such cases, the possibility of calamitous nuclear escalation cannot be ruled out.

On the other hand, of course, awareness of the dangers of catalytic war may make each superpower especially cautious and thus, unlikely to become directly involved in such a manner. If so, then even while deterrence holds, and even if it restrains the superpowers from direct confrontation, it may actually increase the frequency of **proxy wars** taking place under the nuclear umbrella of either superpower, in which the two sides support revolutionaries or counterrevolutionaries in third world countries but rarely employ their own troops.

## NUCLEAR ACCIDENTS

HORATIO: *And let me speak to the yet unknowing world*

**FIGURE 8.3 Missile launch officers at their consoles, which control ICBMs in their underground silos.** (Courtesy of the US Department of Defense.)

*How these things came about: so shall you hear*
*Of carnal, bloody, and unnatural acts,*
*Of accidental judgments, casual slaughters,*
*Of deaths put on by cunning and forced cause,*
*And, in this upshot, purposes mistook*
*Fall'n on th' inventors' heads. (William Shakespeare,* Hamlet, *Act V, Scene II)*

Deterrence is intended to prevent nuclear war arising as a conscious, calculated decision, by making such a war unprofitable for both sides. As we have seen, however, nuclear war could still occur unintentionally, as a result of misperceptions—especially during a crisis—or because of mutual stubbornness while playing nuclear Chicken. Even in such cases, war might be "rational" in the sense that it would have been planned, even if miscalculated. A nuclear war could be said to have occurred unintentionally if it were initiated:

- Independently of any explicit decision to wage war by the legitimate national authorities

- Intentionally and deliberately by these authorities, but as a result of false information

- As a result of escalation not originally envisaged by those who decided to use force in the first place

The likelihood of any of these scenarios would be increased by a variety of possible accidents, which could undermine deterrence. First, let us consider possible accidents involving nuclear weapons themselves, known to the military as **broken arrows.**

## Broken Arrows

Sophisticated "fail-safe" controls consisting of mechanical as well as electronic keys are built into nuclear weapons to prevent accidental detonations. Typically, these controls are redundant, so that the weapons are safe in the event of failure of any one component. There have never been any accidental nuclear detonations, which may be testimony to the effectiveness of such precautions. Moreover, it seems unlikely that an accidental nuclear explosion would in itself trigger nuclear war, although the effects would be indistinguishable for the people locally involved. But just as human fallibility is real, so is machine fallibility. No enterprise can be 100% error-free or truly fail-safe, no matter how many redundant or cross-checking safety systems are built into it. "Multisystems failures" or "common-mode breakdowns" have been known to occur, even when such occurrences are supposed to be impossible. For example, a serious accident at a nuclear power plant at Brown's Ferry occurred because the several different, seemingly independent safety pipes were routed through the same tunnel, so that failure of one system caused failure of them all.

The accident at the Three Mile Island nuclear power plant in Pennsylvania in 1979 was another story. The incident, which assumed crisis proportions, was later attributed in part to the imposition of an overwhelming number of confusing, demanding, time-urgent signals on operators who may not have been adequately trained. Yet the fail-safes and redundancies designed into the system were sufficient to prevent such worst-case scenarios as the explosion of the reactor containment vessel. Given the magnitude of the disruption caused by this internal malfunction at a nuclear power plant, the shock and chaos that would accompany an explosion at a military nuclear facility are hard to imagine. It is always possible, therefore, that such an event would be misinterpreted as a sneak attack, which would then trigger retaliation. It is also possible that following such an explosion, the victimized nation would find it more expedient to blame the other side than to accept responsibility.

There have been a large number of announced American broken arrows; the USSR is much more reticent about comparable events. In many cases, the damage from a nuclear accident involves radioactive contamination from leakage of the unexploded fissile fuel. Occasionally, the conventional high-explosive trigger has also ignited. There have been several dozen broken arrows admitted by the United States government, including the following.

- In 1956 an unarmed B-47 crashed into a nuclear weapons stockpile at the Royal Air Force Lakenheath Base in East Anglia, Britain.

- In 1957 a B-47 accidentally dropped a 1-megaton bomb near Mars Bluff, South Carolina; the conventional explosive detonated, obliterating a farmhouse and killing several people.

- In 1962 a B-52 broke up in midair, causing the accidental release of two bombs. One broke up upon impact with the ground. The other, which descended by parachute and was found hanging in a tree near Goldsboro, North Carolina, was a 24-megaton bomb, equipped with six safety switches; five of them had been tripped.

- In 1968 a B-52 crashed and burned while landing at Thule Air Force Base, Greenland. All four nuclear bombs were destroyed in the fire. (Following this accident, B-52s with nuclear bombs were no longer kept on "airborne alert.")

- In 1968 a B-52 crashed and burned while landing at Thule Air Force Base, Greenland. All four nuclear bombs were destroyed in the fire. (Following this accident, B-52s with nuclear bombs were no longer kept on "airborne alert.")

- In 1980 a mechanic dropped a wrench, which ruptured the tanks of a liquid-fueled Titan II missile near Damascus, Arkansas. The resulting explo-

sion tossed the 9-megaton warhead 200 yards into the air.

The USSR is more reticent about comparable events, but the following Soviet broken arrows seem likely, based on reports in the international press:

- In 1970 one nuclear-armed submarine collided with an Italian cruise liner, and another exploded and sank off the British coast.

- Also in 1970 a large explosion occurred at the Gorki submarine yards, after which the Volga River and Black Sea estuary were radioactively contaminated.

- In 1981 a Soviet submarine, apparently on a spying mission and known to be armed with nuclear-tipped torpedoes, was grounded near the top-secret Swedish naval facility of Karlskrona.

- In 1984 a Soviet nuclear-armed submarine collided with the US aircraft carrier *Kitty Hawk*, in the Sea of Japan.

- Also in 1984, an errant submarine-launched cruise missile overflew Norwegian airspace and later crashed in Finland.

## Unauthorized Use

Many fictional accounts of accidental war have been based on scenarios of unauthorized use, typically by crazed subordinates. Only a very small number of individuals are authorized to order the use of the nuclear weapons of either superpower. Even in the United States, the exact designated responsibility is kept secret, although it is generally agreed that only the president can legally give such orders. Following an attack on the US, authority would be delegated to many different lower level authorities, including the SAC general aloft in the Looking Glass airplane and ballistic missile submarine commanders (Fig. 8.4). Given that the Soviet Union has a highly centralized command hierarchy, it seems likely that responsibility for ordering the use of nuclear weapons is also vested in a very small number of individuals within the Politburo, and perhaps limited to the General Secretary of the Communist Party. It is assumed that as in the case of the United States, procedures exist in the Soviet Union for delegation of launch authority if the political leadership is destroyed in an attack.

Although only a few individuals are officially empowered to order nuclear war, a relatively large

**FIGURE 8.4 Combat operations center at NORAD, deep under Cheyenne Mountain, Colorado. Reported attacks against the US would be analyzed here.** (Courtesy of the US Department of Defense.)

number of people have their fingers on the button. Rather stringent procedures exist to limit the likelihood that nuclear weapons will be used without legitimate authority—although that possibility can never be ruled out entirely. Nuclear weapons themselves are typically outfitted with safeguards that render them inoperable if tampered with. They are also generally outfitted with electronic locking codes such that they cannot be armed except by officially designated authority.

ICBMs are the most securely controlled strategic system and are outfitted with **permissive action links (PALS),** which ensure that the weapons are not armed until they receive electronically coded authorization from higher in the command structure. Strategic bombers are also under **positive control:** after reaching a certain designated flight radius, they must return to base unless they receive a specific "go-code," authorizing them to continue. Missile submarines, as we have seen, are the most invulnerable but also the most difficult to communicate with. It is possible, although unlikely, that following a nuclear attack, the victim nation's submarines would never receive the command to fire. One possibility is therefore to send constant messages during peace, with orders to launch missiles if the message stream is interrupted; this approach has so far been rejected, however, as too susceptible to accidental breakdown. There are efforts under way to solve the problem of inadequate communication with submerged submarines by installing a system known as ELF, for the extremely low-frequency electromagnetic waves it would employ. As mentioned in Chapter 2, the

**ELF system** would use large antennas strung across miles of northern Michigan and possibly Wisconsin to send messages that can penetrate hundreds of meters of water. Because the information-transmitting ability of such a system would be very limited, it could do little more than send the message to fire. Such a system, although ostensibly for strengthening deterrence, also could be interpreted as providing the minimal coordination needed to orchestrate a surprise first strike.

It appears that unlike the case of missile silos and bombers, the capability of arming and firing the nuclear weapons of strategic missile submarines lies with the crew alone. Whereas this may be necessitated by the requirements of secure deterrence, it lends special danger to accidental explosions and/or collisions at sea, which may be falsely interpreted by submarine commanders as preemptive attacks.

The Defense Department, through its Human Reliability Program, routinely scrutinizes all personnel with nuclear weapons responsibility. About 1,500–2,000 people are disqualified annually from the Strategic Air Command alone because of disclosures obtained from this program, often for psychiatric or drug-related problems. After the second year on the job, very few people are disqualified. This may testify to the effectiveness of the program, which screens out high-risk individuals before they have enough seniority to acquire significant authority. Alternatively, it may suggest that individuals learn how to "pass" the screening, and/or that the system may be more forgiving of transgressions by people who are integrated into it. It is widely

**FIGURE 8.5 Crewmen in the missile control room of a US strategic missile submarine.** (Courtesy of the US Department of Defense.)

acknowledged that alcoholism is a very serious problem in the USSR and that the military is not exempt. Whether this extends to nuclear weapons duty officers (the responsibility of the KGB) is a subject of debate.

Even with authorization from the president of the United States or a designated successor, the arming and launching of nuclear weapons requires at least two people. For example, each of two ICBM launch officers must insert his or her launch keys within 2 seconds of the other. Submarine launches are believed to require the participation of the commanding officer, the executive officer, the weapons officer, and the launch officer (Fig. 8.5). Although it is possible that four people who had been passed by the Human Reliability Program could be induced to collaborate in an unauthorized launch, such a prospect is considered very remote . . . but of course it can never be zero.

**Irrational Use**  One can certainly argue that any use of nuclear weapons is by definition irrational, and that no authorization, even if it flows appropriately down the predelegated chain of command, is "legitimate." However, as we have just seen, a distinction can be made between decisions made by duly constituted political/military authority and unauthorized use by subordinates. Furthermore, a distinction may also seem appropriate between rational and irrational orders, even if emanating from legitimate authority. The United States government has no publicized procedures for declaring a president incompetent and relieving him or her

from authority. This is understandable, to avoid legitimizing a *coup d'état* under the guise of psychiatric or medical necessity. But it leaves unanswered the question of whether duly constituted authority can be challenged, under sufficiently extreme conditions.

Insanity and medical incapacitation are not unknown among political leaders: Caligula, Nero, Ludwig of Bavaria, George III, and quite possibly Adolf Hitler and Josef Stalin are believed to have been mad. Woodrow Wilson suffered a nervous breakdown, and Dwight Eisenhower experienced two strokes while in office. During the final days of his administration, President Nixon behaved with increasing irrationality, and Secretary of Defense Schlesinger is said to have taken extraordinary precautions, arranging that he be informed in the event of any unusual orders involving nuclear weapons. When President Reagan was shot, there appears to have been confusion regarding the command structure in Washington; by contrast, when President Reagan underwent elective surgery, procedures were smoothly implemented. It is unclear, however, what legal opportunities, if any, exist for countermanding the orders of a sitting president.

It is also possible that the social isolation and stress of events—especially among personnel in an underground ICBM launch silo or a nuclear submarine—could trigger irrational behavior. A survey of drug abuse in the United States armed forces during 1980 and 1981 was not reassuring (Table 8.1). It seems likely that such levels of drug abuse contribute to conventional acci-

**TABLE 8.1 Percentage of US armed forces personnel who admitted to using drugs and alcohol during the previous month, while on active duty**

| Substance | Service (% admitting to use) | | | |
|---|---|---|---|---|
| | Army | Air Force | Marines | Navy |
| Marijuana/hashish | 38 | 4.5 | 24.3 | 41 |
| Cocaine | 3 | 0 | 3.9 | 3.8 |
| Heroin | 2 | 0 | 0.6 | 0.6 |
| "Uppers" | 9.6 | 0 | 13.7 | 27 |
| "Downers" | 4.6 | 0 | 4.9 | 10.1 |
| Hallucinogens (e.g., LSD) | 2.6 | 0 | 2.2 | 8.8 |
| Alcohol | 28 | 15.7 | 19.4 | 21 |

*Source:* From James Thompson. 1985. *Psychological Aspects of Nuclear War.* New York: John Wiley, quoting from "Select Committee on Narcotics and Drug Abuse" presentation of results obtained in 1981.

dents. The situation regarding personnel with nuclear weapons responsibility is unclear, although it is noteworthy that approximately 5,000 people are removed annually from nuclear weapons duties of various sorts; in about one-third of these cases, alcohol or other substance abuse is cited. There are rumors concerning drug abuse on nuclear submarines in particular, although no firm data are available. We have even fewer details on the situation among the Soviet armed forces. It is generally believed, however, that substance abuse—especially alcohol—constitutes an acute problem, perhaps even more serious than in the United States.

## False Alarms

Of all the possible scenarios for nuclear war by accident, perhaps the most frightening are those involving false alarms. In such cases, an error in its $C^3I$ system causes a nuclear weapons state to believe, falsely, that it is under attack, whereupon it "retaliates," unleashing World War III. In the prenuclear world, nations worried about being the victims of a surprise strategic attack, and indeed, in 1941 Hitler attacked the Soviet Union and Japan attacked the US Pacific fleet at Pearl Harbor. In the Nuclear Age, the danger of surprise attack continues and has if anything increased as the warning time has diminished, just as the potential consequences of such an attack have grown. However, this situation has led to a new and particularly dangerous possibility: that a nation might be so jumpy about being

attacked that it will preemptively attack in response to a false alarm.

False alarms are actually quite common, as one would expect in a far-flung and complex warning system. Just as there have never been any accidental explosions, or unauthorized or irrationally authorized launches, there have never yet been any false alarms that resulted in use of nuclear weapons. This may indicate the effectiveness of the safety features built into the system, in which case our confidence should perhaps be enhanced by the many false alarms that have been caught in time. Or it may indicate that we are treading on rather thin ice.

According to an unclassified report of the Senate Armed Services Committee, there were 151 "serious" nuclear false alarms and 3,703 lesser alarms between January 1, 1979, and June 30, 1980. Between 1945 and 1975 there were 33 SAC alerts. Here are some examples of notable false alarms.

- The Thule, Greenland, Ballistic Missile Early Warning System reported in October 1960 that a missile attack was approaching the US. After about 15–20 minutes, it was found that radar signals were bouncing off the newly risen moon.

- Twice during 1971 US Polaris submarines accidentally released emergency communications transmitter buoys, signaling (incorrectly) that the vessel had been attacked and destroyed.

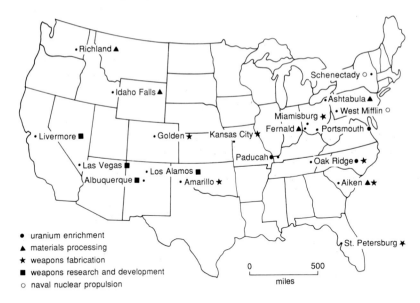

**FIGURE 8.6 Major sites of nuclear weapons fabrication, processing, enrichment, and research in the United States.** (Modified from Dennis, 1984.)

- In October 1975 infrared sensors on an American early warning satellite detected a sudden burst of heat in Siberia, interpreting it as a missile launch; it was, instead, a fire in a gas pipeline.

- In November 1979 a practice war-games tape was fed into a NORAD (North American Aerospace Defense Command) computer. Signals from this tape were taken as a real attack, and fighters were scrambled. After 6 minutes, the error was discovered.

- Twice in June 1980, microchips failed in a NORAD computer, resulting in worldwide nuclear alerts, which again were canceled after a few minutes.

The problem of false alarms is heightened by the growing accuracy of nuclear weapons delivery systems which makes such intelligence increasingly credible, and by the diminishing attack time (30 minutes for ICBMs, even less for SLBMs), which has in turn necessitated the ability to respond quickly. It should be emphasized that in the absence of counterforce weapons, or if such weapons allowed more response time, neither side would be as nervous about possible failures of deterrence; thus neither side would be so sensitive to the need to evaluate reported attacks in a matter of minutes. On the other hand, it has been argued that the high level of responsiveness of national command structures makes a surprise attack less likely and helps maintain the peace.

## TERRORISM

After the 1973 Arab-Israeli Yom Kippur war, the Arab countries, angered by western support for Israel, organized an oil boycott that severely stressed the economies of most petroleum-importing nations. Before that time, very few people had anticipated an "energy crisis." At present, very few people worry about nuclear terrorism, but that too could change quickly.

Nuclear terrorism could take place in several ways. For example, the construction of a nuclear weapon is no longer a secret. All that is needed is sufficient high-technology machining skills and the necessary nuclear materials. An average reactor makes from 5 to 400 pounds of plutonium per year. The Nuclear Regulatory Commission or NRC (successor to the Atomic Energy Commission) keeps track of plutonium stores in the United States. The NRC reports that more than a ton of plutonium is missing and unaccounted for; although it seems likely that much of this is in fact truly missing, it is also possible that a portion has been diverted to unofficial uses, or will be so diverted in the future. (In Chapter 11, we shall discuss nuclear proliferation, including its possible connection with nuclear power as well as its political ramifications.)

Concern has been expressed that plutonium or enriched uranium could be stolen while in transit between reprocessing plants, or that intact bombs could be stolen from their commercial fabricating plants or from military reservations where they are stored (Fig. 8.6). To date, no terrorist groups have made use of nuclear weapons. The possibility is nightmarish, however, because of the potential susceptibility of large, wealthy nations to nuclear blackmail. Some groups have shown themselves capable of suicide missions and have received encouragement and assistance from various governments. It is therefore conceivable that certain governments would provide terrorists with nuclear weapons, which might be used for extortion or for terror. Given that nuclear weapons are currently small

enough to fit in a suitcase, it is not even necessary for would-be nuclear terrorists to have access to missiles or other sophisticated delivery systems.

The possibility also exists that a small number of nuclear bombs, exploded by terrorists, could generate war by inducing nations to think they had been the victims of a major attack. If Washington, DC, were blown up overnight, for example, no one can predict how the surviving governmental authorities would respond, or against whom, since in the confusion it is doubtful whether the culprits could be reliably identified.

---

## Policy Issues

---

### Are nuclear weapons useful instruments of international power and diplomacy?

**Yes:**  Although nuclear weapons have not been detonated in anger since 1945, there have been numerous threats, some of which have been successful. For example, Eisenhower's threat to use nuclear weapons in Korea may have helped end that conflict, Truman's threat to Stalin may have helped expedite Soviet withdrawal from Iran, and Carter's threat to use nuclear weapons if necessary in the Persian Gulf may have averted Soviet expansionism in that region. Moreover, the mere presence of nuclear weapons could well be responsible for the absence of major superpower conflict; after all, there has never been a collision during nuclear Chicken. If the threat of nuclear annihilation did not exist, it is quite possible that wars would be more frequent then they have been since 1945. After all, Europe has been at peace for 40 consecutive years. And finally, perhaps the greatest "usefulness" of nuclear weapons to the United States has been to balance the unilateral advantage that the USSR would possess if we did not have them. If the Soviets had a nuclear monopoly, the rest of the world would doubtless be subjected to nuclear intimidation.

**No:**  Nuclear weapons are not really weapons at all; they lack any military or political utility because they cannot be used, except perhaps to deter an opponent's use of nuclear weapons. Nuclear weapons cannot be translated into political gains. For example, a US nuclear monopoly did prevent the Soviet-

inspired coup in Czechoslovakia (1948), the Berlin blockade (1948), or the success of the Chinese revolution (1949). Similarly, American nuclear weapons did not aid the US in Vietnam and have not helped the US in dealing with Castro's Cuba; they did not deter North Korea from invading South Korea, and they have had no value in coping with unrest in Central America. Soviet nuclear weapons, in turn, have not strengthened the USSR's hand in Afghanistan or Poland. The Soviets could not get their way in the world by incinerating Warsaw or Kabul, just as the US would gain nothing by destroying Hanoi or Managua. Britain's possession of nuclear weapons did not prevent Argentina from seeking to wrest the Falkland Islands in 1982, and in 1969 the USSR and China came to blows across their border; neither side was inhibited by the knowledge that the other possessed nuclear weapons. Nuclear weapons are simply too blunt to be translated into political influence. Just as we cannot repair a computer with a sledge hammer, try as we might, we cannot get our way in the world with nuclear weapons . . . but reliance on nuclear weapons does run the risk that someday, deterrence will fail.

### Should the president be required to consult with others before authorizing use of nuclear weapons?

**No:**  Deterrence relies on the threat of prompt retaliation. If the president had to consult with others, and this procedural necessity were known to the other side, deterrence would be eroded. Even if conventional war were to escalate into possible use of nuclear weapons, any obstacles placed in the way of potential nuclear response would lower the credibility of nuclear weapons as a deterrent.

**Yes:** By requiring that the president consult with, say, a select bipartisan congressional group, the chance of irrational and/or ill-considered acts by an individual would be greatly diminished. Retaliation for a direct nuclear attack on the US might still be permitted without consultation, but there would be time for consultation in all other cases, such as a conventional war in Europe or in the Persian Gulf.

### Should the US maintain its nuclear weapons in a high state of readiness? (Fig. 8.7.)

**Yes:** The more "ready" our weapons, the less likely that they will be challenged. As we place more controls on their use, we make it more likely that if needed, they may not be usable.

**No:** The more "ready" our weapons, the more likely that they will be used accidentally. As we place more controls on their use, we make accidental use less likely.

### Should we consider accidental nuclear war to be a realistic possibility?

**No:** The US government (and almost certainly, the Soviet government as well) has done everything humanly possible to protect against accidental nuclear war. Nuclear weapons bear an array of physical and electronic control systems, making detonation by accident or by terrorists virtually impossible. All false alarms have been detected in time, which is precisely how the system has been designed to function. The chance of nuclear war by accident is effectively zero.

**Yes:** When it comes to the greatest disaster of all times, all that is humanly possible just may not be enough. Nothing is error-free, neither people nor machines. A single error could well be the last error of all time, and this is an unacceptable risk. Moreover, our nuclear weapons policies (especially counterforce) make it more likely that accidental war (especially because of false alarms) will occur.

### Should we consider intentional nuclear war to be a realistic possibility?

**No:** The greatest danger facing the United States and the world today is not nuclear war; rather it is that our fears about nuclear war may rob the free world of the courage and determination to stand up to communist aggression. Given the destructiveness of nuclear war, we can be confident that neither side will go over the brink, as long as the US maintains a sufficient margin of safety to ensure that the Soviet Union will respect American national interests.

**Yes:** Wars do not always start because of rational calculations. More often, in fact, they result from miscalculations and accidents. It is entirely possible that nuclear war will break out between the superpowers despite its not being in the interests of either party, because both sides refuse to swerve aside during a crisis, because one side misinterprets the actions and intentions of the other, and possibly even because one side or the other decides that the consequences of nuclear war are likely to be less severe than the consequences of accepting a loss to personal prestige or geopolitical national interest.

### Must we maintain an ever-expanding arsenal to ensure that deterrence will not fail?

**Yes:** No one knows precisely what it will take to deter the Soviets, but for the sake of prudence, better to err on the side of caution and have more than we need rather than not enough. We can dream about a world free of nuclear weapons, but nuclear weapons exist in the present world, along with a dangerous opponent. The USSR lost 20 million people during World War II and eventually prospered. The Soviets might well find such losses acceptable today; we must therefore be sure that the costs of nuclear war will be unacceptable to them. As President Kennedy once put it, only when our strength is certain beyond doubt can we be certain beyond doubt that it will not be tested.

**No:** McGeorge Bundy has written [that]:

*There is an enormous gulf between what political leaders really think about nuclear weapons and what is assumed in complex calculations of relative "advantage" in simulated strategic war-*

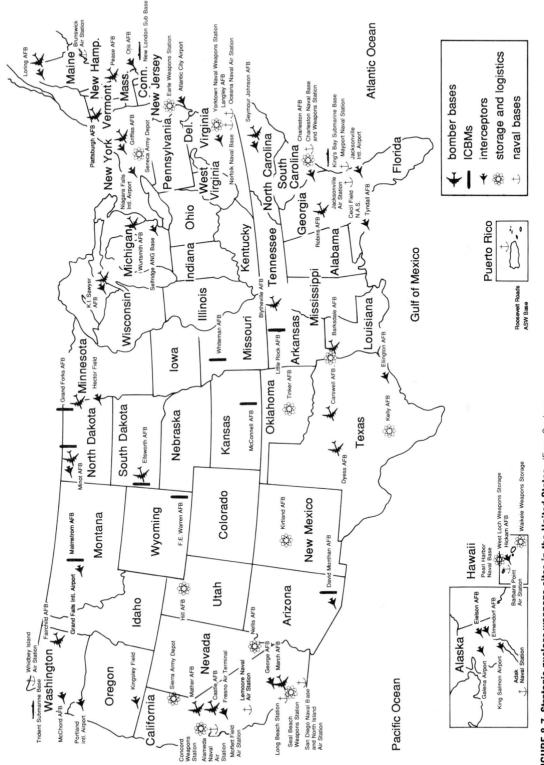

**FIGURE 8.7 Strategic nuclear weapons sites in the United States.** (From Cochran, Arkin, and Hoenig, 1984.)

fare. Think-tank analysts can set levels of "acceptable" damage well up in the tens of millions of lives. They can assume that the loss of dozens of great cities is somehow a real choice for sane men. They are in an unreal world. In the real world of real political leaders—whether here or in the Soviet Union—a decision that would

bring even one hydrogen bomb on one city of one's own country would be recognized in advance as a catastrophic blunder; ten bombs on ten cities would be a disaster beyond history; and a hundred bombs on a hundred cities are unthinkable.*

## KEY TERMS

"boob" attack
Hot Line
interacting alerts
horizontal escalation
catalytic war
proxy wars

broken arrows
permissive action links (PALS)
positive control
ELF system

## STUDY QUESTIONS

1. Compare the likelihood of a counterforce versus a countervalue "boob" attack. Why?

2. Which is more likely to lead to nuclear war, a "broken arrow" or a "false alarm"? Why?

3. Discuss the relationship between speed of delivery vehicles and response time.

4. Distinguish between unauthorized use and accidental use of nuclear weapons.

5. Distinguish between catalytic US–Soviet war and the escalation of a conventional conflict.

6. Describe three different ways in which terrorists could conceivably gain access to nuclear weapons.

## ADDITIONAL READINGS

Beres, Louis René. 1980. *Apocalypse*. Chicago: University of Chicago Press. Many possible scenarios (including terrorism, accidents, and escalations) of how nuclear war might occur.

Bracken, Paul. 1983. *The Command and Control of Nuclear Forces*. New Haven, CT: Yale University Press. A disturbing examination of the problem of managing nuclear forces during a crisis.

Cox, Arthur Macy. 1982. *Russian Roulette*. New York: Times Books. A former CIA official describes what he sees as the dangers of the arms race, especially the prospects of false alarms.

Frei, Daniel. 1982. *Risks of Unintentional Nuclear War*. Geneva, Switzerland: United Nations Institute for Disarmament Research. A UN report that examines various aspects of crisis instability, including accidental nuclear war and other possible failures of deterrence.

Harvard Nuclear Study Group. 1983. *Living Nuclear Weapons*. Cambridge, MA: Harvard University Press. A defense of the current nuclear weapons regime.

*"To Cap the Volcano." 1969. *Foreign Affairs* 48:1.

# Competition and Efforts at Control

Thus far, we have examined nuclear weapons themselves (Part One), their effects (Part Two), and the strategic doctrine that has surrounded them (Part Three). It is clear, however, that the issues raised cannot be understood without examining the way nations have both competed and (occasionally) cooperated with each other in the nuclear arena. In Part Four we shall therefore consider nuclear weapons as a problem of interaction among nations, notably the United States and the Soviet Union. We shall review in turn the history and dynamics of the nuclear arms race (Chapter 9), the past, present and pitfalls of nuclear negotiations (Chapter 10), and the vexing problem of nuclear proliferation (Chapter 11).

# 9 The Arms Race

*[Nuclear weapons are] the rock on which the renaissance of the West since 1945 was based and the foundation for its security.*
Eugene V. Rostow

*The era of armaments has ended and the human race must conform its actions to this truth or die.*
Dwight D. Eisenhower

The nuclear arms race cannot be separated from the history of US–Soviet relations, or from the development of strategic nuclear doctrine (Chapter 6). It is not clear, however, how these factors are related. Do the requirements of strategic doctrine provide the driving force for arms acquisitions? Or do the weapons stimulate the doctrine? Similarly, does the arms race proceed as a result of relations between the US and the USSR, or are US–Soviet relations determined by the arms race? It can also be debated whether there has been a nuclear arms "race" at all, as the term is usually understood.

There are many other questions, as well. What are the roles of science and technology? Of past grievances and public opinion? Can the arms race be accurately described as a sort of huge misunderstanding, or is one nation at fault, and the other innocent and aggrieved? These questions do not yield simple answers; in this chapter, we shall therefore aim for a basic grasp of the questions, looking first at the history of the US–Soviet nuclear competition, and then at the broader phenomenon of arms races.

## EARLY US–SOVIET RELATIONS

Even before nuclear weapons, relations between the United States and the USSR were rarely smooth. As a result of the Bolshevik revolution of 1917, czarist Russia was transformed into the Union of Soviet Socialist Republics. Just as the United States was entering World War I, on the same side as its Russian ally, the recently established Soviet government, led by V. I. Lenin, signed a separate peace treaty with Germany. This hardly endeared the new government in Moscow to the United States. Moreover, communist goals of worldwide revolution and explicit anticapitalist ideology added to the distrust. The US, along with other European nations, even participated—although in a very small way—in the attempted counterrevolution of 1918–1920, supporting the "Whites," who were ultimately defeated by the "Reds." Not surprisingly, this taking of sides contributed to Soviet enmity toward the US and the West generally.

Americans, in turn, objected to Lenin's refusal to pay war debts (incurred by the czar's government), to the forced collectivization of the 1920s and 1930s, and to the heavy-handed dictatorship of Lenin's successor, Josef Stalin. The US government did not recognize the Soviet government until 1933, and even then, Stalin's murderous purges, combined with fear and dislike of communist ideology and its possible inroads into American society, cast a pall on US–Soviet relations throughout the 1930s.

Communism was among Adolf Hitler's most prominent targets, and Stalin, with his foreign minister Maxim Litvinoff, sought to establish antifascist and anti-Nazi agreements with Western governments during the mid- to late 1930s. However, distrust of the USSR impeded any such arrangements, and shortly after Britain and France had concluded the Munich agreements (1938), seeking to appease Hitler by permitting virtual annexation of Czechoslovakia, Stalin shocked the West by signing a nonaggression pact with Hitler. When Hitler invaded Poland later the same year (1939), Russian troops also invaded from the east. During the brief Russo-Finnish War (1939–1940), the USSR acquired additional territory near Leningrad. Stalin also annexed the Baltic states of Latvia, Estonia, and Lithuania, which had been lost to Germany in World War I and subsequently had been granted independence. All this added to an American perception of the USSR as aggressive, untrustworthy, and expansionistic.

After Hitler's surprise attack on the USSR on June 22, 1941, and America's entry into World War II after the Japanese surprise attack on Pearl Harbor on December 7, 1941, the US and USSR were allies against the Axis powers (Germany, Italy, and Japan). This alliance, however, was short-lived.

## WORLD WAR II AND IMMEDIATELY AFTERWARD

Even during the war, tensions developed, despite Soviet gratitude for American lend-lease aid (which was never repaid) as well as American gratitude for Soviet valor and recognition of the immense losses suffered by the USSR. In particular, Soviet leadership objected to the long delay in opening a "second front" in Europe. The Red Army, bearing the brunt of Germany's war effort, eventually overran most of eastern Europe, such that by the war's end in 1945, Soviet forces controlled the previously independent states on the USSR's western borders. Just before the war's end, however, in February 1945, President Franklin D. Roosevelt, British Prime Minister Winston S. Churchill, and Stalin had met at Yalta, on the coast of the Black Sea, where they agreed to divide power, temporarily at least, in postwar Europe. This division corresponded broadly to the positions of the armies at V-E Day, which marked the surrender of Germany, some 12 weeks later, and has continued to the present.

However, disputes arose over the governing of several European countries, since the Western allies expected democracy whereas Stalin insisted on communist governments under his control. In Poland, for example, the Red Army established a communist government, rejecting the Polish government then in exile in London. Virtual civil war broke out in Greece between communist and democratic partisans, although in this case, Britain succeeded in installing a capitalist/democratic government. The growing outlines of competition and conflict were clear. For example, only after substantial Western protest (and possibly nuclear threats) did Stalin withdraw from northern Iran. According to some people, the Soviet Union's behavior at this time was primarily defensive, simply seeking buffer zones to protect itself against future invasions; to others, the USSR after World War II was continuing its old ways

of aggression and expansionism, a continuing step toward its goal of world domination.

Whatever the underlying causes, it soon became clear that the USSR would insist on satellite, communist states along its European borders, with very little internal freedom. While touring the United States in 1946, Winston Churchill made a famous speech:

> From Stettin in the Baltic to Trieste in the Adriatic an iron curtain has descended across the continent. . . . I do not believe that Soviet Russia desires war. What they desire is the fruits of war and the indefinite expansion of their power and doctrines.

In 1947, the following year, President Harry Truman initiated substantial US aid to Greece and Turkey, to counteract communist revolutionary efforts in those nations. The resulting **Truman Doctrine** held that the United States would "support free peoples who are resisting attempted subjugation by armed minorities or outside pressure."

Less than two years after the end of the wartime antifascist alliance, Bernard Baruch, elder statesman and adviser to presidents, announced: "Let us not be deceived, today we are in the midst of a cold war."

## THE COLD WAR AND NUCLEAR WEAPONS

The Manhattan Project was begun in 1942, several years after Albert Einstein, prompted especially by physicist Leo Szilard, wrote to President Roosevelt, briefly describing the possibility of nuclear weapons and warning that Germany might be proceeding with research in this direction (Fig. 9.1). Alarmed by the specter of nuclear weapons in the hands of Adolf Hitler, and also motivated by the excitement of being in the forefront of scientific research, a team of physicists and engineers assembled at a top-secret site at Los Alamos, New Mexico, under the military control of General Leslie Groves and the scientific leadership of physicist J. Robert Oppenheimer (Fig. 9.2). Uranium enrichment was conducted at Oak Ridge, Tennessee, and plutonium was produced at Hanford, Washington.

The resulting crash program detonated the world's first man-made nuclear explosion, code-named Trinity, in July 1945. Germany had surrendered in May, and even before that, it had been apparent that German scientists were not on the verge of attaining nuclear weapons. The project's momentum continued una-

**FIGURE 9.1 Albert Einstein and Leo Szilard recreating their writing of a letter to President Roosevelt, warning of the possibility that Nazi Germany might shortly obtain an atomic bomb.** (Courtesy G. W. Szilard; American Institute of Physics Niels Bohr Library.)

**FIGURE 9.2 A nuclear "odd couple": Dr. J. Robert Oppenheimer (left) and General Leslie Groves examining the site of the first atomic explosion, at Alamogordo, New Mexico.** (UPI photo, courtesy of Los Alamos National Laboratory.)

bated, however, this time with the intent of using the atomic bomb against Japan. Some of the Manhattan Project scientists recommended that atomic bombs not be employed against civilian targets, proposing a demonstration blast instead. Nonetheless, a single atomic bomb was exploded over Hiroshima on August 6, 1945, and another over Nagasaki on August 9. Japan surrendered on August 15.

The atomic bombing of Hiroshima and Nagasaki marked the beginning of a period of clear-cut American nuclear monopoly. President Truman and his advisers, notably Secretary of State James Byrnes, had hoped that this monopoly would make Stalin more tractable and would also compensate for the intimidating strength of the Red Army (Fig. 9.3). As it happened, American nuclear weapons may also, ironically, have been partly responsible for the continued size of that army. Thus, Soviet military and political stubbornness during the years immediately following 1945 may have been Stalin's response to the American military advantage. In any event, the Red Army was not demobilized to the degree that Western armies were, and the resulting conventional military posture of the USSR seemed about as threatening to the West as American atomic bombs did to the East.

The victorious allies had organized the United Nations in the closing days of World War II, hoping to succeed where the League of Nations had failed. In a notable effort to include the United Nations in the new nuclear regime, Bernard Baruch proposed to the international body a plan that had originally been worked

**FIGURE 9.3 The "Big Three" meeting at Potsdam in 1945, after the war with Germany had been won but before the surrender of Japan. President Harry Truman sits between British Prime Minister Winston Churchill (left) and Soviet Premier Josef Stalin. Truman had been informed of the successful US atomic test en route to Potsdam, and it is said that he behaved with more confidence and assertiveness toward Stalin because of it.** (US Army photo; courtesy of the Harry S. Truman Library.)

out by Secretary of State Dean Acheson and David Lilienthal, the director of the Tennessee Valley Authority, who later became the first chairman of the Atomic Energy Commission. The so-called **Baruch Plan** called for complete UN control over all atomic facilities everywhere in the world, from uranium mining to power generators to prospective weapons plants. It also called for "condign punishment" for any violators to be administered by the UN, and not subject to a Security Council veto. Such punishment, although never clearly specified, would presumably have been military, and severe.

The USSR rejected the Baruch Plan. Under its terms, the United States would have surrendered its nuclear weapons to the world organization, but only after all other nations had first surrendered their nuclear facilities. To the Soviets, the Baruch Plan may have seemed intended to preserve exclusive American control of nuclear weapons, and some have suggested that it was merely a propaganda ploy, designed to be rejected. Many Americans, by contrast, saw the Baruch Plan as an offer of extraordinary generosity, in which their country was volunteering to forego a unilateral advantage. Soviet rejection of the Baruch Plan therefore served to underline the USSR's hostility and intransigence. Thus, even before the phrase "cold war" was in vogue, it was clear that nuclear weapons were an important and troublesome part of the US–Soviet equation.

On the political/economic front, the Truman Doctrine was quickly followed by the European Recovery Plan—the Marshall Plan—for channeling financial aid

to the devastated economies of western Europe. Although widely perceived by Americans as humanitarian, this program was also intended to help bolster the nations of western Europe against communism. Indeed, US diplomat George Kennan had warned in 1946, in his famous "long telegram" to Washington DC, that it would be necessary to support the governments of Europe and to help strengthen their economies, if the US were to compete successfully with the powerful presence of Soviet Russia in the postwar world. Thus perhaps not surprisingly, the Soviets perceived the Marshall Plan as a virtual declaration of economic war. The Kremlin engineered a communist coup in Czechoslovakia in 1948 and also blockaded Berlin in the same year, seeking to induce the Western allies to make currency concessions and/or to give up their occupancy of West Berlin, which was (and still is) within the Soviet-occupied sector. (The various occupation zones had been established at Yalta, three years before.) The Berlin blockade was overcome by an airlift and was eventually withdrawn, but by then, the Cold War had become quite frigid.

The success of the communist revolution in China, in 1949, added to Western anxieties, which were enhanced even more when the USSR exploded its first atomic weapon in the same year. The following year, 1950, saw the outbreak of the Korean war, which ended in 1953 in a stalemate that continues to the present. It also marked the appearance of a very important American policy document, National Security Council (NSC) Report number 68. **NSC 68** concluded that the USSR "seeks to impose its absolute authority over the rest of the world," and it identified the USSR as the prime threat to American national security. NSC 68 recommended that the United States maintain vigorous military forces, both nuclear and conventional, to deter the USSR and also to prevent further expansionism. Long before deterrence, **containment** (of the Soviet Union at its present level of strength) became the US foreign policy of the 1950s.

In 1949 the **North Atlantic Treaty Organization,** or **NATO,** was established. Now comprising the United States, Canada, and the nations shown in Figure 3.5, NATO members are pledged to maintain "collective security" by adhering to the principle that an attack against any member of the alliance is an attack against all. NATO membership marked the first US commitment, as part of a peacetime alliance, to fight on behalf of another country. There is no doubt that NATO was intended as a defensive pact; however, it may have seemed more ominous to Soviet leaders, especially when West Germany joined the alliance in 1955. In the same year, the USSR organized the **Warsaw Pact** (WP), which joined the communist nations of eastern Europe under a unified military command. The Soviet Union exercises virtually unquestioned, authoritarian control over decisions by the Warsaw Pact, although Romania, for example, has occasionally charted a somewhat independent foreign policy. By contrast, although the United States is the diplomatic, economic, and military leader of NATO, the organization is composed of independent governments, which can join or leave at will and often disagree among themselves. The United States nonetheless retains control over its nuclear weapons deployed in Europe, and NATO nations hotly debate whether the US has also retained the potential to order use of such weapons, unilaterally if it chooses.

## THE 1950S

The possibility of thermonuclear bombs had been suggested in 1942 by physicist Edward Teller. A scientific advisory committee, chaired by Oppenheimer, recommended against building such weapons, on the grounds that they would not be militarily useful and would precipitate further competition with the USSR. However, shortly after the Soviet atomic test in 1949, President Truman ordered the Atomic Energy Commission to proceed with development. The first thermonuclear explosion was achieved in 1952 by the United

States, followed by the USSR in 1953. Usable H-bombs were available to both sides by the mid-1950s.

Meanwhile, the McCarthy era in American history had begun, and in the domestic anticommunist crusade that followed, Oppenheimer's opposition to the H-bomb was interpreted as verging on treason. Support for nuclear weapons became equated with patriotism.

The Cold War thawed somewhat with the death of Stalin in 1953, which was followed by a period of collective leadership from which Nikita Khrushchev emerged as Soviet leader. Khrushchev initiated a process of "de-Stalinization" in 1956, modified Soviet doctrine to deny the inevitability of war between capitalist and communist states, and also began to show somewhat greater concern for domestic economic growth, as opposed to heavy industry. Foreign policy, moreover, became generally less confrontational.

This was also the era of "massive retaliation," as we have already reviewed (Chapter 6), when the United States enjoyed overwhelming nuclear superiority over the USSR. It may be no exaggeration to say that during this period each side regularly made disarmament proposals intended primarily for propaganda purposes, probably expecting them to be turned down. The United States, far ahead in nuclear weaponry, regularly called for a mutual halt at current levels, which would help preserve the American advantage. The US also insisted on rigorous inspection and verification procedures. The USSR, in turn, called for more drastic disarmament, which would enable it to overcome its disadvantages. The USSR, traditionally a more secretive society than the US, also rejected American demands for inspection as thinly disguised attempts at espionage. The US viewed Soviet resistance to inspection as evidence of their dishonest intentions. As Swedish disarmament advocate and Nobel Peace Prize winner Alva Myrdal put it: "The Soviet government has often felt free to launch broad proposals for disarmament. . . . It can safely rely on the United States to raise demands for controls, which the Soviet Union can then decline."

Two notable diplomatic initiatives by the Eisenhower administration were the **"Atoms for Peace"** proposal in 1953 and the **"Open Skies"** proposal in 1955 (Fig. 9.4). The former gave rise ultimately to the International Atomic Energy Agency, which has had some effect in restraining nuclear proliferation and has also served to promote the peaceful uses of nuclear energy (more about this in Chapter 11). The "Open Skies" proposal—namely, that each side use aerial reconnaissance as a substitute for on-site inspection—was rejected by the USSR. However, overflights of the USSR began around that time anyhow, and in 1960 an American U-2 aircraft, piloted by Francis Gary Powers, was shot down over the Soviet Union, causing a major diplomatic incident.

## THE BOMBER GAP AND THE MISSILE GAP

The USSR unveiled its first intercontinental bombers, a squadron of 10 Bears, at the Soviet Air Show in 1955. These airplanes flew repeatedly around the viewing stand, apparently causing confusion as to their actual numbers. American analysts promptly calculated that within 2 years, 600 such airplanes could be produced. The United States responded with an intensification of its strategic bomber effort, producing about 500 B-52s and more than 1,500 medium-range B-47s. The much-feared **bomber gap** never materialized, however, except in favor of the United States. As we have seen, the USSR has never invested heavily in strategic bombing.

Two years later, in 1957, the Soviets shocked the West by orbiting the world's first artificial satellite, Sputnik, just two months after they had tested their first ICBM (another shock, which had been more significant yet for the strategic community). The Gaither Committee, appointed by President Eisenhower to assess the newfound Soviet missile capability, reported that within 2 years, 100 Soviet ICBMs could be available to attack the US. At that time, the United States was developing the Atlas and Titan ICBMs, but neither class was operational. American anxiety accordingly switched from Soviet bombers to Soviet missiles, and the **"missile gap"** became a major issue in the 1960 presidential campaign, with candidate John F. Kennedy accusing the outgoing administration (hence his opponent, Richard Nixon, who served as Eisenhower's vice president) of being insufficiently attentive to American defense by permitting such a Soviet lead.

The new Kennedy administration quickly learned, however, that the missile gap, like the bomber gap before it, was essentially nonexistent. The U-2 flights had been intended to obtain intelligence about Soviet missile deployments, but beginning in 1961 such information was gathered by spy satellites (see discussion of "national technical means," in Chapter 10). It soon became clear that the USSR never deployed very many of these first-generation missiles: estimates range from 4 to 50. Despite the worrisome missile gap, once again the US had a substantial lead in strategic nuclear

**FIGURE 9.4 President Eisenhower and Soviet Premier Khrushchev at Camp David just before a summit meeting.** (Courtesy Dwight D. Eisenhower Library.)

weaponry, as a result of weapons programs begun during the 1950s. These programs were expanded by the Kennedy administration. By 1962 the liquid-fueled Titan and Atlas missiles were being replaced by the solid-fueled Minuteman 1, and the Polaris submarine fleet was also being deployed along with strategic bombers. None of the weapons, on either side, were MIRVed. Table 9.1 shows Soviet and US strategic forces as of October 1962 (the Cuban missile crisis).

## INTO THE 1960S AND 1970S

During the Kennedy administration, basic decisions were made about the American strategic nuclear posture, decisions that in some ways have remained

**TABLE 9.1 US–Soviet strategic nuclear forces at the time of the Cuban missile crisis**

| Missiles or bombers | US | USSR |
|---|---|---|
| ICBMs | 100 Minuteman I<br>90 Atlas<br>36 Titan | 75 (?)[a] |
| SLBMs | 144 Polaris SLBMs (9 Polaris submarines) | 0 |
| Strategic bombers | 600 B-52s<br>750 B-47s | 70 Bears<br>120 Bisons |

*Source:* International Institute for Strategic Studies, "The Communist Bloc and the Western Alliance: The Military Balance 1962–63" (London, England).
[a]Some authorities claim that at this time the USSR had as few as six operational ICBMs and that this imbalance was a major reason for their attempt to base intermediate-range missiles, capable of threatening the US, in Cuba.

unchanged to the present day. The triad itself was designed, with the decision to place roughly equal emphasis on each leg. The ICBM force was built up rapidly, to 1,000 Minutemen and 54 Titan IIs. Polaris submarines (eventually replaced by Poseidons) were commissioned in large numbers. Production of B-52s ceased, and emphasis switched to qualitative improvements in engines, in electronic countermeasures, and in stand-off missiles as well as the low, ground-hugging approach rather than high-altitude bombardment. Major development programs were initiated, which led in the 1970s to long-range cruise missiles, MIRVing, enhanced radiation warheads, and greatly increased missile accuracy.

The USSR did not begin deploying significant additional numbers of strategic nuclear weapons until the mid-1960s. When the Soviet buildup came, however, it was only slightly less intense than that of the US. This increased deployment may have been partly a response to the American missile buildup that had been initiated in the early 1960s, and/or a result of the Soviet humiliation during the Cuban missile crisis. At the conclusion of that episode, a high-ranking member of the Soviet government is reported to have commented to his American counterpart, "You'll never be able to do this to us again."

It is now widely acknowledged that Khrushchev had bluffed the US into thinking that the Soviet Union possessed substantially more nuclear weapons than it actually did. (Recall that this was before the era of sat-

ellite surveillance.) It is unclear, however, whether such a bluff was in either side's strategic interest, since its ultimate result may have been substantial increases in the arsenals of both. It is also possible, of course, that the Soviet strategic buildup would have occurred independently of American actions, and that the American strategic buildup would have occurred even without Khrushchev's bluffs and the various supposed gaps. There is little doubt, however, that such factors contributed to the arms race.

Clear American nuclear superiority continued through the mid-1960s, when the USSR began to catch up, and, at least in numbers of ICBMs, to surpass the United States. During this time MAD became recognized as American strategic doctrine, the goal of nuclear "sufficiency" came to replace nuclear "superiority," and strategic thinking increasingly emphasized the prospects of mutual stability if not disarmament. The US essentially stopped racing with the USSR, at least with regard to the numbers of deployed missiles, and, in a sense, allowed the Soviets to catch up. But just as US analysts had overestimated Soviet military procurement at the time the bomber gap and the missile gap were proclaimed, they generally seem to have underestimated it during the late 1960s. Just after the United States had obtained its complement of Minuteman ICBMs and built up its Polaris fleet, the USSR began introducing its own nuclear missile submarines, and outproduced the US in ICBMs as well (Fig. 9.5). The US lead in strategic bombers, however, continued to hold. Table 9.2 shows Soviet and US strategic forces by late 1969, by which time nuclear parity had essentially been reached and US–Soviet arms negotiations began in earnest.

**Table 9.2 US–Soviet strategic nuclear forces by late 1969**

| Missiles or bombers | US | USSR |
|---|---|---|
| ICBMs | 1,000 Minutemen<br>54 Titan IIs | 1,200 |
| SLBMs | 656 (16 missiles each on 41 Polaris submarines) | 230 |
| Strategic bombers | 540 | 150 |

*Source:* International Institute for Strategic Studies, "Strategic Survey, 1969" (London, England).

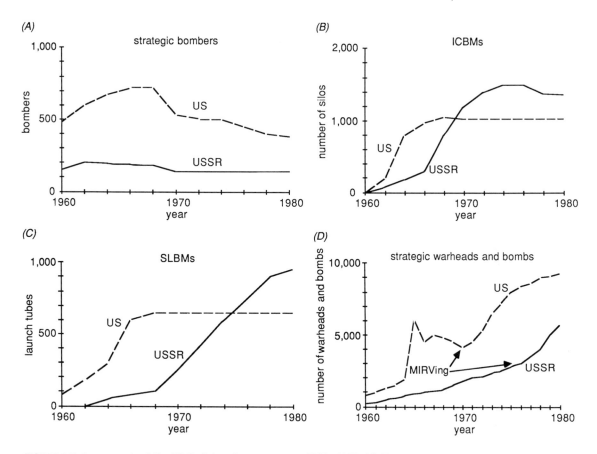

**FIGURE 9.5 Four aspects of the US-Soviet nuclear arms race, 1960–1980. (*A*) The US has always maintained a lead in strategic bombers, although that lead has been quantitatively decreasing. (*B*) The US grabbed an early lead in numbers of ICBMs during the mid-1960s; the USSR responded in the late 1960s and early 1970s, eventually surpassing the US in absolute numbers. (*C*) A similar pattern obtained for submarine-launched ballistic missiles: an early US lead, after which the USSR pulled ahead in sheer numbers. (*D*) The US has led consistently in numbers of strategic bombs and warheads; note the increases on both sides due to MIRVing.** (Modified from Dennis, 1984.)

## IS IT REALLY AN ARMS RACE?

A "race" is generally thought to be a competition in speed, in which each contestant seeks to outpace the other. It also presupposes an end point, and a winner; whoever reaches the finish line first. In some respects, the nuclear arms "race" is a very peculiar race indeed. The finish line is not obvious, and it is clear that neither side has been running at top speed. For example, if either nation simply tried to make as many ICBMs as it possibly could, there would be tens of thousands of such missiles on each side today. However, the pattern has been more like a series of temporary leads held by the US, followed by a halt during which the USSR catches up and in some ways forges ahead, while concurrently both sides (especially the US) seek to invent some other way of competing.

Nuclear competition takes place qualitatively as well as quantitatively. The expression "arms race," although not precisely accurate, is widely used and so we shall continue to employ it. It is important to recognize, however, that it offers an oversimple, sometimes misleading image of a complex, multifaceted process that proceeds at different times in different ways, at different rates, and for differing motivations. Although the US intentionally settled for mutual deterrence rather than clear-cut quantitative advantage, the arms race continued with regard to new models and new technology, even during the "detente" that characterized most of the 1970s.

## A QUICK NOTE ON DETENTE

Beginning with the Nixon administration, and especially under the guidance of Secretary of State Henry Kissinger, the United States and the Soviet Union entered into a period of superpower accommodation and relative harmony known as **detente.** Some critics (notably from China and the third world) viewed detente as a shared umbrella under which the superpowers sought hegemony over the planet, at the expense of other nations. Others (notably from the hawkish right) viewed detente as a misguided US effort to appease the Soviets, during which the USSR gained much and the United States, little. Others (notably from the dovish left and much of Europe) viewed detente as a necessary and if anything insufficient effort on the part of the two superpowers to improve political and economic relations and to learn how to live together—since the alternative in a highly nuclearized world is to die together.

A major aspect of detente was the Strategic Arms Limitation Talks (SALT), as well as other negotiated agreements, which we review in the next chapter. Detente also involved increased scientific and cultural exchanges, as well as a general lowering of superpower tensions. In other respects, however, detente was a disappointment. The Soviets had expected dramatically improved trade relations with the US, but they refused to permit increased Jewish emigration, which the United States had established as a precondition. The United States remained disappointed at the lack of Soviet progress in human rights, while the Soviets were irritated by what they saw as American meddling in their internal affairs.

American hawks pointed increasingly to the Soviet backstage role during the 1973 Arab-Israeli war and to Soviet adventurism in Africa, especially their assistance to Cuban troops in Angola and Ethiopia. Detente unraveled during the latter years of the Carter administration, when: a Soviet brigade was revealed to be stationed in Cuba, the American-backed dictator Anastasio Somoza was overthrown in Nicaragua, and the United States government was chagrined at the Iranian revolution, and angered and humiliated over the taking of American hostages. By the time the USSR invaded Afghanistan, in 1979, detente was effectively dead.

## THE ARMS RACE DURING THE 1970S AND 1980S

Despite detente, both superpowers continued to modify, modernize, and in many ways add to their nuclear arsenals throughout the 1970s. The major developments during that decade involved, on the American side: upgrading the Minutemen both in accuracy and in megatonnage; hardening and then superhardening missile silos; replacing Polaris with Poseidon submarines and developing the Trident; conducting research on possible ballistic missile defense systems; and reducing the numbers of B-52s, along with substantial upgrading of the remaining fleet as well as developing the B-1 bomber and the MX missile (Fig. 9.6). On the Soviet side, there was deployment of three new, large ICBMs (the SS-17s, SS-18s, and SS-19s), increases and improvements in SLBMs, deployment of medium-range SS-20 missiles in Europe (see Chapter 10), as well as deployment of the Backfire bomber.

Also during the 1970s, both sides proceeded with:

- *Modernization* (increases in missile accuracy and, more recently, in explosive yield of the strategic warheads as well).

- *MIRVing of ICBMs and SLBMs* (which has resulted in the addition of thousands of new warheads to existing missiles).

- *Cruise missiles* (especially the long-range models, in which the US is currently estimated to hold about a 5-year lead). The US is actively engaged in programs outfitting B-52s with air-launched cruise missiles and plans to deploy several thousand sea-launched cruise missiles as well, on both submarines and surface ships.

With regard to new ICBMs expected during the 1980s, it is anticipated that the USSR will begin deploying an additional missile, the SS-X-24, by 1986 or so. (The "X" designation, for "experimental," will be removed upon deployment.) Although it will be deployed initially in fixed silos, it is thought that the SS-24 will ultimately be a mobile system. On the US side, deployment of MX missiles is scheduled to begin on a comparable schedule. The USSR is deploying another ICBM, which the US designates the SS-25; the Soviets claim that this is a slight modification of an earlier model, their only operational solid-fueled ICBM, the SS-13 (Fig. 9.7). The United States is also developing a comparable missile (Fig. 9.8), the small, mobile, single-warhead ICBM generally known as "Midgetman."

During the 1980s, 12 Poseidon submarines were retrofitted with Trident missiles, and vessels were launched in a growing fleet of Trident submarines. The last Polaris submarines were retired, some of them converted for use in commando applications or as attack submarines. The USSR launched its new generation, Delta class submarines in the late 1970s and has been developing its newest submarines, the Typhoons, for deployment in the late 1980s. The American B-1B and the Soviet Blackjack strategic bombers are also expected to be deployed in growing numbers, while Advanced Technology (Stealth) cruise missiles and Star Wars/SDI systems will be researched on both sides. Tables 9.3 and 9.4 summarize the major current US and Soviet nuclear weapons programs.

The preceding brief review has touched only some of the highlights of the US–Soviet nuclear arms race. In the next chapter, we shall review the major negotiated agreements between the superpowers and the relationship of these agreements to the ongoing nuclear competition. The nuclear arms race is unique just as any historical sequence is one of a kind. But beyond this, the nuclear arms race is unique in the importance it holds for the human species. The US–Soviet arms race is a specific case of a widespread and longstanding human experience of international military and political competition; therefore, our understanding may be increased by examining its relationship to arms races more generally.

**FIGURE 9.6 The first flight-ready MX missile undergoing developmental testing.** (Courtesy of the US Department of Defense.)

For the remainder of this chapter, we shall use some broad features of arms races to illuminate the specifics of the US–Soviet nuclear competition. In doing so, it is useful to identify two basic factors: first, those resulting primarily from external causes and/or each nation's perception of those external causes, and then, those resulting primarily from internal, or domestic factors.

**FIGURE 9.7 Soviet SS-13 ICBM on display during the May Day parade, 1982.** (Courtesy of the US Department of Defense.)

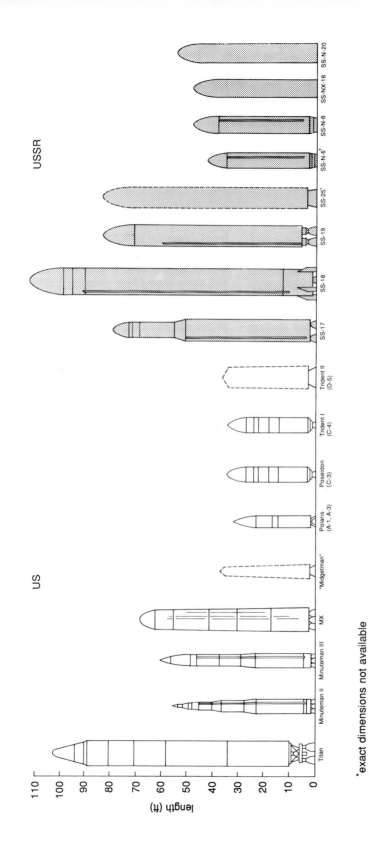

**FIGURE 9.8 Relative sizes of major US and Soviet strategic missiles.** (Modified from Dennis, 1984.)

*exact dimensions not available

†N = naval (submarine) missile

**TABLE 9.3 Major US nuclear weapons programs of the late 1980s**

| Weapon system | Total to be produced | First year operational | Spent by fiscal year 1986 ($ billion) | Requested funding, fiscal year 1986 ($ billion) | Number requested | Proposed funding, fiscal year 1987 ($ billion) | Unit cost, fiscal year 1986 ($ million) | Estimated total cost[a] ($ billion) | Comments |
|---|---|---|---|---|---|---|---|---|---|
| MX missile | ? | 1986 | 14.6 | 4.0 | 48 | 3.2 | 116 | 25.9 | ? (deployed by 1989) |
| Trident submarine | 20–25 | 1982 | 16.8 | 2.0 | 1 | 1.8 | 1,600 | 31–39 | Cost for first 16 subs: $25.1 billion |
| Trident I (C-4) | 595 | 1979 | 8.1 | 0.066 | 0 | 0.047 | 19 | 11.2 | For 12 Poseidons and 8 Tridents, 211 tests and spares |
| Trident II (D-5) | 764 | 1989 | 4.4 | 2.7 | 0 | 3.6 | 49 | 37.4 | For 16 subs; for 20–25, cost would be $42 billion–$48 billion |
| B-1B | 100 | 1986 | 26.4 | 6.0 | 48 | 0.136 | 400 | 40 | 90 operational aircraft |
| Stealth | 132 | 1990s | ? | 0.80 | 0 | 2.272 | ? | 40–50? | One estimate $6.3 billion for fiscal years 1984–1988 |
| B-52 modifications | 263 | Ongoing | 3.3 | 0.480 | — | 0.805 | 20 each | 5.8 | Radar, engines, avionics |
| ALCM | 1,739 | 1982 | 4.1 | 0.049 | 0 | 0.037 | 2.5 | 4.5 | Production stopped |
| GLCM | 565 | 1983 | 2.8 | 0.620 | 95 | 0.243 | 6.5 | 3.7 | |
| SLCM | 4,068 | 1984 | 3.3 | 0.849 | 249 | 1 | 3.2 | 13.0 | |
| Advanced cruise missile | 2,600 | 1988 | ? | ? | 0 | ? | 5–7 | 7.0 | Figures are estimates |
| Pershing II | 325 | 1983 | 2.2 | 0.335 | 70 | 0.007 | 7.0 | 2.9 | |
| Midgetman | 1,000 | 1992 | 0.807 | 0.625 | 0 | ? | 38–70 | 38–70 | 20-year cost could be $107 billion |

*Source:* Modified from SIPRI (1985).
[a] Does not include costs computed by the Department of Energy for nuclear warheads and bombs, which normally are an additional 10–20% of the weapon system cost.

**TABLE 9.4 Major Soviet nuclear weapons programs of the late 1980s**

| Strategic | Theater/tactical |
|---|---|
| SS-18 Mod 5, ICBM | SS-X-28 (replacement for SS-20) |
| SS-18 Mod 4, ICBM | SS-21 |
| SS-X-24, ICBM | SS-22 |
| SS-X-25, ICBM | SS-23 |
| SS-X-26, ICBM | Replacement for SS-21 |
| SS-X-27, ICBM | Replacement for SS-22 |
| SS-NX-23/Delta IV submarine[a] | Replacement for SS-23 |
| New undesignated SLBM | SS-CX-4 |
| Bear G bomber | MiG-27 Frogger J, aircraft |
| Bear H/with AS-15 ALCM | Su-25 Frogfoot, aircraft |
| Blackjack A bomber | 152-mm howitzer |
| Backfire C bomber | SS-N-21, SLBM |
| ABM-X-3, missile | SS-N-22, SLBM |
| | Next-generation SLCM/GLCM |

*Source:* Modified from SIPRI (1985).
[a]N = naval (submarine) missile

## EXTERNAL CAUSES

### Action-Reaction Sequences

As we have seen, the nuclear arms race is an unusual race, if indeed it is a race at all. It is generally recognized that the goal cannot be to win, insofar as there would be no winners in a nuclear war. To some, the goal is to avoid losing, that is, to maintain a stable situation, albeit with some unavoidable competition, perhaps forever. Others claim that by continuing such a balance, and demonstrating resolve to do so indefinitely, it might be possible to convince the Soviets ultimately to agree to substantial reductions. To others, the goal is to win without war. For some hawkish US strategists, this may involve squeezing the USSR so hard and for so long that it collapses economically and/or politically. For some Soviet strategists, this may involve keeping pace with the United States until worldwide capitalism collapses of its own internal contradictions and dynamics. (It is also possible that for a minority of strategists on both sides the goal is in fact to defeat the opponent in a nuclear war.)

In any event, it is clear that whatever the ultimate goals, the accumulation of nuclear weapons on each side has not occurred in a vacuum: there has been awareness—often acute awareness—by each side of the other's future plans, and certainly, of each other's latest deployments. In most cases, the USSR has been playing "catch-up." That is, beginning with the Manhattan Project, the United States has set the pace in most advances related to nuclear weapons (Table 9.5).

The Soviet Union has also initiated some nuclear developments that the United States has not chosen to emulate: very large ICBMs, very large thermonuclear bombs, fractional orbital bombardment systems, and reusable ICBM silos. Moreover, after having caught up, the USSR has tended to forge ahead in sheer numbers of weapons deployed, while the US has tended to remain ahead in overall sophistication and in technological innovation.

There has been some debate over the extent to which the arms race is driven by cycles of action by one side, which generates a reaction by the other, which produces a counterreaction, and so forth. According to advocates of this **action–reaction** interpretation, the US has largely been running a race with itself, escalating the arms race first by achieving a quantitative lead and more recently by qualitative innovations, forcing the USSR to keep struggling to catch up, . . . , which they always do, a few years later. Then the US has reacted to the Soviet reactions, and the sequence has

**TABLE 9.5  Sequence of major new developments in technology and nuclear weapons**

| Event | First place | Date | Second place | Date |
|---|---|---|---|---|
| First sustained chain reaction | US | 1942 | USSR | 1946 |
| Atomic bomb | US | 1945 | USSR | 1949 |
| Intercontinental bomber | US | 1948 | USSR | 1955 |
| Postwar military pact | US (NATO) | 1949 | USSR (WP) | 1955 |
| Tactical nuclear weapons in Europe | US | 1954 | USSR | 1957 |
| Nuclear-powered submarine | US | 1955 | USSR | 1959 |
| ICBM | USSR | 1957 | US | 1958 |
| Orbiting satellite | USSR | 1957 | US | 1958 |
| Supersonic bomber | US | 1960 | USSR | 1975 |
| SLBM | US | 1960 | USSR | 1968 |
| Solid-fueled missiles | US | 1960 | USSR | 1968 |
| MRVs | US | 1964 | USSR | 1968 |
| ABM system | USSR | 1968 | US | 1972 |
| MIRVs | US | 1970 | USSR | 1975 |
| Enhanced radiation warheads | US | 1981 | USSR | [a] |
| Long-range cruise missiles | US | 1982 | USSR | [a] |

[a]As of 1986, these weapons have not been deployed by the USSR. It is widely assumed, however, that they will be, before 1990.

repeated itself. In some respects, the occurrence of action-reaction cycles seems to be undeniable, as with the Soviet development of antiaircraft defenses in the 1950s as a likely reaction to the large United States strategic bomber fleet. This in turn led to the development of electronic countermeasures by the bombers, low-level penetration capabilities, and air-launched cruise missiles, which seem likely to lead in the next round to "look-down" Soviet radar systems analogous to the American AWACS.

Similarly, the American ICBM buildup of the early 1960s may have begun as a reaction to the missile gap. The missile gap, in turn, although misperceived by the United States, did reflect a real, pioneering effort by the USSR that may have been stimulated by the Soviets' recognition that they were hopelessly behind the United States in strategic bombers. It is further possible that the vigorous Soviet ICBM buildup of the late 1960s was a reaction to the prior American buildup earlier in that decade. The action-reaction interpretation does not necessarily imply that each reaction will precisely match the action that stimulated it: the American ICBM buildup was not aborted even after the mis-

sile gap was found to be nonexistent. Similarly, the Soviet deployment of ICBMs, even granting that it was a reaction to the American deployment, did not stop once the US levels had been surpassed.

Because patterns of weapons deployment and doctrinal decisions develop over many years, action-reaction cycles are not readily adjustable. It is therefore possible for a reaction on one side to begin in response to a perceived action by the other, and for this reaction to continue long after the "action" has been recognized to be quite different from what it originally appeared to be. It is also possible for overreactions to occur. The misperceptions that contribute to reactions, and sometimes overreactions, may be honest errors of intelligence; they may also be the result of cautious judgments by people whose professional discipline requires that they assume the worst (see the next section); or they may, on occasion, be cynically manipulated by individuals on each side wishing to stimulate the arms race.

The Soviets deployed the so-called Tallinn air defense system near Leningrad during the 1960s. This "action" was originally considered by the United States to be an ABM system. It gave added impetus to American MIRVing, to the decision to develop and deploy an American ABM system, and even to the Poseidon and Minuteman III programs. It was subsequently learned that the Tallinn system was actually an anti*aircraft* system, itself probably intended as a reaction to American plans to develop and deploy B-70 bombers and/or SR-71 strike–reconnaissance aircraft. Neither was ever deployed, so the Soviet Tallinn "reaction" was an inappropriate overreaction. However, American counterreactions did in fact take place.

In general, the action-reaction interpretation of the arms race is favored by those who argue for greater unilateral restraint: if actions on one side simply produce reactions on the other (and sometimes overreactions), such actions are counterproductive. Both sides probably would have been better off if no action had been initiated in the first place.

On the other hand, many of the decisions to add another rung of escalation to the nuclear arms race must have been made independently of any action-reaction cycle. Thus, the USSR developed hydrogen bombs just a year after the US; clearly, Soviet scientists did not wait until the first American H-bomb test to initiate their own program. Most new weapons and weapon systems require years of research and development, followed by extensive testing before deployment can take place. Action-reaction cycles alone therefore cannot be responsible for weapons that follow each other within just a few years. Nevertheless, graphic presentations of the sequence of weapons system procurement (e.g., Fig. 9.9) can be instructive.

The action-reaction phenomenon almost certainly figures into the arms race, but it is not the only factor. For example, the American decision to proceed with MIRVing was not simply a reaction to Soviet ABM deployment. MIRVs were attractive because they offered the opportunity to increase the number of strategic warheads at minimal cost, without adding to the number of ICBMs and SLBMs. MIRVing also presented the opportunity to exploit a technological advantage over the Soviet Union, as well as the temptation to proceed with an elegant technological innovation, a process that Oppenheimer had earlier described as being "technically sweet."

In many cases, new developments in nuclear weapons occur not so much in response to what the other side has done as in response to estimates of what the other side is likely to do, or—more often—what the other side might do. John S. Foster, Director of Research

and Engineering at the Defense Department under Jimmy Carter, testified as follows to Congress:

> We are moving ahead to make sure that, whatever they do, or the possible things we imagine that they might do, we will respond. . . . We see possible threats on the horizon, usually not something the enemy has done, but something we may have thought of ourselves that he might do, and that we must therefore be prepared for.

Critics charge that this is a route to bankruptcy and competition that is unrealistic, unending, and very dangerous. Supporters maintain that in an imperfect world, it is only prudent to respond to one's opponent, and moreover, to plan ahead—hoping for the best, but expecting the worst.

## Worst-Case Analyses

The job of military strategists is to maintain national security. As a result, security analysts tend to be professional pessimists, since the most conservative—and seemingly, the safest—way to proceed is to assume the worst and prepare to deal with it. Military planners therefore typically try to avoid both underestimating a potential opponent and overestimating their own weaponry. In the resulting approach, known as **worst-case analysis,** national security strategists try to imagine the least desirable consequence of many situations and plan to meet such possibilities.

Intelligence data are rarely exact, and yet, procurement decisions and even decisions on strategic policy are often strongly influenced by each side's perceptions of the other. Let us imagine, for example, that an American analyst seeking to assess the theoretical vulnerability of American missile silos has been given estimates of Soviet missile accuracy that range from a CEP of 150 to 450 meters. An assumption of the more generous estimate (450 meters) or even the average of the two extremes (300 meters) would result in a recommendation very different from the one that would result if the worst were assumed; that is, if Soviet missiles were believed to have a CEP of only 150 meters. When national security is involved, general procedure (on both sides) has been to assume the worst, and then perhaps to be pleasantly surprised if this analysis proves to be overly gloomy. In short, better safe than sorry.

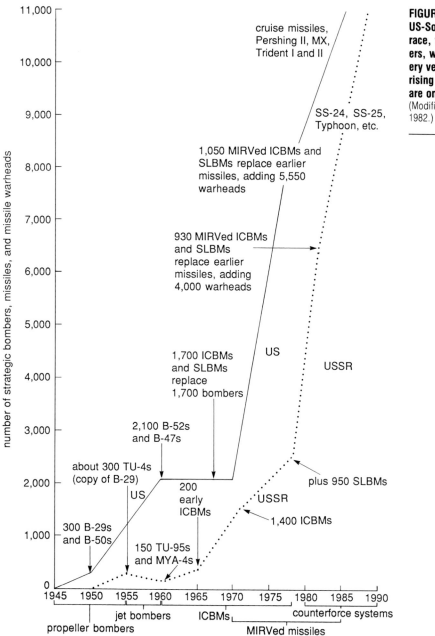

cruise missiles, Pershing II, MX, Trident I and II

SS-24, SS-25, Typhoon, etc.

1,050 MIRVed ICBMs and SLBMs replace earlier missiles, adding 5,550 warheads

930 MIRVed ICBMs and SLBMs replace earlier missiles, adding 4,000 warheads

1,700 ICBMs and SLBMs replace 1,700 bombers

US

USSR

2,100 B-52s and B-47s

about 300 TU-4s (copy of B-29)

US

200 early ICBMs

plus 950 SLBMs

USSR

1,400 ICBMs

300 B-29s and B-50s

150 TU-95s and MYA-4s

number of strategic bombers, missiles, and missile warheads

11,000 — 10,000 — 9,000 — 8,000 — 7,000 — 6,000 — 5,000 — 4,000 — 3,000 — 2,000 — 1,000 — 0

1945  1950  1955  1960  1965  1970  1975  1980  1985  1990

propeller bombers

jet bombers

ICBMs

MIRVed missiles

counterforce systems

**FIGURE 9.9 History of the US-Soviet nuclear arms race, with regard to bombers, warheads, and delivery vehicles. The steeply rising curves after 1982 are only approximate.** (Modified from Forsberg, 1982.)

However, this approach has been criticized. It is claimed that worst-case analysis may in fact contribute directly to the arms race itself because it leads to decisions that stimulate worst-case analysis on the other side, and so forth. In our example of missile accuracy, assumptions that the opponent's missiles are highly accurate lead to decisions that one's own silos should be hardened in response. This in turn can lead the other side to a worst-case conclusion that the silos have actually been superhardened, resulting in a presumed need to increase accuracy yet more, and so on. Thus worst-case analysis can become a self-fulfilling prophecy, generating precisely the "worst case" it seeks to preclude. "It is the business of military strategists to prepare for all eventualities," wrote theologian Reinhold Niebuhr, who was emphatically not a pacifist. Yet Niebuhr concluded that it is the "fatal error of such strategists to create the eventualities for which they must prepare."

Take a hypothetical case of offense/defense competition in a world of deployed ballistic missile defenses. The defending side, observing 1,000 missiles pointed in its direction, makes the worst-case assumption that all 1,000 missiles will perform as intended. Let us say that defense requires 2,000 lasers (two per attacking missile). But in the worst case, the analyst may assume that although all 1,000 of the opponent's missiles will work, only 80% of the defending lasers will function as expected; this would require the defender to deploy 2,000 + (20% × 2,000) or 2,400 lasers. The other side, however, is also making worst-case assumptions. Their analysts assume that all 2,400 of the opponent's newly installed lasers will work and only 80% of their attacking missiles will function as designed. Accordingly, they must plan for yet more missiles, and this strategy is anticipated by the defense, which in turn calls for more lasers.

Similarly, worst-case analysis may stimulate the arms race even when it does not lead directly to an action-reaction sequence. In the cases of the bomber and missile gaps, for example, worst-case analyses resulted in overestimates of Soviet deployment, and of likely future deployments. The predominant American response was to increase the US production of bombers, and then of missiles, respectively. The sequence is not strictly logical: bombers do not counter bombers, nor (in the absence of counterforce) do the ICBMs of one side somehow erase the ICBMs of the other. Nonetheless, worst-case analyses contribute to a feeling of anxiety and to a public perception of the need to "keep up." On the other hand, it can be argued that when it comes to deterrence, perception is everything. Therefore, stability depends precisely on maintaining the perception that both sides are equally vulnerable.

Criticisms notwithstanding, few alternatives to worst-case analysis have been suggested. Although it seems likely that the USSR uses a similar approach in evaluating its nuclear posture with respect to the United States, worst-case analysis is especially characteristic of American strategic decision making. The US is a very open society; reasonably accurate and complete data are publicly available through congressional hearings, widespread media coverage, scientific symposia, and annual reports from the Department of Defense. By contrast, the USSR plays its nuclear cards much closer to its chest. Very little information is made available concerning current deployments or future plans. This situation forces others to rely on estimates, which tend to emphasize the worst case and often err in the direction of excess. It is at least possible that in the long run, Soviet security would be maximized by more openness, which in turn would lead to more accurate—and perhaps less alarmist—projections and analyses by United States officials.

Closely related to the problem of worst-case analysis is the important distinction between **capabilities** and **intentions.** Our discussion of worst-case analysis has focused on assessment of actual military hardware, that is, on capabilities. As susceptible as even these estimates may be to uncertainties, assessments of an opponent's intentions are even more unlikely to be exact. Thus, for example, either side may be developing a nuclear force that is *capable* of a first strike. As we have seen, this can be debated, perhaps endlessly. Even more uncertain, however, is whether the political leadership actually *intends* to make a first strike. And yet, this is the important question. The United States may be capable of destroying a given percentage of Soviet ICBMs; it is crucial for the Soviet leadership to judge whether we actually intend to do so.

It is often argued that since intentions cannot be estimated reliably, judgments must be based on assessments of capabilities, which as we have seen, tend to assume the worst, for the sake of prudence. In the process, each side has a tendency to make an additional, unspoken worst-case analysis here as well: it is tacitly assumed that the other side also has the worst possible intent. Even when the reality of an action is unquestioned, its interpretation is debatable, with hawks and doves typically seeing it as indicating very different intentions. In the West, for example, the Soviet establishment of satellite states in eastern Europe was viewed as primarily offensive by hawks and defensive by doves. Similarly, hawks and doves tend to apply a double standard in judging the intentions of the US and the USSR: doves look with alarm at the US acquisition of first-strike-capable missiles such as the MX and Trident II, which suggest aggressive intent to them. They are less alarmed by Soviet first-strike-capable ICBMs such as the SS-18s. American hawks look with alarm at the prospect of the USSR developing a ballistic missile defense—Defense Secretary Weinberger called it "one of the most frightening prospects imaginable"—and yet, they are untroubled about the strategic consequences for the Soviet Union if the United States developed such a system.

Partisans of each nation see their own intentions as peaceful, and they tend to downplay their capabilities, except when it comes to deterrence. When looking at the other side, they see aggressive intentions, buttressed by increasingly capable and thus threatening nuclear weapons.

## The Prisoner's Dilemma Revisited

In Chapter 6 we considered the relevance of game theory and the games of Chicken and Prisoner's Dilemma to deterrence and crisis stability. Game theory also has been applied to problems of the arms race and arms race stability, since two "players" are often involved, and the payoff to each depends on what the other does. Prisoner's Dilemma seems to be especially appropriate in this regard: the payoff to each side is likely to be high if both agree to reduce their arsenals, or at least to refrain from escalating (mutual "reward" in the terminology introduced earlier). The cost to each side is high if they both build up ("punishment" of mutual defection). But cooperation is inhibited by fear on each side that if it behaves cooperatively and refrains from escalating, or actually begins disarming, the other side will take advantage of this and refuse to disarm, or actually build up. In this case, the cooperative side would get "suckered" by the more aggressive side, which succumbed to the "temptation" of defection.

|  | side 2 | |
|---|---|---|
|  | disarm | build up |
| side 1 — disarm | R, R | S, T |
| side 1 — build up | T, S | P, P |

Caught in this dilemma, each side feels itself forced to escalate the arms race—to the detriment of both sides—out of fear that if it did not, the other side would take advantage of its restraint. So, both sides wind up in the "build-up" quadrant we have been describing in this chapter.

An example of this process may be seen in President Truman's decision to press ahead with development of the hydrogen bomb. It seemed likely that the security of the US and the USSR would ultimately be reduced if these weapons were added to their respective arsenals (mutual punishment). However, the prospect of ensuring cooperation (agreement not to develop H-bombs) was seen as virtually zero, and the danger of being suckered (the USSR developing the bombs and not the US), was considered to be intolerable. So, both sides developed H-bombs and the arms race was ratcheted up another notch.

Presumably in such cases, both sides reason as follows: "If we refrain from doing such-and-such, and they do not, we will be at a disadvantage." It should also be clear how action-reaction sequences would accelerate this process. Furthermore, worst-case analyses tend to modify the reasoning to: "Regardless of whether we do such-and-such, they almost certainly will, so we must."

The logic of Prisoner's Dilemma may also apply to geopolitical issues no less than to specific decisions regarding development and deployment of weapons. Thus, a power vacuum—say, in the Middle East—tends to attract involvement from the superpowers, even though both sides might be better off if mutual noninterference could be arranged. The problem, once again, is that each side fears being suckered if it stays out while the other side, following the temptation to gain influence at the opponent's expense, becomes involved. According to this view, the arms race is driven at least partly by the sad reality that each side is prisoner of a dilemma that forces counterproductive escalation, because of fear that to refrain is to be taken advantage of . . . which would be even worse.

## Good Versus Evil

**(Right-wing View)** Our discussion of action-reaction chains, worst-case planning, and Prisoner's Dilemma tended to place responsibility for the arms race about equally on the two superpowers. It presented each side as the victim of a self-fulfilling dynamic. Although most observers acknowledge that such a view has some validity, this perspective is rejected as naive and incomplete by many partisans of the political right, according to whom the major driving force in the arms race is the Soviet threat. The Soviet Union is seen as a dangerous, aggressive, expansionist power committed to worldwide revolution, and ultimately world domination and the destruction of Western values. The Soviet repression of eastern Europe, their provocative behavior in Berlin, their support of North Korea during the Korean war, their support of Castro's Cuba, of the North Vietnamese, and of the Sandinistas in Nicaragua, their invasion of Afghanistan, and of course, their weapons buildup are all seen as demonstrating aggressive intent and necessitating constant vigilance by the United States.

The USSR, in this view, is a dangerous, determined opponent whose basic values are alien to our own. As a result, the nuclear arms race is forced on us, through no fault of ours. It is regrettable that we are confronted with such a situation, but we have no morally or practically acceptable alternative than to persevere. The arms race is not so much a misunderstanding as it is a result of our correct understanding of Soviet (and to a lesser extent, other communist) aggressive designs. The primary momentum of the arms race is produced by Soviet behavior and our need to defend the free world. In his Farewell Address (better known for its warning about the "military–industrial complex") Dwight Eisenhower gave this explanation: "We face a hostile ideology—global in scope, atheistic in character, ruthless in purpose, and insidious in method. Unhappily the danger it poses promises to be of indefinite duration."

**Left-wing View**  Just as the American far right places most if not all of the blame for the arms race on the Soviet Union, the far left attributes most of the blame to the United States. Although very few are apologists for repressive Soviet behavior, there is a widespread tendency to emphasize the defensive, reactive nature of Soviet foreign policy and the pace-setting role of the US throughout nearly all of the nuclear competition. The United States, according to this view, has never accepted Soviet communism as a legitimate form of government, and yearns to destroy it, by military means if necessary. Moreover, the United States has inherited the mantle of European imperialism. As a result, it seeks to maintain economic and political control over third world nations, and to use its nuclear arsenal to intimidate the Soviet Union and if necessary the rest of the world, into permitting continued American domination. The primary momentum of the arms race is produced by American behavior and our stubborn insistence on military solutions to social, economic, and political problems.

**An Attempt at Balance**  It is difficult and perhaps impossible to know which side is correct in this dispute, or, if the truth lies somewhere in between, where this in-between position might be. It is even difficult to assess the effects that the policies of one nation have on the policies of another, as we have sought to do in discussing the arms race as a dynamic interaction between the two countries. In any event, it seems clear that not all the momentum of the nuclear arms race—or of arms races generally—comes from foreign actions and the perception of external threats. It has been argued that to a large extent the dynamics of arms races are internally generated, quite independent of the supposed external enemy. In this view, participants in arms races are to a large extent autonomous, or even "autistic" in that they behave primarily with reference to internal factors rather than to the outside world. We shall therefore turn to some of these domestic forces that have been seen as making the "arms race" less a race between two nations than a process that is largely internally generated, within each nation.

## INTERNAL CAUSES

### Technology

Much of the arms race seems to ride on the momentum of scientific and technological advances. Einstein once noted that politics was more difficult than physics; certainly, the physicists have been more successful inventing weapons of destruction than politicians have been in controlling them (Fig. 9.10). To some extent, it can be argued that strategic doctrine has not determined the kinds of weapons that have been fielded, but rather, the weapons have determined the doctrine. This would be an obvious case of putting the cart before the horse, since in theory at least, each nation should decide on the weapons it needs to carry out its strategic goals; it should not modify its goals to accommodate the weapons. An alternative view can also be maintained, however: that scientific research and the discoveries that result are largely a consequence of national policies and desires. In this view, technology is the handmaiden of national priorities, rather than a Frankenstein's monster, dangerously out of control.

The first atomic explosion was not the result of a serendipitous discovery by a lonely inventor working weekends in the garage. Rather, the development of nuclear weapons via the Manhattan Project was a massive governmental program, requiring the concerted efforts of thousands of highly trained people and a vast expenditure of resources. (Similarly, the program to develop the hydrogen bomb, the space program, and more recently, Star Wars/SDI research have originated at the federal level.)

This would suggest that government policy, not scientific-technological momentum, was crucially responsible for the invention of nuclear weapons in the first place. Moreover, without immense investment of government funds, it seems likely that much of the technological momentum of the arms race would promptly disappear. This further suggests that at least to some extent, the arms race is not at the mercy of science and technology; rather, government policy provides direction and momentum for each new round of the superpowers' nuclear competition. In a sense, this interpretation suggests that national decision makers can take control of nuclear weapons policy. It also suggests that they are in control today, a contention that may be disputed.

Thus, the **technological determinism** school argues that especially since 1945, science and technology have provided politicians with a never-ending series of Pandora's boxes. Once again, take the invention of the atomic bomb: although developed at the behest of the government, the atomic bomb confronted politicians with a reality for which they had no developed agenda or policies. Such strategies as massive retaliation, assured destruction, counterforce, the various proposed nuances of deterrence, and limited war-fighting can be seen to have followed in the wake of the latest technology: strategic bombers, ICBMs, accuracy improvements, MIRVing, and so on.

In some cases, it is indisputable that science and technology provide what politicians request: SLBMs, for example, were developed because strategists saw a need for them, and scientists and engineers did what they were asked. And if Star Wars/SDI becomes a reality, it will be because politicians and diplomats overcame skepticism in the scientific community and insisted on such a program of research and development. But on the other hand, it can also be argued that if science and technology had not disclosed the theoretical possibility of the various weapons, governments would not have developed them. If fusion technology had not beckoned, President Truman would not

1945: Hiroshima bomb
1 warhead of 12.5 kt

1.2 miles

1970: Minuteman III ICBM
3 MIRVed warheads of 170 kt each

2.2 miles

1986: MX ICBM
10 MIRVed warheads of 350 kt each

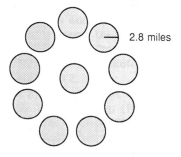

2.8 miles

**FIGURE 9.10 Diagram indicating the increase in destructiveness of nuclear weapons. Each circle indicates the area to be subjected to 3 psi overpressure. For the Hiroshima bomb, this area was about 4 square miles; a single Minuteman III missile, with three MIRVed warheads, can destroy more than 10 times that area; the MX missile, with 10 MIRVed warheads, could destroy more than 50 times the area destroyed at Hiroshima.** (Modified from Dennis, 1984.)

have decided to proceed with it in 1949. Similarly, if directed energy weapons and orbiting satellites were not on the technological horizon, President Reagan probably would not have called for Star Wars/SDI.

Cruise missiles and MIRVs may well have been developed in large part because they represented attractive and challenging technology. For a time, they were "weapons without a mission," produced by the creative genius of researchers. MIRVing, for example, was a spin-off of the domestic space program of the early 1960s, when it was discovered that several satellites could be launched from a single rocket. And the elaboration of the new category of nuclear weapons,

**FIGURE 9.11 Lawrence Livermore National Laboratory, Livermore, California. This multimillion-dollar research complex is one of two weapons design laboratories in the United States; the other is Los Alamos National Laboratory in New Mexico.** (Courtesy of Los Alamos National Laboratory.)

the "long-range theater" missiles such as the SS-20s, GLCMs, and Pershing IIs, has presented diplomats with some thorny difficulties (which we examine in Chapter 10).

In part because of the Prisoner's Dilemma situations we have already explored, governments feel a need to encourage research in a variety of abstruse fields, both in the hope of achieving unilateral advantage and out of fear that they might otherwise be surprised by the other side. Funds for military **research and development,** the creative arm of the military establishment, whose job is to come up with new weapons, consumed less than 1% of military budgets before World War II; it now represents about 15%. Approximately half a million scientists and engineers are employed in military work, which occupies one-third to half of all the world's research efforts. The creative genius of researchers, in short, has been unleashed in the design and production of weapons (Fig. 9.11). Governments often find themselves saddled with weapons not originally intended, or even, in the long run, desired. By a process sometimes known as **technological creep,** such innovations gradually become integrated into the arsenal. And because of the very long lead times—sometimes 10 years or more from research to deployment—weapons programs have a unique momentum of their own. Even despite delays and lags, it generally takes longer yet for diplomats to integrate new weapons into their planning, or alternatively, to ban them, than for weapons specialists to invent them.

Closely tied to technological innovation, strategic doctrine itself can also be identified as a partial contributor to the nuclear arms race. Thus, a national policy of finite or minimal deterrence would not prescribe a continuing accumulation of nuclear weapons; once each side had acquired the ability to destroy the other,

it would stop obtaining more. But in conjunction with the emerging doctrine of counterforce and doubts about vulnerability and second-strike capability—with those worries themselves due to technological innovations, notably MIRVing and accuracy improvements—deterrence policy has called for continuing increases in the weaponry of both sides, reaching levels that exceed the requirements of MAD (Fig. 9.12). And insofar as one side's nuclear weapons serve to deter the nuclear weapons of the other side, such a strategic stalemate has also led to renewed attention to the conventional force levels of both the US and the USSR.

Very little is known about the role of "technological imperatives" in the Soviet Union. It seems likely, however, that such factors are less important than in the United States, since most innovations have originated in the US. But for the same reason, a technological action-reaction imperative may be especially potent within the USSR. Whereas American scientists seek to match imagined Soviet weapons, Soviet scientists strive to match existing American advances. They often do so by begging, borrowing, and/or stealing modern Western technology.

In the United States, both the military and the military's industrial contractors are fond of expensive new weapons: the former because of the hoped-for effectiveness and prestige associated with such weapons, and the latter because of the profits as well as the scientific excitement of new technologies. In the USSR, however, although the Soviet military, too, appears to favor expensive new weapons, industrial managers seem to be more conservative. Technological, scientific, and industrial leaders in the USSR are not rewarded for profits, but rather for fulfilling their quotas. Therefore, they prefer smaller quotas, less imaginative goals, and less innovative weapons. It is generally easier to

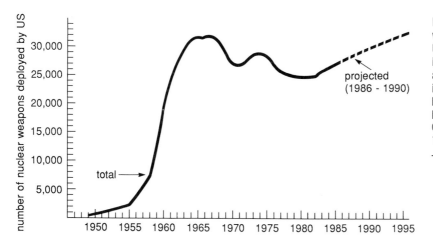

**FIGURE 9.12 The strategic weapons arsenal of the United States. After reaching a peak in 1965, the arsenal declined somewhat in numerical strength, but has been increasing in the late 1980s.** (Modified from Cochran, Arkin, and Hoenig, 1984.)

keep making and remaking a familiar item than to try something new. Hence, the "technological imperative" in the Soviet Union tends to favor incremental changes over radical new departures.

It may be that each case must be examined separately. In some situations, technology has preceded policy, often making headaches for the diplomats; in others, the technology is dependent on policy decisions. However, the two processes—political decisions and technological innovation—are certainly influenced by each other, often in complex ways.

### The Military-Industrial Complex

New weapons go through a predictable sequence, beginning with an investigation of the basic feasibility of the concepts and the underlying technology. After research comes development, the initial efforts to produce a prototype. During the testing stage, models are evaluated, if possible under realistic conditions. In some cases, several competing prototypes, developed by different military contractors, are tested against each other. Then, one or more models are chosen and production begins. Finally comes deployment, the placing of the weapons in the field. As the process continues, a constituency develops as well, consisting especially of the civilian contractors, their employees, the military leadership associated with the particular weapon, and the legislators representing the district within which the weapon or its components are to be produced and/or deployed. These interested parties generate additional pressures for producing the weapon, in large numbers. In general, the farther along in the continuum

from research toward deployment, the more difficult it is to stop a given project.

At each of these stages, an important interaction exists, especially between the federal government and its military services on the one hand, and the scientists and industrial contractors on the other. The "military-industrial complex" was identified by President Eisenhower in his Farewell Address in 1961:

> We have been compelled to create a permanent armaments industry of vast proportions. . . . This conjunction of an immense military establishment and a large arms industry is new in the American experience. The total influence—economic, political, even spiritual—is felt in every city, every Statehouse, every office of the Federal government. . . . In the councils of government, we must guard against the acquisition of unwarranted influence, whether sought or unsought, by the military-industrial complex. The potential for the disastrous rise of misplaced power exists and will persist.

Many observers note that the military-industrial complex is really a military-industrial-governmental-scientific-labor complex, a complicated amalgamation of interest groups, all of which have a stake in the arms race. As a result, this "complex" has become a powerful constituency for weapons acquisition. Such groups have substantial (and perhaps disproportionate) influence in decision making, in part because of the "revolving door" phenomenon, whereby former government and military employees are hired by military contractors, and vice versa.

Just as technological innovations are at least partly responsible for qualitative aspects of the arms race, it seems likely that the military-industrial complex, defined broadly, is at least partly responsible for some of its quantitative aspects, the actual numbers of weapons deployed. Thus, Robert McNamara noted in 1967 that "there is a kind of mad momentum intrinsic to the development of all nuclear weaponry. If a system works— and works well—there is a strong pressure from all directions to procure and deploy the weapon out of all proportion to the prudent level required."

On the other hand, supporters point out that American security depends on an effective system for research, testing, production, and deployment. They emphasize that the military-industrial complex is a creation of American democratic politics and free enterprise, and that whatever its contribution to the arms race, the military-industrial complex plays an even greater role in keeping the United States strong and at peace. After all, they point out, peace is expensive and sometimes wasteful; the only thing more expensive and more wasteful is war.

Although it seems obvious that a corresponding phenomenon exists in the USSR, the exact structure of the Soviet military-industrial complex is not clear. Thus, heavy industry has long had a special place in Soviet economic planning, favored over light industry and consumer goods in priority. In a full-employment economy such as the Soviet Union's, there is no temptation to use military spending to provide jobs in specific communities, as is sometimes the case in the United States (see Chapter 12 for the economic impact of military spending). In addition, the conflicting demand of the military and nonmilitary sectors is particularly acute in the USSR, which is in many ways an economy of scarcity: resources expended on the military are unavailable to the already-pinched civilian economy.

Although profits per se are not a motivating force in the USSR, power and status likely are. And in the Soviet Union, making missiles has long been favored over making sausages. In a communist system, no less than in a capitalist one, people are rewarded in proportion to the control and influence they exert over a large, impressive and, if possible, growing bureaucracy. Soviet managers, no less than their American counterparts, derive position and prestige from maintaining and if possible increasing the size of their operations. This makes it likely that resources—even if scarce—will be funneled toward the Soviet military-industrial complex perhaps even more inexorably than in our own.

This widespread phenomenon leads us to ask, How are resources divided among the different military services?

## Interservice Rivalries

Competition among the branches of the military sometimes seems as intense as rivalry between nations. This competition often involves efforts to maximize appropriations and to procure the newest and most impressive weapons. Moreover, since military appropriations must somehow be divided among the competing services, each branch has tended to disparage the others while arguing for its own role. There is also a tendency for each service branch to claim that its Soviet counterpart is surpassing them . . . which, in turn, requires additional efforts.

A few years after World War II, the US Air Force was established as coequal with the army and the navy and was charged with primary responsibility for strategic nuclear weapons, via the intercontinental bombers of the Strategic Air Command (SAC). For a time, the navy, with no share in the nuclear "action," vigorously opposed the concept of strategic bombing. In the mid- to late 1950s, however, when the Polaris submarine program offered the prospect of a strategic nuclear role for the navy as well, the navy became ardently pronuclear. Navy officers, in fact, became especially critical of potential SAC vulnerability, emphasizing that by contrast, Polaris submarines were invulnerable. The air force, genuinely concerned by the navy's challenge, received a boost in the late 1950s from the bomber and missile gaps, and from the new doctrine of counterforce, which emphasized accuracy—at which ICBMs and bombers exceed SLBMs.

Each service traditionally claims that it needs the newest weapons available, and in very large numbers. At one point, for example, the air force wanted 10,000 Minuteman missiles, claiming this was necessary for them to fulfill their mission of deterrence. Excluded from strategic nuclear weaponry, the army was nevertheless given charge of ABM systems in the mid-1960s, and before that, development of counterinsurgency warfare ("special forces"). Later, when the air force began MIRVing its ICBMs, the navy wanted to MIRV its SLBMs, too. And part of Defense Secretary McNamara's decision to build up the Minuteman force in the early 1960s, even after it was apparent that the USSR had not invested heavily in ICBMs at that time, may have fulfilled a perceived need to compensate the air force for the substantial reduction in the strategic bomber fleet then in progress.

Bureaucratic politics have continued to play a role in the arms race into the 1980s. Thus, cancellation of the B-1 bomber by the Carter administration seems to have been tied to support for giving the air force the MX missile, almost as a consolation prize. The army has been given control of NATO's new Euromissile deployment, and not surprisingly, the military service that has been the most energetic on behalf of the Euromissiles has been the army.

The armed services are organized somewhat differently in the USSR. For example, ICBMs are maintained by a separate, elite service, the Strategic Rocket Forces, rather than the Soviet Air Force. Very little is known about how the Kremlin makes decisions to allocate resources among the military services. In all probability, however, Soviet interservice rivalries are no less intense than in the United States, and equally likely to stimulate the arms race. The USSR also contains several design bureaus, responsible for new weapons research and development; these appear to compete with one another, not directly for profits, but rather, with respect to the prestige and career advancement accorded individuals who meet their quotas and bring acclaim to their service or agency.

## Public Opinion

Public opinion can work to oppose arms races or to support them. Short-term changes in public opinion have relatively little effect on the nuclear arms race, even in a democracy like the United States. This is at least partly because the foreign policy/military acquisitions system is large and cumbersome, often burdened with long lead times; therefore it changes slowly. In the long run, however, if an arms race is to be maintained in a democratic society, public support is necessary. In the absence of international crises or perceived reversals to American pride or national interests, public support for the arms race tends to diminish. And the memory of voters is notoriously short. Support for military spending increased during the war in Korea, the Berlin crisis, and the Iranian hostage situation, and after the shock of Sputnik and the Soviet invasion of Afghanistan. Widespread public perception of a missile gap not only helped elect John F. Kennedy in 1960 but also provided a political climate conducive to the American buildup of the early 1960s. On the other hand, public support for military spending decreased at the end of the Korean and Vietnam wars, and during detente.

The increased US military expenditures that characterized the Reagan administration took place because public opinion supported such an increase, partly as a result of a perception of American policy reversals in Iran and Afghanistan, and before that, in Angola and the Horn of Africa, where Cuban troops assisted in leftist revolutions. A majority of the American public felt that the United States had been insufficiently assertive during the Carter administration, and they elected a government pledged to turn things around. By the 1980s, the US public was also increasingly ready to shake off the defeat in Vietnam and to support a more militarized foreign policy.

By 1980 there was also a widespread public feeling that the USSR had caught and in some respects surpassed the US in military strength, and that remedial actions were needed. In the minds of some people, the goal for the 1980s has been to reestablish the unquestioned military superiority the United States enjoyed during the first decade after World War II. (This was a time, for example, when publisher Henry Luce declared the beginning of an "American century." It didn't last long, and many Americans have sought to recapture it.) For others, the intent is to achieve a "margin of safety," as President Reagan has put it. Opponents of this view question whether the USSR has—or ever had—a "definite margin of superiority" as President Reagan claimed in 1981 and continued to claim during his second term in office. There is also room for doubt whether either side could ever attain such superiority, just as there is debate over whether nuclear weapons can effectively be translated into diplomatic power.

Influential groups such as the Committee on the Present Danger have worked hard since the mid-1970s to alert the country to what they saw as a "spending gap" favoring the USSR, along with a "modernization gap," a "civil defense gap," and so on. There can be little doubt that such efforts contributed significantly to the souring of detente and to the stiffening US posture in the nuclear arms race. Observers differ, of course, about whether this has been an unhealthy development or one that was desperately needed—a risky and unnecessary escalation of the arms race that has increased the chances of war, or the welcome reversal of a dangerous slide toward increasing weakness with respect to the Soviet Union.

American public opinion is notoriously fickle when it comes to foreign policy and arms races. Balancing a sensitivity to foreign threats and a desire for pride and assertiveness in international affairs is a sporadic awareness of the competition between military and domestic spending. As a result, citizen pressure periodically favors a reduction in military expenditures, especially when foreign affairs appear to be going smoothly, or when domestic spending is being curtailed, as occurred within a few years after Ronald Reagan took office, and particularly during his second term.

Thus, we have American public opinion supporting military expenditures as a result of its perception of national security needs, and opposing such expenditures as a result of its perception of the domestic costs of such spending. In addition, "peace movements" have regularly lobbied against arms races, with varying degrees of intensity and effectiveness. During the late 1950s, for example, radioactive fallout from atmospheric nuclear tests was a major rallying point. In the 1960s and 1970s, domestic opposition to the Vietnam war and to ABM systems had a clear effect on ultimate national policy, although the nuclear arms race itself received less public attention. In the 1980s an antinuclear peace movement has once again surfaced in the United States, and in Europe as well. As of 1982, for example, various polls showed that approximately 65–85% of the American public favored a bilateral freeze on nuclear weapons. In the same era, however, Ronald Reagan, who has strongly opposed a freeze and favored a major nuclear weapons buildup, was elected, and reelected by a substantial majority.

Ideological factors are also important in affecting public opinion. Religious fundamentalists generally tend to support the arms race, since they often see the USSR as especially threatening because of its outspoken atheism. Although Democrats are generally thought to be less ideologically antagonistic to the USSR than are Republicans, Democratic presidents have historically been more likely to escalate the nuclear arms race than have Republican presidents. This may be because politicians with relatively liberal domestic inclinations feel a need to demonstrate their patriotism by taking a relatively hard line in foreign affairs, hence the term "Cold War liberal" applied to such influential politicians as Dean Acheson (Fig. 9.13), Hubert Humphrey, and Henry Jackson.

Another contributing factor may be the conservatives' traditional cost consciousness; during the late 1940s and early 1950s, many American conservatives, led by the powerful Republican leader Senator Robert Taft, favored a virtual return to prewar isolationism, whereas Democrats such as Dean Acheson, who was Truman's secretary of state, urged that the US become actively involved as the guarantor of democracy throughout the world, notably in Europe. The latter view prevailed, leading ultimately to a generally bipartisan American consensus in this respect.

NSC 68 was promulgated under President Harry Truman, a Democrat; his administration saw the use of atomic bombs against Japan and the formation of NATO, and made the decision to proceed with the H-bomb. Although John Foster Dulles, Dwight Eisenhower's secretary of state, was vigorously anticommunist, this Republican administration actually sought to reduce military spending by relying on the "New Look." During the Eisenhower years, and despite a more antagonistic Cold War environment, fewer major arms race escalations were initiated than during the administrations of Democrats John Kennedy and Lyndon Johnson. The Republican administrations of Richard Nixon and Gerald Ford were the prime workshops of detente, especially under the direction of Secretary of State Henry Kissinger, who placed great value on cooperative— even if distrustful—relations with the USSR. Democrat Jimmy Carter came into office determined to halt the nuclear arms race, but his final two years were characterized by a return to Cold War rhetoric and the decision to build the MX missile.

The Reagan administration has been an exception to this general pattern, in that a conservative Republican government has vigorously pursued a substantial peacetime military buildup. Critics point out that this indicates the potency of ideology within the Reagan administration: militant anticommunism (or more accurately, anti-Sovietism) combined with a tendency to view the world in simple-minded military and confrontational terms. Supporters, by contrast, see it as a laudable, appropriate, and in fact, overdue response to a potentially shifting balance of world military power. Adherence to one view or the other depends on whether one perceives the current state of the nuclear arms race as enhancing or diminishing American national security.

Once again, we know very little about the role of public opinion as an internal driving force in the USSR. The Soviet government seems to be able to proceed with its chosen policies without much direct regard to public opinion. In the long run, however, even the autocratic and somewhat insulated Kremlin leadership doubtless requires at least some degree of citizen approval, hence the extensive state-run propaganda apparatus. Whatever their disaffection with their government, Soviet citizens appear to be quite supportive of the USSR's role in the nuclear arms race. They take great pride in having won the "Great Patriotic War"

against Germany, in having become a superpower, and they remember acutely and painfully the devastation of World War II. Just like Americans, Soviet citizens generally see their role in the nuclear arms race as overwhelmingly defensive, and thus, a regrettable necessity imposed on them by a puzzling and implacable enemy.

Internal maneuvering within the government doubtless influences Soviet behavior in the nuclear arms race. Their military buildup of the late 1960s and 1970s seems to have been at least partly a response to their humiliation during the Cuban missile crisis, which in turn contributed to Nikita Khrushchev's downfall and the rise of Leonid Brezhnev. The de-Stalinization that began under Khrushchev was accompanied by an effort to de-emphasize heavy industry and military production in favor of consumer goods. In carrying out this policy, Khrushchev ran afoul of the Soviet equivalent of the US military-industrial complex, who blamed him for shortchanging national security, and substituting bluff and bluster for strength and effectiveness. Brezhnev promised to be more supportive of Soviet military needs, and he was.

Finally, there is good reason to think that the domestic costs of the arms race are painfully apparent to Soviet leaders, especially since the USSR's economy is basically one of scarcity, particularly of domestic goods. The USSR, however, is no less capable than the US of investing heavily in the nuclear arms race so long as other factors, both external and internal, keep up the pressure.

## COMBINED INFLUENCES

There are professional partisans of each explanation of the arms race: external causes such as the Soviet threat, the American threat, action-reaction chains, and worst-case planning, as well as such internal domestic causes as the pressure of technology, the military-industrial complex, interservice rivalries, and public opinion. It seems likely that on balance a combination of many if not all of these factors influences the arms race, with different ones having greater importance at specific times.

In one of the best-known attempts to model arms races, the British mathematician and physicist Lewis F. Richardson suggested equations that describe the military effort of two nations. This set of equations describes a **Richardson process,** as follows:

$$\Delta X = r_x Y - f_x X + g_x$$
$$\Delta Y = r_y X - f_y Y + g_y$$

In these equations, $\Delta$ is the change in military expenditures by each nation ($X$ and $Y$), and $r$ is a "reaction coefficient." Thus, for example, $r_x$ is the degree to which nation $X$ reacts to the continuing level of expenditure by nation $Y$. Assuming that the reaction coefficients are positive, this formulation guarantees a continuing, upward-spiral type of action-reaction process. But Richardson's equations also recognize a "fatigue" coefficient that tends to act against military expenditures: $f_x$, for example, is the fatigue coefficient for nation

**FIGURE 9.14 Aerial view of the Pentagon, home of the US Department of Defense.** (Courtesy of the US Department of Defense.)

$X$. It is assumed that the socioeconomic resistance to an arms race will be proportional to the amount actually spent on it; so as the actual level of expenditure by nation $X$ increases, this fatigue effect also increases. Finally, the $g$ terms represent underlying "grievances" by each nation against the other, considerations that tend to increase the military efforts by each.

Richardson's model was tested against the European arms race immediately preceding World War I. In its general outline, it may also be applicable to the nuclear arms race. It is an interesting exercise to identify and define the various relevant terms for the 1980s, including appropriate possible modifications, taking account of such additional factors as "minimal deterrence," counterforce, and the likely role of competition among alliances rather than nations, as well as the impact of other parties (e.g., China) on such equations.

## WHAT IS THE RELATIONSHIP BETWEEN ARMS RACES AND WARS?

In general, doves are more likely to focus on the nuclear arms race as an economic and social evil in itself, and as likely to lead to even greater evil, namely, nuclear war. Doves point out that throughout history, all weapons that have been deployed have eventually been used. They emphasize that the arms race also leads to misunderstandings and to heightened tensions along with their obvious consequence: the accumulation of increasing numbers of weapons, often weapons that are increasingly dangerous as well. They believe that historically, arms races have been more likely to lead to wars than to prevent them. For example, political scientist Michael Wallace analyzed 99 serious international disputes between 1815 and 1965. Twenty-eight of these had been preceded by an arms race and 71 had not. Of the former, 23 (82%) resulted in a war, whereas of the 71 disputes not preceded by an arms race, only 3 (4%), resulted in war. Although this single analysis does not prove that arms races cause war, it does suggest that when a serious dispute occurs in conjunction with an arms race, war is far more likely than when the disputing nations have not also been competing militarily.

By contrast, hawkish opinion tends to point to the motto, *Vis pacem, para bellum* ("If you want peace, prepare for war"). They emphasize "peace through strength," as with President Reagan's assertion that America has never gotten into a war because it was too strong. Hawks (in both the US and the USSR) point to the dangers of showing weakness, and the lessons of Munich. They warn that wars are made more likely by appeasing a would-be aggressor. To some degree, the widespread acceptance of deterrence implies a major conceptual victory for this view, since deterrence presupposes the worst-case assumption that one's opponent is prone to attack and must therefore be "deterred." Hence, it is only prudent to be strong.

In the decades immediately following the discovery of nuclear weapons, a group of influential Americans, including political scientist Hans Morgenthau, theologian Reinhold Niebuhr, and journalist Walter Lippmann maintained that the arms race was a *symptom* of political conflict rather than its *cause*. "Men do not fight because they have arms," wrote Morgenthau, "but they have arms because they deem it necessary to fight."

Such attitudes are important, because if arms races are seen as a major cause of instability, then direct efforts to curb the nuclear arms race are warranted. On the other hand, if arms races are appropriate responses to underlying disaffections between nations, the nuclear arms race can be seen as a bulwark against war, albeit an unpleasant one. It seems likely that the arms race exacerbates tensions but may to some degree also produce caution. It would doubtless be useful to curb the arms race, but such curbs would be ultimately unavailing unless they also led to changes in the super-power relationship.

An enormous literature exists on the causes of war. There is currently little agreement, however, on the spe-

cific causes of arms races in general, of the nuclear arms race in particular, or of the relationship between arms races and war. Certainly, there is dispute over whether the arms race, as it is currently being con-ducted, is increasing or decreasing the likelihood of war (Fig. 9.14).

## Policy Issues

### Should the US seek to restrict the rate of scientific and technological innovation in the nuclear arms race?

**Yes:** Innovations in weaponry drive the arms race and prevent any long-term resolution. One side or the other (usually the United States) initiates some-thing, to which the other side responds, and so on, back and forth, with no end in sight. Negotiators strive to restrict weapons that are already outmoded, while new ones are inevitably on the drawing boards.

**No:** Of all the stages of nuclear weapons produc-tion, research is the most difficult to monitor. Hence, restrictions on research would be extremely diffi-cult—perhaps impossible—to verify. The US has no choice but to continue researching various weapons, not only for the sake of possible achievements, but also to protect against possible Soviet breakthroughs (Table 9.6). At the same time, there have been numerous beneficial civilian spin-offs of such research.

### Did the USSR surpass the US in military spending during the late 1970s? Was the increase in US military spending during the 1980s justified?

**Yes:** The United States responded to "detente" dur-ing the 1970s by scaling down military efforts, under the mistaken impression that the Soviets would do the same. They did not. In fact, a CIA study in 1976 revealed that the USSR had not been spending 5–7% of its gross national product on military pro-curement, as had been thought, but rather 13–15%. The USSR surpassed the US in numbers of deployed SLBMs and has long held a lead in numbers of ICBMs and in megatonnage. The MIRVing of the large Soviet ICBMs opened a window of vulnerability for the Minuteman ICBMs. In short, America had lost ground dangerously, making the world a more

unstable place. The US military buildup during the Reagan administration has accordingly been fully justified and may have occurred just in time.

**No:** The revised estimates of Soviet military spend-ing simply involved a decision that the USSR is only about half as efficient at procuring weapons as had been thought. It did not represent the discovery of a single new missile or bomber, but rather, analysts' opinion that the USSR must have spent more to get what they had. Estimates of Soviet military spending are grossly misleading, since they are based on CIA estimates of what it would cost to procure identical goods and services in the US economy, with US dol-lars. Soviet military salaries, for example, are only about 10% of the US; the Soviets build generally less sophisticated weapons, at much less cost, and yet the CIA estimates Soviet military costs as though they were hiring American volunteer soldiers or build-ing weapons at American pay scales. And even if we take the CIA's own measures, NATO has been out-spending the Warsaw Pact for a long time. As to nuclear strength, each side is ahead in some areas. Neither side has meaningful superiority.

### Should the US seek to win the nuclear arms race?

**Yes:** No one knows what winning might mean, but it certainly is better than planning to lose! Fortunately, American technology continues to surpass the USSR's, and we must not cease to exploit this advan-tage. The Soviet Union engaged in an unprece-dented nuclear weapons buildup during the 1970s and would like nothing better than for us to drop out of this competition and give them a clear field. In addition, the relative positions of our two nations with regard to nuclear weapons exert an important effect on the confidence and effectiveness with which we can work our will in other areas of geopolitical com-

**TABLE 9.6 Comparison of US and Soviet technology in 20 areas having military significance**

| Technological area | US ahead | | | US and USSR equal | USSR ahead |
| | Lead growing | Lead holding | Lead slipping | | |
| --- | --- | --- | --- | --- | --- |
| Computers and software | ■ | | | | |
| Robotics and artificial intelligence | | ■ | | | |
| Life sciences[a] | | ■ | | | |
| Signal processing | | ■ | | | |
| Signature reduction/Stealth | | ■ | | | |
| Submarine detection | | ■ | | | |
| Telecommunications[b] | | ■ | | | |
| Production/manufacturing[c] | | ■ | | | |
| Electro-optical sensors | | ■ | | | |
| Guidance and navigation systems | | | ■ | | |
| Materials[d] | | | ■ | | |
| Optics | | | ■ | | |
| Propulsion | | | ■ | | |
| Radar sensors | | | ■ | | |
| Aerodynamics | | | | ■ | |
| Conventional warheads | | | | ■ | |
| Lasers | | | | ■ | |
| Nuclear warheads | | | | ■ | |
| Power sources | | | | ■ | |

*Source:* Modified from SIPRI (1985).
[a]Human factors and genetic engineering.
[b]Including fiber optics.
[c]Including automated control.
[d]Lightweight, high strength, high temperature.

petition, such as the third world. If we settle for second best, or even for nuclear parity, our leaders will have to become more cautious and less assertive. With a strong, even dominating, nuclear posture, the United States could enforce a regime of world peace by inhibiting Soviet adventurism.

**No:** No one who is familiar with the US buildup in the 1960s can call the Soviet behavior of the 1970s "unprecedented." In fact, even during the 1970s, we added more strategic nuclear warheads than did the USSR. Just as in a nuclear war, there can be no winners in the nuclear arms race: only losers. By continuing to press for unilateral advantage, the US simply ensures that the USSR will continue to react to American developments. Nuclear weaponry does not translate into political leverage, as shown by the US

defeat in Vietnam and the Soviet stalemate in Afghanistan. However, continued competition—driven by either side seeking to "win" the arms race—may result in nuclear war. The only sane end of all this is mutual restraint and abandoning the false goal of victory, either in a nuclear war or in the arms race.

**Can the US cause the USSR ultimately to give up the arms race by pushing the Soviet Union economically in the competition?**

**Yes:** The USSR is economically stagnant and can ill afford the continued expenditure of the arms race. By continuing the competition, perhaps intensifying it and playing to US technological strength, the increased pressure might well make the Soviets more amenable to signing arms agreements that are advantageous to America. There is even the possibility of Soviet economic and political collapse, to be followed by a government compatible with Western values, negating the need for any arms race.

**No:**  The USSR is a tightly controlled economy, and although some might wish to spend less on the military, the Soviets are capable of directing whatever resources they wish in that direction—perhaps more so than in the US, which must respond to domestic opposition. During World War II, the US spent 40% of its gross national product on the military, and Great Britain and the USSR spent up to 60%. It is grossly unrealistic to expect the USSR to collapse; indeed, perhaps the US would collapse first. And if by chance the USSR suffered an overall breakdown, would the world be safer if anarchy reigned in a nation that already has 25,000 nuclear weapons?

### Should we seek to restrict the influence of the military-industrial complex?

**Yes:**  Decisions should be made on the basis of national security considerations, not private profit or career advancement. One possibility is to restrict the cross-hiring of military and industry officials. The legitimate goal of national security is too often subordinated to private and corporate gain.

**No:**  With all its flaws, our system is nonetheless the best the world has seen. We also should not place any additional obstacles in the way of government or industry efforts to hire the best people. And after all, we believe in free enterprise: why shouldn't the enhancement of national security also result in profit for the American public as well?

### Should the US scrutinize each new addition to its nuclear arsenal, evaluating its likely effect on the USSR?

**Yes:**  It is all too easy to arm unilaterally, without regard to the effect of one side's actions in generating a reaction that negates the first and ends up making both sides less safe than they were before. This is an example of what physicist Herbert York called "the fallacy of the last move": assuming that when one side acts, the other side will not react, or when one side counters the other's reaction, this will not lead to another, countering the counterreaction,

and so on. But in fact, the arms race is interactive and mutually stimulating. Especially in a world of nuclear weapons, security must be mutual; it is invariably a losing proposition for either side simply to add to its arsenal, oblivious to the ultimate effect of such actions.

**No:**  As former Secretary of Defense Harold Brown observed: "When we build, they build. When we stop, they build." It is the height of foolishness to think that by restraining itself the US could somehow restrain the USSR. The Soviets build weapons with regard only to achieving influence and if possible, superiority in the world. It would be absurd and dangerous to give the USSR veto power over US national security. When the Soviets become convinced that America has both the will and the ability to pursue the arms race to the extent necessary to achieve peace, then both sides shall be able to achieve peace. As long as the US keeps timidly worrying that the USSR might react or overreact, the Soviets are encouraged to think that they can outbluff or outbuild the West.

### Can the US increase its security by the arms race?

**Yes:**  Not all new developments in the arms race are destabilizing. For example, the deployment of SLBMs has been stabilizing. Maintaining a secure retaliatory second-strike capacity is stabilizing; and as the Soviets develop silo-busting missiles, the US must rely on new developments—notably, an ability to threaten Soviet missiles—to maintain such stability. The US can and must maintain the peace by balancing Soviet weapons with American. Ultimately, such a balance also offers the only hope of getting the USSR to agree to reductions. An imbalance in military strength leads to war.

**No:**  Most US actions, taken in the name of increasing stability and responding to the supposed Soviet threat, have in fact produced and/or escalated that threat. The arms race is a major part of the problem, certainly not the solution. When the US seeks to "balance" Soviet weaponry, they respond by building more; just as they have done in response to the many US escalations. American national security demands that the arms race be halted. Competition in military strength leads to war.

## KEY TERMS

| | |
|---|---|
| Truman Doctrine | missile gap |
| Baruch Plan | detente |
| NSC 68 | action-reaction |
| containment | worse-case analysis |
| North Atlantic Treaty Organization (NATO) | capabilities |
| | intentions |
| Warsaw Pact | technological determinism |
| "Atoms for Peace" | |
| "Open Skies" | research and development |
| bomber gap | |
| | technological creep |
| | Richardson process |

## STUDY QUESTIONS

1. In what way were US-Soviet relations difficult even before 1945? Were there any areas of cooperation?

2. Distinguish between quantitative and qualitative aspects of the nuclear arms race.

3. How is the nuclear arms "race" not a race?

4. Describe the nuclear modernization programs of the 1980s.

5. What is meant by action-reaction sequences? Give some examples and counterexamples.

6. Discuss a relationship between arms races and the Prisoner's Dilemma.

7. Explain how worst-case analyses contribute to arms races. Give examples.

8. Defend the proposition that the nuclear arms race is driven fundamentally by advances in weapons technology. Argue against this proposition.

9. What is the military-industrial complex?

10. How can arms races lead to war? How can they lead to peace?

11. Compare forces driving the arms race within the United States to those within the Soviet Union.

## ADDITIONAL READINGS

Halle, Louis. 1967. *The Cold War as History.* New York: Harper & Row. A superb, accessible account of the major forces at work in the evolution of US–Soviet relations, primarily since World War II.

Sherwin, Martin. 1975. *A World Destroyed: The Atomic Bomb and the Grand Alliance.* New York: Alfred A. Knopf. A historian's view of the role of nuclear weapons in shaping East–West relations.

Smoke, Richard. 1984. *National Security and the Nuclear Dilemma.* Reading, MA: Addison-Wesley. A brief, readable historical account of the American experience in seeking national security in the Nuclear Age.

Wright, Quincy. 1965. *A Study of War,* 2 vols. Chicago: University of Chicago Press. The classic compilation of historical and political background for wars and arms races.

# 10 Negotiated Agreements

*What would you think about a meeting of a town council which is concerned because an increasing number of people are knifed to death each night in drunken brawls, and which proceeds to discuss just how long and how sharp shall be the knife that the inhabitants of the city may be permitted to carry?*
—Albert Einstein (when asked his opinion of the Geneva disarmament conference, 1926)

People have long sought to achieve security not only by unilateral military actions, but also by agreements with potential adversaries. The United States has been party to some notable successes. For example, in 1817 the US and Great Britain (then controlling Canada) signed the Rush-Bagot Treaty. It called for the demilitarization of the Great Lakes as well as actual disarmament—the destruction of some navy vessels. This occurred just 2 years after the conclusion of the War of 1812, at a time when British–American relations were not particularly friendly, and yet, it laid the foundation for the world's longest demilitarized border: between the US and present-day Canada. The Washington Naval Treaty of 1922, signed by the US, Japan, and the major European powers, restricted the production of large naval vessels and also prescribed a ratio of battleships and aircraft carriers to be permitted among the world's major military nations. It almost certainly postponed a worldwide naval arms race for more than a decade.

When it come to nuclear weapons, however, the record of negotiated agreements has been very disappointing. As we have seen, the Baruch Plan and its Soviet counterparts were unavailing. And as anyone can judge simply by looking around in the 1980s, agreements to limit the nuclear arms race have not been notably successful; there are, after all, more than 50,000 nuclear weapons in the world today, and their number is growing. This has led some experts to suggest that the real arms race is not between the United States and the Soviet Union, but rather between the builders of arms on the one hand, and the disarmers or arms controllers on the other. In this race, the builders on both sides have been winning, and by an ever-increasing margin.

The currently huge nuclear arsenals, especially those held by the superpowers, can be seen as a monumental failure of efforts to eliminate—or even to mitigate—the danger posed by nuclear weapons. On the other hand, there have been some successes, if not in ending the nuclear arms race, then in channeling and modifying it. Such efforts should perhaps be judged not against an ideal of mutual disarmament and guaranteed peace, but against an appraisal of what the world would be like if nations sought security by military competition alone.

The great majority of people recognize that unlimited arms competition, especially in a world of nuclear weapons, is an extraordinarily perilous prospect. Accordingly, substantial attention has been given to controlling and possibly even reversing some of its most dangerous aspects. This chapter begins with a historical review of the major nuclear arms agreements. Our discussion will be largely chronological but not strictly so, since it is more coherent to group such agreements conceptually rather than in strict historical sequence. (Discussion of one major negotiated agreement, the Non-Proliferation Treaty, is deferred until Chapter 11, and we considered the ABM treaty in Chapter 7.) After discussing the most important US-Soviet nuclear agreements, we shall attempt a wider treatment of issues related to nuclear negotiations, especially the problem of verification, claims of cheating or noncompliance, as well as some general principles and cautions of negotiated agreements.

## DISARMAMENT AND ARMS CONTROL

Although both sides have typically given lip service to disarmament as a goal, neither side seems to have pursued it seriously. It can be argued that during the late 1940s and early 1950s, neither the US nor the USSR was really interested in disarmament or in seriously restricting the development of nuclear weapons. Both nations were making basic nuclear weapons discoveries and developing and deploying the weapons themselves. The goal of "general and complete disarmament" was often proclaimed, but no real movement in that direction took place. Perhaps because it was far behind in nuclear weapons, the USSR often called for such radical steps, but proposals foundered on Soviet refusal to permit "on-site inspection" which the United States claimed was necessary to verify that agreed disarmament steps had actually been taken.

The United States, in turn, typically proposed measures that would essentially freeze the nuclear arsenals of both sides at their existing levels (i.e., with the US ahead), suggestions that were unacceptable to the USSR. Similarly, the USSR regularly proposed more dramatic reductions in nuclear arsenals than the US would accept; in addition to the problem of verification, the USSR maintained superior conventional military forces, which made reduced reliance on nuclear weapons a more acceptable option from the Soviet viewpoint.

By the end of the 1950s, however, the climate had changed somewhat, leading to a number of negotiated agreements. This change was due, among other things, to some thawing of the Cold War after Stalin's death, to the growing sophistication of verification technology, and in two different respects, to the growing nuclear arsenals of both sides. First, the ongoing arms accumulation heightened citizen anxiety and generated growing pressures for cessation; and second, the growth of the Soviet arsenal appears to have made the USSR more willing to enter into equitable agreements.

Eventual disarmament nonetheless remained the ultimate hope: In 1961 John J. McCloy (representing the United States) and Valerian Zorin (representing the Soviet Union) presented a "Joint Statement of Agreed Principles for Disarmament Negotiations" to the UN General Assembly. Among other things, it called for multilateral negotiations to design and then implement general and complete disarmament, in concert with a standing UN peacekeeping force. This document, which became known as the **McCloy–Zorin Agreement,** was adopted unanimously. President Kennedy established the **Arms Control and Disarmament Agency (ACDA)** in 1961, specifically to oversee negotiations for the US government. However, the fine ideals of the McCloy–Zorin Agreement proved difficult to pin down in specifics. Perhaps as a result, strategic analysts began increasingly to turn their attention from the seemingly unattainable ideal of disarmament to the more modest goal of **arms control.**

To dovish critics, arms control is a thinly veiled excuse for continuing the arms race, aimed more at managing it than at ending it. To hawkish critics, arms control is a delusion whereby a nation allows itself to be outmaneuvered at the bargaining table by its adversary. To analyst Thomas Schelling, the goals of arms control are essentially threefold: (1) reduce the likelihood that war will break out; (2) if war does occur, reduce the level of destruction that results; and (3) regardless of whether war occurs, reduce the cost of preparing for it. Increasingly, sound arms control is being considered to be an essential aspect of a nation's search for security, since the alternative appears to be a system of international anarchy and unrestrained competition. However, as we shall see, this is not to say that the successes of arms control have been especially impressive or that arms control through negotiations has not been criticized.

The negotiating styles of the US and the USSR tend to differ in consistent ways. For example, the US is more likely to make proposals; the USSR, to respond to them. The US gives its negotiators substantially more flexibility and authority than is the case with the USSR; as a result, Soviet negotiators must often refer to Moscow for specific details. Both sides, however, engage in tough "positional" bargaining, in which initial stands are typically strongly biased toward one's own side, with begrudging compromises reached later, if at all.

## TEST BAN TREATIES

### History of the Partial Test Ban Treaty

During the mid- to late 1950s, the public had become increasingly concerned about radioactive fallout from atmospheric nuclear testing, which was being conducted by the two superpowers (Fig. 10.1). In particular, the strontium isotope Sr-90 was appearing in large amounts in milk and in children's bones and teeth. Many scientists warned about a possible increase in cancer rates as well as genetic defects, and a worldwide movement to ban all nuclear testing gained momentum. Finally, in 1958, both sides agreed to a moratorium on testing while formal negotiations for a mutual test ban treaty were under way in Geneva.

Consistent with their previous positions on disarmament provisions, however, the two sides disagreed because of Soviet refusal to permit on-site inspection, combined with American insistence on strict verifiabil-

**FIGURE 10.1 Army troops take part in an exercise involving an atmospheric nuclear explosion at Yucca Flat, Nevada, in 1951.** (Courtesy of the US Department of Defense.)

ity. The USSR resumed testing in 1961. To some, this further proved Soviet unreliability. On the other hand, the US had previously announced that it no longer felt bound by the moratorium, and France had exploded its first nuclear weapon shortly thereafter, in 1960. Given that France was an American ally, certain elements in the Soviet leadership may have found it intolerable for the USSR to refrain from testing during seemingly fruitless negotiations while such tests were being carried out by another adversary. Among these Soviet tests

was the largest H-bomb ever exploded: 57 megatons. The US also resumed testing in 1961.

The Cuban missile crisis of October 1962 may well have had a sobering effect on both sides. The test ban negotiations at this point were still floundering over the question of verifying a ban on underground nuclear tests. In December 1962 Nikita Khrushchev offered to permit three seismic stations on Soviet soil, as well as three annual on-site inspections in the event of suspicious events (i.e., underground tremors that did

**FIGURE 10.2 President John F. Kennedy signing the Partial Test Ban Treaty in 1963. Going clockwise, the dignitaries surrounding him include John Pastore, W. Averell Harriman, J. William Fulbright, Dean Rusk, George Aiken, Hubert Humphrey, Everett Dirksen, and Lyndon Johnson.** (Courtesy of the John F. Kennedy Library.)

not appear to be earthquakes). The US rejected this offer, insisting that eight to ten such inspections were needed, whereupon the USSR angrily withdrew its concession.

Then in June 1963, President Kennedy made one of the most important speeches of his career. In the famous "Strategy of Peace" address at American University, Kennedy praised the USSR for its sacrifices and accomplishments, and announced that the United States was unilaterally initiating a test ban and would not resume testing unless the Soviet Union did so. The USSR followed suit, and the **Partial Test Ban Treaty (PTBT),** also sometimes known as the **Limited Test Ban Treaty (LTBT)** was signed just two months later, in August (Fig. 10.2).

The PTBT called for a halt to all testing of nuclear weapons in the atmosphere, in space, or underwater. It was only a partial success, since it did not prohibit underground testing. It did not involve any agreements regarding on-site inspection or on-site monitoring equipment, since it was generally agreed that except for underground tests, violations would be readily apparent. The PTBT was therefore a compromise, less than the doves on each side had hoped for, and more than the hawks had wanted.

## Effects of the Partial Test Ban Treaty

The PTBT has had several positive effects, and some negative ones as well. The most notable benefit has been in dramatically reducing contamination of the environment by fallout. Throughout the world, background atmospheric radiation has diminished virtually to pretesting levels (Fig. 10.3). Those who did not live through the era of fallout from aboveground testing, or for whom it is but a dim memory, may find it difficult to appreciate the relief brought about by the PTBT.

The PTBT has had other beneficial effects. It was the first treaty that explicitly limited a direct aspect of the nuclear competition, and it has been adhered to. It is therefore important both as a precedent and as a demonstration of feasibility. In addition, and paradoxically, by keeping both sides in the dark about some important nuclear weapons effects, the PTBT may contribute directly to strategic stability. For example, the precise nature of EMP effects cannot be determined without testing nuclear weapons above the atmosphere; in the absence of such information, worst-case analysis may make both sides less likely to chance a surprise attack because of the many uncertainties involved. The precise effectiveness of silo hardening

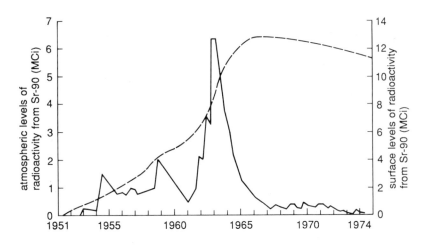

**FIGURE 10.3 Changes over time in atmospheric and ground contamination with Sr-90. The data are presented in units of radioactivity, megacuries (MCi). Note that atmospheric levels (solid line) have declined precipitously since 1962, whereas surface levels (dotted line) have declined much more slowly.** (Modified from Glasstone and Dolan, 1977.)

must also remain unknown, since weapons cannot be tested against them. Finally, a successful counterforce attack would almost certainly require cross-targeting of two warheads at each silo. But because of the PTBT, there is uncertainty about the exact details of "fratricide": planners cannot count on the effectiveness of two explosions at the same target because of the likelihood that the first might disrupt the accuracy of the second. There may be some optimum spacing between incoming warheads that would minimize fratricide, thus making such an attack more feasible. Because of the PTBT, however, uncertainty exists, and along with it, a reduced likelihood that either side will chance such an attack.

Despite these benefits, the PTBT has not been a complete triumph. To obtain military and political support for the treaty, President Kennedy had to promise that technology not prohibited by the treaty would be vigorously pursued. (As we shall see, this has become a frequent correlate of nuclear agreements.) In particular, underground nuclear testing was permitted by the treaty, and both sides tested more after it was signed than before: between 1945 and 1963 the US and USSR together made 488 nuclear tests (about 80% aboveground); during the same number of years, between 1963 and 1981, the two nations exploded more than 700 nuclear weapons, all underground. In short, the PTBT did nothing to halt the nuclear arms race; it simply drove testing underground where its pace actually increased (Fig. 10.4). If this treaty had been comprehensive instead of partial, MIRVing and the development of neutron bombs would have been severely

hampered. Alternatively, of course, it is also possible that either side could have cheated and gained a unilateral advantage.

Much of the public outcry that preceded the PTBT had been directed primarily at radioactive fallout rather than at nuclear testing itself, and when atmospheric testing was halted, public concern diminished rapidly. It is therefore possible that as a result of the PTBT, citizen awareness of the continued arms race is less than it would otherwise be. To some extent, then, the PTBT simply drove the nuclear arms race underground, where it has continued, out of sight and largely out of mind (Fig. 10.5).

The PTBT has been signed by 112 nations. China and France are not signatories, although in 1974 France bowed to international pressure and suspended atmospheric testing. However, an underwater testing program that is maintained in French Polynesia has been the subject of substantial criticism.

### The Threshold Test Ban Treaty and the Peaceful Nuclear Explosions Treaty

In 1974 the US and the USSR agreed not to exceed a threshold of 150 kilotons in their underground tests. Although signed by President Ford, the **Threshold Test Ban Treaty (TTBT)** has not been ratified by the US Senate; hence it is not formally in effect. The treaty may constrain the development of high-yield warheads, although computer simulations now permit accurate estimations of likely yields without actual testing. The TTBT has been criticized by doves as being a travesty

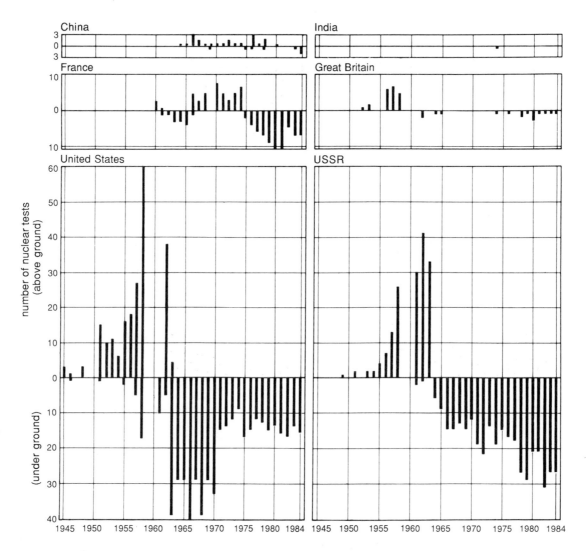

**FIGURE 10.4 Nuclear explosive tests by the six nuclear nations, 1945–1984. Above-ground tests are indicated above the 0 line, underground tests, below. The 33 above-ground tests conducted by the USSR in 1963 occurred before the PTBT was signed. Note that more tests have been conducted underground after the PTBT than above-ground, before it.** (Modified from Epstein, 1985.)

of arms control—after all, 150 kilotons is more than 10 times the power of the Hiroshima bomb. It has also been criticized by hawks as being difficult to verify and not in the US national interest. Nonetheless, both sides have agreed to adhere to its limits, although there has been some controversy in the United States over whether the USSR has exceeded 150 kilotons in some of its

tests. (We shall review the general issue of verification later in the chapter.)

The TTBT allowed the testing of so-called peaceful nuclear explosions (Fig. 10.6), without restriction as to yield. Nuclear enthusiasts claim that nuclear explosives could be helpful in enlarging harbors, digging canals, improving gas and oil well performance, and

**FIGURE 10.5 Preparations for an underground nuclear test at the Nevada test site. The electronic cables spread on the ground will be lowered into the deep drilled shaft at center, to relay scientific data to the monitoring trailers at the surface.** (Courtesy of the US Department of Energy.)

so on. However, none of these benefits have yet been found to outweigh the costs, and of course, the distinction between peaceable and warlike technology is difficult to make. Accordingly, the **Peaceful Nuclear Explosions Treaty (PNET)** was signed by the US and the USSR in 1976, applying the same 150-kiloton limit to peaceful as to warlike explosions. Like the TTBT, the PNET has not been ratified by the US Senate.

## The Comprehensive Test Ban Treaty

The initial debate over the PTBT was notable in that for the first time, scientists publicly discussed a significant nuclear weapons issue. (The debate over whether to develop the H-bomb, by contrast, had been conducted almost entirely in secrecy.) While biologists pointed to the harmful effects of fallout, and some politicians and strategists argued that a test ban would help retard the arms race, others were strongly opposed to the treaty. Supporters of continued nuclear testing maintained, for example, that the treaty would retard scientific advance and that it would inhibit the development of needed weapons. It was also argued that the Soviets might secretly test nuclear weapons on the far side of the moon, or in huge foam-filled underground caverns, and that they may have already gained information from their tests that would be unavailable to us if we stopped testing. Leading figures from the two US laboratories responsible for designing

**FIGURE 10.6 Crater produced by the "Sedan" test, a "peaceful nuclear explosion" conducted in 1962 as part of an earth-moving experiment during Operation Plowshares. The 100-kiloton explosion was detonated under 635 feet of ground; it displaced 12 million tons of earth and produced a crater 320 feet deep and 1,280 feet in diameter.** (Courtesy of the US Department of Energy.)

new nuclear weapons—Los Alamos and Lawrence Livermore—vigorously opposed the treaty.

Because of such opposition, and the uncertainty about whether a ban on underground tests could be adequately verified, the PTBT fell short of banning all nuclear tests. Continued efforts to achieve a complete, "comprehensive" ban on all testing, that is, on underground tests as well, encounter similar opposition more than 20 years later.

As part of their obligations under the PTBT of 1963, the nuclear powers agreed to seek "the discontinuance of all test explosions of nuclear weapons for all time" and pledged themselves "to continue negotiations to this end." Indeed, at the time of the PTBT, the US and the USSR came close to banning all nuclear testing; that is, they nearly agreed to a **comprehensive test ban treaty (CTBT).** The USSR had been willing to permit no more than three on-site inspections: the United States insisted that this was inadequate to verify treaty compliance. The PTBT was therefore a compromise, reached in part because atmospheric, underwater, or outer space nuclear tests would be readily detectable.

Discussions of a CTBT continued fitfully through the 1970s and were resumed seriously in the latter part of that decade. At one point, the USSR agreed to allow 10 on-site monitoring devices to operate within its territory, plus an unspecified number of on-site, "challenge" inspections in the event of suspect findings. But in the United States at least, the CTBT received lower priority than SALT II, and talks on a comprehensive test ban were broken off following the Soviet invasion of Afghanistan. The Reagan administration has chosen not to resume these discussions, citing problems of verification and the argument that weapons modernization is necessary for US security. In addition to the weapons laboratories, the Joint Chiefs of Staff have long opposed such a ban. However, a comprehensive test ban treaty remains high on the agenda of many peace groups and arms controllers, and it promises to be a source of continuing controversy. In August 1985, on the fortieth anniversary of the bombing of Hiroshima, Soviet leader Gorbachev announced a unilateral moratorium on underground nuclear tests and invited the US to reciprocate; the US refused.

## GEOGRAPHIC TREATIES

A number of treaties have established certain regions as off limits to nuclear weapons. Whereas none of these are accorded overwhelming significance, some are of substantial value in themselves and others might serve as useful precedents for agreements that may be even more useful in the future.

The Austrian State Treaty of 1955 is not a nuclear weapons agreement or a disarmament treaty (or even an arms control treaty). However, it is a useful example of superpower collaboration, to the benefit of all. In this treaty, the postwar occupation zones established by the victorious allies in Austria were dissolved and an independent, neutral nation of Austria was reestablished. (By contrast, it is noteworthy that artificially divided nations such as North and South Korea, North and South Vietnam, East and West Germany have been among the world's trouble spots.)

The Antarctic Treaty, signed in 1959, prevented any military bases, fortifications, maneuvers, or testing, conventional or nuclear, in the Antarctic region. The 1967 Outer Space Treaty establishes a variety of rules regarding the peaceful use of space (rescue and return of astronauts, etc.), and it prohibits the placing of nuclear weapons or any other weapons of "mass destruction" on celestial bodies, in orbit, or in outer space. Space itself, however, is not denuclearized by this treaty, since nuclear-armed ballistic missiles are permitted to travel through it. Moreover, signatories are still permitted to employ nuclear weapons placed in orbit and traveling less than one full revolution: so-called **fractional orbital bombardment systems (FOBS).** The deployment of conventional weapons in space is not constrained in any way, thereby permitting antisatellite warfare and other Star Wars/SDI programs not explicitly prohibited by the ABM treaty.

The Sea-Bed Treaty of 1971 prohibits emplanting nuclear weapons or other weapons of mass destruction on or below the ocean floor. It does not apply within each nation's 12-mile territorial limit; nor does it forbid submarines bearing SLBMs from loitering on the seabed, or prohibit ground-moored mines, servicing facilities, or antisubmarine warfare activities.

The foregoing treaties are not usually considered to be major accomplishments, since they prohibit activities that neither side planned to carry out anyhow. Nonetheless, such agreements may have prevented wasteful competition of the Prisoner's Dilemma type.

The Treaty of Tlatelolco (1967), named after a suburb of Mexico City, is the only agreement establishing a large part of the inhabited earth as a zone free of nuclear weapons testing, manufacture, or deployment. Nuclear power plants and research reactors are permitted, however, along with the transit of nuclear weapons belonging to other nations. This treaty has been considered to be a possible model for preventing nuclear competition in major geographic regions. It is greatly weakened, however, by the failure of Argentina, Brazil, Chile, and Cuba to ratify it. There is also some uncertainty about whether the treaty permits the acquisition of "peaceful" nuclear explosives. Nonetheless, it remains in force for an area of more than 8 million square kilometers, inhabited by about 150 million people.

## NONNUCLEAR WEAPONS TREATIES

Several treaties in recent years have sought to restrict or outlaw nonnuclear weapons. Perhaps the most important of these is the Biological Weapons Convention of 1972, which updated the Geneva Protocol of 1925. The Geneva Protocol was not ratified by the US until 1974; it does not prevent the development and stockpiling of such weapons, only their use in war. In 1968 an accidental release of nerve gas resulted in the death of thousands of sheep in Utah and heightened public awareness of the possible dangers of **chemical and biological warfare,** or **CBW.** The use of tear gas and chemical defoliants by the United States in Vietnam raised additional awareness and concern.

Scientists had also long been worried about the likely effectiveness of biological warfare, fearing that it might not be possible to direct it accurately against a targeted enemy. In addition, there has been concern that biological warfare poses a substantial risk to civilians because of the possibility of accidental release of lethal pathogens. Shortly after taking office, President Nixon announced a unilateral American halt to biological warfare technologies, and in 1972 both sides agreed not to develop, produce, or stockpile biological (primarily viral and bacteriological) weapons. Chemical weapons are not included in this treaty, which leaves certain gray areas, such as chemical toxins that are produced by biological processes (e.g., botulinus, which produces botulism, or the various fungal toxins that the USSR has been accused of using in Afghanistan and Kampuchea).

The Environmental Modification Convention of 1977 prohibits the hostile use of techniques to alter the environment of an adversary. The inducement of long-lasting, widespread, and severe effects, including climate modification, is explicitly forbidden. (It is an interesting question whether the use of nuclear weapons is also prohibited by this treaty, because the prospect of nuclear winter was not contemplated at the time the convention was signed.)

The major powers have been engaged in fruitless **mutual and balanced force reduction (MBFR)** talks in Vienna since 1973. Aimed at achieving reductions in NATO and Warsaw Pact conventional forces in Europe, these negotiations have been deadlocked over disagreements about troop levels in Europe, with the Soviets insisting that there are fewer Red Army troops in Europe than are claimed by the US. The West wants reductions to equal levels of deployed troops and equipment, whereas the Soviets want reductions of equal numbers of troops and equipment . . . which the West claims will then result in unequal levels.

The MBFR negotiations commenced after the US Senate began seriously contemplating the **Mansfield Amendment,** which was based on the proposition that by the early 1970s western Europe was economically strong enough to defend itself. The Mansfield Amendment would have brought several hundred thousand American troops home from Europe. Ironically, the Soviet Union may have been more negative than our NATO allies about the prospect of such an American withdrawal, because of fear that it might lead to a compensating increase in the military forces of West Germany. Whatever their prospects of eventual success, the MBFR negotiations effectively ended the prospect of a United States withdrawal, since such a unilateral act by the US would undercut the negotiations.

It is also at least possible that Soviet intransigence on this issue is a result of the USSR's desire to maintain forces in eastern Europe, not so much in response to any perceived threat from the West or even from any desire to conquer the West, but rather, to maintain control over their putative Warsaw Pact allies.

## AGREEMENTS TO COMMUNICATE AND TO AVOID MISUNDERSTANDINGS

There have been a number of other agreements intended to improve communication between the US and the USSR and to reduce the danger of misunderstandings leading to war. Best known among these is the "Hot Line" agreement, signed several weeks before the PTBT in 1963, which established a teletype communications link between Washington and Moscow. Satellite circuits were added in 1971, and serious proposals have been made for upgrading this system as of the mid-1980s. Also in 1971, a Nuclear Accidents Agreement was signed to provide for immediate notification of the other side in the event of possible acci-

**FIGURE 10.7 President Lyndon Johnson (right) meeting with Soviet Premier Alexei Kosygin at Glassboro, New Jersey, in 1967. This meeting set the stage for the first series of SALT negotiations.** (Courtesy of the Lyndon B. Johnson Library.)

dental or unauthorized nuclear detonations. A High Seas Agreement of 1972, together with its Protocol of 1973, seeks to establish rules of conduct to reduce the likelihood of ocean collision and to prohibit simulated attacks on each other's vessels.

A 1972 Agreement of Basic Principles, along with the 1973 Nuclear War Prevention Agreement, pledged the US and USSR to the peaceful resolution of disputes and to urgent consultations in the event of a nuclear crisis. These two agreements are largely symbolic, and also indicative of a spirit of detente, but they lack specific provisions.

A moderately important agreement was reached in 1975: the Final Act of the Conference on Security and Cooperation in Europe, often known as the **Helsinki Accords.** The NATO and WP signatories pledged to give each other advance notification in the event of any major military maneuvers in Europe, exercises that might otherwise be dangerously misinterpreted. The Helsinki

Accords also essentially ratified the postwar political division of Europe, as sought by the USSR, over the objections of US conservatives, who feel that it legitimizes the Soviet domination of eastern Europe. [Interestingly, some peace groups, such as END (European Nuclear Disarmament) have also been critical of the Helsinki Accords because they believe that one way to end the Cold War is to terminate the current division of Europe into Soviet and US spheres of influence.] In the Helsinki Accords, signatories also pledged to respect certain basic principles of human rights—a promise the Soviet Union has not kept, especially since the late 1970s.

## SALT I

The centerpiece of nuclear negotiations has been the strategic arms agreements between the US and the USSR, and to a lesser extent, the jockeying over nuclear

**FIGURE 10.8 President Richard Nixon and Soviet leader Leonid Brezhnev shaking hands after signing the SALT I treaty.** (Courtesy of the US Arms Control and Disarmament Agency.)

weapons in Europe. We now turn to these momentous issues.

## History and Terms

As the 1960s advanced, both the US and the USSR were on the verge of deploying ABM systems of great expense and questionable effectiveness. In addition, the superpowers had reached essential equivalence in their strategic nuclear forces: although each side led the other in certain categories, each was capable of destroying the other in a retaliatory strike. Following several overtures by President Johnson, notably during his meeting with Soviet leader Alexei Kosygin in Glassboro, New Jersey (Fig. 10.7), the first round of **Strategic Arms Limitation Talks,** or **SALT I,** was scheduled for the summer of 1968. However, the USSR invaded Czechoslovakia in that year in response to the "Prague spring" of liberalization. In reaction to this, SALT I was not convened until 1969, when Richard Nixon had become president.

The chief US negotiator was Gerard Smith, director of the ACDA, and his deputies included Paul Nitze

(later US chief negotiator at the Euromissile talks) and Harold Brown (later secretary of defense under Jimmy Carter). It is widely acknowledged that in addition to this "front door" of direct negotiations, substantial assists were provided via "back door" channels to the Soviet leadership opened by then national security adviser Henry Kissinger.

Two major agreements were reached under SALT I, and they were signed by Richard Nixon and Leonid Brezhnev in Moscow in May 1972 (Fig. 10.8). We have already considered the most important of these instruments: the ABM treaty, which prohibited the testing and deployment of air-, space-, or mobile land-based ABM systems and limited each side to no more than two ABM sites. The ABM treaty is of unlimited duration and remains in force, despite considerable pressure for abrogation on the part of the US.

The other component of SALT I, the Interim Agreement on the Limitation of Strategic Arms, generally known simply as the **Interim Agreement,** established numerical ceilings for each side's ICBMs, SLBMs, and missile-carrying submarines, as shown in Table 10.1. This agreement, which expired in 1977, was to have been replaced by a subsequent offensive arms limitation agreement, SALT II, which both sides expected to negotiate promptly.

Several things are apparent from the data of Table 10.1. First, the Interim Agreement did not set any limits that were lower than the existing deployments of either side. Moreover, it permitted the Soviet Union higher ceilings than the United States. Not surprisingly, this caused great consternation among hawkish critics in the US, and for a time, Senate ratification was in doubt. Senator Henry Jackson offered an amendment requiring that no future SALT agreement provide for the US having intercontinental strategic forces in any category that were numerically inferior to those of the USSR. The Interim Agreement was then ratified.

It is important to understand why American negotiators agreed to these less-than-equal numerical ceilings. For one thing, American weaponry was qualitatively far superior to Soviet counterparts, although quantitatively the US was behind in certain categories. For example, the USSR had more SLBMs and more strategic submarines, but the US models were greatly superior and carried many more warheads, largely because of MIRVing. Similarly, although the American ICBM force consisted of fewer and smaller missiles, it was more accurate, it was technologically superior, and, unlike the Soviet force, it was MIRVed. The USSR also complained about US **forward-based systems:** nuclear

**TABLE 10.1 Basic terms of the SALT I Interim Agreement, showing the number of missile launchers deployed in 1972 and the numbers permitted by the agreement**

| Launching system | United States | USSR |
|---|---|---|
| *ICBMs* | | |
| Deployed | 1,054 | 1,618 |
| Permitted | 1,054 | 1,618 |
| *SLBMs* | | |
| Deployed | 656 | 740 |
| Permitted | 710 | 950 |
| *Strategic submarines* | | |
| Deployed | 41 | 56 |
| Permitted | 44 | 62 |

*Source:* From Richard Smoke. 1984. *National Security and the Nuclear Dilemma* Reading, MA: Addison-Wesley.

weapons that are stationed in Europe and on aircraft carriers and can reach the USSR (Fig. 10.9). By contrast, Soviet "tactical" nuclear weapons were not able to reach the US homeland and still lack this capability.

The result was a compromise. The US agreed to accept lower numerical limits on its ICBMs, SLBMs, and strategic submarines. The USSR agreed to exclude forward-based systems from the Interim Agreement. As a further concession, the USSR agreed that strategic bombers, in which the US held a commanding lead, would not be counted in SALT I. The USSR was granted a continuing monopoly of "heavy" ICBMs but was not permitted to add to the number already deployed at the time of the agreement.

It was also agreed that both sides would monitor compliance with both the Interim Agreement and the ABM treaty by **national technical means** (i.e., by spy satellites) rather than by means of on-site verification and that neither side would interfere with the ability of the other to achieve such long-distance verification. Another important and often overlooked accomplishment of SALT I was the establishment of a **Standing Consultative Commission (SCC)** composed of representatives of both nations. The SCC was intended as a way for each side to satisfy concerns about possible treaty noncompliance and to resolve ambiguities without the glare and likely distortion of public recriminations, which often degenerate into propaganda battles.

**FIGURE 10.9 An FB-111 medium-range bomber. Deployed in Europe, such aircraft are capable of reaching the USSR. Soviet negotiators have sought to have them included within the limits established for strategic systems; the US has successfully opposed this proposed restriction.** (Courtesy of the US Department of Defense.)

## Weaknesses of SALT I

The Interim Agreement set ceilings on some aspects of offensive arms. However, it did not encompass bombers or the newly developing technology of cruise missiles. Perhaps most important, it did nothing to inhibit the spread of MIRVs. Many experts, worried about the ultimately destabilizing effects of MIRVing on both sides, had hoped that MIRVs would be forestalled at SALT I. This failure may have been due at least partly to timing: by the opening of SALT I, MIRVs were being tested for both the Minuteman and Poseidon missiles. Having reached this stage, any new military procurement, especially one involving a large number of civilian contractors and military officials, is very difficult to stop— and MIRVs were no exception.

Nonetheless, the US offered a ban on the flight testing of MIRVs, but the Soviet Union refused. This was because by 1970–1971 the US had essentially completed its testing program, whereas the USSR was just beginning. Not surprisingly, the Soviet Union would not agree to ban a technique that only the US had perfected. Even given the distinct US lead in this technology, however, it is widely agreed that some sort of MIRV prohibition could have been reached if the United States had pushed for it. As concluded, however, the Interim Agreement referred only to missiles (more accurately, missile launchers) and did not count warheads or make any mention of MIRVing. The United States began MIRVing in 1970, while the SALT I negotiations were under way, and the USSR followed suit in 1975, after the talks were concluded (Fig. 10.10).

Dovish critics point out that the "window of vulnerability" that has so bedeviled American strategic planning since the late 1970s—and has given rise to the MX missile, among other things—was a direct result of the failure to ban MIRVing in SALT I. Hawkish critics point out that the same "window" is also a direct result of American willingness to allow the USSR to retain a large number of heavy missiles, which, when MIRVed, began to constitute a theoretical threat to strategic stability.

In addition, hawks were concerned about the Soviet "reload capacity," since many of the USSR's ICBMs have been designed to be cold-launched, as a result of which silos can be reloaded with missiles and fired a second or even third time. Theoretically, since SALT I banned launchers rather than missiles, the USSR could accumulate a substantial "warehoused" arsenal for use in a prolonged nuclear war. Doves counter that a prolonged nuclear war is not realistically possible and that,

moreover, transporting and loading a large liquid-fueled rocket is a tricky procedure even during peacetime: it would be impossible in the chaos of nuclear war. To hawks, the reload problem (which recurs in SALT II) is an example of the US being hoodwinked in negotiations; to doves, it is an example of hawks opposing arms control by pointing to a red herring: a concocted problem that distracts attention from the real issue.

## THE VLADIVOSTOK ACCORDS

After SALT I, negotiations continued for the next phase of the SALT process, beginning in 1972. A further compromise was reached: the United States agreed to permit strategic bombers to be included in the overall permitted totals, while the Soviet Union agreed to continue excluding American forward-based systems. By doing this, the negotiators were able to adhere to the Jackson amendment's stipulation of "essential equivalence" in the strategic nuclear forces of both sides, since the American advantage in bombers almost precisely made up for its relative deficit in missiles.

In 1974 presidents Ford and Brezhnev met in Vladivostok, a Soviet city on the Pacific Ocean, to sign a bridging agreement between SALTs I and II that became known as the **Vladivostok Accords** (Fig. 10.11). This agreement called for equal numbers of offensive strategic nuclear weapons, specifically, 2,400 strategic launch vehicles for each side. Unlike the SALT I Interim Agreement, strategic bombers as well as ICBMs and SLBMs were to be counted in these totals, with each side having **freedom to mix:** either could substitute additional bombers, for example, if it were willing to forego an equal number of missiles. The Vladivostok Accords allowed the US to build 258 more launchers than were permitted by the 1972 Interim Agreement, whereas the USSR was required to scrap 99.

A limit was also set on the number of MIRVed vehicles. Thus, of the 2,400 strategic delivery vehicles permitted to each side, no more than 1,320 could be MIRVed (in the case of missiles) or outfitted with cruise missiles (in the case of bombers). In addition, the ABM treaty was modified by mutual agreement at Vladivostok, permitting only one ABM site for each nation.

Most critics were dismayed by the very high ceilings established at Vladivostok, which accommodated all the newer strategic weapons deployed by both sides. Moreover, the Vladivostok Accords did not inhibit any plans for additional nuclear weapons that either superpower had in mind. On the other hand, it may have

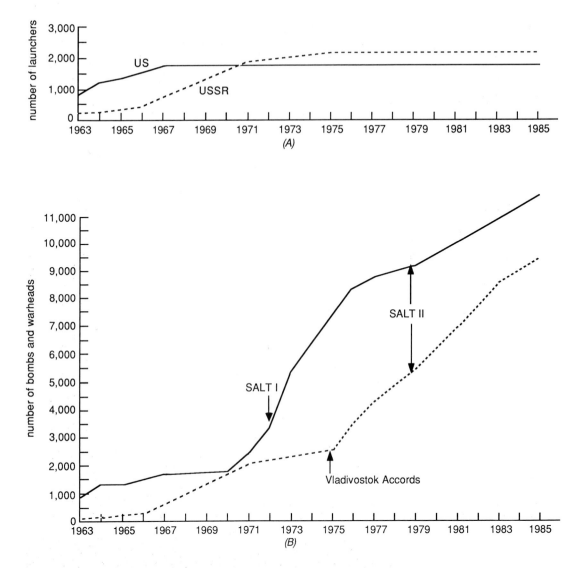

**FIGURE 10.10** Changes in the numbers of launchers (*A*) and of warheads and bombs (*B*) in the strategic arsenals of the US (solid curves) and the USSR (dashed curves) since 1963. Note that the USSR exceeded the US in total number of launchers during 1970, and that the US has never been behind in numbers of bombs and warheads; also note that neither SALT I nor any subsequent agreement has materially diminished the increase in weaponry on either side.

**FIGURE 10.11 Gerald Ford and Leonid Brezhnev signing the Vladivostok Accords in Okeansky Sanitarium, Vladivostok, USSR, in November 1974. Partially visible, above President Ford, are (left to right) Secretary of State Henry Kissinger, Soviet Foreign Minister Andrei Gromyko, and Soviet Ambassador to the US Anatoly Dobrynin.** (Courtesy of the Gerald R. Ford Library.)

represented an important step toward compromise and agreed equivalence. Those dissatisfied with the SALT I process were urged to withhold their judgment until SALT II.

## SALT II

### History and Initial Maneuvering in the Second Round of Strategic Arms Limitation Talks

At the signing of the Vladivostok Accords, presidents Ford and Brezhnev announced that a SALT II agreement would be reached no later than early summer of 1975 and that before it expired, both sides would begin for the first time to seek serious arms reductions. This sequence of events, of course, did not occur. Some observers have suggested that if Richard Nixon had not resigned in the wake of the Watergate scandal, he and Brezhnev might have reached a SALT II agreement in 1973 or 1974. (In fact, in the Soviet interpretation, Watergate was a plot by American hawks to sabotage detente and arms control!) In any event, SALT II was a partial casualty of the American obsession with Watergate.

The SALT negotiations dragged on nonetheless, slowed also by two new developments in weaponry: cruise missiles on the US side and the Backfire bomber (Fig. 10.12) on the part of the USSR. The United States

enjoyed a substantial lead in long-range cruise missile development; the USSR not surprisingly wanted all cruise missiles with ranges exceeding 600 kilometers to be considered "strategic launch vehicles," hence equivalent to an ICBM or SLBM in the SALT II counting rules. The US refused. The US negotiators, in turn, pointed to the Backfire as a strategic bomber, since with midair refueling, or by landing in Cuba, this aircraft could reach the United States. Negotiators for the United States therefore insisted that it be counted as a strategic launch vehicle along with the Soviet Bear and Bison, and the American B-52. The USSR refused, countering that the Backfire bomber was only a medium-range aircraft, comparable to the FB-111, which was not included in the SALT totals.

Meanwhile, conservative pressure within the US was making the SALT process increasingly unpopular, especially because of vigorous lobbying from hawkish groups, one of the most influential of which was called the Committee on the Present Danger. Under strong political pressure from the right, particularly from candidate Ronald Reagan during the election campaign of 1976, President Ford found it politically impossible to push strongly for SALT II.

Jimmy Carter entered office in 1977 determined to make substantial cuts in the nuclear forces of both sides (Fig. 10.13). He promptly sent Secretary of State Cyrus Vance to Moscow with a rather dramatic proposal for "deep cuts," including a unilateral reduction in Soviet "heavy" ICBMs from 308 to 150 and also fea-

**FIGURE 10.12 A Tu-26 Backfire bomber in flight. Without midair refueling, this aircraft could not attack the US from the USSR and return to home base. The US has argued that the Backfire should be counted as a strategic weapon, whereas the USSR resisted, successfully, in SALT II.** (Courtesy of the US Department of Defense.)

turing a limit of 550 MIRVed ICBMs (the number in the US arsenal). The Soviet leadership indignantly rejected this proposal, which they considered to be unacceptably one-sided. However, it also called for restrictions on long-range cruise missiles and on new flight testing and missile modernization. If accepted, it would have prevented the MX missile, as well as Soviet counterparts. But it was not. (Part of the problem may have been procedural: the Carter proposals were aired publicly before being shown to the Soviets, a breach of diplomatic etiquette. In addition, the USSR tends to be conservative in negotiating treaties, and its leaders may have been genuinely offended by this radical departure from the established tenor of SALT II negotiations.)

When the furor died down, both sides returned to painstaking negotiations, with the American team led by ACDA director Paul Warnke. A **SALT II** treaty was eventually arrived at and signed in Vienna in 1979 (Fig. 10.14). It did not differ dramatically from the Vladivostok Accords, although it was much more precise and detailed. However, by this time SALT II was in serious trouble. It was criticized by doves for not going far enough and once again setting excessively high limits; it was criticized by hawks for having made too many concessions to the Soviets. Increasingly, detente seemed to have evaporated in American anger over Soviet adventurism in Africa, alarm over a Soviet "combat brigade" in Cuba, and Soviet anger over American insistence on linking improvements in trade relations with increased emigration of Soviet Jews, as well as Soviet resentment over President Carter's focus on the Soviet human rights record. With the Soviet invasion of

**FIGURE 10.13 President Jimmy Carter (head of table) conferring with his national security team. To his right: Secretary of State Cyrus Vance, ACDA director and SALT II negotiator Paul Warnke, and White House chief of staff Hamilton Jordan; to his left, national security adviser Zbigniew Brzezinski and Secretary of Defense Harold Brown.** (Courtesy of the Carter Presidential Library.)

**FIGURE 10.14 Jimmy Carter and Leonid Brezhnev signing the SALT II treaty. Onlookers include Gen. David Jones, Zbigniew Brzezinski, Harold Brown, Leslie Gelb, Cyrus Vance, Andrei Gromyko, and Anatoly Dobrynin.** (Courtesy of the Carter Presidential Library.)

Afghanistan in 1979, it was clear that the SALT II treaty would not be ratified by the US Senate, and it was withdrawn from consideration.

In 1980 candidate Ronald Reagan campaigned hard against the SALT II treaty, calling it "fatally flawed" and announcing that if elected, he would begin a new round of strategic arms negotiations rather than resubmit the existing draft. However, as of 1986, both the US and the USSR had pledged to abide by the terms of SALT II, as long as the other continues to do so. For this reason, and also because it helps reveal the shape of agreements reached to date, we shall briefly review the major terms of SALT II.

### Terms of SALT II

SALT II consisted essentially of a protocol that expired at the end of 1981 and a treaty that expired at the end of 1985. The protocol banned mobile ICBMs, limited certain new models of ICBMs, and placed several restrictions on long-range cruise missiles. Neither side claims to be abiding by this protocol any longer. The treaty was a complex document, including numerical limits for various offensive weapons, as well as certain qualitative restrictions and clarifications. Its major quantitative features (Fig. 10.15) are as follows.

1.  The Vladivostok ceiling of 2,400 strategic launchers (ICBMs, SLBMs, and bombers combined) was reaffirmed until 1982, at which time this number was reduced to 2,250.

2.  Of the 2,250 strategic launchers, no more than 1,320 could be MIRVed (a bomber armed with cruise missiles is to be counted as a strategic vehicle, equivalent to an ICBM or an SLBM).

3.  Of this subtotal of 1,320 MIRVed vehicles, no more than 1,200 may be ballistic missiles. An additional restriction holds that of this maximum of 1,200 MIRVed missiles, no more than 820 can be ICBMs (Fig. 10.15).

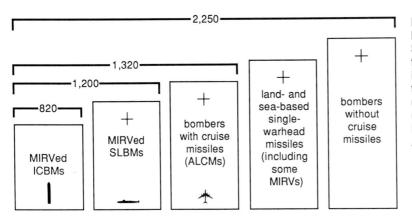

**FIGURE 10.15 Major arms limitation terms of the SALT II treaty, which called for a nested series of ceilings, as shown, with limitations placed specifically on the numbers of launchers and of MIRVed launchers.**

4. Each side may deploy one additional ICBM.

5. The USSR is not permitted more than 308 heavy ICBMs—its current number of SS-18s.

6. The USSR is prohibited from testing or deploying its large, ground-mobile SS-16 ICBM.

The SALT II treaty includes a number of other important points relating to qualitative aspects of the nuclear arsenals of both sides.

1. Rapid reload capability is prohibited.

2. Modifications of existing missiles cannot involve changing size, launch weight, or throw weight by more than 5%.

3. Fractionally orbiting nuclear weapons (FOBS) are prohibited.

4. Bombers carrying cruise missiles may not have more than an average of 28 cruise missiles apiece and must be clearly distinguished from bombers not carrying them.

5. By a formal exchange of letters, the USSR pledged that the Backfire bomber would not be outfitted for midair refueling, nor would its production rate (approximately 30/year) be increased.

6. Although the SALT II treaty does not restrict overall numbers of warheads as such, it does restrict each deployed missile to the number of MIRVed warheads for which it has been tested. Thus, the Minuteman III cannot be deployed with more than three warheads, or the SS-18 with more than 10. By these "counting rules," missiles will be tallied as having the maximum of warheads with which

they have been tested, even though in fact they might be carrying fewer.

7. During routine missile tests, each side gets information about its missiles' performance from radio signals; each side monitors the other's **telemetry** (rate of fuel consumption, burn times, acceleration patterns, etc.), as well. Both sides are prohibited from "encrypting" these signals (i.e., using code) if the disguised information would have been relevant to verifying the terms of the SALT II agreement.

No restrictions are established on missile accuracy, on antisubmarine warfare, or on the military balance in Europe. Throughout the SALT negotiations, the US had attempted to restrict the number and size of the Soviet Union's heavy, MIRVed ICBMs and if possible, to induce the USSR to rely relatively more on SLBMs. Because they are less accurate than ICBMs and also somewhat less vulnerable, Soviet SLBMs are considered to be less destabilizing. The USSR has resisted these pressures for several reasons: in submarine technology and in ASW capability the USSR is behind the US; the USSR is ill-suited geographically to maintain a large, efficient fleet of strategic submarines; and the USSR has a large investment in ICBMs. Replacement of existing Soviet ICBMs with other systems would be formidably expensive, and moreover, neither side responds well to demands that it destroy efficient and capable systems once they have been deployed.

For its part, the USSR sought persistently and unsuccessfully to place restrictions on cruise missiles and on American forward-based systems, and for the US to acknowledge the Soviet right to compensate for any increases in British, French, and Chinese arsenals.

## START

For more than a year after entering office, the Reagan administration did not begin strategic arms talks with the USSR, leading many to conclude that it was more interested in a military buildup than in negotiated limits or reductions. Then, in May 1982, largely in response to the increasingly vigorous peace and freeze movements in the United States, President Reagan proposed the resumption of a new round of talks, to emphasize reductions rather than limitations, and therefore known as **START,** for **STrategic Arms Reduction Talks.**

President Reagan publicly offered the following proposal:

1. A limit of 5,000 strategic warheads for each side, on SLBMs and ICBMs combined.

2. Of this total, a subceiling of 2,500 warheads on ICBMs.

3. Neither side would have more than 850 ICBMs and SLBMs combined.

4. Subsequent negotiations would seek to establish a limit on missile throw weight and would include strategic bombers.

The USSR—as well as the large number of American and European critics—complained that START was unfairly one-sided and so clearly loaded against the Soviet Union that it might have been designed to be rejected. For example, point 1, the limit on strategic warheads, did not constrain bombers or cruise missiles, two areas of enormous American advantage. Regarding point 2, the United States already had more than half its warheads on SLBMs, whereas the USSR had three-quarters of its warheads on ICBMs. The proposed shift would require a radical restructuring of Soviet strategic forces. (President Reagan later said he hadn't known that this was the case.) A cutback to 850 ballistic missiles (point 3) would require that the US eliminate about 800 missiles, and the USSR, about 1,500. Finally, throw weight (point 4) is an area of long-standing Soviet advantage, compensating for greater American accuracy and reliability, as well as other technological asymmetries.

On the positive side, the Reagan START proposals were innovative in the size of the suggested reductions and also in seeking to restrict numbers of warheads rather than number of missiles and/or "launch vehicles." START negotiations began in 1982 in Geneva,

with a retired army general, Edward Rowny, heading the American delegation. The United States continued to seek sizable reductions in Soviet heavy ICBMs, either directly in numbers, or indirectly, via limits on throw weight. The USSR favored an agreement along the lines of SALT I and II, with lower ceilings and "freedom to mix" within those limits. There is also some indication that the Soviets were willing to modify their traditionally negative view of on-site verification. No real progress had been made in 18 months, however, when the talks were suspended shortly after the Soviet Union walked out in protest against the beginning NATO deployment of new Euromissiles.

## EUROMISSILES

### Background

As we saw in Chapter 3, neither the nuclear nor the conventional balance in Europe is straightforward. Many of the smaller, tactical aircraft fielded by both NATO and the Warsaw Pact are "dual capable," that is, able to carry either conventional or nuclear munitions. Especially complex has been the question of **Euromissiles,** which can refer to any missiles deployed in or targeted on Europe. During the 1980s, however, Euromissiles has referred specifically to Soviet SS-20s and US Pershing IIs and GLCMs.

Since the late 1950s, the Soviet Union has deployed hundreds of SS-4 and SS-5 missiles in the western USSR, targeted on the cities of western Europe. The US first countered with Thor and Jupiter missiles, deployed in Britain and Turkey. By the early 1960s, it was felt that these missiles were outmoded, whereupon they were removed (following the Cuban missile crisis) and replaced with Polaris submarines assigned to NATO. The USSR kept its SS-4s and SS-5s, however, and both sides continued to maintain an array of shorter range missiles as well as very short range nuclear artillery.

In 1977 the USSR began phasing out its aged SS-4s and SS-5s, replacing them with a newer model, the SS-20 (Fig. 10.16). Unlike its predecessors, the SS-20 is solid-fueled, mobile, and armed with three MIRVed warheads. There was very little immediate response to this move, largely because the SS-20s seemed to be understandable as modernization rather than escalation and because they did not differ from the SS-4s and SS-5s in terms of military threat. However, shortly after the deployment of the SS-20s, President Carter decided to defer production of neutron warheads. European

**FIGURE 10.16 Artist's conception of an SS-20 mobile intermediate-range ballistic missile launch. These Soviet missiles are MIRVed, with three warheads, and have been deployed since 1977, facing both Europe and Asia.** (Courtesy of the US Department of Defense.)

leaders had generally opposed such weapons, fearing that with neutron weapons, the nuclear threshold would be too easily crossed. The European NATO leaders eventually acquiesced to such deployment, however; whereupon President Carter did an about-face. With the SALT II negotiations also pending, Chancellor Helmut Schmidt of West Germany was concerned that European security interests might be shortchanged. In an influential speech, he pointed to the Soviet deployment of SS-20s with some alarm.

In fact, NATO had no weapons in the same theater or intermediate category as the SS-20. But the US did have two new missiles to offer, both just being perfected: ground-launched cruise missiles (GLCMs) and Pershing II missiles (Figs. 10.17 and 10.18). Pershing IIs are single-warhead ballistic missiles with a longer range and greater accuracy than the Pershing I missiles already deployed by NATO. At a meeting in 1979, NATO decided on a **two-track strategy.** Track 1 was to deploy 464 GLCMs in Britain, Italy, Belgium, and Holland, as well as 108 Pershing IIs in West Germany, beginning in December 1983. Track 2 was to use this threat of deployment to help reach a negotiated agreement with the Soviets that would reduce or eliminate their SS-20s and thereby make NATO's Euromissile deployment unnecessary.

The US claimed that the SS-20s had upset the European nuclear balance and that the new NATO deployments would be necessary unless the Soviets unilaterally dismantled what was, after all, a unilateral escalation on their part. The USSR claimed that European nuclear forces were already balanced and

that additional NATO missiles would represent an unacceptable NATO advantage.

Another factor that hangs heavily over the Euromissile controversy is the difficult question of Soviet–German relations. Given their searing experiences in World War I and World War II, the USSR profoundly distrusts Germany and has endeavored to maintain a convincing nuclear capability against the Federal Republic of Germany (i.e., West Germany). In large part, therefore, the SS-20 deployments are directed at the Federal Republic; approximately a third of the USSR's SS-20s are also directed at China (Figs. 10.19 and 10.20).

The impending NATO Euromissile deployments generated immense opposition from many western Europeans as well. Marches and demonstrations during 1980 and 1981 attracted hundreds of thousands of protesters, who worried that the NATO missile deployment was increasing the chances of war and that, moreover, the superpowers were scheming to have such a war limited to the European "theater." Anxieties were stimulated further by statements such as President Reagan's remark that he could imagine such a war occurring without either side pushing "the button." Secretary of State Alexander Haig also discussed the possible use of "demonstration" nuclear blasts. Production of neutron warheads was resumed in the United States.

As we saw in Chapter 6, Europeans had long been ambivalent about the American nuclear guarantee. On the one hand, many welcomed it as a deterrent to conventional war, of which Europe has had more than its

FIGURE 10.17 Ground-launched cruise missile (GLCM) being test-fired from its transporter/erector/launcher vehicle. This weapon is a variant of the US Navy's Tomahawk sea-launched cruise missile; each vehicle is capable of launching four missiles and the vehicles are grouped in units of four, each associated with two launch control center vans. (Courtesy of the US Department of Defense.)

FIGURE 10.18 This Pershing II missile, test-fired in 1982, malfunctioned in flight and destroyed itself. There are 108 Pershing IIs deployed in West Germany. (Courtesy of the US Department of Defense.)

share. As we have already described, European public opinion has encouraged the presence of American troops less for their fighting effectiveness than as a "tripwire" to inhibit Soviet aggression by assuring that any attack would trigger an American military response. (As we have also seen, there is even some evidence that the USSR welcomes the presence of US servicemen in the Federal Republic, since their removal might mean an increase in the size of the West German army, or *Bundeswehr,* which the Soviet Union finds especially abhorrent.)

European proponents of deterrence have consistently supported measures designed to couple the defense of Europe to the strategic interests of the American homeland: to guarantee upping the ante in

the event of any Soviet attack . . . and thereby, to deter such an attack. However, there was growing fear that the more pronounced American military posture of the 1980s, epitomized by strident anti-Soviet rhetoric and the vigorous military buildup of the Reagan administration, might drag Europe into a war between the US and the USSR. In the view of leaders of the European peace movement, such a war might well be generated by a Soviet false alarm, reporting an attack by highly accurate Pershing II missiles, which were to be deployed (ominously, in the Soviet view) on German soil within 6–9 minutes of Soviet command and control centers. Not surprisingly, the USSR also sought to stimulate and encourage European objections to the forthcoming NATO missile deployments.

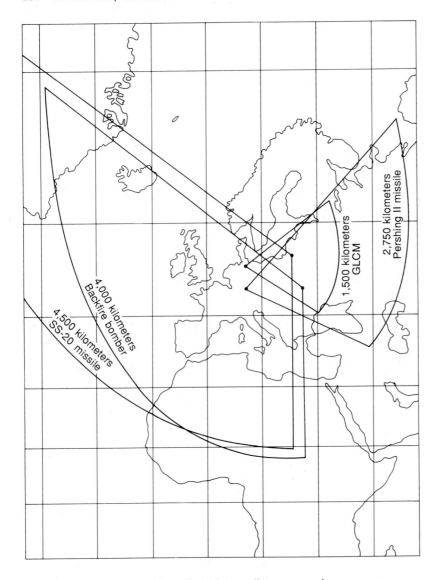

**FIGURE 10.19 Likely ranges of two Soviet intermediate-range nuclear weapons systems, the SS-20 missile and the Tu-26 Backfire bomber, and of the US Pershing II and GLCMs. Note that the Soviet systems have longer range; however, the US systems can reach the USSR, whereas the Soviet systems cannot reach the US.** (Modified from Lewis, 1979.)

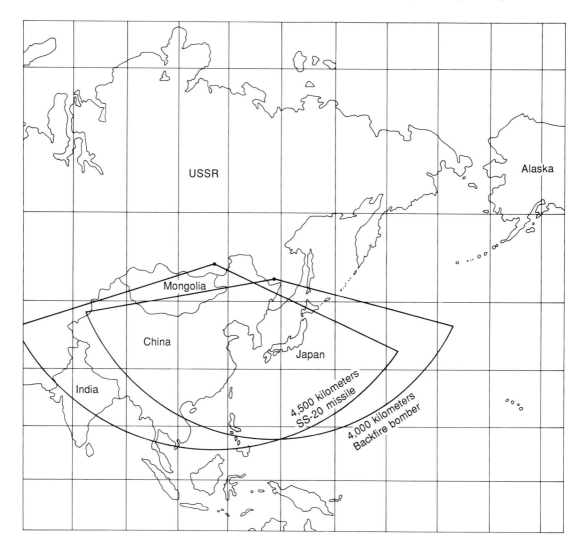

**FIGURE 10.20 Likely ranges of SS-20 missiles and Tu-26 Backfire bombers in the Far East. About a third of these systems are deployed in Asia. No US deployments of GLCMs or Pershing IIs are contemplated for this theater, although there is some anxiety that SS-20s withdrawn from Europe could be redeployed against US allies in Asia, including Japan, Pakistan, or the Philippines.** (Modified from Lewis, 1979.)

Supporters of NATO's Euromissile deployment claimed that it would be a better deterrent because it would help achieve a closer coupling of Europe to the American strategic nuclear forces. Opponents pointed out that ample coupling is achieved by the presence of 350,000 US troops in Europe. Supporters also maintained that NATO's Euromissiles would provide for the option of retaliation in kind: if the USSR fired its SS-20s, the West could respond with its GLCMs or Pershing IIs without having to employ strategic forces. This would make for a more credible deterrent. Opponents emphasized that this presumed benefit is exactly the opposite of the previous one; that is, it would involve some degree of decoupling. Moreover, it is unlikely that the Soviet leadership would discriminate between an American missile fired from Europe and one fired from North Dakota.

Perched atop this complex morass of fear, history, and weaponry, negotiations were resumed in Geneva in 1982, parallel to START. The chief American negotiator at these **INF (intermediate-range nuclear forces)** talks was a veteran, Paul Nitze, who had been involved in authoring NSC 68 more than 30 years before and had resigned from the SALT II delegation to campaign, successfully, against the SALT II treaty.

## The INF Talks

The INF talks began in Geneva in June 1982, at the same time as the START negotiations. They focused on systems with a range of 1,000–5,500 kilometers. As with START, no agreement was reached, and the INF talks were terminated in December 1983, when the Soviet delegation walked out—as they had said they would—after the first NATO Euromissile deployments began.

The opening position for the United States, as announced by President Reagan, was the **zero option,** whereby NATO offered to forego all its proposed missile deployments if the Soviet Union would dismantle all its SS-20s. This suggestion appealed to the widespread public desire to eliminate nuclear weapons, and in fact, it resulted in a decrease in antinuclear protests in Western Europe. Critics claimed, however, that the Reagan administration was simply seeking deployment and that the negotiations were a smokescreen and a sham to quiet European opposition. The Soviet objection to the zero option was essentially threefold. The USSR claimed that the zero option (1) demanded unilateral disarmament by the USSR, since the Soviets had already dismantled most of their older SS-4 and SS-5 missiles, (2) required that the USSR scrap existing weapons in return for a NATO pledge to refrain from doing something in the future, and (3) would leave the Soviet Union with no counters to British and French intermediate-range nuclear weapons.

The question of British and French nuclear forces was to become a continuing source of disagreement during the INF talks. The United States claimed that it could not negotiate for its allies and pointed out that France is not even in NATO's military command. An additional, but unstated objection once again concerned the Federal Republic of Germany: the British and French nuclear forces are considered to be "independent" (i.e., not under direct NATO control). Since

neither Britain nor France will give it an explicit nuclear guarantee, the Federal Republic is without a clear, visible nuclear "umbrella" unless NATO deploys ground-based missiles on its soil.

The Soviet Union claimed in turn that it must be concerned with all nuclear weapons arrayed against it, no matter what their national flag. Britain has four Polaris submarines, with 16 missiles apiece. (These missiles each carry three warheads, but they are MRVs, not MIRVs, so each is counted as a single warhead.) Added to these 64 British SLBM warheads, France has five submarines (80 SLBM warheads) plus 18 intermediate-range, land-based ballistic missiles. Britain and France together, therefore, have 162 intermediate-range missiles, generally also counted as 162 warheads (not counting the dual-capable British Vulcan and French Mirage bombers, both of which have range sufficient to reach the USSR). Both nations are planning to MIRV their forces—France with six warheads per missile, and Britain by purchasing US-built Trident submarines and C-4 missiles, probably MIRVed with eight warheads apiece.

As we have seen (Chapter 3), the US and the USSR disagree somewhat over the actual forces present in Europe. In addition, there is the vexing problem of which weapons to count: each side argues against counting certain of its aircraft. The US has deployed 72 short- to medium-range Pershing I missiles in the Federal Republic; these missiles are in German hands, whereas the nuclear warheads are under US control. The United States also maintains 560 aircraft in the European theater, composed of F-4, A-6, and A-7 fighter-bombers, and medium-range F-111 and FB-111 bombers. The USSR agreed to count 461 of its medium-range aircraft, composed of Badger and Blinder fighter-bombers, and Backfire bombers. However, the US also wanted to count 2,700 SU-17s ("Fitters"), SU-24s ("Fencers"), and MiG-27s ("Floggers"). The Soviets refused, claiming that these were short-range interceptors intended for defensive purposes only. The Soviets also objected to the US insistence on counting all SS-20s, given that about a third of these are targeted on China. The US, in turn, objected to counting its carrier-based aircraft, as well as British and French forces. As of 1985, the USSR had deployed a total of 414 SS-20 missiles and had declared a moratorium on further deployment; all the SS-5s have been withdrawn and the SS-4s are on the verge of being decommissioned. In addition, six "Golf II" class submarines, each carrying three warheads, have been deployed in the Baltic Sea since 1976.

Another asymmetry caused continuing difficulty: the United States claimed that NATO needed strong nuclear defenses to offset Soviet conventional superiority in Europe. The Soviet Union claimed that whereas the US considers GLCMs and Pershing IIs to be tactical nuclear weapons, to the USSR, they are strategic weapons; that is, the US weapons can reach the Soviet homeland whereas SS-20s cannot reach the United States. A truly comparable situation would exist if the USSR were to deploy SS-20s in Cuba. The US, in turn, pointed out that the SS-20 is actually an SS-16 ICBM with one stage removed and could readily be refitted to achieve intercontinental range. The mobility of the SS-20s also caused controversy, since the US expressed concern that if these missiles were withdrawn out of range of western Europe, they could always be brought back. It also would not be acceptable if Soviet SS-20s, brought out of range of Europe, were redeployed against Japan or China (especially since the latter has increasingly emerged as a semially of the US).

Eventually, there was some give on each side, but not enough to reach agreement. Yuri Andropov, who was named General Secretary of the Soviet Communist Party in 1982, after the death of Brezhnev, offered to reduce the number of SS-20s to equal the number of deployed British and French missiles. Eventually, this offer was modified to involve an equal number of warheads. (The unspoken implication was that the number would automatically increase as Britain and France begin MIRVing.) The US refused to accept such an arrangement, which, although it would produce East-West equality in intermediate-range missiles, would result in US–Soviet inequality, since the US would be left with no European intermediate-range missiles while the USSR had many. The US, in turn, modified its zero option, proposing that the two superpowers have equal numbers of intermediate-range nuclear forces. But this was unacceptable to the Soviets, once again because it involved no compensation for British and French forces.

Both sides came closest to an agreement during a private meeting between Ambassador Nitze and his Soviet counterpart, Yuli Kvitsinski, their so-called walk in the woods. This informal understanding called for the Soviet Union to deploy 75 SS-20s (225 ballistic missile warheads) and for the US to deploy 300 GLCMs (300 cruise missile warheads). This would have foreclosed deployment of Pershing IIs, which had been the major Soviet worry. Pershing IIs are the world's first ballistic missiles with terminal guidance, and thus, the most accurate; accordingly, they are potentially effec-

tive counterforce weapons (e.g., if used against Soviet command and control centers in the western USSR). Given this accuracy, combined with the short flight time from launch to target—estimated at 6–9 minutes—Pershing IIs are considered by Soviet officials and peace movement leaders to be highly destabilizing.

US and NATO officials, by contrast, emphasize that 108 Pershing IIs would not constitute a serious first-strike threat. In any event, the tentative "walk in the woods" agreement was rejected by national leaders, apparently on both sides. About this time, British Prime Minister Margaret Thatcher and West German Chancellor Helmut Kohl, both advocates of the NATO deployment, were reelected. As of this writing in 1986, deployment of NATO's Euromissiles is virtually complete; the USSR has responded by deploying new, shorter range SS-22 and SS-23 missiles in Czechoslovakia and East Germany (Fig. 10.21). These missiles are also capable of reaching most of the west European targets threatened by the SS-20s, and they may further complicate future Euromissile negotiations.

## THE GENEVA TALKS OF 1985

Following the Soviet walkout, Yuri Andropov died and was succeeded by Konstantin Chernenko. Mikhail Gorbachev succeeded Chernenko, who also died after a short time in office. President Reagan was resoundingly reelected in 1984, and in March 1985, US-Soviet nuclear arms negotiations resumed in Geneva. This time they consisted of three parallel sets of talks: INF, strategic weapons, and a new category concerned with Star Wars/SDI. The Soviet Union has insisted that any progress in the first two discussions must be linked to an agreement to ban the militarization of space, that is, severe restrictions on Star Wars/SDI. The United States has been equally insistent that Star Wars/SDI is a research program only and is not subject to negotiation. Both sides have endorsed, in principle, the concept of a 50% cut in offensive missiles. The USSR insists, however, that this category must include US GLCMs and Pershing IIs deployed in Europe, whereas the US insists that Soviet SS-20s must also be counted. As of early 1986, it was expected that an "interim" agreement on theater nuclear missiles in Europe might be achieved.

Following a Reagan-Gorbachev summit meeting in Geneva during late 1985, the USSR announced in early 1986 a three-part proposal, purportedly leading

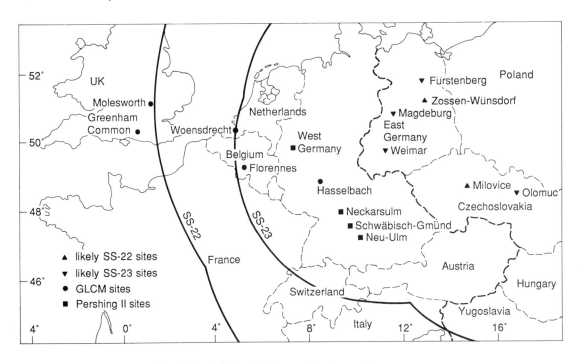

**FIGURE 10.21 Missile sites in England and continental Europe, showing maximum range of Soviet SS-22 and SS-23 missiles from their new sites in Czechoslovakia and East Germany. An additional GLCM site, not shown, is at Comiso, Sicily.** (Modified from SIPRI, 1985.)

to the elimination of nuclear weapons by the year 2000. The basic terms are as follows.

1. Over the next 5–8 years, each side would reduce by 50% the number of nuclear weapons capable of reaching the other's territory, and would renounce development, testing, and deployment of "space-strike" weapons. US and Soviet medium-range missiles would be removed from Europe; Britain and France would agree not to increase their arsenals. In addition, the US would join the USSR in the moratorium on nuclear testing begun unilaterally on August 6, 1985. (The US has refused to carry out this part of the proposal, claiming that verification is uncertain, that the Soviet moratorium is merely a ploy, undertaken during a lull in their testing, and that testing is needed to maintain the reliability of the US arsenal and to develop the X-ray laser for Star Wars/SDI. Also, the US is leery of Soviet SS-20s remaining in Asia.)

2. Beginning in 1990, other nations would freeze their nuclear arsenals and agree not to deploy them beyond national borders. All nuclear testing would cease. US–Soviet reductions would continue, to a total for each of 6,000 warheads and bombs capable of reaching the other nation. Medium-range nuclear weapons would be eliminated, along with tactical nuclear weapons with a range of less than 1,000 kilometers. (The US maintains that such an arrangement requires separate decisions by France, Britain, and China and that removal of nuclear weapons from Europe would favor superior Warsaw Pact conventional forces there.)

3. All remaining nuclear weapons would be eliminated between 1995 and 2000, with "a universal accord that such weapons should never again come into being."

Figure 10.22 summarizes the major nuclear negotiations and agreements, to date.

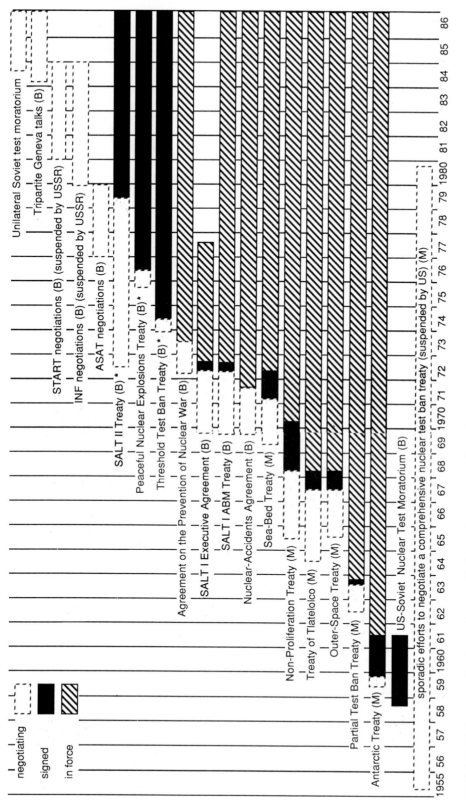

**FIGURE 10.22 Summary of major nuclear negotiations and agreements since 1955.
Dashed rectangles indicate negotiating periods; asterisks indicate instruments
signed by US president but not ratified by Senate; B = bilateral (US–USSR), M =
multilateral.** (Modified from York, 1983.)

In the early summer of 1986, President Reagan announced that the US no longer considered itself bound by the provisions of SALT II. Specifically, when the 131st B-52 bomber was outfitted with ALCMs (scheduled for December 1986), this would place the US over the SALT II limit of 1,320 MIRVed missiles plus bombers with ALCMs (Fig. 10.15). US government officials maintained, however, that this decision was not irrevocable, but was contingent on full Soviet compliance with SALT II, and/or progress in arms control. The Soviets, and many American critics of this decision, maintained that if the US abandoned SALT II, the result would be an unrestricted arms race with massive escalation on both sides.

## VERIFICATION

### General Considerations

Verification has long been a major stumbling block to nuclear negotiations. The United States in particular has insisted on strict means of verification, to ensure that the Soviet Union will comply with any agreements. The Soviet Union has typically opposed on-site verification, complaining that such activities will facilitate espionage. To some degree, these differences reflect differences between the two nations: The United States is historically an open society, such that relatively little that goes on within its borders is entirely secret to an adversary. By contrast, the Soviet Union is historically a closed society, highly controlled and suspicious. The effect is twofold. Soviet officials are typically uncomfortable that verification will involve spying. As a result of this asymmetry between the two nations, the United States may well have a particular need for verification, since it cannot rely on the same sort of information about the USSR that the USSR readily obtains about the United States.

Fortunately, technological advances during the past 25 years—especially in satellite surveillance—have made verification possible to a degree previously unknown. Both sides have agreed to such procedures, known in treaty language as "national technical means." Disagreements nonetheless persist regarding the degree of confidence with which critical events can be verified. Since doves are generally eager for arms control and disarmament agreements, they tend to emphasize the capability of either side to verify activities of the other. On the other hand, hawks are more skeptical of such agreements and are more inclined toward arms races, so they are more likely to warn about the possibility of undetected cheating. As of 1986, the USSR has indicated greater willingness than ever before to permit on-site inspection.

Disagreement also exists about the degree of verifiability necessary to render a treaty acceptable. Thus, one can insist on **absolute verifiability,** which amounts to a guarantee that any violation whatever would be detected. The probability of obtaining absolute verifiability would seem to be very low, almost zero. Or one can settle for **functional verifiability,** whereby violations that might materially degrade US national security would be detected, whereas lesser violations might not. Hawks favor absolute verifiability and are very sensitive to allegations of Soviet noncompliance; doves favor functional verifiability and are more inclined to give treaty compliance the benefit of the doubt, as long as national security is not compromised.

Closely related to such concerns is the confidence level with which violations can be detected. Guaranteed, 100% detection of every violation probably is impossible. Does this mean, therefore, that no agreements can be acceptable? The smaller the violation, the harder it is to detect, but also, the less likely it is that such a violation will significantly decrease the potential victim's security. Larger violations, of the sort that might conceivably endanger the national interests, would be more readily detected, however.

In addition, it has been argued that nations would be deterred from violating a treaty as long as the probability of detection were high enough and the benefits gained from such violation too low to merit the risk of detection. It remains uncertain, however, what these probability levels must be. It is generally acknowledged that nations do not adhere to agreements because of the niceties of international law per se; rather, if it is in the interest of both sides to adhere to an agreement, compliance can be expected. The benefits of cheating must be outweighed by the benefits of adherence or, alternatively, the costs of cheating and being caught must exceed the potential benefits to be gained from undetected cheating. Most weapons programs require numerous tests over a period of years before they can be relied on, and it is unlikely that an effective testing program could be carried to its conclusion without arousing suspicions great enough to lead the potential victim to abrogate the treaty.

Hawks on both sides worry not only that their adversaries might violate an agreement clandestinely, but also that there would be hesitancy to publicize violations even if they were detected, to help maintain an atmosphere conducive to further negotiations, as well as to save face for those who had negotiated and supported the treaty. For some hawks, verification can never be good enough: after all, we have never found anything that the USSR has successfully hidden from us! On the other hand, doves charge that hawks use an insistence on strict, ironclad verification as a way to block any arms agreements. National leaders on each side also tend to worry that the other might continue to push on the margins of allowable activities, perhaps supplemented with some clandestine activities as well, and then break out of the agreement, having gained some sort of unilateral advantage. Fear of breakout is thus a major driving force leading to insistence on strict verifiability.

## Verification of Nuclear Explosions

A nuclear explosion is a large and significant event, not easily hidden. The United States verifies compliance with the PTBT primarily through its Vela satellites (Figs. 10.23 and 10.24), which are highly sensitive to electromagnetic radiation of the sort given off by nuclear explosions, especially infrared (heat), light, and EMP. These will shortly be supplemented by data from the IONDS system of NAVSTAR satellites (Chapter 2). Atmospheric nuclear explosions in particular give themselves away by their characteristic double flash (Chapter 4). However, despite the acknowledged high confidence level of Vela detection, the system is not perfect: in 1979, for example, there were some mysterious flashes off South Africa that showed many of the characteristics of nuclear explosions, but confirmation has been elusive.

The technology for detecting underground nuclear explosions, which is critical for achieving a comprehensive test ban, has been improving steadily. The challenge is twofold: to detect an anomalous underground event, and then to discriminate between a nuclear explosion and a naturally occurring earthquake. Verification of any CTBT—and of adherence to the Threshold Test Ban Treaty—therefore involves seismic monitoring devices. There are several ways to distinguish underground explosions from natural phenomena. One simple discriminant is depth: earthquakes often occur deep underground, with about 30% originating below 100 kilometers. Drilling technology rarely allows underground explosions to be placed deeper than a few kilometers. However, some shallow earthquakes could be mistaken for explosions, and vice versa.

**FIGURE 10.23 Atlas rocket carrying a Vela nuclear test detection satellite, readied for launching at Vandenberg Air Force Base, California.** (Courtesy of the US Department of Defense.)

The location of the event is another discriminant: seismic events occurring near a known nuclear test area would be suspect, whereas those in seismically active nontesting areas would be less so. Nonetheless, some tests could in theory be conducted in seismically active areas, or in nontraditional sites. Fortunately, explosions and earthquakes are also discriminable by the kinds and pattern of energy they release: both phenomena produce two types of seismic disturbance, **ground waves,** which travel through the body of the earth, and **surface waves,** which have their effects primarily on the earth's crust. Ground waves consist of movement progressing directly away from the seismic event, compressing the ground, and of movements at right angles

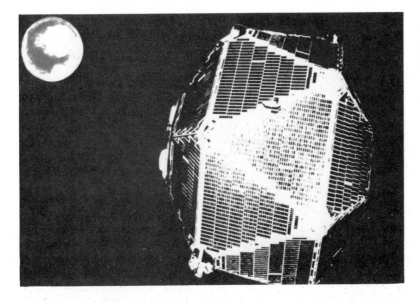

**FIGURE 10.24 Close-up of Vela satellite, designed for detecting aboveground nuclear explosions.** (Courtesy of the Sandia National Laboratory.)

to the event, exerting a shear effect (the P and S waves, respectively, Fig. 10.25). Surface waves (the Love and Rayleigh waves of Fig. 10.25) are caused by complex interactions of the ground waves.

Earthquakes and explosions differ in the ratio of magnitudes of these two kinds of wave: earthquakes produce relatively large amounts of shearing, whereas explosions produce large amounts of compression, directed radially outward from the point of detonation. Since earthquakes are relatively "spread-out" events, they transmit acoustic energy at long wavelengths, whereas nuclear tests, being more abrupt, release their energy in shorter waves with higher frequencies (Fig. 10.26). But, since high-frequency waves don't travel far through the earth's crust, a high confidence of detection requires seismometers placed relatively close to the suspected source—ideally, within the US and the USSR.

Detection and discrimination is more reliable—that is, the signal-to-noise ratio is higher—when there are many seismic monitoring stations and when these facilities are close to the events in question. Not surprisingly, the ability to detect and discriminate nuclear tests is highest for large explosions and declines for smaller ones. It would also be more difficult to verify a test ban if testing facilities were located in earthquake-prone regions, as opposed to areas that seldom experience earthquakes.

Much of the controversy over underground test ban verification has involved the prospects of evading verification. In particular, it has been suggested that a nation could wait for a natural earthquake and then test its weapons, partially disguise the signal by exploding weapons in soft soil, and muffle the signal yet more by using excavated underground caverns, such as abandoned salt mines. As it happens, the Soviet underground test sites are in regions of relative earthquake rarity, while the US underground test site, in Nevada, is more earthquake prone. The nature of the ground material is also critical: hard rock such as granite transmits seismic events much more efficiently than does soft alluvial soil, for example. The United States contains more soft, potentially absorbent underground formations than does the USSR. It is also noteworthy, however, that whereas soft, alluvial soils may lend themselves somewhat to undetected underground tests, they are also likely to collapse above the explosion's focus, resulting in visible cratering of the surface . . . which might prove highly embarrassing to a CTBT signatory!

It is customary to be concerned about whether a party wishing to monitor compliance would be able to detect clandestine efforts at cheating. That is, how confident can one side be that if the other cheated in a significant way, the violation could be detected? It is also worthwhile, however, to consider the issue from the perspective of any would-be cheaters: if they

P wave

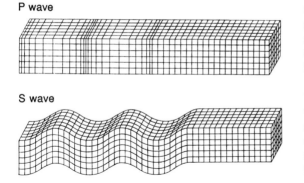

S wave

Love and Rayleigh waves

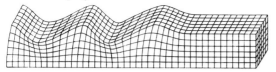

**FIGURE 10.25 Three major types of seismic wave. Compressive body waves (known as primary or P waves) travel most rapidly and reach a seismograph first; they are the major wave generated by an underground nuclear explosion. The slower body waves (known as shear or secondary, or S waves) travel more slowly and vibrate in a direction at right angles to their propagation; they are the major seismic wave form generated by an earthquake. Love and Rayleigh waves are caused by the complex interaction of P and S waves, reflected by the earth's crust.** (Modified from Sykes and Evernden, 1982.)

attempted to cheat, how confident could they be of getting away with it? For the record, a plot of underground nuclear explosions detected up to 1982, versus earthquakes identified in the same period, is presented in Figure 10.27.

Many geophysicists believe that tests as low as 10 kilotons can be detected and discriminated, even without a seismic network located within the USSR. With such a network, it is claimed that the absence of tests down to 1 kiloton could be verified. Others, notably scientists associated with the armed forces and the two US weapons laboratories, disagree.

Previous administrations, from Eisenhower to Carter, affirmed a comprehensive test ban treaty as a long-term policy goal, and indeed, the US has five unmanned seismic stations, intended to verify compliance with such an agreement, operating in this country and in Canada (Figs. 10.28 and 10.29). The Reagan administration has departed from this posture, however, and it appears that the prime issue is no longer verification, but rather, the desirability of continued US testing, to maintain stockpile reliability and facilitate the development of Star Wars/SDI.

## Verification of Production, Testing, and Deployment

Treaty verification, especially by "national technical means" (i.e., satellites) provides the most dramatic example of technology serving to help restrain the arms race and to enhance superpower stability. Satellites are unobtrusive and much less provoking than manned overflights in the atmosphere. By tradition and, more recently, by solemn treaty declaration, satellites are

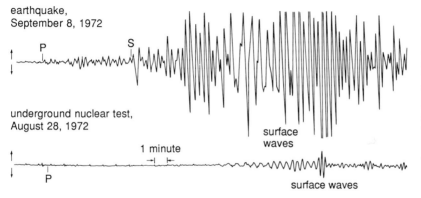

earthquake, September 8, 1972

P    S

underground nuclear test, August 28, 1972

surface waves

1 minute

P

surface waves

**FIGURE 10.26 Seismographic records of an earthquake and an underground nuclear test of comparable magnitude. The explosion produced virtually no S waves, and much smaller Rayleigh surface waves.** (Modified from Sykes and Evernden, 1982.)

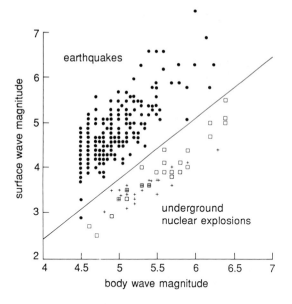

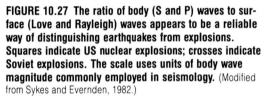

**FIGURE 10.27 The ratio of body (S and P) waves to surface (Love and Rayleigh) waves appears to be a reliable way of distinguishing earthquakes from explosions. Squares indicate US nuclear explosions; crosses indicate Soviet explosions. The scale uses units of body wave magnitude commonly employed in seismology.** (Modified from Sykes and Evernden, 1982.)

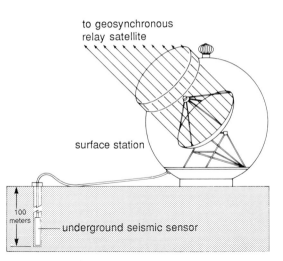

**FIGURE 10.28 Diagram of an unmanned seismic station, (designed at Sandia National Laboratory) intended to help verify compliance with a CTBT.** (Modified from Hafemeister, Romm, and Tsipis, 1985.)

acknowledged to be mutually acceptable means of treaty verification.

The earliest stages of the weapons process—especially research and development—are the most difficult ones to monitor by satellites. Hence, they have generally not been restricted by treaty. On the other hand, according to William J. Perry, Undersecretary of Defense for Research and Engineering, "We monitor the activity at the [Soviet missile] design bureaus well enough that we have been able to predict every ICBM before it even begins its tests." Testing is easier to monitor, whereas production is somewhat more difficult. The production facilities belonging to each side are large, complex operations, well known to the other. It is nonetheless very difficult to determine the precise number of items produced, and of course, the smaller these items, the more elusive they are. The final stage, deployment, is moderately verifiable (Fig. 10.30), although small weapons such as cruise missiles pose special problems, just as without direct inspection it is not possible to monitor accurately the number of MIRVs

in each missile's nose cone. It is the step before deployment—testing, especially field testing—that is widely recognized to be the most verifiable.

New weapons typically require many field tests, often 10 or more, and since these must occur in the atmosphere and/or in outer space, they can be detected and followed with a high degree of confidence. Phased array radars, operated by both nations, are capable of detecting and tracking dozens of basketball-sized objects simultaneously. US and Soviet test sites and launching ranges are known: the US typically tests its missiles by launching them from Vandenberg Air Force Base (California) toward Kwajalein Island in the South Pacific, whereas the USSR launches from its test facilities at Tyuratam and Plesetsk to the Kamchatka Peninsula and the central Pacific.

Launch of every Soviet test missile is detected by US Vela satellites, and the trajectory is monitored by radar. (US radar installations in Iran, lost following the overthrow of the Shah, have been replaced by others.) The radar tracking stations, in China and Turkey, provide information about trajectories, MIRVing patterns, and accuracy. "Big Bird" satellites photograph the missile in flight. In addition, "Ferret" satellites eavesdrop on the telemetry data sent from a missile being tested to its ground stations.

**FIGURE 10.29 Unmanned seismic station, operating in upstate New York.** (Courtesy of Sandia National Laboratory.)

Photographic reconnaissance is also widely employed by each side, to examine military installations on the other's territory: deployment sites of missiles and bombers, stockpiling depots, and to some extent, even production facilities are under regular surveillance. Three types of US surveillance satellites are shown in Figure 10.31. Low-resolution photography is used for examining large areas, then detailed, high-resolution photographs are taken of items of special interest. Electro-optical arrays can transmit images to ground directly, in "real time," without the delay imposed by film developing, and without the disadvantages of running out of film. Television cameras can scan film that is developed automatically aboard the satellite. Ground personnel then decide whether a closer look is warranted. For more detailed resolution, exposed film is ejected from the satellite; it descends through the atmosphere by parachute and is intercepted by reconnaissance aircraft.

The ability to resolve images is critical to verification and has been improving steadily. Just as with nuclear explosions, larger items are easier to detect (Fig. 10.32). When conditions are right, it is currently possible to detect license plates on the streets of Moscow; some enthusiasts claim that it is possible to read them as well! Computer-aided contrast enhancement also promises to increase ground resolution even further. It is generally acknowledged that ground resolution on the order of 10 cm is regularly achieved.

Objects about eight times this size can be recognized (e.g., as either a tank or a missile), and objects about 12 times this size can be identified (e.g., as an SS-18 vs. an SS-19 missile). To some degree, multispectral photography permits penetration of cloud layers, and infrared sensing can detect changes in worker patterns within a factory. However, the ability of satellite surveillance to detect possible treaty violations, especially during bad weather, is a matter of controversy. In addition, authorities are faced with the daunting prospect of having to evaluate enormous amounts of irrelevant information, combined with the possibility that important information may be camouflaged. Underground facilities are virtually impossible to monitor with much confidence. On the other hand, it is reemphasized that the production, storage, testing, and deployment facilities of each superpower are generally well known to the other, and covert sources of information are presumably available to each side.

## CLAIMS OF CHEATING

There were relatively few claims of treaty noncompliance during the 1960s and 1970s. Those arising on both sides were satisfactorily resolved by the Standing Consultative Commission. Since 1980, however, both the US and the USSR have accused each other of

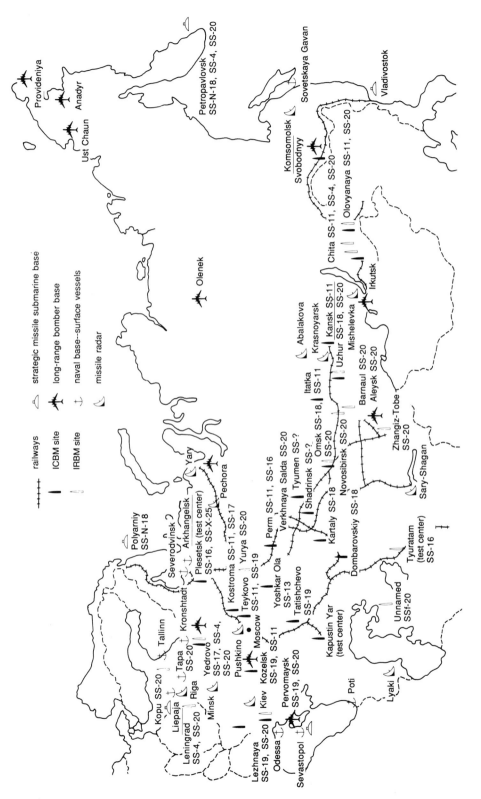

**FIGURE 10.30 Major nuclear weapons deployment sites in the USSR. Soviet nuclear weapons activities, and their locations, are well known to the United States, just as US activities and their locations are well known to the USSR.** (Modified from IISS, 1984.)

(A)

(B)

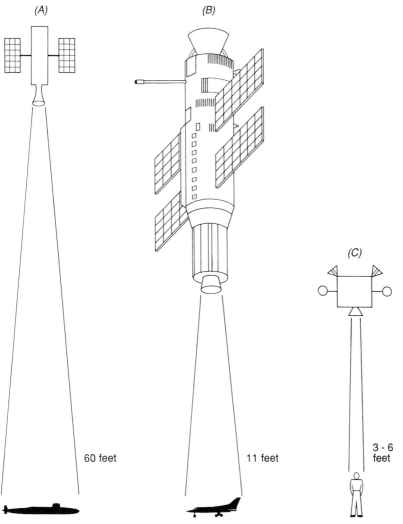

60 feet

11 feet

(C)

3 - 6 feet

**FIGURE 10.31 Three types of US national technical means of verification, showing the ground resolution and detectable targets of these spy satellites. (*A*) KH-11, (*B*) "Big Bird," (*C*) USAF high-resolution satellite.**

growing numbers of violations, and these have received more attention than ever before. Doves claim that this effort, largely initiated by the United States, was a result of the Reagan administration's antipathy to arms control, part of a campaign intended to create widespread public distrust both of arms control and of the Soviet Union, and also to pave the way for unilateral American abrogation of the ABM treaty, and possibly of SALT II compliance as well. Hawks claim that real violations have occurred and that we must realistically face up to this fact and to its implications.

Claims of cheating are generally of two kinds: those involving allegations of specific violations of existing treaties (ratified or not), and those relating to alleged intentions to abrogate or circumvent such treaties. Most of the US complaints are of the first sort; most of the Soviet complaints are of the second.

Some of the most important US complaints are that the Soviet Union has been using biological warfare ("yellow rain") in Laos, Kampuchea, and Afghanistan (Biological Weapons Convention); constructing a phased array radar at Krasnoyarsk, potentially suitable for area defense (ABM treaty); encrypting missile test telemetry (SALT II); testing a second ICBM, the SS-25, whereas the SS-24 had been identified as the USSR's only allowed new ICBM (SALT II); preparing to deploy

FIGURE 10.32 US satellite photograph of a Soviet aircraft carrier under construction at drydock on the Black Sea. In 1984 this and two other photos were published in *Jane's Defense Weekly*, and the navy analyst who provided them to the magazine was convicted of espionage a year later. The government claimed that release of these photos compromised security by informing the USSR about US satellite information-gathering capabilities.

the SS-16 missile (SALT II); and testing weapons in excess of 150 kilotons (Threshold Test Ban Treaty).

The USSR, in turn, has accused the US of constructing shelters over certain ICBM silos, notably the Minuteman IIs, which could hide their upgrading to MIRVed status; intending to violate SALT II by developing both the MX and the Midgetman missiles; engaging in a strategic weapons program of unprecedented dimensions, seeking to achieve coercive military superiority over the USSR; circumventing SALT II by deploying in Europe new land-based weapons that have a strategic role; actively preparing to break out of the ABM treaty by the research and development of large-scale ABM systems; and threatening to violate the ABM treaty by deploying large radars on Shemya Island in the northwest Pacific, as well as other new phased array radars.

The merits of these claims are disputed. Many—perhaps all—are susceptible to different interpretations. The United States, for example, claims that it has sought to permit verification despite the need to shelter silo construction crews from bad weather, that Euromissiles are not of sufficient range to be counted by SALT II, that research is permitted by the ABM treaty and that Star Wars/SDI is a research program. On the other hand, because Soviet test sites are geologically "harder" US counterparts, seismic signals from Soviet tests are less attenuated; it is claimed that when correction factors for such rocky substrates are used, Soviet tests have not exceeded 150 kilotons. The USSR claims, in addition that the SS-25 is permitted under SALT II

because it is not a new missile, but rather a minor modification of the SS-13. The Krasnoyarsk radar station is described by the Soviets as a satellite-tracking station—permitted under the ABM treaty—rather than an ABM component, and so forth.

In many cases, even the side claiming a violation identifies it as "possible," or "probable." There is uncertainty about how to respond to such accusations, apparently stemming in part from attempts by each side to exploit ambiguities in treaty language as possible loopholes. There has been active debate, for example, about whether Star Wars/SDI involves development of ABM "components" (in which case it would be in violation of the ABM treaty), or "subcomponents" (in which case it would not). Each side also tends to hold the other accountable for actions that qualify as violations under its own interpretation of treaties. For example, some representatives of the US intelligence community were angered at the Soviet Union's deployment of the SS-19 missile, which was a violation of the American expectation of how the USSR would interpret SALT I, but not a violation of the Interim Agreement itself. Similarly, the USSR has been upset at the American insistence on deploying Euromissiles, which threaten the Soviet homeland and yet do not constitute literal violations of SALT II.

In general, the USSR has greater opportunity to cheat on its treaty obligations than does the United States, since as we have seen, Soviet society is closed and secretive, whereas the US is comparatively open. It would therefore be more difficult for the United

States to conceal treaty violations. But even a massive "breakout" would almost certainly be irrelevant, insofar as mutual deterrence is concerned. Even if one party were to violate agreements successfully and in secret, given the large number of nuclear weapons on each side, it is arguable whether either side could suddenly unveil anything that would confer a unilateral advantage.

Disagreements about treaty compliance appear thus far to be more in the realm of legalistic argumentation than of real military or strategic significance. However, they carry enormous political impact and their resolution can have substantial implications for future arms control efforts. Many of these disputes seem to be resolvable by on-site inspection, although others involve interpretation of treaty wording rather than observable data.

## PITFALLS OF NEGOTIATIONS

There are many problems associated with negotiated agreements, even beyond the occasional difficulties of verification and compliance. Here are a few.

### Slowness

Negotiations take a long time: 3 years for SALT I and 7 years for SALT II, which wasn't ratified. When such negotiations overlap changes in the US executive branch, real discontinuity is introduced into the process. In addition, for reasons of pride and ideology, each new president is inclined to discard what his predecessor has accomplished and start anew. This happened to some extent when Carter and Reagan assumed office in 1977 and 1981, respectively. Each new administration sought in its own way to reinvent the wheel, but at the same time weapons designers were plunging ahead from ever higher thresholds, with new and often destabilizing technologies.

### Numerical Obsessions

Treaties necessarily involve things that can be counted. As a result, they may cause an inappropriate focus on quantitative rather than qualitative factors. Arms negotiators become modern-day Scholastics, arguing over how many warheads can dance on the head of an ICBM. By encouraging concern with nuclear parity, negotiations discourage concern with nuclear sufficiency, which is much more difficult to count or measure.

### Asymmetries

The US and the USSR are huge military and political systems that differ in their strengths and weaknesses. If each side insists on equality in the areas in which it is behind, while demanding to stay ahead in areas of advantage, no agreements can be reached. There is no easy way, for example, to compare the US advantage in bombers, cruise missiles, and SLBMs with the USSR's advantage in ICBMs, theater missiles, and conventional forces. It has been said that there are two rules for negotiators: don't negotiate when you are behind, and don't negotiate when you are ahead. If this is true, then nuclear negotiations are impossible, since the two superpowers have fundamental asymmetries—in arsenals, in allies, even in geography.

### "Leveling Up"

Decisions to build more weapons are made unilaterally and are relatively easy. Bilateral decisions to reduce, or even constrain both sides' arsenals are much more difficult. Rather than agree on reducing armaments, both sides are more prone to agree to accept the level of the side that is currently higher. Since neither wants to destroy any of its own weapons, there is a tendency to set treaty limits as high or higher than the actual level of armaments. Such "ceilings" may thus become production goals instead, permissible levels that stimulate participation in the arms race on the part of the side that sees itself as behind, rather than constraining the nuclear competition for both and for the benefit of both.

### The "Balloon" Principle

As political scientist George Rathjens has pointed out, negotiating restrictions in the nuclear arms race is like squeezing a balloon: constrict it in one place, and it pops out somewhere else. For example, the frequency of nuclear testing increased after the PTBT took effect, and there was an enormous increase in the overall number of warheads on both sides after SALT I, which did not limit MIRVing. The US has vigorously resisted efforts to curtail its advantage in cruise missiles, just as the USSR has jealously guarded its advantage in heavy ICBMs.

## Bargaining Chips

**Externally Generated Problems** It is widely felt that negotiations will be more successful if each side enters from a "position of strength." This has meant that weapons may be produced that, in the absence of negotiations, might not be justified. Then, if the negotiations fail, the weapons are often retained. Or alternatively, the weapons may develop an internal constituency of contractors, politicians, and military officers who come to cherish them and oppose any move to bargain them away. (For something to be a bargaining chip, it is necessary for each side to assert that under no circumstances is it a bargaining chip!) Cruise missiles were initially justified at least in part as providing leverage for the US in SALT II, although SALT II did not effectively restrict them. At a time when even proponents of the MX missile acknowledged that it was not supportable on its merits, limited production was approved in 1985 by appeal to the Geneva negotiations just under way at that time.

**Internally Generated Problems** It is less widely recognized that to obtain military support for a treaty limiting some aspect of military competition, it is typically necessary for governments to offer compensations to military and political constituencies that might feel slighted by the restrictive provision. For example, in return for support from the Joint Chiefs of Staff for the PTBT, President Kennedy had to promise a vigorous underground testing program. In return for SALT I, President Nixon had to proceed with MIRVing. In return for support for SALT II, President Carter had to support the MX missile and the Trident program. Also, since a two-thirds majority in the Senate is needed for treaty ratification, a minority of 34 can hold any treaty hostage, insisting on other weapons programs in exchange.

## Bargaining Leverage

Bargaining chips are by definition intended to be traded—for example, a possible offer to cancel the MX in return for Soviet agreement to cancel the SS-24. By contrast, **bargaining leverage** refers to the proposition previously alluded to that one has more influence at negotiations by entering into them from a position of strength. This in itself generates momentum for a military buildup: "We arm to parley," said Winston Churchill. On the other hand, critics of the negotiating process point out that perhaps the situation has reversed itself, and we now parley to arm; that is, the Reagan administration (and perhaps its Soviet counterparts as well) may be using nuclear negotiations as a way of generating support for further weapons. Some within the United States Congress, at least, justify weapons that would be unsupportable on their merits as part of the nation's commitment to arms control.

Since 1981, a related type of bargaining leverage has been especially prominent in debates over military funding: Congress has used its constitutional "power of the purse" as a source of leverage, not with the Soviets, but with the Reagan administration. Thus, since the executive branch during the 1980s has been widely seen as antagonistic to arms control, approval of the MX missile in particular was explicitly linked in 1983 to a demonstrated "good faith" effort at seeking an arms control agreement with the USSR. Reagan administration officials have claimed consistently that we must build up now in order to build down eventually. The USSR, they maintain, understands only force; they claim that America's military buildup of the 1980s has been primarily responsible for bringing the Soviets to the bargaining table.

## Legitimating the Arms Race

As analyst Richard Smoke puts it, "If the arms race is visualized as something like a freight train speeding down the tracks, then the SALT process is best visualized as something running *alongside* it. SALT has not succeeded in getting out in front, as it were, to push in the opposite direction and thereby slow it down significantly." In fact, critics of both the left and the right point out that arms control negotiations have served to legitimate and validate the arms race, rather than to stop it.

## False Confidence

Some right-wing critics point out that two decades of arms control efforts have failed to enhance American national security. They claim that such efforts have distracted national attention from the need to make greater military efforts. Reagan administration Assistant Secretary of Defense Richard Perle, for example, has emphasized that arms control agreements tend to generate a false sense of security and to anesthetize the public to the need for constant vigilance and a posture of military strength: "Democracies will not sacrifice to protect their security in the absence of a sense of danger. And every time we create the impression that we and the Soviets are cooperating and moderating the competition, we diminish that sense of apprehension." Advocates of this viewpoint sometimes favor negotiated agreements nonetheless, but they tend to emphasize strict verifiability and genuine reductions—especially in areas of Soviet advantage. They also point to the large Soviet military buildup during the 1970s as proof that detente was a dangerous delusion.

## ADVANTAGES OF NEGOTIATIONS

As Winston Churchill pointed out, "Jaw, jaw, jaw is better than war, war, war." Whatever the dangers, liabilities, and drawbacks of negotiations, they should be compared with the disadvantages that would result if no such efforts were made, and if each side relied on uncontrolled, unilateral arms escalation. Since the nuclear arms race is not a zero-sum game, it must be possible for both superpowers to identify outcomes in which both would be ahead. "We have a choice between the quick and the dead," said Bernard Baruch, when addressing the UN in 1946. "Behind the black portent

of the new atomic age lies a hope which, seized upon with faith, can work out salvation. If we fail, then we have damned every man to be the slave of fear. Let us not deceive ourselves: we must elect world peace or world destruction."

Negotiated agreements, if mutually adhered to and fair to both sides, can be mutually beneficial in preventing dangerous worldwide pollution (the PTBT), inhibiting potentially ruinous and destabilizing competition (the ABM treaty), eventually achieving real arms reductions, and perhaps most important of all, establishing the political and diplomatic climate necessary if war is to be avoided. In his Farewell Address, President Eisenhower urged:

*The conference table, though scarred by many past frustrations, cannot be abandoned for the certain agony of the battlefield. Disarmament, with mutual honor and confidence, is a continuing imperative. Together we must learn how to compose differences not with arms but with intellect and decent purpose.*

---

## Policy Issues

### Should the United States link arms control to Soviet behavior?

**Yes:**  It is absurd and dangerous to reward the USSR for its aggression in Afghanistan, its trouble-making in Africa and the Middle East, and its repression of Poland and of Soviet dissidents by entering into arms control agreements at the same time. We have a moral obligation to insist on basic standards of international decency; if we ignore Soviet misbehavior and proceed to negotiate regardless of their actions, we will have virtually no leverage over them. We postponed the SALT I talks for a year after the Soviet invasion of Czechoslovakia, and our refusal to ratify SALT II in the wake of the invasion of Afghanistan is equally appropriate.

**No:**  "Linkage" is misguided. Arms control is not a gift that we provide to them, or they to us; rather, it is an effort to reach mutually beneficial agreements. SALT I was in fact negotiated during the Vietnam war. "A sea wall is not needed when the seas are calm," wrote President Kennedy.

*Sound disarmament agreements, deeply rooted in mankind's mutual interest in survival, must serve as a bulwark against the tidal waves of war and its destructiveness. Let no one, then, say that we cannot arrive at such agreements in troubled times, for it is then that their need is greatest.\**

### Should we agree to a comprehensive test ban treaty?

**No:**  We do not have the technical abilities to verify Soviet compliance, and in any case, the USSR would find it much easier to cheat than we would. In addition, the US and the Soviet Union are not the only nations in the world; we must maintain our nuclear capability against possible threats from China, Libya, Pakistan, and so on, or even our current allies. Continued testing is also necessary for us to develop the latest generations of enhanced radiation warheads, to investigate the complexities of ballistic missile defense, and to maintain the reliability of our stockpiles.

---

\*Quoted by Sen. Edward Kennedy, speech to Arms Control Association, 1978.

**Yes:** Underground tests can be verified down to the level of military significance: a few kilotons. What is lacking is not technical capacities but rather, political will. A CTBT would be a real step toward ending the arms race, since it would inhibit new, destabilizing developments. And by decreasing stockpile reliability, a CTBT would make each side less likely to initiate a first strike, since a disabling first strike would require that a very high proportion of the attacker's warheads function as expected; by contrast, a much lower level of confidence is needed for deterrence.

### Should the United States continue to observe the terms of the SALT II agreement, which expired on December 31, 1985, unratified by the Senate?

**No:** SALT II is not a good arms control agreement. It sets allowed limits too high on both sides. The total strategic warheads on both sides grew from 5,500 in 1969 to more than 20,000 in 1985, all in compliance with SALT II. Most important, SALT II permits the USSR to maintain a monopoly in heavy ICBMs, in particular, its SS-17s, SS-18s, and SS-19s. It also permits the USSR to maintain its SS-20 missiles, which can be converted into intercontinental-range SS-16s by adding one rocket stage, as well as its Backfire bombers, which can reach the United States if they use midair refueling and/or land in Cuba. Many aspects of SALT II, such as the pledge not to increase MIRVing above tested levels, cannot be reliably verified. It might be in the interest of the US to continue observing the terms of SALT II as long as the USSR does the same, although the recent record of their violations suggests that America may be the only party adhering to it. Rather than ratifying SALT II, the US would be better off continuing with the defense modernization program. To keep with SALT II, it has already been necessary to retire 10 Polaris submarines, and it is now becoming necessary to dismantle perfectly good Poseidon submarines as the Trident program continues. The US would be better off to retain these weapons and depart from the artificial constraints of SALT II altogether. A vigorous rearmament program of this sort may very well induce the Soviets to agree to real nuclear reductions, whereas under SALT, they can simply retain the threatening weapons they were allowed to possess. If no such divestiture occurs, the US at least will have guaranteed its own security through its own strength and will continue doing so until a sound agreement can be reached.

**Yes:** SALT II isn't perfect, but it does provide many useful controls. Without SALT II, for example, Soviet SS-18s could be MIRVed with 20, 30, or perhaps even 40 warheads apiece, greatly increasing their counterforce threat. Under SALT II, the SS-16s were banned altogether, and some restrictions were achieved on the Backfire. US FB-111s and forward-based aircraft, as well as British and French nuclear forces, were not constrained. SALT II provides restrictions on the number of new missiles either side could introduce, and in fact, the USSR is much better poised than is the US to expand its nuclear arsenal if the SALT II restrictions are lifted. The US is not alone in dismantling weapons because of SALT II. The limitations cut both ways: while deploying new missiles and submarines (like the US), the USSR has dismantled 1,027 ICBMs and 14 submarines since 1972, so as to remain within the SALT limits. SALT II also represents a concerted effort to talk to each other and to reach arms accords, negotiated by three different US administrations. Thus, it is not only a result of superpower relationships but also a signal of the superpowers' attitude toward each other; the US refusal to ratify SALT II has in itself strained US-Soviet relations. By adhering to SALT II, it could be possible to achieve meaningful reductions by working down from the various ceilings that the treaty established. Otherwise, the superpowers are left with chaos.

### Should the US insist on a significant NATO Euromissile deployment?

**Yes:** It would not be acceptable for the USSR to have hundreds of SS-20s in Europe while the United States had nothing comparable to offset them. Such a situation could lead to the "Finlandization" of Europe, that is, the hypothetical case of the countries of Europe becoming so intimidated by Soviet military strength that they essentially gave up their independence in foreign affairs. The deployment of Euromissiles was a major triumph of NATO solidarity and diplomacy, and should be continued. By reestablishing the nuclear balance in Europe, such deployment also would reduce the chance of war.

**No:** There is no military significance to an "INF gap," especially since NATO's existing weapons plus the immense US strategic arsenal provide more than adequate deterrence. It is not necessary to have precise equivalence at every identifiable level of nuclear arms. Moreover, the widespread deployment of unverifiable cruise missiles might well condemn future generations to an unstoppable arms race, while the Pershing IIs, because of their first-strike characteristics, which make the Kremlin leadership so nervous, could lead to nuclear war by false alarm. With the SS-4s and SS-5s retired and even a moderate SS-20 force in place, the USSR would have fewer warheads targeted at western Europe than it had 20 years ago. The Euromissile deployment is not a triumph but a tragedy. It was supposed to make the Soviets more tractable; it made them less so. It has seriously strained NATO's internal unity. In addition, it precipitated additional Soviet missile deployments, as a result of which the structure of peace is even more fragile than before.

### Is it important to have "bargaining chips" during negotiations?

**Yes:** Ask any negotiator. If you give away the store before the negotiations begin, you are going to end up with a very unfavorable agreement. The stronger you are at the commencement of bargaining, the stronger you will be when you conclude the agreement, partly because your strength makes the other side more tractable, and partly because the stronger you are, the more you can bargain away . . . and still have something credible left. For example, the Soviets resisted the ABM treaty for a long time; they became receptive only when the US began constructing its own ABM system.

**No:** ABMs were not banned simply because each held them as bargaining chips; after all, each side has held ICBMs, SLBMs, and so on for a longer time but neither has agreed to cash in these weapons

systems. Rather, ABMs were banned because it was mutually recognized that they would not work, that they were destabilizing, and that such a treaty would be in the interests of both sides. Bargaining chips typically are never bargained away; they simply represent a way of adding to the arsenal. They do work in one way, however: they stimulate the other side to match or even exceed them, thereby turning the nuclear arms race up another notch. With 30,000 bombs and warheads, the US has plenty to bargain away if it were serious about it, without having to build more as bargaining chips.

### Should the US insist on absolute verifiability of agreements?

**Yes:** Nuclear weapons are too important for any nation to settle for any agreements that cannot be verified with absolute confidence. Moreover, the Soviets have repeatedly shown themselves to be unreliable and untrustworthy, willing to cheat and deceive when it suits their interest. If America cannot be absolutely confident that the Soviets are adhering to a treaty, it would be better off trusting to its ability to enhance deterrence and continue achieving peace through strength.

**No:** Large-scale cheating would be readily detectable and, with thousands of nuclear weapons on each side, small-scale cheating would be irrelevant. The greatest danger is not cheating, but rather, the continued destabilizing momentum of the arms race. The risks either side would take in negotiating arms agreements, even if only partially verifiable, are small compared to the risks run if both sides continue in their present course.

---

## KEY TERMS

McCloy–Zorin Agreement

Arms Control and Disarmament Agency (ADCA)

arms control

Partial Test Ban Treaty (PTBT)

Limited Test Ban Treaty (LTBT)

Threshold Test Ban Treaty (TTBT)

Peaceful Nuclear Explosions Treaty (PNET)

Comprehensive Test Ban Treaty (CTBT)

fractional orbital bombardment systems (FOBS)

chemical and biological warfare (CBW)

mutual and balanced force reduction (MBFR)

Mansfield Amendment

Helsinki Accords

Strategic Arms Limitation Talks (SALT I)

Interim Agreement

forward-based systems

national technical means

Standing Consultative Commission (SCC)

Vladivostok Accords

freedom to mix

SALT II

telemetry

Strategic Arms Reduction Talks (START)

Euromissiles

two-track strategy

intermediate-range nuclear forces (INF)

zero option

absolute verifiability

functional verifiability

ground waves

surface waves

asymmetries

"leveling up"

"balloon" principle

bargaining chips

bargaining leverage

## STUDY QUESTIONS

1. Distinguish between disarmament and arms control.

2. What relationships exist between negotiated agreements regarding conventional weapons and those regarding nuclear weapons?

3. What are some of the most important negotiated geographic restrictions on nuclear weapons?

4. What are some of the major agreements seeking to enhance communications and reduce the risk of accidental war?

5. Review briefly the history of the PTBT.

6. Why did the United States agree in SALT I to permit higher numerical ceilings for the USSR than for itself?

7. Distinguish between the SALT I Interim Agreement and the ABM treaty.

8. What are some of the major restrictions that SALT II placed on the USSR? On the United States?

9. What is meant by a "comprehensive test ban treaty?" Why is this idea so controversial?

10. Describe some arguments for and against the deployment of Euromissiles by NATO.

11. Why is the US generally more worried about treaty verification than is the Soviet Union?

## ADDITIONAL READINGS

Barton, John H., and L. Weiler (Eds.). 1976. *International Arms Control: Issues and Agreements.* Stanford, CA: Stanford University Press. A scholarly volume containing contributions on theoretical and practical aspects of international arms agreements.

Jacobson, Harold K., and Eric Stein. 1966. *Diplomats, Scientists and Politicians: The United States and the Nuclear Test Ban Negotiations.* Ann Arbor: University of Michigan Press. A well-balanced description of the major factors involved in the 1963 PTBT negotiations.

Krass, Allan. 1985. *Verification: How Much is Enough?* London: Taylor & Francis. A readable discussion of the politics and technology of treaty verification, emphasizing its feasibility.

Newhouse, John. 1973. *Cold Dawn: The Story of SALT.* New York: Holt, Rinehart & Winston. An excellent account, by a knowledgeable journalist, of the personal and public diplomacy associated with SALT I.

Sloss, Leon, and M. Scott Davis (Eds.). 1985. *A Game for High Stakes.* Cambridge, MA: Ballinger. A collection of accounts of participants' experiences during the US–Soviet negotiating process, with lessons learned, things to avoid, and problems encountered.

Talbott, Strobe. 1984. *Deadly Gambits.* New York: Alfred *SALT II.* New York: Harper & Row. A detailed account of the SALT II negotiating process.

Talbott, Strobe. 1984. *Deadly Gambits.* New York: Alfred A. Knopf. A detailed accounting of the diplomatic and personal maneuvering associated with the INF and START talks.

## UPDATE ON THE GENEVA NEGOTIATIONS

By midsummer 1986, the USSR had modified its negotiating position as follows: (1) an overall limit of 8,000 bombs and long-range warheads for each, with no more than 60% deployed in any one way (e.g., ICBMs); (2) each side having no more than 1,600 delivery systems (missiles and bombers); (3) allowing long-range cruise missiles on submarines but not on surface ships; (4) freezing US forward-based systems at current levels, but not counting them against the US total; (5) both superpowers agree to prohibit antimissile tests in space and mutually commit themselves to the ABM Treaty for at least 15 years; (6) increased flexibility on verification, including on-site inspection and techniques for monitoring the deployment of mobile long-range missiles, such as the new SS-24s and SS-25s; (7) freeze SS-20 deployments in Asia, with Britain and France freezing their forces at current levels. The USSR also proposed a possible limit of 6,000 bombs and warheads, but only if the the US agrees to forego all Star Wars/SDI research, including laboratory work.

# 11 Proliferation

**B**etween them, the United States and the Soviet Union have about 98% of the world's nuclear weapons. This is why they are considered nuclear superpowers and why we have focused almost exclusively on them so far. However, because of the extraordinary destructive potential of even a very small number of nuclear weapons, it is appropriate to consider all the world's nuclear weapons, whatever their number and whoever has them. As we shall see, there are also reasons to fear that nuclear weapons are more likely to be used if **proliferation** takes place; that is, if these weapons become widespread among many different nations.

## THE NUCLEAR CLUB

### Members

The United States was the charter member (1945) of the nuclear club. It was joined 4 years later by the Soviet Union. Scientists from the US, Canada, and Britain had collaborated during the Manhattan Project. However, such international atomic cooperation was terminated in 1946 with the passage of the McMahon Act by the United States Congress. Britain thereupon pursued the development of its own nuclear weapons, becoming the third nuclear weapons state in 1952. France was next, in 1960 (Fig. 11.1). Unlike the case of Britain, with which the United States has resumed nuclear collaboration, France independently developed its nuclear weapons, and delivery systems as well.

The People's Republic of China had been receiving some nuclear assistance from the Soviet Union during the 1950s but was frustrated by Soviet unwillingness to share the most sensitive and up-to-date technology. This failure to cooperate fully in the realization of China's nuclear ambitions may have contributed to the Sino–Soviet antagonism that became pronounced after 1960. In any event, China joined the nuclear club in 1964.

The nuclear delivery systems of Britain, France, and China are summarized in Table 11.1. To these totals one should add that both Britain and France are planning to MIRV their ballistic missile forces, which will multiply the numbers of British and French warheads by 8 and 6, respectively, toward the end of the 1980s. In addition, Britain is beginning to receive delivery of dual-capable Tornado bombers, and both nations have several kinds of nuclear-capable intermediate-range aircraft, including several hundred Buccaneers, Jaguars, and Harriers (Britain) and several hundred Jaguars, Mirage IIIs, and Super-Étendards (France). The Chinese land-based missiles are clearly targeted on the Soviet Union; however, China has also tested a long-range ICBM capable of reaching the United States, and has now launched at least two ballistic missile submarines as well.

India must also be counted a member of the nuclear club, having detonated an underground nuclear explosion in 1974. This was described as a "peaceful" nuclear "device." India has not followed up by accumulating a nuclear arsenal, but its ability to do so is undoubted. Some reports hold that India could activate a small stockpile in a very short time.

### Suspected and Near-nuclear Nations

In addition to the nations discussed above, several are widely acknowledged to have nuclear weapons, although they may not have tested any. Foremost among

**FIGURE 11.1 French nuclear test in the South Pacific (early 1960s).** (United Nations photo.)

**TABLE 11.1 Strategic nuclear weapons of Britain, France, and China**

| Delivery system | Warheads | Range (km) | Number |
| --- | --- | --- | --- |
| *Britain* | | | |
| Vulcan bomber | 2 | | 48 |
| Polaris submarines | 16 (3 × 200 kt MRVed) | 4,600 | 4 |
| *France* | | | |
| Mirage IV bomber | 1 | 1,400 | 34 |
| MSBS submarines | 16 × 1 Mt | 4,600 | 5 |
| SSBS silo-based | 1–2 Mt | 2,880 | 18 |
| Pluton land-mobile missiles | 15–25 kt | 100 | 42 |
| *China* | | | |
| CSS-1 (land-based) | 20 kt | 1,100 | 40–60 |
| CSS-2 (land-based) | 2–3 Mt | 2,600 | 85–125 |
| CSS-3 (silo-based) | 1 Mt | 7,000 | 10 |
| CSS-4 (silo-based) | 5–10 Mt | 12,000 | 10 |
| B-4 and B-5 bombers | 1 Mt | 1,800–6,000 | 40 |
| Submarines | 26 × 200 k–1 Mt | 3,300 | 2 |

these is Israel, which is generally assumed to have an arsenal of perhaps 200 weapons, which are either ready to use or in components that could be assembled very quickly. South Africa is also believed by many experts to be a covert member of the nuclear club. (It has been suggested that a mysterious, possibly nuclear explosion in 1979 off the southern tip of Africa may have been a result of Israeli–South African cooperation.) Taiwan is another nation that may have developed a covert nuclear weapons capability.

The identification of other nations as "near-nuclear" is partly a matter of definition. Thus, many nations (e.g., West Germany, Japan, Canada, Sweden, Switzerland, Australia, Italy, the Netherlands) undoubtedly have the resources and technological skill to produce nuclear weapons very quickly if they choose to do so. However, there is very little anxiety that these nations might join the nuclear club, because they have relatively little motivation to "go nuclear," and often, powerful political reasons for refraining.

Other near-nuclear nations are apparently seeking to develop nuclear weapons and may well do so in the 1980s. These include Pakistan, Argentina, Brazil, Iraq, and possibly South Korea. It is emphasized that estimates of this sort are controversial and not universally agreed upon (Fig. 11.2).

In any event, the decision to acquire nuclear weapons is a complex one. We can identify two major components: technological means and political motivation. This distinction is similar to the difference between capabilities and intentions, as used in our treatment of arms races.

## TECHNOLOGICAL MEANS OF PROLIFERATION

### The Front End

There are several undeniable connections between civilian nuclear power reactors and research reactors on the one hand, and nuclear weapons on the other. For one thing, the basic nuclear physics is the same. There aren't two different atoms—one peaceful and the other warlike—but rather, just one. As we have already seen (Chapter 1), nuclear reactors operate via the controlled nuclear fission of uranium fuel. Atomic bombs are the uncontrolled, explosive nuclear fissioning of uranium or plutonium fuel. The techniques used in handling radioactive materials are the same whether the goal is civilian, scientific, or military. And most important, the operation of nonmilitary reactors nec-

essarily involves the use of fissionable fuel as well as the production of highly radioactive waste, which could serve as the components for nuclear weapons. On the other hand, the practical and political connections between nuclear power and nuclear weapons are still being debated. Among the superpowers, and Britain and France as well, nuclear weapons were not developed as a spin-off from nuclear power, but rather, vice versa.

The **front end** of the nuclear fuel cycle involves uranium mining and then various processes for enriching its U-235 content: raw uranium ore contains 0.7% of this isotope, but 3% is needed for use in reactors. The process can be continued further, yielding the 90% or so U-235 needed for military-grade explosives (Fig. 11.3). Indeed, by conducting their own uranium enrichment, nations can obtain sufficient quantities of purified U-235 to construct atomic bombs of the sort that was dropped on Hiroshima.

As we have seen (Chapter 1), gaseous diffusion, which yields relatively large amounts of U-235, is the predominant method of uranium enrichment. However, it is a very costly process, requiring a massive investment of funds and technological resources. Enrichment plants of this sort currently exist in the United States, the Soviet Union, China, France, and Great Britain. Such enterprises are beyond the reach of any but the wealthiest and most industrialized nations.

Other techniques exist for uranium enrichment; although these produce smaller quantities of U-235, they are also cheaper, hence presumably more attractive to a would-be nuclear proliferator. One of these "poor man's uranium enrichment techniques" uses gas centrifuges, and plants have recently been built in the Netherlands, by a German company, and in Pakistan (Fig. 11.4). Another technique involves so-called nozzle enrichment, and is used in West Germany, with plants under construction in Brazil and already operating in South Africa. Laser enrichment is also being investigated and may be on the technological horizon.

### The Rear End

Although enrichment technology is clearly "sensitive" in that it can lead to weapons-grade U-235, the **reprocessing** of depleted reactor fuel is more sensitive yet, because it provides the opportunity of obtaining a plutonium isotope (Pu-239), which is even more readily fissionable than U-235 (Fig. 11.5). Moreover, reprocessing can be done at relatively low cost, and because reprocessing facilities are smaller and cheaper to build

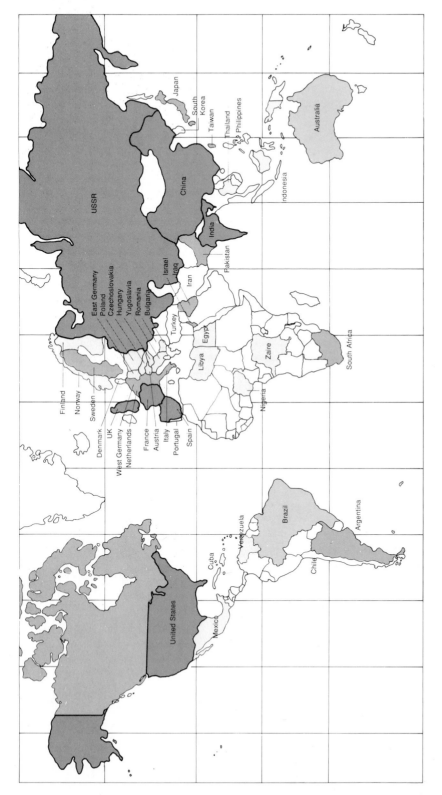

**FIGURE 11.2 Nuclear-armed nations and potential nuclear nations. Those heavily outlined currently possess nuclear weapons or in the case of India, have demonstrated the ability to construct them. Those colored dark gray are capable of developing nuclear weapons very rapidly, should they elect to do so; progressively lighter shades indicate less immediate likelihood of going nuclear. It is widely believed that both Israel and South Africa have nuclear arsenals, although neither nation acknowledges this.**

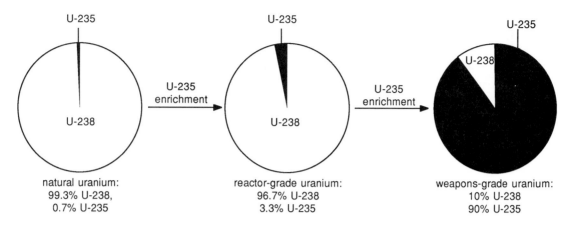

**FIGURE 11.3 The proportions of U-235 and U-238 found naturally and in enriched sources.** (Modified from Epstein, 1980.)

**FIGURE 11.4 Installation of gas centrifuge enrichment facilities in Pakistan.** (Courtesy of the Oak Ridge National Laboratory.)

and to operate, there is a greater likelihood that reprocessing can be carried out in secret. Thus the **rear end** of the nuclear fuel cycle provides an even more tempting opportunity for a nation to obtain bomb-grade, fissionable material.

The **light water reactor,** developed particularly in the United States, uses natural, nonisotopic (i.e., "light") water to remove heat from the nuclear reactor core and turn electric turbines. Light water reactors, using either pressurized (Fig. 11.6) or boiling water, are now in operation worldwide and are the most abundant kind of nuclear reactor. A second kind of reactor uses water containing "heavy hydrogen" (deuterium). The best known **heavy water reactor** is the **CANDU** (CAnadian Deu-

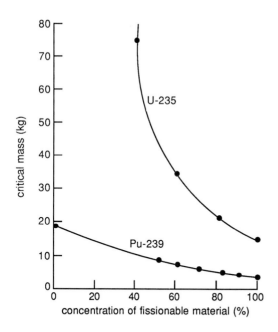

**FIGURE 11.5 Concentration of fissionable material needed to attain critical mass. For both U-235 and Pu-239, the critical mass is smallest when the fissile material is in pure isotopic form. Note that critical mass for Pu-239 is less than for U-235 and that U-235 is much more sensitive to the presence of contaminants.** (Modified from Epstein, 1980.)

terium Uranium) reactor, which is unusual in that it uses natural, unenriched uranium fuel.

When a reactor "burns" fissionable U-235, large amounts of neutrons are emitted, some of which strike U-238, the major component of uranium ore, which is always present in large quantities. Although U-238 is not fissile in a reactor, it is **fertile,** that is, it can absorb a neutron and thus be transformed into the fissionable isotope Pu-239.

The plutonium contained in the spent fuel in a standard nuclear reactor is too dilute to be used to build bombs, or even to fuel other reactors. However, by the 1960s, the nuclear power industry was looking ahead to retrieving this plutonium via reprocessing, then using it for commercial purposes. Such procedures have been developed and could yield plutonium that is suitable for military purposes as well.

By extracting the plutonium from spent reactor fuel, therefore, it is possible to obtain enough explosive for a bomb. The technology of reprocessing is not simple, especially since purified plutonium will burn on exposure to air and is highly toxic. However, plutonium reprocessing is much cheaper and more easily accomplished than is uranium enrichment. It has been estimated, for example, that a reprocessing plant

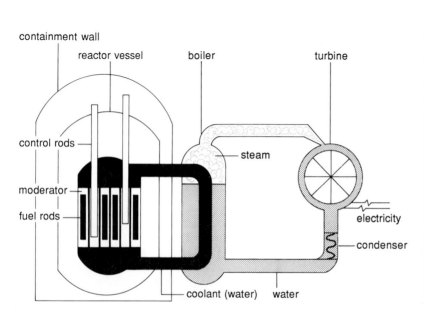

**FIGURE 11.6 Diagram of a typical pressurized water reactor. Control rods (typically cadmium or boron) absorb excess neutrons; the moderator (typically graphite or water) converts high-energy neutrons to low-energy forms more suitable for a sustained reaction. The high temperatures generated in the reactor vessel are diminished somewhat by the coolant, which is greatly heated and in turn heats another circulating system of water. The heated water is transformed into steam, which is used to turn a turbine and generate electricity. The coolant typically operates at very high temperatures and pressures.**

capable of separating 15–20 kilograms of plutonium per year (enough for several bombs) could be built for a few million dollars.

Because they are relatively economical, reprocessing plants are now more widely distributed than are enrichment plants; reprocessing installations are either planned or in operation in Japan, Belgium, Italy, Spain, Argentina, Brazil, and Pakistan. (They are not nearly as abundant as nuclear reactors, however.) It is widely acknowledged that Israel maintains a plutonium reprocessing plant at its top-secret Dimona facility. The Indian nuclear test in 1974 was made possible by plutonium obtained by reprocessing the radioactive material produced in a small CANDU research reactor (Fig. 11.7), using uranium supplied by the United States.

Plutonium reprocessing plants in themselves do not unambiguously indicate the intention of building bombs. Japan, for example, has an active reprocessing effort, but is not considered to be a proliferation risk. Sometimes reprocessing is motivated simply by a desire to produce plutonium for use as an economic supplement to the reactor fuel itself. In addition, for nations not desiring to build nuclear weapons, the plutonium present in spent reactor fuel constitutes **high-level nuclear waste,** which is a public health menace. This, in turn, has led to the suggestion that reprocessing may be desirable as a means of concentrating and recycling a material that is a menace to public health.

There are hundreds of nuclear reactors operating or under construction worldwide—more than 200 in the US alone. It is impossible to operate such facilities without making plutonium. The amount produced, of course, depends on the size and design of the reactor. Power reactors, for example, are much larger than research reactors, and therefore they typically produce more more plutonium. A typical power reactor will yield about 200 kilograms of plutonium per year, easily enough for about 20 bombs, if the plutonium is adequately separated from the radioactive waste. The connection between reactor operation and the production of plutonium was made clear to the world in 1981, when Israeli fighters destroyed a French-built research reactor in Iraq because of concern that the Iraqis planned to use it for the production of nuclear weapons.

As the newly produced plutonium remains within a reactor, it absorbs an additional neutron and is transformed into Pu-240. However, this isotope is so much more radioactive than Pu-239 that it is less suitable for bomb-building: the spontaneously released neutrons tend to initiate a chain reaction before full supercriticality is reached. As a result of such "preignition," Pu-

**FIGURE 11.7 Workers monitor the reactor at the Bhabba Atomic Research Center in Trombay, India. If it is desired to reprocess plutonium in a CANDU reactor, the fuel rods can be readily removed before they become contaminated with excessive amounts of Pu-240. Hence such facilities lend themselves to bomb-building via the "rear end" of the nuclear cycle.** (United Nations photo.)

240 (and other even-numbered plutonium isotopes) cause bombs to blow apart prematurely, resulting in a "fizzle yield." It has therefore been suggested that reactor fuel could be denatured by contaminating it with such isotopes; however, the feasibility of such a fail-safe mechanism may have been exaggerated, and it is now widely recognized that although the plutonium obtainable from spent reactor fuel may be less than ideal for bomb-building, it would nonetheless suffice.

The United States currently engages in plutonium reprocessing for the spent fuel of military reactors, but not for that from commercial power plants. This reflects an effort to maintain some distinction between peaceful and military applications of nuclear energy. In the early days of nuclear technology, before reprocessing became feasible, natural supplies of uranium were considered to be especially important. In addition to the United States, nations with such supplies include the Soviet Union, China, Australia, South Africa, France, Canada, and Niger. However, many routes now exist for obtaining the fissile materials necessary to construct atomic bombs, even for countries lacking both indigenous uranium supplies and the economic and technological base for uranium enrichment: (1) steal U-235 or plutonium, (2) steal bombs or warheads, (3) purchase bombs or warheads, and (4) operate one or more nuclear reactors and then divert and reprocess the plutonium that is produced.

Figure 11.8 charts the nuclear fuel cycle from the mine through the refining and production steps to fabrication, use, and storage as radioactive waste. Note that the "fuel elements" shown here going into reactors could, with suitable enrichment, be used in nuclear weapons. Similarly, the box labeled "reprocessing plant" could accommodate material to be used for bombs as well as for fuel.

Although plutonium reprocessing is considerably less expensive than uranium enrichment, it is cheaper yet to buy enriched uranium from one of the "nuclear supplier" countries, such as the United States or France. Such material, however, is not suitable for bomb-building without further enrichment. Despite the oil crisis of 1973–1974, the cost of uranium has remained relatively low during the 1970s and 1980s. Electricity demand has also been lower than anticipated, and safety concerns have increased the costs of nuclear power reactors. The United States, in particular, has hoped to discourage the widespread occurrence of plutonium reprocessing by making enriched uranium available to nations that want it.

Traditional nuclear reactors produce plutonium as a (presumably) unwanted but unavoidable by-product. **Breeder reactors,** however, are designed to produce plutonium, which they accomplish by generating (i.e., "breeding") more fissile fuel than they consume. These reactors differ from nonbreeder reactors in that the fuel is more tightly packed; as a result, neutron capture by U-238 is more efficient and so, breeder reactors produce more plutonium. They also produce higher operating temperatures, necessitating the use of liquid sodium instead of water as the cooling medium. This property leads to the technical name **liquid metal fast breeder reactors** (or **LMFBR**s). Breeder reactors are therefore closely tied to plutonium reprocessing. They are also especially attractive to high-tech nations lacking their own supplies of uranium, such as Japan and the countries of northern Europe.

The use and possible abuse of breeder reactor technology has been very controversial, especially in the United States, which for years has debated a proposal to build such a facility at a site near Oak Ridge, Tennessee—the Clinch River project. Breeder reactors are also considerably more expensive than their nonbreeder counterparts. France, West Germany, Britain, Japan, and the Soviet Union are all pursuing breeder technology.

It should be emphasized that there is no nuclear "secret" any more, at least not with respect to the construction of a basic atomic bomb. Given sufficient quantities of fissile fuel, it is not very difficult to design a workable explosive. The necessary engineering and machining skills remain formidable, but certainly they can be acquired. Perhaps the biggest hurdle to nuclear proliferation lies not in the technology, but in the will to acquire nuclear weapons. We shall therefore turn to the question of political motivation.

## THE POLITICAL MOTIVATIONS FOR PROLIFERATION

It is easier to be confident of the technology involved in proliferation than of the various possible political motivations. More than 220 tons of plutonium has been produced by commercial power reactors in the noncommunist world alone. Of this, about one-fifth has been reprocessed, which in itself would yield the equivalent of more than 5,000 Nagasaki-sized atomic bombs. Clearly, then, "to build or not to build" is a significant question.

As we have already seen, most of the world's more technologically advanced nations, although capable of building nuclear weapons, have renounced this prospect. In many cases, the most likely proliferators are to be found among third world nations whose technology is less advanced but whose political motivation is more compelling. What, then, are some of the reasons for going nuclear, and conversely, for abstaining?

A major reason for acquiring nuclear weapons, at least in the past, was fear of being beaten to the punch; the prime motivation for the invention of nuclear weapons was the American worry that Nazi Germany might develop nuclear weapons first. Since the 1940s, a more frequent motivation has been concern that one's

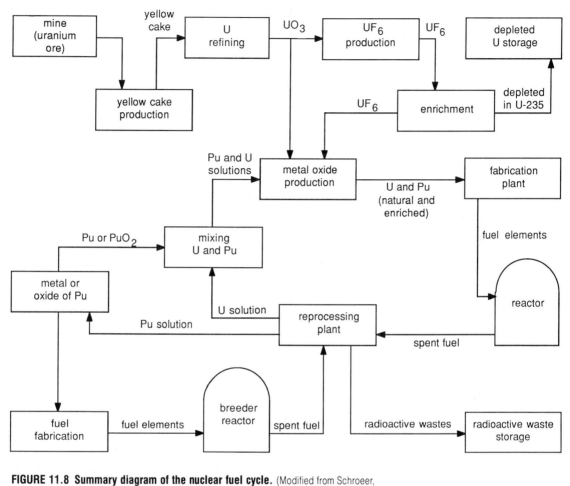

**FIGURE 11.8 Summary diagram of the nuclear fuel cycle.** (Modified from Schroeer, 1984.)

adversary has nuclear weapons, and that a national arsenal must be obtained either to deter a nuclear attack or to prevent nuclear blackmail and intimidation by the nuclear-armed adversary. This concern apparently motivated the Soviet decision to acquire nuclear weapons. It may also have been involved in China's decision to join the nuclear club, since in the early 1960s it viewed not only the US as an enemy, but also the USSR.

The possession of nuclear weapons generates what has come to be called the *n*th-nation problem, a sort of domino effect manifested as follows: the US developed nuclear weapons because of Germany; the USSR developed nuclear weapons because of the US; China developed nuclear weapons because of the US and the USSR; India developed nuclear weapons because

of China; and now Pakistan apparently seeks to develop nuclear weapons because of India.

However, security concerns may motivate nations to go nuclear even when their adversaries are not armed in this fashion. For example, Israel and South Africa, both suspected of having covertly developed nuclear capacity, consider themselves to be isolated and beleaguered, surrounded by enemies that are conventionally armed but nonetheless very threatening. Taiwan, which might have opted for the small nuclear arsenal believed by some analysts to exist even if mainland China were not a nuclear power, is a similar case. South Korea is regarded as a possible future proliferator, especially if the security guarantee provided by the United States is somehow doubted, and if the South Koreans come to feel especially threatened by the hostile North.

In addition, some analysts, particularly in the third world, believe that the proliferative activities of the US and the USSR have set a bad example. K. Sabrahmonyam, the former director of India's Institute for Defence Studies and Analyses wrote that the superpowers, by their behavior, had served "to convert the nuclear issue into a confrontation between North and South, and make the development of nuclear technology a symbol of declaration of autonomy from neo-colonial dependence."*

The technologically advanced countries of western Europe, by contrast, may be disinclined to seek independent nuclear arsenals because of their membership in NATO, which provides a security guarantee that might be considered more reliable than any bilateral assurance the United States might extend to Israel, Taiwan, or South Africa. West Germany renounced nuclear weapons for itself in the 1950s and shows no signs of reneging on this policy; to do so would be immensely provocative to the Soviet Union. The decision of the Bonn government to forego nuclear weapons, although doubtless stabilizing in itself, is also partly a cause of the Euromissile crisis: namely, the perception on the part of the NATO countries of the need to extend to a member state a nuclear guarantee which that state has chosen not to provide for itself.

Other technologically advanced nations—Sweden, Switzerland, Australia—could easily acquire nuclear weapons but are not politically motivated to do so. These nations may have decided to forego the nuclear option because they do not feel themselves to be immediately and directly threatened, either by nuclear- or conventionally armed opponents. Or, they may perceive that if they were to obtain nuclear weapons, they would promptly become prospective targets of other nuclear powers.

Beyond perceived threats to security, national pride may be an important factor motivating the development of nuclear weapons. Thus, when India detonated its nuclear explosion, the world's response (except for Pakistan, which protested vigorously) was muted or openly congratulatory.

It is entirely possible that the role of nuclear weapons as status symbol was involved in the decisions of

Britain and France to go nuclear several decades ago. Both nations were then relinquishing their once-mighty colonial empires, hence were losing their status as preeminent world powers. Nuclear weapons were a way of retaining national self-respect and, perhaps, greater weight in world councils as well. Religious pride may play a role as well: the late Pakistani leader Zulfikar Ali Bhutto, for example, once announced that since there was a Christian bomb, a Jewish bomb, and a Hindu bomb, there should be an Islamic bomb as well, and that his people would "eat grass, if necessary" to build one. In other cases, there may be the straightforward desire to make trouble: it is widely rumored that Libya has attempted (unsuccessfully) to purchase atomic bombs, especially from China.

In addition to the incentives for acquiring nuclear weapons, there are disincentives, however. The cost and sheer difficulty of developing a nuclear weapons program might be a real consideration, especially for an already beleaguered economy. Domestic opposition, too, may be a potent force. It would be politically impossible, for example, for any government in Japan to push for the development of nuclear weapons. In other cases, the expectation of international opposition seems to constitute an effective deterrent: West Germany, for example. The acquisition of nuclear weapons also would deprive a nation of whatever moral authority it had enjoyed by virtue of being a nonnuclear state. And some nations may even be deterred from obtaining nuclear weapons because of the belief that to do so would be morally wrong, regardless of the political merits or demerits.

On a more practical level, many leaders recognize that acquiring nuclear weapons would in the long run make their nations less secure rather than more. In particular, the decision to go nuclear might well induce one's adversaries to do the same. The result would be a "lose-lose" situation that is very similar to a kind of Prisoner's Dilemma. Each side would find itself forced to acquire nuclear weapons because the other side had done so. The end result? Each side would be more endangered than it was before. Both sides would thus be better off if neither one went nuclear . . . assuming of course that appropriate verification can be obtained.

The preceding discussion assumes that a proliferated world really is disadvantageous. But if the presence of nuclear weapons has helped keep the peace between the superpowers, why shouldn't it deter war among third world nations as well? Let us therefore ask about the likely consequences of nuclear proliferation.

---

*B. Russett and B. Blair. 1979. *Progress in Arms Control?* San Francisco: Freeman.

## THE CONSEQUENCES OF PROLIFERATION

There is a school of thought—a minority one, to be sure—holding that nuclear proliferation may be a stabilizing influence on international affairs. Just as nuclear deterrence can be at least partly credited with the absence of any post-1945 European or US–Soviet war, it is conceivable that the presence of nuclear weapons has induced national leaders to be more prudent in their foreign relations. This has been described as the **porcupine theory** of proliferation: just as porcupines walk peacefully through the forest, with little fear of being molested, nuclear-armed nations might well treat each other with well-founded respect, resulting in world peace.

However, it is more widely believed that a world of many additional nuclear nations would be even more hazardous than today's situation. Some of the concerns are as follows.

### Many Fingers on the Button

The laws of chance alone suggest that as the number of fingers on "the button" increases, the probability necessarily increases that someone, somewhere, will someday press it.

### Irresponsible Leaders

The more nations with nuclear weapons, the greater the chance that an irresponsible, unstable individual will have authority to use nuclear weapons. Such a person is less likely to be deterred by moral considerations, or even by the logic of deterrence. The specter of former Ugandan dictator Idi Amin and the present danger of Libya's Khadafy are often raised in this respect. To some people, this argument is thinly veiled racism, implying that dark-skinned people are likely to be less responsible than Caucasians. Perhaps the light-skinned superpowers have acted "responsibly"; after all, they have not blown up the world. However, given that they have accumulated tens of thousands of nuclear weapons, they may have little moral authority with which to accuse other nations of potentially irresponsible behavior.

### Accidental War

The nuclear powers, because of their relative wealth and technological sophistication, have been able to invest quite heavily in various "fail-safe" mechanisms that greatly diminish the probability of accidental war via unauthorized use, false alarms, and so on. By contrast, a nation that is straining its resources to acquire a nuclear arsenal might be tempted to save money by doing without the various sophisticated controls that characterize current nuclear arsenals and make accidental war less likely.

### Strategic Instability

Given the size and complexity of both Soviet and US nuclear arsenals, each side is basically assured an invulnerable second-strike capability, even against a possible first strike involving thousands of warheads. Imagine, by contrast, that a third world nation has a total arsenal of 10 atomic bombs. This would likely be highly provoking to its adversaries, who might be tempted to eliminate the danger in a preemptive first strike. Moreover, the temptation would be even greater since a small arsenal of this sort might be vulnerable to a surprise attack. As a result, deterrence might be quite unstable in the case of small arsenals, especially if two adversaries have nuclear arms—since striking first might be perceived as less risky than doing nothing. That is, applying the small-arsenals condition to the payoff matrix on page 124, the "attack" option might be seen as more favorable than "wait."

### Active Conflicts

The US and the USSR are not actively engaged in mutual hostilities or simmering border disputes with each other. By contrast, certain potential proliferators are adjacent to each other—North and South Korea, Israel and some of her Arab neighbors. Given that many would-be proliferators share common borders without buffer zones, conventional skirmishes here might be more likely to escalate to nuclear conflict than in the case of the superpowers, which typically confront each other in various "theaters" rather than in their own backyards.

In many of the world's trouble spots, too, current antagonisms and/or historic grudges would permit war to arise quickly. Once at war, nations tend to use whatever weapons are at hand, unless their conventional forces are adequate (as Britain's were in the Falklands war). It can be argued that nuclear weapons would not benefit the user even in a one-sided conflict—if, for example, the USSR were to use them in Afghanistan or Poland or the US in Nicaragua or El Salvador. However, nations do not always act in their own best interest. If nuclear warheads were available to both sides, it is certainly possible that the conflict would cease. But it is also possible that the powerful weapons would be used.

## THE NONPROLIFERATION REGIME

### The Non-Proliferation Treaty

In view of the threats just described, there is widespread consensus that nuclear proliferation constitutes a real danger. What has been done to try to prevent or limit it?

Efforts to prevent nuclear proliferation are known generally as the **nonproliferation regime.** The centerpiece of the nonproliferation regime is the **Non-Proliferation Treaty,** or **NPT.** Original impetus for the NPT came from several nonnuclear nations, in appeals to the United Nations in 1960. The two superpowers were interested but not wildly enthusiastic. A major stumbling block consisted of plans by the United States to develop a "multilateral force" within NATO, which would give the various NATO members joint control over nuclear weapons maintained by the alliance. The Soviet Union was especially upset at the prospect of German hands on the nuclear trigger and the plan was eventually dropped, after which a Non-Proliferation Treaty was negotiated without too much difficulty—largely because both superpowers felt that their security interests were enhanced by such an agreement.

The NPT was first open for signing in 1968 (Fig. 11.9); it entered into force in 1970. Basically, the NPT divides the world into "have" and "have-not" nations with respect to nuclear weapons. Its most significant nonproliferation items are as follows.

- Nuclear weapons states agree not to transfer nuclear weapons to nonweapons states, or to help nonweapons states make their own weapons.

- Nonweapons states agree not to receive nuclear weapons, and not to manufacture their own. They also agree to accept inspection safeguards on their nuclear facilities to be monitored by the **International Atomic Energy Agency (IAEA),** an agency of the United Nations.

Not surprisingly, some of the nonweapons states objected to the NPT, feeling that it was discriminatory: they were being asked to give up the possibility of acquiring nuclear weapons without receiving any tangible benefit in return. As a result, they insisted on the following additional provisions.

- The weapons states agree to share peaceful nuclear technology with the nonweapons states.

- The weapons states agree to begin serious bargaining to end the arms race and to undertake efforts at nuclear disarmament.

The NPT is to be reviewed every five years (1975, 1980, 1985, etc.). At these review conferences, the nonweapons states have expressed anger at what they see as the superpowers' failure to live up to their agreement to work seriously toward an end to the arms race. They emphasize that nuclear proliferation occurs not only "horizontally," when new nations acquire nuclear weapons, but also "vertically," as the nuclear nations—especially the two superpowers—accumulate larger and more deadly arsenals. The nonweapons states have insisted that **horizontal proliferation** cannot be prohibited indefinitely while **vertical proliferation** continues at the hands of the nuclear weapons states.

Swedish disarmament expert (and Nobel Peace Prize winner) Alva Myrdal was particularly vehement in her 1976 book, *The Game of Disarmament: How the United States and Russia Run the Arms Race.* "Between their outwardly often fierce disagreements," she charged, ". . . there has always been a secret and undeclared collusion between the superpowers. Neither of them has wanted to be restrained by effective disarmament measures." Myrdal reflected much of the anger and disillusionment of nonnuclear nations when she argued that "Military competition results in an ever-increasing superiority—militarily and technologically—of the already overstrong superpowers, thus sharpening the discrimination against all lesser powers." According to such critics, the United States and the Soviet Union play a game of "duopoly," while at the same time demanding that other nations of the world do as they say, not as they do. American and Soviet exhortations that other nations refrain from going nuclear may ring hollow while the two superpowers cling to their own nuclear arsenals. On the other hand, it is debatable whether even serious disarmament by the two superpowers would necessarily induce other nations to respond in kind. And it may be encouraging that at least with respect to inhibiting proliferation, the US and the USSR seem to recognize that their security interests coincide.

The NPT is generally considered to have been relatively successful in halting and preventing nuclear

**FIGURE 11.9 Dean Rusk signing the Non-Proliferation Treaty for the United States, in 1968. President Lyndon Johnson, to his left, looks on.** (Courtesy Lyndon B. Johnson Library.)

proliferation. As of 1985, 128 nations have signed it, officially renouncing any intent of obtaining nuclear weapons. Especially during the 1960s and early 1970s, many authorities were quite worried that dozens of nations would shortly acquire nuclear weapons. This has not happened; as we have seen, the nuclear club has grown very slowly in recent decades, much more slowly than most experts had feared. However, the NPT's effectiveness has been retarded by the failure thus far of some important nations to sign or ratify it. Both France and China have refused, although France has announced that it intends to behave as though it were party to the treaty, and so far as is known, China has refused to aid other nations in acquiring nuclear weapons. Beyond this, several important nonweapons nations have also refused to join the NPT, and included among these are some suspected and/or likely proliferators: Israel, India, Pakistan, Argentina, Brazil, Cuba, Spain, South Africa, and Taiwan (Fig. 11.10).

In addition, critics of the NPT point out that a would-be proliferator can ratify the NPT, receive substantial assistance (including reactors and the necessary technological expertise), and then, when it is on the threshold of building bombs, withdraw from the treaty and construct its arsenal. As we shall now see, the NPT itself is not entirely foolproof and proliferation-resistant.

## Safeguards and Problems

The NPT is an explicit bargain in which the nuclear nations have committed themselves to provide civilian nuclear technology to the nonweapons signers. According to its supporters, this is the only possible way to restrict proliferation, since nations desiring nuclear technology will somehow acquire it. Under the NPT, such acquisition will be at least supervised and therefore less likely to result in new nuclear arsenals.

According to critics, however, there is no such thing as nonmilitary nuclear technology; every reactor is a potential bomb factory. Moreover, the inclusion of reprocessing technology as "nonmilitary" further blurs the line between civilian and military.

Even aside from the problem of nonsigners, who are not bound to the NPT in any way, the nonproliferation regime has a number of weaknesses.

- The nuclear safeguards, overseen by the IAEA, are of questionable reliability, since they include no means of enforcing compliance or of preventing diversion of plutonium for military use. Rather, IAEA inspectors are empowered to report any possible violations they are able to detect. The intent is that a negative inspection report will constitute "timely warning," after which it is up to the nations of the world to respond as they see fit, possibly with sanctions.

- IAEA inspectors may examine only nuclear facilities that have been "declared" by the host country. They may not search for undeclared or secret facilities. Hypothetically, a nation could be maintaining both safeguarded and unsafeguarded facilities at the same time.

- Compliance is verified by allegedly tamperproof remote-control cameras, fuel components with special seals, and accounting checks, procedures that may nonetheless offer loopholes for would-be violators. It has been estimated that the "annual detection threshold" for plutonium may be as high as 18 pounds: that is, it may be possible to divert as much as 18 pounds (about one bomb) per country per year without being detected.

- Although a nation's nuclear facilities are to be open for inspection at all times, IAEA inspectors must

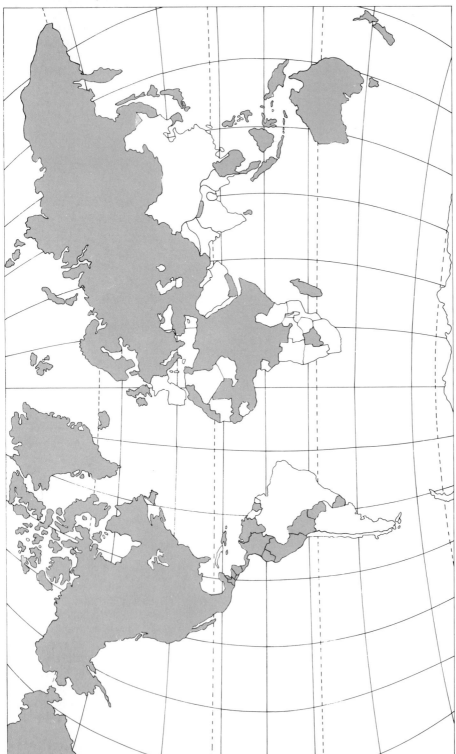

**FIGURE 11.10 Signers of the Non-Proliferation Treaty are shown in gray, nonsigners in white. Certain nonsigners, such as China and France, have nonetheless pledged to observe the terms of the Treaty.**

announce their visits weeks in advance, giving the host operators ample opportunity to prepare for such events. Moreover, host countries can veto inspectors from nations they consider unfriendly.

These weaknesses derive from a reluctance on the part of host nations to give up the prerequisites of national sovereignty. They do not necessarily indicate an intent to circumvent the terms of the NPT. It rankles many nonweapons states that the requirements of inspection are discriminatory: the nuclear weapons states are not obligated to have their facilities inspected. Both the US and Britain have voluntarily permitted inspection of their civilian reactors, however, and as of 1985, the Soviet Union has followed suit.

Supporters of the safeguards and inspection system, while acknowledging its weaknesses, point out that it is better than no system at all. And it bears repeating that although many people have expressed alarm about nuclear proliferation, its rate has in fact been relatively modest. It was widely feared that the Indian nuclear explosion of 1974 signaled the imminent unraveling of the nonproliferation regime; however, there have been no declared additions to the nuclear club since then (Fig. 11.11).

## The Role of the United States in the Nonproliferation Regime

In 1953 President Eisenhower announced his "Atoms for Peace" program in a major speech to the United Nations. Critics point out that this occurred just after the US and the USSR had exploded the first hydrogen bombs and that it was simply an effort to render nuclear energy more acceptable to world opinion. In addition, it represented a great financial gain for the firms—all of them initially American—seeking to sell nuclear reactors to other nations. Supporters maintain that it was a noble effort to share America's nuclear expertise, for the peaceful benefit of the world.

"Atoms for Peace" involved the declassification of much nuclear information, and a willingness—even, eagerness—on the part of the United States to collaborate with other nations in exploring the peaceful uses of nuclear energy. Much of the secrecy that had characterized the US nuclear program was eliminated (Fig. 11.12). Nuclear power was uppermost, but medical applications were also included; at that time, some scientists and many politicians were enthusiastic about the prospects of peaceful nuclear explosions as well, eventually resulting in such (unsuccessful) efforts as

Operation Plowshares. During the late 1950s and throughout the 1960s, the United States signed many bilateral agreements for nuclear cooperation, most of them involving the transfer of light water nuclear reactors, along with promises to supply reactor fuel.

President Eisenhower's "Atoms for Peace" plan also stimulated the United Nations to establish the IAEA in 1957, to handle safeguards and inspections. Nuclear supplier nations tended to favor stricter safeguards than recipient nations deemed appropriate. The IAEA was also charged with the job of promoting peaceful uses of nuclear energy, a role many critics feel poses a conflict of interest with its job as watchdog against proliferation. With the Non-Proliferation Treaty, the IAEA achieved an enhanced and designated role as part of the worldwide nonproliferation regime.

Concern about nuclear proliferation dramatically increased after the Indian test explosion in 1974. The major nuclear suppliers—15 nations making up the "nuclear suppliers group"—met in London between 1975 and 1977. They agreed to increase the physical security at nuclear facilities, and also to ensure that certain "sensitive" items could be exported only under IAEA safeguards. President Ford announced that the United States would temporarily forego reprocessing of spent fuel and would also prohibit the export of enrichment technology. Nuclear proliferation was an issue of even higher priority for President Carter, who deferred reprocessing indefinitely and sought to terminate the breeder reactor program. President Carter also urged other nations to follow the lead of the United States in vigorously opposing the worldwide "plutonium economy" that reprocessing and breeder technology threatened to initiate. Other supplier nations, however, were less enthusiastic, and many—especially in Europe—declined to follow the American example; they pointed out that whereas the United States had ample supplies of uranium, they did not; hence, reprocessing was economically appropriate for them.

In 1978 the US Congress passed the Non-Proliferation Act, which required strengthening of safeguards and the seeking of agreements among supplier nations to reduce the prospects of nuclear proliferation, as well as further investigation into nonnuclear ways of meeting the world's energy needs. It also forbids US vendors from dealing with other countries, whether or not they are signatories to the NPT, whose nuclear facilities have not been placed under full-scope IAEA inspections and safeguards. (Under conditions of **full-scope inspection,** all a nation's nuclear facilities are included, whether they were produced indige-

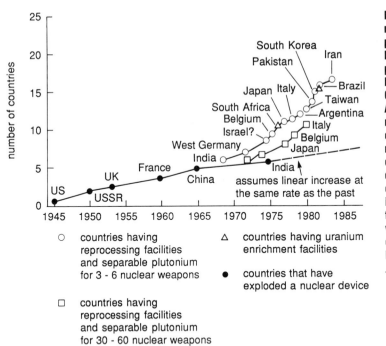

**FIGURE 11.11 Slightly modified version of a chart prepared by nuclear analyst Albert Wohlstetter as part of "Moving toward Life in a Nuclear Armed Crowd," a report to the Arms Control and Disarmament Agency (1976). Anxiety regarding the spread of nuclear weapons has generated concern about the dangers of exporting enrichment and reprocessing technology, although the proliferation of nuclear weapons to date has not occurred as rapidly as had been feared.**

nously or acquired with outside assistance.) With the Non-Proliferation Act, the United States also sought to discourage uranium enrichment and plutonium reprocessing by other nations.

The Reagan administration has taken a rather different view of nuclear technology and its transfer to other nations. During the 1980s, the United States has accordingly relaxed several of its controls on nuclear exports and has sought to lift restrictions on plutonium reprocessing and to encourage, once again, the development of breeder reactors. It has emphasized that the technological opportunity to go nuclear exists for any nation wanting to proceed in this direction. Accordingly, restrictions on such opportunities are considered to be misplaced. Reagan administration officials maintain that proliferation would be made less likely if the United States were seen to be a reliable supplier of nuclear technology, as well as a provider of dependable security guarantees.

The various nonproliferation strategies currently discussed and available to the United States are as follows:

- Nuclear proliferation, especially to US allies, is in our security interest and should be encouraged.

- Nuclear proliferation is none of our business, and we should avail ourselves of any commercial opportunities to profit from nuclear exports. After all, nations wanting such technology will buy it somewhere, so it may as well be from us.

- Nuclear proliferation will be minimized if the United States permits access to nonsensitive nuclear technology and establishes a record as a reliable supplier. As a result, nations will be able to meet their energy needs without relying heavily on Middle East oil or developing their own reprocessing or enrichment operations.

- Nuclear proliferation will be minimized if the United States, in conjunction with other prospective nuclear suppliers, insists on rigorous IAEA safeguards, with enforcement options as well.

- Nuclear proliferation will be minimized if the United States does everything within its power to see that nuclear technology is not spread to other nations.

It is noteworthy that the United States and the Soviet Union typically find themselves more closely allied on issues of nonproliferation than on other aspects of nuclear weaponry. The USSR provided early nuclear

**FIGURE 11.12 President Eisenhower turning on the first commercial nuclear reactor, at Shippingport, Pennsylvania, by remote control.** (Courtesy Dwight D. Eisenhower Library.)

assistance to China and Egypt, but has generally been less active in providing nuclear technology to other nations than has the United States and its western European allies (Fig. 11.13). Although all the Warsaw Pact countries have research and/or power reactors, there are fewer of these than in the West, they are not exported, and they include neither enrichment nor reprocessing facilities. Spent fuel is rigorously monitored and returned to the USSR.

## NUCLEAR FREE ZONES

**Nuclear free zones** represent another possible way of dealing with the proliferation problem: nations within a given geographic region are ensured by treaty that no nation within the region covered by the agreement will go nuclear. Establishing a nuclear free zone by mutual agreement can be a way of bypassing the Prisoner's Dilemma situation in which political pressure to go nuclear is generated by fear that nearby potential adversaries will do so, reaping some unilateral advantage in the process. If properly verified, a nuclear free zone is thus a way of ensuring that each participant receives the "reward" of staying nonnuclear, and that no one is "suckered."

Nuclear free zones can be defined in different ways. Among United States antinuclear activists, a nuclear free zone is often taken to be a city or municipality in

**FIGURE 11.13 The Syr-Darya nuclear power station under construction in the USSR. Although the Soviet Union makes substantial use of nuclear power, it has been more circumspect than the West about exporting nuclear technology to other nations.** (United Nations/Tass photo by A. Orokrik.)

which all activities associated with nuclear weapons and nuclear power are banned. At the international level, the phrase refers more often to a ban on nuclear weapons alone.

The only populated, multinational region that has been rendered nuclear free by treaty is Latin America, via the Treaty of Tlatelolco, as we have seen in Chapter 10. Serious proposals have been made for a Balkan nuclear free zone, which would encompass Romania, Bulgaria, Turkey, Greece, Albania, and Yugoslavia, and for a Nordic nuclear free zone, to include Finland, Sweden, Norway, and Denmark. Proposals are regularly made for an African nuclear free zone, but these are stymied by concern about South Africa's likely nuclear capability. Suggestions have also been made for the denuclearization of central Europe, including notably East and West Germany, Poland, and Czechoslovakia, along the lines of the **Rapacki Plan,** named for the Polish diplomat who first raised the possibility, during the 1950s. Such plans for nuclear free zones in Europe are typically supported by the Soviet Union and opposed by the United States, a disagreement that is consistent

with a Western distrust of Soviet treaty compliance, as well as the higher reliance that the United States and NATO place on the possible use of nuclear weapons to deter and if necessary, fight, any future war.

Nuclear free zones have been proposed for other regions, including Southeast Asia and the Middle East. It is also worth noting that the following NATO nations do not permit the basing of nuclear weapons on their soil during peacetime: Canada, Denmark, Iceland, Luxembourg, Norway, Portugal, and Spain. Greece has announced its intention of joining this group. Nuclear weapons belonging to the United States have been ousted from France, Greenland, Libya, Morocco, Okinawa, the Philippines, Taiwan, and Thailand, where they were once deployed. (In the case of the Philippines, the prohibition is on paper only, since it is tacitly understood that nuclear weapons are stored at Clark Air Force Base and Subic Bay Naval Base.) In 1985 New Zealand angered the United States by declaring itself a nuclear free zone and prohibiting the docking of nuclear-armed or nuclear-powered ships.

## Policy Issues

### Should the United States phase out nuclear power and encourage other nations to do the same?

**No:**  The world needs energy, and nuclear power is a good way to provide it. In fact, world stability is enhanced and the likelihood of war is diminished if nations can obtain cheap and reliable sources of energy, especially if this involves a reduction of dependence on oil imported from the Middle East and the Persian Gulf. Even if the US sought to discourage other nations from using nuclear energy, in all probability they would simply purchase nuclear power plants from other nations. The United States is a relatively energy-rich nation and perhaps can afford to rely on nonnuclear sources (coal, oil, hydroelectric power, etc.), but other countries are not so fortunate. Besides, if the US does not continue to pursue nuclear power, it will have turned its back on the technological future.

**Yes:**  Nuclear power is not a good way to meet the world's energy needs. It is intolerably dangerous, producing waste that will remain fiendishly toxic for

thousands of years. The 1986 disaster at the Soviet nuclear power plant at Chernobyl further underscores the risks of accident. Nuclear power is also unacceptably expensive. Moreover, it produces a very limited form of power, namely, electricity. This is not really a substitute for oil: less than 10% of the world's oil is used to make electricity. Nuclear power is not even commercially viable today. Once we were told that nuclear power would provide electricity "too cheap to meter," and now the nuclear power industry is being kept afloat only by irrational faith, as well as government subsidies and preferential tax and rate structures. Its risks and dangers far outweigh its benefits. Energy needs can be met by enhanced conservation combined with decentralization and such safe energy sources as solar power, wind, tide, and biomass.

### Should the US seek to inhibit the spread of advanced civilian nuclear technology?

**No:**  No one wants to see nuclear proliferation on a vast scale. But advanced nuclear technology is here to stay; as with the atomic bomb, there is no "secret," and the US cannot prevent nations who want bomb-building technology from acquiring it. America can and should address itself vigorously to the more important question, the political motivations for going nuclear. If the US denies nuclear technology to other nations—as happened to some extent during the late 1970s—nations will purchase it from other suppliers, as we learned from experience. So not only did the US fail to stem proliferation, but it allowed other nations to profit from exporting the relevant technology. America will do more to control nuclear proliferation in the long run by being a reliable supplier of nuclear technology and the necessary fuel to run nuclear power plants than by denying such services. Otherwise, nations may feel all the more pressured to develop their own enrichment and/or reprocessing plants, which would render the nonproliferation regime even more shaky than it is at present.

**Yes:** Nuclear technology involves much of the same instrumentation, training, and facilities needed for building nuclear weapons. With the addition of reprocessing or enrichment, it provides the necessary fissile materials. Clearly, the decision to acquire nuclear weapons is political, but it is one that the US can influence and make more difficult by vigorously denying nuclear technology to would-be proliferators. In addition to being environmentally dangerous and unnecessary, advanced nuclear facilities provide a convenient smokescreen behind which a nation can amass a nuclear arsenal. In a denuclearized world, developing such facilities would be a clear statement of intent, whereas nations now can deny having military goals while still pursuing a nuclear weapons capability. Finally, the US cannot continue vigorously promoting nuclear technology and expect that other nations will refrain from developing nuclear weapons as well.

### Should the US and the USSR seek to induce other nations to refrain from horizontal proliferation by curbing their own vertical proliferation?

**No:** The superpowers have an obligation to get the nuclear arms race under control, but they must proceed as seems best to them. They cannot allow themselves to be blackmailed or suckered by other nations in the process. Nor can they permit themselves to be intimidated by threats from would-be proliferators.

**Yes:** We cannot assume that other nations will remain patient indefinitely while the US and USSR fail to live up to their NPT obligations. If we keep claiming that nuclear weapons are essential to our security, other nations cannot be blamed for making the same argument. And then the security of all nations will be gravely diminished.

---

## KEY TERMS

proliferation

front end (of the nuclear fuel cycle)

reprocessing

rear end (of the nuclear fuel cycle)

light water reactor

heavy water reactor

CANDU

fertile

high-level nuclear waste

breeder reactor

liquid metal fast breeder reactor (LMFBR)

*n*th-nation problem

porcupine theory

nonproliferation regime

Non-Proliferation Treaty (NPT)

International Atomic Energy Agency (IAEA)

horizontal proliferation

vertical proliferation

full-scope inspection

nuclear free zone

Rapacki Plan

## STUDY QUESTIONS

1. What is the nonproliferation regime?

2. Describe the "front end" connection between nuclear reactors and nuclear weapons. How has this been changing because of technology?

3. What is plutonium reprocessing? Why is it a cause of concern?

4. How does the Prisoner's Dilemma relate to the political motivation of going nuclear?

5. Distinguish between the technological and motivational hurdles to acquiring nuclear weapons.

6. Describe some of the major incentives and disincentives for going nuclear.

7. In what way is the Non-Proliferation Treaty a bar-

gain between the nuclear weapons states and the nonweapons states?

8. What are IAEA safeguards?

9. Why is it generally thought that a world in which nuclear weapons have been allowed to proliferate is likely to be more dangerous than a world in which nuclear weapons are held by only a small number of nations?

## ADDITIONAL READINGS

Epstein, William. 1976. *The Last Chance*. New York: Free Press. A former UN official describes some of the dangers of proliferation, the workings of the nonproliferation regime, and suggests ways to strengthen it.

Fisher, David, and Paul Szasz (Eds.). 1985. *Safeguarding the Atom*. Philadelphia: Taylor & Francis. An evaluation of the IAEA safeguards system, with suggestions for strengthening it.

Goldblat, Jozef (Ed.). 1985. *Nonproliferation*. Philadelphia: Taylor & Francis. A careful examination of the political motivation in deciding whether to go nuclear.

Lovins, Amory B., and L. Hunter Lovins. 1980. *Energy/War: Breaking the Nuclear Link*. New York: Harper & Row. A strong and controversial indictment of the connection between nuclear power and nuclear war, including suggestions for alternative energy sources.

Wohlstetter, Albert (plus six others). 1977. *Swords from Plowshares: The Military Potential of Civilian Nuclear Energy*. Chicago: University of Chicago Press. An influential and rigorous analysis of the potential for proliferation via nuclear power.

# Part Five

# Domestic Aspects

In the next three chapters, we focus on some unilateral domestic aspects of the nuclear arms race: economic, ethical, and psychological. A warning seems appropriate, however. Much of the preceding material on nuclear hardware, effects, strategy, history of the arms race, and so forth has been subject to different interpretations depending on one's political orientation. But at least the facts should be reasonably clear. By contrast, discussions of nuclear economics, ethics, and psychology are unusually dependent on opinions. As we shall see in exploring these areas, some facts are generally acknowledged, but their significance is often controversial. Although crucial decisions regarding nuclear weapons are rarely made on the basis of economics, psychology, or ethics, it is hoped that the student will emerge from these chapters with a deeper appreciation of the issues, and a better ability to interpret the ongoing public debate.

# 12 Nuclear Economics

*Every gun that is made, every warship launched, every rocket fired signifies, in the final sense, a theft from those who hunger and are not fed, those who are cold and are not clothed. The world in arms is not spending money alone. It is spending the sweat of its laborers, the genius of its scientists, the hopes of its children.*
Dwight D. Eisenhower

Advocates of a large military budget typically base their arguments on their perception of the "Soviet threat," not on the possible economic benefits of such spending. Similarly, opponents of military spending typically base their opposition more on their perception of the political and military dangers of the weapons than on the possible economic costs of such spending. Thus, both hawks and doves recognize that on questions of nuclear weapons, economic considerations are secondary. The possible economic costs and benefits of military spending are nonetheless important issues affecting nuclear weapons decisions, especially since they must often be voted on annually in the context of congressional budget decisions. At such times, the annual battle over the federal budget and its military component becomes a conspicuous time for examining alternative directions in public policy. Critics then emphasize the economic costs of military expenditures, whereas supporters often take advantage of the political leverage provided by any local and visible economic benefits resulting from such programs. In certain cases, it may even be that the economic tail wags the political dog. We shall therefore next examine the basic economics of nuclear expenditures.

## HOW IS MILITARY EXPENDITURE DECIDED?

Unlike a family budget, in which expenses are relatively straightforward, the federal military budget comes in many different parts. A distinction must be made between (1) **budget authority,** sometimes referred to as **total obligational authority,** which is congressionally granted permission to expend a given amount (even though not all the authorized budget will be used during a given fiscal year), (2) **obligations incurred,** which are the expenditures to which the federal government has committed itself during a given year (salary obligations, contracts signed with various defense contractors, etc.), and (3) **outlays,** which are direct, out-of-pocket expenditures.

According to the US Constitution, Congress controls the federal purse strings, including all military expenditures. In brief, the budget process is as follows:

1. The **first budget resolution** (March or April) establishes target levels for spending.

2. The **defense authorization bill** (June or July) is written by the Senate and House Armed Services committees. This bill specifies how much may be spent on individual programs and it may set additional conditions (e.g., no funds for testing of a particular weapon if the USSR agrees not to test a counterpart or unless the president certifies that good-faith efforts are under way to ban such weapons on both sides).

3. The **defense appropriations bill** is acted on by the Defense subcommittees of the House and the Appropriations Committee of the Senate before it reaches each legislative body (September or October). The appropriations bill actually approves the spending of money for military programs. If—as often happens—the appropriations bills passed by the two houses of Congress differ, these differences must be ironed out by a joint committee of representatives from both chambers. As with all federal legislation, such spending bills require the president's signature and are subject to presidential veto.

Budget authority covers the estimated total cost of any military procurement or construction, although the actual expenditures and even the obligations incurred may take place over a number of years. Budget authorization figures are therefore larger than actual expenditures. During any given year, the federal government's direct expenditures are only partly taken up with spending money appropriated for use that year; some of the money spent annually goes toward meeting obligations incurred in previous years. For example, in fiscal year 1982, $57 billion in military spending (30% of the budget of the Department of Defense) was for commitments from prior years; in fiscal year 1984, this figure was $77 billion, which was not only a large absolute increase but also a proportional increase to 35% of the total. This also shows the effects of raising the part of the budget used for procurement, as happened in the early 1980s: the bills come due in the future.

Particularly when military spending has been increasing rapidly, as during the 1980s, budget authority is considerably greater than actual outlays. This has been described as the **bow-wave** or **wedge effect,** since the out-of-pocket expenses for a new weapons system may be relatively low during the first few years, when it is still in the research, development, or testing stage. Costs often become much larger in succeeding years, when production begins.

## HOW IS MILITARY SPENDING DEFINED?

As we shall see later in this chapter, it is difficult to compare the military expenditures of the United States and the Soviet Union. Surprisingly, perhaps, it is difficult to agree on what constitutes military expenditure in the United States alone.

Several definitions are often used, each yielding different total estimates, because each includes somewhat different items.

1. The Department of Defense (DoD) estimate of military spending is limited to spending by that agency. It includes personnel costs (as well as retirement pay), procurement (weapons and other equipment), maintenance and operations, research and development, and military construction (bases as well as housing).

2. The so-called national defense budget category includes, in addition to the more narrowly defined DoD figures, certain related expenditures by other agencies and other departments: the costs of civil defense planning (FEMA), the Selective Service System, and various military expenses incurred by the Department of Energy, notably the design and production of nuclear warheads and bombs, the production and maintenance of naval reactors, and maintenance of the strategic stockpile. This estimate, defined in the US budget as the **"national defense function,"** is the most widely used official estimate of military expenditures. Unless otherwise stated, it will be synonymous with "the military budget," "military spending," or "military expenditure" cited throughout this chapter.

3. The Department of Commerce provides annual data on military purchases of goods and services, as part of the **National Income and Product Accounts (NIPA).** This estimate excludes military retirement pay, but does include foreign military assistance. In addition, NIPA estimates do not count military purchases until the final products are delivered. As a result, for example, the billions of dollars expended for research and development of the MX missile would not appear as part of the NIPA estimates until the missiles were actually produced.

4. Different military budget estimates are made for the purposes of evaluating burden sharing among NATO nations. This estimate also includes foreign military assistance, and the training of police and paramilitary forces. Expenditures for civil defense and veterans' pensions are not included.

In addition, the following costs are not included in any official government estimate of military spending:

1. Retirement pay for civil service (nonuniformed) DoD employees. Of about 2 million civilian federal government employees, nearly 900,000 work for DoD and another 200,000 for the Veterans Administration. In 1980 retirement pay for all civil service employees was about $14.5 billion; taking half of this as military related adds about $7.2 billion to the military's share.

2. The continuing costs of previous military activities, notably veterans' benefits, amounting to $21 billion in 1980.

3. The budget for the National Aeronautics and Space Administration (NASA). Originally described as a civilian space agency, with ASAT and SDI/Star Wars research, NASA has become increasingly militar-

ized. A conservative estimate, allotting 50% of NASA's budget to the military, adds $2.6 billion to the military budget in 1980.

4. Interest costs on the federal deficit, a sizable proportion of which is due to military expenditures. It is typically argued that the costs of financing any endeavor are part of its real costs, and yet, these are not normally calculated in estimating military expenditures. On the other hand, interest costs for other federal expenditures—for, say, the National Park Service—are not considered to be part of the Interior Department's annual budget (Fig. 12.1).

If the goal in calculating military expenditures is to assess the total financial burden of such expenditures on the economy, the costs of retirement pay, veterans' benefits, and so on seem to be relevant. However, if it is to compare expenditures in terms of their contribution to military preparedness, only the NASA budget seems to warrant inclusion. Veterans' benefits, for example, are a past obligation; they do not contribute to the current military posture (except perhaps insofar as a nation's ability to recruit volunteers varies with its reputation for caring for its veterans). Table 12.1 presents a breakdown of various components of military spending during the 1980s.

Finally, in addition to the different ways of defining military expenditures, there are several ways of presenting military budgets, which differ substantially in the impression produced. Not surprisingly, techniques that make the military budget appear large are used by dovish critics seeking to emphasize the burden of military expenditures, or by politicians seeking credit for a substantial military effort when speaking to hawkish groups. In turn, statistical techniques that make the military budget appear small are used by politicians criticizing those in power for neglecting the nation's military strength, as well as by others arguing for an increase in that budget.

For example, absolute numbers may be used. By presenting budget figures as so-and-so billion dollars, not adjusted for inflation, military budgets can be made to appear enormous, and especially large in recent years. To adjust for inflation, it is often more meaningful therefore to present such data in **constant dollars,** reflecting the purchasing power of money as it was in a specified past year. (Thus, $100 million in 1955 may be the equivalent of $400 million in 1985.) **Current dollars,** by contrast simply refers to the actual amount of money at a given time. Even in these cases, when a recent year price level is selected, this has the statis-

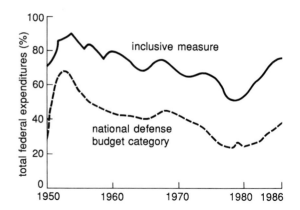

**FIGURE 12.1 Two measures of US military expenditures in relation to total federal expenditures. The inclusive measure includes veterans' benefits as well as the national defense budget category; it also is calculated by subtracting trust funds and interest on the federal debt attributable to military spending from the total federal outlays. Portions of curves after 1980 represent estimates.** (Modified from DeGrasse, 1982.)

tical effect of making recent increases seem less abrupt than those of the past. Military budgets are also often presented as a percentage of some previous period or year. For example, a decline in military spending—in **absolute,** or current, **dollars**—can be described as occurring in the 1970s, compared with the late 1960s, but this can be misleading because the baseline chosen was a time of very high military spending because of the Vietnam war (Fig. 12.2).

Relative spending levels are therefore popular, especially as a measure of national military effort. These typically involve the total military budget, m, as a percentage of gross national product: **m/GNP.** (The term gross domestic product, or GDP, which is identical to GNP except that imports and exports are excluded, is sometimes used.) Israel, for example, averages an m/GNP ratio of about 30%; many other mideastern nations average about 15%; NATO nations, between 3 and 10%; the US, about 7%; and the USSR, about 10–15%. Obviously, nations with smaller GNPs will have larger m/GNP ratios, if they maintain comparable absolute levels of military spending (Fig. 12.3).

Such ratios, although useful, can be misleading even when evaluating military spending within one nation. They tell different tales depending on how they are presented. For example, following the winding down

**TABLE 12.1  US government expenditures, 1982–1984, and projected budget estimates, 1985–1988 (billions of dollars), for six principal components of military spending**

| | Year | | | | | | |
|---|---|---|---|---|---|---|---|
| | 1982 | 1983 | 1984 | 1985 | 1986 | 1987 | 1988 |
| Department of Defense | 218.7 | 245.5 | 280.5 | 330.0 | 364.8 | 397.0 | 432.7 |
| Interest attributable to national defense[a] | 50.8 | 53.3 | 61.9 | 68.5 | 73.6 | 78.2 | 80.6 |
| Veterans' benefits | 25.0 | 25.0 | 26.1 | 26.9 | 27.8 | 26.8 | 29.5 |
| International affairs | 15.3 | 17.1 | 16.8 | 16.3 | 15.8 | 15.6 | 16.1 |
| Science, space, and technology | 7.1 | 7.9 | 8.5 | 8.4 | 7.7 | 7.7 | 6.8 |
| Department of Energy | 3.3 | 3.7 | 2.9 | 3.1 | 3.1 | 3.2 | 3.7 |
| Total | 320.2 | 352.5 | 396.7 | 453.2 | 492.8 | 530.3 | 569.4 |

Source: From J. Joseph, "The Economic Impact of Military Spending," in P. Joseph and S. Rosenblum, *Search for Sanity,* Boston: South End Press, 1984.
[a]Estimated at 60% of total interest.

of the Vietnam war by 1974, the US military budget declined as a percentage of gross national product, giving rise to claims of a "decade of neglect." As a percentage of GNP, US military budgets during the 1970s were in fact at the lowest level of any time during the postwar era—but this was at least partly because expenditures can be expected to go down after a war, and also because total GNP continued to rise. It can be debated whether a nation's military effort should necessarily rise automatically with its GNP. Rather, should it be judged against the function to be served by military forces? In the latter case, what relationship, if any, should be expected between military spending and GNP?

In a sense, GNP is a measure of the total national budget, the value of all goods and services produced

**FIGURE 12.2  US military spending, in billions of constant 1982 dollars.** (Congressional Budget Office.)

in a nation during a given year. Alternatively, military spending can be stated as a percentage of the total federal budget. Since the nation's budget, the GNP, is much larger than just the federal government's budget, military spending can be made to look much lower when it is presented as a percentage of the GNP rather than as a percentage of the federal budget. On the other hand, the federal government, not private corporations or the domestic consumer, is the entity that purchases military forces. Not surprisingly, critics of military spending tend to look at military spending as a percentage of the federal budget, while supporters often point to a much smaller figure, military spending as a proportion of the GNP.

Even the ratio of military spending to the total federal budget can itself be misleading. This is because the total, "unified federal budget" includes large expenditures for such items as interest on the federal debt, as well as Social Security and other transfer payments. These latter expenditures are relatively uncontrollable and also relatively large. As a result, military expenditures seen as a percentage of the unified budget appear smaller than when they are taken as a percentage of the "controllable" or "discretionary" federal budget, which includes programs that are optionally budgeted during any given year. During 1984, for example, US military expenditures were 27.8% of the unified federal budget (Social Security and Medicare were 28.1%, interest on the debt, 12.7%, and other discretionary programs were 31.4%). Taken as a percentage of total discretionary spending, however, the 1984 military budget constituted 40%. Even within the military budget, some funds are uncontrollable if they are tied to contracts from earlier years. For example, 27.2% of the total military budget during 1980 was already obligated from previous years; this figure will rise to about 38% in 1986 because of increases in weapons procurement during the 1980s.

The student is therefore advised to look hard and long at any numbers purporting to show military expenditures, remembering Disraeli's observation that there are three kinds of lies: lies, damned lies, and statistics!

## THE SIZE AND GROWTH OF THE MILITARY BUDGET

In constant 1980 dollars, the DoD budget has gone through numerous fluctuations. Definite peaks correlated with World War II, the Korean war, and the Vietnam war. President Reagan took office in 1981 with a strong

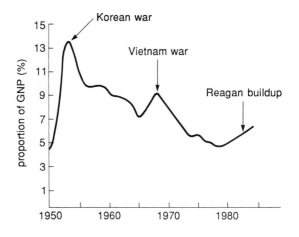

**FIGURE 12.3 US military spending as a share of the gross national product between 1950 and 1985.** (Congressional Budget Office.)

commitment to increasing the military budget (Fig. 12.4). He has done so, and the largest peak yet has been occurring in the 1980s (see Fig. 12.2).

It is estimated that during the period 1982–1989, the US military budget will be approximately $2.6 trillion, whereas in the preceding 35 years (including the Korean and Vietnam wars), it totaled $2.3 trillion. During fiscal year 1985, the military budget request was for $313 billion, equivalent to $860 million per day, $36 million per hour, and almost $10,000 per second. This is 18% more than the request for fiscal year 1984, and 72% more than in 1981. Since 1979, the *rate of increase* in US military spending, above inflation, has never been less than 2.6% and has averaged about 5%.

Although absolute amounts of military spending are approaching an all-time high, as a percentage of GNP directed to the military, the US buildup of the 1980s has been less dramatic. The spending ratio, m/GNP, has been larger than during the Vietnam war but smaller than during the Korean war (Fig. 12.3), and much smaller than during World War II. Higher manpower costs accounted for a large proportion of the increased military expenditures during the Korean and Vietnam wars. By contrast, the Reagan administration's buildup has occurred during peacetime and has especially involved increases in military contracting to private industry. For example, while the overall military budget doubled from 1980 to 1986, spending on procurement, research and development (R&D), and military construction almost tripled, from $52.7 billion in 1980 to $156.4 billion in

**FIGURE 12.4 President Ronald Reagan, with Vice President George Bush. President Reagan has presided over a substantial increase in US military spending during the 1980s.** (Courtesy of the US Department of Defense.)

1986. Because of the long lead times for such expenditures, the actual outlays will continue to rise more slowly than the obligated spending, which will come due in future years.

## THE NUCLEAR COMPONENT OF THE MILITARY BUDGET

No official figures are available on the percentage of the military budget attributable to nuclear weapons. Since the 1950s and the "New Look," however, it has been recognized that nuclear weapons provide more "bang for the buck." They constitute a relatively small proportion of the nation's military expenditures, estimated in the past at between 10 and 15%. Since 1980 or so, it seems likely that this figure has increased to 20–25%, as a result of increased emphasis on nuclear weaponry and on new nuclear weapons programs.

It is difficult to estimate the nuclear component to military expenditures partly because nuclear weapons are so closely integrated into military operations. Nuclear bombs, nuclear warheads, nuclear missiles, strategic bombers, and strategic submarines clearly fall into this category, but many other weapons such as F-15 or F-18 fighters are "dual capable," designed to employ both nuclear and conventionally armed munitions. Attack submarines carry nuclear-armed torpedoes; guided missile cruisers are heavily nuclearized, along with air-

craft carrier battle groups and revitalized, SLCM-carrying battleships; so are US Army units in Europe, supported by nuclear artillery as well as a variety of short-range missiles.

Most dramatic, and easily identified, are the so-called big-ticket items: strategic nuclear systems that are being developed and initially deployed during the 1980s. As we have seen, expenditures for many of these systems are being obligated during the mid-1980s, with the bills coming due toward the end of the 1980s and during the 1990s. Costs for these systems—the MX, Trident II, Pershing II, and Midgetman ballistic missiles, Trident submarines, cruise missiles, and Star Wars/SDI—have increased from $1.2 billion in 1980 to $20 billion in 1986. Table 12.2 shows basic data on some of these big-ticket items.

**Cost overruns,** which occur when the cost of an item turns out to be substantially more than originally projected, are frequent in military contracts. Cost overruns often are blamed on inflation, and indeed, while the US economy was suffering from 9–10% inflation during the late 1970s, inflation of military items was on the order of 15%. It is rare for "big-ticket" military items to be delivered at the price originally quoted. In some cases (for example, the C-5A transport plane), costs multiply several times.

While the overall military budget has been growing during the 1980s, increases for the nuclear component of this budget seem to have grown even more

**TABLE 12.2 "Big-ticket" nuclear items in the US military budget[a]**

| Weapon system | Number | First year operational | Money spent through 1983 ($ billions) | Money requested 1984 ($ billions) | Number requested 1984 | Money proposed 1985 ($ billions) | Unit cost ($ millions) | Estimated total cost ($ billions)[b] | Remarks |
|---|---|---|---|---|---|---|---|---|---|
| MX missile | 223? | 1986 | 6.7 | 6.2 | 27 | 5.3 | 123 | 27.4 | 100 deployed by 1989, balance test and spares |
| Trident submarine | 20–25 | 1982 | 13.0 | 1.8 | 1 | 2.0 | 1,600 | 31–39 | Cost for first 15 subs: $23.6 billion |
| Trident I missile | 595 | 1979 | 7.4 | 0.6 | 52 | 0.210 | 19 | 11.2 | For 12 backfitted subs and first 8 Trident subs with 211 test and spares |
| Trident II missile | 740 | 1969 | 0.682 | 1.5 | 0 (R&D) | 2.3 | 50 | 37.6 | For 15 subs; for 20–25 subs cost would be $45–$53 billion |
| B-1B bomber | 100 | 1986 | 11.5 | 6.9 | 10 | 8.5 | 400 | 40 | 90 operational aircraft to be deployed at four bases |
| Stealth bomber | 132 | Early 1990s | ? | 0.292 | 0 (R&D) | 1.05 | ? | 40–50 | Classified program; one estimate $6.3 billion for 1984–1988 |

| Program | Number | Operational[a] | | | | | | | Comments |
|---|---|---|---|---|---|---|---|---|---|
| B-52 bomber modifications | 263 | Ongoing | 2.5 | 0.720 | — | 0.752 | 20 per plane | 5.8 | Radar, engines, avionics, and other improvements |
| Air-launched cruise missile | 1,739 | 1982 | 3.5 | 0.493 | 240 | ? | 2.7 | 4.7 | Production canceled at 1,739 of original 4,348 |
| Ground-launched cruise missile | 565 | 1983 | 1.5 | 0.801 | 120 | 0.544 | 6.3 | 3.6 | 464 for Europe, 1983–1988 |
| Sea-launched cruise missile | 4,068 | 1984 | 2.1 | 0.528 | 124 | 0.768 | 2.8 | 11.5 | Total is for all versions; includes 74 for R&D, 758 for nuclear attack |
| Advanced cruise missile | 2,600 | 1987/88 | ? | ? | 0 (R&D) | ? | 5–7 | 7 | Classified program, figures are estimates |
| Pershing II missile | 380 | 1983 | 1.4 | 0.455 | 95 | 0.447 | 7.0 | 2.7 | 108 for West Germany, 1983–1985 |
| Command, control, communications, and intelligence | Many programs | Ongoing | ? | 7.5 | — | 9 | — | 40–50 | Hundreds of programs |
| Air defense | Many programs | Ongoing | ? | 0.482 | Various | 1 | — | 7.8 | Radar, F-15 aircraft, AWACS aircraft |
| Midgetman missile | 1,000? | 1992 | 0 | 0.604 | 0 (R&D) | 0.604 | 38–70 | 38–70 | 20-year costs could be $107 billion |

Source: Center for Defense Information, Washington, D.C.
[a] Budget data given for fiscal years; "operational" category gives calendar years.
[b] Does not include Department of Energy costs for nuclear weapons and bombs, which normally are an additional 10–20% of the weapon system cost.

dramatically. According to the Center for Defense Information (a private organization), it is reasonable to estimate that nuclear expenditures constitute 100% of the DoD budget's strategic forces category, 5% of general-purpose forces, 40% of intelligence and communications, 30% of research and development, and 10% of all other programs. Based on US government budget figures, the results are as follows:

| Year | Nuclear weapons spending |
|------|--------------------------|
| 1980 | $29.8 billion |
| 1984 | $58.1 billion |
| 1986 | $77.5 billion |

Nuclear weapons programs are also very R&D intensive; the R&D component of the strategic nuclear weapons budget grew 350% from 1980 to 1984.

Taking official DoD figures for strategic forces alone, the budget is substantially smaller; nonetheless, it increased from $15.3 billion in 1982 to $28.1 billion in 1984 (up 87%). The nuclear weapons budget of the Department of Energy (DoE), the agency charged with the design and actual production of nuclear explosives, has increased as follows:

| Year | Amount | Proportion of total DoE budget |
|------|--------|-------------------------------|
| 1979 | $2.3 billion | 23% |
| 1984 | $6.2 billion | 55% |

Figure 12.5 shows the history of nuclear energy military expenditures.

The actual costs of nuclear explosives themselves, as shown in the DoE budget, represent only a small proportion of the nation's total nuclear-related expenditures. During the initial decades of the Nuclear Age, from 1940 to 1985, the United States made the following expenditures directly related to nuclear weapons:

| Item | Cost (current dollars) | (1986 dollars) |
|------|------------------------|----------------|
| Bombs and warheads (including expenses of the Manhattan Project) | $82 billion | $209 billion |
| Nuclear delivery systems (including support costs and construction) | $650 billion | $1.7 trillion |

Note that delivery systems and their associated costs involved about eight times the money actually spent on nuclear explosives.

Finally, it is interesting to compare military budget priorities in the late 1950s, following the winding down of the Korean war and during the period of Cold War military expansion, with the mid-1970s, following the winding down of the Vietnam war and during the period of detente. The absolute expenditures were comparable: about $135 billion per year. Of this, personnel costs were comparable during the two decades. Weapons procurement costs were lower in the 1970s than in the 1950s, whereas operations and maintenance (O&M) and R&D costs were higher in the 1970s. During the 1980s, these trends have changed once again: military pay and operations and maintenance have received a steadily declining share of the military budget, while at the same time, procurement costs and R&D have increased steadily as a percentage of the military budget:

| | 1980 | 1985 |
|---|------|------|
| Military pay (O&M) | 54% | 44% |
| Procurement (R&D) | 35% | 45% |

This shows a change in federal military priorities, with increased emphasis on new weapons programs as opposed to readiness and reliability. From 1980 to 1986, the overall military budget doubled; at the same time, spending on procurement, R&D, and military construction tripled, from $52.7 billion in 1980 to a projected $156.4 billion in 1986.

Supporters of this increase emphasize that the procurement of new weapons and the large increase in R&D expenditures have been a crucial part of the Reagan administration's program to "rearm America," necessitated by a post-Watergate, post-Vietnam tendency to shortchange America's military forces. Critics claim that such expenditures represent a wasteful obsession with weapons that are unnecessary and dangerously provocative. In addition, it is often said that Pentagon procurement decisions favor weapons that are extremely expensive and complicated. Such "gold-plated" weapons confer prestige on their users and profit their producers; qualified observers, however, have questioned the practicality and effectiveness of some of these state-of-the-art systems. In terms of cost alone, the M-1 Abrams main battle tank (Fig. 12.6) and the B-1B bomber offer striking examples. The Congressional Budget Office has predicted that the complete fleet of 100 B-1Bs will cost $40 billion, not counting additional related expenses: about $5 million per year for maintenance and training.

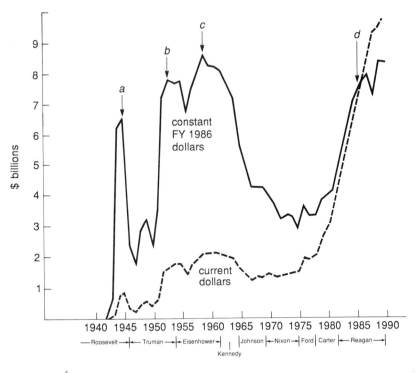

**FIGURE 12.5 US expenditures devoted specifically to military applications of nuclear energy. Note increases associated with (***a***) the Manhattan Project, (***b***) hydrogen bombs and tactical nuclear forces in Europe, (***c***) the bomber and ICBM buildup of the late Eisenhower and Kennedy years, and (***d***) the Reagan buildup.** (Modified from Adams and Weiss, 1985.)

**FIGURE 12.6 The M-1 Abrams main battle tank. During 10 years, the single-unit procurement cost of this weapon increased from $500,000 to $2.8 million.** (Courtesy of the US Department of Defense.)

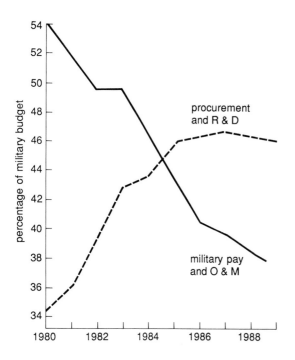

**FIGURE 12.7 Percentages of the military budget directed to procurement and research and development and to military pay and operations and maintenance, respectively, during the 1980s.** (From "The Defense Monitor," Center for Defense Information.)

Cuts in the O&M sector of the military budget have long been a favored way to satisfy demands for "less military spending." This is partly because such activities are less glamorous than major new weapons. In addition, cuts in O&M have a direct effect in reducing outlays, whereas because of the wedge effect already described, only a proportion of cuts in procurement reduce the military budget during a given year, since such costs are typically spread over a number of years. In dollars expended, the O&M portion of the military budget almost doubled from 1980 to 1986; however, as a percentage of the DoD budget, O&M actually declined, from 33% in 1980 to 26% in 1986. Critics of this pattern note that O&M correlates with the actual readiness of military forces and suggest that although decreases in O&M are relatively easy to achieve, both politically and budgetarily, such cuts may be more likely to degrade national military strength than would failure

to purchase a new and expensive weapons system (Fig. 12.7).

Another favored technique for reducing the military budget is to stretch out the actual delivery of contracted weapons, accepting the total number in relatively small annual quantities rather than all at once. This reduces the annual cost but increases the unit cost (the cost per item) because of production inefficiencies; it therefore increases the total cost once delivery has been completed.

## COMPARING THE MILITARY BUDGETS OF THE UNITED STATES AND THE SOVIET UNION

The United States makes an enormous amount of military budget information public (witness all the data in the preceding section). Nonetheless, as we have seen, there are many difficulties and ambiguities in assessing the country's military budget. Not surprisingly, it is virtually impossible to make meaningful comparisons with the Soviet Union, which merely announces a single, undefined figure for its military budget: approximately 17 billion rubles annually. This amount is so unrealistic that it is not generally taken seriously. Several US intelligence agencies, notably the CIA, are therefore charged with estimating Soviet military expenditures. Governmental authorities usually consult the CIA's Annual Intelligence Estimate of Soviet military spending for purposes of US–Soviet comparison. These figures are obtained by counting up all military goods and services believed to have been purchased by the Soviet government during a given year and calculating equivalent costs to the US government, if comparable goods and services were to be purchased with US dollars, in the US economy. The result, however, may be somewhat misleading, tending to exaggerate Soviet expenditures.

For example, to calculate the Soviet military budget for ICBM production, information on each Soviet missile or each new modification is given to US contractors, which estimate the costs if they were to build a comparable item. There is reason to think that US military contracting costs are exceptionally high, which would result in an inflated US view of what the USSR is spending. And in any event, such figures may have little bearing on what the items actually cost the Soviet government. The Soviet Army, for example, is composed largely of conscripts, who are paid the ruble equivalent of less than $100 per year. However, when calculated on the US pay scale—which averages about $14,000 per capita—the cost of Soviet military salaries alone is estimated at about $50,000 billion. Whenever the US gives its soldiers a raise, our estimate of the Soviet budget is automatically increased. National economies tend to emphasize the resource dimension that they have to greatest advantage: in the US, where salaries are high and technology quite advanced, most military activities are machinery intensive, using relatively little manpower. In the USSR, where salaries are low and technology is relatively backward, large numbers of soldiers are employed.

An alternative to the official US government technique for estimating Soviet military expenditures is to convert the USSR's estimated ruble expenditures directly into dollars. This yields figures for Soviet military spending that are considerably lower, and comparable to those for the US military budget. (On the other hand, it may be inappropriate to grant the USSR 140 soldiers at the cost of one soldier for the United States.)

In any event, in 1983, the CIA revised its estimates of the rate of growth in Soviet military expenditures, judging that during the period 1976–1981 such spending increased at a steady rate of 2% per year, which is less than half the rate of increase that had been estimated previously.

Much attention is typically given to comparisons of US and Soviet military spending, although it would seem more appropriate to consider what each side gets for its money, rather than how much is spent. This is especially true given the uncertainties and misleading aspects of such financial comparisons. On the other hand, the willingness of a nation to spend money on its military may also be seen as a convenient benchmark for its society's military efforts, and an index of the willingness of its public officials, and its taxpayers, to meet such a burden. Hawks see a large Soviet military budget as evidence of aggressive intent; doves see it as evidence of defensive, even paranoid anxiety. Hawks point out that given the inefficient Soviet economy, the USSR may be unable to keep up with America's pace in armaments. Doves point out that given the authoritarian nature of Soviet society, the USSR is willing and able to devote whatever resources are necessary to avoid falling behind militarily. It is generally acknowledged that the USSR spends a larger proportion of its GNP on the military than does the United States; however, this does not necessarily indicate a greater absolute military effort, since the Soviet GNP is only about half that of the US, and in fact the military investments of the two nations are about comparable.

## MILITARY KEYNESIANISM

### Theory

The famous British economist John Maynard Keynes was a renowned advocate of using national expenditures, largely in the civilian sector, to stimulate a lagging economy. There are many, however, who claim that military spending by the federal government can benefit the economy as a whole, and contemporary economist John Kenneth Galbraith has termed this position **military Keynesianism.** One of the fundamental assumptions of military Keynesianism is that economic stagnation is often caused by insufficient "aggregate demand" in the economy. That is, when domestic buyers do not make sufficient requests for new goods and services, the available resources of a national economy are not mobilized as fully as they could be. According to the supporters of military Keynesianism, aggregate demand can be created by having the federal government purchase military goods and services from private contractors. When the capacity of an economy is being underutilized, military expenditures can stimulate it in a helpful manner.

Supporters of military Keynesianism argue that military spending is more likely to be an economic stimulant than a drag, and that the US economy does not have to sacrifice butter (i.e., domestic priorities) for guns (military priorities). Furthermore, it is claimed that when guns are being produced, the extra boost this provides to the economy makes it easier for everyone to buy butter.

In addition, given the classic Keynesian assumption that balanced budgets are not terribly important, federal expenditures can be used to produce artificial demand that will compensate for the cycles of stagnation that periodically plague market economies. Military spending yields profits for contractors and subcontractors, and also jobs with these firms (as well as direct employment with the various military-related agencies of the federal government). Finally, it is assumed that military–industrial production, stimulated by government demand and especially through subsidies to high-technology research and development, as well as production, further contributes to innovation and thus, to future economic growth.

To some extent, such stimulation could be accomplished by any federal expenditure. Military spending, however, lends itself especially to direct stimulation of the economy, for the following reasons:

1. Because military spending does not meet a clear-cut domestic need, it can be increased, decreased, or reshuffled among different sectors, as desired. We could eventually have too many schools or hospitals, but according to certain aspects of military and strategic theory, never too many missiles or bombers.

2. The domestic political consensus generally favors military expenditures for reasons of national security. As a result, such spending is usually approved by Congress.

3. Unlike domestic spending, military spending does not compete with the private sector. If the government was to provide national medical care, for example, many physicians and other health care workers would feel undercut, and would object. But when the federal government purchases missiles and warheads, private enterprise is benefitted.

4. Military spending acts directly to stimulate the economy. By contrast, other ways of stimulating the economy, such as cutting taxes or increasing transfer payments, act more slowly, especially when it comes to generating employment.

5. Military spending is especially appropriate for stimulating the "capital goods" sector of the economy, which tends to be especially stagnation prone. This is because a relatively high proportion of military expenditure involves construction as well as the purchase of industrial items, in comparison with government social programs or increases in personal, disposable income; which take longer to work their way through the economy.

The USSR, by contrast, is an economy of scarcity: when steel is used to manufacture Soviet tanks, waiting lines for automobiles become longer in Moscow. The Soviet Union does not suffer from insufficient demand, but rather from insufficient supply to consumers; hence, military spending is more likely to be economically costly for the USSR. And since unemployment is not an issue for the Soviet economy, military spending is not looked on as a beneficial source of jobs. As we have seen, the Soviet Union has many reasons for its military spending, but Keynesian thinking does not appear to be influential.

## History

World War II had a beneficial economic effect on the United States, enabling it to recover finally from the Great Depression of the 1930s. GNP rose rapidly during the war, as did personal consumption. Civilian employment also rose from 46 million in 1939 to 53 million in 1945, while the military employed an additonal 11 million persons. Nonetheless, even after World War II, the conventional economic and political orthodoxy did not support military Keynesianism. There was strong emphasis on the value of a balanced federal budget, and on the following liabilities of heavy government involvement in the economy: the distasteful necessity of choosing between inflation and higher taxes, the diversion of labor and materials from other purposes, the need for odious semisocialist government controls on the civilian economy, as well as the so-called opportunity costs of military spending. (As discussed further in the section entitled "Unmet Domestic Needs," when a nation's economic capacity is fully utilized, expenditures on the military necessarily carry with them an opportunity cost in that domestic expenditures must be foregone.)

Insulated by oceans east and west, and friendly neighbors to the north and south, the United States has historically relied on the maintenance of relatively small peacetime armed forces and a primarily civilian economy. Both the armed forces and the economy could be mobilized quickly and effectively in emergencies. When nuclear weapons appeared at the end of World War II, and especially when the Soviet Union acquired them, this tradition changed and the United States began to rely increasingly on large forces-in-being, that is, a permanent, ongoing military economy. Because of their potency and short response times, nuclear weapons have the peculiar effect of requiring that a nation be on a continuing emergency and alert status. It is not feasible for a nuclear superpower to rely on a powerful military–industrial effort to be mounted only after a declaration of war.

This transition to a chronic semiwartime economy in the United States was enunciated in political and military terms by NSC 68, before the Korean war. The authors of this document called for a program of vigorous military spending. They also addressed the likely economic consequences of a more militarized economy, noting, for example, that:

> From the point of view of the economy as a whole, the program might not result in a real decrease in the standard of living, for the eco-

*nomic effects of the program might be to increase the gross national product by more than the amount being absorbed for additional military and foreign assistance purposes.*

It was argued that the US can have both enhanced military security and economic gains if (1) there is sufficient unused capacity in the economy, (2) military spending stimulates additional growth in that economy, and (3) higher levels of military spending produce sufficient growth to offset the costs of such spending.

As US participation in the conflict in Korea mounted in the early 1950s, rearmament proceeded rapidly, although conservatives worried that the economic costs of the buildup would bankrupt the nation and serve Stalin's purposes. (Thirty years later, things have changed considerably: although conservatives want to reduce government spending on the domestic front, they generally favor enhanced military outlays, whereas liberals, who generally supported large military budgets in the early 1950s, tend to oppose them in the 1980s.) The Truman administration still practiced fiscal (non-Keynesian) orthodoxy, even with the Korean buildup, which was financed virtually on a pay-as-you-go basis. Tax increases produced a $6 billion budget *surplus* in 1951, and in 1952 a deficit of only $1.5 billion.

Still in the early 1950s, the Bureau of the Budget, disagreeing with the rosy predictions of military Keynesianism, had concluded:

*The implications of higher military expenditures are of course mainly a matter of degree. It cannot be said that at any point such expenditures are "too high." They must be sufficient to meet minimum requirements for the security of the nation. But security rests in economic as well as military strength, and due consideration should be given to the tendency for military expenditures to reduce the potential rate of economic growth, and at an advanced stage to require measures which may seriously impair the functioning of our system.*

President Eisenhower generally shared these sentiments, striving to keep military expenditures as low as possible. In fact, the growing reliance of US strategy on nuclear weapons that began in the 1950s fit in with this rejection of military Keynesianism, since nuclear weapons tend to be less expensive than their conventional counterparts. It was not until the Kennedy administration that military Keynesianism was widely and publicly embraced as government policy.

Federal expenditures increased sharply in the early 1960s, partly as a result of the missile, strategic submarine, and space programs, and later because of the Vietnam war. Even then, Eisenhower spoke for the previous economic orthodoxy during the early Kennedy years, when he observed:

*There is no way in which a country can satisfy the craving for absolute security—but it can easily bankrupt itself, morally and economically, in attempting to reach that illusory goal through arms alone. The military establishment, not productive in itself, necessarily must feed on the energy, productivity and brainpower of the country, and if it takes too much, our total strength declines.*

But a sea-change in the structuring of the national economy had nonetheless occurred. Military Keynesianism had arrived as a fact of life, in the federal budget as well as in the national economy.

It is reemphasized, however, that even in the minds of most supporters, large military expenditures were justified primarily because of their supposed contribution to national security rather than to a strong economy. Thus, military spending can be seen as a public good, one whose benefits are "externalized"—that is, consumption by one person does not detract from consumption by another. Supporters of military spending argue that unlike the provisioning of individual, private goods such as medical care or school lunches whose benefits are "internalized," military spending provides a wider societal benefit (national security) that is not immediately obvious and is really apparent only if it is gone . . . at which point it is too late to worry that not enough of this particular public good had been provided!

In any event, military spending almost certainly has effects on a nation's economy, even if the detonators never go off. Many different sorts of positive and negative effects have been identified. In the next few sections we shall examine some of them.

## THE EFFECTS OF MILITARY SPENDING

### Employment

There is no doubt that military spending creates jobs. First, there are the members of the uniformed armed services as well as the civilian employees of the Department of Defense and other, military-related agencies (DoE, NASA, etc.). All such employees receive paychecks directly from the federal government as a result of military expenditures. In addition, others are "indirectly employed"; that is, their jobs are in the private sector, but they work for military contractors or subcontractors. When federal contracts are let out, they go to various industrial firms, consulting groups, and so on, which in turn use a portion of the money they receive to hire workers and produce the final product—whether a missile, a warhead, or a report. Beyond this, estimates of jobs created by military spending typically include a **multiplier effect,** by which additional jobs are created as the stimulus from introduced capital and labor income filters through the economy. Multiplier effect estimates for military spending range from 1.5 to 2.0; at 2.0, for example, it is assumed that for every job created either directly or indirectly by military spending, one additional job is ultimately generated somewhere in the economy.

For 1983, military-related employment in the United States can be estimated as follows:

| | |
|---|---|
| Uniformed armed services | 2.2 million |
| Defense-related civilian employment | 1.3 million |
| Private industry employment | 2.9 million |
| Total government and private | 6.4 million |
| Multiplier effect of employment (1.5–2.0) | 3.2–6.4 million |
| Total military-related employment | 9.6–12.8 million |

Members of Congress typically compete to attract federal funding to their constituencies, and military expenditures are especially coveted. Corporate lobbyists as well as Pentagon officials also publicize the job-related benefits of such expenditures, thereby increasing national appreciation of these endeavors. For examples, it is said that one reason for the broad bipartisan support enjoyed by the B-1B bomber is that some component of this airplane is being made in every state in the union; the prime contractor, Rockwell International, circulated material pointing out the state-by-state benefits that would result.

On the other hand, critics point out that although military spending undeniably produces some jobs, it is likely to be a very inefficient way of generating employment. For one thing, military products tend to be "capital intensive," requiring that relatively large amounts of money be spent for expensive processes, elaborate technology, and a relatively small number of highly skilled and hence, highly paid workers (Fig. 12.8). By contrast, other forms of government expenditure are likely to be more "labor intensive," which means that more people are hired per dollar spent. The result is that military spending makes jobs at the cost of a net loss in employment, since additional jobs would have been created if the federal government had spent the same amount of money in the civilian sector instead.

Military expenditures are highly concentrated in a relatively small number of very large private firms, many of which are largely or even wholly dependent on military contracts. For example, the 25 top military contractors accounted for nearly 43% of the value of all military contracts. The industries affected are strongly biased toward electronics, aircraft, aerospace, shipbuilding, and scientific instruments.

Elaborate methodology is needed to obtain exact estimates of the actual number of jobs produced by military spending, and even here, the results are subject to debate. Figures on how many alternative jobs would be created if an equivalent amount of federal money were devoted to civilian expenditures are therefore even more uncertain. However, estimates are available, suggesting for example that for every billion dollars spent in the overall military budget, approximately 45,000 jobs are created. According to the Coalition for a New Foreign and Military Policy (a private, nongovernmental organization), if that billion dollars were spent instead on energy and conservation programs, it would produce 65,000 jobs; on mass transit, 79,000 jobs; and on day care, 120,000 jobs.

Analyses of specific weapons programs have yielded similar results. For example, according to a 1982 study by the Council on Economic Priorities, 58,591 jobs could be created for every billion dollars spent on the B-1B bomber. Even more jobs would result if that money were spent in other ways:

| Programs | Jobs created per $1 billion |
|---|---|
| B-1 bomber | 58,591 |
| Army Corps of Engineers | 69,384 |
| Law enforcement | 74,601 |
| Sanitation | 78,954 |
| Mass transit | 83,536 |
| Public housing | 84,524 |
| Highway construction | 84,933 |
| Conservation and recreation | 88,415 |
| Welfare payments | 99,406 |
| Social Security | 108,196 |
| Education | 118,191 |

Similar studies have been conducted for the MX missile, with similar results.

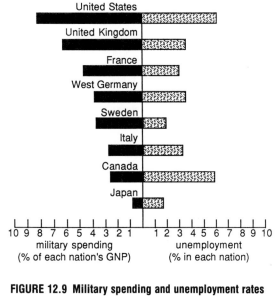

**FIGURE 12.8 Assembly of Pershing II missile components.** (Courtesy of Martin Marietta Corporation.)

**FIGURE 12.9 Military spending and unemployment rates in eight industrialized nations.** (Modified from DeGrasse, 1982.)

In addition to questions about the number of jobs created by alternative forms of government spending, there are issues relating to the location of these jobs and the nature of the jobs supported. Thus, military spending tends to be concentrated in the South Atlantic states (from Delaware to Florida) and in the West and Southwest, whereas "Frost Belt" states tend to receive less than their share of military-related employment. Such employment also tends to favor highly skilled professionals, notably machinists, scientists, and engineers. Research and development costs, for example, make up about 35% of military procurement outlays; by contrast, R&D constitutes only about 2% of the costs incurred in civilian production. Such R&D-intensive expenditures tend to favor the highly skilled over the unskilled worker: nearly 50% of the work force in the aerospace industry are scientists and engineers. In the guided missile industry, for example, only 28% of employees are production workers, as compared to 90% for US industry as a whole. Thus, military spending—especially the procurement of new weapons systems—tends especially to benefit people who are qualified for white collar jobs, at the expense of blue collar workers.

Finally, any consideration of the employment effects of military spending must also recognize that alternative scenarios for military spending are truly hypothetical; it is not at all clear, for example, that money not spent on purchasing submarines would be spent on hospitals instead. It might go toward reducing the federal deficit, or to support a reduction in taxes. Either of these would presumably also have positive employment effects, but their exact nature is very difficult to predict. In the meantime, advocates of reduced military spending are faced with the need to balance the loss of real jobs against the *possibility* of creating more jobs in an alternative system of national priorities. A comparison of eight industrialized nations reveals no clear correlation between military spending and unemployment (Fig. 12.9).

## Unmet Domestic Needs

A dollar spent on the military cannot be used to meet domestic needs. Of course, it is equally true that money spent in any way cannot be used for something else: money spent on hospitals is not available for education, and so on. But given the lack of obvious domestic utility for military spending, as well as the immense quantity of resources involved, it seems appropriate to consider the alternative uses to which military expenditures might be put.

In economics, **opportunity costs** refer to profits foregone by virtue of decisions to invest in one way rather than another. Since the resources of any nation are finite, the use of such resources in any one direction precludes their use in another. These opportunity costs are especially apparent with regard to the allocation of federal money, particularly when—as during the 1980s—the government has been seeking to increase military spending while reducing overall expenditures. The result must be a reduction in domestic expenditures, although it should be noted carefully whether these reductions are: (1) in absolute dollars, (2) after inflation, (3) relative to increases in the military sector, (4) compared to previous proportions of domestic spending to GNP, (5) compared to previous proportions of domestic spending to the total federal budget (whether complete or "controllable"), and (6) relative to domestic need, however defined.

Table 12.3 shows budget shifts in 16 areas of expenditure from 1981 to 1985.

Overall, while military expenditures (including a proportion of DoE, NASA, etc.) increased from 5.8 to 7.4% of GNP from 1980 to 1984, domestic expenditures declined from 15% of GNP to 14%. The tradeoff has been more dramatic in terms of direct resource allocation: by 1987, approximately 10% of the budget since 1980 will have been shifted from domestic to military programs. If nondiscretionary federal expenditures are removed from this estimate, the shift exceeds 20%. In 1983, for example, the federal government reduced the following programs: Medicaid; child nutrition; food programs for women, infants, and children; legal services; supplemental security income; elementary and secondary education; guaranteed student loans; energy and conservation; community development grants; mass transit; food stamps, and aid to families with dependent children—at a total savings of $6 billion. During the same year, military spending increased by $33 billion.

If the economy were expanding greatly, or if the federal government elected to offset military expenditures by levying additional taxes, it might be possible to meet both military and domestic expenditures. Otherwise, and especially in recent years, large increases in one sector occur at the expense of expenditures in others. Economist Émil Benoit, for example,

found that for every 1% of a nation's GNP expended on the military, there was a 0.25% decrease in the overall GNP. And political scientist Bruce Russett has determined that every military dollar expended by the United States between 1939 and 1968 decreased personal consumption by 42¢ and reduced fixed civilian investment (a much smaller fraction of the economy) by as much as 29¢.

There is no simple tradeoff between military and civilian government spending, however. The **substitution effect** refers to the observed fact that funds spent in one sector tend to be deleted from the other (e.g., guns *or* butter, rarely both). This link between military and domestic spending, however, is not so much an economic law as a political decision; hence, a reduction in military spending in no way guarantees increases in domestic spending. When Russett analyzed the pattern of US government spending during the period 1941–1971, he found a negative association—but only a weak one—between military and domestic spending by the federal government. The clear tradeoff between these two that seems to be characteristic of the 1980s therefore appears to be a recent phenomenon, but one that may become familiar as we approach the twenty-first century. In times of domestic economic belt-tightening, especially when legislators hesitate to raise taxes, there can be substantial competition for budgetary priority between guns and butter. The degree of confrontation between Congress and the administration over the size of the military budget during the 1980s has also been relatively new to the American experience—previously, military budgets have been rather easily agreed upon, based on bipartisan consensus. Such items as the MX missile or the B-1B bomber, as well as nonnuclear items of proposed military procurement, have generated vigorous and critical debate of a sort that had been quite rare. This almost certainly reflects not only some doubts about the wisdom of the Reagan administration's military buildup, but also a growing sensitivity to the domestic opportunity costs of military spending.

As already mentioned, the Soviet Union's economy tends to be one of insufficient supply rather than insufficient demand. As a result, whatever the possible benefits of military spending in the US, such effects are more likely to be felt as liabilities in the USSR, since the Soviet Union does not need to create demand, but rather, to satisfy existing demand, which is often unmet. It appears, in fact, that Soviet citizens have paid dearly for their nation's military programs: during the period 1972–1982, for example, the life expectancy of men

**TABLE 12.3  Recent shifts in federal expenditures in selected military and nonmilitary areas**

| Area of expenditure | Shift ($ billions) | | Change (%) |
| --- | --- | --- | --- |
| | 1981 | 1985 | |
| Military | 159.7 | 272.0 | +70 |
| Veterans' medical care | 6.9 | 9.6 | +38 |
| Consumer occupational health and safety | 1.0 | 1.2 | +12 |
| Transportation | 17.1 | 18.6 | +9 |
| Higher education | 6.8 | 7.2 | +6 |
| Nutrition | 16.2 | 17.0 | +5 |
| Elementary, secondary, and vocational education | 7.1 | 7.1 | 0 |
| Community development | 5.0 | 4.8 | −5 |
| Recreation | 1.6 | 1.5 | −6 |
| Revenue sharing | 5.1 | 4.5 | −11 |
| Pollution control | 5.2 | 4.2 | −19 |
| Veterans' education and rehabilitation | 2.3 | 1.3 | −41 |
| Energy conservation | 0.7 | 0.4 | −44 |
| Job training and employment | 9.2 | 4.9 | −47 |
| Energy supply | 5.2 | 1.6 | −70 |
| Conservation/land management | 1.2 | 0.3 | −73 |

Source: Congressional Budget Office and Center for Defense Information.

in the USSR has declined from 66 years to 62, and infant mortality has increased from 23 per 1,000 live births to more than 40.

Finally, it must be noted that while the nations of the world continue to spend vast and increasing quantities of money on armaments, enormous social needs are met poorly and sometimes not at all, especially in nations not currently possessing nuclear weapons. On average, the world spends about $450 to educate each of its children, and about $25,600 to support each of its soldiers. Approximately 500 million people suffer from malnutrition, 2 billion people do not have safe drinking water, and the World Health Organization estimates that someone dies every 2 seconds from a disease that could be prevented if a fraction of the money and effort now spent on armaments were instead directed toward enhancing the quality of life on earth. According to the Brandt Commission of 1980, 0.5% of the world's military expenditures would pay for the farm equipment needed to make the nations that are currently unable to feed themselves self-sufficient in food

by 1990. One of the greatest challenges of politics and diplomacy is therefore to redirect the world's economic resources, so much of which are now devoted to military activities, toward humanitarian purposes (Fig. 12.10).

## Productivity and Growth

Just as critics point out that there must be a substitution effect, a tradeoff between military and domestic spending, it is also argued that military spending occurs at the cost of long-term investment in the domestic economy; if so, there may be a relation between military budgets and overall economic vitality as well as growth.

Economist Seymour Melman, a persistent critic of military spending, has suggested that rather than examining military expenditures as a percentage of GNP, it would be more meaningful to take the ratio of military spending to **total fixed capital formation**—that is, the financial resources invested annually in new and

**FIGURE 12.10 A refugee mother and her severely undernourished child in an emergency famine camp in Jijiga, Ethiopia.** (United Nations photo by O. Monsen.)

potentially productive ways. This emphasizes the opportunity costs of military expenditures in terms of possible, alternative uses in the national economy. Melman points out, for example, that in 1977, when the military budget of the United States constituted 4.9% of the GNP, it represented 46% of fixed capital formation that year; by contrast, corresponding figures for West Germany and Japan were 18 and 3.7%, respectively. This highlights an important criticism of military spending, the inverse correlation between a nation's military spending and its economic growth: the nations that have invested heavily in the military have grown the least economically in recent years, whereas low military expenditure correlates with high economic growth (Fig. 12.11).

There are several reasons for this correlation, the first being the straightforward substitution effect or opportunity cost, of military expenditures, which we have already considered. In short, the low level of capital investment by the US and Britain in particular can be attributable to these nations' high levels of military spending: funds spent in one way are not available to be expended in another. Supply bottlenecks also tend to develop, with regard to raw materials as well as research and labor talent. Materials, effort, and talent devoted to military innovation and production are not available for innovation and production of domestic goods. During 1962, for example, the United States accounted for 22.6% of the international automobile market; in 1979, this figure had declined to 13.9%. Much of this is due to increased competitiveness from Japan, which, compared to the US, has invested much less in the military and much more in modernization of its domestic industrial plant.

Military expenditures can be financed either by borrowing from the public (i.e., by creating budget deficits) or by raising taxes. In the first case, growth is inhibited because increased demand for money drives up interest rates, increasing the cost of capital to would-be borrowers outside the federal government. In the second, money is withdrawn directly from would-be personal and corporate investors.

As presented in Russett's book *What Price Vigilance?,* during the period 1938–1969, increases in military spending (as a percentage of GNP) were correlated with drops in personal consumption, in investment in housing, and in purchases of productive equipment. Every billion dollars of military spending caused, on average, a decline of $293 million in fixed investment and a decline of $110 million in investments in durable equipment. Critics accordingly point to the decline in traditional American preeminence in steel, automobiles, and electronics as a result of the competitive benefits being reaped by Japan and West Germany, in particular, since their military spending is less and their domestic productivity correspondingly greater. Products that are successful in the civilian marketplace tend to be standardized, efficiently produced, and relatively inexpensive. By contrast, military products tend to be highly specialized. Although cost is not irrelevant, it is not a major consideration, especially since military contracting practices tend to guarantee a certain profit to industries, beyond any overhead costs.

On the other hand, although US military spending has been increasing in absolute terms since the early 1950s, it has generally declined as a percentage of GNP. And since the early 1970s, the rate of growth of the economies of most industrial nations has tended to decline, at the same time as military expenditures (as a percentage of GNP), have also declined. It is therefore at least possible that the relatively slow rates of economic growth since the early 1970s are due to factors other than military spending. Supporters of military spending point out that during World War II, the US devoted up to 30% of its GNP to the military, and not surprisingly, domestic investment declined during this period. However, during the Korean war, the ratio of military spending to GNP was down to 13%, and during the Vietnam war, 9%. During neither of these periods was there a clearly negative effect of such spending on domestic investment. In addition, if military spending helps contribute to an increase in overall GNP, it would be wrong to attribute the decline of investment as a percentage of GNP to military spending alone.

Military spending in the Nuclear Age involves a disproportionate emphasis on R&D. For example, during 1975, R&D constituted 43% of the costs of military production, as compared with only 2.3% for total manufacturing output. This means that military products are nearly 20 times more R&D intensive than civilian products. One-third of all R&D funds expended by the US as a whole go for military purposes; and of R&D funds spent by the federal government, the military accounts for about 70%. During the 1980s, the proportion of federal R&D funds directed to military rather than civilian programs has more than doubled (Fig. 12.12). Military R&D tends to be highly specialized, producing items of little or no value in the domestic economy. In addition, during 1984 for example, 88% of military R&D went to "D" (i.e., development) and only 12% to research; compared with research, development is even less likely to benefit the economy as a whole, since it involves fine-tuning "dedicated" military hardware. Military R&D also emphasizes high-level performance characteristics; by contrast, successful domestic products tend to be more forgiving of performance (e.g., it is not necessary for a stereo set to function at 50 degrees below zero) and to be more cost sensitive. Whereas the US used to be the world leader in percentage of nonmilitary R&D expended as a function of GNP, supremacy has been taken by other nations, notably Japan and West Germany (Fig. 12.13). During the period 1971–1981, the number of US patents granted to US citizens fell 40%. Whereas in 1966, 21% of all US patents went to foreign nationals, in 1982 this figure had grown to 42%. Perhaps not coincidentally, in 1982 the National Science Foundation found that approximately 42% of the US scientific work force had been employed in the military-related economy. (A comparable, or even

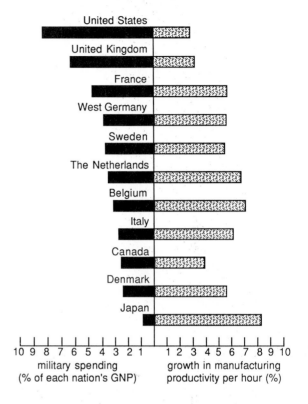

**FIGURE 12.11  Military spending in 11 industrialized nations, and economic productivity in the same nations. Percentages are averages for 1960–1979.** (Modified from DeGrasse, 1982.)

higher proportion, is likely to be similarly employed in the USSR.)

Supporters of military spending point to the various civilian spin-offs available from military R&D: satellites, nuclear reactors, radar, microwave ovens, early advances in computers, jet technology, medical CAT scans, flame-retardant clothing, and artificial intelligence. Such advances are undeniable. In other areas, such as lasers, there are numerous civilian implications—notably in industry and medicine—although the innovations of particular military interest, such as long-range propagation of high-intensity beams (as for Star Wars/SDI) are much less likely to have domestic relevance. It is undeniable that if the R&D effort expended on military products were instead directed toward the achievement of civilian breakthroughs, the domestic "spin-offs" would be much greater yet. But, as with the debate over the effects on military spending on

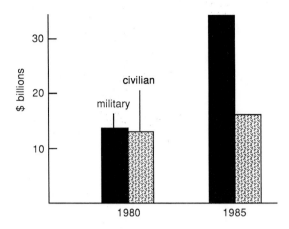

**FIGURE 12.12 Federal expenditures for military (solid bars) versus civilian (shaded bars) R&D, comparing 1980 with 1985 (in constant 1985 dollars). Although the amount of federal funds expended on civilian R&D remained about the same, the amount spent on military R&D more than doubled.** (Modified from "The Defense Monitor," Center for Defense Information.)

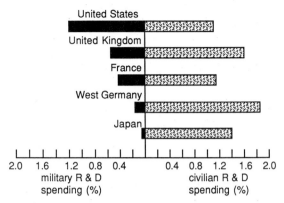

**FIGURE 12.13 Correlations of military R&D/GNP and civilian R&D/GNP, for five industrialized nations (average percentages for 1960–1976). Note that the US, with relatively high military R&D expenditures, expends proportionately less on civilian R&D, whereas the UK, France, West Germany, and Japan, with relatively low military R&D expenditures, expend proportionately more on civilian R&D.** (Modified from DeGrasse, 1982.)

employment, it cannot be known precisely how funds released from military use might otherwise be spent.

It is noteworthy that approximately 33% of US military R&D goes toward electronics (an additional 55% goes for aerospace); however, less than 3% of US national income derives directly from electronics. At the same time, it is ironically true that even in electronics and aerospace—areas stimulated by military expenditures—the US has become less competitive, not more, on the international market. This may have occurred partly because military secrecy impedes domestic application. In addition, whereas military R&D emphasizes "product technology" (the innovation itself), nations with more civilian industrial focus emphasize the design and modification of items specifically for civilian consumption. Their R&D efforts emphasize the "process technology" necessary for making the product cheaply and in large quantities.

On balance, it is impossible to come up with precise, quantitative statements about the impact of military expenditures on economic growth and productivity, although the direction of the relationship seems clear: especially when one compares the US with other nations, military spending is on balance more likely to injure a nation's economic strength than to enhance it (Fig. 12.14).

However, substantial economic growth and productivity are not necessarily incompatible with a high level of military expenditure. Supporters of military spending also point out that the mere existence of competition between military spending and domestic investment does not necessarily prove that the former is excessive, since it must be evaluated in another arena, that of national security. Moreover, not all nonmilitary spending is likely to stimulate growth, just as not all military spending necesarily will limit growth. Finally, there is nothing as potentially disruptive and harmful to a nation's economy as a destructive war on its own soil. The ultimate justification for military expenditures, especially in the Nuclear Age, is the hope that they will help prevent war.

## Federal Deficits

The Truman administration financed the military spending of the Korean war almost entirely by increased taxes. The president's economic report of 1951 noted that "the real economic cost of this defense effort is that we must work harder, reduce consumption, and forego improvements in farm, business, and household equipment." By contrast, the Johnson administration

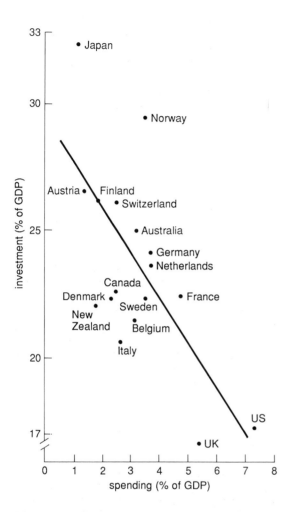

**FIGURE 12.14 Correlation between military spending and domestic investment as percentages of gross domestic product for 17 industrialized nations (data averaged for 1960–1980). Comparable data for Warsaw Pact nations are not available.** (Modified from Joseph, 1984.)

to finance its activities in Vietnam by raising taxes produced the inflationary spiral that continued through the 1970s.

As long ago as 1820, the British economist David Ricardo had advised a different policy, one that is closer to US policy during the Korean war. Believing that political leaders should be restrained from their tendency to engage in unnecessary wars, Ricardo urged that wars be financed in a manner that makes their economic costs immediately apparent: "When the pressure of the war is felt at once, without mitigation, we shall be less disposed wantonly to engage in an expensive contest, and if engaged in it, we shall be sooner disposed to get out of it unless it was a contest of some great national interest." The converse of Ricardo's advice might also hold: in the absence of a shooting war, the public is especially unwilling to shoulder the economic burden of military preparedness. Such unwillingness can be finessed, however, by making the burden less clear.

It is uncertain whether the American public during the 1980s would have been willing to support the added tax burden of the Reagan administration's military buildup in the absence of an accompanying hot war. But that option was not presented, since the Reagan administration followed Ricardo's converse and chose not only to increase military spending but also to *reduce* taxes, in the expectation that this would stimulate the economy sufficiently to permit such expenditures. Moreover, government spending in the civilian sector was to be cut back or at least severly limited, thereby effecting additional savings. In fact, the economy did recover from a severe recession suffered during 1981–1983. Any government surplus accumulated by the improving economy, however, was eliminated by the tax reductions and the large military expenditures of the early 1980s. Being greater than the initial cuts in domestic spending, the tax reductions led to a net deficit in themselves; increased military spending was essentially financed via this deficit.

The federal deficit, as a percentage of GNP, exceeded 5% in 1982, for the first time ever. The combined federal deficit, for the decades of 1950 and 1960, was about $75 billion. In 1983 alone, the operating deficit was $208 billion, which also exceeds the total 5-year World War II deficit of $175 billion. As of 1985, the total accumulated US federal debt has exceeded $2 trillion. At such levels, interest on the federal deficit alone ($53 billion in 1980, $97 billion in 1983) will soon constitute one of the largest components of the federal budget.

elected not to raise taxes to meet the costs of the war in Vietnam. Moreover, during the 1960s the US pursued both an increase in military spending as well as the "Great Society" program, that is, guns as well as butter. Reluctance to raise taxes at this time appears to have been largely a political decision: unlike the situation during the Korean war, the US government hesitated to ask the American people to shoulder a direct tax burden for an increasingly unpopular war. Economists are generally agreed that the failure of the United States

Military spending is government financial outlay, just like any other type of spending; thus, military spending contributes to the federal deficit no more and no less than any other type of spending. Once again, however, it seems inappropriate to count trust fund expenditures (Social Security, Medicare, unemployment insurance) as adding similarly to the federal debt, since these are paid for themselves by designated contributions, which are earmarked for such use upon collection. General revenue funds have never been used to finance these social welfare payments. In effect, then, just as the Korean war was financed by increased taxes, and the Vietnam war was financed by eventual inflation, the Reagan administration's buildup of the 1980s has been financed by unprecedented increases in the federal deficit.

## Inflation

Inflation is an economic situation in which the value of currency declines. As a result, more money is required to purchase the same products. The causes of inflation are controversial. Similarly, the exact contribution of military spending to inflation is debatable. Before the Vietnam war, for example, inflation in the US economy averaged only about 2%, increasing to 4.8% in 1969. But on the other hand, during the late 1970s, when military spending was relatively low, inflation rose to 10 and 11%. The increased military spending of the 1980s coincided with a period of greatly diminished inflation. Nonetheless, it is widely acknowledged that military spending is inflationary, although the effect is often delayed. Thus, inflation doubled from about 2% to 4.1% in 1968, and 4.8% in 1969. It is generally agreed that President Johnson's decision not to raise taxes during the war in Vietnam gave rise to the inflationary spiral of the 1970s.

The following relationships have existed between inflation in the United States and wars during the twentieth century.

| Start of military buildup | Inflation rate in 3 prior years (%) | Inflation rate in 3 subsequent years (%) |
| --- | --- | --- |
| 1917 (World War I) | 8.7 | 16.0 |
| 1941 (World War II) | 1.5 | 6.2 |
| 1950 (Korea) | 2.6 | 5.6 |
| 1965 (Vietnam) | 1.4 | 3.3 |

The experience with the Reagan administration buildup of the 1980s forms an exception to this pattern, since inflation has gone down in the face of an ongoing military buildup. This is apparently due in part to three factors: (1) the decision to finance the buildup by deficit spending, combined with strict monetary policies by the Federal Reserve, (2) the severe recession of the early 1980s, which idled many industries and produced substantial unemployment, as a result of which the economy could absorb increased military spending without the usual inflationary consequences, and (3) a period of oil oversupply and good agricultural harvests, which tended generally to keep petroleum and food prices down.

Economic theory generally identifies three major causes of inflation, and military spending makes a contribution to each. First, **monetary inflation** occurs when the supply of money and credit increases without corresponding increases in economic output: in short, too much money chasing too few goods. Insofar as it contributes to the federal deficit, military spending contributes to monetary inflation, since federal deficits are generally financed by expanding the money supply, as when the federal treasury issues notes, bills, and bonds.

Second, **demand-pull inflation** occurs when active demand exceeds supply, pulling prices upward. Military spending is a major source of a nation's economic demand, especially in the sectors in which military spending is concentrated: high-tech industries, metal alloys, shipbuilding, munitions, aircraft, and highly skilled manpower. Except for military goods that are sold to foreign governments, most military procurements do not add to the purchasable goods in the domestic economy. By contrast, resources expended to produce automobiles, for example, increase the number of automobiles available for purchase. Inflationary pressures are balanced by the increased supply, and as a result, the price per automobile is kept down. But no consumer can purchase a B-1 bomber or an MX missile. At the same time, military procurement makes demands on certain resources, especially metal alloys: when the makers of both toasters and missiles bid for aluminum, for example, the price of aluminum goes up. Insofar as military spending uses resources, creates demand, and does not add correspondingly to the supply that can be purchased and consumed, it contributes to demand-pull inflation. The existence of unused capacity in an economy becomes crucial here. When such capacity exists, military expenditures need not generate demand–pull inflation; when it does not, the added demand for limited resources increases the price of these resources.

Finally, **cost-push inflation** occurs when production costs are driven up, either because actual costs have risen or because of the perceived opportunity to increase wages and profits. Military spending often leads to cost-inefficient management, hence to cost-push inflation, in several ways. For one, military contracts are often let on a **cost-plus** basis, which means that the contractor is guaranteed to recover costs plus an agreed-upon profit. This gives no incentive to keep costs down and contributes to the notorious cost overruns that sometimes multiply many times the price of military items. In addition, government money is typically expended with less strict oversight than would be the case for private expenditures, leading to such debacles as $200 hammers and $650 toilet seats. Cronyism may also play a part, since many high-level government and military officials ply their trade knowing that they can expect to be hired ultimately by the firms they are supposed to be holding accountable. Since many military items are produced by only one contractor, competitive bidding is not possible: "sole source" purchasing of this kind is insensitive to forces that might cause lower prices (and perhaps, even, better products) in a free, competitive market. In addition, the military economy tends to be concentrated in a rather small number of large firms, some of which specialize almost entirely in military contracting and are insulated from the normal cost consciousness of the civilian economy.

It may also be argued, however, that despite their large size, military expenditures nonetheless constitute only about 6–8% of the GNP, and about 10% of manufacturing output. In addition, the military is not the only recipient of nonproductive government expenditures—that is, goods and services that lack a corresponding product. Military spending can be distinctly noninflationary if financed by increased taxes or by economic growth, although as we have seen, there is reason to believe that if anything, military spending inhibits growth . . . and taxation is politically unpopular and may sometimes be economically counterproductive. Military expenditure comprises by far the largest discretionary part of the federal budget, and because it is so prominent, it exerts an important psychological effect on inflationary expectations as well. With regard to inflationary psychology, therefore, it is possible that a kind of "multiplier effect," analogous to the one used to assess employment, should be applied to military spending.

In summary, there are ways to mitigate the inflationary effects of military spending. It seems undeniable, however, that military spending has a strong inflationary bias.

## ECONOMIC CONVERSION?

It disarmament ever occurs, whether nuclear or conventional, it would almost certainly take place gradually rather than suddenly. Although **economic conversion,** the process of changing from a military to a civilian economy, might well benefit the economy in the long run, it would probably be painful in the short run. This is because as we have seen, many industries and many jobs depend directly and indirectly on military spending. Planning for such conversion therefore seems desirable, if only to mitigate immediate stresses if and when the opportunity for disarmament arrives. In addition, the prominence of military spending in the American economy raises numerous political obstacles to disarmament. A national strategy for economic conversion would help make disarmament more acceptable domestically, hence, more likely to occur. Even without general and complete disarmament, a winding down of military expenditures could have potentially severe economic effects, especially in regions (e.g., much of California) that are particularly dependent on military spending.

The American economy has had some experience with becoming less dependent on military expenditures and military employment, following World War II, Korea, and to a lesser extent, Vietnam. The economy boomed after World War II, profiting from the pent-up consumer demand that was released. For example, new automobiles had not been produced during the war years, and as a result, the major auto makers were able to start selling cars as soon as their assembly lines were retooled from making tanks and other military vehicles. Consumers picked up the demand that military spending had provided. This might not happen today. On the other hand, following World War II, the US economy had to cope with a very large number of quickly demobilized servicemen, a massive influx of job seekers that would not occur in the present day, since military manpower is significantly reduced.

Economic conversion in the Nuclear Age would involve primarily retooling of high-tech industries and retraining of the employees of industrial contractors. It may well be, in fact, that at least in the short term, any denuclearization of America's military posture would involve an increase rather than a decrease in conventional weaponry and manpower needs.

There is no rule of *macroeconomics* (the study of large-scale economic effects) requiring that national economies engage in any military expenditures whatever; such spending could, in theory, go to zero. On the other hand, there would be a pressing need to take account of the short-term effect of shifting priorities in the national economy, to avoid massive dislocations. It should also be emphasized that personnel costs comprise a large proportion of military spending (roughly 25% of the DoD budget); such costs could—again, in theory—be transferred to the domestic sector without major changes, since the personal spending patterns of military families and of civilian families supported by military contracts are not greatly different from those of nonmilitary families.

At the national level, the financial savings of economic conversion probably would lead to reductions in individual and/or corporate taxes, and/or reductions in the federal deficit, and/or expansion in government-sponsored civilian programs (health, education, social welfare, housing, etc.). Federal loan and monetary policies would presumably be adjusted to stimulate private investment and consumption, to make up for decreases in military-industrial demand.

At the local level, planning could focus on the readjustment of industrial plants from the production of military goods to items desired in the domestic sector. It has been proposed that local conversion plans be developed for every military-industrial plant, including identification of appropriate domestic products or services that could alternatively be produced. In theory, assembly lines now producing missiles could just as well produce mass transit. Scientists and engineers now working on warhead design or on Star Wars/SDI could, in theory, work on techniques of waste management or on new energy sources. Many of the design, machining, and production skills now used in military assembly lines are similar to those used in domestic products. Nonetheless, substantial job retraining would doubtless be necessary, especially for mid- and high-level management personnel who have grown accustomed to military contracting and competitive procedures that are quite different from those found in the private sector.

Military contracting tends to reward high costs and of course, it has only a single customer—but one whose regulations and preference are very detailed and complex. Successful domestic managers, instead of know-

ing the Armed Services Procurement Regulations in minute detail, lobbying Congress, and developing personal relationships with Pentagon officials, must be attuned to costs, marketing, and the vagaries of consumer demand. Compared with military contracting, the civilian market is more risky, with many prospective customers, no guaranteed markets, and, generally, lower profit margins. Cost consciousness would have to replace high-level performance consciousness among product designers and promoters. Instead of meeting the requirements of military procurement officers and the desires of Congress (which are often motivated by "pork barrel" concerns somewhat removed from military necessity), it would be necessary to meet the requirements and preferences of the consumer. In the conversion to a domestic economy, firms and those workers producing highly specialized military items would clearly need a disproportionate share of assistance.

At present, when scientists and engineers who are accustomed to military contract work are laid off, they typically either remain unemployed until finding other military-related work, or they move geographically, in search of similar work elsewhere. This reluctance on the part of military-industrial employees to accept employment in the domestic sector may indicate a lack of domestic demand for their skills, perhaps because these skills are so specialized. Or it may reflect unwillingness to settle for less than the salaries they have grown accustomed to in the military-industrial sector.

Thus far, planning for economic conversion in the United States has been undertaken by some private peace groups, and occasionally by labor unions. No serious federal effort is under way. However, an Economic Adjustment Office has long existed in the Department of Defense, helping individual communities and industries cope with local curtailment and redistribution of defense spending. A stepped-up effort on the national level would also seem possible.

No serious national planning for economic conversion appears to have been carried out in the Soviet Union, either. As we have seen, there is reason to believe that the USSR devotes a larger percentage of its GNP to military purposes than does the United States (about 14% vs. 7%). In addition, the system whereby resources are allotted to various industries in the USSR strongly favors military activities, and the status and benefits associated with military work generally exceed those accompanying civilian activities. It therefore seems likely that the disruption of economic conversion would be at least as great in the Soviet Union as in the United States. On the other hand, since the Soviet economy is centrally planned—as befits a communist nation— it presumably would be somewhat easier for the USSR to initiate the requisite planning and also to implement the necessary adjustments.

---

## Policy Issues

### Should the US match the USSR in military budgets?

**Yes:**  Military budgets are a good way to assess military effort. They are important for their psychological as well as their practical significance: it would be ruinous for the US to be perceived as unwilling to shoulder the necessary burden for its own defense. The USSR has been outspending the US in the military sector.

**No:**  Military budgets are notoriously difficult to determine, even in our own country; comparisons between the US and the USSR in this respect are almost meaningless. The US should strive for military sufficiency, concerning itself with what it needs, not how much it costs, or how much the other side appears to be spending. Comparisons of US and Soviet spending are misleading; even going by these figures, however, NATO outspends the Warsaw Pact.

### Should the US strive to reduce its reliance on military spending?

**No:**  First, the appropriate amount of military spending is determined not by its economic impact, but rather by the magnitude of the Soviet threat and what the US needs to do to counteract that threat. But aside from this, there is sufficient unused productive capacity in the US economy to absorb the demands of a military economy. Morever, military demand stimulates the economy and will lead to growth and greater prosperity. Even if defense spending were entirely a drain on the national economy—which it is not—the US would be obliged to make every effort necessary to secure its freedom. Fortunately, defense expenditures can also be used to stimulate the economy when needed, to reduce pockets of unemployment, to create demand in some sectors, and/or to reduce excess supply in others.

**Yes:**  "The whole army and navy are unproductive laborers," wrote Adam Smith in *The Wealth of Nations.*

> They are the servants of the public, and are maintained by a part of the annual produce of the industry of other people. Their service, how honorable, how useful, or how necessary soever, produces nothing for which an equal quantity of services can afterwards be produced.

Thus, even the most renowned exponent of democratic capitalism recognized that military budgets can be ruinous. Military spending is an albatross around the neck of the US economy, leading to economic stagnation, inflation, reduced international competitiveness, waste of resources that are desperately needed in the domestic sector, and fewer jobs than would exist if the money were spent in the civilian economy. A nation's security depends not only on its military capability, but also on the strength of its economy, and military spending saps this strength. All this is in addition to the larger fact that in the Nuclear Age military obsession makes the US less safe, not more.

---

## KEY TERMS

| | | | |
|---|---|---|---|
| budget authority | outlays | defense appropriations bill | National Income and Product Accounts (NIPA) |
| total obligational authority | first [congressional] budget resolution | bow-wave (wedge) effect | constant dollars |
| obligations incurred | defense authorization bill | national defense function | current dollars |

absolute dollars

m/GNP

cost overruns

military Keynesianism

multiplier effect

opportunity costs

substitution effect

total fixed capital formation

monetary inflation

demand-pull inflation

cost-push inflation

cost-plus

economic conversion

## STUDY QUESTIONS

1. Describe several different ways of calculating the military budget of the United States. Describe several different ways of evaluating the total size of this budget—that is, comparing military spending in one year with spending in another.

2. What is meant by military Keynesianism? Under what circumstances could military spending be a prop to the economy rather than a burden?

3. Why is it difficult to compare the military budgets of the US and the USSR? How is such comparison accomplished?

4. What is the difference between obligated spending and actual spending in the military budget? How does this difference become especially apparent in the process of procurement?

5. In what ways does military spending contribute to total employment? In what ways does it detract from total employment?

6. In what ways does military spending add to a nation's economic productivity? In what ways does it detract from productivity?

7. Discuss the relationship between military spending and inflation.

8. Contrast the American experience with economic conversion after World War II with the potential experience of economic conversion in the 1980s.

## ADDITIONAL READINGS

Hitch, Charles, and Roland McKean. 1965. *The Economics of Defense in the Nuclear Age*. Cambridge, MA: Harvard University Press. The bible of military economics, written with an orientation supportive of military spending; also analyzes such issues as how to allocate resources among the various military programs.

Melman, Seymour. 1974. *The Permanent War Economy*. New York: Simon & Schuster. An influential evaluation of the costs—mostly in lost potential productivity—of military expenditures, by one of the most articulate critics of military spending.

Mosley, Hugh. 1985. *The Arms Race: Economic and Social Consequences*. Lexington, MA: D. C. Heath. A scholarly yet accessible evaluation of the economic impact of military spending; up to date and reasonably evenhanded.

Russett, Bruce, 1970. *What Price Vigilance?* New Haven, CT: Yale University Press. An acclaimed account of the economic and social costs of military spending.

# 13 Nuclear Ethics

*The task before us is . . . to consider anew whether and how our religious-moral tradition can assess, direct, contain, and, we hope, help to eliminate the threat posed to the human family by the nuclear arsenals of the world.*
U.S. Catholic Bishops Pastoral Letter, 1983

In the preceding chapter, we saw that nuclear weapons make up only a part of the larger question of military spending. Similarly, when examining the ethics of nuclear weaponry and nuclear war, we shall find that *nuclear* ethics comprise only a small part of a lengthy and complex tradition concerning itself with the morality of war. But given the enormous consequences of their potential use, nuclear weapons occupy a special place in ethical considerations.

## WESTERN RELIGIOUS TRADITIONS AND WAR

Each of the world's religions has its own attitude toward war; such attitudes and the teaching they inspire are, not surprisingly, diverse and often contradictory. Most important for our purposes are the views of Western religions, notably Christianity. This is not to deny the separation of church and state, as imposed by the U.S. Constitution; rather, it simply recognizes that religious traditions, especially the Judaeo-Christian tradition, have a particularly strong influence on American attitudes toward war in general and nuclear war in particular. It is possible to identify three basic threads in the Western religious tradition as it relates to war: at one extreme are the "commanded" or "righteous" wars of the Old Testament and at the other, pacifism; between them lies an intermediate zone, characterized by what has been called "Christian realism" and the so-called *Just War* doctrine.

The Old Testament contains numerous references to wars in which God took the part of the ancient Israelites. Typically, there were few if any limits to the actual conduct of such wars: "When the Lord your God has given them over to you, and you defeat them, then you must utterly destroy them; you shall make no covenant with them, and show no mercy to them" (Deuteronomy 7:2).

This condonement of unrestrained war, justified entirely by the belief that one is doing God's will, has its counterpart in later tradition as well, notably during the Crusades of the Middle Ages. For example, consider the following excerpt from a twelfth-century sermon by Saint Bernard of Clairvaux.

*A new sort of army has appeared. . . . It fights a double war; first, the war of the flesh and blood against enemies; second, the war of the spirit against Satan and vice. . . . The soldier of Christ kills with safety; he dies with more safety still. He serves Christ when he kills. He serves himself when he is killed.*

Not surprisingly, wars that were believed by both sides to be justified as the fulfillment of God's will tended to be more vicious than secular wars, since each side considered that its belligerency was sanctioned directly by the deity and neither side felt constrained in the manner in which it conducted the war.

Such "Holy Wars" are not an important part of modern geopolitics, although the Islamic *jihad* retains some adherents, especially in opposition to Israel and even during intra-Islamic wars (e.g., between Iran and Iraq). It is noteworthy, however, that some fundamentalist Christians interpret literally the prophecies of the End Times contained in the Book of Revelation. According to this view, the world will come to an end in war, fire, and upheaval, as part of the final battle between good and evil, and as a prelude to the second coming of Christ. To those who carry this view to its most extreme conclusion, a nuclear war between the

US and the USSR could constitute the will of God, as anticipated in the Bible; hence it need not necessarily be something to abhor, or even to try to prevent.

If the Crusades of the Middle Ages represented the Holy War tradition, it seems likely that the early Church was intensely pacifist (many Christian martyrs died rather than serve in the Roman legions). In the twentieth century, Christian pacifists cite the admonitions of Jesus to love one's neighbor and to turn the other cheek, and they point to the scriptural proclamation that the meek shall inherit the earth. Such views are currently maintained by the so-called Peace Churches within Christianity, including notably the Mennonites and the Quakers, as well as certain pacificist traditions within other Protestant denominations and within Roman Catholicism as well.

By the fourth century AD, however, with the conversion of the emperor Constantine, Christianity gained acceptance and recognition as the state religion of the Roman Empire. Around this time, there developed a new tradition within Christianity, one that took a more practical and political view of the use of violence. This change of attitude is consistent with the new-found role of Christianity as a defender of governmental and societal values rather than as a minority movement. This new attitude sought to establish a middle ground between the commanded wars of the Old Testament and the uncompromising pacifism of the Gospels. It sought, particularly, to establish careful rules by which "just wars" could be identified and fought.

## THE JUST WAR TRADITION

Efforts to identify the conditions for **Just Wars**—that is, those that Christians can engage in—are especially found among Roman Catholic writings. However, they have also received much support from other religious denominations. In a secular form, dating from the medieval writings of DeVittoria, Suarez, and Grotius, they also embody most of the organized ethical and legal perceptions of warfare. The Just War tradition derives particularly from the writings of St. Augustine, early in the fourth century. Augustine was especially concerned with justifying Christian participation in the defense of Rome. In *The City of God*, for example, Augustine maintained that "it is the wrong-doing of the opposing party which compels the wise man to wage just wars," and that "war with the hope of peace everlasting" to follow was preferable to "captivity without any thought of deliverance." However, anyone seeking

recourse to arms was under a heavy responsibility to demonstrate that violence was justified by the circumstances. The presumption is in favor of peace and peaceful resolution of conflict. Augustine explicitly excluded self-defense, allowing only the defense of others. The argument is based essentially on "Christian charity," wherein nations might go to war in the defense of a neighbor who has been unjustly attacked. Later thinkers have justified both self-defense and the defense of others. Just War doctrine was further developed by St. Thomas Aquinas, and more recently it has been brought into the Nuclear Age.

Just War theory can readily be divided into two major concerns: first, whether a war may legitimately be fought in the first place—that is, the justification for going to war—and second, how that war might be fought—that is, justifiable acts in wartime. The Latin phrase that applies to the former is **jus ad bellum,** law [for going] *to* war; the latter is referred to as **jus in bello,** law *in* war. A Just War (one that meets *ad bellum* criteria) may be fought unjustly, if it does not follow the appropriate *in bello* restraints. Similarly, an unjust war (one that fails to meet *ad bellum* criteria) can nonetheless be fought justly, if the protagonists adhere to the *in bello* rules of war.

Let us next apply the traditional Christian criteria to the concept of *jus ad bellum*, to determine the conditions under which a war could be called a Just War.

1. *Last resort.* War is legitimate only if all other possible means of resolution have been explored and found unsatisfactory.

2. *Legitimate authority.* The decision to go to war must not be made by disgruntled groups or individuals; it must come from duly constituted state authorities. This also provides the opportunity for a state to declare itself a neutral or nonbelligerent, which at least in theory confers immunity against attack.

3. *Just cause* and *right intention.* War must not be motivated by revenge or by aggressive designs; it must somehow be consistent with Christian charity and/or post-Augustinian self-defense.

4. *Chance of success.* Hopeless or futile resistance cannot be justified.

5. *Goal of peace.* The ultimate prospect of a Just War must be a peace preferable to that which would prevail if the war were not fought.

Considerations 3-5 are sometimes summarized as the **principle of proportionality:** the overall moral benefit likely to derive from the war must be greater than its overall moral cost. The principle of proportionality therefore recognizes that war is an evil, and often, a very great evil. It suggests, however, that evil can sometimes be tolerated if it leads to a greater good.

Next, we turn to the question of *jus in bello*; how wars may and may not be fought. There are two fundamental issues here. The first is a more specific application of proportionality, often known as the **doctrine of double effect.** Many actions during war may have the "good" effect of helping to defeat the opponent, hence, to bring the war to a successful conclusion, but they also have the "bad" effect of producing death and suffering, among combatants and innocent civilians alike. So the doctrine of double effect maintains that for a war to be fought justly, the good results of any specific act (an invasion, a bombing, etc.) must be proportionately greater than the bad. In short, military means must be proportional to a discrete military end. These means themselves must also be proportional to the overall legitimate goals of the war.

The second aspect of *jus in bello* restraint concerns the so-called **principle of discrimination.** This is often synonymous with **noncombatant immunity,** the doctrine that civilians must not be the direct object of any intentional military attack. In truth, noncombatants have often been grossly abused during war, as armies have traditionally looted, plundered, ravaged, and murdered. The ability to engage in such acts has been limited, however. But in recent times, as war has become increasingly "total," ethicists have become concerned to establish limits on permissible behavior during war. Military casualties were roughly comparable during World Wars I and II, but there were many times more civilian deaths and injuries in the latter than in the former. And projecting to the future, the vast majority of casualties during a nuclear war seem likely to be civilian.

Writing on "Morality of War" in the 1967 edition of the *New Catholic Encyclopedia*, one authority has commented that:

> It is a fundamental moral principle [unanimously accepted by Catholic moralists] that it is immoral directly to take innocent human life except with divine authorization. "Direct" taking of human life implies that one performs a lethal action with the intention that death should result for himself or another. Death therefore is deliberately willed as the effect of one's action. "Indirect" killing refers to an action or omission that is designed and intended solely to achieve some

other purpose(s) even though death is foreseen as a concomitant effect. Death therefore is not positively willed, but is reluctantly permitted as an unavoidable by-product.*

Thus, noncombatant immunity specifies that innocent civilians must not be the direct targets of military attack. However, this is generally interpreted to mean that *in bello* restraints are not violated as long as the killing of civilians is indirect—that is, if the victims were not directly targeted. In practice, the *jus in bello* restraints are that the actual or potential killing of innocents may be done only if every effort is made to minimize it, in the context of other Just War restrictions.

For example, catapults were frequently used during medieval sieges of castles. The express intent of these weapons was to break down the castle's defenses, but not uncommonly, civilian bystanders were injured as well. This was considered regrettable, but since it was an "unavoidable by-product" of legitimate military means, a "concomitant effect," and as long as every effort was made to minimize this effect, and civilians were not the direct targets of such armed force, the use of catapults was not considered to violate *in bello* restrictions.

There are obviously some difficulties with the specifics of noncombatant immunity, especially in recent years when the economies of entire nations tend to be mobilized for a war effort. For example, is a civilian employed in manufacturing munitions or designing weapons a noncombatant? What about a uniformed soldier who was conscripted against his will?

The original designers of Just War theory obviously did not have nuclear weapons in mind. Before turning specifically to nuclear war, however, we shall look briefly at some high points (or low points) of efforts to enforce *in bello* restraints during conventional warfare.

## SOME *IN BELLO* RESTRAINTS

Several efforts were made during medieval times to agree on restrictions on belligerent activities. Notable among these were the "Truce of God," which defined certain days as unacceptable for fighting, and the "Peace of God," which prohibited direct attack against certain persons: merchants, travelers, clergy and reli-

---

*R. A. McCormick. 1967. Morality of War. *New Catholic Encyclopedia*. New York: McGraw-Hill. Reprinted with permission of The Catholic University of America Press.

gious, and farmers. The chivalric code of knighthood established rules of who might legitimately fight with whom and regarded the treatment of prisoners (especially prisoners who were members of the nobility). In 1139 the Second Lateran Council even banned the use of certain weapons, notably the crossbow. Significantly, however, the restriction applied only to use of the weapon against other Christians; crossbows could still be used against the forces of Islam, in the Crusades. This prohibition eventually faltered altogether, and in fact, there have been no examples of militarily effective weapons whose use has been prevented by the agreement that they were unethical. The closest case may be the use of poison gas in the twentieth century, although as we have seen, the argument has been made that the restraint showed during World War II was more a result of mutual deterrence than an example of moral behavior.

Of the various failures of *in bello* restraint, perhaps the most notable have involved persistent violations of noncombatant immunity, a trend that has been accelerating in modern times. This acceleration seems to be due largely to two factors: (1) the progressively greater involvement of entire civilian populations in the war effort, thereby making them combatants of a sort, and (2) the invention of progressively more destructive and often less discriminating means of killing, which typically operate at a great distance as well.

Before the French Revolution, most conflicts were "sovereign's wars," limited by an individual ruler's personal income and by the number of soldiers that could be bribed or coerced into fighting. By the time of Napoleon, however, wars became "national wars," involving the mobilization of a nation's resources. To some extent, the American Civil War turned an additional page in the strategy and ethics of warfare; Sherman's march through Georgia, for example, was directed not so much against the Confederate Armies as against the morale and war-making potential of the Confederacy as a whole.

Some civilians were attacked directly, from dirigibles and aircraft, during World War I. However, it was still felt that attacking noncombatants was wrong. Indeed, American outrage over the German sinking of the civilian ocean liner *Lusitania*, helped precipitate the United States' entry into that war in 1917. The slaughter of World War I was so appalling that military theorists, also encouraged by advances in aircraft technology, looked increasingly at the potential of ending wars quickly by strategic bombardment of the enemy's homeland. Between World Wars I and II, the Italian general Giulo Douhet especially developed the theory of

strategic airpower: "the air arm . . . will strike against entities less well able to resist, and helpless to act or counteract. It is fated, therefore, that the moral and material collapse will come about more quickly and easily." Ironically, then, some of the most fearsome aspects of modern war, and a general relaxation of *in bello* restraints, were brought about by the desire to reduce the overall destructiveness of war.

The ethical legitimacy of such actions could still be maintained by appeals to "double effect"—the greater benefit of ending a war quickly could be said to make up for the bad effect of targeting civilians. Under such conditions, it can be argued that even civilian morale, for example, is of military significance; hence attacks against the civilian population can be justified under the doctrine of double effect. (Nonetheless, many ethicists maintained, and still maintain, that it is immoral to target civilians directly, for any reason, ever.)

Strategic bombing of civilians occurred with increasing frequency during World War II; it also provoked diminishing outrage as people came increasingly to accept such behavior as unavoidable. The bombing of the city of Guernica during the Spanish civil war was something of a prelude to Japanese bombing of Chinese cities, and the German bombing of Warsaw and Rotterdam early in World War II. However, Britain, France, and Germany refrained from bombing each other's cities until August 1940, when some German bombers—apparently by accident—bombed London. The British retaliated against Berlin, the Germans responded with the London "blitz," and countercity warfare was a reality. Restraints against targeting civilian populations deteriorated rapidly, and raids originally directed against war industries were redirected at civilian population centers. Because cities are relatively large and "soft," whereas military targets are relatively small and "hard," it is easier to hit the former than the latter, especially with bombs dropped at night. (Although in the 1940s day bombing was more accurate, night bombing was much safer for the bombers.) Tens of thousands of civilians died in the nighttime firebombing of Dresden, Hamburg, Tokyo, and Osaka (Fig. 13.1). At such times, munitions were used that specifically increased the probability of creating fire storms, and bombing patterns were intentionally employed to create a ring of fire, entrapping civilians within.

Lewis Mumford denounced such saturation bombing of civilian targets as "unconditional moral surrender to Hitler," and David Lilienthal, later the first chairman of the Atomic Energy Commission, warned:

"The fences are gone. And it was we, the civilized, who have pushed standardless conduct to its ultimate." Others claimed that during the supreme national emergency of all-out war, such tactics were legitimate as a way of hastening the war's end. Much debate persists, however, about whether strategic bombing was in fact effective in this regard: until the final months of World War II, for example, German war production appeared to be unaffected by the generally inaccurate Allied bombing, and civilian morale may well have been stiffened rather than weakened.

Moral standards were not entirely abandoned. It is noteworthy, for example, that a plaque in Westminster Abbey comemorates the brave RAF pilots of Fighter Command who died during the Battle of Britain, whereas no comparable memorial exists to the equally brave pilots of Bomber Command who died while bombing the cities of Germany. There appears to be some recognition that the former action was morally superior to the latter. Even by the end of World War II, with all its carnage, some moral compunctions remained about the deliberate targeting of civilians. Thus, in announcing the dropping of an atomic bomb on the city of Hiroshima, President Truman described the target as "an important military base." In fact, evidence now suggests that Hiroshima was selected because it had not previously been attacked; had it truly been an important military base, it should have been attacked long before, since at that time B-29s had been bombing Japanese cities with virtual impunity. The city of Hiroshima was chosen because it was an intact city, and as such, it offered a clear demonstration of the atomic bomb's power.

## NUCLEAR WAR AND JUST WAR

The bombings of Hiroshima and Nagasaki have been debated extensively, with critics arguing that they were unnecessary and immoral, while supporters claim they were regrettable, but necessary and moral. This ongoing controversy provides an example of the use of Just War criteria, and the difficulty of coming to firm conclusions. Thus, it is debated whether the atomic bombings were truly last resorts. Some claim that the Japanese government had unequivocally rejected US calls for unconditional surrender; others maintain that the Japanese government was on the verge of surrender, waiting only for assurance that the Emperor would be retained. The casualties of both bombings were overwhelmingly civilian, although there was an army head-

**FIGURE 13.1  The city of Tokyo burning, after a (conventional) firebombing in the spring of 1945.** (USAF Photographic Collection, National Air and Space Museum, Smithsonian Institution.)

quarters at Hiroshima, and the Mitsubishi naval shipyards were located in Nagasaki. Most important, it has been claimed that the atomic bombings were carried out in a proportionate manner; that is, the death of about 200,000 people, although horrible, was proportionately less evil than the death of perhaps a million or more people if the war had continued and the islands of Japan had had to be directly invaded. In addition, a cruel and destructive war was taking place, and many Americans were dying. US authorities were also painfully aware of Japanese atrocities to American prisoners of war, notably during the Bataan "death march." Under such conditions, it can be argued that the prime responsibility for American leaders was to end the war as quickly as possible and with a minimum loss of life —especially American lives.

On the other hand, it may well be that Japan was essentially defeated anyway and that a bloody invasion would not have been warranted, even without the atomic bombings. The official US government *Strategic Bombing Survey,* conducted after the war, concluded:

*Certainly prior to 31 December 1945 and in all probability prior to 1 November 1945 Japan would have surrendered, even if Russia had not entered the war, and even if no invasion had been planned or contemplated.*

In addition, the actual aim point was undeniably a civilian one: a major bridge, in the center of the city. Thus, civilians were targeted directly, in clear contravention of the principle of discrimination. (It appears that no serious consideration was given to the possibility of exploding a "demonstration blast" over unpopulated areas, although this option had been suggested by physicists involved in the Manhattan Project.) If the main reason for the bombings was a desire to intimidate the Soviet Union and make Stalin more tractable — as many critics allege — then the slaughter of thousands of women, children, and elderly people at Hiroshima and Nagasaki was clearly immoral. Others have also argued that whereas the bombing of Hiroshima may have been ethically defensible, the follow-up destruction of Nagasaki is less justifiable. In any event, such killing of civilians was not without precedent, since even more people had died earlier in the firebombing of Tokyo, for example. What was unprecedented, however, was the relative ease with which the carnage was accomplished.

The world's arsenals have grown enormously since 1945, both in number of bombs and warheads, and in the size of the larger ones. It should be emphasized that whereas small atomic bombs such as those used at Hiroshima and Nagasaki are measured in kilotons, hydrogen bombs are measured in megatons of destructive power: a thousandfold increase. With the addition of possible atmospheric effects, especially nuclear winter, it seems clear that nuclear war poses the gravest possible consequences, raising perhaps the most serious ethical and moral issues ever confronted by humanity.

Whatever the justice or injustice of past wars, the presence of nuclear weapons now threatens to render any future nuclear war "unjust." According to political philosopher Micheal Walzer, "nuclear weapons explode the theory of Just War. They are the first of mankind's technological innovations that are simply not encompassable within the familiar moral world." It is widely agreed that nuclear war would necessarily fail to meet the major Just War criteria:

1. *Last resort.* The fact that nuclear weapons have not been exploded in anger since the bombing of Nagasaki suggests a real hesitation to employ them. However, each side has been accumulating "first-strike" weaponry, and NATO, at least, continues to maintain a first-use policy; that is, it is explicit doctrine that a conventional Warsaw Pact invasion of western Europe could well precipitate "first use" of tactical nuclear weapons by NATO. Supporters of this policy claim, however, that such use would constitute a last resort.

2. *Legitimate authority.* In the case of nuclear retaliation, the period in which the decision to use nuclear weapons must be made may be very brief (perhaps a matter of minutes). As a result, there will be insufficient time to consult with Congress or obtain a declaration of war. Supporters maintain, however, that the president or his or her designated successors constitute legitimate authority in such cases.

3. *Reasonable chance of success.* Given the possibility that use of nuclear weapons will escalate into nuclear holocaust, the chance of success appears to be unreasonably low. On the other hand, no one can accurately predict the course of events in advance: whether it will be possible to keep a nuclear war limited, or whether the long-term effects will in fact be globally catastrophic.

4. *Ultimate goal of peace.* If nuclear war results in the destruction of most or all of humanity, it is difficult to defend the assertion that a legitimate goal of peace has been achieved. It seems likely that the number of people killed would include most if not all of those for whom the war had been fought.

5. *Proportionality.* It is questionable whether any social, political, economic, or philosophical differences between the US and USSR could justify the destruction of nuclear war. Whereas one body of opinion holds that certain things are worth fighting for, and if need be, "better dead than Red," other opinion maintains that nothing is worth the destruction of civilization and possibly, the human species itself (not to mention the rest of the biosphere, which is entirely innocent and yet might also be at risk).

6. *Noncombatant immunity.* In their pastoral letter of 1983, the American Catholic bishops noted that "no Christian can rightfully carry out orders or policies deliberately aimed at killing noncombatants." Given the enormous destructive power of nuclear weapons, it seems impossible for nuclear war to meet this important requirement of *in bello* restraint. Thus, the Second Vatican Council had concluded that "Any act of war aimed indiscriminately at the destruction of entire cities or of extensive areas along with their populations is a crime against God

and man itself. It merits unequivocal and unhesitating condemnation." In their pastoral letter two decades later, the American bishops added that "this condemnation, in our judgment, applies even to the retaliatory use of weapons striking enemy cities after our own have already been struck. No Christian can rightfully carry out orders or policies aimed at killing noncombatants."

In response to this, government officials have repeatedly noted that it is not official policy to target civilian populations as such. In a celebrated speech in 1962, Defense Secretary Robert McNamara stated that "principal military objectives, in the event of a nuclear war stemming from a major attack on the Alliance, should be the destruction of the enemy's military forces, not of his civilian population." And as we have seen, US targeting doctrine, as formalized in Presidential Directive 59, emphasizes the destruction of Soviet military forces, political leadership, and command and control facilities. Thus, any destruction of the general civilian population would be "collateral damage," incidental to attacking legitimate military targets. As a response to this, however, critics point out that according to government reports, there are more than 60 "military" targets in Moscow alone, making it irrelevant whether noncombatants are directly targeted; they would be destroyed in any case, making the distinction meaningless, a travesty of ethics.

In their unequivocal rejection of arguments in favor of the morality of nuclear war-fighting, the American bishops emphasized what they see as the very great possibility that a nuclear exchange, once initiated, could not be limited or controlled but would almost certainly escalate into all-out destruction that would necessarily be disproportionate to any possible "good" outcome. Hence, they have the gravest reservations about the morality of ever using nuclear weapons, although they stop short of absolute prohibition. Supporters of a counterforce, war-fighting strategy claim, in contrast, that it may well prove possible to fight limited, controlled nuclear wars, and that moreover, it is precisely by developing this capability that we shall ensure that it will never be used.

Strategist Albert Wohlstetter, for example, asks rhetorically, "Can we deter a restricted nuclear attack better by threatening an 'unlimited,' frankly suicidal, and therefore improbable attack on the aggressor's cities, or by a limited but much more probable response suited to the circumstances?"

Others, notably Jonathan Schell in his influential and moving book *The Fate of the Earth,* point out that since nuclear war carries with it the possible end of human experience and the death of the unborn, it simply cannot be justified or tolerated in any way. They argue that human beings who hold in their frail hands the power of life and death over an entire planet, do not have the right to keep the future hostage to their own whims, angers, and possible error. Human beings have never had to confront the moral implications of an act that might prove to be both overwhelmingly destructive and irrevocably permanent. It seems to be a dramatic case in which our technological inventiveness has outpaced our moral and ethical precepts. According to the Catholic bishops, "nuclear weaponry has drastically changed the nature of warfare, and the arms race poses a threat to human life and human civilization which is without precedent." As a result, they conclude that "our No to nuclear war must, in the end be definitive and decisive."

## THE MORALITY OF DETERRENCE

*The first and most vital step in any American security program for the age of atomic bombs is to take measures to guarantee to ourselves in case of attack the possibility of retaliation in kind. The writer in making that statement is not for the moment concerned about who will win the next war in which atomic bombs are used. Thus far the chief purpose of our military establishment has been to win wars. From now on its chief purpose must be to avert them. It can have almost no other useful purpose. (Bernard Brodie, 1946.)*

Most authorities seem to be agreed that nuclear war would be profoundly immoral and unethical, hence unacceptable. However, there is substantial disagreement about the acceptability of deterrence as a means of preventing nuclear war. It is one thing to agree that nuclear war itself would be deeply wrong, but what about the morality of threatening nuclear war? Even granting that there may be no rational purpose served by carrying out the threat of nuclear war, there could be "method to the madness" of making the threat, in order to deter wars—both nuclear and conventional. But rationality aside, are such threats ethical? Among the most influential thinkers in this regard is the Protestant ethicist and philosopher Paul Ramsey. He has described the ethical dilemma of deterrence in the following metaphor:

> *Suppose that one Labor Day weekend no one was killed or maimed on the highways, and that the reason for the remarkable restraint placed on the recklessness of automobile drivers was that suddenly every one of them discovered that he was driving with a baby tied to his front bumper! That would be no way to regulate traffic* even if it succeeds *in regulating it perfectly, since such a system makes innocent human lives the* direct object *of attack and uses them as a mere means for restraining the drivers of automobiles.\**

Ramsey is consistent with standard ethical (and legal) teaching by emphasizing that if the performance of an action is immoral, then so is the threat of it. This is based on the well-established ethical principle that moral error lies first in the intention to do wrong, and only later in the act itself; unintended wrong is therefore generally considered a lesser immorality than intended wrong, and similarly, doing the right thing for the wrong reason is an ethical error. Perhaps an even more accurate metaphor for the (im)morality of deterrence would be the following: imagine a legal code prescribing that when a murderer is apprehended, the society would execute not only the murderer but also all his relatives and friends. Such a deeply immoral system would be unacceptable as a way of regulating conduct.

Yet, Ramsey nonetheless winds up defending the moral legitimacy of deterrence, as long as the direct, explicit threat is of retaliation against military targets rather than cities as such. He recognizes that the threat of collateral civilian damage might also serve to restrain a would-be aggressor but judges that to be moral as long as it is a by-product, not the direct goal. Thus if an adversary is deterred by the recognition that our legitimate, discriminate retaliation would also have serious collateral consequences, so much the better.

Paul Ramsey speaks for many ethicists (both religious and secular) when he defends the moral legitimacy of counterforce targeting and condemns countercity targeting. Certain strategists have long maintained the same, basing their argument not so much on ethical considerations but on their view of practical, power politics. In particular, it has been pointed out

that countercity strategies are inherently lacking in credibility, since they do nothing to diminish the ability of the attacker to annihilate the victim, and would simply increase the probability that the retaliating nation's population would itself be devastated in counterretaliation. Morever, it is also argued that history shows that the Kremlin leadership is not necessarily averse to sacrificing large numbers of civilians. According to this argument, the only way to deter the USSR successfully is to maintain a threat against the assets the Soviet leadership values most: its military forces.

Strategic implications aside, there seems to be little doubt that counterforce targeting is ethically superior to countercity targeting. On the other hand, ethical critics of counterforce targeting point out first that counterforce targeting will likely result in civilian casualties that are almost indistinguishable from those accompanying countercity targeting. Second, they emphasize the paradox that even if counterforce is, narrowly speaking, the more ethical policy, it may also be the more dangerous one. That is, it may also be more likely to precipitate nuclear war, since it could lead to a hair-trigger situation in which the actions of one side might be interpreted as an effort to preemptively destroy the other side's ability to retaliate. To compound the irony, weapons with smaller yields and more accurate delivery systems—those that are likely to be ethically more acceptable—are also precisely those that logically would be perceived by the opponent as being more likely to be used in a first strike, hence, more provocative. If so, the more ethical posture is also more dangerous.

The American bishops end up with a similar position, although one that is yet more uncomfortable about deterrence. They seem to accept the idea that one must sometimes threaten a wrong to prevent a greater wrong. They wind up accepting nuclear deterrence, but only in a very limited manner, echoing Pope John Paul, who said in a speech at Hiroshima that "in current conditions 'deterrence' based on balance, certainly not as an end in itself but as a step on the way toward a progressive disarmament, may still be judged morally acceptable." However, critics have questioned whether deterrence has been employed as a step toward progressive disarmament, rather than an excuse for driving the arms race. And as we have seen, the bishops emphasize that the actual use of nuclear weapons against cities would be an intolerable wrong under any circumstances. They accept the morality of possession —in a limited way, and only insofar as it leads to progressive disarmament. Moreover, the Catholic bishops

---

\*Paul Ramsey. *The Just War.* Copyright © 1968 Paul Ramsey. Reprinted with permission of Charles Scribner's Sons.

rejected the morality of using nuclear weapons against an opponent's population.

This leaves the nation in a paradoxical position, since the essence of deterrence is to maintain the peace by threatening intolerable retaliation; but nuclear weapons can fulfill their purpose only if one's adversary believes that one fully intends to use them. Yet, holding that intention is supposedly unethical and immoral. Some people have suggested that to avoid this dilemma, it might be possible to establish a distinction between **declaratory policy** (what we say we would do under certain circumstances) and **action policy** (what we actually would do). According to this viewpoint, there can be some rational and moral justification for making a nuclear threat, even if there can be no justifications for carrying it out. But if it ever becomes established that we will not use nuclear weapons, this will undermine deterrence and may make war more likely. Deterrence works in proportion to the firmness of the other side's belief that one's threat is credible. Moreover, given the many thousands of individuals and the complex systems, all of which must be tested, drilled, and kept in constant readiness, it is difficult to imagine that a nation that could effectively declare and appear ready to implement a policy of nuclear retaliation (or first-use against a conventional attack), would be able to turn off this machinery if push came to shove.

Many objections to nuclear deterrence involve what are known to moral philosophers as "consequentialist" arguments: nuclear deterrence is described as immoral because it is likely to lead, ultimately, to nuclear war. Thus, perhaps one can argue with equal persuasiveness that deterrence is leading the world to nuclear war or toward lasting peace. Another moral objection, however, is less concerned with the possible consequences of deterrence than with its fundamental moral legitimacy. Philosopher Raymond Perkins, for example, has argued that there must be limits on the means that a moral society can employ, no matter how ethical its ends:

> The leaders of one country threaten, and prepare to commit, the mass murder of the civilian population of another country in order to deter its leaders from initiating future aggression. Neither the US nor the Soviet leadership has the moral right to threaten the lives of the people on the other side in this way. In accepting the policy of nuclear deterrence, we promote a moral (and probably legal) heresy which makes a mockery of our claim to uphold the principles of justice

> and decency. And each side confirms the other's official propaganda that it really is led by the very sort of morally reprehensible beings that only an equally reprehensible policy can protect against. Even if such a policy could be guaranteed to succeed for another 40 years, it could never be morally justified.*

Deterrence has come under double attack, from hawkish critics on the political right as well as dovish critics on the left. Both extremes agree that deterrence is immoral. Hawks feel that it should be replaced with a clearly counterforce strategy (augmented with Star Wars/SDI); doves feel it should be replaced by either minimal deterrence, conventional deterrence, and/or more strenuous efforts at bilateral arms agreements or, if these fail, unilateral initiatives toward disarmament.

The more extreme views on this difficult and delicate question are the pacifist (or the more restricted, nuclear-pacifist) position, and the more confrontational viewpoint that supports the legitimacy of nuclear threats and even, if necessary, nuclear war. The first view has been eloquently expressed, as we have already seen, by Jonathan Schell. It is also reflected in these words by George F. Kennan:

> The readiness to use nuclear weapons against other human beings—against people whom we do not know, whom we have never seen, and whose guilt or innocence it is not for us to establish—and in doing so, to place in jeopardy the natural structure upon which all civilization rests, as though the safety and the perceived interests of our own generation were more important than everything that has ever taken place or could take place in civilization; this is nothing less than a presumption, a blasphemy, an indignity—an indignity of monstrous dimensions—offered to God!†

The other extreme seeks to derive its legitimacy from the use of nuclear weapons to defend Western, and often Christian, values. It has been expressed well by Charles Krauthammer:

---

*R. Perkins. 1985. Deterrence is immoral. *Bulletin of the Atomic Scientists*, *41*, 32–34. Copyright © 1985 by the Educational Foundation for Nuclear Science, Chicago, IL 60637. Reprinted with permission of the publisher.

†1982. A Christian's view of the arms race. *Theology Today*, *39*, 2. Reprinted with permission of the publisher.

*(1) There are values more important than survival, and (2) nuclear weapons are necessary to protect them. The second proposition is, of course, true. The West is the guarantor of such fragile historical achievements as democracy and political liberty; a whole constellation of ideals and values ultimately rests on its ability to deter those who reject these values and have a history of destroying them wherever they dominate. Unilaterally to reject deterrence is to surrender those values in the name of survival. The rub comes with the first proposition. Are there values more important than survival? [Philosopher] Sidney Hook was surely right when he once said that when a person makes survival the highest value, he has declared that there is nothing he will not betray. But for a civilization, self-sacrifice makes no sense since there are not survivors to give meaning to the sacrificial act. In that case, survival may be worth betrayal. If this highly abstract choice were indeed the only one, it would be hard to meet Schell's point that since all values hinge on biological survival, to forfeit that is to forfeit everything. It is thus simply not enough to say (rightly) that nuclear weapons, given the world as it is today, keep us free; one must couple that statement with another, equally true: they keep us safe.* *

Of course, others would dispute the contention that nuclear weapons keep us safe.

Generally speaking, hawkish supporters of nuclear deterrence and, *in extremis* of resort to nuclear war, are prone to dwell on the horrors of communism, especially Soviet communism, and to emphasize the virtues of courage and the values of the "free world" to which they feel that Soviet communism is inimical. Thus, conservative journalist George Will, on the morality of nuclear weapons: "It is reckless to decree that any use, even any possession is necessarily a larger evil than the long night of centuries that would follow the extinguishing of Western cultural values by armed totalitarianism." Nuclear hawks also are likely to emphasize the possibility that nuclear war might be limited, controllable, and even, perhaps, won. And for them, the threat to initiate nuclear war (i.e., deterrence) may be distasteful but it

is clearly moral. Dovish opponents of nuclear deterrence and of the potential resort to nuclear war are likely to dwell, by contrast, on the immorality of making lethal threats, on the likely horror of nuclear war itself, and on the possibility that it will be uncontrollable and globally suicidal.

Few people seem to believe seriously that the choices are as stark as "Red or dead," and as we shall see in Chapter 15, there are numerous courses of action, intermediate between oblivion and capitulation. Nonetheless, it is an interesting exercise to pretend that there are only two alternatives. In this (admittedly hypothetical) case, many hawks would presumably choose to die rather than surrender, considering death to be the moral stance. Or at least, they argue that it is appropriate to be prepared to die, so as to be able to live freely. The antinuclear response is typically that although an individual may have the right to choose his or her own death rather than life under communism, it is presumptuous and immoral for any person—or any government—to decree a nuclear death for someone else, especially others who might feel differently, as well as children, and the generations yet unborn.

## INTERNATIONAL LAW

Law is relatively well established at the local, state, and national levels; it is less known and generally less clear at the international level. This may be due partly to the absence of a clearly identified authority to enforce legal agreements and to punish violators. In many ways, nations tend to view themselves as the highest authorities in assessing their own actions. However, a tradition of international law does exist, and on occasion, it has substantial impact. For example, nations customarily enter into legal relations with each other regarding such transnational issues as maritime affairs, international trade, postal service, and (more recently) dealing with hijackers. There is no reason, in theory, for nations not to be equally bound in other respects, even where their supreme military and political interests are at stake.

The "realist" school of international law tends to be skeptical of the validity and potential of legal restrictions on the belligerent behavior of nations. And indeed, when the supreme interests of a national entity are at stake, recourse to international law has not been an effective counter to the overriding justification of *raison d'état (reasons of state)*. Perhaps the clearest state-

*1983. On nuclear morality. *Commentary,* 48–50. Reprinted with permission of the publisher and author.

ment of this view was chronicled by Thucydides, in the *Melian Dialogues,* when mighty Athens announced to the inhabitants of tiny Melos that "the strong do what they have the power to do and the weak accept what they have to accept." This is perhaps the earliest statement of the position that when it comes to international affairs, might makes right. As the political philosopher Michael Walzer has pointed out in our day:

> For as long as men and women have talked about war, they have talked about it in terms of right and wrong. And for almost as long, some among them have derided such talk, called it a charade, insisted that war lies beyond (or beneath) moral judgement. War is a world apart, where life itself is at stake, where human nature is reduced to its elemental forms, where self-interest and necessity prevail. Here men and women do what they must to save themselves and their communities, and morality and law have no place. Inter arma silent leges: *in time of war the law is silent.**

On the other hand, there has developed a large and growing body of principles of international legal conduct, principles that have been widely followed, if not universally. And the violation of these principles has at least sometimes resulted in severe punishments. Even lacking a world authority with clear enforcing power, two or more nations can—and do—regularly agree on important issues relating to national power and sovereignty, promising to abide by such agreements. Typically, in such cases, it is further agreed that any disputes are to be determined by some independent body, such as an international court. The nations are then party to a legal agreement and are subject to the conditions to which they have agreed. This applies to international treaties, conventions, declarations, and protocols, although of course problems may arise when one side or the other refuses to be bound by the agreement, and when no enforcing authority exists.

In addition to these formal contractual agreements between nations, another source of international law is recognized, although it is more controversial. This is, simply, whatever has become customary and accepted standards for international conduct. After World War II, for example, the victorious Allies con-

*1977. *Just and Unjust Wars*. New York: Basic Books. Reprinted with permission of the publisher.

vened the International Military Tribunal at Nuremberg, Germany, to prosecute many Nazi officials for alleged war crimes, violations of international law based on the norms and expectations of appropriate international behavior, even in the absence of explicit legal obligations and treaties.

The International Military Tribunal at Nuremberg recognized three classes of war crimes:

- *Crimes against peace.* Planning, initiating, and/or waging a war of aggression or against international treaties, or conspiring to do so.

- *Crimes against humanity.* Murder, extermination, enslavement, deportation, and other inhumane acts, whether or not in violation of the domestic law of the country within which the act was perpetrated.

- *War crimes.* Violations of the laws or customs of war, including "wanton destruction of cities, towns, or villages, or devastation not justified by military necessity."

The crucial point here is not that war, as such, is illegal or against international law. Wrongly or rightly, nations have had recourse to war throughout history. Rather, there is a growing secular body of concepts and rules of conduct by which people have sought to regulate what is permissible and what is not permissible during war. The Nuremberg tribunal acquitted some Nazi officials; others were executed as war criminals. Similar trials were held for many Japanese military officials. In all, more than 1,000 persons were executed following these proceedings. These events can be interpreted, perhaps cynically, as "victor's justice," merely thinly disguised revenge. Or they can be seen as evidence that the international community is serious about enforcing sanctions relating to permissible and forbidden behavior . . . even during war.

On one level, war is the very opposite of restraint; accordingly, it is meaningless to establish rules for "humane" warfare. Yet, people have historically recognized that the rights of combatants to injure one another (and especially, innocent bystanders) are not unlimited. There have been numerous international conferences seeking to establish rules for the conduct of warfare. The first such meeting resulted in the Declaration of St. Petersburg in 1868, wherein nations agreed that "the right to adopt means of injuring the enemy is not unlimited" and also that "the only legitimate object which States should endeavor to accomplish during a war is to weaken the military forces of the enemy." As a result, it was agreed that weapons causing unnecessary suffering should be outlawed as contrary to the laws of humanity. France, Great Britain, and Russia were among the signatories, which agreed to renounce the use of small-scale exploding projectiles. (Consistent with its policy at the time of avoiding entangling alliances, the United States did not sign.) At the First Hague Peace Conference of 1899, agreements were reached prohibiting expanding (dum-dum) bullets and poison gas. At the Hague Convention of 1907, it was agreed to forbid "the attack or bombardment, by whatever means, of towns, villages (and even individual) dwellings or buildings which are undefended."

But what about nuclear weapons, which of course did not exist before 1945? The 1907 Hague Convention included the so-called **Mertens clause**, which stated that the various rules for "humane warfare" would apply to other technology not yet known or in use at the time of that agreement. According to the Mertens clause, in the event of new developments (such as, presumably, nuclear weapons), "the inhabitants and the belligerents remain under the protection and the rule of the principles of the laws of nations, as they result from the usages established among civilized peoples, from the laws of humanity, and the dictates of public conscience."

The Geneva Protocol of 1925 begins as follows:

*Whereas the use of asphyxiating, poisonous, or other gases, and of all analogous liquids, materials, or devices, has been justly condemned by the general opinion of the civilized world; and whereas the prohibition of such use has been declared in Treaties to which the majority of Powers of the world are Parties; and to the end that this prohibition shall be universally accepted as a part of International Law, binding alike the conscience and the practice of nations . . .*

The mention of "analogous materials or devices" has been interpreted by some people as applying to nuclear weapons (not yet a reality in 1925). This follows the general tradition of applying laws from an earlier time to specific cases not directly mentioned and not even contemplated by the originators of the regulations. The relevance and applicability of the United States Constitution, two centuries after its drafting, for example, depends on such flexibility. On the other hand, it can be maintained that prohibitions of particular weapons cannot be extrapolated from older documents because the weapons are so complex and the details of their

banning so specific that only clearly specified agreements relating to individual cases can be valid.

In 1948, motivated in part by the holocaust of World War II, an UN Genocide Convention defined genocide as specific acts committed with the intent of destroying, in whole or in part, a national, ethnic, racial, or religious group as such. It was also made illegal to conspire, incite, or attempt to commit genocide, or to be in any way complicit in genocide. One year later, at the 1949 Geneva Convention of the International Red Cross, various provisions were agreed serving to protect civilian populations in time of war, and it was further agreed that "the civilian population can never be regarded as a military objective." Although the United States is not currently party to these treaties, more than 130 nations have signed the 1949 convention.

There have been numerous condemnations of nuclear weapons by the United Nations, including General Assembly Resolution 1,653 (in 1961), which declared that "any State using nuclear or thermonuclear weapons is to be considered as violating the Charter of the United Nations, as acting contrary to the law of humanity, and as committing a crime against mankind and civilization." No one seriously expects that in times of severe national emergency, the hands of political leaders will be stayed by treaties or UN resolutions, or even by the details of ethical argumentation. However, such declarations are important not only in helping to make up the body of precepts by which nations are expected to govern their conduct, but also as statements of widespread attitudes and expectations.

It can be argued that by international consensus, nuclear warfare contradicts the fundamental humanitarian principles on which international law rests. However, it should also be noted that the United States has frequently voted against or refused to ratify such agreements, whereas the Soviet Union has typically signed them, often lobbying for explicit prohibitions against the use of nuclear weapons. For example, in 1981 the United States voted against a General Assembly resolution that would have committed all nations to forego the use of nuclear weapons under any circumstances. In signing the Geneva Protocol of 1977, which placed restrictions on the use of conventional weapons against civilian populations, the United States made the explicit reservation that for its part, the rules established "were not intended to have any effect on and do not regulate or prohibit the use of nuclear weapons."

This hesitancy to identify nuclear weapons as illegal may indicate that the United States is less opposed to nuclear war than is the USSR. Alternatively, it may be that the USSR does not scruple to enter into agreements with the cynical intent of violating them if need be but reaping a signatory's propaganda benefits in the meantime. Or it may be a partial result of the fact that the United States relies more heavily on nuclear weapons and the threat of initiating nuclear war (i.e., deterrence) than does the USSR, especially with regard to possible war in Europe.

It is at least debatable whether international treaties can be considered binding on nations that have not signed them: the priority of national sovereignty would suggest that they are not. Moreover, most nuclear weapons states claim explicitly that the use of nuclear weapons, under certain conditions (such as retaliation), would not violate international law. On the other hand, it is not necessary for every citizen to subscribe personally to a law in order for him or her to be bound by it. Germans and Japanese were held responsible by international tribunals for violating standards of humanitarian conduct to which they had not explicitly agreed.

Most nuclear weapons states see no prohibition against the possession of such weapons. But if one assumes that the use of nuclear weapons would be illegal, then any preparation to use them would be a criminal conspiracy. (Supporters of deterrence, of course, maintain that by keeping nuclear weapons, a state is prepared *not* to use them!) Under widely recognized national law, persons may use various means—including noncompliance or even reasonable force—to prevent a crime. This line of argument is often used by those who protest the development, testing, manufacture, storing, and/or deployment of nuclear weapons, sometimes using tactics of civil disobedience. They maintain that nuclear weapons are contrary to international law and that opposition to them is therefore legal and moreover, the only moral recourse.

Not suprisingly, national authorities maintain to the contrary that nuclear weapons are moral in that they help keep the peace. Nuclear deterrence is thus justified by claiming that it serves to prevent a greater crime, aggression and nuclear war. The underlying purpose of law, in fact, is to maintain public order. In the absence of a universally agreed structure for keeping international peace, especially between the superpowers, one view of nuclear weapons is therefore that they are peacekeepers, hence fundamentally lawful.

The Charter of the United Nations enjoins all states to "refrain in their international relations from the threat or use of force against the territorial integrity or political independence of any state. . . ." But this does not preclude the legitimate use of force in self-defense or in preventing greater wrong. It is often difficult, in a basically anarchic world composed of many powerful and independent nations, to distinguish between aggressive and defensive uses of force. Accordingly, supporters of nuclear deterrence claim that there must be a strong presumption favoring the states whose use of force is oriented around self-defense. They also claim that violations of local or national law—for example, by antinuclear protesters—must be dealt with as acts that are illegal and possibly immoral as well.

## Policy Issues

**Should the United States announce a policy of strictly counterforce targeting, because it is more ethical than countercity (or countervalue) targeting?**

**Yes:** It is wrong to aim military force at civilians. By targeting the aspects of the USSR that the Soviet leadership values most, the US would also be most likely to deter the Soviets from instituting hostilities. In addition, the US might have some coercive leverage that would not otherwise be available, as well as a more credible deterrent posture.

**No:** It is indeed wrong to target civilians, but in fact, it is even more wrong to target weapons, since this could be destabilizing and could lead to nuclear war, especially during an international crisis. Just as there is no ethical way to blind babies, there is no ethical way to plan to use nuclear weapons, so we may as well do it in the way least likely to lead to war.

**Are the niceties of *in bello* restraints meaningful once war has broken out?**

**No:** War is violent, cruel, and awful. As the great Prussian strategist Karl Von Clausewitz pointed out, it is absurd it introduce a principle of moderation into such business. Moreover, knowledge that one party is likely to be restrained might make recourse to war more likely. A British military official, commenting on the firebombing of Dresden, observed:

> It is not so much this or the other means of making war that is immoral or inhuman. What is immoral is war itself. Once the full-scale war has broken out it can never be humanized or civilized, and if one side attempted to do so it would most likely be defeated. So long as we resort to war to settle differences between nations, so long will we have to endure the horrors, barbarities, and excesses war brings with it. That, to me, is the lesson of Dresden.*

Our goal must be to prevent all war, not just nuclear war, and for better or worse, the threat that any superpower confrontation might escalate to nuclear war serves to deter each side from initiating such a confrontation. As long as our adversary knows that war will result in his certain destruction, that adversary will be deterred. If we reassure the USSR that we will refrain from a nuclear response, we virtually invite a provocation.

**Yes:** All is not fair in love or in war. Restraints on humane conduct, even during war, have been helpful in controlling some of our penchants for violent excess. Now that nuclear war carries the prospect of destroying entire societies and perhaps human life on earth, we have a special responsibility to exert whatever moral leverage we can to see that human beings stop short of the final abyss. Some people survived the destruction of Dresden; it may well be that no one will survive World War III and therefore, the stakes are simply too high. As the American Catholic bishops put it in the pastoral letter of 1983:

> We do not perceive any situation in which the deliberate initiation of nuclear warfare, on however restricted a scale, can be morally justified. Nonnuclear attacks by another state must be resisted by other than nuclear means. Therefore, a serious moral obligation exists to develop nonnuclear defensive strategies as rapidly as possible.

### Does Christianity require a definite rejection of the prospect of war in general and of nuclear war in particular?

**Yes:** As theologian John Yoder sees it:

> Christians whose loyalty to the Prince of Peace puts them out of step with today's nationalistic world, because of a willingness to love their nation's friends but not to hate the nation's enemies, are not unrealistic dreamers who think that by their objections all wars will end. The unrealistic dreamers are rather the soldiers who think that they can put an end to wars by preparing for just one more. . . . Christians love their enemies not because they think the enemies are wonderful people, nor because they believe that love is sure to conquer those enemies. . . . The Christian loves his or her enemies because God does, and God commands His followers to do so; that is the only reason, and that is enough.†

An international religious convocation held in 1982 addressed itself specifically to the threat of nuclear war, and concluded:

> We have different points of view on realities. We uncompromisingly adhere to our different religious convictions. But in spite of these differences we can be together in asserting the many things that we all hold dear. . . . A new factor that exists in the world today is that for the first time in history a nuclear catastrophe threatens all life and that a nuclear war can only lead to a universal catastrophe. Therefore our religions all agree on this very obvious point: there can never and under no circumstances be any justification for a nuclear war, which represents the gravest threat to mankind today.

**No:** The British theologian Edward Norman expresses another viewpoint, as follows:

> The development of the Old Covenant between God and the Jewish people was characterized by military struggle to gain possession of the promised land. . . . Christendom, for its part, has always employed military strategy in order to

---

*Air Marshall Sir Robert Saundby quoted in D. Irving. 1963. *The Destruction of Dresden*. New York: Holt, Rinehart & Winston.

†J. Yoder. 1982. Living the disarmed life. In J. Wallis, ed. *Waging Peace*. New York: Harper & Row. Reprinted with permission of the publisher.

*preserve its values and to extend its boundaries. . . . It is not even clear whether the pursuit of peace is, as is now so often asserted, actually a fundamental Christian principle. The "peace" of the Scriptures was inner peace, interior serenity. . . . But it was not "peace" in the global sense; it was not regarded as a Christian principle that peace between nations, in the great cosmic battle of good and evil, was a priority over "righteousness." Indeed, the Scriptures speak of righteousness as an active condition of things, which men seek to preserve in the real world of contests and moral rivalries—a world in which war has always played a part. . . . As far as the question of nuclear defense is concerned, the problem is of some moment, for those Christians who do approve of the practice of nuclear deterrence are precisely those who have some sense of Christianity's spiritual values and of their unique claim to preservation . . . mankind has inventive genius endowed by God which he has used in a flawed manner due to his inherent frailty as a spiritual being. He creates, in the one moment of his being, the mechanics and medicines of healing, and in the next, thermonuclear weapons. This is not an aberration but a characteristic of Man. Warfare is as much a part of his pursuit of genius as great art, or whatever. It is token both of his ability to discern ultimate purposes and of the crudity of his delivery. Fallen men need the coercion that government supplies, and the international coercion that in the end entails war. In this scheme of things Christians are caught up.* *

### Are nation-states sovereign in their behavior relative to nuclear weapons?

**Yes:** World government may be desirable, but it is a long way off. Until such a time, there is no better recourse than to rely on the behavioral norms agreed by each nation; in this respect Americans are fortunate to be inhabiting a nation whose principles are established by democracy, rule of law, and informed by deep-seated religious convictions as well.

**No:** A welcome trend in international law and human affairs has been to restrain the sovereign prerogative of nations. This is especially important with the advent of nuclear weapons. As attorney Elliot Meyrowitz has written:

> *For centuries* raison d'état *was used to cloak horrendous crimes. The world witnessed the culmination of this idea in the justification of the policies of Hitler's Germany. Yet are there not values more important than honoring sovereign prerogative? Were . . . [such] legal reasoning to be applied to the policies of Nazi Germany, those policies would enjoy the status of a sovereign right.†*

National sovereignty cannot be used to justify the extinction of the human species.

---

## KEY TERMS

Just War
*jus ad bellum*
*jus in bello*
principle of proportionality
doctrine of double effect

principle of discrimination
noncombatant immunity
declaratory policy
action policy
Mertens clause

## STUDY QUESTIONS

1. Distinguish between the pacifist, "realist," and Holy War religious traditions.

2. What are the major components of Just War doctrine?

3. In what ways does the principle of proportionality apply to both *ad bellum* and *in bello* considerations?

---

\*1983. E. Norman, The churches and the nuclear debate. In E. Norman, ed. *Ethics and Nuclear Arms.* London: Institute for European Defence and Strategic Studies. Reprinted with permission of the publisher.

†1985. Nuclear weapons are illegal threats. *Bulletin of the Atomic Scientists, 41,* 35–37.

4. Why is there generally more debate about the ethics of nuclear deterrence than about the ethics of nuclear war?

5. What is the ethical irony regarding counterforce versus countercity targeting?

6. What is the relevance or irrelevance of the Mertens clause to the legality of nuclear war?

7. Protesters against nuclear weapons sometimes base their legal defense on international law. Try to summarize their arguments.

8. Summarize the arguments that might be made by a prosecutor seeking to convict such protesters.

## ADDITIONAL READINGS

Cohen, Arnes, and Steven Lee (Eds.). 1984. *Nuclear Weapons and the Future of Humanity,* Totowa, NJ: Rowman and Allenheld: A collection of papers emphasizing the philosophical issues raised by the specter of nuclear war.

Levine, Herbert M., and David Carlton (Eds.). 1986. The *Nuclear Arms Race Debated.* New York: McGraw-Hill. A useful compendium of alternative viewpoints, including the major provisions of the US Catholic bishops' pastoral letter.

Ramsey, Paul. 1983. *The Just War.* Lanham, MD: University Press of America: A recent version of an important and influential work by one of the most respected advocates of the ethics of nuclear deterrence.

Sterba, James P. (Ed). 1985. *The Ethics of War and Nuclear Deterrence.* Belmont, CA: Wadsworth. A recent compilation of ethical and religious arguments regarding nuclear war and nuclear deterrence; includes a balanced treatment of many different perspectives.

Walzer, Michael. 1977. *Just and Unjust Wars.* New York: Basic Books. A modern classic, examining the Just War doctrine and its various permutations, both religious and secular, from ancient times up to and including nuclear deterrence.

# 14 Nuclear Psychology

*Whether science—and indeed civilization in general—can survive depends upon psychology, that is to say, it depends upon what human beings desire.*
Bertrand Russell

When we examine the psychological dimensions of the arms race and nuclear war, we encounter a paradox. On the one hand, psychological issues are diffuse and difficult to grasp firmly, lacking in clear-cut data (although not lacking, as we shall see, in theories!). "Nuclear psychology" is therefore easy to dismiss, since it is less real than the weapons themselves, less obviously relevant than the political process, less definitive than strategic policy. But on the other hand, it can be argued that the entire problem of nuclear weapons is a problem of human perceptions, human attitudes, and ultimately, human behavior. In this chapter, we shall not seek to review the abundant literature on human aggressiveness or the psychology of war; rather, we shall focus on some of the aspects of psychology that are peculiarly relevant to the arms race and especially, nuclear war. Our understanding of human psychology, and our even more limited grasp of nuclear psychology, may be the weakest link in our search for nuclear literacy. Ironically, however, this link may be the most crucial.

In a sense, the present chapter is the least "balanced" of any in this book, because the relevance of psychological processes to the arms race and nuclear war is itself controversial. Attempts to apply psychology to the arms race have, thus far, tended to be overwhelmingly from the dovish perspective. Nuclear hawks, by contrast, generally do not blame the arms race on psychological processes, perceptions, or misperceptions, but rather, on the Soviet threat. If this view is correct, and if the arms race and nuclear war are problems thrust on us by the Soviet menace, then it is not so much a psychological phenomenon as one of politics, military power, and strategy. There may, of course, be legitimate psychological issues raised by this per-

spective, insofar as deterrence itself is a psychological strategy—(e.g., How much does it take to deter a ruthless enemy?). And there may be other psychological dimensions as well—for example, the idea that human beings are innately aggressive; accordingly, the Soviets can be expected to behave aggressively (since that is how people have presumably always been) and the US must be prepared to respond in kind, or at least to deter them. Nuclear hawks, however, are more inclined to use the language of psychology to account for the views of those who oppose the arms race. Such opposition, for example, has been attributed to the presumed susceptibility of members of the peace movement to Soviet propaganda and disinformation, perhaps a lack of adequate patriotic zeal and love for the United States, perhaps an inordinate, neurotic fear of nuclear war, and/or perhaps a degree of straightforward cowardice that makes some people reluctant to maintain and if necessary, to use adequate military force to deter the evil Soviet empire, and if need be, to defend themselves and others.

It is not our task here to assess the validity of these notions, which must be decided by each student, and each citizen, individually. But we note in passing that such ideas have not given rise to a body of psychological thought. This may be (1) because they are unworthy, (2) because of a lack of attention to such issues by psychologists (perhaps owing to a dovish bias on their part), or (3) because they reflect common sense, hence make further "psychologizing" unnecessary. When we consider the arms race as a psychological problem, we tend to delegitimize the arms race itself and the underlying US-Soviet political conflict. By psychologizing the arms race, we are likely to see it as less a problem in itself and more a creator of second-order metaproblems that lend themselves to psychological interpretation. Students should accordingly be forewarned.

## IMPRESSIONS OF DANGER

> *It does not do to leave a live dragon out of your calculations, if you live near him. (J.R.R. Tolkien,* The Hobbit.*)*

It seems that most people, wherever they live, leave nuclear war out of their calculations. Sigmund Freud pointed out that every human being lives under a fearsome personal cloud: the certainty of his or her eventual death. To make this tolerable, we practice **denial,** the mental process of refusing to confront facts that would cause us pain or otherwise disrupt our daily lives. It may well be that for large numbers of people in the late twentieth century, a similar process of denial operates with regard to the nuclear threat. It is exceedingly painful to contemplate nuclear war; accordingly, most people do not. Unless directly confronted with gruesome evidence or dire predictions, they tend to go on with their lives as though there were no potential mushroom clouds on the horizon.

Other factors are likely involved here. Pain, after all, indicates that the organism is subject to danger. Thus, the avoidance of pain is a primitive and appropriate behavior pattern. By avoiding pain, we generally avoid danger; since pain can be emotional as well as physical, we may be inclined to avoid the emotional pain of thinking about nuclear war. This may contribute further to denial.

In addition, psychologists identify the phenomenon of **habituation,** or learning not to respond to something, which is the simplest form of learning. The stimuli that normally impinge on a living creature are of practical significance insofar as they indicate that something is about to happen. If nothing happens after awhile, the stimulus can readily be ignored, and it typically is. Thus, we quickly stop hearing the hum of a refrigerator, and we become insensitive to a new odor, as long as there is no significant change, and no obvious consequence. To some degree, most of us appear to have habituated to the presence of thousands of nuclear weapons. Although there is some correlation between the growth of arsenals and the growth of antinuclear sentiment, the latter seems more related to readily apparent events, such as atmospheric testing or the emplacement of Euromissiles (Fig. 14.1).

Nuclear weapons cannot generally be seen, felt, heard, or smelled, and so, for most people, it is as though they do not exist. This lack of psychological reality has been facilitated by governmental policy "neither to confirm nor deny" the presence of nuclear weapons, anywhere. Officially justified as necessary to deny information to potential adversaries, including would-be nuclear terrorists, this policy also contributes—intentionally or otherwise—to the psychological unreality of nuclear weapons themselves.

This unreal aspect of nuclear weapons is further reinforced, ironically, by their power. Thus, human psychology is attuned to the intensities typically encountered during everyday life on the planet Earth: a world of medium-sized objects moving at medium speeds and medium temperatures. In short, our psychology is adjusted to a Newtonian environment, whereas the nuclear world is Einsteinian. We can understand 212 degrees Fahrenheit, the boiling point of water, but not 100 million degrees, the inside of a thermonuclear explosion. We can, at some level, understand the death of one person, or a family, or perhaps even an entire village. But we are out of our psychological element when asked to contemplate the death of millions, or the possibility of planetary extinction. To some degree, it is not so much that we are unwilling to make the mental leap needed to confer psychological reality to the threat of nuclear war, but rather that we are unable to do so.

Such tendencies are reinforced by a widespread human reluctance to think about anything negative. "The more people can avoid thinking about negatives (like there being no more fuel for cars or a nuclear holocaust)" wrote social psychologist Charles Osgood,

> *—particularly when they seem remote in time and are highly symbolic in nature—the less likely they are to try to do anything about them until it's too late. Seated in the backyard on a nice spring day, watching the kids at play, and sipping a beer, the Neanderthal within us simply cannot conceive of the trees suddenly blackened and the voices of the children stilled—or there being no more beer.*

The impression, or misimpression, of danger in the Nuclear Age is also influenced by the psychological phenomenon of the **just-noticeable difference.** In a quiet room, for example, a very soft sound—less than

---

*1981. GRIT: A strategy for survival in mankind's nuclear age? In W. Epstein, and B. Feld, eds. New Directions in Disarmament. *New York: Praeger.*

one decibel—can be detected. However, when the background sound level is 100 decibels, an increase to 101 decibels or even to 105 decibels, may be undetectable: that is, the increase is less than the just-noticeable difference. Obviously, perception of a change depends on the type and intensity of background stimulation. It has therefore been argued that during the late 1940s, when there were only a few dozen nuclear weapons in the world, the addition of a few thousand, or even a few hundred, would have been readily noted as a very dramatic event. During the 1980s, however, with the holdings of both sides totaling more than 50,000 such weapons, even large additions to the superpowers' arsenals barely make a just-noticeable difference.

## IMPRESSIONS OF SECURITY

Human beings crave and seek security. Early in life we find security in a mother-infant or parent-infant bond; as we grow older, we associate ourselves with peer groups and larger social entities: tribes, villages, nations. A useful distinction can be made between **security** (the psychological perception of safety) and **safety,** which is the condition of being protected from possible harm. The phenomenon of nationalism has been interpreted as an exaggerated susceptibility to primitive security-seeking impulses. It is arguable, however, whether in the Nuclear Age, national identification increases or decreases the actual safety of individual citizens, especially since it is the nation-state, not the individual, that possesses nuclear weapons, and it is typically "national security" that is announced as the ultimate goal of national policies. Supporters of nationalism, on the other hand, point to its connection to such laudable human emotions as love, compassion, devotion, and self-sacrifice, emphasizing also that freedom and liberty have often been achieved by wars of national liberation.

Once the individual has made the association of self with nation, he or she is likely to personalize international relations as analogous to interpersonal squabbles. Psychoanalysts have even suggested that the modern obsession with nuclear missiles may reflect, at least in part, their phallic nature; worry about whose missiles are bigger has been interpreted similarly. Note that such transference would be particularly likely after individuals have made the association of self with nation, and moreover, it should be especially prevalent among men rather than women (which it is).

There is also a strong tendency to attribute wholly benevolent motives to one's own nation (as people typ-

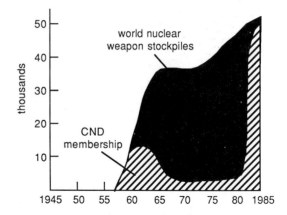

**FIGURE 14.1 Changes in membership of CND, a British antinuclear organization, compared with growth of world nuclear weapons stockpiles. Antinuclear membership increased rapidly along with increases in nuclear arsenals in the late 1950s, and again in the early 1980s, but declined dramatically in the mid-1960s following the Partial Test Ban Treaty and throughout the 1970s, even though world nuclear weapons remained high and even increased during that time.** (Modified from SIPRI, 1985.)

ically rationalize their own actions) and to be readily motivated by such emotions as fear and pride, expanded to reflect alleged threats or insults to one's nation, just as people commonly respond to threats or insults to one's family or one's self (Fig. 14.2). Hence, Soviet boastfulness during the Khrushchev era and the taking of American hostages in Iran during 1979 led to strong feelings of personal anger and frustration among the American people. Similarly, it appears that Soviet humiliation during the Cuban missile crisis led to a determination on the part of the USSR not to be pushed around in the future.

The tendency to accept and often adore national leaders can also be described as the exaggeration of primitive security-seeking tendencies, notably the human inclination to revere one's parents. Just as children feel more secure (and often are more safe) when they entrust their lives to benevolent, loving parents, citizens of a nuclear-armed nation apparently feel more secure when they entrust nuclear policy to national leaders who are perceived as wise and benevolent. Whether as a consequence the citizens actually are more safe, once again, can be debated. In any event, there is a strong psychological tendency to "leave it to the experts."

**FIGURE 14.2 President Reagan and Defense Secretary Weinberger flank Congressional Medal of Honor winner Roy Benavidez during a White House award ceremony. Political and military leaders, especially those of right-wing inclination, traditionally extol the military virtues of patriotism and heroic self-sacrifice.** (Courtesy of the US Department of Defense.)

Psychiatrist/psychologist Jerome Frank has written: "When humans are faced with an entirely new and unprecedented problem, such as the abrupt emergence of nuclear weapons, they try to make it appear like a familiar one and handle it by methods that worked in the past." We might call this **"Procrustean thinking,"** after the mythical Greek highwayman who used to force people onto his iron bed, stretching them if they were too short, or amputating limbs if they were too tall. It can be argued that national leaders are being Procrustean when they think of nuclear weapons as simply a larger form of artillery, or as the World War II blockbuster magnified many times. Such attitudes help give rise to the further perception that nuclear weapons can be used just as conventional weapons were used in the past: to obtain security, to get one's way, and if war breaks out, to win.

Political scientist Hans Morgenthau wrote about what he saw as the dangerous tendency to "conventionalize" nuclear weapons, to think of them as conventional weapons, only larger, more powerful, therefore, more desirable. Similarly, Albert Einstein noted that "the splitting of the atom has changed everything except our way of thinking, and hence, we drift toward unparalleled catastrophe." If human beings derived security in the past from accumulating more weapons, it is not surprising that they are inclined to do so still, no less in the Nuclear Age than in the age of bows and

arrows, or gunpowder. Doves argue that such a tendency is a dangerous delusion, since everything (but our way of thinking) has changed, and accumulating more nuclear weapons makes us less safe rather than more. Hawks, by contrast, argue not only that it might be lethal to fall behind one's opponent, but also that human perceptions being what they are, it is crucially important not to be perceived as having fallen behind.

This leads us to one of the few psychological concepts typically embraced by pronuclear hawks: what has been called perception theory.

## PERCEPTION THEORY

According to the advocates of perception theory, it may well be true that nuclear weapons are new and utterly unconventional, and that as a result, traditional concepts of equality or superiority may not apply. However, it is argued that the important thing is not reality as such, but rather, the way reality is perceived. And, according to **perception theory,** nuclear reality is widely perceived as not differing substantially from the reality of conventional weapons, a reality in which superiority was a realistic goal and more weapons generally brought greater influence and, ultimately, greater security. In his 1975 fiscal report to Congress, for example, Defense Secretary James Schlesinger said: "There must be essential equivalence between the strategic forces of the United States and the USSR—an equivalence perceived not only by ourselves but by the Soviet Union and third audiences as well." He further emphasized that there is "an important relationship between the political behavior of many leaders of other nations and what they perceive the strategic nuclear balance to be." Schlesinger concluded that "to the degree that we wish to influence the perception of others, we must take appropriate steps (by their lights) in the design of the strategic forces."

Building weapons beyond those needed for deterrence can, according to this view, serve a very important psychological purpose: creating the perception of strength and resolve. Large, threatening, ground-based missiles (a Soviet specialty, as we have seen) are therefore especially important, not so much for their alleged counterforce capability, but for their visibility and the degree to which they contribute to an image of power that might be intimidating.

The distinction between reality and perception, and the importance of the latter, was further underlined by Defense Secretary Harold Brown in his 1979 report to Congress:

*The United States and its allies must be free from any coercion and intimidation that could result from perceptions of an overall imbalance or particular asymmetries in nuclear forces. . . . Insistence on essential equivalence guards against any danger that the Soviets might be seen as superior—even if the perception is not technically justified.*

Although advocates of perception theory generally recognize, for example, that neither side has a first-strike capability and that neither side is ahead in any meaningful sense, they argue that we must adjust our nuclear weapons programs not to reality, but to perceptions of reality . . . because these are in effect, the real realities. The argument is that in the field of international affairs, perceptions tend to produce reality; hence we are obliged to treat perceptions—even misguided ones—as though they were real. If we fail to do so, we might lose the support of our allies, as well as possibly inviting aggression from our opponents. Perception theory was invoked by the Scowcroft Commission, appointed by President Reagan to advise on US strategic nuclear weapons. This commission recommended the deployment of the MX missile even though this weapon could not be justified on its technical, stra-

tegic, or military merits, precisely because of the belief that failure to deploy the MX would result in a perception that the United States was unwilling to compete militarily with the USSR. The commission stated that the missile was needed as a "demonstration of national resolve," and a way of proving to the Soviet Union and our allies that we mean business: "The overall perception of strategic imbalance . . . has been reasonably regarded as destabilizing and as a weakness in the overall fabric of deterrence."

A similar justification has been suggested for the NATO Euromissile deployments, even by officials who publicly doubt the military utility of such weapons: cruise missiles and Pershing IIs are needed, they claim, so that the world will perceive that NATO is militarily equal to the Warsaw Pact in medium-range, ground-based missiles. This holds even though such equality may be meaningless given the saturation parity of both sides' strategic forces; as we have seen, such deployments may also be needed to give the West Germans the perception that the US is committed to their defense. Writing about the Euromissile controversy in 1983, former Defense Secretary McNamara commented that "the Europeans are operating on a misperception, but as long as it is held, it must be treated as a reality."

Defenders of perception theory are also likely to be impatient with antinuclear critics who point out the absurdities of overkill, for example. According to perception theory, it is naive to ignore differing levels of overkill, or differing missile sizes between the superpowers, because people's perceptions are in fact influenced by such comparisons. Perception theorists thus typically have such respect for certain nuclear illusions that they end up defending and even actively promoting them.

Psychologist Steven Kull, in an article titled "Nuclear Nonsense" appearing in the journal *International Security,* offered the following analyses of the consequences of perception theory:

*In international power relations, perceptions of the superpower military balance are the coinage of international affairs even though all the key parties involved seem to recognize that the coins are counterfeit. The situation resembles nothing so much as a drawing-room comedy. All of the key characters know a certain secret— that strategic asymmetries are militarily irrelevant in an age of overkill—but because they think that others do not know the secret they act* *as if they do not know the secret either. A farcical quality emerges as all the characters, more or less unconsciously, collude to establish a norm of behavior based on a failure to recognize the secret. What is particularly striking, though, is that when the main character—in this case the Defense Department—is informed that, in fact, everybody knows the secret, it stiffens its resolve to maintain the charade.\**

The argument applies, for example, with regard to war-winning doctrine and capacity: if the Soviets had a theoretical war-winning capability, they might use it to intimidate us. If this fails, perhaps they would threaten to intimidate us; that is, they might be *perceived* as able to intimidate us, even if they were not able to do so in fact!

In his 1984 annual report, Defense Secretary Weinberger stated:

*History has shown us all too often that conflicts occur when one state believes it has a sufficiently greater military capability than another and attempts to exploit that superior strength through intimidation or conflict with the weaker state.*

Perception theory has its weaknesses, however, beyond its air of unreality. For one, the presumed need to augment military forces (to engender the perception that one is ahead, or at least, not behind) often requires that political leaders claim publicly that the United States is in fact, behind, to stimulate Congress to appropriate the requested funds. But this "poor-mouthing" process itself goes against the recommendations of perception theory, which would prescribe that if anything, leaders should behave with swagger and perhaps even braggadacio, to contribute to the perception that we are strong, not weak. It can also be argued that instead of playing the "perception game," leaders who know better have an obligation to try educating their allies, their opponents, and also their own populace regarding the likely errors of misperception in the Nuclear Age. Although perceptions do in fact influence reality, this does not necessarily mean that we must play this psychological game; it might even be possible to rectify false and dangerous perceptions by—of all things!—telling the truth.

---

*1985. Nuclear nonsense. *Foreign Policy, 58,* Spring 1985, 28–52. Copyright 1985 by the Carnegie Endowment for International Peace. Reprinted with permission of the publisher.

## MIRROR IMAGING

Perceptions play a large role in the nuclear arms race, beyond perception theory in the narrow sense. Thus, psychologist Urie Bronfenbrenner has reported a phenomenon known as **mirror imaging,** in which citizens of the US and the USSR maintain inverted but otherwise identical perceptions of each other.

On the individual level, Americans tend to see their own nation as overwhelmingly defensive and righteous, and the Soviet Union as aggressive and malign, whereas for most Soviet citizens, perceptions of defenders and aggressors are reversed. Americans believe that the Soviet government exploits and deludes its populace and that the actions of the Soviet government do not accurately reflect the will of the citizens; Soviets believe the same about the United States. Recently, Americans have heard often about the Soviet invasion of Afghanistan, whereas Soviet citizens heard that the Red Army was going to the aid of a neighbor in distress, at the request of the Afghan government; similarly, in the 1960s and 1970s Soviet citizens heard about an American invasion of Vietnam, whereas to many Americans, the United States was responding to a friendly ally in distress. As noted above, the psychological term for this phenomenon is "mirror imaging."

On the governmental level, mirror imaging is shown in booklets titled *Soviet Military Power* and *Whence the Threat to Peace,* published by the US Department of Defense and the USSR Ministry of Defense, respectively. Each focuses on the military forces of the other, painting a picture of the other as aggressive, threatening, and dangerously powerful (Figs. 14.3 and 14.4).

Closely related to mirror imaging is the phenomenon of **cognitive dissonance,** which is manifested in a symptom known as the **strain to consistency.** People who are experiencing cognitive dissonance try very hard to maintain consistent images, to avoid the intellectually painful position of simultaneously subscribing to incongruent views. However, when people must strain to impose consistency on beliefs that are not mutually consistent, they tend to have a restricted worldview, in which heroes (Us) and villains (Them) are easily identified. For example, when the United States deployed medium-range Jupiter and Thor missiles in Turkey and Great Britain during the early 1960s, the government called the action "defensive," but the USSR's attempt to emplant medium-range missiles in Cuba shortly thereafter was considered to be intolerably provocative.

Cognitive dissonance and the strain to consistency also make images of the enemy resistant to modi-

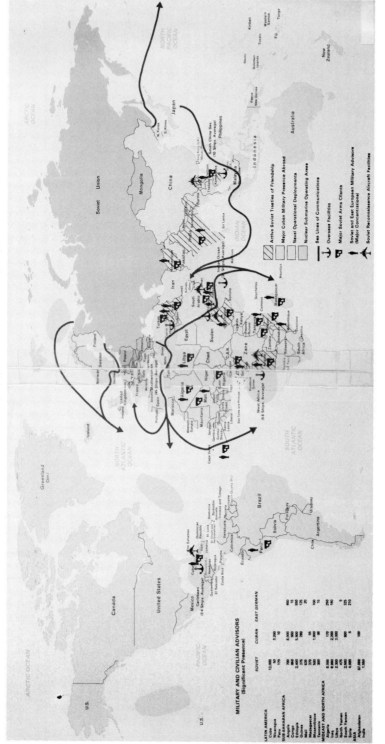

SOVIET GLOBAL POWER PROJECTION

**FIGURE 14.3 "Soviet global power projection."** (Illustration from the US government publication *Soviet Military Power*.)

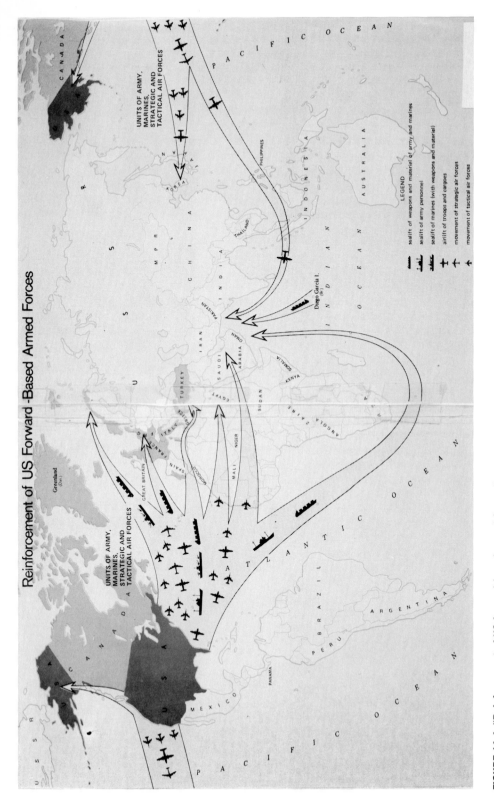

**FIGURE 14.4 "Reinforcement of US forward-based armed forces."** (Illustration from the English-language Soviet government publication *Whence the Threat to Peace.*)

fication by experience. For example, it has become widely assumed that any refusal of an American proposal by the USSR demonstrates Soviet intransigence, whereas Soviet acceptance is taken to show that the proposal confers a one-sided advantage on them.

In short, according to theorists of this persuasion, mirror imaging combined with the strain to consistency results in a mental set whereby We are good and right, They are bad and wrong. Moreover, this impression is necessarily confirmed by whatever We and They subsequently do, even if our behavior is virtually identical.

In the past two decades, social psychologists have been concerned with what they call **attribution theory,** which involves analysis of the factors to which people ascribe their own behavior and that of others. There is a tendency to make a distinction between one's own motivation for a particular action, and the motivation of someone else, even when the behaviors in question are identical. This may lead to the **attribution error,** whereby each nation excuses its own unsavory behavior on the basis of the press of external events, while asserting that the behavior of its opponent reflects that nation's evil nature or nasty intentions. Thus, the US claims that it does not want nuclear weapons but is forced into having them by the Soviet Union. The USSR's nuclear arsenal, by contrast, is not seen as a response to the US; rather, it is attributed to Soviet aggressiveness, desire to intimidate, and so on.

However, many qualified observers argue that there really are important differences between the behavior of the US and the USSR, and that no amount of psychological theorizing can obscure this fact or apologize for the persistent immorality of the other side. Is this a further confirmation of the potency of mirror-imaging, or a legitimate statement of the way things really are?

## DEHUMANIZATION AND THE IMAGE OF THE ENEMY

In the languages of certain nontechnological peoples, the same words are used for "tribe" and for "human being." As a result, because members of a different tribe are not defined as being people, they are in a sense dehumanized. All societies have rules that govern what is and is not permissible within the group: killing, for example, except under very special circumstances, is nearly always prohibited. Once the psychological process of dehumanization has taken hold, however, such prohibitions cease to apply. Members

of an "in group" are able to behave toward members of the "out group" in ways that would not otherwise be acceptable. The phenomenon of **in-group amity, out-group enmity** is well established throughout most of the human species.

It has been proposed that a similar process operates in technological societies as well, especially during war and periods of national antagonism. Propaganda tends to caricature the opposing side, picturing leaders, soldiers, and even common citizens as inhuman or subhuman. The result is a heightened antagonism and quite possibly, a loosening of restraints with respect to the use of lethal force.

For better or worse, such images are also susceptible to change. Thus, for example, a Gallup poll during World War II revealed that the adjectives preferred by Americans to describe the Germans and Japanese included "warlike," "treacherous," and "cruel," none of which were applied to the Soviets, who were our allies at the time. By 1966, West Germany and Japan were US allies, and none of these terms were used in describing their citizens; however, both "treacherous" and "warlike" were applied to the "Russians." The Chinese had also been our allies during World War II and were described favorably by contemporary respondents, but by 1966 they were our enemies and were "warlike," "treacherous," and "sly." Shortly after President Nixon's visit to China and the normalizing of US-Sino relations, however, the Chinese became "hard-working," "practical," "intelligent," and "artistic."

The psychologist Carl Jung emphasized that people tend especially to hate and fear what they cannot tolerate in themselves. Accordingly, he claimed that human beings are likely to project their "dark side" onto others and to then respond negatively to such images.

## THE SANITIZATION OF NUCLEAR LANGUAGE

People use words to signify and to communicate. But words have many other roles as well, sometimes intended and sometimes not. When discussing nuclear weapons and nuclear war, we have no choice but to use words, just as when discussing anything! However, words are rarely neutral in their effect; at times, for example, they heighten emotion, and at others they tend to obscure it. It has been argued that the language associated with nuclear weaponry does the latter. Thus, nuclear language is sometimes called "nukespeak," after "newspeak" in George Orwell's novel *1984.* Like Orwell's caricature, nuclear language has been criticized as being dishonest and dangerous, and also artifically sanitizing in that it tends to drain the horror from the subject. This in turn encourages people to approach the issue of nuclear weapons and nuclear war intellectually, ignoring other important avenues such as feeling.

The following list includes some prominent examples of nuclear language:

| Nuclear language | Blunt language |
|---|---|
| Nuclear exchange | Nuclear war |
| Countervalue | City destroying |
| Collateral damage | Killing of innocent civilians |
| Delivery vehicle | Bomber or missile |
| Reentry vehicle | Nuclear warhead |
| Hardware | Weapons |
| Taking out a target | Destroying a target |

Shortly after the end of World War II, the War Department was officially changed to the Department of Defense; it is easy to oppose war but difficult to object to defense. There may be as much difference between a "defense budget" and a "military budget" as there is between "national security" and "national suicide."

Defenders of nuclear language point out that every discipline has its own vocabulary, necessary to maintain precision of thought. Furthermore, they maintain that when it comes to nuclear weapons and nuclear war, thought is precisely what is needed; therefore, it is appropriate to employ language that is precise, intellectual, and not throbbing with emotion. Indeed, throughout this book we have used many examples of nuclear language, in part to introduce students to words and phrases they are likely to encounter and in part because it is easier to discuss such material in cerebral rather than emotional terms. To some extent, therefore, "nukespeak" may be unavoidable, and even desirable. Critics point out, however, that one of the dangers of such use (some would say, abuse) of language is that it permits—even encourages—people to deal calmly and coolly with possibilities that should instead be handled with dread. In any event, you may want to keep track of nuclear jargon, to be readily able to translate it into blunter language.

## CRISIS BEHAVIOR

We have already reviewed some of the possible ways in which nuclear war could occur, with special emphasis on accidents, including issues of human fallibility—

which may be exaggerated by drug and alcohol abuse. It should be emphasized that no battery of psychological tests can guarantee that a given person will not, at some time in the future, behave irrationally. Does, then, the nuclear weapons regime, as currently constituted, demand perfection? In a sense, it does not, in that there are multiple levels of interactive checking and cross-checking, designed as backups to prevent accidents or human error. But in another sense, nothing less than perfection is acceptable as the end product, since a single failure could be catastrophic.

Another appropriate area for psychological concern is the behavior of people, especially political and military leaders, during crisis situations. Studies of the behavior of decision makers during international crises have attempted to reveal the dynamics of such periods as the months immediately preceding World War I, and more recently, the much briefer Cuban missile crisis. The former is often cited as an example of events "getting out of hand." Looking with hindsight at the events of 1914, one is entitled to blame the pathology of the situation itself, rather than a pathology of individuals. It is also clear, however, that in times of crisis, acting under stress, human beings tend to behave in ways that are less rational and more rigid than otherwise. At such times, there is often a stubborn refusal, or even inability, to consider evidence that runs counter to preconceptions. For example, it has been suggested that immediately before World War I, Kaiser Wilhelm ignored reports from the German ambassador in London that Britain was prepared to join the war. Similarly, certain US officials seem to have ignored indications of Japan's impending attack on Pearl Harbor in 1941, just as, the previous June, Stalin had been insensitive to evidence suggesting an imminent German attack on the Soviet Union.

The Cuban missile crisis, by contrast, is typically seen as an example of carefully exercised crisis behavior in which accurate information was monitored and acted upon, and the situation was prevented from going out of control, because of a combination of cool-headedness, willingness to consider alternative options, and recognition of the importance of providing the other side with some opportunity to save face.

Certain common crisis patterns have been identified:

1. Time pressure is generally felt to be acute.

2. Anxiety is raised by the perception that the stakes involved are very high.

3. Decisions must often be made on the basis of very limited information.

4. Very few or limited options are perceived to be available.

5. The decision makers are often operating with very little sleep or rest.

It seems likely that during nuclear crises, all these conditions would exist, if anything in exaggerated form compared to the situations that obtained before 1945. "Substandard performance by decision makers in crisis situations is particularly common," writes political scientist Daniel Frei.

> More than two decades of crisis research have provided ample evidence of all kinds of individual and organizational failures, such as misperceptions, erratic behavior under stress, the improper handling of information, the escalation of hostilities by mirror-image mechanisms . . . the failure to implement decisions due to their overwhelming complexity, confusion due to organizational bottlenecks and the inflexibility of standard operating procedures. . . . Decision makers may become victims of urgency and commit all kinds of mistakes, miscalculations, and misperceptions.*

Psychologists D. Kahneman and A. Tversky, for example, have documented some of the perceptual distortions and elementary errors in statistical reasoning that occur when people seek to make judgments under conditions of uncertainty.

Research in social psychology has also found that under stressful conditions, most people resort to relatively simple, stereotyped responses, and are notably uncreative and unimaginative. An additional result of stress is that the ability to process complex information tends to be reduced, and people rely on habitual behavior patterns. Tolerance for ambiguity declines, and there appears to be a kind of intellectual tunnel vision, in which available options are narrowed. Cognitive rigidity is particularly likely, as well as repetitive thinking. Preprogrammed routines, such as those involving a limited sequence of retaliatory actions, are likely to be especially appealing and to be seen as the only available options. These effects are enhanced when people are deprived of sleep and behaving for very

high stakes, under intense pressure. As psychiatrist Lester Grinspoon has put it:

> It is possible that any use of nuclear weapons would not escalate into a war of extinction. But the fact is that a limited degree of rationality and morality has been displayed so far in nuclear matters. Taking into account the conditions that would probably prevail during a nuclear attack, anyone whose confidence ultimately depends on a belief in reliable human functioning at all levels, and in the prudence and restraint of national leaders in an unprecedented situation, is merely avoiding anxiety by indulging in wishful thinking.†

There is an ongoing debate over whether human decision making should be removed from the nuclear retaliatory posture. In this debate, ironically, the seemingly dovish argument regarding human fallibility (as expressed by Grinspoon, above) is used to reinforce the otherwise hawkish viewpoint favoring increased reliance on computers and possibly, launch on warning (see Chapter 6).

## GROUPS, CONFORMITY, AND OBEDIENCE

During international crises, leaders will be advised by a group of close associates, both civilian and military. Common sense suggests that decisions made in such groups are likely to be more moderate and careful than those made by a single leader. However, research suggests just the opposite: psychologist Irving Janis, for example, has coined the phrase **"group-think"** for the process whereby decisions made in small war cabinets tend to be influenced by the group process itself. He concludes that group decision making, especially under conditions of stress, is likely to be quite fallible and prone to ratifying irrational and even dangerous actions. This is because the group process fosters: (1) an illusion of invulnerability, (2) social pressures that discourage any disagreement, (3) collective attempts to ignore or rationalize away information that runs counter to the group's consensus, and (4) a diminution of personal responsibility (since it becomes difficult to identify one person as the ultimate decision maker). Group-think typically leads therefore to the taking of greater risks than would be ventured by a smaller number of individuals. There clearly is an advantage in hav-

---

*1982. *Risks of Unintentional Nuclear War*. Geneva: UN Institute for Disarmament Research.

†1984. Crisis behavior. *Bulletin of the Atomic Scientists, 40*, 25–28.

ing a variety of inputs, and the phenomenon of group-think strongly suggests the need for active efforts to ensure that numerous opinions—especially those contrary to the preference of the group—are favorably presented.

Social psychologist Solomon Asch investigated the related phenomenon of social conformity by asking subjects to tell which of two lines is longer. When tested alone, people tended to be quite accurate at this simple task. Asch then tested people in groups, asking them to vote; unknown to one subject in each case, the other group members were cooperating with the experimenter, intentionally voting for the wrong answer. In these conditions, under the pressure of other people's (wrong) opinions, many subjects willingly changed their votes, going against the evidence of their own eyes.

In another now-famous experiment, sociologist Stanley Milgram designed a situation in which subjects were ordered to administer what they thought were dangerously powerful electric shocks to other subjects (who in fact were assistants of the experimenter). The disturbing result was that fully two-thirds of apparently normal subjects were willing to administer what they thought were lethal dosages of electric shocks, as long as the "experimenter" assumed responsibility and also ordered the subject to continue with the procedure. "Perhaps the most fundamental lesson in our study" wrote Milgram, "is that ordinary people, simply doing their jobs, and without any particular hostility on their part, can become agents in a terrible destructive process."

The philosopher Hannah Arendt, reflecting on the behavior of Adolf Eichmann, who had a special role in Hitler's program of genocide, wrote about the "banality of evil." According to Arendt, evil frequently appears as mild-mannered obedience to accepted authority, rather than in fiendish or diabolical form. Military preparedness typically involves almost interminable war-games, practice sessions, and drills, which are intended to make the appropriate responses virtually automatic. Especially for lower level personnel, the goal is generally to minimize the amount of thinking, feeling, or worrying, and also to increase reliability. Such training might be especially likely to produce obedience when behavior toward a distant, dehumanized enemy is called for, in response to the dictates of accepted leadership and group process, under crisis conditions (when the most likely behaviors are those that have been carefully rehearsed).

There is, of course, another view of the prospect of unconditional obedience. Willingness to plunge the world into nuclear war may indeed be seen as an immense evil, potentially the greatest evil of all history. However, supporters of deterrence claim that such willingness—hence the psychological process of obedience to authority—must be cultivated if we are to avoid disaster. In a 1964 article titled "The Test: Are We the Tougher?" presidential adviser Walt Rostow wrote that "credible deterrence in the Nuclear Age lies in being prepared to face the consequences if deterrence fails—up to and including all-out nuclear war." According to this view, willingness to kill, and to do so in immense numbers, remains a necessary cornerstone of today's nuclear policies, on both sides. Whatever one thinks of the morality or desirability of such a posture, and whatever one thinks of the possibility of replacing or modifying it in the future, it should be clear that the current situation has psychological as well as political and strategical components.

## GOING TO WAR

There is room for debate over whether human aggressiveness as such is meaningfully related to warfare. Some scholars maintain that war is a social phenomenon, motivated primarily by geopolitical, economic, and social issues, such that personal angers are only secondarily aroused. Proponents of this view, in which the "aggression" of one nation against another is really quite different from the "aggression" of one human being against another, often quote the well-known dictum of von Clausewitz: "War is the continuation of politics by other means."

On the other hand, the constitution of UNESCO states: "Wars begin in the minds of men." If so, then at some level war-making (and war-preventing as well) should be psychological phenomena. Wars may occur for a variety of complex reasons, but they reflect decisions made by people, often a relatively small number of people in positions of authority. In addition, a system that ultimately gives rise to a specific war must receive at least some support from the populace. And once the decision to engage in war has been made, acquiescence—even if it results from coercion—must be achieved. Otherwise, the question would never be asked: "What if they had a war and no one came?" It must be emphasized, however, that in the case of nuclear war, decisions could be made and the war "fought" with essentially no behavioral involvement, aggressive or otherwise, on the part of more than 99% of the populace. In this sense, as well as in its destructiveness, nuclear war would be unique in human experience. However, even here it seems undeniable that everyday citizens, by virtue of their actions or their inaction, do play a role in nuclear events. (Hence, this book.)

Archaeological and anthropological evidence suggests that warfare was an ancient human endeavor. For nontechnological human beings, it appears that warfare was also adaptive in the biological sense: that is, it contributed to social and personal success. In the absence of advanced technology, the costs of war were much lower than they have become in recent times, while the benefits may have been substantial, including prestige, mates, living space, food, plunder, and other valuable resources. War was almost exclusively an enterprise for young males, not yet fully integrated into the social system; the rest of the population was at least somewhat insulated from its direct effects. Even for the combatants, moreover, primitive war was closer to a series of skirmishes than to the all-out war of modern nations. It has therefore been suggested that the inclination to resort to war, especially under conditions of intense competition, is a primitive and widespread human tendency, with which relatively few inhibitory factors are associated. As we have seen, there is much in human psychology that seems to incline us to fight, and to fight lethally, at certain times.

In modern times, however, and especially with the dawning of the Nuclear Age, the actual consequences of warfare have become much more severe. It seems unlikely that the benefits of nuclear war could ever exceed its costs, even if one side or the other could be said to have "prevailed." Yet the same psychological stirrings that motivated our ancestors may operate within modern-day citizens, as well as leaders of the most advanced industrial nations. Although this line of argument (like most efforts in nuclear psychology) lends itself especially to a dovish perspective, it can also be used to make a hawkish case: if, in fact, our opponents are motivated by primitive and dangerously inappropriate behavioral tendencies—once adaptive but now outmoded in a world of nuclear weapons—it is all the more important that we be vigilant and prepared to defend ourselves if need be, and better yet, that we be able to deter such behavior.

## SELF-FULFILLING PROPHECIES AND PARANOIA

Psychologists have emphasized that when two individuals, or two groups of individuals, confront each other in the absence of trust, each side is likely to behave competitively and with a high degree of cognitive rigidity. As a result, each side tends to behave as a "cheater" or "noncooperator" in a game of Prisoner's Dilemma (see Chapter 6). Under experimental conditions, at least, such actions almost invariably produce "cheating" or "noncooperating" behavior in the other side, which in turn serves to reinforce the seeming wisdom of the original antagonism. Under such conditions, mistrust and ill will therefore serve as **self-fulfilling prophecies,** predictions about the future that become true insofar as one believes them. Applying this model to the arms race, when one side assumes that the other will be antagonistic, and behaves antagonistically in return, this produces precisely the behavior that was predicted . . . and which, rationally, each side actually hopes to avoid. In a sense, a kind of worst-case planning (see Chapter 9), operating on a psychological level, might in fact generate the worst case.

Such behavior typically appears rational—and often, unavoidable as well—to the person engaged in it, although to an outside observer it can seem quite crazy. "The superpowers are involved in a crazy social process," wrote psychologist Morton Deutsch,

> which, given the existence of nuclear weapons, is too dangerous to allow to continue. Perfectly sane and intelligent people, once they are enmeshed in a crazy social process, may engage in actions which seem to them completely rational and necessary, but which a detached, objective observer would readily identify as contributing to the perpetuation and intensification of a vicious cycle of interactions.*

In such a situation, the participants typically see no way of extricating themselves, without danger to their nations and/or to their personal reputations.

When individuals consider themselves to have been persistently and unjustly persecuted, and especially if such views are somewhat exaggerated, they are often described as "paranoid." **Paranoia** often is based on real inadequacies or on a history of having suffered actual wrongs, and it can be a personal style or a psychological stance, (i.e., it is not necessarily symptomatic of being "crazy" or psychotic). Typically, paranoia is augmented by feelings of **centrality**—of being the focus of events, with even seemingly insignificant details directed toward one's self—and grandiosity (the

---

*1983. The prevention of World War III: A psychological perspective, *Political Psychology, 4,* 3–31.

sense of great individual power). When paranoids act on perceptions that others are aggressive and about to cheat or defect, they are especially inclined to cheat or defect themselves. In so doing, however, they set in motion the "vicious cycle" noted by Deutsch and others, and each subsequent act of cheating or aggression virtually guarantees reciprocal behavior by the other party. Thus the set of beliefs that led to the label "paranoid" can be described as a self-fulfilling prophecy.

Nations sometimes act as though they are paranoid (e.g., in 1983 the Soviets shot down a civilian airliner in their airspace). But this does not mean that the behavior is completely irrational, since paranoids typically have more than their share of enemies because of their paranoid behavior. The paranoid typically thinks that his or her vital interests are constantly threatened, and then behaves in a manner that serves to ensure that such dangers exist: threatening a neighbor with a gun for fear that the neighbor is an enemy, for example, thereby making the neighbor an enemy, perhaps for the first time, and often winding up in jail or a mental hospital as well. The diagnosis of "national paranoia," however, must be performed with some care, at least partly because it is unclear whether nations can be seen as embodying a psychology in the same sense as an individual. In addition, such terms can be used either as an explanatory diagnosis, or as an exercise in derogatory finger-pointing.

## THE PSYCHOLOGY OF DETERRENCE

Deterrence itself can be seen as a psychological ploy, since it aims to influence the behavior of the other party by inducing the expectation that particular acts (an attack, or substantial trespass on a nation's commitments or vital interests) will provoke certain responses (i.e., retaliation). On the other hand, a critical psychological view of the whole process suggests that by amassing a deterrent arsenal—and especially, one that is increasingly destructive and accurate—each side threatens the other, provoking a (justified) degree of paranoia, and nurturing the antagonism to which the process is supposed to be solely a response. For example, official statements by both US and Soviet leaders claim that the other side has amassed military forces in excess of the amount needed for self-defense; and to some degree, both sides may be right, with this state of affairs attributable to the behavior of the other, and thus, ultimately, to itself.

In addition, the psychological appeal of deterrence may be augmented by the phenomenon of Procrusteanism, discussed earlier. It is frequently stated that deterrence "works" because nuclear weapons have apparently kept the peace between the superpowers. The observation that something has not yet happened is generally a good indicator that it will not happen; at least, this is the way things have generally been in the past. However, it can also be argued that some events—like nuclear war—will be singular if they ever occur. That is, since they will only occur once, the fact that they haven't yet taken place should not be considered to be evidence that they never will. Finally, most psychological views of deterrence hold that for a process to be effective, it must be based on positive reinforcement (i.e., encouragement), not just negative reinforcement (the threat of punishment).

It must be emphasized, however, that this view is by no means universal. According to many people, the arms race is less a "crazy social process" than a regrettable necessity, forced on the United States. Thus, President Reagan informed the National Association of Evangelicals in 1983:

> Let us be aware that while [the Soviets] preach the supremacy of the state, declare its omnipotence over individual man, and predict its eventual domination of all peoples of the earth—they are the focus of evil in the modern world. . . . I urge you to beware the temptation of pride—the temptation blithely to declare yourselves above it all and label both sides equally at fault, to ignore the facts of history and the aggressive impulses of an evil empire, to simply call the arms race a giant misunderstanding and thereby remove yourselves from the struggle between right and wrong, good and evil.

That Soviet leaders have made similar statements about the United States can be interpreted as confirming the mirror-image, vicious cycle interpretation suggested earlier. Or, alternatively, it is possible that only one side is correct and the other is misled or simply dishonest.

## PSYCHOLOGICAL RESPONSES TO DISASTER

In evaluating the possible effects of nuclear war (Chapters 4 and 5), we focused on its physical dimensions. Psychological effects, however, should also be considered. When it comes to evaluating these psychological consequences, we encounter the same difficulty discussed in the course of our earlier examination of possible physical effects of nuclear war: since large-scale nuclear war would be an unprecedented event, it is at least questionable whether we can legitimately use extrapolations from previous events in our analysis.

Certain general patterns, at least, have been identified, based on studies of nonnuclear disasters, as well as the Japanese experience at Hiroshima and Nagasaki. The usual human response to severe disaster is initially an outcry of rage, fear, and grief, typically followed by a state of dazed shock. This is the beginning of the psychological process of denial of the event, which apparently allows the individual to come to grips with his or her shattered world at a tolerable pace. During the following period, which may last for months or even years, this blocking process alternates with intrusive awareness of the tragedy, as the victim gradually encompasses the full truth. Long-term psychological effects may also result, apparently due to severe disruption of an individual's basic assumption of trust and self-worth. Thus, it is widely acknowledged that the process whereby a child acquires confidence and a positive self-image is closely tied to his or her faith in the reliability, predictability, and benevolence of the surrounding world. When this faith is shattered, people of any age can become profoundly mistrustful, both of their environments and of themselves.

For example, survivors were studied after the dam collapse at Buffalo Creek in southern West Virginia, which killed 125 people and left 4,000 homeless in 1972. Even in this relatively mild disaster, all survivors were found to be psychologically impaired, in varying degree, by their experience. Apathy, despair, and depression were frequent, and many people suffered as well from "survivor guilt," a feeling of unresolved and sometimes paralyzing responsibility for having lived through a disaster that killed many friends and loved ones. (A comparable syndrome has been described for concentration camp survivors.)

Sociologist Kai Erikson also found that survivors of communal disasters, unlike those who have overcome personal catastrophe, suffer a peculiar disorientation because of destruction of the social fabric: most people are accustomed to investing in the community, and drawing on communal resources when in need. When that communal whole was destroyed at Buffalo Creek (and as it almost certainly would be in a nuclear war), people not only were unable to profit from the greater society, they also felt disinclined to invest any further in it.

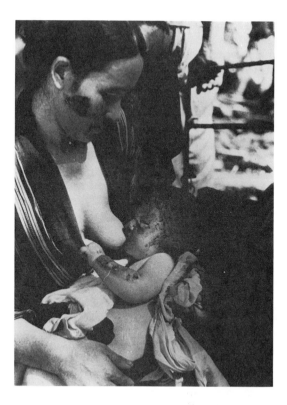

**FIGURE 14.5 Woman nursing her burned child the day after the bombing of Hiroshima. The blank, expressionless look on the mother's face is suggestive of "psychic numbing."** (United Nations photo by Yosuka Yamahata.)

In the cases of Hiroshima and Nagasaki, psychological impairment was severe. Psychiatrist Robert Lifton studied the Japanese survivors of Hiroshima and Nagasaki, known as **hibakusha** ("explosion-affected person"). They suffered from what has been called **psychic numbing,** a deadening inability to show and feel emotion (Fig. 14.5). Lifton proposed that this resulted from their overwhelming encounter with death and destruction. Just as anesthesia is a medical technique for ensuring that a person does not experience excruciating physical pain, psychic numbing may be a widespread human response to intense emotional pain. Psychic numbing may be very long-lasting, however, in which case it seriously impairs one's ability to function sensitively, with joy and effectiveness.

On the other hand, supporters of civil defense and of crisis relocation planning—as well as many nuclear hawks generally—point out that Hiroshima and Nagasaki eventually recovered and were rebuilt. They also emphasize that studies of the response to disaster evacuations (because of floods, hurricanes, etc.) show that in most cases panic is rare and people tend to behave responsibly, so long as: (1) they have confidence in the government, and (2) they are provided with understandable and reliable guidelines for coping with the emergency.

However, it is also noteworthy that in the cases of Hiroshima and Nagasaki, as well as in various conventional disasters, there has always been an outside world to which survivors could turn. Also, because of the relatively small size of the Hiroshima and Nagasaki bombs, there were survivors in the first place. And finally, no one knows whether people would respond to an imminent threat of nuclear war, not to mention its onset, in the same ways that they have responded to other, more limited disasters in the past. When preparing for a flood or hurricane, people can also anticipate an eventual return to normality, which may facilitate their willingness to cooperate with authorities and to behave responsibly. Also, there is a body of experience, accumulated from past floods, hurricanes, and so forth, that is helpful and to some extent comforting by its mere existence. But no one knows how people will behave when anticipating a nuclear war or even in the uncertainty associated with a serious, deteriorating international crisis.

## CHILDREN'S FEARS OF NUCLEAR WAR

After the detonation of a hydrogen bomb and the acquisition of strategic bombers by the Soviet Union, American school children in the 1950s began to participate in "duck and cover" and shelter drills. It is not clear whether this experience reduced or heightened the anxiety of children or of their parents. (It is also unclear what effect these maneuvers would have had on their safety, in the event of attack.) In any event, nuclear anxiety increased substantially again in the late 1950s and early 1960s, largely because of concern about radioactive fallout from aboveground nuclear tests. Such anxiety surfaced once more in the late 1970s and early 1980s, this time directed toward nuclear war itself.

Survey studies, conducted in the US, the USSR, and even neutral countries, have shown that a high proportion of children and adolescents are deeply worried about the prospect of nuclear war. One such study disclosed that whereas 7% of adolescent Americans

worried about nuclear war in 1975, about 30% worried about it in 1984. A large proportion of people surveyed, children as well as adults, typically report that they think nuclear war is probable during their lifetimes: commonly about 50%. It is interesting, however, that a much smaller percentage (typically around 10–15%) generally indicates that nuclear war is their major worry about the future. This inconsistency may reflect the widespread workings of denial, and/or the popular tendency to ignore a problem that one feels helpless to do anything about. In any event, some psychiatrists have emphasized that nuclear anxieties may be responsible for high levels of drug use, apathy, pessimism, refusal to plan for the future, and lack of respect for society's values, as well as feelings that one's parents—and adults generally—are not trustworthy. It has also been proposed that the threat of nuclear war has induced a kind of "radical futurelessness," which is responsible for widespread societal refusal to delay gratifications, to accumulate personal savings, or to plan for the future, including the decision not to have children.

Most of the data regarding childhood nuclear fears have been used to support antinuclear sentiment by emphasizing the degree to which the nuclear threat is destructive to everyday lives, even without nuclear war occurring. Nuclear anxiety seems to be most pronounced among the children of white, upper middle class, liberally inclined parents. Thus it remains to be seen whether it is a deeply rooted phenomenon, with serious long-term effects, and also, to what extent it is present in society as a whole. It is also possible, however, that nuclear anxiety is more significant than currently is realized. Indeed, the relatively few in-depth psychological studies of this phenomenon have shown that such concerns typically are not revealed during a superficial interview or survey, at least partly because the issue itself makes people anxious and causes them to repress their true feelings about it.

## THE PSYCHOLOGY OF ACTIVISM

Most people are not directly involved as either pronuclear or antinuclear activists. The reasons for this are unclear, but they may well be related to several psychological phenomena. For one thing, people tend to ignore issues about which they feel helpless. And given the size of the national bureaucracies, the imposing dimensions of the weapons themselves, and last but not least their effects, most people are inclined to feel

**FIGURE 14.6 Marchers demonstrating in support of a nuclear freeze in 1982. Antinuclear activism reached a relative peak about that time.** (Courtesy of Nuclear War Graphics Project.)

dwarfed and inadequate. They therefore are likely to direct their time and energy in ways that are more immediately productive and effective, such as their families or careers. In addition, involvement in issues relating to the arms race and nuclear war are widely considered "too depressing." Activists point out, however, that by admitting that they anticipate that the issue will be depressing, people acknowledge that it has already been affecting them; becoming active, if only with a small proportion of one's time and energy, then feels very good, coming as a great relief.

As a general rule, partisans of the political right and left tend to be relatively pronuclear and antinuclear, respectively. This appears to be largely because nuclear weapons have come to be associated, at least in the Western world, with defense against communism. To some degree, hawkish opinion tends to hold that nuclear war is a lesser threat than Soviet communist domination. Comparably, dovish opinion holds that the real danger faced by the United States, and the world, is not the Soviet Union, or even communist ideas in general, but rather nuclear war (Fig. 14.6). This divergence may reflect a difference in the way in which people identify an enemy: in the former case, a tendency to personify danger and one's opponent, and therefore to fear and often to hate individuals and foreign social systems; in the latter, to focus on more impersonal events and often on the dangers posed by error and bad judgment rather than intentional ill will (Fig. 14.7).

**FIGURE 14.7 Summit meeting between President John F. Kennedy and Soviet Premier Nikita S. Khrushchev in Vienna, in 1961. Soviet Foreign Minister Andrei Gromyko is at the far right. It is generally acknowledged that Khrushchev dominated Kennedy at this meeting, which contributed partly to Khrushchev's (incorrect) assumption that he could successfully deploy missiles in Cuba the following year.** (Courtesy of the John F. Kennedy Library.)

## Policy Issues

### Should the US abandon perception theory and treat nuclear weapons as their reality dictates?

**Yes:**  By assuming that the important thing is not the weapons themselves but rather the psychological and political impact of those weapons, we essentially guarantee a never-ending arms race, since there can be no answer to the question, How much is enough? It might be possible to begin to dismantle the nuclear arms race if the US government would only stop playing the game of perception theory and start informing its citizenry—as well as the other people of the world—that nuclear superiority is unobtainable and in fact, meaningless, and that additional nuclear weapons make even the side obtaining them less safe rather than more. At least, it would be more feasible to adopt a policy of minimum deterrence.

**No:**  The reality of nuclear weapons dictates that everyone recognize the crucial role of political perceptions. Such perceptions, in fact, become reality. Thus, deterrence is basically an effort to coerce the behavior of the Soviet leadership, and the effectiveness of such coercion increases in proportion to the emphasis placed on the image of usability and if possible, superiority. In addition, it is crucially important that the NATO allies perceive the US as willing to defend not only itself, but also them if necessary. Toward that end, not only must the US be militarily capable, but also it must be perceived to be capa-

ble. The same applies, with slight modification, to third world nations as well.

### Can psychology help the world out of its current nuclear dilemma?

**Yes:**  The problem of the nuclear arms race is in large part a result of human perceptions, and all too often, misperceptions. It would therefore be very useful if everyone could better understand the significance of mirror imaging, vicious cycle processes, human fallibility, the image of the enemy, and so forth, in placing the US and the Soviets in a position that neither party wants, which endangers us all.

**No:**  Psychological insights may be worthwhile in this respect, but only to a very limited extent. Thus, it might well be useful to better understand the mentality of the Kremlin leadership, and how best to make deterrence more effective—for example, what assets the Soviet government particularly values, how far the leaders could be trusted in certain cases, and how far they could safely be pushed in others. It would also be in the American interest to make maximally effective use of propaganda, to appeal to third world nations as well as people behind the Iron Curtain. But the arms race itself is not a result of human psychology gone awry. The arms race goes on not because of a misunderstanding on America's part; rather, because the US leadership understands the necessity for it, just as it should.

## KEY TERMS

denial

habituation

just-noticeable difference

security

safety

Procrustean thinking

perception theory

mirror imaging

cognitive dissonance

strain to consistency

attribution theory

attribution error

in-group amity

out-group enmity

group-think

self-fulfilling prophecy

paranoia

centrality

*hibakusha*

psychic numbing

## STUDY QUESTIONS

1.  What is meant by (psychological) denial? How might it influence attitudes toward nuclear war?

2.  What is habituation? How might it influence attitudes toward nuclear war?

3.  What are some of the hallmarks of crisis decision making?

4.  What is group-think?

5.  What is psychic numbing? Can one argue that even people who are not *hibakusha* are victims of psychic numbing?

6. What is the possible relationship between cognitive dissonance and mirror imaging?

7. In what way can deterrence be seen as a self-fulfilling prophecy?

8. Can you attempt to develop a psychological interpretation of antinuclear anxiety? Of pronuclear suppport?

## ADDITIONAL READINGS

Barash, David P., and Judith Eve Lipton. 1985. *The Caveman and the Bomb: Human Nature, Evolution and Nuclear War.* New York: McGraw-Hill. A book for the layperson, developing the thesis that the underlying psychological basis of the arms race can be found in the application of outmoded ways of thinking (and sometimes, not thinking) to the very new problem of nuclear war.

Frank, Jerome. 1982. *Sanity and Survival in the Nuclear Age.* New York: Random House. A reprinting of a classic examination of the psychology of the arms race and nuclear war, with material ranging from personal aggressiveness to social psychology.

Thompson, James. 1985. *Psychological Aspects of Nuclear War.* New York: John Wiley. A brief but information-packed volume that served as an official report of the British Psychological Association, emphasizing issues in human fallibility and the psychological assumptions behind civil defense planning.

White, Ralph. 1984. *Fearful Warriors.* New York: Free Press. A psychological profile of US–Soviet relations, emphasizing the role of fear and national pride in generating past wars and in stimulating the nuclear arms race today.

# 15 Some Possible Futures

*Success is relative: It is what we can make of the mess we have made of things.*

T. S. Eliot (*The Family Reunion*)

---

It may be significant that after 14 chapters examining various aspects of the arms race and nuclear war, we conclude with only a single, rather brief chapter on possible solutions. Mark Twain once commented that it was easy to stop smoking: he had done it hundreds of times! Similarly, perhaps it would be easy to end the arms race and solve the problem of nuclear war: there have been hundreds of suggestions! Many ways out of the nuclear dilemma have been proposed: some involve long-term strategies and others, short-term fixes. Predictably, some are hawkish and are characterized by a relatively aggressive, somewhat confrontational attitude toward the Soviet Union, along with continued or even heightened reliance on military preparedness; others are dovish, hence more conciliatory, with emphasis on reducing the role of nuclear weapons. Others, less easily categorized, focus instead on reducing the likelihood of misunderstanding and miscalculation, and on improving communication.

We have already considered some suggestions—such as no first use, Star Wars/SDI, and a comprehensive test ban—as "policy issues" associated with preceding chapters. In this chapter, we shall review some of these as well as other proposals. It is hoped that by this point, each reader has enough nuclear literacy to evaluate such proposals and perhaps enough motivation to become involved on behalf of one possible future or another.

In many ways, this has been a traditional textbook, presenting an introduction to the arms race and nuclear war in much the same way as one might be introduced to psychology, physics, or world history. However, in other ways, it has been unique, because the subject matter itself is unique: to a degree not found in most introductory textbooks, the issues raised here have direct application to the real world of immediate politics, and

quite possibly, the future of the United States and all human beings. The writer of every textbook hopes that students will be inspired to become involved and possibly, someday, to make contributions to the field, whether that field be ancient literature, economics, or advanced nuclear physics. It is not expected that every reader of this book will become a nuclear strategist, politician, peace activist, or pronuclear apologist. However, it is certainly hoped that all will go beyond understanding the basic issues to define a vision of the future that they, as responsible individual citizens, would like to see enacted. To a degree that is not shared by other, more strictly academic or scholarly endeavors, future directions of the nuclear arms race may well have direct impact on every one of us.

## BUILDUP AND MODERNIZATION

One strategy long advocated by nuclear hawks recommends the continued development of nuclear weapons, especially emphasizing improvements in reliability, accuracy, and invulnerability—in short, build up and modernize.

**PRO:** Today, just as the Red Queen advised Alice, the world is moving so quickly that we must keep going just to stay where we are, and run if we wish to get anywhere. By continuing the present nuclear competition with the USSR, we will be able to counter their advances and in the process, maintain our world position and national security. To let down our guard, or allow the Soviets to outresearch, outproduce, or outdeploy us in nuclear weapons, is to invite disaster. On the other hand, the scientific ingenuity and industrial potential of the United States is such that we can effectively defeat the USSR in an ongoing arms race. Negotiations are not to be trusted. Our negotiators are accountable to a democratic process whereas theirs are not, and our leaders often seek the most moral and balanced agreements whereas theirs seek only one-sided advantage; as a result, negotiations with the Soviets generally leave them ahead. We can engage cautiously in negotiations—always from a position of strength so that we will never have to make concessions—but we should rely primarily on our own inventiveness and military capabilities to keep us free and safe. Perhaps nuclear weapons will be abolished in some future utopia, but for the foreseeable future, we must continue to compete vigorously.

**CON:** In a world of nuclear weapons, security must be mutual; it simply cannot be obtained unilaterally, and definitely not by unilateral military actions. Each side can destroy the other, and this is not likely to change by the accumulation of more weaponry. In fact, the present course of the nuclear arms race is for the deployment of weapons that make war more likely rather than less. "Modernization" is a buzzword that really means dangerous and unnecessary escalation. There is nothing but hopelessness and ultimate destruction waiting for us down the path of continued arms racing; this strategy offers no hope for a resolution of the crisis, and is therefore not really a solution at all, but rather a proposal that we continue multiplying the problem. We do not increase our safety by further escalating the arms race, and we cannot defeat the USSR in this regard. History shows that they always catch up. By building more, we simply ensure that they also will build more, which not only makes negotiated agreements more difficult, but leaves both sides in a more dangerous situation.

## NUCLEAR FREEZE

The nuclear freeze movement was founded by Randall Forsberg in 1979, although it has historical antecedents. The freeze proposal calls for "a mutual and verifiable freeze on the testing, production, and deployment of nuclear warheads, missiles, and delivery systems." A nonbinding freeze resolution was passed by the House of Representatives and numerous state and local referenda, and according to various public opinion polls, it is favored by 65–85% of the American people.

**PRO:** A mutual, verifiable freeze would effectively end the arms race. It would prevent the next generation of destabilizing weapons, on both sides—it would equally inhibit, for example, the Soviet SS-24 and SS-25 missiles, the Typhoon submarines, and the Blackjack bomber, as well as the MX, Midgetman, and Pershing II missiles, the B-1 bomber, and the Trident II (D-5) missiles. This would make the current nuclear balance more stable, since it would block the highly accurate, provocative weapons that both sides will otherwise deploy. On balance, neither side is ahead now—the US leads in some areas, the USSR in others; therefore, a freeze would be appropriate and should be acceptable to both sides. In fact, given the enormous and grotesque levels of mutual overkill, it scarcely matters who is ahead: both sides are behind. The freeze is also simple enough to be understandable to the public, and yet it would be profoundly effective. It will be mutual, and it can be verified. Although small violations might occur unnoticed, major violations will be detectable. A freeze would also save hundreds of billions of dollars, meet our mutual obligations under the Non-Proliferation Treaty, and set the stage for meaningful reductions. It would not solve all our problems, but it is a crucial step in the right direction: stopping the lethal, ongoing nuclear arms race. Opponents who claim that a freeze does not go far enough are being either naive or intellectually dishonest: it is a basic physical principle that if you want to change direction by 180 degrees, first you must come to a halt, then go the other way.

**CON:** Not surprisingly, because it would be in the Soviet interest more than that of the US, a freeze is supported by the USSR. The Soviets currently have a "definite margin of superiority" in strategic weapons, as President Reagan has said. To freeze now would be to concede to them unacceptable advantages in ICBMs and in megatonnage. It would also hobble scientific and technological innovation, which is precisely the arena in which the US has an advantage. A freeze would be difficult to verify; a ban on production of missiles and warheads would in fact be almost impossible to police, especially if the Soviets continue to balk at on-site inspection. We can be assured, however, that the USSR will cheat wherever possible, and some time after agreeing to a freeze, they may unveil a new weapon and demand concessions from the United States. A freeze will not permit replacement of weapons when they become obsolete, and by inhibiting the deployment of Midgetman, it will prevent the move toward less provocative, single-warhead missiles that will help stabilize the nuclear balance. Finally, a freeze does not go far enough: we don't simply need a freeze, we need substantial reductions in offensive weapons on both sides. If the US agrees to a freeze at current levels, it removes any incentive for the Soviets to agree to such reductions.

## STAR WARS/SDI

Many hawks, in and out of the Reagan administration, have urged that the US vigorously pursue Star Wars/SDI, seeking to establish a regime whereby the United States will be protected against nuclear attack.

**PRO:**   There is virtually no limit to scientific ingenuity, and furthermore, many of the basic technologies for SDI are almost ready for deployment today. Deterrence, on the other hand, is an obsolete, immoral concept. As President Reagan has asked, wouldn't it be preferable to save lives rather than to avenge them? With a space-based defensive shield, the US would not be susceptible to nuclear coercion. The Soviets, seeing that their weapons were no longer effective, would be more amenable to suggestions that they make dramatic reductions. Ultimately, a situation of threatening, offensive weapons can be replaced by defensive, nonthreatening shields. It will be necessary, of course, to phase in such a system carefully, to ensure that its installation is not provocative to the other side. Even if SDI were not 100% effective, it would greatly complicate any Soviet planning for a first strike, thereby making such a first strike less likely. The first choice of the US should be to provide complete protection for the entire country. But even if a defensive system did not prove reliable enough to guarantee protection for the civilian population, by selectively defending American retaliatory weapons, the SDI would enhance deterrence and thus promote stability.

**CON:**   Star Wars is wishful thinking. Closer to science fiction than to science, it would be a monumental waste of time and of huge amounts of money. The federal government could just as well seek to build a missile that goes faster than the speed of light as seek to build a system that will, with reliability, shoot down incoming missiles. Star Wars would be suscep-

tible to a wide array of Soviet countermeasures, and such countermeasures are much easier, cheaper, and more reliable than Star Wars itself could ever be. Even without countermeasures, there are overwhelming problems of providing the energy needed for defensive weapons, tracking and battle management computer software, response times, and so on; no responsible government could ever be confident that such a system, even if it were theoretically ready, could be relied on. Yet we can be assured that the Soviet leadership, making worst-case assumptions, would see Star Wars as very threatening and provocative. In the face of a US commitment to Star Wars, they would be most unlikely to reduce their offensive weapons, since they would see a need for more firepower to assure that Star Wars could be overwhelmed and that the US would be deterred. If the US were to engage in a Star Wars crash program, this almost certainly would stimulate a Soviet counterprogram, as well as making it likely that the Soviets would increase rather than decrease their offensive arsenal. Star Wars would only provoke military competition in space, leading to greater anxiety and even a possible preemptive strike. In addition, it would complicate any possible reductions in current weapons and probably lead to an escalating arms race on earth.

## GRIT

Psychologist Charles Osgood has proposed a strategy known as GRIT (*graduated and reciprocated initiatives in tension reduction*), based on the idea that it is possible for two sides to move down the tension ladder just as they often move up. Thus, Osgood recommends that the US engage in a series of unilateral initiatives, intended to reduce tension. A strategy of GRIT would have the following components.

1.  Deterrence would be preserved throughout. GRIT would not be unilateral disarmament; rather, we would always retain the ability to inflict unacceptable damage on any aggressor, but we would make concrete steps toward defusing tension.

2.  GRIT initiatives would not be accompanied by threats, since threatening an opponent is a sure way of maintaining an adversary relationship. The initiator might invite reciprocation from the other side, but no demands should be made.

3. The initiatives should be publicly announced, and maximum attention directed toward the goal of reducing tension and diminishing the sense of mutual threat.

4. Each action should be real and meaningful—not involving, for example, the dismantling of weapons recognized to be obsolete and slated for removal.

5. GRIT should be maintained, unilaterally if necessary for some time, to bring maximum pressure to bear on the other side.

**PRO:** GRIT offers a viable strategy for getting out of the present superpower impasse, and at no risk, since the US nuclear arsenal is already so grossly excessive. GRIT was used successfully by President Kennedy in 1963, when he initiated a unilateral nuclear test moratorium and invited the Soviets to join. Premier Khrushchev responded positively and also announced a halt in plans for strategic bomber production. Within weeks, there was the Hot Line agreement as well as the Partial Test Ban Treaty, a large wheat sale, and a dramatic lowering of East-West tensions. President Nixon also used GRIT successfully when he announced a unilateral halt to the production of biological weapons in 1969, leading eventually to another treaty. All that is needed is a little imagination, combined with confidence in the deterrent value of US strategic forces (remember that a single Poseidon submarine carries 160 MIRVed warheads, equaling the explosive power of about 500 Hiroshima bombs). Perhaps the only good thing about having more than 30,000 nuclear weapons is that the United States can begin to dismantle many of them, improving the international climate greatly, without compromising its national security in the slightest. For example, the US can unilaterally dismantle its ICBMs, its nuclear missiles in Europe, and so forth, one by one, all the while inviting the Soviets to reciprocate, but proceeding on its own if need be. This could lower tensions and generate a new climate in which it is very likely that the Soviets would participate in arms reductions. If they did not, the US could always stop, but it is certainly worth a try.

**CON:** GRIT doesn't always work. Sometimes one side or the other makes offers that have more propaganda value than real significance. The Soviets would love it if the US began unilaterally disarming, but if so, what incentive would the USSR have to

reduce its own oversized arsenal? Once the United States began such a series of actions, it would be very difficult for American leaders to recognize that GRIT had failed, especially once public expectations had been raised. There might therefore be a very dangerous momentum to continue disarming to the point that US national security is endangered. Although world opinion may perceive the US as seeking to be peacemakers, it would also be seen as weak-willed and eventually, much weaker than its opponent. Such perceptions would work against the US in many ways. The Soviets, who understand strength and assertiveness, are all too eager to take advantage of any sign of conciliation, which they interpret as weakness. Far better to maintain a position of strength and then seek to obtain concessions.

## STEADY AS WE GO

Although not usually stated as a distinct strategy, "steady as you go" is in fact the current policy of the United States and has been for decades. In the absence of some other strategy, it also seems likely to be the direction the US will take in the future as well. The basic notion is to continue the evolution of new weapons systems, with newer generations replacing older ones, while also seeking (with varying degrees of eagerness) to reach mutual, verifiable agreements to halt certain aspects of the superpowers' nuclear competition that seem to be especially destabilizing and/or wasteful.

**PRO:** The technological momentum of the arms race cannot be stopped, and the nuclear "secret" cannot be unlearned. Rather than entrust US security to the benevolence of the other side, America must continue the basic policies of the past (which include both a reasonable level of military preparedness and a readiness to reach certain agreements) that modify the superpower competition, channeling it away from areas likely to be especially wasteful and destabilizing. Given the seriousness of a mistake, it seems especially unwise to make any radical new departures. We know that US nuclear policies have kept the peace between the superpowers; we do not know that any dramatic changes will not upset the applecart. Hence, the US should move very cautiously from its current stance, if indeed it should move at all.

**CON:** The policies of the past have been "successful" in only a very limited way—they have not yet blown us up. But they have been enormously wasteful of resources, and unforgivably dangerous. Several decades of unimaginative, occasionally bellicose nuclear policies have put both sides where they are today: admittedly at peace, but in the midst of a rapidly escalating and almost uncontrollable arms race, and quite possibly on the verge of World War III. There are always risks; indeed, there are risks in seeking to freeze and ultimately reverse the arms race. But these risks are insignificant compared with the risks of continuing as we are today. The Chinese have a proverb: "If you do not change direction, you will end up where you are going."

## SOVIET COLLAPSE

By putting unrelenting pressure on the USSR, including a vigorous arms race and other forms of economic and political competition, the Soviet government may be caused to collapse outright, or at least to embark on a program of liberalization at home and abroad.

**PRO:** The USSR is suffering from many internal difficulties including a stagnant economy, social disaffection as revealed in alcoholism and low job performance, tensions stemming from the presence of a large and growing Moslem minority, as well as simmering resistance from the satellite states of eastern Europe. Once the Soviet leadership recognizes that they cannot win the arms race, and that their economy is being sorely injured by the competition, they will seek to mitigate it by agreeing to terms more favorable to the US. Furthermore, by pressuring the Soviets sufficiently, it might be possible to force a significant change in their system. Such a change would offer the best possible long-term prospect of world peace: imagine, for example, that the Soviet Union became a democracy, even a socialist democracy like India or the nations of western Europe!

**CON:** There is no evidence that the Soviet government is on the verge of collapse—and if it were, the world would be even more dangerous than it is today: imagine a situation of anarchy in a nation with 25,000 nuclear weapons! The arms race simply cannot be "won," either by one side defeating the other with military force, or by wishful thinking that either can induce the other to disappear. Moreover, if the US sought to pressure the Soviets, they will simply devote more effort to their military sector. In fact, since they are a centralized, controlled economy without the democratic accountability that exists in the United States, the USSR would be able to devote a much larger proportion of its GNP to the military, with less controversy, than would the United States. Rather than leading to collapse, intensified pressure is likely to cause a stiffening of Soviet resolve, among both the leadership and the citizenry, resulting in a worse situation for everyone. During the height of detente, for example, about 50,000 Soviet Jews were permitted to leave the country annually; with the renewed Cold War of the 1980s, Jewish emigration has slowed to a mere trickle. When the Soviet leadership feels pushed, they respond by being more repressive and more dangerous. Such pressure is thus counterproductive.

## A COMPREHENSIVE TEST BAN TREATY (CTBT)

Under the terms of a comprehensive test ban treaty, test explosions of all kinds, including those now being conducted underground, would be banned. Other suggestions are for a very low threshold (say, 1-kiloton) treaty.

**PRO:** A CTBT could be adequately verified, with a very high level of confidence, and down to the explosive levels that would be militarily significant. Such a treaty would greatly slow down the arms race. It would retard the continuing momentum for new bomb and warhead design. Some authorities claim that it would not diminish confidence in the effectiveness of existing stockpiles as a deterrent, since weapons can be evaluated without actually blowing them up. Others maintain that such confidence would necessarily be eroded somewhat, and that this would actually have a stabilizing effect, since a much higher level of confidence would be needed for either side to mount a first strike; with diminished warhead reliability, neither side would be likely to strike first, and in addition, each side could be more assured that the other would be similarly restrained. The result would be a relaxation of the hair-trigger situation we now have, which is otherwise likely to grow more dangerous. Also, the US now has a substantial lead over the USSR in miniaturization of nuclear warheads; a CTBT would lock in this advantage. In

August 1985, the USSR announced a unilateral testing moratorium; we should join it.

**CON:** The US needs continued nuclear testing to complete its ongoing modernization program, including research on the H-bomb pumped X-ray laser, necessary for Star Wars/SDI. A test ban would also effectively shut down the great weapons labs; skilled scientists would find jobs elsewhere, leaving America unable to resume such activities if and when a test moratorium were abrogated. The Soviets are also much more likely to cheat than is the US, and given the large size of their country as well as the much tighter control of information that they maintain, they would be more able to conduct such tests without being detected. For something as important as the future development of nuclear weapons, iron-clad verifiability is needed. This is not now available, nor is it likely to be developed in the foreseeable future, unless and until the USSR permits complete on-site inspection. If the Soviets were not planning to cheat, what do they have to hide?

## STRATEGIC BUILDDOWN

Modernization of each side's strategic forces would be permitted, but with the proviso that for every new warhead added, two old ones would have to be dismantled. Other variants on the builddown call for a different ratio of replacement, depending on the basing mode for the new bombs and warheads: for example, to encourage a move toward (relatively stabilizing) submarine-based missiles, it has been suggested that two new submarine-based warheads be replaced for every three that are scrapped.

**PRO:** This would permit needed modernization while also resulting in a drawdown of both sides' arsenals. It would also promote a shift toward a more stable configuration of forces on both sides—notably, lesser reliance on ICBMs. It is in the US national interest to try to encourage the USSR to rely less on ICBMs and more on submarines, or even bombers.

**CON:** The real danger is not so much the total number of nuclear weapons, but rather, their kinds and delivery vehicles. "Modernization" is precisely what is so dangerous and should be prevented: if either side, for example, had only half its current arsenal but if this supply consisted of fast, highly accurate weapons, the situation would be more unstable than it is today.

## TEST FLIGHT MORATORIUM

Both sides should enter into a moratorium in flight-testing of new delivery systems. Some people prefer a total ban on all new flight testing, whereas others favor a very limited number of permitted flight tests; say, six per nation per year.

**PRO:** New delivery vehicles are the real destabilizing danger in the arms race, and every new missile or bomber must be flight-tested many times before it is deployed. These tests are easily monitored, so a ban could be verified with confidence. A test flight moratorium would therefore prevent the development, and ultimately the deployment, of most of the destabilizing new missiles—on both sides—that are currently on the horizon.

**CON:** The Soviets could test new weapons in the laboratory, or behind shielding, and then deploy something new and very threatening. The US could never be confident that the Soviets have not been cheating in other ways, and besides, testing is needed to bring forth the next generation of weapons and to keep US military research and development facilities operating at high efficiency.

## CRISIS CONTROL CENTER

The US and the USSR should establish a crisis control center, jointly manned by high-ranking military officials of both nations. Such a center would monitor suspicious events, especially during times of international tension and crisis.

**PRO:** Some of the most likely scenarios for nuclear war involve misunderstandings, false alarms, and various errors, occurring particularly during times of mistrust and tension. It would therefore be very helpful to have immediate access to data and viewpoints from the other side, to enhance communication and avoid possibly lethal misunderstandings.

**CON:** It is precisely during times of crisis that each side would distrust the other, particularly the government representatives at such a center, who would be likely to spread misinformation, and perhaps conduct espionage as well. A crisis control center could be very expensive and also could raise false expectations of cooperation and diminished danger.

## SUBSTANTIAL CUTS IN EXISTING ARSENALS

There have been many proposals to slash existing arsenals. The most notable are as follows.

1. Diplomat/historian George Kennan has proposed the elimination of half the bombers, ICBMs, and strategic submarines possessed by each side. Then the remaining forces should similarly be reduced by another two-thirds.

2. The Federation of American Scientists has proposed that both sides continue to adhere to SALT II, and then draw down their arsenals by annual percentage cuts—say, 10% per year, with each side able to select the weapons it will eliminate. (Presumably, they will forego the weapons that are especially vulnerable first, saving their secure deterrent forces.)

3. Admiral Noel Gaylor, retired commander of the US Pacific fleet, has suggested that each side turn in the explosive nuclear material from its weapons, on a one-for-one basis. A central receiving station would be located in a neutral site and observed carefully by experts from both sides, as well as the international media.

**PRO:** The two sides have reached essential equivalence in nuclear forces, such that further wrangling among the experts and the politicians is unnecessary and also likely to prolong the resolution. Rather than worrying about how to equate submarines with ICBMs, and so on it would be simpler and more effective to diminish the forces of both sides as they exist today. The specific details vary with the proposal, but the basic principle remains: nuclear forces are excessive and provocative, and it is time to cut through the Gordian knots of strategic analysis and political grandstanding.

**CON:** Complicated problems do not admit of simple solutions, no matter how appealing these solutions may appear to be. Both sides would insist on iron-clad guarantees, for example, that the materials being destroyed were in fact derived from current weapons in the Soviet arsenal and that these mate-

rials were not simply being replaced via clandestine production. In addition, there is currently an unacceptable imbalance in nuclear forces, and it would be dangerous to continue this relative imbalance at levels that were merely lower than before.

## UNILATERAL NUCLEAR DISARMAMENT

The United States should dismantle its nuclear forces unilaterally, regardless of what the Soviet Union does.

**PRO:** Nuclear weapons constitute an unacceptable threat to Americans and to the world. It is only because of the presence of American nuclear weapons that the USSR might possibly use nuclear weapons against the US. If the US were to disarm, there would be no motivation for the Soviets to attack: even aside from the problem of nuclear winter, where would they buy their wheat? As to Soviet invasion, the US could still maintain adequate conventional forces and also be prepared for civilian defense and resistance.

**CON:** It is quite possible that if American deterrent forces were eliminated, the USSR would destroy the US immediately; this is simply not an acceptable risk to take. Even if the Soviets refrained from doing this, they could easily dictate terms to the US, which would have no choice but to obey. Unilateral nuclear disarmament would be tantamount to surrender.

## VICTORY IN A NUCLEAR WAR

The US should be prepared to fight and win a nuclear war.

**PRO:** Nuclear war might occur, and the US must therefore be prepared to emerge with minimal casualties and with sufficient remaining nuclear forces to be able to assure that it will not be subject to coercion from any remaining Soviet forces, or for that matter, from any other nation. While perhaps America should not seek such a war directly, there is an obligation to fight it successfully if need be, and to establish a postwar world that is consistent with the Western values of freedom, justice, and democracy.

**CON:** There probably will be no values, Eastern or Western, after a nuclear war. The prospects of catastrophe are so great, and the likelihood of keeping such a war limited so remote, that it is profoundly irresponsible to consider fighting a nuclear war to be a viable option. The differences between the US and the USSR simply do not justify the carnage of nuclear war. In addition, not only would victory in a nuclear war be unattainable, but planning for one is necessarily provocative and likely to precipitate such a conflict. The only answer must be prevention.

## MINIMAL DETERRENCE

The United States should reduce its arsenal to a level consistent with minimal deterrence—several guided missile submarines and perhaps a handful of strategic bombers, dispersed throughout the country.

**PRO:**  As Robert McNamara has pointed out, nuclear weapons are not useful as weapons, except, perhaps, for one purpose: to deter an opponent from using nuclear weapons against us. Given that a single Poseidon submarine could obliterate the USSR, and two submarines could destroy all of Eurasia, the United States does not need anything like the large arsenal it is currently maintaining. Such an arsenal is more than wasteful: it is increasingly provocative, leading strategists on our side to plan for "winnable" and "limited" nuclear wars—both of which are illusions—and leading strategists on the Soviet side to worry that the US may be planning a first strike. If the US reduced its forces to what is strictly needed for deterrence, America could then sit back, assured of its ability to destroy any opponent that attacked it, but no longer stimulating the dangerous arms race.

**CON:**  No one knows what it really takes to deter the USSR. Better, therefore, to err on the side of safety, by maintaining a large deterrent force. A "minimal deterrent," since it involves fewer weapons, could more easily be targeted by an opponent. Therefore it would run a greater danger of being destroyed in a first strike than would a larger, more dispersed and more varied force posture. In addition, it is important that the United States have the capability of responding in precise and controlled ways to various levels of provocation. If the US had only a "minimal deterrent," a president may some day be faced with the decision of whether to retaliate with everything available—which would necessarily be targeted at Soviet cities and probably would bring about a devastating

countervalue retaliation from the Soviets—or do nothing in the face of an attack.

## REGULAR US-SOVIET SUMMITS

The leaders of the United States and the Soviet Union could arrange to meet regularly, perhaps at least once per year.

**PRO:**  Much misunderstanding could be avoided if the leaders of the two superpowers met regularly, got to know each other, and exchanged ideas and information. The enhanced communication that would result would lead to greater mutual understanding, hence would decrease the likelihood of war.

**CON:**  Personal meetings can result in animosity as well as friendship, in misreading of the other as well as greater cooperation. It has been suggested, for example, that after their Vienna summit meeting, Soviet Premier Khrushchev felt that President Kennedy could be pushed around, which led in turn to the Cuban missile crisis a year later.

## TRANSARMAMENT

"Transarmament" refers to a shift in emphasis, from potentially offensive weapons to those that are defensive only, and thus nonprovocative. For example, short-range interceptors are defensive, long-range bombers are potentially offensive; tank traps and mines are defensive, tanks are potentially offensive.

**PRO:**  It is only realistic to recognize that nations have a need to defend themselves. All too often, however, weapons are two-edged swords: even if they are intended to be purely defensive, they often have offensive capabilities. Not surprisingly, such weapons are typically perceived by an adversary as being offensive. National security would be greatly enhanced if military effort were switched to emphasize nonprovocative defense—that is, not disarmament, but rather transarmament. This would be especially appropriate for Europe, and if successfully implemented, could spread to the US and the USSR.

**CON:**  Such a strategy might work for small nations (like Switzerland or Finland) that do not have global interests and are not involved with nuclear weapons.

But for the superpowers, there is not yet any defense against nuclear weapons, so the US has no choice but to emphasize a retaliatory capacity (i.e., the ability to attack an adversary if need be). This posture might be considered by some adversaries to be offensive, but in fact it is not. As to Europe, the Warsaw Pact's advantage in conventional forces is so great that NATO has no choice but to make use of whatever strategies (including recourse to nuclear weapons) might deter the USSR.

## A MORE JUST WORLD

According to the "more just world" view, the security of the United States does not rest on nuclear weapons, but rather, on the establishment of worldwide political, social, and economic justice, which would remove the causes of war.

**PRO:**   The US would be well advised to shift its focus from military security to other, less tangible but no less real aspects of security. America is not now endangered by any current or potential military imbalance between East and West—nuclear weapons have made these factors irrelevant anyhow—but rather, by the social and resource imbalances between North and South, and within its own society as well. American security would therefore be enhanced if the nation spent less money on the military and more on economic development and social justice.

**CON:**   There are varying opinions about the responsibility of the United States government for righting injustice and promoting equality, both within the US and internationally. However, it seems clear that starvation in a third world country does not directly threaten the citizens of the United States. The threat comes from nuclear weapons in the hands of its enemies, and no amount of food-growing or promotion of worldwide hygiene will change that. America has no choice but to see to its military defenses.

## CONFIDENCE-BUILDING MEASURES

Since significant advances toward nuclear disarmament have been so elusive, the superpowers might be well advised to concentrate instead on agreements that are less controversial, notably a series of confidence-building measures (CBMs) such as: improved communication at all levels, improved "transparency" of military plans and forces (to avoid surprise and miscalculation), advance notification of any military exercises, exchange of accurate military information and of observers, establishment of tank-free zones, and ultimately nuclear weapons–free zones in various areas of contention where each side fears an attack from the other, and the mutual pullback of tactical nuclear weapons in Europe.

**PRO:**   Simple, yet cautious, such actions speak for themselves. They could initiate a gradual turnabout in superpower relations, with increasing momentum toward goodwill and eventual nuclear reductions as well.

**CON:**   The US must beware of being too gullible, never forgetting that the USSR will employ any ruses available to lull its enemies into a false sense of security. In addition, each suggestion must be evaluated carefully on its merits.

## A NO-FIRST-USE POLICY

Current NATO doctrine calls for the first use of tactical nuclear weapons in the event that the alliance is found to be losing a conventional war in Europe. Under a "no-first-use" policy, this would be changed and NATO would rely instead on conventional forces.

**PRO:**   Current NATO policy is either a colossal bluff or a suicide pact. Because of reliance on this policy, Europe is now crowded with nuclear weapons, and in the event of hostilities, the pressure to use these weapons would doubtless be immense. The Soviets have made it clear that they would not engage in a carefully orchestrated limited nuclear war, whether in Europe or anywhere else, so the US intention of using nuclear weapons—if carried out—probably would result in nuclear holocaust. With a relatively small investment, NATO could beef up its conventional forces in a nonprovocative way. Given the USSR's already precarious hold over eastern Europe, and the economic and military strength of the West, combined with the USSR's overwhelmingly defensive orientation, there is virtually no danger that the Warsaw Pact would be willing to suffer the immense pains of an invasion of the West. There is a much greater danger, on the other hand, that the profusion of nuclear weapons in Europe will lead to a war that no one wants.

**CON:**  A "no-first-use" policy would essentially decouple Europe from its existing American nuclear umbrella. Europe has had peace for more than four decades under the current policy; it would be foolhardy to exchange it for reliance on Soviet forbearance rather than on fear of our nuclear retaliation. The Warsaw Pact's conventional superiority over NATO is such that without the threat of nuclear retaliation, an attack by this alliance might not be deterred. And it is most unlikely that either the Western Europeans or the Americans would be willing to make the large-scale investment in additional conventional forces that would be needed to replace nuclear weapons in the European theater.

There have been numerous other suggestions, many of them dealing with specific weapons systems: notably either supporting or opposing the MX, Trident, or Pershing II missiles, cruise missiles, launch-on-warning strategies, and the militarization of outer space. Above, we have concentrated on those likely to have more far-reaching effects. Other proposals range from such "far-out" suggestions as US withdrawal from the United Nations to consolidating the present system of nation-states into a single world government. Specific suggestions regarding nuclear weapons policy involve various schemes for mutual pullbacks in tactical nuclear weapons in Europe, a multilateral cutoff in the production of plutonium and highly enriched uranium, the establishment of oceanic sanctuaries for each side's strategic submarines, US-Soviet nonintervention pacts regarding third world nations, and efforts to break down the East-West "bloc system" and establish a neutral Europe. There have also been numerous suggestions for domestic policies, including the establishment of a US Peace Academy, increased stature and funding for the Arms Control and Disarmament Agency, increases

(or alternatively, reductions) in US–Soviet scientific and cultural exchanges including "sister city" relationships and pen pals, national planning for economic conversion, and increased civil defense and crisis relocation planning. Every citizen has the opportunity—some might say, the responsibility—to make a judgment on each of these proposals, to oppose some and support others as he or she sees fit, perhaps to suggest new ones as well, and then to work for their implementation.

## ADDITIONAL READINGS

Allison, Graham, Albert Carnesale, and Joseph Nye, Jr. (Eds.). 1985. *Hawks, Doves and Owls: An Agenda for Avoiding Nuclear War.* New York: W. W. Norton & Co. An edited collection of various suggestions for reducing the probability of nuclear war. Evaluates 51 different proposals from a centrist perspective.

Dyson, F. 1984. *Weapons and Hope.* New York: Harper & Row. A noted physicist stakes out a position between hawk and dove, recommending a "live and let live" policy.

Kennedy, Edward, and Mark Hatfield. 1982. *Freeze!* New York: Ballantine Books. Two prominent US Senators make the case for a bilateral US–Soviet nuclear freeze.

Osgood, Charles. 1961. *An Alternative to War or Surrender.* Urbana: University of Illinois Press. The now-classic book that introduced the concept of GRIT.

Pipes, Richard. 1985. *Survival Is Not Enough.* New York: Simon & Schuster. A hawkish view, arguing for continued and even enhanced US pressure on the Soviet Union, to induce the Soviet government to reform itself or even collapse.

Urey, William. 1985. *Beyond the Hotline.* Boston: Houghton Mifflin. A discussion of techniques for improving US–Soviet communication, including the establishment of a crisis control center.

# Journals and Organizations

This book is now finished, but the arms race is not. The future is ours (that means yours) to determine. Anyone wanting to have some direct input into that future—and especially into the structure of the arms race and the probability of nuclear war—is urged to continue learning about the subject and to become active in whatever way he or she sees fit. To this end, it is especially advisable to subscribe to one or more magazines that provide updated information, and also to join one or more organizations that could help organize and coordinate your activities.

Here is a very small sampling, for both hawkishly and dovishly inclined individuals.

## MAGAZINES

### Hawkish

- *Commentary*
  165 East 56th Street
  New York, NY 10022

- *Conservative Digest*
  7777 Leesburg Pike, Suite 317
  Falls Church, VA 22043

- *Human Events*
  422 First Avenue SE
  Washington, DC 20003

- *National Review*          —
  150 East 35th Street
  New York, NY 10016

- *Public Opinion*
  1150 17th Street NW
  Washington, DC 20036

### Dovish

- *The Bulletin of the Atomic Scientists*
  5801 South Kenwood Avenue
  Chicago, IL 60637

- *The Nation*
  72 Fifth Avenue
  New York, NY 10001

- *Nuclear Times*
  298 Fifth Avenue
  New York, NY 10001

- *The Progressive*
  408 West Gorham Street
  Madison, WI 53703

- *World Policy Journal*
  777 United Nations Plaza
  New York, NY 10017

## ORGANIZATIONS

### Hawkish

- American Conservative Union
  38 Ivy Street SE
  Washington, DC 20003

- American Enterprise Institute
  1150 17th Street NW
  Washington, DC 20036

- American Legion
  National Security Division
  1608 K Street
  Washington, DC 20036

- The American Security Council
  P. O. Box 8
  Boston, VA 22713

- Committee on the Present Danger
  1800 Massachusetts Avenue NW, #601
  Washington, DC 20036

- Conservative Caucus
  501 Church Street NE, Room 317
  Vienna, VA 22180

- Heritage Foundation
  214 Massachusetts Avenue NE
  Washington, DC 20002

- High Frontiers Foundation
  1010 Vermont Avenue NW, Suite 1000
  Washington, DC 20005

- National Conservative Political Action Committee
  1001 Prince Street
  Alexandria, VA 22314

- United States Defense Committee
  3238 Wynford Drive
  Fairfax, VA 22631

## Dovish

- American Friends Service Committee
  1501 Cherry Street
  Philadelphia, PA 19102

- Arms Control Association
  11 Dupont Circle NW
  Washington, DC 20036

- Center for Defense Information
  122 Maryland Avenue NE
  Washington, DC 20002

- Coalition for a New Foreign and Military Policy
  712 G Street SE
  Washington, DC 20003

- Federation of American Scientists
  307 Massachusetts Avenue NE
  Washington, DC 20002

- Nuclear Weapons Freeze Campaign
  3195 South Grand
  St. Louis, MO 63118

- Physicians for Social Responsibility
  639 Massachusetts Avenue
  Cambridge, MA 02138

- SANE
  514 C Street NE
  Washington, DC 20002

- US Committee Against Nuclear War
  P. O. Box 33554
  Washington, DC 20033

- Women's Action for Nuclear Disarmament (WAND)
  P. O. Box 153
  Boston, MA 02258

# Sources for Figures and Tables

Adams, G., and L. Weiss. 1985. Military spending boosts the deficit. *Bulletin of the Atomic Scientists, 41,* 26–27.

Bethe, H., R. Garwin, K. Gottfried, and H. Kendall. 1984. Space-based ballistic-missile defense. *Scientific American, 25,* 39–49.

Carter, A. 1985. The command and control of nuclear war. *Scientific American, 252,* 32–39.

Cochran, T., W. Arkin, and M. Hoenig. 1984. *US Nuclear Forces and Capabilities.* Cambridge, MA: Ballinger.

DeGrasse, R. 1982. *The Costs and Consequences of Reagan's Military Buildup.* New York: Council on Economic Priorities.

Dennis, J. (Ed.). 1984. *Nuclear Almanac.* Reading, MA: Addison-Wesley.

Ehrlich, R. 1984. *Waging Nuclear Peace.* Albany, NY: SUNY Press.

Epstein, W. 1980. A ban on the production of fissionable material for weapons. *Scientific American, 243,* 43–51.

Epstein, W. 1985. A critical time for nuclear nonproliferation. *Scientific American, 253,* 33–39.

Fetter, S., and K. Tsipis. 1981. Catastrophic release of radioactivity. *Scientific American, 244,* 41–47.

Forsberg, R. 1982. A bilateral nuclear-weapons freeze. *Scientific American, 247,* 52–61.

Glasstone, S., and P. Dolan. 1977. *The Effects of Nuclear Weapons.* Washington, DC: Government Printing Office.

Gottfried, K., H. Kendall, and J. Lee. 1984. "No first use" of nuclear weapons. *Scientific American, 250,* 33–41.

Hafemeister, D., R. Romm, and K. Tsipis. 1985. The verification of compliance with arms-control agreements. *Scientific American, 252,* 39–45.

Harwell, M. 1984. *Nuclear Winter.* New York: Springer-Verlag.

IISS (International Institute for Strategic Studies). 1984/1985. *The Military Balance.* London.

Joseph, J. 1984. The economic impact of military spending. In P. Joseph and S. Rosenblum (Eds.). *Search for Sanity.* Boston: South End Press.

Kaplan, F. 1978. *A Skeptical Look at the Soviet Threat.* Washington, DC: Institute for Policy Studies.

Katz, A. 1982. *Life after Nuclear War.* Cambridge, MA: Ballinger.

Lewis, K. 1979. The prompt and delayed effects of nuclear war. *Scientific American, 241,* 35–47.

Lewis, K. 1980. Intermediate-range nuclear weapons. *Scientific American, 243,* 63–73.

Office of Technology Assessment. 1979. *The Effects of Nuclear War.* Washington, DC: Government Printing Office.

Rathjens, G. 1969. The dynamics of the arms race. *Scientific American, 220,* 15–25.

Schroeer, D. 1984. *Science, Technology, and the Nuclear Arms Race.* New York: John Wiley.

Scoville, H. 1977. The SALT negotiations. *Scientific American, 237,* 24–31.

SIPRI (Stockholm International Peace Research Institute). 1984 and 1985. *World Armaments and Disarmament.* London: Taylor & Francis.

Sykes, L., and J. Evernden. 1982. The verification of a comprehensive test ban. *Scientific American, 247,* 47–55.

Tsipis, K. 1981. Laser weapons. *Scientific American, 245,* 51–57.

Turco, R., O. Toon, T. Ackerman, J. Pollack, and C. Sagan (TTAPS). 1983. Nuclear winter: Global consequences of multiple nuclear explosions. *Science, 222,* 1283–1292.

Witt, J. 1981. Advances in antisubmarine warfare. *Scientific American, 244,* 32–41.

York, H. 1983. Bilateral negotiations and the arms race. *Scientific American, 248,* 149–160.

# Index